Adolescent Behavior

READINGS & INTERPRETATIONS

To my husband, Richard Berman
and my children, Joshua and Anna

About the Author

Elizabeth Aries is a professor of psychology in the Department of Psychology at Amherst College in Amherst, Massachusetts. She received her M.A. and Ph.D. in social psychology in the Department of Social Relations at Harvard University and joined the faculty at Amherst College in 1975. She has been teaching a popular course on the psychology of adolescents for 25 years and has taught an interdisciplinary seminar on growing up in America to freshman students. It focuses on the impacts of gender, race, and class on coming of age in America. She is the author of *Men and Women in Interaction: Reconsidering the Differences* (Oxford University Press, 1996) and numerous articles and book chapters on gender differences in communication and on identity development at adolescence.

Adolescent Behavior

READINGS & INTERPRETATIONS

ELIZABETH ARIES
AMHERST COLLEGE

McGraw-Hill/Dushkin

A Division of The McGraw-Hill Companies

Book Team

Vice President and Publisher *Jeffrey L. Hahn*
List Manager *Theodore Knight*
Developmental Editor *Ava Suntoke*
Copy Editor *Tracy Benedict*
Production Manager *Brenda S. Filley*
Director of Technology *Jonathan Stowe*
Designer *Charles Vitelli*
Typesetting Supervisor *Juliana Arbo*
Permissions Editor *Rose Gleich*
Proofreading Editor *Elizabeth Stevens*
Copier Coordinator *Larry Killian*

McGraw-Hill/Dushkin

A Division of The **McGraw-Hill** Companies

Cover © Photex/CORBIS

Cover Design *Charles Vitelli*

The acknowledgment section for this book begins on page 577 and is considered an extension of the copyright page.

Library of Congress Control Number 00-136004

ISBN 0-07-244813-X

Printed in the United States of America

2345678FGRFGR54

http://www.mhhe.com

Preface

Looking at adolescence through history and across cultures, we find that adolescent behavior does not always take the form it does in contemporary American society. Nor are there universals to the adolescent experience within contemporary American society. The study of adolescence helps to explain why adolescent behavior takes its many forms, and it is my hope that the readings in this book will broaden the reader's understanding of the adolescent experience and its diversity.

The plan of this book derives from the Psychology of Adolescence course I have been teaching for the past 25 years at Amherst College. Part I addresses major influences on adolescent behavior. The first two chapters consider the impact of the historical and cultural context on adolescent behavior by looking at the adolescent experience in previous centuries and in societies very different from our own. The following two chapters examine the ways in which the physiological changes of puberty and the development of new cognitive capacities influence adolescent behavior. An exploration of the development of personal and social identity is the focus of Part II. The chapters in this section address the theoretical foundations for the study of identity, and the importance of race, ethnicity, social class, gender and sexual orientation in identity development. Part III focuses on social contexts and contemporary social issues. The opening chapters consider the importance of family and peer relationships, school, and work in shaping adolescent behavior. The final chapters examine three contemporary adolescent issues: gangs and violence, teenage pregnancy, and eating disorders.

Plan of the Book
Each chapter of the book begins with a general introduction to the topic and includes Web site addresses (URLs) for further information and exploration. Introductions have been written to each of the readings to set them in context, provide background information, and summarize the content. These introductions are followed by a set of questions for further thought and discussion, as well as suggested readings.

A Word to the Instructor
Suggestions on how to generate classroom discussion around the themes raised in each article, as well as multiple-choice questions to test for comprehension are presented in the *Instructor's Manual for Adolescent Behavior: Readings and Interpretations,* which is available from the publisher.

Acknowledgments

As a graduate student in the Department of Social Relations at Harvard University, I had the opportunity one semester to work as a teaching assistant in a course on the Psychology of Adolescence taught by George W. Goethals. George Goethal's course was uniquely his own. He did not use a traditional textbook. He had drawn together readings that reflected the interdisciplinary department in which he taught and his own interest in the analysis of case material using psychological theory and research. When I joined the faculty in the Department of Psychology at Amherst College in 1975, I modeled my Psychology of Adolescence course on the syllabus developed by George Goethals, and I am truly grateful for the influence he has had in shaping my understanding and teaching about adolescence.

I am thankful to many people for helping this project become a reality. First, I want to thank my students. I am privileged to teach a group of bright, talented undergraduates who read course assignments thoroughly and critically and are eager to share their responses and debate ideas with others in class. My students have taught me much about adolescence. I am deeply grateful to Richard Halgin, who advised, encouraged, instructed, counseled, and supported me along the way. Without Rich I could never have written this book. I want to thank Rose Olver, who has been my closest colleague and collaborator throughout the years. Her wisdom, encouragement, support, and friendship continuously enrich my life. Special thanks go to two undergraduate students who spent many long hours working on this book: Alessandro Piselli, who searched the Web for relevant sites, and Brian Larivee, who researched information about the contributing authors. My deepest thanks go to my husband, Richard Berman, whose love inspires my life, and whose life is profoundly entwined in my own. His belief in me never falters, and his love and companionship is the bedrock of my life. Thanks go to my two children, Anna and Joshua, who have brought me so much joy, and who keep me in touch with adolescent life. And finally, my sincere appreciation goes to Ted Knight for his enthusiasm and support of this book, to Ava Suntoke for her superb editorial work and her commitment and dedication to this project, and to the rest of the staff at McGraw-Hill/Dushkin who did a wonderful job seeing this book through to production.

Elizabeth Aries

Understanding
Adolescent Behavior

Adolescence is the developmental period that falls between childhood and adulthood, and it is defined by biological, social, and cultural variables. The biological changes of puberty are often taken to denote the beginning of adolescence (see chapter 3), but considerable variability exists in the onset of puberty within a single culture, across cultures, and throughout history (Reading 1.2). Thus no precise chronological age marks the onset of adolescence. Nor can physiological maturation alone be taken as the beginning of adolescence. Girls as young as 8 or 9 show evidence of breast development, as a rule the first sign of puberty, yet most people would not consider these girls to be adolescents. Therefore, additional criteria must be considered in defining adolescence as a distinct stage of life.

Another marker of the onset of adolescence is the acquisition of new cognitive capacities: specifically, the acquisition of formal operational thought (Piaget, 1972). With formal thought, adolescents develop the capacity to think abstractly, to understand that a belief they may hold is not a truth but simply a hypothesis. They develop the capacity to deal with many attributes simultaneously, and to assume a relativistic view. These new cognitive abilities enable adolescents to formulate their own beliefs and values as different from those they may have internalized during childhood (Reading 4.1). Cognitive advances enable adolescents to take account of the thoughts of others and to see the world from different perspectives (Reading 4.2), and contribute to considerable shifts in adolescents' self-concepts (Reading 4.3). Adolescents can begin to think about who they were in the past, who they are now, and who they might become in the future. But the acquisition of formal thought is not achieved by all adolescents. This acquisition depends upon the environmental context in which a person develops and whether or not there is demand for the use of these formal structures (chapter 4). Thus the attainment of formal thought is not a universal marker of adolescence.

The onset of adolescence is determined also by changing societal expectations. Societies expect adolescents to behave differently from children or adults. Adolescents are expected to accomplish a unique set of developmental tasks that will prepare them for adulthood, and these tasks vary from one culture to another. Adolescence, then, can be defined as a transitional period during which individuals progress toward the accomplishment of the developmental tasks specified by a particular society. In American society, several complex and interrelated tasks are associated with adolescence, including the attainment of individuation and autonomy from the family, the establishment of a sense of identity, and the development of intimate relationships.

Autonomy entails a psychological and behavioral independence from parents. It includes taking responsibility for oneself and one's actions, making one's own decisions about friends, activities, employment, and lifestyle; and becoming independent from parents behaviorally. Autonomy is not necessarily related to residential status. While many young people leave home by the end of their teen years for college, they do not take on full responsibility for independent living at that point in time. Many young people move in and out of their parents' homes during their late teens and 20s as well, before establishing a more permanent home base separate from parents (Arnett, 2000). Autonomy involves, rather, a psychological differentiation and individuation from parents (chapter 10).

The task of identity consists of establishing a set of personal beliefs and values, and finding a fit between who one is, what one is good at, and the social roles and opportunities that are available in society (Reading 5.1). Some youth engage in extensive exploration of possible roles, trying out different options before coming to a vocational identity and a set of beliefs by which to live. College students, for example, may explore different majors and try on possible occupational futures through summer jobs and internships, but not all adolescents are afforded the opportunity for such exploration. Adolescents raised in poverty generally find they have fewer opportunities for exploration and fewer options available for adult roles (chapter 6).

Another developmental task of adolescence is the establishment of intimate relationships (chapter 11). Adolescents begin to develop deeper same sex friendships, providing the skills for later romantic relationships. They must deal with emerging sexuality, come to know themselves sexually, perhaps discover their sexual preferences, and develop the capacity to integrate sexuality into their love relationships (chapter 9). Before a firm sense of identity is established, friendships and dating may serve the purpose of identity exploration (Erikson, 1968). Many adolescents' explorations in love are transient as they try to figure out the kind of persons they are and the kinds of persons with whom they want to spend their lives (Reading 11.3).

The end of adolescence is as difficult to ascertain as the beginning because it has no biological markers, and because what it means to be an adult is socially constructed and may vary from one community and society to another. Sociologists have taken transition events such as entry into the labor force, marriage, and parenthood as social markers of adulthood. Major demographic shifts have occurred over the last 50 years, and the median ages of marriage and childbirth are now occurring in the mid- to late 20s. Using such transition events as markers of entry into adulthood, adolescence could continue until the mid-20s. Adolescence can also be considered to end when an individual has established autonomy, a sense of identity, and intimate relationships, but using these criteria, adolescence may continue well into the 20s as well.

Several researchers have hypothesized that there is a stage of life that falls between adolescence and adulthood. Kenneth Keniston (1971) postulated that there is a stage of youth, marked by continued role experimentation, that falls between adolescence and adulthood. More recently Jeffrey Arnett (2000) has postulated a stage of emerging adulthood covering the ages of 18 to 25. He defined this as a period marked by change and uncertainty, when demographic status is unpredictable, when individuals' lives are marked by residential instability, and enduring choices in love and work have not yet been made.

Sources and Methods

Before examining how our knowledge and understanding of adolescent behavior has developed and changed over the course of the last century, it is important to look first at our sources of information about adolescence, the methodological approaches that have been used in studying adolescence, and the limitations of those methods. What we know about adolescence depends upon where we get our information, the methods by which we gather that information, and the quality of that information. Our knowledge of adolescent behavior comes from a variety of sources.

Historical and Anthropological Data

An important source of data comes from historians and anthropologists (chapters 1 and 2). By looking at the patterning of development between childhood and adulthood at different moments in time throughout history and across different cultures, historians and anthropologists are able to provide a perspective on whether or not there are universals to the adolescent experience. Historians have demonstrated that adolescence as we know it in America today has not existed in the same form in societies in previous centuries, and they have also shown that societal conditions at a particular moment in time shape the existence of a period of adolescence, strongly influencing its form, duration, and intensity (Readings 1.1 and 1.2). Anthropologists have studied numerous preindustrial societies and have likewise found that cultural conditions play an important role in determining the kind of adolescence that unfolds (Readings 2.1 and 2.2). Data from historians and anthropologists have greatly enriched our understanding of the contemporary adolescent experience by helping to illuminate the societal conditions that play a role in determining the form adolescence assumes in America today.

Clinical Data

A primary source of data comes from therapists who have worked with adolescents and adults in therapy (adults provide retrospective accounts of their adolescent experiences). Therapists generally work with only a small number of individuals, but often have the opportunity to work with them over a period of time and can attain a depth of understanding of their experiences and the factors that have shaped their experiences. Some of the most important theoretical contributions to our understanding of adolescent development come from clinicians such as Anna Freud (1937/1966; 1958), Erik Erikson (1968), and Harry Stack Sullivan (1953), who have used their therapeutic work with troubled individuals and adults to make inferences about the normal pressures of adolescence (Reading 5.1). They have developed theoretical frameworks to account for the behavior they observed and have thereby provided hypotheses to be tested on larger samples of normal adolescents.

Empirical Studies

Empirical research studies on samples of normal adolescents provide the bulk of our data on adolescence. These studies furnish us with detailed observations, measurements, and descriptions of adolescent behavior. The empirical studies include samples of adolescents that range in magnitude from less than a hundred (Reading 7.1), to large-scale surveys of over a thousand participants (Reading 12.2). Most of the empirical studies employ questionnaires in which adolescents report on their behavior, for example, sleep patterns and dating experiences (Readings 3.2 and 11.3). Some studies include not only self-reports by adolescents, but also reports by observers, such as peers, teachers, or parents (Reading 3.3), an important addition because often the information provided by adolescents is discrepant with information given by others. Observational studies or life-history interviews of adolescents are rarer, because such studies are very expensive and time consuming (Readings 7.1 and 9.2).

First-Person Accounts

A final source of data comes from first-person accounts by adolescents of their own experience. All of the approaches discussed above involve viewing adolescence through the eyes of another, be it a clinician or researcher. In those cases adolescent experience has been abstracted through a particular lens, and may be distorted in some way. Thus an important source of information about adolescence comes from the voices of adolescents themselves (Reading 7.2).

Strengths and weaknesses exist in all forms of data. Researchers draw conclusions from their data about adolescent behavior, but the validity of those conclusions depends entirely on the quality of data upon which they are based. A number of issues need to be considered in assessing the merits of the information we have about adolescence.

Generalizability of Findings

The results of a study may be valid for the particular sample upon which they were based, but the results may not generalize to all adolescents. For example, clinicians see troubled adolescents and do not have the opportunity to work with adolescents who are coping successfully with the challenges in their lives, have high self-esteem and self-confidence, have a sense of who they are and what they want, are academically successful, and have successful relationships. Such individuals do not seek the help of a therapist. Therefore, findings based on clinical samples must be interpreted with caution as the adolescent behavior they describe may not be representative of the norm.

The vast majority of research on adolescence has been conducted on white middle-class samples. Our understanding of normal developmental processes based on these samples in many cases may not generalize to nonwhite, non-middle-class populations (chapters 6 and 7). In America, race and class define the parameters of people's lives: where they live, how they are perceived and treated by others, and what opportunities are available to them. Adolescents who go to college are confronted with a multitude of choices and options, and often have a great deal of control over the molding of their own lives. Adolescents from low-income neighborhoods are less likely to attend college or to be confronted with an array of options or opportunities, and seem to have less control over the molding of their futures. Minority adolescents may face prejudice and discrimination—barriers to achieving their goals that white adolescents do not encounter. Thus, the pathway through adolescence and the resultant adolescent behavior may be markedly different based on a person's race or socioeconomic status, and caution must be exercised before taking the white middle-class adolescent experience to be universal (Montemayor, Adams, & Gullotta, 2000).

Correlation and Causality

Many of our research studies on adolescence are correlational studies that compare contrasting groups of adolescents and examine differences in outcomes for these groups. For example, comparisons are made of adolescents whose parents did or did not divorce, adolescents who did or did not become pregnant, and adolescents who are white or nonwhite. It is impossible to conclude from these studies, however, that divorce, teenage parenthood, or race produced any differences in outcomes that occurred between the groups, because the groups were not likely to have been equivalent from the start. For example, studies have compared teenage mothers to mothers who delayed childbirth. Teenage motherhood has been found to have negative effects on educational attainment, as having a child makes it difficult for a teenage mother to continue her education. However, those adolescents who bear children as teenagers tend to have lower educational attainment before they become pregnant than those who defer childbirth. Thus teenage childbearing is not the cause of the difference in educational outcomes; rather, the effect is due to preexisting differences (Reading 14.2). It is important to be careful in assessing the results of research studies to determine whether the results could be produced by prior differences in the groups, or by variables highly correlated with the independent variable that may cause differences in the outcomes between the two groups.

Group Representatives

Often the behavior of a minority of adolescents is taken to be representative of the whole group. The popular press is filled with accounts of adolescents who are harming themselves and harming others. Reports of gang violence, drug dealing, drug and alcohol abuse, school shootings, and eating disorders make headlines. Adolescents are portrayed as hostile, angry, and defiant of authority; as depressed, suicidal, or disengaged, and as engaged in conflictual relationships with their parents. Such behavior clearly characterizes the experience of some adolescents, but it does not characterize the experience of the majority of adolescents (see "Normality and Abnormality," below). Caution needs to be exercised in determining the extent to which a particular portrayal of adolescents reflects the behavior of the majority of adolescents.

Magnitude of the Findings

Empirical studies generally report results that are statistically significant. Statistically significant findings can result, however, even when the relationship between two variables is small in magnitude, particularly if the number of participants in the study is large. With very large sample sizes, extremely small differences will be statistically significant. It is important to pay attention to the actual magnitude of the findings that are reported. For example, significant associations have been found between hormone levels in early adolescence and negative moods (Brooks-Gunn & Warren, 1989). Brooks-Gunn and Warren found, however, that the endocrine system factors that related to moods accounted for no more than 4% of the variance in negative emotional expression. Thus, while a statistically significant relationship exists between hormones and negative moods, to say that adolescents are the victims of raging hormones may be unwarranted because the effect is quite small, and the occurrence of negative affect at adolescence may be better explained by other nonbiological variables (chapter 3).

Replicability of Results

A result that has been found once may be compelling, but we should have less confidence in the finding if it has not been replicated by other studies. Quite often results from one study of adolescents are not consistent with results from another study due to differences in the samples studied, or due to the methodological approach or particular measures used. For example, the American Association of University Women carried out a study of how schools shortchange girls (AAUW, 1992). Their report revealed that girls show a drop in self-esteem at adolescence, a result that has been widely cited in both the popular press and the scholarly literature (chapter 8). The gender differences reported by the AAUW are much larger, however, than the differences reported in a recent meta-analysis of gender and self-esteem (Kling, Hyde, Showers, & Buswell, 1999) based on a notably larger sample of almost 100,000 adolescents.

The Study of Adolescence

Our knowledge and understanding of adolescent behavior has changed over the course of the last century. In a groundbreaking two-volume work published in 1904, G. Stanley Hall sketched out the dimensions of adolescent experience and established adolescence as an area of scientific study. Hall drew on nineteenth-century biologist Ernst Haeckel's fundamental law of development that ontogeny, the sequence of growth that an organism follows in the womb, recapitulates phylogeny, the sequence of development the organism's ancestors followed during evolution. Hall extended Haeckel's principle to postnatal development, claiming that stages of a child's development are a passive unfolding that repeats the history of the species. Adolescence is the recapitulation of a stage of human history that falls somewhere between the primitive and the civilized. Hall believed, however, that development becomes more sensitive to outside influences at adolescence. He proposed that adolescence is inherently a developmental period of storm and stress, of emotional turbulence and instability, and that this stress is further magnified by sociocultural influences.

Many of Hall's observations are now out of date, and his notion that life is governed by the principle of recapitulation has been attacked and thoroughly discredited. His depiction of adolescence as a period of storm and stress, however, gained further credence from psychoanalyst Anna Freud whose writings on adolescence in the decades that followed echoed and perpetuated his views (Freud, 1937/1966; 1958). The psychoanalytic perspective implicates sexuality as the cause of the upheaval of adolescence. Anna Freud argued that with the upsurge in libido or sexual energy at puberty, the ego (the rational part of personality) must redouble its defenses to keep the sexual impulses (the id) in check. In addition, oedipal fantasies (sexual feelings toward the opposite sex parent) come out of repression, and they are more dangerous at adolescence than they were during childhood because they can now be acted upon.

Thus adolescents must detach from parents and direct their love to other individuals outside the family. Anna Freud wrote, "I take it that it is normal for an adolescent to behave for a considerable length of time in an inconsistent and unpredictable manner; to fight his impulses and to accept them; to ward them off successfully and to be overrun by them; to love his parents and to hate them; to revolt against them and to be dependent on them" (Freud, 1958, p. 275). Anna Freud argued that those who by age 16 show no evidence of inner unrest, and who remain good children wrapped up in their family relationships in accordance with ideas and ideals with which they were raised, are experiencing a delay of normal development.

Anna Freud's notion that sexuality is the driving force behind development, like Hall's theory of recapitulation, has been largely discredited. Her depiction of adolescence, however, as a time of storm and stress, of detachment from parents, and of emotional turmoil, has held to the present day. Many mental health professionals and adults still believe that adolescence is a time of storm and stress for most teenagers. Studies find that both parents and teachers believe that early adolescence is a challenging time of life, and that hormonal changes make this period difficult (Buchanan, Eccles, Flanagan, Midgley, Feldlaufer, & Harold, 1990).

Normality and Abnormality

In recent decades large-scale studies have been carried out on normal adolescents to determine whether or not the depiction of adolescence as a time of storm and stress is accurate (Csikzentmihalyi & Larson, 1984; Douvan & Adelson, 1966; Offer, 1969; Offer & Offer, 1975). These studies have demonstrated that adolescence is not a time of serious disturbance for the majority of adolescents. Studies show that 80% of adolescents do not experience adolescent turmoil. Twenty percent of adolescents do, however, show mental health problems, but the prevalence rate is almost identical to that of adults (Offer & Schonert-Reichl, 1992).

Researchers who have reviewed the literature on adolescent behavior have reached different conclusions about adolescent storm and stress. A review of the literature by Jeffrey Arnett on adolescent storm and stress, focusing on relationships with parents, mood disruptions, and risk behavior, concludes:

> Adolescent storm and stress is not simply a myth that has captured the popular imagination but a real part of life for many adolescents and their parents in contemporary American society. . . . In their conflicts with parents, in their mood disruptions, and in their higher rates of a variety of types of risk behavior, many adolescents exhibit a heightened degree of storm and stress compared with other periods of life (Arnett, 1999, p. 324).

Weiner (1992), on the other hand, in a review of literature on normality during adolescence, concludes that the cases in which turmoil emerges are infrequent:

> Contrary to the popular belief that adolescents normally pass through a period of psychological upheaval and alienation, empirical evidence demonstrates that adolescence is typically an adaptive phase of growth characterized by developmental continuity rather than disruption, emotional stability rather than disorder, gradual identity formation rather than disabling crisis, and generational harmony rather than conflict (p. 86).

Adolescence is associated with antisocial, risk-taking behavior (substance abuse, delinquency, early sexual activity, risky driving), behavior that can affect the health, well-being, and life course of an adolescent. Indeed, rates of risk behavior are higher at adolescence than in childhood or adulthood. But this does not mean that all adolescents engage in risk-taking behavior. Many adolescents refrain from drugs and sexual activity, are committed and connected to school, do not engage in delinquent activity, and are cautious drivers. Research reveals that the cluster of high-risk problem behaviors is found to occur in 20% or less of youth studied. In commenting on the studies on risk behavior in a recent volume, Hagan (1998) concludes, "The picture that therefore emerges is of a large plurality of youth who are developing with relatively restricted exposure to and experience with high-risk behaviors, even in declining urban neighborhoods, in contrast with the much smaller but much higher-risk groupings" (p. 501).

Changing Research Focus

In his work on adolescence, G. Stanley Hall included chapters on topics such as sexual development, adolescent love, and intellectual development and education, topics covered today in all textbooks on adolescence. But while some subjects have remained topics of research throughout the past century, research interests have shifted with the social changes that have occurred. The Vietnam War and student protest movements of the 1960s gave rise to the study of the parent–child relationship in terms of the existence and extent of a generation gap. The rise of the women's movement was followed by intensive research on gender differences, the costs of adapting to societal gender roles, and the ways that gender shapes the developmental tasks of adolescence differentially for male and females. The civil rights and Black Power movements of the 1960s and 1970s gave rise to an interest in racial identity. A focus on drug and substance abuse, religious cults, and alienation arose in the 1970s. With each decade as new social problems arise, our research agenda changes. In the last two decades the study of eating disorders, AIDS, minority youth, gay and lesbian youth, and violence have been added to our research agenda.

Some topics, such as teenage pregnancy and substance abuse, have stayed on the research agenda over the decades, but our understanding of these issues has changed as societal values have changed, our conceptualization of the relevant variables have changed, and our research methods have become more sophisticated. Our studies of substance abuse, for example, reflect more general changes in our research studies on adolescence. Recent studies of substance abuse have given greater weight over time to biological factors in the etiology of adolescent substance abuse, and more attention to populations that are not white and middle class. They have given more attention to social contexts, such as neighborhoods and communities, which may shape drug use, to factors that protect an adolescent against substance abuse, as well as to risk factors (Kandel, 1998).

After decades of research based almost exclusively on white middle-class samples, focus is now being placed on understanding the role of race, ethnicity, and social class on adolescent behavior (Montemayor, Adams, & Gullotta, 2000). Thirty years ago, research centered on finding the universals of adolescence. Little attention was paid to the backgrounds of the individuals studied, and samples were predominantly white and middle class because such samples were conveniently available to researchers. The demographics of the adolescent population are changing. By the middle of the twenty-first century, according to some estimates, non-Latino whites will no longer be in the majority; rather they will account for barely half the American population. Thus it has become imperative that research be extended to understanding the impact of race and social class on adolescent development. As such research has begun, it is clear that what was taken to be the universal adolescent experience does not capture the experience of a growing number of adolescents in this society (chapters 6 and 7).

Finally, in the past a great deal of research on adolescents growing up poor or nonwhite focused on problem behavior, such as teenage pregnancy, use of drugs and alcohol, and gang membership. Some research is now shifting to an adaptation model. Researchers are beginning to focus, for example, on the competencies that are developed by urban adolescents living in poverty (Yoshikawa & Seidman, 2000), and on the factors that promote healthy adjustment among racial and ethnic minority youth (Castro, Boyer, & Balcazar, 2000; Taylor, Jacobson, & Roberts, 2000).

Social Context

Increasing research attention is also being given to the social contexts that shape adolescent development (Crockett, & Crouter, 1995; Graber, Brooks-Gunn, & Petersen, 1996). Until the 1970s research studies tended to ignore the broader context in which adolescent behavior occurred. Today adolescent experience is seen as being shaped by the interaction of personal characteristics, opportunities, and environmental influences. Social-contextual influences are now being assessed and integrated into studies along with data at the level of the individual (Readings 13.2 and 14.1).

The family provides the first context that molds the life of the growing individual. As adolescents move out of the matrix of family into the wider community, their lives are shaped by a widening radius of people, by friends, peer groups, and adults, as well as by social institutions, such as schools and religious institutions. As adolescents move from community elementary schools often to more diverse secondary schools, they are exposed to a larger number and diversity of individuals and role models. Adolescents select companions and contexts for interaction and their development, in turn, is influenced by them. Family, school, and peers have been the major contexts that have gained research attention in terms of their influence on adolescent behavior. But family and peer interactions are in turn shaped by broader social influences. Neighborhoods and communities impact families and provide important contexts for interaction. Because of their race or social class, some adolescents are in schools and neighborhoods that offer a limited range of social niches and have restricted opportunities to select alternative settings.

Other contexts may also play an important role in the pathway through adolescence (Fine, Mortimer, & Roberts, 1990). Many adolescents participate in organized activities that structure their time outside of school—sports teams, religious youth groups, or part-time jobs. Each of these activities or settings provides a context for interaction and plays a role in adolescent socialization. Finally, adolescents spend a significant portion of their time in media-related activities that transmit cultural messages. Adolescents spend time watching television and movies, playing video or computer games, going online, listening to the radio or to music, reading newspapers and magazines. Social contexts do not have the same impact on all adolescents. What an adolescent takes from each of these contexts depends upon what that adolescent brings to them. In addition, the question is not simply what impact these contexts have on adolescents, but why adolescents are drawn to certain contexts.

The study of social contexts has been accompanied by understanding adolescence as a developmental pathway from childhood to adulthood. Laurence Steinberg holds that three sets of factors shape developmental pathways through adolescence, "(a) characteristics of the developing adolescent, (b) influences of the immediate environment, and (c) opportunities and constraints in the broader context" (Steinberg, 1995, pp. 248–249). Today, adolescence is studied as a period of growing into adulthood, a preparation biologically, socially, and emotionally for adulthood. The focus of study is on understanding both the continuity between childhood development and what occurs developmentally at adolescence, and the continuity between adolescent development and what must follow in adulthood (Crockett & Crouter, 1995). Developmental research studies have become increasingly sophisticated over the decades to reflect the complexity of adolescent behavior as determined by multiple influences, and these studies have been facilitated by statistical advances and increased computer capacity.

Conclusion

Fifty years ago anthropologist Margaret Mead claimed that as a society we anticipate adolescence with apprehensiveness. Society, she wrote, "has all the tensity of a roomful of people who expect the latest arrival to throw a bomb" (Mead, 1952, p. 537). As a culture we continue to view adolescence with anxiety and concern for a variety of reasons. Adolescents arouse anxiety because their lives can be so separate from those of adults. Adolescents appear to be in a world of their own, segregated by age, spending little time with their families and other adults. Adolescents arouse anxiety because they are seen as the victims of raging hormones and of energies they cannot control; because they are sexually alluring; and because they are not fully developed and are vulnerable to many risks like substance abuse, pregnancy, AIDS, sexually transmitted diseases, and driving accidents. They arouse fear because they engage in delinquent activity, carry weapons to school and on the street, commit increasingly violent and deadly acts, harm themselves as well as others, starve themselves, binge drink and binge eat, cut themselves, and kill themselves. Adolescents are also envied by many adults because they are young, and their lives are believed to be full of possibility in terms of love and work, and because they are allowed to act out and break societal rules, to have fun, and to enjoy their freedom from adult responsibilities. They arouse hope because they are not fully formed and there is still a chance to redirect them in positive ways, to perfect them.

Many of the anxieties, beliefs, and hopes about adolescence are based on behaviors that are representative of only a minority of adolescents, and may, in turn, have the power to become self-fulfilling prophecies, to create exactly the adolescent behavior we expect. As our research and understanding of the actualities and diversity of adolescents increases, we can move away from the myths of adolescence and closer to the realities and complexities of the transition to adulthood.

References

American Association of University Women (1992). *The AAUW report: How schools shortchange girls.* Washington, DC: American Association of University Women.

Arnett, J. J. (1999). Adolescent storm and stress, reconsidered. *American Psychologist, 54,* 317–326.

Arnett, J. J. (2000). Emerging adulthood: A theory of development from the late teens through the twenties. *American Psychologist, 55*(5), 469–480.

Brooks-Gunn, J., & Warren, M. P. (1989). Biological and social contributions to negative affect in young adolescent girls. *Child Development, 60,* 40–55.

Buchanan, C. M., Eccles, J. S., Flanagan, C., Midgley, C., Feldlaufer, H., & Harold, R. D. (1990). Parents' and teachers' beliefs about adolescents: Effects of sex and experience. *Journal of Youth and Adolescence, 19*(4), 363–394.

Castro, F. G., Boyer, G. R., & Balcazar, H. G. (2000). Healthy adjustment in Mexican American and other hispanic adolescents. In R. Montemayor, G. R. Adams, & T. P. Gullotta (Eds.) *Adolescent diversity in ethnic, economic, and cultural contexts* (pp. 141–178). Thousand Oaks, CA: Sage.

Crockett, L. J., & Crouter, A. C. (Eds.) (1995). *Pathways through adolescence: Individual development in relation to social contexts.* Mahwah, NJ: Lawrence Erlbaum.

Csikzentmihalyi, M., & Larson, R. (1984). *Being adolescent.* New York: Basic Books.

Douvan, E., & Adelson, J. (1966). *The adolescent experience.* New York: John Wiley.

Erikson, E. (1968). *Identity: Youth and crisis.* New York: W. W. Norton.

Fine, G. A., Mortimer, J. T., & Roberts, D. F. (1990). In S. S. Feldman, & G. R. Elliott (Eds.) *At the threshold: The developing adolescent* (pp. 225–252). Cambridge, MA: Harvard University Press.

Freud, A. (1937/1966). *The ego and the mechanisms of defense* (Rev. ed.) New York: International Universities Press.

Freud, A. (1958). Adolescence. *Psychoanalytic Study of the Child, 13,* 255–278.

Graber, J. A., Brooks-Gunn, J., & Petersen, A. C. (Eds.) (1996). *Transitions through adolescence: Interpersonal domains and context.* Mahwah, NJ: Lawrence Erlbaum.

Hagan, J. (1998). Life course capitalization and adolescent behavioral development. In R. Jessor (Ed.) *New perspectives on adolescent risk behavior* (pp. 499–517). Cambridge: Cambridge University Press.

Hall, G. S. (1904). *Adolescence: Its psychology and its relation to physiology, anthropology, sociology, sex, crime, religion, and education* (Vols. I & II). Englewood Cliffs, NJ: Prentice Hall.

Kandel, D. B. (1998). Persistent themes and new perspectives on adolescent substance use: A lifespan perspective. In R. Jessor (Ed.). *New perspectives on adolescent risk behavior* (pp. 43–89). Cambridge: Cambridge University Press.

Keniston, K. (1971). *Youth and dissent: The rise of a new opposition.* New York: Harcourt Brace Jovanovich.

Kling, K. C., Hyde, J. S., Showers, C. J., & Buswell, B. N. (1999). Gender differences in self-esteem: A meta-analysis. *Psychological Bulletin, 125*(4), 470–500.

Mead, M. (1952). Adolescence in primitive and in modern society. In Society for the Psychological Study of Social Issues (Ed.) *Readings in social psychology* (Rev. ed.) (pp. 531–539). New York: Henry Holt.

Montemayor, R., Adams, G. R., & Gullotta, T. P. (Eds.) (2000). *Adolescent diversity in ethnic, economic, and cultural contexts.* Thousand Oaks, CA: Sage.

Offer, D. (1969). *The psychological world of the teenager.* New York: Basic Books.

Offer, D., & Offer, J. B. (1975). *From teenage to young manhood: A psychological study.* New York: Basic Books.

Offer, D., & Schonert-Reichl, K. A. (1992). Debunking the myths of adolescence: Findings from recent research. *Journal of the American Academy of Child and Adolescent Psychiatry, 31*(6), 1003–1014.

Piaget, J. (1972). Intellectual evolution from adolescence to adulthood. *Human Development, 15,* 1–12.

Steinberg, L. (1995). Commentary: On developmental pathways and social contexts in adolescence. In L. J. Crockett, & A. C. Crouter (Eds.) *Pathways through adolescence: Individual development in relation to social contexts* (pp. 245–253). Mahwah, NJ: Lawrence Erlbaum.

Sullivan, H. S. (1953). *The interpersonal theory of psychiatry.* New York: W. W. Norton.

Taylor, R. D., Jacobson, L., & Roberts, D. (2000). Ecological correlates of the social and emotional adjustment of African American adolescents. In R. Montemayor, G. R. Adams, & T. P. Gullotta (Eds.) *Adolescent diversity in ethnic, economic, and cultural contexts* (pp. 208–234). Thousand Oaks, CA: Sage.

Weiner, I. B. (1992). Normality during adolescence. In McAnarney, E. R., Kreipe, R. E., Orr, D. P., & Comerci, G. D. (Eds.) *Textbook of adolescent medicine* (pp. 86–90). Philadelphia: W. B. Saunders.

Yoshikawa, H., & Seidman, E. (2000). Competence among urban adolescents in poverty: Multiple forms, contexts, and developmental processes. In R. Montemayor, G. R. Adams, & T. P. Gullotta (Eds.) *Adolescent diversity in ethnic, economic, and cultural contexts* (pp. 9–42). Thousand Oaks, CA: Sage.

Contents in Brief

Contents

Part 1
Influences on Adolescent Behavior

Chapter 1

Historical Context

The life course is marked by a progression from childhood through adulthood with no clearly defined markers in between. Within each society at any moment in history, however, the period between childhood and adulthood is given a uniformity, and passage through that phase in the life cycle is shaped by the social conditions in which it unfolds.

A striking contrast appears between the form that adolescence in America takes at the turn of the twenty-first century and the form it took over 200 years ago. In the late 1700s America was predominantly an agricultural society with the population scattered in village communities. The lives of adolescents reflected patterns of farm youth everywhere. Children labored beside their parents and learned their adult occupational roles from their parents or through apprenticeships. Models of adult roles were visible and present from childhood. Schooling took place primarily during the winter months when adolescents were not needed for planting, haying, or harvesting. Children and adolescents were integrated into the lives of parents and the larger community.

Considerable change took place during the nineteenth century due to increasing urbanization and industrialization. Parents were no longer able to provide youth with models for adult work or with the same degree of guidance in learning adult roles. Decisions that had formerly been made for youth by families about occupation, residence, friends, and ultimately spouses became a matter of individual choice. With the twentieth century came compulsory education, which in turn separated the lives of adolescents from those of their parents and the larger community. Today, with compulsory education, adolescents who had formerly been producers have become consumers, and now make little contribution to the larger communities in which they live. While many adolescents hold jobs, these are part-time jobs and are often used to obtain money to support an active leisure life.

Thus by looking back historically it becomes apparent that adolescence as we understand it in America today has not always taken the form it does. We take certain regularities of adolescent life for granted, like compulsory schooling and age segregation, but these regularities have only come into being in the last century. Thus a historical perspective can enable us to better ascertain the larger societal forces that shape the social experience and behavior of adolescents.

Additional Resources

References and Suggested Reading

Demos, J. (1986). *Past, present, and personal: The family and the life course in American history*. New York: Oxford University Press.

Demos, J., & Demos, V. (1977). Adolescence in historical perspective. In T. J. Cottle (Ed.) *Readings in adolescent psychology: Contemporary perspectives* (pp. 16–22). New York: Harper & Row.

Modell, J., & Goodman, M. (1990). Historical perspectives. In S. S. Feldman, & G. R. Elliott (Eds.) *At the threshold: The developing adolescent* (pp. 93–122). Cambridge, MA: Harvard University Press.

On the Internet

http://www.charterfriends.org/adolescence.html

Questioning the Whole Notion of Adolescence
An article by Ted Kolderie, which challenges the underlying concept of adolescence in light of growing concern nationally about isolation of young people and their disconnection from adults and their communities.

http://webster.commnet.edu/hp/PAGES/DARLING/connections/violato.htm

Images of Adolescence in English Literature: The Middle Ages to the Modern Period
Modern images of adolescence are reflected in English literary tradition. The main theme of adolescence throughout the works of major English literary figures—that it is a time of turbulence, excess, and passion—is in consonance with the modern-day view of adolescence as a time of storm and stress.

1.1   David Bakan, 1971

Adolescence in America: From Idea to Social Fact

David Bakan, Ph.D., is a professor emeritus of psychology at York University, Toronto. He is author of many books including *Sigmund Freud and Jewish Mystical Tradition* (1958), *The Duality of Human Existence: An Essay on Religion and Psychology* (1966), *Disease, Pain, and Sacrifice* (1968), and *Slaughter of the Innocents: A Study of the Battered Child Phenomenon* (1971).

David Bakan argues that adolescence arose in America in response to the shift that occurred at the end of the nineteenth century from an agricultural to an urban industrial society. Bakan contends that three social movements developed during the period from 1890 to 1920 that gave form to adolescence as we know it today. These movements include compulsory education, child labor legislation, and separate legal procedures for juveniles. These changes provided a standardization to the experience of adolescence and, by effectively delaying the achievement of adult status, created a period of adolescence.

Compulsory education, child labor legislation, and separate legal procedures for juveniles arose out of a mixture of practical and humanitarian concerns. It was not until the late nineteenth century that a more prolonged, formal education became an important determinant of a person's economic prospects. A more educated labor force was needed for industry, and thus more schooling became necessary for improved job opportunities. Apprehension about the hazards of the workplace for children and the demand for more skilled and reliable workers in industry contributed significantly to restrictions in child labor. In addition, increasing immigration raised concerns about the acculturation of immigrant children, and public schools were seen as a vehicle for teaching American values and customs. With the movement of the population to urban areas, parental control over the lives of adolescents weakened. Homeless, crime-prone youth populated the streets in urban slums in the later part of the nineteenth century. Some youth, whose parents had died, moved away, or deserted them, formed gangs and terrorized neighborhoods. Many adolescents were seen as potential delinquents and in need of supervision. Thus juvenile courts were set up to provide corrective treatment for youth rather than punishment, along with reform schools and settlement houses to redeem children.

The end result of these three movements was that adolescence was set apart as a distinct phase of life during which adolescents were unable to be full-time workers, were required to spend time with age mates in school, and were set outside the adult code of justice. While depriving adolescents of certain rights, we have granted them "the promise" that if they do what they are "supposed to do" they will achieve the American dream of success, status, and wealth. Bakan argues that "the promise" has sustained adolescence as a social fact.

The Idea of Adolescence

(O)ften a technical term is invented in order to create a social condition and a social fact; such has been true with respect to the term "adolescence." The idea of adolescence as an intermediary period in life starting at puberty and extending to some period in the life cycle unmarked by any conspicuous physical change but socially defined as "manhood" or "womanhood" is the product of modern times. The *Oxford English Dictionary* traces the term to the fifteenth century. Prior to that, if we follow the thought of Philip Aries,[1] the notion of childhood hardly existed, let alone the idea of the prolongation of childhood beyond puberty, as the term adolescence suggests.

Meaningful ascription of serious role characteristics for this period of life occurs, perhaps for the first time, in Rousseau's *Émile*, in which he characterized the period of adolescence as being beyond the earlier period of weakness of childhood and as a second birth. "We are born, so to speak, twice over; born into existence, and born into life; born a human being and born a man."[2] His aim was explicitly to prolong childhood, including the condition of innocence, as long as possible.

Although *Émile* has had considerable influence since its publication, the conversion of the idea of adolescence into a commonly accepted social reality was largely associated with modern urban-industrial life. Rousseau may have *invented* adolescence, as maintained by Musgrove,[3] but the notion as it is commonly understood in contemporary thought did not prevail prior to the last two decades of the nineteenth century and was "on the whole an American discovery."[4] The idea received an important stamp of reality from G. Stanley Hall in his monumental two-volume work on *Adolescence,* which he proudly presented to the reader as "essentially the author's first book" in 1904.[5] In point of fact he had introduced the idea as a special stage of development earlier.[6] In *Adolescence* he complained that we in America, because of our history, "have had neither childhood nor youth, but have lost touch with these stages of life because we lack a normal developmental history . . . Our immigrants have often passed the best years of youth or leave it behind when they reach our shores, and their memories of it are in other lands. No country is so precociously old for its years."[7] The giving of social reality to adolescence would, as it were, youthen the nation.

By reviewing some of the history, I will attempt to show in this essay that the invention or discovery of adolescence in America was largely in response to the social changes that accompanied America's development in the latter half of the nineteenth and the early twentieth century, and that the principal reason was to prolong the years of childhood. Adolescence was added to childhood as a second childhood in order to fulfill the aims of the new urban-industrial society which developed so rapidly following the Civil War.

Historical Background

From the days of the early settlement of America to the second half of the nineteenth century, America suffered a chronic labor shortage. It sought to overcome this labor shortage through slavery, the encouragement of immigration, and industrialization. The incompatibility of slavery and industrialization plagued America during much of its early history, and that incompatibility remained until the Civil War, the Emancipation Proclamation, and the Thirteenth Amendment resolved it in favor of industrialization. But with development of urban-industrial society, the nation became possessed of new contradictions characteristic of modern technological society, most serious among them the presence of a large number of persons who were mature by historical standards but immature in the new context.

The country changed dramatically during the second half of the nineteenth century. In 1880 the railroad network was completely integrated; there was no longer a frontier; the number of cities that had populations of more than 8,000 almost doubled in the decade from 1880 to 1890. By the year 1900 more than a third of the population was living in cities and more than half the population of the North Atlantic area lived in cities of more than 8,000 persons. In 1890 more than a third of the American population were people of foreign parentage. The question of property was becoming increasingly salient, as testified to by the proliferation of criminal laws designed to protect property rights—a not unimportant fact when we consider the question of juvenile delinquency, because most juvenile crimes are crimes against property, such as burglary, larceny, robbery, and auto theft.

The low level of "morality" of the new occupants of the burgeoning cities was a matter of frequent comment. Drinking, sexual immorality, vagrancy, and crime were not only intrinsically threatening to orderliness, but were also particularly distressing influences on the young. The rapid breeding, the continuing threat of "street Arabs," evoked a strong cry that the state intercede in restraining and training the young. In an address before the American Social Science Association in 1875, the influential Mary Carpenter said that if the parents of the young fail in their duty, then the whole society suffers; it was therefore the duty of the state to intercede and "stand in loco parentis and do its duty to the child and to society, by seeing that he is properly brought up."8 Not the least of the dangers was the presence of un-American ideas and ideologies brought by the new immigrants, which were considered threatening to the basic fiber of American life. Even private education, as compared with public education, was regarded as a threat, the fear being that the children would not be sufficiently socialized and "Americanized." The Ku Klux Klan, for example, took a firm stand against private education.

As a result of these conditions, three major social movements developed, all of which conspired to make a social fact out of adolescence: compulsory (and characteristically public) education, child labor legislation, and special legal procedures for "juveniles." By the explicit citation of a precise chronological age, the legislation associated with these three areas essentially removed the vagueness of all previous ideas of the time at which adolescence terminates. Thus adolescence became the period of time between pubescence, a concrete biological occurrence, and the ages specified by law for compulsory education, employment, and criminal procedure.

There is no doubt that these movements were strongly motivated, at least on the conscious level, by humanitarian considerations. The rhetoric in defense of these three types of law was always cast in terms of the benefit and the saving quality that they would have for the young. The presumption that the various child welfare laws were principally created for the benefit of youth must, however, be confronted with the fact that there has been only a small degree of legal attention to the serious problem of child abuse in our society. The so-called "battered child" was not discovered until the late 1940's and early 1950's, and to this day appropriate protective and social support legislation is still quite negligible in contrast to the magnitude of the problem and the frequency of cases of cruelty to children.9 The confluence of humanitarian considerations with the major economic, social, and political forces in the society needs to be clearly recognized. Indeed, the recognition of these underlying forces may help us to understand some of the failures to fulfill humanitarian aims and the disabilities which currently prevail with respect to that period of life that we call adolescence.

Compulsory Education

In the late nineteenth century, public compulsory education for children between six and eighteen, characteristically to age sixteen, was introduced widely in the United States. English common law had given parents virtually complete control over the education of the child, a principle prevalent in colonial America and throughout most of our early history. However, the general legal position later became that: "The primary function of the public school . . . is not to confer benefits upon the individual as such." Rather "the school exists as a state institution because the very existence of civil society demands it. The education of youth is a matter of such vital importance to the democratic state and to the public weal that the state may do much, may go very far indeed, by way of limiting the control of the parent over the education of his child."[10]

In the case of a father who had violated the compulsory attendance law, the court stated in its opinion:

> The course of study to be pursued in the public school of our state is prescribed either by statute or by the school authorities in pursuance thereof. These schools include not only elementary schools, but high schools as well . . . A parent, therefore, is not at liberty to exercise a choice in that regard, but, where not exempt for some lawful reason, must send his child to the school where instruction is provided suitable to its attainments as the school authorities may determine.[11]

It has been held that even a competent parent may not engage in domestic education on the following grounds:

> We have no doubt many parents are capable of instructing their own children, but to permit such parents to withdraw their children from the public schools without permission from the superintendent of schools, and to instruct them at home, would be to disrupt our common school system and destroy its value to the state.[12]

At the same time the school authorities have been granted virtually complete discretionary powers with respect to suspension, expulsion, and punishment.[13] Such power rests in the hands of school authorities even in cases where the pupil has violated no rules. In one case, for example, a pupil was expelled for general misbehavior. In holding that the board of education had power to expel the pupil, the court said:

> It matters not whether rules have been announced by either the directors or teachers. If the conduct of the pupil is such as reasonably to satisfy such school officers that the presence of that pupil is detrimental to the interests of the school, then the power of expulsion is conferred.[14]

Thus, it has turned out that the power of the state in America is such that it can, through its officials, not only compel school attendance, but also bar a pupil access to educational resources. Certainly there have been numerous legislative acts and court actions which would qualify particular cases. However, the total thrust of the various steps that have been taken since the middle of the nineteenth century has been in the direction of increasing the power of the state rather than protecting the rights of young people and their parents.

At the same time as the legal power of school authorities over pupils and their parents has been great, the schools have been derelict in the teaching of law—instruction which some regard as essential for people living in a democracy. In a society that is heavily dependent for its functioning on law, it is important that an appreciation of law, how it works, and its limits be taught in the public schools. One critic of this aspect of American education, in discussing the matter of education on due process, indicates that it is taught as though it applies only to criminals and that it fails to reflect itself in procedural fairness in school disciplinary matters. The idea of freedom of the press is characteristically not brought to bear in connection with school newspapers. "One of the difficult problems," he laconically comments, "is whether [proposed] law courses will be permitted to ventilate these issues, given the anxiety about them."[15]

Although from time to time there have been steps to increase the knowledge of law among educators, the emphasis has been on the kind of legal knowledge that an educator might require to deal with relationships of the school to outside institutions and individuals rather than on teaching law to students. One article along these lines, for example, deals with the legal structure of education, pupil personnel policies, control of pupil conduct, staff personnel policies, curricula, and liability. Illustrations are that: physical education coordinators should be expert in the law of liability for pupil injuries; guidance teachers should be familiar with compulsory educational laws and their enforcement; curriculum coordinators should understand the legal position of parents in relation to school studies and activities; business administrators should understand contract law; personnel administrators should understand the legal aspects of employing and discharging teachers; and teachers of the history or philosophy of education should be acquainted with the relevant judicial opinions.[16]

Child Labor

The movement to restrict child labor in the United States also provided a definition of the termination of adolescence. Though there is a considerable amount of variation from state to state, the laws with respect to employment give specific minimum ages for definitions of maturity of different kinds: eighteen, minimum age for work in "hazardous occupations"; under eighteen, eight-hour day and forty-hour week; under eighteen, employment certificate required; under sixteen, limited hours of night work; sixteen, minimum age for factory work and employment during school hours; fourteen, minimum age for work outside of school hours. These are fairly typical laws governing age and employment.

The regulation of child labor has been one of the most controversial issues in this country since the nineteenth century. The harm to children from work in factories has been stridently declaimed. On the other hand, the virtues of work, the harm associated with idleness, and even the economic discriminatory effect of such legislation have also been consistently indicated, As an example, Senator Alexander Wiley, in questioning the representative of the American Federal of Labor before a Senate subcommittee to investigate juvenile delinquency said: "To me when I see the youth of this country in idleness, walking the streets of the cities, [I feel] we are meeting a challenge to our common sense because we know idleness breeds not only crime but everything else."[17] There have been repeated charges that the legal regulation of child labor is partly responsible for the widespread unemployment among young people, particularly Negroes.[18]

Adolescents in the labor force were a common occurrence throughout American history. In 1832 about 40 percent of the factory workers in New England were children. Starting a few years after the Civil War the major historical trend of a chronic labor shortage began to reverse itself, with ever-increasing evidences of labor surplus. With the changes in the kinds of work needed in the growing cities in the second half of the nineteenth century, an increasing proportion of females sought gainful employment. Indeed, the possibility of a close relationship between the various movements in connection with "child saving" and female employment has been seriously suggested.[19] Labor began to organize. The Knights of Labor, the precursor of the American Federation of Labor, was founded in 1869. In 1885 it had a membership of 100,000; a year later it could boast a membership of 730,000. Virtually from its founding, the Knights of Labor began its campaign for the prohibition of child labor. In spite of its efforts, child labor increased. The participation rate of youth between the ages of ten and fifteen in the labor force increased until 1900 and then began to decline. Indeed, in the decade which ended in 1900, the number of child laborers in the canneries, glass industry, mines, and so forth in the South tripled. The effort to control the labor supply in the United States was evident also in legislation to restrict immigration. In 1882 the Chinese Exclusion Act, barring immigration of Chinese laborers, was passed and was followed by other laws which severely restricted immigration.

Among employers there was a polarization. On the one hand there were certainly those employers who were in favor of having access to the cheap labor of young people and new immigrants; on the other hand the nature of industrial requirements was changing rapidly in favor of more skilled, and especially more reliable, workers. One of the most serious interferences with the reliability of labor was alcohol, and the prohibition movement grew simultaneously with the efforts to remove young people from the labor market and to restrict immigration. The prohibition movement gained increasing support from industrial leaders, "who were not unaware of the economic implications of the trade in intoxicants."[20]

The belief, common during the early part of the nineteenth century, that the children of the poor should work and that education of the children of the poor was filled with social danger tended to decline in the course of the century. The enlightened leaders of industry, taking ever longer views of history, recognized the dependence of industry on the existence of a reasonably educated labor force, educated not only with respect to knowledge and skill, but also with respect to bureaucratic subordination and reliable work habits.[21] At the same time, organized labor sought not only reforms in the conditions of child labor, but also education for their own children, to increase the likelihood of vertical social mobility. The continuing interest of both industry and labor in the education of the young is evidenced by the clear agreement on this on the part of both the National Association of Manufacturers and organized labor.[22]

One of the classic conflicts in connection with child labor was that between the textile manufacturers of the North and those in the South. The northern manufacturers charged that the South had a competitive advantage from its greater use of young workers.[23] Among the factors that eventually led to a resolution of the conflict was the later discovery, resulting in part from the changed nature of manufacture and experience of some restrictive legislation, that, as the *Textile World Journal* in 1918 put it: "The labor of children under fourteen years of age is not only inefficient in itself, but tends to lower the efficiency of all departments in which they are employed; also children of fourteen to sixteen years, worked on a short time basis, are scarcely less efficient and have a disorganizing effect in the departments where they are utilized. Because of these facts, and entirely apart from humanitarian considerations, large number of southern mills will not re-employ children of these ages."[24]

Juvenile Delinquency

Quite analogous to the "invention of adolescence," as Musgrove put it, was the "invention of delinquency," as Anthony M. Platt puts it in his book on the history of the notion of delinquency in the United States.[25] The humane motivation associated with the development of the notion of the juvenile delinquent was the desire to remove young people from the rigidities and inexorabilities associated with criminal justice and to allow wide discretionary powers to authorities in dealing with juveniles. The new legal apparatus was intended to separate young offenders from older offenders, and to provide corrective rather than punitive treatment. The first Juvenile Court Act was passed by the Illinois legislature of 1899 and brought together for single consideration cases of dependency, neglect, and delinquency. The hearings under the act were to be informal, the records were to be confidential, the young people were to be detained separately from adults. The aims were to be investigation and prescription rather than the determination of guilt or innocence. Lawyers were to be unnecessary. The definition of the "juvenile delinquent" in the various laws which multiplied after the model legislation in Illinois now vary for the upper limit from sixteen to twenty-one. The United States Children's Bureau had recommended nineteen, and this has been followed in about two-third of the states.[26]

Although the juvenile acts tended to free the courts from the obligation of imposing punishments associated with the criminal codes, they also had the effect of suspending the fundamental principle of legality, that one may not be punished for an offense unless a definite law in effect at the time when the act in question was committed has been broken. Considerations of due process were not obligatory. Guilt did not have to be established beyond a reasonable doubt. Among the acts reported under the heading of juvenile delinquency may be found the following: immoral conduct around schools, association with vicious or immoral persons, patronizing public pool rooms, wandering about railroad yards, truancy, incorrigibility, absenting self from home without consent, smoking cigarettes in public places, begging or receiving alms (or in street for purposes of).[27] As Harvery Baker of the Boston juvenile court put it in 1910:

> The court does not confine its attention to just the particular offense which brought the child to its notice. For example, a boy who comes to court for such a trifle as failing to wear his badge when selling papers may be held on probation for months because of difficulties at school; and a boy who comes in for playing on the street may . . . be committed to a reform school because he is found to have habits of loafing, stealing or gambling which can not be corrected outside.[28]

Questions have been raised as to whether the procedures of such courts adequately protect the rights of young offenders and whether they are consistent with constitutional rights.[29] In some states corrective legislation has been attempted by providing for legal defense of persons who come under the jurisdiction of the juvenile courts. However, the evidence is that this is not common. Indeed, treatment by officials tends to be more kindly toward young persons who admit guilt and indicate that they will mend their ways than toward those who are defensive or those whose parents are defensive.[30] The failure of the juvenile court to achieve its avowed objectives is notorious.

Suggestions that the aim of the juvenile court is to introduce a middle-class child-rearing orientation to the courtroom are apparent in the opinion of Judge Ben Lindsey of Denver, one of the pioneers in the juvenile court movement, and in the findings of Melvin L. Kohn. In an introduction to a book called *Winning the Boy* by Lilburn Merrill, Lindsey stressed the importance of "character," rather than the act itself.

> You have not really a safe citizen until there comes into the boy's heart the desire to do right because it is right . . . I ask the boy why he will not steal again and he invariably replies, "Because I will get in jail." He is afraid of jail; he is not afraid to do wrong . . . Conscience is the moral director; without it character is impossible, and character is the greatest need, for it means that the pure in heart shall see and know and act the truth, as surely as they shall see God.[31]

Kohn has been able to show, on the basis of comparative data which he has collected, that there are differences in corrective actions between working-class and middle-class parents. Working-class parents tend to punish the external consequences of an action, as contrasted with middle-class parents who tend to punish on the basis of intention, rather than the action itself.[32] The latter mode is clearly suggested in Judge Lindsey's comment. Thus one way of interpreting the development of juvenile delinquency practices is as an effort to bring middle-class child-rearing practices into play, even when they involved the suspension of the principle of legality.

The legal disability of those who come under the juvenile laws is not limited to a small minority of youth in our society. "Statutes often define juvenile delinquency so broadly as to make virtually all youngsters delinquent . . . Rough estimates by the Children's Bureau, supported by independent studies, indicate that one in every nine youths—one in every six male youths—will be referred to juvenile court in connection with a delinquent act (excluding traffic offenses) before his 18th birthday."[33] As soon as the young person gains what may be called the animal sufficiency that comes with puberty, and may enter public places without an attendant, he becomes subject to extraordinary powers of the state until the legal definition of his maturity comes into being. This power of the state differs dramatically from the power of the state over adults in our society. The great discrepancy between adult justice and juvenile justice and the legal vulnerability of juveniles has been one of the major factors associated with the conversion of the idea of adolescence into the social fact of adolescence.

The Study of Adolescence

Starting with the work of G. Stanley Hall, adolescence became the subject of a considerable amount of investigation. There can be no doubt about the value of such investigation. . . . Nonetheless, this body of literature articulated with the cultural forces in the society at large. Although the intention of people like Hall to draw attention to an extremely important age period significant to the history of civilization generally, and the United States in particular, and thereby to create greater concern with proper development at that state, was meritorious, there was another effect which needs to be pointed out. By stressing, for example, the presumptive emotional instability and unformed nature of people of that age—the work of Margaret Mead and others suggests that such phenomena of adolescence may be extrinsic rather than intrinsic[34]—Hall and others tended to put a gloss of psychopathology on this age period. Since it has long been a principle in our society that persons regarded as psychologically pathological are to be relieved of rights,[35] the effect of this literature has been to serve the general disability of persons under legal ages. In this way, the workers in the field of adolescence have tended to conspire, certainly unwittingly, with some of the forces depriving adolescents of their rights.

The Promise

A major factor which has sustained the social fact of adolescence in our society has been the belief, so pervasive in our success-oriented culture, in "the promise." The promise is that if a younger person does all the things he is "supposed to do" during his adolescence, he will then realize success, status, income, power, and so forth in his adulthood.

A study by Arthur L. Stinchcombe[36] may help us to understand the operation of the promise. He studied the attitudes, behavior, and perceptions of the labor market among high school students, and found a direct and dramatic relationship between the images of the future that the students have and their rebellious attitudes and behavior. His data bear out the hypothesis "that high school rebellion, and expressive alienation, are most common among students who do not see themselves as gaining an increment in future status from conformity in high school."[37] In elaborating on the dynamics of the hypothesis, he writes: "When a student realizes that he does not achieve status increment from improved current performance, current performance loses meaning. The student becomes hedonistic because he does not visualize achievement of long-run goals through current self-restraint. He reacts negatively to a conformity that offers nothing concrete. He claims autonomy from adults because their authority does not promise him a satisfactory future."[38] Stinchcombe's hypothesis is derived from considerations of the legitimacy of bureaucratic authority as developed by Max Weber. Among the interesting derivations Stinchcombe makes from the hypothesis is an explanation of the difference between the sexes in various categories of expressive alienation. Girls are less likely to be rebellious because they perceive at least the possibility of marriage as a viable "career." He points out that the relatively high delinquency rate among Negroes is associated with the perception of the employment discrimination against Negro adult males.

As the creditability of the promise declines, the willingness of young people to accept the varieties of disabilities of adolescence equally declines. The profoundly pervasive metaphor of appropriate behavior in adolescence as a form of capital investment for the realization of returns in the future necessarily falters in cogency as the likelihood of such returns declines. The problems of order in the schools, juvenile delinquency, and other forms of expressive alienation cannot readily be solved by making small changes in the schools, Stinchcombe says.[39] It would appear that the schools cannot promise much because the society cannot promise much.

A study by William Westley and Frederick Elkin[40] of young people in an upper-class suburb of Montreal in 1951 attempted to explode the notion of the adolescent period as being one of storm and stress, nonconformity, gang formation, struggle for emancipation, and the like. The data collected in that place and time indicated considerably greater harmony and positive social adjustment by conventional standards than one might expect. However, the characterization of these young people would clearly indicate that they expected that the promise would be fulfilled. The typical youth in the study "internalizes aspirations for a professional or business career; he learns the expected patterns of language and breeding; he learns to resolve disputes by peaceable means; he learns to defer many immediate gratifications for the sake of future gains."[41]

The major question in our society today is whether, for youth of *all* social classes, the promise has continued credibility. Unemployment among manual workers is increasingly patent. The public service advertisements directed at potential drop-outs to remain in school in order to get better jobs later are met with increasing cynicism.[42] The poor acceptance rates of college students into the labor market predicted in the early sixties[43] are rapidly materializing. Even for scientists with Ph.D.'s the possibilities for employment are extremely dismal.[44] And few young people are ignorant of the fact that a career in "free enterprise" is virtually impossible without access to capital.[45] The idyllic vision of Erik Erikson that adolescence "can be viewed as a *psychosocial moratorium* during which the individual through free role experimentation may find a niche in some section of his society, a niche which is firmly defined and yet seems to be uniquely made for him,"[46] must increasingly be viewed cynically if that niche in life is contingent upon an appropriate niche in the labor force.

One of the likely consequences of these trends will be a strong move on the part of youth and their parents to dissolve the social fact of adolescence and to remove the historical disabilities which have been created by the state and sustained by the promise. Albert K. Cohen, in 1965, indicated that he thought it was sad that youth accepted their disabilities without protest.[47] The picture soon changed. Jerry Farber's critique of what he calls America's "Auschwitz" educational system, "The Student as

Nigger," originally published in 1967 in the Los Angeles *Free Press,* quickly became one of the most widely distributed underground documents in history—reprinted, reduplicated, recopied many times by student groups all over America and Canada.[48] A national clearing house of anti-public school thought has been formed in Washington, D.C., which puts out a regular biweekly newsletter called *FPS (the letters don't stand for anything).* Ellen Lurie has written what is fast becoming a standard manual for parents seeking to reduce state control over their children's education in the public schools.[49] This book is consistent with the United Nations Universal Declaration of Human Rights, adopted in 1948, that "Parents have a prior right to choose the kind of education that shall be given to their children."[50] The crime statistics mount at an exponential rate. Demonstrations become ever more strident. The "underground revolution"[51] gets new recruits daily.

The future? My assignment was to discuss history. The future must be left to time and other occasions.[52]

Notes

1. P. Aries, *Centuries of Childhood* (New York: Knopf, 1962).
2. Jean Jacques Rousseau, *Émile,* trans. Barbara Foxley (New York: Dutton, 1966; originally published 1762), pp. 128, 172.
3. F. Musgrove, *Youth and the Social Order* (Bloomington, Ind.: Indiana University Press, 1964). Musgrove titles one of his chapters "The Invention of the Adolescent," pp. 33–57.
4. John Demos and Virginia Demos, "Adolescence in Historical Perspective," *Journal of Marriage and the Family,* 31 (1969), 632–638, 632.
5. G. Stanley Hall, *Adolescence: Its Psychology and Its Relations to Physiology, Anthropology, Sociology, Sex, Crime, Religion, and Education* (New York: D. Appleton and Company, 1904).
6. G. Stanley, Hall, "The Moral and Religious Training of Children," *Princeton Review* (January 1882), pp. 26–48.
7. Hall, *Adolescence,* p. xvi.
8. As cited in Grace Abbot, ed., *The Child and the State* (Chicago: University of Chicago Press, 1938), II, 372.
9. See M. G. Paulsen, "The Law and Abused Children," in R. E. Helfer and C. H. Kempe, *The Battered Child* (Chicago: University of Chicago Press, 1968), pp. 175–207; and D. Bakan, *Slaughter of the Innocents: A Study of the Battered Child Phenomenon* (San Francisco: Jossey-Bass, 1971; Toronto: Canadian Broadcasting Corp., 1971).
10. Newton Edwards, *The Courts and the Public Schools: The Legal Basis of School Organization and Administration,* rev. ed. (Chicago: University of Chicago Press, 1955), p. 24.
11. *Miller v. State,* 77 Ind. App. 611, 134 N. E. 209, as cited by Edwards, *The Courts and the Public Schools,* p. 524.
12. *State v. Counort,* 69 Wash. 361, 124 Pac. 910, 41 L.R.A. (N.S.) 95, as cited by Edwards, *The Courts and the Public Schools,* p. 522.
13. Edwards, *The Courts and the Public Schools,* pp. 601ff.
14. *State v. Hamilton,* 42 Mo. App. 24, as cited by Edwards, *The Courts and the Public Schools,* p. 603.
15. Alex Elson, "General Education in Law for Non-Lawyers," in The American Assembly, Columbia University, *Law in a Changing America* (Englewood Cliffs, N.J.: Prentice-Hall, 1968), pp. 183–191, 189.

16. E. E. Reutter, Jr., "Essentials of School Law for Educators," in Harold J. Carter, ed., *Intellectual Foundations of American Education* (New York: Pitman Publishing Corporation, 1965), pp. 216–225.

17. *Juvenile Delinquency: Hearings before the Subcommittee to Investigate Juvenile Delinquency,* Senate, 1955 (New York: Greenwood Press, 1968), p. 86.

18. See, for example, the effort to counter these charges by H. M. Haisch of the U.S. Department of Labor: H. M. Haisch, "Do Child Labor Laws Prevent Youth Employment?" *Journal of Negro Education,* 33 (1964), 182–185.

19. "Although child saving had important symbolic functions for preserving the prestige of middle-class women in a rapidly changing society, it also had considerable instrumental significance for legitimizing new career openings for women. The new role of social worker combined elements of an old and partly fictitious role—defender of family life— and elements of a new role—social servant. Social work and philanthropy were thus an affirmation of cherished values and an instrumentality for women's emancipation." Anthony M. Platt, *The Child Savers: The Invention of Delinquency* (Chicago: University of Chicago Press, 1969), p. 98.

20. John Allen Krout, *The Origins of Prohibition* (New York: Russell and Russell, 1967), p. 302.

21. For an analysis of relations between education and industry see John Galbraith, *The New Industrial State* (Boston: Houghton Mifflin, 1967).

22. See Charles R. Sligh, Jr., "Views on Curriculum," *Harvard Educational Review,* 4 (1957), 239–245; Walter P. Reuther, "What the Public Schools Should Teach," *Harvard Educational Review,* 4 (1957), 246–250.

23. Stephen B. Wood, *Constitutional Politics in the Progressive Era: Child Labor and the Law* (Chicago: University of Chicago Press, 1968), p. 9.

24. Cited by Wood, *Constitutional Politics,* p. 172.

25. Anthony M. Platt, *The Child Savers: The Invention of Delinquency* (Chicago: University of Chicago Press, 1969).

26. Robert W. Winslow, ed., *Juvenile Delinquency in a Free Society: Selections from the President's Commission on Law Enforcement and Administration of Justice* (Belmont, Calif.: Dickenson Publishing Company, 1968), pp. 119–120.

27. Winslow, *Juvenile Delinquency,* pp. 166–167.

28. Cited in Platt, *The Child Savers,* p. 142.

29. See Lewis Mayer, *The American Legal System* (New York: Harper and Row, 1964), pp. 146–149.

30. Winslow, *Juvenile Delinquency,* pp. 140, 150.

31. Cited in Bernard Wishy, *The Child and the Republic: The Dawn of Modern American Child Nurture* (Philadelphia: University of Pennsylvania Press, 1968), p. 134.

32. M. L. Kohn, "Social Class and Parent-Child Relationships: An Interpretation," *American Journal of Sociology,* 68 (1963), 471–480; M. L. Kohn, "Social Class and the Exercise of Parental Authority," *American Sociological Review,* 24 (1959), 352–366; M. L. Kohn, *Class and Conformity: A Study in Values* (Homewood, Ill.: Dorsey Press, 1969).

33. Winslow, *Juvenile Delinquency,* p. 2.

34. Margaret Mead, *Coming of Age in Samoa* (New York: W. Morrow and Co., 1928).

35. See Thomas S. Szasz, *Law, Liberty and Psychiatry* (New York: Macmillan, 1963).

36. Arthur L. Stinchcombe, *Rebellion in a High School* (Chicago: Quadrangle Books, 1964).

37. *Ibid.,* p. 49; see especially chaps. 3 and 4, pp. 49–102, titled "The Labor Market and Rebellion I; II."

38. *Ibid.,* pp. 5–6.

39. *Ibid.,* passim.

40. William A. Westley and Frederick Elkin, "The Protective Environment and Adolescent Socialization," in Martin Gold and Elizabeth Douvan, eds., *Adolescent Development; Read-*

ings in *Research and Theory* (Boston: Allyn and Bacon, 1969), pp. 158–164; reprinted from *Social Forces,* 35 (1957), 243–249.

41. *Ibid.,* p. 158.
42. See, for example, the stress on the employment advantages of school in the *National Stay-in-School Campaign Handbook for Communities* (Washington, D.C.: Government Printing Office, 1957). The campaign was sponsored jointly by the Department of Labor, Department of Health, Education and Welfare, and Department of Defense.
43. J. Folger and C. Nam, "Trends in Education in Relation to the Occupational Structure," *Sociology of Education,* 38 (1964), 19–33; R. Havighurst and B. Neugarten, *Society and Education,* 2d ed. (Boston: Allyn and Bacon, 1962).
44. Allan Cartter, "Scientific Manpower for 1970–1985," *Science,* 172 (1971), 132–140.
45. Such has been the case at least since 1885 when Andrew Carnegie, the great exponent of the idea that any able and energetic young man could "rise to the top," told a group of students that "There is no doubt that it is becoming harder and harder as business gravitates more and more to immense concerns for a young man without capital to get a start for himself." Cited in H. J. Perkinson, *The Imperfect Panacea: American Faith in Education, 1865–1965* (New York: Random House, 1968), p. 120. Ironically, one of the few spheres in which "free enterprise," with relatively little capital and high returns on investment, is still possible is in the illegal merchandising of drugs.
46. Erik H. Erikson, "The Problem of Ego Identity," in Gold and Douvan, *Adolescent Development,* p. 19; reprinted from *Identity and the Life Cycle* (New York: International Universities Press, 1959).
47. In his foreword to Musgrove, *Youth and the Social Order,* p. xix: "Do they really believe that all preparation for life must, in the nature of things, take for its model the process of becoming a thirty-second degree Mason?"
48. Jerry Farber, *The Student as Nigger* (New York: Pocket Books, 1970).
49. Ellen Lurie, *How to Change the Schools: A Parents' Action Handbook on How to Fight the System* (New York: Vintage Books, 1970).
50. Article 26–3.
51. Naomi Feigelson, ed., *The Underground Revolution: Hippies, Yippies and Others* (New York: Funk and Wagnalls, 1970).
52. Since the time that I wrote this the amendment reducing the voting age to eighteen has been ratified. I am of the opinion that it will have important consequences bearing on the considerations in this essay.

Questions

1. How did a shift from an agricultural society to an urban industrial society alter the experience of coming of age (finding an identity, becoming autonomous from parents, choices, and opportunities available)?
2. How did compulsory education, child labor laws, and separate laws for juveniles create adolescence?
3. Would a period of adolescence continue to exist if compulsory education, child labor laws, and separate laws for juveniles were abolished?
4. How is "the promise" important to defining adolescence, and what are the consequences of failing to believe in it?

References and Further Reading

Kett, J. F. (1977). *Rites of passage: Adolescence in America 1790 to the present.* New York: Basic Books.

Teeter, R. (1988). Coming of age on the city streets in nineteenth-century America. *Adolescence, 23*(92), 909–912.

1.2   Michael Mitterauer, 1993

Puberty—Adolescence—Youth

Michael Mitterauer, Ph.D., is a professor of sociology at the Institute for Economic and Social History, University of Vienna, Austria. He is author of *The European Family: Patriarchy to Partnership from the Middle Ages to Present* (1982) and *A History of Youth* (1993).

Pubertal maturation is often taken as a marker of the beginning of adolescence. Puberty is a biological occurrence that is universal; it takes place for individuals across all cultures and in all historical periods. While the sequences of physical growth and sexual maturation are regular and highly regulated processes that have altered little over time, the timing of these processes has changed dramatically over the course of the last two centuries. In Western Europe in the early nineteenth century, for example, menarche occurred at an average age of 15 to 17, but by the late twentieth century had dropped to an average age of 12 to 13. Thus by looking at puberty historically, we see that the timing of physiological maturation has not been static and unchanging and may be influenced by the societal context in which it unfolds.

Michael Mitterauer contends that both the biological and the psychological dimensions of adolescence are socially conditioned and historically changeable. He begins his book, *A History of Youth*, by examining how the processes of physical growth and sexual maturation have changed over time. He presents data on physical and sexual maturation over the last few centuries, examining the age of menarche for girls and of the breaking of the voice and the attainment of adult height and muscular strength for males. These data consistently reveal that physical growth and sexual maturation have been occurring at an earlier and earlier age. Mitterauer examines a variety of societal factors that may cause earlier sexual maturation. Mitterauer then extends the discussion from pubertal maturation to the larger question of whether or not there are any psychological universals to the adolescent experience, any aspects of the experience of adolescence that are predetermined and manifested in all adolescents throughout history. It is widely assumed in contemporary American society that adolescence is a period of unrest and increased emotionality, that inherent to the stage of adolescence is a struggle for individuality and distance from parents. But an examination of the historical data indicates that while we often assume that certain attitudes and behaviors are characteristic of all adolescents, the psychological development of adolescents is shaped by contemporary societal conditions.

The idea of treating youth as a theme in social history requires to be clarified by a number of basic questions. How can this academic discipline contribute to our treatment of the topic? Is youth a legitimate theme in historical studies in any case? Social history is concerned with the processes of social change. At first sight, however, youth appears to be an anthropological constant. In all human societies there is a transitional phase between childhood and adulthood. All humans undergo a process of physical growth and sexual maturing. Sexual development is a physiological experience which, though it affects boys and girls in different ways, is common to all. It would appear to belong in the field of human biology, not of history.

However, it needs to be stressed that, while we shall certainly be concerned with processes of physical development, the theme of youth is also deeply linked to social phenomena. We can see this clearly in the concept of 'adulthood', the ultimate goal of the process of youth. Originally, the word 'adult' comes from a Latin term meaning 'grown up', having completed the process of growth. Today, however, this definition, with its focus on external physical features, is no longer prominent. Far more important is the sense in which the word highlights personality. The concept 'adult' refers to the completion of emotional and social development. At the same time, it signals a role in society which differs from that of the adolescent. So youth, as a phase in the cycle of life which leads into the role of adulthood, embraces physical, emotional and social processes which are causally related to each other. For the sociologist, and therefore also for the historian, those aspects which can be connected with social conditions will stand in the foreground of any analysis.

It is of the greatest importance to see youth not only in its biological determinants, but also as socially conditioned and historically changeable. In this respect, youth bears a similarity to other themes with biological components, such as male and female roles, sexuality, and family: if a study deals only with natural forces and data, the impression is given that the theme is static and unchanging. Such supposedly 'anthropological constants' are dangerous, for they hide the possibility of variation. A historical-sociological approach, on the other hand, admits the concept of change. What appeared to be the natural order turns out to be socially shaped. In this respect, social history may be able to contribute to the development of our understanding of youth in the present day.

If we pursue the question of how nature relates to socially conditioned aspects of youth, we find that social factors play a considerable part even in what appear to be purely biological phenomena, such as the age of attaining sexual maturity, the period and extent of bodily growth, the development of physical strength, or the age at which the voice breaks. In all these respects, striking variations frequently emerge between different periods of history or different parts of Europe, between urban and rural, and most of all between different social classes. These variations cannot be satisfactorily explained by the facts of the natural environment, such as climate. The causes must be sought in the social conditions prevailing.[1]

The effect of social differences on the course of puberty was observed by scholarship long ago. As early as 1620 a doctor named Guarinonius established that peasant girls in the Tyrol reached sexual maturity significantly later than the daughters of bourgeois and noble families. In 1798 Buffon pointed out differences in age at the start of menstruation between the French urban and rural populations. A survey taken in 1857 found unmistakable class-related differences within the population of Vienna. At that time, the average age for the beginning of menstruation was 15.7 among the middle bourgeois, 16.2 among manual workers and domestic servants and 16.8 among day labourers. In Berlin, a study made in the 1860s calculated an average age of 15.2 for 'women of higher standing' and 16.1 for 'women of lower standing'. Countless other nineteenth-century investigations into menarche rates confirm this class-related distinction.[2]

The data obtained in the nineteenth century for the sexual maturity of girls makes wider comparisons possible. We can illustrate the rate of change by comparing some of the early averages for menarche with equivalents for the present or recent past.[3]

Germany	1808:	16.8	1981:	12.5[4]
France	1830:	15.3	1979:	13.0
England	1832:	15.7	1973:	13.0
Denmark	1850:	17.3	1968:	13.2
Sweden	1844:	16.2	1976:	13.1
Finland	1883:	16.6	1971:	13.2
Netherlands	1873:	16.1	1976:	13.4
Norway	1839:	17.0	1973:	13.2

These data show that in some parts of Europe female maturity has been brought forward by more than four years since the first half of the nineteenth century. Furthermore, the rate at which these figures are falling has shown a marked acceleration during the twentieth century.

The more recent results show smaller variations between the different countries of Europe than do those from the nineteenth century. Even in class-related comparisons, a levelling-out of the data can be established. This suggests that the conditions which determine the rate of sexual development among children and juveniles have become more uniform, both within and between the industrial nations of Europe.

The general drop in the average age of physical maturity in the last couple of centuries raises the question whether we should assume a high average age in the old European societies, or whether the decline in recent times was preceded by a rise in previous centuries. This question has the greatest importance for any conclusions about the factors involved. In Roman law girls came of age at 12 (boys at 14), and some writers have linked this with sexual maturity. It must, however, be remembered that this age was a minimum, not an average, since the law had to take account of the earliest possible advent of sexual maturity. The distribution of ages of first menstruation was extremely wide in the populations of the past: it not infrequently preceded 12, yet it occasionally exceeded 20.

The acceleration of male youth in recent times is less well documented than that of females. The available data relates more to height than to genital development. Measurements taken by the military provide a starting point for comparisons over longer periods of time. Norway provides sources stretching back to 1741. These show that adults in 1830 were only slightly taller than in the mid-eighteenth century. Between 1830 and 1875 average height increased by 1.5 cm (0.3 cm per decade), between 1875 and 1935 by about 4 cm (0.6 cm per decade).[5] What seems particularly important is that until the early twentieth century men continued growing until their mid-twenties. Between the ages of 20 and 26 they grew by 3.5 cm in Norway in 1813, by 2 cm in Great Britain in 1880, and by 1 cm in Sweden in 1900.[6] By contrast, young men in the better-off populations of Western Europe today are fully grown by the age of about 18. Nowadays we are 'grown up' in the biological sense many years earlier than in centuries past. Complete development of muscular strength does not run quite parallel to growth in height. Generally it comes about one year later.[7] A French encyclopedia of the mid-sixteenth century actually places this at the 28th year of life.[8] The relatively late development of muscle power in old European societies is of the greatest importance since it has definite social consequences. Work, particularly in an agricultural setting, requires physical strength. Generally, it would only be possible to become a farmer when one was strong enough. Where the norms of an agrarian society linked marriage to the holding of a proper farm job, this in turn meant that men would be married at a relatively late age.

Information regarding height and muscular strength provide important clues about the period of growth in young men, which was much longer than it is today. We can chart the changing age of puberty from the albeit sporadic information available about the breaking of the voice. We know the ages at which the great composers had to leave boys' choirs. In the case of Haydn it was 18, Schubert 16, Bruckner 15, but in the twentieth century it is often as early as 14 or 13.[9] These figures display clearly the acceleration of male development in the last 200 years.

What were the reasons for such a wide variation in the time-scale of sexual maturity and of the somatic phenomena which accompany it? It is a problem which has certainly not been exhaustively researched. However, there are two socially conditioned factors which undoubtedly provide an important starting point: nutrition and work-load. As far as food is concerned, we are thinking less of the quantity or the calorie count than of the composition. The consumption of meat, fat, sugar, fruit and vegetables seems to be particularly significant for the acceleration of physical growth.[10] Meat consumption has always been far higher in the cities than among the rural population, and much more prevalent among the upper classes than among the lower ones. Throughout Europe it has increased sharply since the first half of the nineteenth century. Likewise, sugar is historically a typically urban commodity which has become more important since the nineteenth century. However, the changing nutritional situation does not form a linear process. In particular, the two world wars represent serious interruptions. As a consequence, obvious delays in the pubic development of young people can be observed in each case.[11] The retarding effect of heavy physical labour was acknowledged last century.[12] It helps especially to explain the differences in physical processes between upper and lower classes, and to some extent also between city and country. This can clearly be seen in the stunted development of the children of mountain peasants, who were given a particularly strenuous work-load. The accelerated development since the nineteenth century could no doubt be seen as a result of the technological revolution, against the background of the abolition of child labour and the decline of heavy labour generally. The development of schooling in the twentieth century has, after all, led to the majority of young people being unavailable for work. In these ways, fundamental processes of social change have exerted a profound influence on physical development in the last two centuries. In view of such thoroughgoing changes, it is clearly not possible to regard the processes of physical maturity as anthropological constants. The phenomenon of youth is by no means a one-sided interaction of the somatic and the social in which the former is the constant and the latter the variable.[13] Obviously, there are also influences in the opposite direction. In this sense, the development of the human body is indeed a subject for historical study.

The way in which the biological and the social interact becomes even clearer if we attempt to approach youth from the psychological angle. It is usual to refer to psychological development in youth by the term adolescence, as opposed to puberty, which represents the physical processes.[14] The same question which we asked about puberty must now be asked about adolescence: to what extent is it endogenous and to what extent exogenous? The answer is to some degree predetermined if we define adolescence as 'a psychological coming to terms with sexual development', or 'a child's personality adjusting to puberty'.[15] The psychological mastering of other problems of youth, particularly those which arise from the sociological framework and its historical flux, are thus pushed into the background. In this concentration of interest on the physical aspect there is a danger that adolescence, too, might be interpreted as an anthropological constant.

Non-historical, static conceptions of adolescence have their roots principally in two fields of scholarship: developmental psychology and psychoanalysis. Of particular importance in developmental psychology was the book by Eduard Spranger, *Psychologie des Jugendalters,* published in 1924. Its influence on ideas about the psychological character of youth went far beyond its own field. In hindsight, it is easy to see how far this image of young people, with its pretensions to universal validity, is in fact based on the upper-class high-school pupils of the author's own acquaintance.[16] Likewise, the influence of the *Jugendbewegung,* the German Free Youth Movement of the 1920s, is unmistakable, for example, when the awakening of a feeling for nature is seen as typical of the beginning of adolescence, or especially when it is postulated that a 'sharp distinction between erotic and sexual experience' is a characteristic of the early years, whereby eroticism is defined as an 'aesthetic form of love, which devotes itself without desire—with inner satisfaction—to the beauty of human body and soul.'[17] The Free Youth Movement was by and large responsible for the view commonly held throughout the German-speaking world that certain attitudes and behaviour, which actually belonged to a particular period and class, were to be regarded as the universal, unchanging pattern of youth. The large number of educationalists who emerged from the Movement and the influence they have exerted on educational theory have contributed to the spread of this idea. By contrast, thinking which links adolescent development with social conditions has wielded less influence. Such thinking was indeed to be found among Spranger's contemporaries. Siegfried Bernfeld pointed to the class-related factors in the moulding of young people's emotional development. Charlotte Bühler demonstrated, by a study of girls' diaries through three generations, how the psychological processes are subject to historical change.[18] In his study *Flegeljahre,* the theorist Hans Heinrich Muchow was clearly critical of the 'anthropological constant' strand of development psychology when he later summed up the problem:

> We may therefore hypothesize that in conditions not complicated by civilization, neither emotional puberty nor the so-called *Flegeljahre* (rebellious years) would be recognized or recognizable. Consequently, these do not appear to spring from rules of psychological development which would apply then too. Nor do they seem, as was in the past assumed, to be caused by physiological changes. Rather, they appear to represent symptoms and expressions of the particular historical-cultural setting of a young person. If this hypothesis is correct, it must be possible to demonstrate that in so-called primitive societies, youth may run its course without emotional puberty or teenage rebelliousness.[19]

A more thorough treatment of these 'historical-cultural settings', which would explain specific forms of emotional development in the lives of young people, has, however, only recently been begun.[20]

However, despite the fact that the static non-historical concepts of classical developmental psychology can no longer be maintained, their underlying mode of thinking continues. This becomes clear if we look at an example. Among the 'endogenous developmental mechanisms' which are regarded by psychology as bases for youthful behaviour, several authors mention juvenile wanderlust.[21] Without referring to these authors, but obviously with unquestioning faith in the validity of such generally accepted assumptions, one medievalist sees behind the migrations of the journeymen a 'factor which in popular thinking might be classed as a "thirst for adventure", or an "interest in tourism" '. He writes: 'This reveals a feature of youth in the Middle Ages which remains to be satisfactorily researched. Between childhood and full integration into the adult world, they went on journeys.'[22] Such statements throw up a plethora of questions. If we are dealing with 'a feature of youth', why was it that so many young men, but so few young women, went on journeys? Why did the lads who had learned a trade wander vast distances, while farm lads travelled only short distances, if at all? Why did sons who stood to inherit nothing take to the road, while those who could hope for an inheritance stayed at home? Was it really pleasure which drove them forth? One might think of the Swiss boys in early modern times who served as mercenaries, of whom it was said that their most common complaint was homesickness. Can the migrations of young tradesmen really be classed as 'travel' in the same sense that twentieth-century developmental psychology speaks of, 'wanderlust' as an 'endogenous developmental mechanism'? Certainly, the social historian will wish to state that in European history youth has always been a particularly mobile time of life. But this statement will then have to be linked with specific social considerations: with working conditions, such as farm and domestic service; with family structures, such as neolocal residential patterns; with educational opportunities; and also with moral concepts, such as the way in which various ideas about virginity restricted the freedom of girls to leave home. The elucidation of social factors of this kind should do more to explain the historical facts of the mobility of young people than recourse to the endogenous forces of a supposedly universal psychology of youth.

Similar observations identified a vast number of other attitudes and patterns of behaviour which were, and continue to be, regarded as 'typically youthful' by scholarly writers. We might point here to such stereotypes as the tendency towards idealism, a strong value-system, a strong sense of justice, revolutionary attitudes, the rejection of parents, the quest for alternative role-models, enthusiasm, introspection, the need for solitude, a tendency to brood, a tendency to philosophize, and so on.[23] With all of these typically teenaged characteristics, we must ask how far they can be conceived as constants in the light of comparisons between different social classes, different cultures, and most of all, different epochs. For the majority of the phenomena which developmental psychology has regarded as endogenous, a comparison with the traditional rural situation is enough to show that they cannot be generalized. For the most part they are abstractions drawn from the experience of the urban middle class. Endogenous explanations connected with pubic development are therefore far less plausible than socio-historical explanations. Yet it has to be said that social historians have also been guilty, with very few exceptions, of making too little effort to find sociological explanations for the psycho-structure of youth.

Notes

1. J. M. Tanner, *Wachstum und Reifung des Menschen* (Stuttgart, 1962); A. Schumacher, 'Die sexuelle Reifung', in G. W. Müller (ed.), *Geschlechtsreife und Legitimation zur Zeugung* (Freiburg, 1985), pp. 17ff.; H. Ch. Ehalt, 'Über den Wandel des Termins der Geschlechtsreife in Europa und dessen Ursachen', in *Saeculum*, 36 (1985), pp. 226ff.
2. Cf. the tables in Ehalt, 'Über den Wandel des Termins', pp. 260ff.
3. Thus ibid., pp. 273ff.
4. Thus *Jugend '81* (Opladen, 1982), p. 180.
5. Tanner, *Wachstum und Reifung*, p. 161.
6. Ibid., p. 163.
7. Ibid., p. 218.
8. P. Ariès, *Geschichte der Kindheit,* (Munich, 1975), p. 76.
9. M. Rassem, 'Entdeckung und Formierung der Jugend in der Neuzeit', in *Jugend in der Gesellschaft* (Munich, 1975), p. 98.
10. Ehalt, 'Über den Wandel des Termins', p. 241.
11. Tanner, *Wachstum und Reifung,* pp. 136ff.
12. Friedrich Engels, for example, established this in England. Cf. H. Kreutz, *Soziologie der Jugend* (Munich, 1974), p. 135.
13. The assumption that 'growing up is a universal, clearly defined biological event, and therefore a constant' is to be found in T. Brocher and D. Eckensberger, 'Zur psychoanalytischen Theorie des Jugendalters', in F. Neidhardt et al., *Jugend im Spektrum der Wissenschaften* (Munich, 1970), pp. 121ff.

14. P. Blos, *Adoleszenz. Eine psychoanalytische Interpretation* (Stuttgart, 1973), p. 13.
15. Brocher and Eckensberger, 'Zur psychoanalytischen Theorie', pp. 121ff.
16. See B. Schäfers, *Soziologie des Jungendalters* (Opladen, 1982), pp. 74ff.
17. E. Spranger, *Psychologie des Jugendalters* (Heidelberg, 1924; 1963 edn), p. 85.
18. C. Bühler, *Drei Generationen im Jugendtagebuch* (Jena, 1934).
19. H. H. Muchow, *Flegeljahre: Beiträge zur Psychologie und Pädagogik der 'Vorpubertät'*, 2nd edn (Ravensburg, 1953), pp. 11ff.
20. Cf. U. Herrmann, 'Probleme und Aspekte historischer Ansätze in der Sozialisationsforschung', in K. Hurrelmann and D. Ulrich (eds.), *Handbuch der Sozialisationsforschung* (Weinheim, 1980), pp. 227ff.; U. Herrmann, 'Was heisst "Jugend"?: Jugendkonzeptionen der deutschen Sozialgeschichte', in H. G. Wehling (ed.), *Jugend—Jugendprobleme—Jugendprotest* (Stuttgart, 1982), pp. 11ff.
21. R. Bergius, 'In Richtung auf Eine Psychologische Theorie des Jugendalters', in Neidhardt et al., *Jugend im Spektrum,* p. 62.
22. W. Reininghaus, *Zur Entstehung der Gesellengilden im Spätmittelalter* (Münster, 1980), p. 164.
23. The attempt by developmental psychology to apply such categories to all times and to all social classes can be found, for example, in H. Bertlein, *Jugendleben und soziales Bildungschicksal. Reifungsstil und Bildungserfahrung werkätiger Jugendlicher 1860–1910* (Hanover, 1966).

Questions

1. According to Mitteraur, what factors contribute to the age at which puberty occurs?
2. If puberty occurred in the late teens in early nineteenth century Europe, was there a period of adolescence between childhood and adulthood?
3. What is the impact of puberty on behavior?
4. Many girls in America today show breast development before the age of 10. Does this mean their parents should start reading about how to cope with an adolescent?
5. How are gender and social class important in shaping the adolescent experience?

References and Further Reading

Muuss, R. E. (1970). Adolescent development and the secular trend. *Adolescence, 5,* 267–284.
Mitterauer, M. (1993). *A history of youth.* Oxford: Basil Blackwell.

Chapter 2

Cultural Perspective

In the early 1900s, G. Stanley Hall characterized adolescence as a period of life marked by storm and stress. While this view of adolescence has been the subject of considerable debate, many researchers hold that storm and stress is more likely during adolescence than at other ages (Arnett, 1999). The question that arises is whether the adolescent storm and stress observed by American researchers during the past century is inherent to the period of adolescence itself, or whether it is due to being an adolescent within a particular social context within American society.

Early in the twentieth century anthropologist Margaret Mead noted the omnipresent symptoms of unrest among American adolescents. But she also recognized that "In American civilization, with its many immigrant strains, its dozens of conflicting standards of conduct, its hundreds of religious sects, its shifting economic conditions, this unsettled, disturbed status of youth was more apparent than in the older, more settled civilization of Europe" (Mead, 1974, p. 2). Mead decided to go to another very different civilization to see if adolescent upset was universal to the period between childhood and adulthood.

Mead chose Samoa, an island in the South Sea, as the focus of her field research. Like most anthropologists she selected a simple, preliterate society. She carried out her research in 1924, focusing on 50 adolescent girls. In *Coming of Age in Samoa* (Mead, 1928/1974), Mead reported on the lives of these girls as they came of age. Mead claimed that adolescence in Samoa was not characterized as a period of storm and stress. No great differences set the group of girls who were passing through puberty apart from those who would reach puberty in a few years, or had passed through puberty a few years before. The sole difference Mead noted was that those who were taller were able to do heavier work, or more adult tasks. Girls were faced with few choices, were unhurried, and slipped painlessly from childhood to adulthood doing their share of family work while engaging in casual love affairs. Mead reported that adolescence in Samoa was perhaps the most pleasant stage of the life cycle. While her account may have been a bit idealized (see introduction to Reading 2.3), the tranquility of adolescence in Samoa provides a striking contrast to the stress that is associated with adolescence in American society.

Studies by other anthropologists similarly reveal that adolescence takes a very different form in preindustrial societies from the form it takes in contemporary American society. In preindustrial cultures adolescents do not spend the majority of their time in schools, or in interaction primarily with people of their own age. They spend the majority of their time with adults, with their parents and other kin. Thus the anthropological perspective, like the historical perspective, reveals that adolescent behavior as we know it in America today is not universal, and provides us with a deeper understanding of the societal conditions that may make the period of adolescence a time of stress in our culture.

Additional Resources

References and Suggested Reading

Arnett, J. J. (1999). Adolescent storm and stress, revisited. *American Psychologist, 54*(5), 317–326.

Hall, G. S. (1904). *Adolescence: Its psychology and its relation to physiology, anthropology, sociology, sex, crime, religion, and education (Vols. I & II)*, Englewood Cliffs, NJ: Prentice-Hall.

Mead, M. (1952). Adolescence in primitive and modern society. In Society for the Psychological Study of Social Issues (Ed.) *Readings in social psychology* (Rev. ed.) (pp. 531–539). New York: Henry Holt.

Mead, M. (1928/1974). *Coming of age in Samoa.* New York: William Morrow.

Schlegel, A. (1995). A cross-cultural approach to adolescence. *Ethos, 23*(1), 15–32.

On the Internet

http://www.mead2001.org/

The Margaret Mead Centennial 2001
This Web site has links to all aspects of Margaret Mead's life and work, as well as to other media resources.

http://people.goplay.com/iiviv/

Margaret Mead, Derek Freeman, and the Samoans
The controversy surrounding Margaret Mead and Derek Freeman and their analyses of life in Samoa is presented in this Web site.

Continuities and Discontinuities in Cultural Conditioning

Ruth Benedict, Ph.D., was one of America's leading anthropologists after Franz Boaz's death. She served on the faculty at Columbia University from 1923 to 1948. She was author of numerous books including *Patterns of Culture* (1934) and *Race: Science and Politics* (1943). During World War II she worked for the Bureau of Overseas Intelligence. She died in 1948.

In this classic paper anthropologist Ruth Benedict examines the cultural contribution each society makes in shaping the pathway from childhood to maturity. While it is a fact of nature that an inherent discontinuity exists between the role of child and adult, the way in which this transition occurs varies from one culture to another. No one path is more natural than the next. Our culture is marked by clear extremes between the role demands of children and adults. For example, children are conditioned to assume a submissive role, to show respect and obedience, but once they become adults they are expected to assume the opposite response, to be assertive and controlling. Benedict argues that in our culture contrasts also exist between the nonresponsible and asexual role of children and the responsible, sexual role of adults.

In some cultures the path from childhood to maturity is marked by cultural continuity. Margaret Mead's study of adolescent girls coming of age in Samoa in the 1920s reveals a culture that had little discontinuity between the role of child and adult. Puberty did not bring with it a change in status; a girl was treated no differently after puberty than before puberty. Preadolescent girls had important responsibilities including the care of the young children, and changes in responsibilities were slow and continuous. The transition to becoming a sexual person was marked by continuity. Girls were exposed to adult sexual behavior as children, were knowledgeable about sex, and had their first sexual experiences with a sexually experienced person. Also, sexual experimentation was permitted during adolescence.

Discontinuities that must be bridged at adolescence between two contrasting roles may be a source of stress at adolescence. Some cultures show marked discontinuities between the roles of children and adults, yet have techniques, which our culture lacks, to bridge the discontinuity and ease the strain. In these cultures adolescents are able to swing between incredible extremes of opposite behavior without maladjustment and personality upheaval because the transition is marked by a rite of passage. Upon completion of these rituals, the young person is recognized as a member of adult society, and the young person's duties, responsibilities, and privileges change dramatically. Often the ceremonies leave visible marks of adult status as well, such as circumcision, mutilation, or tattooing. Thus cultural institutions can provide the support necessary to bridge the discontinuity from one role and set of behaviors to another. Benedict argues that our culture lacks such rites or social institutions to bridge the discontinuities between child and adult roles, and then blames adolescents for their failure to pass through this transition in a nonproblematic fashion.

All cultures must deal in one way or another with the cycle of growth from infancy to adulthood. Nature has posed the situation dramatically: on the one hand, the new born baby, physiologically vulnerable, unable to fend for itself, or to participate of its own initiative in the life of the group, and, on the other, the adult man or woman. Every man who rounds out his human potentialities must have been a son first and a father later and the two roles are physiologically in great contrast; he must first have been dependent upon others for his very existence and later he must provide such security for others. This discontinuity in the life cycle is a fact of nature and is inescapable. Facts of nature, however, in any discussion of human problems, are ordinarily read off not at their bare minimal but surrounded by all the local accretions of behavior to which the student of human affairs has become accustomed in his own culture. For that reason it is illuminating to examine comparative material from other societies in order to get a wider perspective on our own special accretions. The anthropologist's role is not to question the facts of nature, but to insist upon the interposition of a middle term between "nature" and "human behavior"; his role is to analyse that term, to document local man-made doctorings of nature and to insist that these doctorings should not be read off in any one culture as nature itself. Although it is a fact of nature that the child becomes a man, the way in which this transition is effected varies from one society to another, and no one of these particular cultural bridges should be regarded as the "natural" path to maturity.

From a comparative point of view our culture goes to great extremes in emphasizing contrasts between the child and the adult. The child is sexless, the adult estimates his virility by his sexual activities; the child must be protected from the ugly facts of life, the adult must meet them without psychic catastrophe; the child must obey, the adult must command this obedience. These are all dogmas of our culture, dogmas which in spite of the facts of nature, other cultures commonly do not share. In spite of the physiological contrasts between child and adult these are cultural accretions.

It will make the point clearer if we consider one habit in our own culture in regard to which there is not this discontinuity of conditioning. With the greatest clarity of purpose and economy of training, we achieve our goal of conditioning everyone to eat three meals a day. The baby's training in regular food periods begins at birth and no crying of the child and no inconvenience to the mother is allowed to interfere. We gauge the child's physiological make-up and at first allow it food oftener than adults, but, because our goal is firmly set and our training consistent, before the child is two years old it has achieved the adult schedule. From the point of view of other cultures this is as startling as the fact of three-year old babies perfectly at home in deep water is to us. Modesty is another sphere in which our child training is consistent and economical; we waste no time in clothing the baby and in contrast to many societies where the child runs naked till it is ceremonially given its skirt or its public sheath at adolescence, the child's training fits it precisely for adult conventions.

In neither of these aspects of behavior is there need for an individual in our culture to embark before puberty, at puberty or at some later date upon a course of action which all his previous training has tabued. He is spared the unsureness inevitable in such a transition.

The illustration I have chosen may appear trivial, but in larger and more important aspects of behavior, our methods are obviously different. Because of the great variety of child training in different families in our society, I might illustrate continuity of conditioning from individual life histories in our culture, but even these, from a comparative point of view, stop far short of consistency and I shall therefore confine myself to describing arrangements in other cultures in which training which with us is idiosyncratic, is accepted and traditional and does not therefore involve the same possibility of conflict. I shall chose childhood rather than infant and nursing situations not because the latter do not vary strikingly in different cultures but because they are nevertheless more circumscribed by the baby's physiological needs than is its later training. Childhood situations provide an excellent field in which to illustrate the range of cultural adjustments which are possible within a universally given, but not so drastic, set of physiological facts.

The major discontinuity in the life cycle is of course that the child who is at one point a son must later be a father. These roles in our society are strongly differentiated; a good son is tractable, and does not assume adult responsibilities; a good father provides for his children and should not allow his authority to be flouted. In addition the child must be sexless so far as his family is concerned, whereas the father's sexual role is primary in the family. The individual in one role must revise his behavior from almost all points of view when he assumes the second role.

I shall select for discussion three such contrasts that occur in our culture between the individual's role as child and as father: 1. responsible—non-responsible status role, 2. dominance—submission, 3. contrasted sexual role. It is largely upon our cultural commitments to these three contrasts that the discontinuity in the life cycle of an individual in our culture depends.

1. Responsible—Non-Responsible Status Role

The techniques adopted by societies which achieve continuity during the life cycle in this sphere in no way differ from those we employ in our uniform conditioning to three meals a day. They are merely applied to other areas of life. We think of the child as wanting to play and the adult as having to work, but in many societies the mother takes the baby daily in her shawl or carrying net to the garden or to gather roots, and adult labor is seen even in infancy from the pleasant security of its position in close contact with its mother. When the child can run about it accompanies its parents still, doing tasks which are essential and yet suited to its powers, and its dichotomy between work and play is not different from what its parents recognize, namely the distinction between the busy day and the free evening. The tasks it is asked to perform are graded to its powers and its elders wait quietly by, not offering to do the task in the child's place. Everyone who is familiar with such societies has been struck by the contrast with our child training. Dr. Ruth Underhill tells me of sitting with a group of Papago elders in Arizona when the man of the house turned to his little three-year old granddaughter and asked her to close the door. The door was heavy and hard to shut. The child tried, but it did not move. Several times the grandfather repeated, "Yes, close the door." No one jumped to the child's assistance. No one took the responsibility away from her. On the other hand there was no impatience, for after all the child was small. They sat gravely waiting till the child succeeded and her grandfather gravely thanked her. It was assumed that the task would not be asked of her unless she could perform it, and having been asked the responsibility was hers alone just as if she were a grown woman.

The essential point of such child training is that the child is from infancy continuously conditioned to responsible social participation while at the same time the tasks that are expected of it are adapted to its capacity. The contrast with our society is very great. A child does not make any labor contribution to our industrial society except as it competes with an adult; its work is not measured against its own strength and skill but against high-geared industrial requirements. Even when we praise a child's achievement in the home we are outraged if such praise is interpreted as being of the same order as praise of adults. The child is praised because the parent feels well disposed, regardless of whether the task is well done by adult standards, and the child acquires no sensible standard by which to measure its achievement. The gravity of a Cheyenne Indian family ceremoniously making a feast out of the little boy's first snowbird is at the furthest remove from our behavior. At birth the little boy was presented with a toy bow, and from the time he could run about serviceable bows suited to his stature were specially made for him by the man of the family. Animals and birds were taught him in a graded series beginning with those most easily taken, and as he brought in his first of each species his family duly made a feast of it, accepting his contribution as gravely as the buffalo his father brought. When he finally killed a buffalo, it was only the final step of his childhood conditioning, not a new adult role with which his childhood experience had been at variance.

The Canadian Ojibwa show clearly what results can be achieved. This tribe gains its livelihood by winter trapping and the small family of father, mother and children live during the long winter alone on their great frozen hunting grounds. The boy accompanies his father and brings in his catch to his sister as his father does to his mother; the girl prepares the meat and skins for him just as his mother does for her husband. By the time the boy is 12, he may have set his own line of traps on a hunting territory of his own and return to his parent's house only once in several months—still bringing the meat and skins to his sister. The young child is taught consistently that it has only itself to rely upon in life, and this is as true in the dealings it will have with the supernatural as in the business of getting a livelihood. This attitude he will accept as a successful adult just as he accepted it as a child.[1]

2. Dominance—Submission

Dominance—submission is the most striking of those categories of behavior where like does not respond to like but where one type of behavior stimulates the opposite response. It is one of the most prominent ways in which behavior is patterned in our culture. When it obtains between classes, it may be nourished by continuous experience; the difficulty in its use between children and adults lies in the fact that an individual conditioned to one set of behavior in childhood must adopt the opposite as an adult. Its opposite is a pattern of approximately identical reciprocal behavior, and societies which rely upon continuous conditioning characteristically invoke this pattern. In some primitive cultures the very terminology of address between father and son, and more commonly, between grandfather and grandson or uncle and nephew, reflects this attitude. In such kinship terminologies one reciprocal expresses each of these relationships so that son and father, for instance, exchange the same term with one another, just as we exchange the same term with a cousin. The child later will exchange it with his son. "Father—son," therefore, is a continuous relationship he enjoys throughout life. The same continuity, backed up by verbal reciprocity, occurs far oftener in the grandfather-grandson relationship or that of mother's brother-sister's son. When these are "joking" relationships, as they often are, travellers report wonderingly upon the liberties and pretensions of tiny toddlers in their dealings with these family elders. In place of our dogma of respect to elders such societies employ in these cases a reciprocity as nearly identical as may be. The teasing and practical joking the grandfather visits upon his grandchild, the grandchild returns in like coin; he would be led to believe that he failed in propriety if he did not give like for like. If the sister's son has right of access without leave to his mother's brother's possessions, the mother's brother has such rights also to the child's possessions. They share reciprocal privileges and obligations which in our society can develop only between age mates.

From the point of view of our present discussion, such kinship conventions allow the child to put in practice from infancy the same forms of behavior which it will rely upon as an adult; behavior is not polarized into a general requirement of submission for the child and dominance for the adult.

It is clear from the techniques described above by which the child is conditioned to a responsible status role that these depend chiefly upon arousing in the child the desire to share responsibility in adult life. To achieve this little stress is laid upon obedience but much stress upon approval and praise. Punishment is very commonly regarded as quite outside the realm of possibility, and natives in many parts of the world have drawn the conclusion from our usual disciplinary methods that white parents do not love their children. If the child is not required to be submissive however, many occasions for punishment melt away; a variety of situations which call for it do not occur. Many American Indian tribes are especially explicit in rejecting the ideal of a child's submissive or obedient behavior. Prince Maximilian von Wied who visited the Crow Indians over a hundred years ago describes a father's boasting about his young son's intractibility even when it was the father himself who was flouted; "He will be a man," his father said. He would have been baffled at the idea that his child should show behavior which would obviously make him appear a poor creature in the eyes of his fellows if he used it as an adult. Dr. George Devereaux tells me of a special case of such an attitude among the Mohave at the present time. The child's mother was white and protested to its father that he must take action when the child disobeyed and struck him. "But why?" the father said, "he is little. He cannot possibly injure me." He did not know of any dichotomy according to which an adult expects obedience and a child must accord it. If his child had been docile he would simply have judged that it would become a docile adult—an eventuality of which he would not have approved.

Child training which brings about the same result is common also in other areas of life than that of reciprocal kinship obligations between child and adult. There is a tendency in our culture to regard every situation as having in it the seeds of a dominance-submission relationship. Even where dominance-submission is patently irrelevant we read in the dichotomy, assuming that in every situation there must be one person dominating another. On the other hand some cultures, even when the situation calls for leadership do not see it in terms of dominance-submission. To do justice to this attitude it would be necessary to describe their political and especially their economic arrangements, for such an attitude to persist must certainly be supported by economic mechanisms that are congruent with it. But it must also be supported by—or what comes to the same thing, express itself in—child training and familial situations.

3. Contrasted Sexual Role

Continuity of conditioning in training the child to assume responsibility and to behave no more submissively than adults is quite possible in terms of the child's physiological endowment if his participation is suited to his strength. Because of the late development of the child's reproductive organs continuity of conditioning in sex experience presents a difficult problem. So far as their belief that the child is anything but a sexless being is concerned, they are probably more nearly right than we are with an opposite dogma. But the great break is presented by the universally sterile unions before puberty and the presumably fertile ones after maturation. This physiological fact no amount of cultural manipulation can minimize or alter, and societies therefore which stress continuous conditioning most strongly sometimes do not expect children to be interested in sex experience until they have matured physically. This is striking among American Indian tribes like the Dakota; adults observe great privacy in sex acts and in no way stimulate children's sexual activity. There need be no discontinuity, in the sense in which I have used the term, in such a program if the child is taught nothing it does not have to unlearn later. In such cultures adults view children's experimentation as in no way wicked or dangerous but merely as innocuous play which can have no serious consequences. In some societies such play is minimal and the children manifest little interest in it. But the same attitude may be taken by adults in societies where such play is encouraged and forms a major activity among small children. This is true among most of the Melanesian cultures of Southeast New Guinea; adults go as far as to laugh off sexual affairs within the prohibited class if the children are not mature, saying that since they cannot marry there can be no harm done.

It is this physiological fact of the difference between children's sterile unions and adults' presumably fertile sex relations which must be kept in mind in order to understand the different mores which almost always govern sex expression in children and in adults in the same culture. A great many cultures with preadolescent sexual license require marital fidelity and a great many which value pre-marital virginity in either male or female arrange their marital life with great license. Continuity in sex experience is complicated by factors which it was unnecessary to consider in the problems previously discussed. The essential problem is not whether or not the child's sexuality is consistently exploited—for even where such exploitation is favored in the majority of cases the child must seriously modify his behavior at puberty or at marriage. Continuity in sex expression means rather that the child is taught nothing it must unlearn later. If the cultural emphasis is upon sexual pleasure the child who is continuously conditioned will be encouraged to experiment freely and pleasurably, as among the Marquesans;[2] if emphasis is upon reproduction, as among the Zuni of New Mexico, childish sex proclivities will not be exploited for the only important use which sex is thought to serve in his culture is not yet possible to him. The important contrast with our child training is that although a Zuni child is impressed with the wickedness of premature sex experimentation he does not run the risk as in our culture of associating this wickedness with sex itself rather than with sex at his age. The adult in our culture has often failed to unlearn the wickedness or the dangerousness of sex, a lesson which was impressed upon him strongly in his most formative years.

Discontinuity in Conditioning

Even from this very summary statement of continuous conditioning the economy of such mores is evident. In spite of the obvious advantages, however, there are difficulties in its way. Many primitive societies expect as different behavior from an individual as child and as adult as we do, and such discontinuity involves a presumption of strain.

Many societies of this type however minimize strain by the techniques they employ, and some techniques are more successful than others in ensuring the individual's functioning without conflict. It is from this point of view that age-grade societies reveal their fundamental significance. Age-graded cultures characteristically demand different behavior of the individual at different times of his life and persons of a like age-grade are grouped into a society whose activities are all oriented toward the behavior desired at that age. Individuals "graduate" publicly and with honor from one of these groups to another. Where age society members are enjoined to loyalty and mutual support, and are drawn not only from the local group but from the whole tribe as among the Arapaho, or even from other tribes as among the Wagawaga of Southeast New Guinea, such an institution has many advantages in eliminating conflicts among local groups and fostering intratribal peace. This seems to be also a factor in the tribal military solidarity of the similarly organized Masai of East Africa. The point that is of chief interest for our present discussion however is that by this means an individual who at any time takes on a new set of duties and virtues is supported not only by a solid phalanx of age mates but by the traditional prestige of the organized "secret" society into which he has now graduated. Fortified in this way, individuals in such cultures often swing between remarkable extremes of opposite behavior without apparent psychic threat. For example, the great majority exhibit prideful and nonconflicted behavior at each stage in the life cycle even when a prime of life devoted to passionate and aggressive head hunting must be followed by a later life dedicated to ritual and to mild and peacable civic virtues.[3]

Our chief interest here, however, is in discontinuity which primarily affects the child. In many primitive societies such discontinuity has been fostered not because of economic or political necessity or because such discontinuity provides for a socially valuable division of labor, but because of some conceptual dogma. The most striking of these are the Australian and Papuan cultures where the ceremony of the "Making of Man" flourishes. In such societies it is believed that men and women have opposite and conflicting powers, and male children, who are of undefined status, must be initiated into the male role. In Central Australia the boy child is of the woman's side and women are tabu in the final adult stages of tribal ritual. The elaborate and protracted initiation ceremonies of the Arunta therefore snatch the boy from the mother, dramatize his gradual repudiation of her. In a final ceremony he is reborn as a man out of the men's ceremonial "baby pouch." The men's ceremonies are ritual statements of a masculine solidarity, carried out by fondling one another's *churingas,* the material symbol of each man's life, and by letting out over one another blood drawn from their veins. After this warm bond among men has been established through the ceremonies, the boy joins the men in the men's house and participates in tribal rites.[4] The enjoined discontinuity has been tribally bridged.

West of the Fly River in southern New Guinea there is a striking development of this Making of Men cult which involves a childhood period of passive homosexuality. Among the Keraki[5] it is thought that no boy can grow to full stature without playing the role for some years. Men slightly older take the active role, and the older man is a jealous partner. The life cycle of the Keraki Indians includes, therefore, in succession, passive homosexuality, active homosexuality and heterosexuality. The Keraki believe that pregnancy will result from post-pubertal passive homosexuality and see evidences of such practices in any fat man whom even as an old man, they may kill or drive out of the tribe because of their fear. The ceremony that is of interest in connection with the present discussion takes place at the end of the period of passive homosexuality. This ceremony consists in burning out the possibility of pregnancy from the boy by pouring lye down his throat, after which he has no further protection if he gives way to the practice. There is no technique for ending active homosexuality, but this is not explicitly tabu for older men; heterosexuality and children however are highly valued. Unlike the neighboring Marindanim who share their homosexual practices, Keraki husband and wife share the same house and work together in the gardens.

I have chosen illustrations of discontinuous conditioning where it is not too much to say that the cultural institutions furnish adequate support to the individual as he progresses from role to role or interdicts the previous behavior in a summary fashion. The contrast with arrangements in our culture is very striking, and against this background of social arrangements in other cultures the adolescent period of *Sturm und Drang* with which we are so familiar becomes intelligible in terms of our discontinuous cultural institutions and dogmas rather than in terms of physiological necessity. It is even more pertinent to consider these comparative facts in relation to maladjusted persons in our culture who are said to be fixated at one or another pre-adult level. It is clear that if we were to look at our social arrangements as an outsider, we should infer directly from our family institutions and habits of child training that many individuals would not "put off childish things"; we should have to say that our adult activity demands traits that are interdicted in children, and that far from redoubling efforts to help children bridge this gap, adults in our culture put all the blame on the child when he fails to manifest spontaneously the new behavior or, overstepping the mark, manifests it with untoward belligerence. It is not surprising that in such a society many individuals fear to use behavior which has up to that time been under a ban and trust instead, though at great psychic cost, to attitudes that have been exercised with approval during their formative years. Insofar as we invoke a physiological scheme to account for these neurotic adjustments we are led to overlook the possibility of developing social institutions which would lessen the social cost we now pay; instead we elaborate a set of dogmas which prove inapplicable under other social conditions.

Notes

1. Landes, Ruth, *The Ojibwa Woman,* Part 1, Youth—Columbia University Contributions to Anthropology, Volume XXXI.
2. Ralph Linton, class notes on the Marquesans.
3. Henry Elkin, manuscript on the Arapaho.
4. Spencer, B., and Gillen, F. J., *The Arunta;* N. Y., Macmillan, 1927 (2 vols.). Róheim, Géza, Psycho-Analysis of Primitive Cultural Types. *Internat. J. Psychoanal.* (1932) 13: 1–224—in particular, Chapter III, on the Aranda, The Children of the Desert.
5. Williams, Francis, E., *Papuans of the Trans-Fly;* Oxford, 1936.

Questions

1. Benedict wrote this paper in the 1930s. Is her characterization of American society true today in terms of the discontinuities she describes in dominant/submissive, responsible/nonresponsible, contrasted sexual roles? Is it true for some adolescents?
2. What is the function of a rite of passage?

3. Do we have any rites of passage in this society?
4. How do the rites of passage we have differ in function from the rites Benedict describes?

References and Further Reading

Barry, H., III, & Schlegel, A. (1980). Early childhood precursors of adolescent initiation ceremonies. *Ethos, 8,* 132–145.

Burton, R. V., & Whiting, J. W. M. (1961). The absent father and cross-sex identity. *Merrill-Palmer Quarterly of Behavior and Development, 7,* 85–95.

Mead, M. (1928/1974). *Coming of age in Samoa.* New York: William Morrow.

Muuss, R. E. (1970). Puberty rites in primitive and modern societies. *Adolescence, 5,* 109–128.

Whiting, J. W. M., Kluckhohn, R., & Anthony, A. S. (1958). The function of male initiation ceremonies at puberty. In E. E. Maccoby, T. M. Newcomb, & E. L. Hartley (Eds.). *Readings in social psychology* (pp. 359–370). New York: Holt, Rinehart & Winston.

Young, F. W. (1962). The function of male initiation ceremonies: A cross-cultural test of an alternate hypothesis. *American Journal of Sociology, 67,* 379–396.

2.2   Alice Schlegel and Herbert Barry III, 1991

Looking at Adolescent Socialization Across Cultures

Alice Schlegel, Ph.D., is a professor of anthropology at the University of Arizona. She is currently investigating adolescent socialization and the evolution of social forms. She is author of *Adolescence: An Anthropological Inquiry* (with Herbert Barry III, 1991).

Herbert Barry III, Ph.D., is a professor of anthropology at the University of Pittsburgh. He wrote *Actions of Alcohol* (with Henrik Wallgren, 1970), and *Adolescence: An Anthropological Inquiry* (with Alice Schlegel, 1991). His research interests include ethnology and political psychology.

Apart from Margaret Mead's classic study, *Coming of Age in Samoa,* anthropologists have devoted relatively little time to the study of adolescence. The most comprehensive work on the topic was written by Alice Schlegel and Herbert Barry, *Adolescence: An Anthropological Inquiry,* based on a worldwide representative sample of 186 preindustrial societies. (Details of this standard cross-cultural sample can be found in Murdock & White, 1980).

Schlegel and Barry begin their examination of adolescence by addressing the question of whether or not a social adolescence—a period between childhood and adulthood in which adolescents are treated differently and behave differently from children or adults—exists in all societies. Schlegel and Barry found that adolescence as a social stage does exist across cultures, but not in the same form that we know it in this society, and it is not of the same duration. Adolescence is relatively short in preindustrial societies, as marriage often takes place much earlier, and it is shorter for girls than for boys because girls may be moved into marriage at an earlier age than boys.

Schlegel and Barry did not find commonalities to the experiences of persons aged 12–17 across the preindustrial cultures. They argue that, "the behavior and treatment of adolescents varies according to subsistence needs and constraints, property ownership or its absence, the structure of the family and the community, and anticipations of adult life" (Schlegel & Barry, 1991, p. 200). They found wide variation to exist in adolescent behavior both among preindustrial societies and among modernizing societies (societies of formerly traditional people undergoing a transition to industrial production).

Adolescents do not assume the same roles in our society as they do in preindustrial societies. Adolescents in our society are not full-time workers and are required to attend school. Thus they spend most of their time apart from parents and family members in the company of their peers. Schlegel and Barry found, by contrast, that adolescents in preindustrial cultures spend their time in the home working alongside adults of the same sex, and they are contributors to a larger system of social organization. Also, their lives are fully integrated into those of their families and communities. While in this culture adolescence is marked by uncertainties, self-doubts, and stress, these characteristics are not found in preindustrial societies.

Parameters of Adolescence

Information is available on the presence or absence of an adolescent social stage for 173 societies for boys and for 175 for girls. Of these, all societies have this stage for boys; only one society may lack it for girls, this being the Gros Ventre (Flannery 1953), where girls are married by about age 10. Because the Gros Ventre believe that sexual intercourse is necessary for menstruation to begin and expect wives to be virgins, marriage must occur before menarche. The child bride is reported to have the legal and social status of a woman and is expected to perform the tasks of an adult. If she is a junior wife in a polygynous household, her older co-wives are likely to be her sisters or close kin. While she may have adult status in the community and is alleged to take her turn sleeping with her husband, her co-wives treat her as a little sister, which softens the abruptness of the change for so young a child. (The information is inadequate to confirm the one brief report on the Gros Ventre girl.) All other societies in the sample recognize an adolescent stage for both sexes.

The boundaries and descriptive characteristics of adolescence must be established. To do this, coders were asked to determine beginning and ending ages of adolescence for each society, rituals marking beginning and ending, if any, and whether adolescence was followed by an intervening youth stage before full adulthood.

A difficulty encountered in any anthropological study of the life cycle is that ages of people are rarely given in ethnographic monographs. In fact, they are often unknown by the people themselves, social role being determined more by level of maturity than by chronological age. To avoid this difficulty, this study relates social adolescence to biological adolescence rather than to any specific age. Starting age of social adolescence is measured as beginning before puberty, at puberty, or after puberty, and ending age is in early adolescence (up to about two years after puberty), mid-adolescence (about two to four years after), or late adolescence (about four to seven years after).

It is possible to make some very rough estimates of age of puberty, defined as first menstruation for girls and first ejaculation for boys. Puberty usually occurs about two years later for boys than for girls in modern industrial societies.[1] If ages of adolescence are given, but no typical age of menarche is estimated by the author, the coders were instructed to estimate 14 as age of girls' puberty unless there is evidence to the contrary. This age is derived from Eveleth and Tanner (1976: 214–215), Table 15. The populations in that study closest in characteristics to the populations in the Standard Sample, peoples in Africa, Asia, and India, range from about 13 to 15 in median age of menarche.[2] We make no attempt to specify any particular chronological ages for social adolescence, nor does the study depend upon such specification. As beginning and ending ages for every society were coded by the same pair of coders, who arrived at consensus during the training period, we have every confidence that the *relative* ages in the study are correct assessments of the variation among cultures and the difference between girls and boys. By these criteria, starting age for both sexes is predominantly at or just about at puberty, 72 percent (173) for boys, 82 percent (175) for girls; the remainder start before puberty, except for one case for girls after puberty.

The movement into adolescence is often marked ritually. Data on this code, combined with that of earlier studies by Schlegel and Barry (1980a, 1980b) using the same sample, show that either a public adolescent initiation ceremony is conducted or the transition is signified in some other ritual form in 68 percent of 130 societies for which there is information on boys and in 79 percent of 126 societies with information on girls. The ceremonies are often major public events, more often for boys but occasionally for girls. Their themes express the important contribution to society the young person is expected to make in his or her future life: productivity is the most common theme among foragers, although fertility is also an important theme in girls' ceremonies, while fertility is a primary theme for both sexes in horticultural societies. (Advanced agricultural societies tend not to have public initiation ceremonies.) Thus, for about half the cases in this sample, the break between childhood and adolescence is given ritual recognition and may be the basis for communitywide ceremonies.

Ending age for boys is most commonly about two to four years after puberty, with 35 percent of 178 cases falling there and another 31 percent within two years after puberty. This estimate places the ending age for most societies at between 16 and 18, coming later for the remainder. For girls, 63 percent of 178 societies end adolescence within two years after puberty, or by about age 16. Because marriage almost always marks the end of adolescence in this sample, moving the individual into adult productive and reproductive relationships, it is safe to assume that adolescence is rather short in most societies in the sample, particularly for girls.

Modern society has nothing that corresponds to a full adolescent initiation ceremony that marks the total social transformation out of childhood. One could argue that transition rituals exist within certain domains, however. For example, the modern bar mitzvah has little effect on the way the adolescent boy is treated in society, but it does mark the end of childhood within the religious sphere of Judaism. Modern society pays more attention to the end of adolescence. For Americans, graduation from high school serves as a ritual of graduation from adolescence. Young people who do not graduate must enter the next stage without ritual recognition, although induction into military service may signify this transition for some.

In most societies, adulthood follows adolescence, but in a minority there is a youth stage before full adulthood is reached: 25 percent of 168 societies have this for boys, and 20 percent of 166 societies have it for girls. This stage exists in some traditional societies, notably those in which there is a postadolescent age-grade for young men serving in the army of the traditional state. Eisenstadt (1956: 142ff.) discussed such age grading for African militaristic states like the Swazi, Zulu, and Tswana, whose young men spent a period of years soldiering and performing public works. He contrasted Sparta, which had such an age-grade for men between ages 20 and 30, with Athens, which had only a short period of service between ages 18 and 20.

Though a youth stage appears to be most common in traditional or modern states, some evidence exists for such a stage in certain tribal societies such as the Abipone of South America (Dobrizhoffer 1822), nomads with no political organization beyond the small local community. Unfortunately, the data are sparse and indicate only that young men do not marry until about age 30, at which time they become full social adults. Very little is known about the content of this stage. Given the frequency of warfare among the Abipone, full adulthood is probably delayed to facilitate the establishment of a warrior-class of unmarried men, as in the more complex traditional states.

A youth stage characterized many segments of early modern Europe as well. After a period of apprenticeship during the teenage years, young townsmen aspiring to be master craftsmen went through a period as journeymen, typically between the ages of about 18 and 26. Not yet married, they were granted neither productive nor reproductive adult status; such status came not at a specific age but rather when they were able to assume the tasks and responsibilities of full adulthood (cf. Burke 1978). In contemporary society the youth stage occurs between high school and the concomitant or sequential events of full employment and marriage. The social timetable (Elder 1975b) for modern society is to complete one's education, settle into a job, perhaps after a period of experimentation with several occupations or a stint in military service, and then marry. Research indicates that people who experience these events out of sequence may suffer adverse effects in terms of decreased lifetime earnings (Hogan 1980).

A fair bit of ink has been spilled concerning the term *adolescence*. Although the *Oxford English Dictionary* traces it to the 15th century (Bakan 1972), it may have differed in meaning then. However, the residents of 14th century Montaillou, a village in the French Pyrenees, did use the term in its modern sense. Between the ages of 12 and 14, children ceased being referred to as *puer* and became *adulescens* or *juvenis* in the records. They kept these terms until adulthood, which came at marriage for girls, not long after menarche, and after age 18 or so for boys (LeRoy Ladurie 1978: 215–216).

Contrary to Bakan (1972), we do not believe that adolescence as a social condition and a social fact has been created by the term *adolescence*. Nor do social facts inevitably give rise to classificatory labels, although labels may increase the awareness of social facts and contribute to the ease of discourse about them. In other words, adolescence as a social fact can exist without a term to distinguish adolescents as a definable class of social beings. Nevertheless, it is of interest to know whether only Western society applies such a label.

Information is limited in the ethnographies, as ethnographers are more likely to report the presence of such terms than their absence. The fact that terms are reported for 14 out of 39 societies for which there is information on boys and for 17 out of 41 societies for girls does not indicate widespread terminological recognition of this stage. However, it does indicate that such recognition is not limited to modern society.

One example comes from the North American Navajo, who call a girl *ch'ikééh* and a boy *tsilkééh* between childhood and marriage. Another comes from the Trobriand Islands of Melanesia, whose adolescent life was richly described by Malinowski (1932: 60). In the Trobriand Islands, the large breaks come between the periods of life characterized by different reproductive status: *wadi*, prereproductive children of both sexes; *ta'u* (male) and *vivila* (female), persons of reproductive capacity; and the post-reproductive elderly (no term given). Within these major periods, stages are designated, each with its name. The boy from puberty to marriage is known as *to'ulatile*, the girl as *nakapugula*.

In addition to labelling the adolescent stage, the Trobrianders see it as highly distinctive, a time when young people are "the flower of the village" (Malinowski 1932: 64). However, the Kalapalo of Brazil, who also regard their adolescents as the epitome of beauty, have no terms for adolescence (Ellen Basso, personal communication). Further, there is no evidence that the Navajo, who do have such terms, consider this period as being in any way special. It appears that some peoples are more concerned about labelling life stages than others, for reasons having less to do with the distinctiveness of the life stages than with ideas about the need to delineate cosmic or social order. Labelling or not labelling social facts may be more reflective of the symbolic structure of the culture than the social structure of the society.

Labelling can be done visually as well as verbally. One signifier of social distinction is distinctiveness in dress, hair style, face painting, or ornamentation, all visual markers. For boys, changes in visual markers from childhood occur in 86 percent of 102 societies, while for girls they occur in 88 percent of 118 societies. Such markers may exist for one sex only. Among the Chatino Indians of Oaxaca, Mexico, girls move out of childhood when they receive a large rebozo, a kind of shawl, to replace the small rebozo of childhood. The large one enables them to carry babies about, a primary task of adolescent girls. Boys, however, do not change their appearance; their exit from childhood is signified only behaviorally, by their entering the ceremonial organization of the village where they act as pages to the adult men (Eva Zavaleta Greenberg, personal communication).

Visual markers to distinguish adolescents from adults are less common, being coded for only 32 percent of 100 societies for boys and 35 percent of 118 societies for girls. An example of distinctive adolescent appearance, differing from that of either children or adults, is the change in hairstyle of the Hopi girl. As a child, she wears the miniature version of the butterfly hairstyle, for which the hair is formed into bunches on each side of the head like butterfly wings. After a small private adolescent initiation ceremony, she puts her hair into large butterfly wings, set with the aid of wicker hoops. This is, in fact, a visual announcement that she is ready for courtship. Upon marriage, she assumes the hairstyle of adult women, in which the hair is worn in two braidlike ropes. Boys have no such visual markers. Incidentally, the Hopi have no terms for adolescence, the adolescent being classified terminologically with the child until the girl marries and the boy undergoes his initiation into a men's society. Nevertheless, visual markers for girls and certain behaviors for both sexes are distinctive of this stage.

Relations with the Family

In most societies of this sample, adolescents spend the majority of their waking hours with adults of the same sex—in 66 percent of 161 cases for boys and in 84 percent of 160 cases for girls—and the setting for most of their activities is the home. Relations with family members are assessed in separate segments of the code and were independently coded by different sets of coders, with the results of each supporting the other. One segment ranks agents of socialization in the family by their importance in teaching adolescents and having some control over their activities. For boys, the father is the single most important agent in 79 percent of 173 cases, while the mother is most important for girls in 85 percent of 171 cases. The other segment measures contact, intimacy, subordination, and conflict on an 11-point scale. The data reflect both the nature of the human family as an integrated unit comprising both sexes and the fact that some degree of sexual separation is widely present, even in the home. Of the societies in this sample for which there are data, girls have both more contact and greater intimacy with older female kin (excluding sisters), mothers, and grandmothers than boys have with older male kin (excluding brothers), fathers, and grandfathers. Contact and intimacy with older siblings of the same sex are similar for girls and boys.

Relations with the Community

Adolescents are quite commonly closely integrated in adult family activities, and many participate substantially in adult community life, assuming new roles in the community. Out of 78 societies for which there is information on boys, new roles are undertaken in 64 (82 percent). These roles are economically productive, military, religious, or contributive to community welfare; no cases were recorded of new political roles. Girls are shown to have less community involvement: out of 45 societies, they take on new roles in 27 (60 percent), these being new religious roles in 14 cases. Examples of new community roles are the military activities that adolescent boys perform in a number of tribal groups. In the South and East African age-graded societies, adolescent boys are not generally warriors themselves, as the warrior grade comprises slightly older youths, but adolescent boys typically receive military training.

Adolescents of both sexes may for the first time take a meaningful part in community rituals. This is the case for the Chatino boys mentioned earlier, who enter the cargo system—the system of religious obligations—at this time. For a small number of societies, there is information on the response of the community to adolescents' new roles. Recognition can be given through such rewards as payment, feasts, or public praise. In a few cases, there is conscious selection or training for community leadership during adolescence.

In the modern world, we expect a certain portion of our adolescents to be delinquents, i.e., to exhibit behavior that violates social standards. However, what may be delinquent in European or American nations might not be so in traditional societies. Information on the question of regular, expected antisocial behavior—not including the occasional deviant—has been coded, framed in terms of what the society itself considers disruptive. Out of 54 societies for which there is information, patterned antisocial behavior of boys occurs in 24, and it occurs in 6 out of 34 societies for girls. It occurs among adolescent boys more than among younger boys in 61 percent of 31 cases and among adolescent boys more than among adult men in 59 percent of 29 cases. For boys but not for girls, adolescence tends to be the stage during which antisocial behavior most often occurs, if it occurs at all. Violence against persons and theft are more common than destruction of property. Punishment for misbehavior of any kind is fairly evenly divided between mild and severe, although it is ignored or only mildly admonished in 23 percent of 69 cases for boys and in 25 percent of 61 cases for girls.

One form of disruptive behavior is running away, and ethnographers are more likely to note its presence than its absence. For societies with information on this feature, it has been recorded for 61 percent of 36 cases for girls and for 55 percent of 31 cases for boys. Nisa, a !Kung adolescent, attempted to avoid a distasteful marriage by running into the forest and remaining there overnight in order to convince her parents of her feelings (Shostak 1983). The first author has been told of several cases of Hopi girls who used this tactic to gain relief from a tense relationship with their mothers. In these cases, they took shelter with relatives, who finally persuaded them to return.

Another form of antisocial behavior, widespread among tribesmen, is the practice of witchcraft, malevolence through magical means. In general, adolescents seem no more likely to be either victims or practitioners of witchcraft than persons of other ages.

Relations with Peers

[We have found that] the peer group is more salient for boys than for girls. This hypothesis is supported by the frequency distributions of the data. Although for both sexes most time is spent with adults of the same sex, the peer group is the single primary locus of boys' waking hours in 17 percent of 161 cases with information but in only 5 percent of 160 cases for girls. The importance of peer groups relative to the family and other social groups has been rated in 91 societies for boys and in 68 societies for girls. For boys, the figures are: more important, 27 percent; equal, 40 percent; and less important, 33 percent. For girls, the comparable figures are 7 percent, 24 percent, and 69 percent respectively. Evidence from other ratings leads us to suspect that this rating overestimates the "more important" category for boys. Nevertheless, peer groups clearly seem to be more important in boys' lives than in girls', while involvement with older kin of the same sex is greater for girls. Data on contact with peers, coded independently from importance of peer group, support this: the mean score for boys is 6.1 for 126 cases, whereas it is 5.0 for 101 cases for girls.

Peer group size also varies between the sexes. Boys' peer groups are large, numbering about 14 or more, in 52 percent of 88 cases with information and are small, about three to six, in 20 percent. Girls' groups, however, are large in 37 percent of 68 cases and small in 34 percent. Boys' peer groups more often have names than do girls' groups. For both sexes, time with peers is most commonly spent in leisure activities. Recreational activities are not confined to peer groups, however; both boys and girls are rated as "often" participating with children and with adults. Young people may get together in work groups. Several Hopi girls, for example, sometimes take the corn they have to grind over to one girl's house and have a grinding party, thus lightening the burdensome task with talk and laughter. Adolescent herd boys in African cattle-owning societies commonly herd together, away from the eyes of the village.

Sexuality and Reproduction

For the large majority of societies, marriage choice is made during adolescence. Age of first marriage relative to puberty tends to differ between girls and boys. In 60 percent of 124 societies with information, girls are married within two years after puberty. Boys are married between two and four years after puberty in 45 percent of 132 societies, earlier than that in 33 percent. This puts the most common chronological ages of marriage roughly at 14 to 16 for girls, 16 to 20 for boys, if our estimates of age of puberty are accurate.

Unless young people are married at or before puberty, the question of adolescent sexuality arises. Ethnographers give fairly extensive accounts of premarital sexual activity. In the majority of societies in this sample, heterosexual intercourse is either tolerated or expected with a limited number of partners: in 65 percent of 155 societies with information for boys and in 60 percent of 163 societies for girls. Some controls are exerted, however; only a few societies tolerate promiscuity, and the partner is most frequently expected to be another adolescent: in 61 percent of 141 cases with information for boys and in 61 percent of 140 cases for girls.

Homosexual activity is also permitted in some societies, although these data are less complete; instances of such activity are more likely to be reported by ethnographers than the absence or prohibition of homosexuality. There is evidence in 25 societies for boys and in 17 for girls that homosexual relations are tolerated or expected.

The Self

Adolescence is a time of new or intensified learning for both sexes in the skill areas identified: work, warfare (boys only), religion, arts and games, cognition, and social interaction. Adolescents tend to do work similar to that of adults and to dress like them but to have different leisure-time activities. Adolescence is also a time when young people are given more productive property to manage than previously in 44 percent of 102 societies with information for boys, 31 percent of 74 societies for girls. Success in adolescence is preponderantly in the area of work. The good worker gets social acclaim and is also likely to attract a satisfactory spouse later. However, physical skill is also important in determining success for boys; the activities are likely to be wrestling or competitive games. For girls, sexual attributes assume importance.

If adolescence is a time during which various skills and social roles are being learned, it is also a time during which the inculcation of character traits continues from childhood or is intensified. The traits selected for measurement were fortitude, impulsiveness, aggressiveness, obedience, sexual expression, sexual restraint, self-reliance, conformity to group, trust, competitiveness, responsibility, and achievement. Mean scores for these traits are primarily of interest in comparing girls with boys. For most, the difference is less than one point on an 11-point scale. The traits with a greater difference are aggressiveness, self-reliance, and competitiveness, with boys receiving higher mean scores in all cases. These distributions argue against radically different socialization of the sexes for most societies.

Adolescents in this sample are not free from social pressures. There is a widespread belief that adolescence in tribal or peasant communities flows smoothly, without competition for resources (which can include a desirable spouse and powerful in-laws) and without areas in which choice must be exercised. This notion is belied by the data from this study. In only a small minority of societies is there no increase over childhood in responsibility. Occupational choice must be made by at least some boys in 65 percent of 150 societies with information and by some girls in 43 percent of 141 societies. An adolescent may have to decide whether to become, for instance, a shaman, midwife, berdache (institutionalized transvestite), or master carver. Because training for a specialized role often means a longer period of apprenticeship to a master, this choice can be costly in terms of time and goods. It is not made lightly. In many societies, there is pressure for excellence rather than mere competence.

Young people may also have to take the initiative in finding a spouse, even though the choice often has to be approved by others. This is the case in 58 percent of 174 societies with information for boys and in 47 percent of 169 societies for girls. Courtship in tribal societies can be as frustrating and as shadowed by fear of rejection as it is for modern Western teenagers.

Adolescence is a time during which adult character is established in the large majority of societies. Memories are long in small communities, and one carries one's adolescent reputation into adulthood.

* * * *

The frequency distributions of the data strongly suggest that an adolescent social stage is very widespread and possibly universal for boys. Such a stage is usual for girls, although there are exceptions. Early marriage, even before menarche, does not necessarily preclude social adolescence, however; the married girl's activities may differ markedly from those of older women, and sexual relations may be delayed until some time after puberty. For any particular societies that schedule life events in a sequence different from that followed by the majority of societies, analysis has to be done on a case-by-case basis.

Compared to modern Western society, the societies in this sample tend to display a rather brief adolescence, particularly for girls. It is necessary to prolong adolescence when adult roles require lengthy training, and role training in many societies may be easier for girls than for boys. Whether in the homes of their fathers or their husbands, women remain subordinate to men in most of the societies in this sample. As women age, they assume considerable autonomy and authority within their domains, but the sphere within which they make decisions is generally more restricted than that of men. When men hold power, adolescent boys are preparing to make the transition from child subordinates to adult peers. Girls, however, move from greater to lesser subordination within the society at large, even in those cases in which a middle-aged or elderly woman is the family matriarch. For role training, then, boys may often need a longer adolescence than girls.

The brevity of the adolescent stage for girls is related to another factor. In many places, nubile girls are political capital for the people who control their marriages, usually their fathers. Fecundity is a critical issue in these societies, for it is through his own increase—via his wife or wives—that a man assures himself of loyal supporters in his middle and later years. He expands his network of social alliances through the marriages of his children. Furthermore, in many horticultural societies and some pastoral ones, multiple wives are an economic asset: polygyny has been demonstrated to be significantly associated with high female contribution to subsistence (Schlegel and Barry 1986). For social reasons, and often economic ones as well, marriageable women are in high demand. Delaying the marriage of a daughter for many years after puberty would be letting an asset go to waste, unless there are compelling reasons to postpone marriage.

The adolescent stage itself not only is midway between childhood and adulthood but also shares some characteristics of both stages. While the adolescents in this sample are childlike in their domestic subordination and lack of political involvement in the community, they are likely to dress like adults and to perform adult productive tasks. Their absence from community decision-making does not indicate that they fail to contribute to the community, for they may take on responsibilities, particularly in religious or military activities. Although they may be sexually active, they are not reproductive.

The pattern of relationships with family, community, and peers among adolescents in this sample follows the model offered [elsewhere]. The greater contact and intimacy shown by girls with adult female kin, compared to that of boys with adult male kin, indicates greater involvement among females of all ages and greater segregation of men from boys. Conversely, involvement with peers is generally greater for boys than for girls. Although for both sexes the family is undoubtedly the most important social group and the peer group secondary in the majority of societies in the sample, a gender difference appears in the degree of involvement in these two social units.

How characteristic this gender difference is of modern society is hard to say. In the United States, for example, there may be considerable variation among ethnic groups and social classes. In the middle and upper classes, where child labor is not needed at home or in family enterprises, adolescents of both sexes are likely to spend a good deal of time with their age-mates, and the difference between boys and girls may be less marked. In working-class households or in families of Hispanic or of recent Middle Eastern or Asian extraction, girls may be expected to spend their after-school hours at home while boys may be away from home, working or at leisure with their peers.

Although adolescence worldwide might not have the *Sturm und Drang* quality attributed to it in some of the more florid 19th and 20th century literature, adolescence in this sample displays points of stress that may be widely characteristic of this stage. Life becomes a serious business at this time, for young people are under the observation of their elders as future children-in-law. Decisions made during these years can have far-reaching consequences. In small closed societies, adolescence is not just a period of training for adult life; it is the time during which the ground is prepared for adult social relations with the same people who are currently one's peers. There is no escape, no chance to begin anew somewhere else. What one will be in 10 years is strongly colored by what one is today. It is likely that adolescents are aware of this as they struggle to cope with the social pressures to conform and often to excel.

Questions

1. What are the difficulties that arise in studying adolescence in another culture?
2. How does adolescence differ in preindustrial cultures from adolescence as we know it in America today in terms of:
   a. length of adolescence
   b. autonomy from the family
   c. involvement with peers
   d. development of an identity
   e. integration into the adult community
3. How does gender define the adolescent experience?
4. Autonomy, identity, and intimacy are developmental tasks of adolescence in American society. Are they developmental tasks of adolescence in preindustrial societies?

5. What cultural conditions make adolescence more stressful in our society than in preindustrial societies?

References and Further Reading

Köbben, A. J. F. (1973). Comparativists and non-comparativists in anthropology. In R. Naroll, & R. Cohen (Eds.) *A handbook of method in cultural anthropology* (pp. 581–596). New York: Columbia University Press.

Mead, M. (1928/1974). *Coming of age in Samoa.* New York: William Morrow.

Murdock, G. P., & White, D. R. (1980). The standard cross-cultural sample and its codes. In A. Schlegel and H. Barry (Eds.) *Cross-cultural samples and codes* (pp. 3–44). Pittsburgh: University of Pittsburgh Press.

2.3   James E. Côté, 1994

Coming of Age in Contemporary Samoa

James E. Côté, Ph.D., is professor of sociology at the University of Western Ontario, Canada. He has authored *Adolescent Storm and Stress: An Evaluation of the Mead-Freeman Controversy* (1994), *Generation on Hold: Coming of Age in the Late Twentieth Century* (1994), and *Arrested Adulthood: The Changing Nature of Maturity and Identity* (2000). With his colleague Anton Allahar, he coauthored *Richer and Poorer: The Structure of Inequality in Canada* (1998).

For many decades Mead's images of coming in age in Samoa were widely popularized and accepted (Mead, 1928/1974). In 1983 an Australian anthropologist, Derek Freeman, published a book, *Margaret Mead and Samoa: The Making and Unmaking of an Anthropological Myth*, attacking Mead's conclusions, and claiming she was fundamentally in error about the nature of coming of age in Samoa. Considerable controversy ensued, but because Freeman published his book after Mead's death, Mead herself was unfortunately unable to participate in the debate in her own defense.

James Côté (1994) wrote a book analyzing the Mead-Freeman controversy in which he points out several important facts to consider in evaluating both Mead's and Freeman's conclusions. First, Mead did her field work in the 1920s. She spent 9 months in Samoa studying 50 girls from three neighboring villages, and focused most of her time on the households in which adolescent girls lived. Freeman did his research in Samoa decades later, beginning in the 1940s. He spent 2 years in Samoa where he was adopted by a titled family head, or chief, and was given access to the village assemblies of family heads who have responsibility for daily economic and social activities, work projects, food distribution, and meting out punishment. Freeman's reference group was the village chiefs.

Freeman did further field work in Samoa in the 1960s. There has been a trajectory of social change in Samoa over the course of the twentieth century, set in motion by contact with the West and the impact of missionaries. Côté argues that "sociological investigation of the history of adolescence in Samoa reveals a fascinating yet depressing saga of the demise of a well-structured and meaningful adolescence before contact with the West, and the creation of a conflictual and alienating adolescence after a century and a half of contact with the West. By denying the relevance of social change in Samoa for the Mead-Freeman controversy, Freeman overlooked the possibility that the turmoil he witnessed among Samoan youth in the 1960s was a product of this change" (Côté, 1994, p. 65–66).

Mead described Samoan society as casual and unhurried. Adolescent-parent relationships were not marked by conflict. Adolescent girls faced few choices in terms of belief systems or what adult roles they might assume in society. Côté's description of Samoa in the 1990s provides a stark contrast to Mead's description of coming of age in Samoa. By examining the factors that changed over the course of the century, we get a better understanding of the cultural conditions that produce stress and conflict at adolescence.

Western Influence and the Cultural Disenfranchisement of Samoan Youth

What has been forgotten in the furor surrounding [Derek] Freeman's critique of [Margaret] Mead's study is the plight of young Samoans currently struggling to come of age. As we have seen, the young people of Samoa have lost most of the institutions that once guided them on a sure path from childhood to adulthood. The degeneration of these institutions began when the missionaries took it upon themselves to drive "Satan" from the islands. Inadvertently acting as the "shocktroops of capitalism," many missionaries set out to instill values and attitudes conducive with wage labor and capital accumulation.

The changes they set in motion have been accelerating in [the] latter part of the 20th century with the entrenchment of mass consumption, mass production, mass education, and mass communications. Moreover, mass transportation has removed protective barriers from Samoan culture, both physical and psychological, so the basic conception of the realm of possibility has been drastically altered for the young Samoan. Most certainly, missionary influences are not responsible for all that has happened in the past 150 years to young Samoans, but the part they played in setting the stage is significant nonetheless.[1]

In a sense, the crux of the current "youth problem" in Samoa is that although the *conception* of the realm of possibility has changed for many young people in Samoa, the *reality* of what is possible has not changed significantly. What emerged from the sociohistorical analysis . . . is that at the heart of these changes is a "cultural disenfranchisement" of young people by which they have been robbed of their rich cultural heritage, and given poor "Western" economic prospects in return.

For example, the propitious institution that once saw to the coming of age of young women (the *aualuma*) was stripped of its mandate soon after the missionaries were securely established, probably because it offended missionaries' puritanical and patriarchal values regarding the autonomy of women—sexual and otherwise. Young women of contemporary Samoa are not only denied this aspect of their heritage, they also face a denial that there was anything different for Samoan women before contact with the West. Thus, they have lost part of their cultural heritage and been misled about their loss. As is seen in this [selection], there is now a "crisis" in gender roles in contemporary Samoa associated with a loss in the status of women introduced by Western religious and economic influences. Interestingly, it is this turn of events in which Mead's work has been caught, because Freeman took up the cause of a denial of Samoa's non-Christian past.

In addition, changes initiated by the missionaries that set the stage for the introduction of the wage economy eventually led to the disintegration of the auspicious institution that saw to the coming of age of young men (the *'aumaga*). In 1928, Mead predicted that should the *'aumaga* ever be disbanded "Samoan village life would have to be entirely reorganized," because the entire village depends on their work and support of ceremonies (p. 76). Moreover, Mead (1928) predicted that Western influences would be devastating for Samoan culture:

> economic instability, poverty, the wage system, the separation of the worker from his land and his tools, modern warfare, industrial disease, the abolition of leisure, the irksomeness of bureaucratic government—these have not yet invaded an island without resources worth exploiting. (pp. 276–277)

It is difficult to say what the ultimate outcome of these changes will be, but it is hard to be optimistic about how well things will turn out in the short run. What is clear, as is seen later, is that many young people in contemporary Samoa no longer have the benefit of the benign transition from childhood to adulthood described by Mead. The structures that have replaced the traditional coming-of-age institutions leave much to be desired in terms of guiding the young from childhood to adulthood. Unfortunately, along with other Western practices, Samoan society has increasingly adopted the practice of making childhood and adolescence into a period of emotional and economic dependency. In doing so, many of the basic rights and privileges of its youngest people have been taken away. Meanwhile, many adults themselves have become dependent on Western economic, social, political, and religious institutions. Consequently, the *quid pro quo* (reciprocal exchange) that existed between young people and adults in precontact culture has been upset. Indeed, as we see, young people have lost much in the span of a few generations, particularly much of the cultural heritage that once saw to their basic emotional and material needs. What they have lost has been replaced for many with unfulfillable dreams imported through Western institutions.

Analysis is restricted [here] to the situation currently facing young people in Western Samoa. It is necessary to consider Western Samoa separate from American Samoa because the two countries are distinct political entities. As such, they have experienced different economic and political forces over the century. The islands of Samoa were divided between the colonial powers of Germany and the United States in 1900. Upolu and Savai'i (now Western Samoa) went under German rule, whereas Tutuila and the Manu'a Group went under American rule. The latter constitute American Samoa, still a U.S. territory, while the former passed under New Zealand rule during World War I, and became an independent state in 1962.

In terms of the extent of Western influence, although no region is untouched, in Western Samoa, the island of Savai'i has been less affected by the modern wage economy than has the island of Upolu. The greatest Western influence on Upolu is in Apia area, the capital city (and only city) with a population of 45,000. American Samoa has been highly "Americanized," especially around Pago Pago harbor, the capital area—there are no cities per se in American Samoa, rather parts of the island of Tutuila are becoming "suburban." More remote villages and islands in the Manu'a Islands (comprising Ofu, Olesega, and Ta'u) retain some of their traditional lifestyle, but less so than in more remote areas of Western Samoa.

The common thread of their joint Samoan heritage remains, but at present they are on two distinct trajectories into the future. In many respects, those coming of age in American Samoa are far better off materially than their "poorer cousins" in Western Samoa. There are more educational opportunities, including free primary and secondary education as well as opportunities to attend U.S. universities. Because all American Samoans are also American nationals, there is the option of emigrating to the United States, especially Hawaii or California. In addition, many males join the U.S. armed forces (cf. North, 1991). In contrast, Western Samoa ranks close to Bangladesh in terms of gross national product (GNP), although its largely intact subsistence economy makes the comparison invidious (Meleisea & Meleisea, 1980).

In terms of social problems, there does not appear to be an unusually high suicide rate (King, 1981) or crime rate in American Samoa. Among those who emigrate, some develop problems associated with living in U.S. inner cities, and those who have returned recently have brought back the gang mentality found among some minority youths in the United States. Consequently, there is some current concern on Tutuila about an increase in violence associated with this gang mentality. Incidentally, some of the gang mentality is now finding its way to Western Samoa via American Samoa.

In view of these differences, I am not dealing in detail with the problems of coming of age in contemporary American Samoa because these problems now very much resemble those found among the young in many parts of the United States. Coming of age in American Samoa certainly has changed dramatically since the time of Mead's study, and consequently any research conducted there now would not shed much light on the controversy over her work. But, in choosing between which "coming of age" to discuss . . . I have selected the situation in Western Samoa because the problems facing the young there appear more pressing than those facing the young in American Samoa. For a treatment of the situation in contemporary American Samoa, see Holmes and Holmes (1992).

Coming of Age in Western Samoa, 1990

One hundred and sixty years of contact with the West has dramatically altered daily life in Western Samoa, even in remote villages. As was seen earlier, the missionaries set out beginning in the 1830s to change the values and attitudes associated with fundamental notions like individualism versus collectivism, and profit versus sharing. Then, with some difficulty, entrepreneurs introduced practices such as wage labor, making way for capital accumulation (see Oliver, 1961, for Samoan resistance to these influences). As we also saw, generational replacement has facilitated the process of social change, for it was by gradually affecting each subsequent generation that the "heathen" traditions of old Samoa were gradually transformed or eradicated. This gradual change meant that Mead still witnessed many precontact practices in the 1920s. Now, many struggle with the contradictions of trying to honor the remnants of old values from *fa'a Samoa* while simultaneously living with the realities of the new practices.

O'Meara (1990, pp. 69–70) provided a detailed account of how life has changed over the span of just one generation in a village he recently studied on the island of Savai'i. Included in these changes are: an increase in population,[2] less isolation, more travel (to Apia, American Samoa, and New Zealand), "new needs and desires," a "perception of scarcity" of material goods, more theft, and more family dispersion.[3] Many of these changes have led to a decreased sense of morale and an increased sense of frustration, particularly among the young who find certain aspects of village life less than satisfactory. As Meleisea and Meleisea (1980) argued, each "year thousands of young people graduate from secondary school but few find jobs and most feel that village farming is a poor return for their years in school" (p. 37).

In reference to how the "new" religion has transformed life in the village he studied on the island of Savai'i, O'Meara provided the following description of life in one of the more "fundamentalist" villages:

> Some church rules have a significant effect on village life. The Methodists are rather puritanical compared to most other denominations in Samoa. They allow precious little in the way of entertainment. The Church does not permit dancing at night (and discourages it during the day). It bans card playing of any kind, day or night, and strictly forbids the drinking of alcohol. . . . During the Christmas and New Year's holidays . . . several entrepreneurial families ran bingo games . . . by the light of gas lanterns in their homes or on the cricket pitch. The pastor banned the popular games after only two nights. (p. 44).

Admittedly, this village represents an extreme to which religious influence has transformed life in some villages, and the extent to which Samoans no longer enjoy various forms of carefree activity and physical releases—such as dancing. Still, there are almost 24,000 practicing Methodists in Western Samoa (Meleisea, 1987a, p. 67).

It is interesting to note in this context that Mead devoted a chapter to the importance of the *siva* (dance) "in the development of individuality and the compensation for repression of personality in other spheres of life" (p. 121).

Despite the prohibitions on hedonistic activities, some young people still engage in these emotional and physical outlets as part of a village "underground." O'Meara described some of this:

> All of these prohibitions apply to villagers wherever they are, but slackness some-times creeps in when people travel to Salelologa, Apia, or overseas. Young men sometimes even hold clandestine poker games or drinking parties behind the vil-lage, though *matai* almost never attend these affairs. Villagers are generally willing to overlook breaches of proper conduct *as long as violators remain discreet.* If mis-conduct leads to a public outburst or to fighting, however, the village council imposes heavy fines on offenders. (pp. 44–45, italics added)

Many young people experience these restrictions as oppressive, particularly those who compare their own lives with the lives of young people in Western culture as portrayed in movies and magazines. For example, apparently many find the nightly curfew that has been instituted in most villages to be unreasonable (cf. Freeman, 1983, pp. 261–262). To violate the curfew brings a sometimes heavy fine for all except the *matai,* who are exempt because it is their duty to patrol the village (it begins at 9 or 10 p.m., depending on the village). O'Meara recorded that the curfew is in place "to assure that schoolchildren get to bed early; to prevent theft, *clandestine meetings of unmarried people,* and other elicit behaviors that might go undetected in the darkness . . ." (p. 56, italics added).

In relation to "Mead's Samoa," then, life in contemporary Samoa is obviously quite different—more repressive—as Freeman inadvertently brought to our attention. He also inadvertently brought to our attention the *deteriorating* situation facing young people there. . . . [T]he *'aumaga* and *aualuma* now exist in name only, with few ex-ceptions. Consequently, the primary village supports that once gave a sense of meaning and future purpose to the lives of the young have weakened. And, increasingly, the generations that once lived together in cooperation and mutual benefit now find family relationships increasingly strained. As Leacock (1987) argued, "the immediate source of stress for many young people is a perceived lack of empathy and concern on the part of stern and demanding parents, while parents who become angry over the per-ceived lack of proper respect on the part of the young may be excessively abusive" (p. 182).

Hence, many of the young are in no-win situations. They are formally educated, and informally socialized, to expect certain material and emotional gratifications, but their prospects for realizing these expectations are often not good. There is now less opportunity for those who try to take the nontraditional, wage-labor route. For those who do take the traditional route, a less than satisfactory situation is increasingly encountered. In 1980, Meleisea and Meleisea characterized these problems in the fol-lowing manner:

> The greatly increased educational facilities which have been available for Samoan children since the 1950s have created rising expectations among the younger gen-

eration, a dissatisfaction with village life and a longing for wage employment in
Apia or a chance to emigrate . . . Returning migrants are another source of dissatisfaction with village life and the predominantly subsistence economy, as well as
a source of new values and aspirations. (p. 37)

More recently, O'Meara (1990) summarized these problems by saying that "the
cycle of *tautua* is broken" (p. 162). With this expression he meant that the traditional
quid pro quo that existed in precontact society between the "young" and the "adult"
has disintegrated, as he explained:

> The system of authority and service is organized largely on seniority—those who
> are younger serve and obey those who are older. Ironically, this kind of system is
> stable only as long as the participants are sure that it will continue. As long as the
> system is closed and the cycle secure, young people perceive their service as a
> tolerable burden, knowing that one day they will, in their turn, command the
> service of others.
>
> The cycle of *tautua* has been broken in the minds of many young people today.
> *New technology and a market economy make individual production, profit, and accu-
> mulation of wealth possible.* Many young people seek their futures in wage labour
> outside the village or even overseas, and they doubt that their own service will
> ever be repaid by a younger generation. In these circumstances, they no longer
> serve so gladly. (p. 162, italics added)

One attempt to augment the sense of meaning and identity among young males
was to increase the number of *matai* titles granted. According to O'Meara (1990), the
"number of *matai* has been growing rapidly over the last three decades, so that now most
adult men hold titles. In rural areas such as Savai'i, 75 percent of all men 21 years and
older are matai.[4] That is more than double the percentage of thirty years ago" (p.
151). But apparently this "oversupply" has had the effect of diminishing the importance of, and respect for, these titles. For example, many young men have been given
titles without the traditional "apprenticeship" and therefore lack many of the skills
necessary to exercise their power wisely. Evidently, some of these less qualified *matai*
are involved in more conflicts with both elder *matai* and younger untitled men, in
part because some of these young *matai* apparently do not conform to the consensus-
building conventions of *fa'a Samoa* (cf. Leacock, 1987).

So, where does this leave the young person who is coming of age and looking
to develop a sense of identity as an adult?

Freeman would have us believe that young people in Samoa have always had
problems with their adolescence because of the nature of traditional Samoan society,
but many observers disagree with him (Leacock, 1987). In her analysis of the problems
facing young people in contemporary Samoa, Leacock argued that Freeman has been
remiss in his "failure to deal seriously with the complexities of recent socio-historical
change" (p. 177). In addition, she contended that "it is a serious misrepresentation
of the situation to say that youth difficulties simply follow from the authoritarianism
of the Samoan past. *Instead they follow from the fact that the nature of youth as a life
period has been transformed in many ways*" (p. 186, italics added). Similarly, in response
to Freeman's citation of suicide statistics, Shankman (1983) argued that a "more plausible
explanation might lie in the modernization of Western Samoa and its interaction with

traditional Samoan culture, since there are different rates of suicide for Western Samoa and American Samoa, where the suicide rate is considerably lower" (p. 52).

The issue of suicide and its recent rise in Western Samoa strikes at the heart of the dilemma facing those now coming of age in Samoa. Moreover, when we examine the nature of the suicide problem, we see more clearly a principal flaw in Freeman's critique of Mead's coming-of-age thesis.

The most comprehensive analyses of suicide in Western Samoa were conducted by Bowles (1985) and MacPherson and MacPherson (1985). According to Bowles, the suicide rate was low in the early 1960s (about 2 per 100,000) and it rose slowly until the mid-1970s (about 10 per 100,000). After this, it rose dramatically in the early 1980s and began a decline again by the mid-1980s. Averaged between 1981 and 1983, Bowles reported a rate of 22.6 for the entire population, with the following breakdown based on age and gender: For males, the total rate was 31.3, but for males 15 to 24 years of age it was 71.0 and for males 25 to 34 it was 75.6; for females the total rate was 13.3, but for females 15 to 24 years of age it was 35.8 and for females 25 to 34, it was 20.4 (note that the actual total number of suicides is 106 for 3 years). More recent figures reveal that in spite of a prevention program and an apparent decline, the problem persists. In 1990, there were 27 confirmed suicides, constituting a rate of 16.9 for a population of 160,000 (Aiavao, 1991).

Based on their sociohistorical analysis of Samoan culture, MacPherson and MacPherson (1985) concluded that although forms of suicide have probably existed throughout the history of Samoan culture, "suicide . . . does not seem to have been an institutionalized response" (p. 37) to problems. They also concluded that the recent suicides constitute forms of "anomic" suicide. In a similar vein to the analyses presented here, MacPherson and MacPherson developed a "blocked opportunity model" that argues that suicides since the mid-1970s can be explained in terms of rising expectations regarding affluence and personal freedom produced by mass education, the media, the wage economy, and emigration prospects. These expectations have been unmet for large numbers of youth who face limited opportunity for paid employment, and who in the mid-1970s had their emigration possibilities severely limited. But, instilled psychologically with alternative conceptions of what life could be like, many are now forced to live in villages with limited economic prospects as well as with families demanding a blind obedience to traditional customs. Accordingly, many of the cases that MacPherson and MacPherson examined involved a thwarted attempt by a young person to exercise some type of autonomy disapproved of by a parent or a *matai*. Hence, many of the suicides and attempted suicides appear to constitute a "statement" by a frustrated individual against what is perceived as an intransigent traditional authority figure. Evidently, much of this desire to exert independence has been stimulated by exposure to Western influence, especially education and the mass media. It is of interest to note Mead's predictions regarding the problems that would emerge in Samoa when individual choice was demanded by the young (e.g., 1928, pp. 169–171).

O'Meara provided a similar explanation for the recent rise in suicide:

> The correlation of the suicide epidemic with the rapid modernization of the post-independence era in Western Samoa is no accident. The desires and expectations of young people are changing very fast. Radios, movies, television, videos, and New

Zealand-style education all give people new ideas and new dreams. . . . The closeness of that other world sometimes makes patience difficult, yet the actual pace of social and economic change makes the fulfilment of these expectations very unlikely. Rapid change alone is not the problem. Suicide is uncommon in American Samoa, where change has been far more rapid and dramatic than in Western Samoa, and where half the population is made up of migrants from Western Samoa. The real problem appears to be *uneven* change, specifically the lag between young people's growing expectations and the social and economic realities in which they live. (p. 111)

Given the no-win situation that many young Samoans face, in a sense it is surprising that there have not been more suicides. It is also estimated, however, that about twice as many *unsuccessful* suicide attempts take place (Bowles, 1985, p. 17). More recent reports suggest that the frustration among the young is being manifested in other ways. For example, marijuana smoking has become "a problem in Western Samoan schools, especially in rural areas . . . Some schools [report that] drug abuse has replaced cigarette smoking and beer drinking as the main offence leading to expulsion" ("Drug Abuse Hits Schools," 1991). Foreboding a more serious problem, it has been reported that "Western Samoa's Police Commissioner . . . has called for the establishment of a special jail for young people" ("Special Youth Jail?," 1992).

We can put the problem of suicide in Samoa into perspective in two other ways.

First, it appears to have the qualities of an epidemic, which means that potentially there is no "cure." The peak of this epidemic in the early 1980s appeared to represent a "contagion" of collective behavior from which it became "fashionable" to drink the weedkiller "paraquat."[5] The death from this poison is agonizing and prolonged (sometimes more than a week), thereby ensuring that the authority figures "responsible" are made to suffer also. Of the 49 known suicides in 1981, 39 were from paraquat poisoning; in 1990, 19 of the 27 suicides were from paraquat (Aiavao, 1991). It is believed that many of the attempts are not genuine suicide attempts, but simply either a means of challenging authority or a passive–aggressive attempt to hurt someone. Apparently, some suicide victims take only a small amount, thinking that they will just get sick, but even a small amount of paraquat can result in death. Access to paraquat has still not been restricted, despite 277 known deaths from it since 1973 (Aiavao, 1991).

Second, we can compare Samoan suicide rates with those from other countries, and take lessons from this comparison. It is often said that Western Samoa has the highest rate in the world; in fact, even some guidebooks now make reference to it (e.g., Swaney, 1990). But, Samoa should not be singled out so readily. In point of fact, the suicide rate for young people increased in many countries around the world between the 1960s and the 1980s, including major industrialized nations. In Canada, for example, it rose from 5.3 per 100,000 for 15- to 19-year-olds in 1960 to 20.2 in 1986, and from 12.3 for 20- to 24-year-olds in 1960 to 32.8 in 1986 (Beneteau, 1988). Moreover, if we look at Canada's indigenous population, we find a rate of 100 per 100,000 among Native Canadian men ages 15 to 19. This rate is stable and is clearly above the rate for Samoan men of the same age. No doubt, similarly high rates can be found among groups that have been disenfranchised in some way. But the rates should also be particularly high among those who have been culturally disenfranchised and who are attempting to come of age, as is the case with both Samoan and Native Canadian young people (cf. Rubinstein, 1985, on suicide in Micronesia).

From these two perspectives we can see that Samoa is not alone with its suicide problem, and that the remedy to this epidemic somehow lies with a lack of a "franchise." To effect a "cure," the questions that must be answered pertain to the exact nature of the relationship between suicide and the lack of a franchise, including how to "re-enfranchise" the young, given that without a franchise the young have no representatives of their own to speak for them on policy matters. . . .

These suicide statistics likely represent the "tip of the iceberg" with respect to the lack of personal meaning and sense of alienation experienced by many of the young. The alienation associated with this lack of meaning has been expressed by a number of Samoa's poets (Malifa, 1975; Petaia, 1980; A. Wendt, 1974). A. Wendt's (1973, 1977, 1979) novels capture some of this alienation and despair, as does a recent movie based on one of his novels (*Flying Fox and the Freedom Tree;* see Robie, 1991, for a review). The poem "Kidnapped" especially captures some of the feelings produced by an "alien" and alienating educational system (Petaia, cited in A. Wendt, 1974):

I was six when
Mama was careless
she sent me to school
alone
five days a week

One day I was
kidnapped by a band
of Western philosophers
armed with glossy-pictured
textbooks and
registered reputations
"Holder of B.A.
and M.A. degrees"

I was held
in a classroom
guarded by Churchill and Garibaldi
pinned-up on one wall
and
Hitler and Mao dictating
from the other
Guevara pointed a revolution
at my brains
from his "Guerilla Warfare"

Each three month term
they sent threats to
my Mama and Papa

Mama and Papa loved
their son and
paid ransom fees
each time

Each time
Mama and Papa grew
poorer and poorer
and my kidnappers grew
richer and richer
I grew whiter and
whiter

On my release
fifteen years after
I was handed
(among loud applause
from fellow victims)
a piece of paper
to decorate my walls
certifying my release

As just mentioned, one way in which many young people once "escaped" the frustrations of living in contemporary Western Samoa was to emigrate. Emigration from Western Samoa has been primarily to New Zealand, its colonial "ruler" since

1914. The Samoan community in New Zealand now numbers some 100,000 (Meleisea, 1987a, p. 161). For some time, the young could freely move to New Zealand to work temporarily, but in the mid-1970s the New Zealand government became concerned about "overstayers," and have since restricted work permits. Since then, immigration has been restricted to those who "have a guarantee of a job in New Zealand," or who qualify under a special quota system that allows 1,100 Western Samoans per year on family or humanitarian grounds (Immigration Division, New Zealand, 1982). The resulting work scheme has led to a trickle of persons being admitted for temporary employment: 11 permits in the first year of the program (1977), none in 1983, and 3 in 1984 (Labour Department, Western Samoa, 1984). According to MacPherson and MacPherson (1985), this move by New Zealand has constituted a serious blow for many young people in terms of their plans and expectations, particularly because this period in New Zealand had come to constitute something of what E. Erikson (1968) called an "institutionalized moratorium," in this case a *Wanderschaft,* in much the same fashion that traveling to Europe constitutes one for young North Americans (cf. Norton, 1984).

[I] began with the assertion that young people have been largely forgotten in the furor among social scientists over the Mead-Freeman controversy. But, of the limited attention given young people, young women have been given even shorter shrift. Indeed, there is an irony in the fact that Mead's study of a few female adolescents in the 1920s has led to so much attention being paid to the reputations of social scientists and so little attention being paid to young women struggling to come of age under the conditions just described. Moreover, in relation to young men, young women appear to have lost even more.

. . . [Y]oung women have lost the organization—the *aualuma*—that, in precontact Samoan culture, gave them solidarity and semi-autonomous sexuality. In what appears to have been an attempt by missionaries to establish a patriarchal nuclear family structure with its associated morality, the role of women in Samoa was targeted for dramatic change. By the time of Mead's study, the chosen few who maintained their chastity were trained to be pastors' wives in the boarding schools, whereas the remainder were left mainly on their own, forced to face an adult world that evidently was increasingly hostile to expressions of their autonomy and individuality. According to O'Meara (1990):

> contemporary Samoans apply a familiar 'double standard' toward unmarried males and females. Young, unmarried men are allowed (or even encouraged by each other) to have affairs (though only with unmarried women). The same activity is forbidden of girls, whose virginity and reputations are social assets as well as moral virtues. (pp. 107–108)

Young women also seem to have lost much of the moratorium period that Mead described, where they could enjoy themselves with a "time out" before taking on adult responsibilities and family commitments. O'Meara (1990) wrote that in the religiously conservative village he studied "young women are . . . closely guarded by other family members" (p. 104) and that "women's daily activities are delineated partly with an eye on keeping [them] close to home" (p. 101). He also noted that most "families go to great lengths to guard and restrain their young girls. In the face of such constant chaperoning, most girls have to actively conspire in order to meet privately with a lover or a suitor" (p. 108). However, he also noted instances of premarital affairs and births, and he speculated that much of this constitutes a form of rebellion against parental authority and an attempt to hurt parents in a passive-aggressive manner, similar to the suicide attempts discussed earlier. His sources in that village told him that "sexual escapades of this kind are an increasing problem" (pp. 108–109).

O'Meara also gave us a glimpse of what daily life is now like for women living in Western Samoan villages in terms of the division of labor that has evolved:

> Males of all ages find more time to play or rest than females. In the late afternoons the young men and boys can usually be found relaxing or playing cricket on the village green, playing rugby on a sand flat exposed by the tide near the lagoon shore, or playing volley ball at the school grounds. A few young women join in the volleyball, but most remain at home, cooking and tending to the many children or countless household chores. Even into advanced middle age, women are expected to keep busy (though not all do). Meanwhile, their husbands often sleep, play dominoes, or discuss the intricacies of the latest social or political manoeuvre, leaving their own household duties half-completed. Women sometimes express resentment towards men for this unequal division of labor. (p. 70)

We can see evidence that as power shifted in social relations over this century, at the microlevel of domestic roles, men appear to have gained at the expense of women. Furthermore, at the more macrolevel of political participation and power, women appear to have gained little from recent cultural change. Again, O'Meara gave us a glimpse of this:

> Like men, women gain more control over their lives as they grow older. Even if a woman outlives her parents, however, she still may not fully control her own life until she is an elderly widow. There are exceptions, of course, when a woman rises to authority in her own household, her extended family, or even in village affairs. I know of no such cases in Vaega, however [the village he studied]. A very few women ever rise to national political prominence, but even though these women are exceptionally talented, they usually gain their initial opportunities through genealogical or marital relationships with powerful men. (p. 70)

With few women in positions of formal power to speak for them, it is unlikely that the rights—the franchise—of young women coming of age will improve. Thus, we can identify a "crisis" in gender roles, whereby the gulf or disparity between the status of women and men in Samoa has widened, with women experiencing a sharp decline in status. This crisis seems to be contributing to the growing social malaise there, particularly among young women.

Notes

1. See Oliver (1961) for a broader, political-economy discussion of historical influences in Western Samoa. Gailey (1987) provided a similar discussion of Tonga, bringing out gender issues, as did Lockwood (1993) in reference to Tahiti.

2. Meleisea and Meleisea (1980) noted that "the population of [Western Samoa] has grown from early 19th century estimates of 40,000 to approximately 160,000 in 1977, with something like a 3% annual increase. The consequence is a growing strain on land and inner reef marine resources" (pp. 36–37). From more recent records it is evident that the rate of population growth is declining. Between 1966 and 1971, the population increased by about 12%; between 1971 and 1976, the increase was only 4%; between 1976 and 1981, the increase was 3%; and between 1981 and 1986 it was only 1% (cf. Department of Statistics, Western Samoa, 1989). Although this "plateauing" should relieve some strain, it means that there is a population "bulge" now coming of age. In 1966, only 24% of the population were between the ages of 15 and 29 (31,510 people). As of 1986, 31% of the population were in this age range (48,495 people).

3. O'Meara noted that a "generation ago families were still united, in good times and in bad. . . . Today migration is often expected and in many cases desired—yet it is also feared. Parents become separated from their children, friends are lost, and brothers and sisters scatter as they disappear into awaiting airplanes" (p. 70). He also noted that some of this family separation is caused by the necessity of family members going off to engage in wage labor to support their families. It is not uncommon for fathers, and especially sons, to work in Apia or American Samoa, but to only visit their families every few weeks.

4. According to O'Meara (1990) "less than 0.02% of all *matai* are women" (p. 33).

5. There is considerable evidence from U.S. studies that when a suicide is publicized by the media, the rate of suicide increases among people with similar characteristics to the person who committed suicide (Phillips, 1979; Stack, 1987).

Questions

1. What sociocultural changes have made coming of age in Samoa so stressful today?
2. A number of social institutions helped guide adolescents to adulthood. What institutions have been lost in Samoa? What role do social institutions such as schools or the Church play in making adolescence less carefree today?
3. How has the process of finding an identity changed in Samoa? What factors have led to this change?
4. How has the parent-child relationship changed in Samoa? What factors have led to increased parent-child conflict at adolescence?
5. How is Bakan's idea of "the promise" relevant to understanding adolescence in Samoa today?
6. How is Benedict's notion of coping with discontinuities in development relevant to understanding adolescence in Samoa today?

References and Further Reading

Caton, H. (1990). *The Samoa reader: Anthropologists take stock.* Lanham, MD: University Press of America.

Côté, J. E. (1994). *Adolescent storm and stress: An evaluation of the Mead-Freeman controversy.* Hillsdale, NJ: Lawrence Erlbaum.

Freeman, D. (1983). *Margaret Mead and Samoa: The making and unmaking of an anthropological myth.* Cambridge, MA: Harvard University Press.

Mead, M. (1928/1974). *Coming of age in Samoa.* New York: William Morrow.

Chapter 3

Biological Development

One marker of the onset of adolescence is puberty, a series of interdependent biological events that result in the appearance of secondary sex characteristics (characteristics that have no reproductive significance) and the attainment of adult stature and reproductive maturity. Great individual variability exists in the timing of various physiological changes, and research has shown that the timing of an adolescent's physical maturation in relation to peers in many cases may have more of an effect on the youth's psychological outlook and behavior than physical status per se (Buchanan, Eccles, & Becker, 1992).

Promoted by the popular press, a widespread belief exists in our society that adolescent behavior is governed by "raging hormones," and that hormones have a particularly large impact on aggression, moods and emotions, and sexual urges. Studies of parents and teachers show that both groups endorse the belief that hormonal changes make early adolescence a difficult period of life (Buchanan et al., 1990). Surprisingly, until the 1980s, evidence about the activating effects of hormones on adolescent behavior was primarily anecdotal (Susman & Petersen, 1992). While research is now being conducted, studies looking at hormonal effects on affect and behavior are not easy to carry out for a variety of reasons. To demonstrate experimentally a causal relationship between hormones and behavior, it would be necessary to manipulate hormone levels in adolescents and then look at their impact on specific behaviors such as moods or sexuality. Such studies would be unethical and as a result the research studies that have been carried out are nonexperimental. Thus while studies may demonstrate a correlation between hormone levels and behavior, hormones may not be the cause of those behaviors.

The endrocrine system is difficult to study. The endocrine system is integrated and hormones interact with each other, rather than acting in isolation. The possible hormonal effects on behavior may be due to different combinations of hormones rather than to the effect of any one hormone in particular. Thus, any hormonal influence needs to be studied by looking both at the impact of individual hormones and the impact of various combinations of hormones. In addition, episodic changes occur in hormone levels during the day, as well as monthly cyclic variations in hormone levels for girls. Daytime concentrations of hormones are lower in adolescents than nighttime concentrations, but studies tend to use measures at a single point of time during the day rather than multiple samples across the 24-hour period. Ideally studies should be based on repeated measures of hormones and behavior in the same individuals to assess any changes that occur in behavior as hormone levels increase and decrease, but most studies have not done this. Furthermore, results tend to differ depending on how hormone levels are measured, and no best way to assess hormone concentrations has been established. While blood measurements of hormone concentrations are considered to be precise, it is technically difficult to obtain blood measures from large samples of adolescents. Some studies assess hormone concentrations in saliva or urine, each of which has its advantages. Finally, hormonal contributions may be nonlinear, having their greatest effect when the endocrine system is undergoing its greatest change in early adolescence, or alternatively, it may take prolonged exposure to a particular hormone to see its effects (Buchanan, Eccles, & Becker, 1992).

It is also difficult to disentangle hormone effects on behavior from other variables. The physiological changes at puberty carry psychological meaning both to adolescents and to those around them. With the onset of puberty and the development of secondary sex characteristics, adolescents begin to think about themselves differently and develop a new image of themselves. A rise occurs in self-consciousness and self-focus (Readings 4.1 and 4.2). Similarly, parents, peers, and others respond to postpubertal individuals differently from prepubertal individuals (Reading 3.3) and expect different behavior from them. Thus, while hormones produce physical changes, the changes themselves then become a stimulus for other reactions and for changing expectations for behavior, and these variables may produce behavior that we attribute to hormones. The physiological changes at puberty are difficult to disentangle from other social factors and events that change at early adolescence, such as changes in schools to junior high school (Reading 12.1) and changing sex role pressures (Readings 8.2 and 8.3). Finally, hormone levels themselves depend partly on social and contextual factors. Living in a dangerous neighborhood or residential mobility can increase the production of stress hormones. Sleep, food ingestion, sexual activity, and exercise can also influence hormone levels.

Given all these complexities, it should not be surprising that research results for the effects of hormones on adolescent behavior are inconsistent and contradictory, and that hormone-affect associations when found are small in magnitude. Thus caution is in order when encountering the claim that adolescents are the victims of raging hormones. It is still an open question and considerably more research is needed to bolster the claim. What is clearer is that physiological maturation and its timing have an impact on how adolescents think about who they are and how they relate to others and also on how they are responded to by others.

Additional Resources

References and Suggested Reading

Brooks-Gunn, J., & Warren, M. (1989). Biological and social contributions to negative affect in young adolescent girls. *Child Development, 60,* 40–55.

Buchanan, C. M., Eccles, J. S., Flanagan, C., Midgley, C., Feldlaufer, H., & Harold, R. D. (1990). Parents' and teachers' beliefs about adolescents: Effects of sex and experience. *Journal of Youth and Adolescence, 19*(4), 363–394.

Buchanan, C. M., Eccles, J. S., & Becker, J. B. (1992). Are adolescents the victims of raging hormones? Evidence of activational effects of hormones on moods and behavior at adolescence. *Psychological Bulletin, 111,* 62–107.

Susman, E. J., & Petersen, A. C. (1992). Hormones and behavior. In E. McAnarney, R. Kreipe, D. Orr, & G. D. Comerci (Eds.) *Textbook of adolescent medicine* (pp. 125–130). Philadelphia: W. B. Saunders.

On the Internet

http://parentingteens.about.com/parenting/parentingteens/

About.com: Parenting of Adolescents—Puberty
The About.com Network consists of over 700 Guide sites covering more than 50,000 subjects with over 1 million links to resources on the Net and a fast-growing archive of original content. Search for "Puberty" in the About.com Network and links will be provided to topics such as Puberty in Boys, Puberty Questions and Answers, and Puberty and Teen Sexuality Glossary.

http://www.personal.psu.edu/faculty/n/x/nxd10/biologic2.htm

Adolescence: Change & Continuity—Biological Transitions
This site was produced by Pennsylvania State University students taking Human Development and Family Studies 433: The Transition to Adulthood; and Human Development and Family Studies 239: Adolescent Development.

http://www.upledger.com/wwwboard/messages/229.html

Brain Continues to Mature in Adolescence
The Upledger Institute, Inc., recognized for its continuing education programs, clinical research, and therapeutic services, posted this paper on continued brain maturation at adolescence from *Nature Neuroscience* (1999), 2, 859–861, 861–863.

http://www.hhdev.psu.edu/hdfs/grad/adoles.htm

Puberty: Hormones and Behavior
This is the Web site for Graduate Study on Adolescent Development at Penn State's College of Health and Human Development. It provides links to current research on puberty, hormones, and behavior.

Adolescents: Lives of Emotional Flux

Reed Larson, Ph.D., is a professor of human development and family studies at the University of Illinois, Urbana-Champaign's Department of Human and Community Development. He is coauthor of *Being Adolescent: Conflict and Growth in the Teenage Years* (with Mihaly Csikzentmihalyi, 1984) and *Divergent Realities: The Emotional Lives of Mothers, Fathers, and Adolescents* (with Maryse Richards, 1994). His research interests include adolescents, experience in the after-school hours; youth activities; and the daily family dynamics of activity and emotion.

Maryse H. Richards, Ph.D., is an associate professor of psychology at Loyola University. She is coauthor, (with Reed Larson), of *Divergent Realities: The Emotional Lives of Mothers, Fathers, and Adolescents* (1994).

Psychoanalyst Anna Freud (1966) described adolescence as a period of psychic disequilibrium filled with contradictions, with moods veering between optimism and the blackest pessimism, and between enthusiasm and apathy. This depiction of adolescent mood states gives rise to two questions. First, was Freud correct that adolescence is marked by fluctuations in moods? Second, if adolescence is a time of emotional instability, are the mood fluctuations attributable to the biological changes of puberty or to factors in the social context of the lives of adolescents?

Reed Larson and Maryse Richards address both of these questions through data collected in two studies: a study of 55 white, middle- to upper-middle-class mother-father-young adolescent triads from two-parent families, and a study of 483 fifth to ninth graders. The focus of their research study was on assessing changes in daily life that come at the ages of puberty. Larson and Richards employed the Experience Sampling Method (ESM), a powerful research approach by which research participants agreed to carry electronic pagers and self-report booklets for a one-week period. Over the course of that week they received eight signals at random moments throughout the day from 7:30 A.M. to 9:30 P.M. Each time participants were signaled, they immediately filled out a self-report form recording what they were doing, who they were with, what they were thinking and feeling, and their mood or emotion. The strength of the ESM is that it captures people in situ and does not rely on remembering past experience which is subject to distortion. Larson and Richards also collected self-reports of pubertal status using established instruments to examine the relationship between adolescents' pubertal status and their moods.

Using the ESM, Larson and Richards were able to compare the emotional ups and downs of adolescents to that of their parents as they moved through a typical week. Adolescents reported more extreme mood states than their parents did, but that variability in emotional experience was not related to pubertal stage. Larson and Richards, however, do note in a footnote and in a more detailed write-up of this study (Richards & Larson, 1993) that while no association was found for girls between pubertal development and emotional experiences, they did find that for boys pubertal development was related to feelings of being in love. These findings could be due to the result of hormone increases, but they could also be explained by the enhanced social stimulus value of having a more developed body shape. Boys with more visibly developed bodies, for example, could attract greater attention from girls, contributing to the feelings of being in love.

In an earlier study using the ESM to compare the emotional states of children and adolescents, Larson and Lampman-Petraitis (1989) also reported that "the onset of adolescence is not associated with appreciable differences in the variability of emotional states experienced during daily life" (p. 1257). Larson and Lampman-Petraitis found that older adolescents reported more negative mood states, but again, this result may be attributable either to pubertal maturation or to contextual changes in the lives of older adolescents.

At the same moment that Sara is hemming her husband's new suit, her son Selman is angrily changing clothes in the school locker room. Selman's friend is denigrating his basketball ability, "he's saying stuff about me," and Selman is hurt. As a short, late-maturing seventh grader, Selman is particularly sensitive about such matters. Only minutes later, however, his anger is forgotten as he jokes and laughs with teammates about their upcoming game; and later that day he is ecstatic over an A he receives on a social studies exam. Selman's emotional state shifts frequently from extreme upset to extreme happiness and back again in a matter of a few hours.

Anne's stylishly dressed eighth-grade daughter, Amy, demonstrates similar emotional changeability. At one moment she is joyful while alone in her room doing her hair and listening to a song by Cyndi Lauper; at another, she is annoyed with her dad because "he is chewing too loudly; he's eating too much and needs to lose weight." Later she is happier watching a soap opera with her mother, but then gets intensely distressed talking with a friend about who will be at a party that night. Selman's life is usually upbeat, but Amy frequently worries about how others see her; in fact, she expresses a feeling of accomplishment one evening that "I went all day without becoming so anxious about fitting in."

Adolescents have a reputation for strong and changeable emotional states. According to stereotype, they are not quite in control of their passions, swinging between extremes of joy and anger, happiness and despair, abandon, and acute self-consciousness. Believed to be prey to "raging hormones," adolescents are considered "unstable," "impulsive," and "wild." Even Aristotle claimed that youth "are heated by Nature as drunken men by wine."

Is this stereotype really true? There is indeed a lot happening in young adolescents' lives in our society. The period of youth covered by our study, ages ten to fourteen, is a transitional time, when the easy life of childhood comes to an end and formidable hazards begin to appear. The fifth graders in our study are sometimes identified as "preadolescent" or "latency"-aged, a comparatively calm period when children have achieved mastery over their limited social world. But within their bloodstreams, the hormonal changes of puberty have already begun to course. In late fifth grade or shortly thereafter, girls' bodies start changing into those of women and, somewhat later, boys' bodies start becoming those of men. On top of these physical changes come a whole set of other transitions, such as entry to junior high school, growing independence from family, and greater exposure to the darker side of life, which make their world more complicated and challenging.

Although the major problems of adolescence—delinquency, drug use, suicide, and pregnancy—do not reach their peak until the high school years, more and more scholars are recognizing that these problems have their roots in how kids respond to these many changes of early adolescence. It is in early adolescence that a child establishes a healthy orientation to life, or begins a downward spiral leading to these difficulties.

Which path children take, we believe, is determined by how they survive day to day. Their emotional well-being is shaped by how they fare in the competitive environment of school, the highly charged world of friends, and the reconfigured terrain of the contemporary family. Getting through the day is often the biggest challenge. As a young person passes from home to class to lunch period, do his or her emotions career out of control, or can some kind of rhythm and order be maintained? The answer to this question shapes adolescents' well-being, which in turn affects the emotional lives of their families.

The Emotional Teenager

Before looking at the specific organization of adolescents' daily reality, let us address the issue of adolescent emotionality or "moodiness." The reports we gathered on adolescents' hour-to-hour feelings provide an opportunity to look closely at this age-old issue. Do teenagers experience wider emotional swings than adults? Than children? Do they experience their lives as out of control? And if so, why?

Selman's Highs and Lows

Selman's emotional experience on Saturday provides a dramatic picture of what it feels like to be a twelve-year-old. Eating breakfast with the family at 9:06 A.M., Selman reported feeling glum and fat. He felt left out at times and had a lisp that reflected his wavering self-confidence. But only a little while later, at 10:58, he was very happy and cheerful, playing catch with his four-year-old brother. In this situation his insecurity was forgotten; he was the leader and felt proud. "I am having fun," he wrote.

Selman's emotions rarely stayed in one place for very long. At 1:13 P.M. he felt very irritable and "grouchy" because "my older brother made me play football." His fifteen-year-old brother drafted Selman as a much needed extra player, then kept him in his place with teasing and ridicule. "He makes fun of my lisp," Selman complained. An hour later, they were still playing football, but Selman was happy again, just because he had been included.

Fluctuating relations with his father filled out the rest of Selman's day. At 3:42 he was happy cheering the Michigan football team with his dad. But at 6:12 he was angry and upset at his imperious father. "I joke around with him a lot. He doesn't like that." Later that night, his mom and dad went out to visit friends, leaving Selman to baby-sit. Selman felt happier watching *To Kill a Mockingbird* on the VCR, but had residual feelings of anger toward his father. This roller coaster of emotions continued throughout his week, at home and at school, with friends and with family.

But the question is, Are Selman's emotional fluctuations really different from those experienced by his parents? Selman's mother, Sara, you may recall, also had ups and downs: she was despondent discussing her father's illness and in high spirits when sharing personal experiences with close friends. Are teens really more emotional and out of control than adults, or is this just a convenient stereotype?

We can begin to investigate this question by comparing how Selman and his parents reacted to a common sequence of family events. On Sunday evening the family held a discussion about the fate of their elderly cat, Chestnut, who was dearly loved by all family members. Chestnut was limping badly from an injury and the family reached the decision that Chestnut needed to be put to sleep. The decision was painful for Selman's mother and father; Sara wrote, "I will miss her, she's been *my* cat." However, the emotions they reported were nowhere near as extreme as Selman's: he was devastated. Similarly, the next day, when the veterinarian determined that Chestnut did *not* need to die, Selman's report of euphoria far outstripped his mother's and father's.

Both Selman and his parents were reacting to the same events regarding a cat they all loved, yet Selman reacted more extremely. This suggests that adolescents like Selman may be more emotional; that they react more intensely to daily events. But might adults like Sara and her husband have *different* events in their lives that elicit equally strong feelings, perhaps events at work or with friends?

Our research indicates that adolescents *are* more emotional than their parents. Across the thousands of times they recorded their feelings, our sample of adolescents reported many more extreme emotional states than their parents did. They reported many more euphoric highs than their parents; in fact, they felt "very happy" *five times* more often. Likewise, they reported many more extreme lows than their parents; they felt "very unhappy" *three times* more often (see Figure 1). Additional evidence leads us to believe that this is not just what psychologists call a "response set"—a tendency of adolescents to use more superlative language about everything. Rather, teenagers genuinely experience their internal lives as swinging between greater extremes of joy and distress.

Figure 1

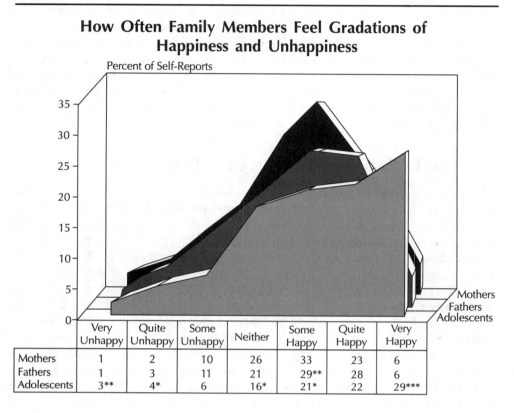

How Often Family Members Feel Gradations of Happiness and Unhappiness

Percent of Self-Reports

	Very Unhappy	Quite Unhappy	Some Unhappy	Neither	Some Happy	Quite Happy	Very Happy
Mothers	1	2	10	26	33	23	6
Fathers	1	3	11	21	29**	28	6
Adolescents	3**	4*	6	16*	21*	22	29***

Significance tests compare mother with father and child with same-sex parent.
*p < .05; **p < .01; ***p < .001

This emotionality is also apparent when we look at adolescents' reports for a wider palette of psychological states. They reported feeling "self-conscious" and "embarrassed" two to three times more often than their parents did; they more often reported social discomfort on a wide range of dimensions: awkward, lonely, nervous, and ignored—a whole array of painful feelings that remind us adults why we never want to be adolescents again.

These teenagers, however, were not more intense on all psychological states. Adolescents like Selman felt "in control" much less often than their parents did. They also reported feeling strongly "interested" less frequently, and they more often said they wished they were doing something else. These teens appeared to experience themselves as less in command and less invested in their immediate lives than their parents did. Perhaps for this reason, they reported feeling bored much more often; they also felt tired, weak, and drowsy more frequently than their parents did. In spite of their youthful bodies and their less harried lives, these adolescents went through the day with more lapses in energy and motivation.

We can conclude, then, that young adolescents live in an emotional reality that differs greatly from their parents'. As adolescents look back on the last twenty-four hours, or anticipate the next, they see themselves hurtling through a more rugged emotional terrain. Teens experienced themselves ascending higher peaks of rapture and tumbling into deeper crevasses of dejection; the adults traversed a more moderate and controlled set of hills and valleys. Given these differences, it is easy to envision why adolescents and parents often misunderstand each other—they are on different wavelengths. But now we need to look at how adolescents' emotionality is related to their immediate lives. Why are they more emotional?

The Evolution of Adolescents' Family Role

The daily emotional experience of teens in our society, no less than that of their mothers and fathers, has been shaped by cultural and historic forces. In the agrarian life of the past, the time and energies of young people were much more tied up with their families. Young people assumed major responsibilities on the farm or were apprenticed in a trade, with the family receiving much of their income. In fact, laws in many states committed the wages of children under twenty-one to their parents.

The introduction of secondary education, however, changed what we expect of young people, and how they spend their time. High schools marked off a separate category of minors, more privileged and worldly than children but with none of the obligations young people previously had assumed on the farm. They were now bound by fewer norms and responsibilities, especially within the family; as early as 1943, Talcott Parsons commented on adolescents' "roleless role." They also spent less time with the family, or with other adults. The channeling of adolescents into junior and senior high schools meant they spent much of their day with same-age peers, and this led to the emergence of the peer group as an important element in teens' lives. As we will see, it has become a major focus of their emotional energy, as well as a major counterweight to their allegiance to their families.

Unfortunately, at the same time that history has been establishing adolescence as a unique stage of life, this stage has been arriving earlier and earlier for each new generation. Because of improved nutrition, puberty, which used to occur at fifteen or even seventeen, now begins as young as nine or ten for girls and eleven or twelve for boys. Since World War II we have also seen the development of a separate "youth culture" which inducts younger and younger children into styles and values distinct from, and sometimes antagonistic to, those of adult society. Other markers of adolescence—questioning of identity, conflicts with parents, and sexual intercourse—are occurring earlier than they did even a generation ago. While Tom Sawyer and Huck Finn were unquestionably children, today they would be five-and-a-half-foot adolescents, with blaring Walkmen and sexual interests.

The result of this evolution has been the compression of multiple life changes within the early adolescent years. Kids from ten to fourteen now experience a concentrated set of personal transitions, often before they are developmentally ready. In addition to normal, expected life changes, such as puberty and the move from elementary to junior high school, they are more likely to encounter a set of idiosyncratic personal crises that can come with adolescence, such as trouble in school, worry about AIDS, and encounters with gangs. This pileup of change is evident among the 483 young people in our larger sample.

This recent compression of stressful changes, of course, affects some teens more than others. Some youths, like Selman, are lucky—events are spaced out, allowing them time to adjust to each one, then get ready for the next. Other teens, like Anne's daughter Amy, however, experience a deluge of stressful events and life changes all at once. Amy, an intelligent and resourceful fourteen-year-old, was coping not only with the uncertainty and conflict surrounding her family's potential move: she had just had a falling-out with her group of friends; she had recently had a major illness; and she was distraught about the new body puberty had just given her. Research shows that teens like Amy, who encounter a pileup of life changes, are much more at risk for psychological problems.

The paradox is that during the same historical period when adolescents are free from the responsibilities assigned to young people of the previous era, they are now burdened with an unpredictable array of major life changes at an earlier age. Young adolescents have more freedom, but also more stress. They have less defined responsibility, yet face increased undefined responsibility—for dealing with these indeterminate personal crises. Not surprisingly, this situation is a crucial factor in their emotional lives.

The Fall from Grace

Prior to adolescence, before this pileup of changes, many children actually have quite enjoyable lives. The elementary-age youngsters in our study basked in a kind of naive happiness. For a remarkable 28 percent of the random times they were signaled, they reported feeling "very happy." One mother expressed astonishment at how exuberant her sixth grader seemed to be when he came home from school; in fact, she even asked us whether she shouldn't "pop his bubble" sometimes.

Part of the reason for these preadolescents' joie de vivre is that their emotional lives were quite simple. When we asked them in the interview whether they ever felt two different things at once, the fifth graders were much more likely than the older youths to say no. They also claimed to know nearly always the reason *why* they were feeling happy or sad: they suffered few of the amorphous, free-floating moods that were more common among the older students. Life was uncomplicated. On the beeper reports, their principal explanation for their negative emotions was concrete immediate events, like getting scolded by parents or losing a game, events that quickly pass and are forgotten.

By seventh grade, however, daily life gets more difficult. The mother of a seventh grader lamented, "She used to be such a happy person. She's become more depressed and intense. It's like someone turned up the volume." These older students felt "great" and "proud" much less often; the ninth graders felt "very happy" only 14 percent of the time, a substantial drop from the 28 percent rate for the fifth graders. This deflation of childhood happiness occurs for both boys and girls. The older students of both sexes also felt "in control" much less than the fifth graders did, and they reported a level of motivation that appeared to be a low point for the entire life span.

Lest the picture seem too bleak, we must emphasize that these adolescents reported feeling happy for the majority of time, and their average mood state was not worse than their parents'. Nonetheless, from their point of view, their experience of negative emotions had increased substantially from just a few short years before. Parents of older students said more often that their children got sulky, raised their voices, and acted violent than parents of younger students reported. Daily life in the middle-school years brings more worry and anger than in the elementary years.

According to the stereotype, these strong adolescent emotions are due to puberty, to "raging hormones." But our findings suggest a more complex set of causes. Contrary to folk wisdom, we found little relationship between pubertal stage and negative emotion or variability in emotion. Rather, we found that adolescents' negative states were related to the pileup of transitions and life events they encountered. Those who were inundated by the most transitions and stressful life events were most likely to be "moody adolescents." Individuals like Amy who encountered multiple, simultaneous personal crises were more likely to report high rates of anger, worry, and sadness. While her parents may dismiss her moods as a product of puberty, they are more likely attributable to the many changes she is trying to cope with.

But it is not just *what* adolescents experience, it is also *how* they interpret these experiences that accounts for their increased emotionality. This is an age when young people develop abstract and critical reasoning skills, described by Jean Piaget and others. And, although these skills represent psychological growth, they actually heighten children's sensitivity to difficult circumstances. These advanced reasoning skills allow them to see beneath the surface of situations and envision hidden and more long-lasting threats to their well-being. As a consequence, adolescents are often troubled by nuances and implications of daily life that do not enter the minds of preadolescents.

We can witness this heightened vulnerability in adolescents' relationships with friends. David Elkind, a student of Piaget, argues convincingly that adolescents' new reasoning skills allow them to imagine what their peers think of them, and this becomes a source of distress. Before adolescence, friends' thoughts and feelings were opaque; teens become able to conjecture what they might be. The result in Amy's case was that she was continually and painfully self-conscious about how others viewed her. The capacity for deeper analysis of her relationships undermined her self-confidence.

Elkind also proposes that these new skills create a growing awareness of the politics of peer relationships, which also makes teenagers more vulnerable to being hurt. One eighth-grade girl in our study reported feeling worried because "I don't want Stacey to know I like Greg." A boy felt torn apart because a girl he liked preferred his friend. Such anxieties over triangular relationships were never reported by the preadolescents in our study. Only in adolescence do children begin to conceive a complex political world in which a network of peers exchange good and bad feelings about each other.

These new reasoning skills, then, magnify adolescents' sensitivity to events at home as well as with friends and at school. Teens begin to form theories about what their parents feel, and they speculate on how these feelings may play out over time.

When a fight raged between the parents of Roger, a fifth grader, his emotional states were unaffected by it. When Amy's parents' fought, however, she was acutely aware of what was happening and responded with gloom and depression. Whereas Roger experienced his parents' fight as an isolated event, Amy perceived the long-lasting implications of her parents' quarrel.

Thus not only do adolescents encounter more stressful events, they are also more likely to be deeply affected by them.

Questions

1. What is the relationship between pubertal stage and emotional states?
2. Why might adolescents report more extreme mood states than their parents do?
3. Why might adolescents report more negative moods than younger children do?
4. Why might adolescents report that they are less in control, and more self-conscious, embarrassed, tired, and bored than parents are?

References and Further Reading

Csikszentmihalyi, M., & Larson, R. (1984). *Being adolescent: Conflict and growth in the teenage years.* New York: Basic Books.
Freud, A. (1966). *The ego and the mechanisms of defense* (Rev. ed.) New York: International Universities Press.
Hall, G. S. (1904). *Adolescence: Its psychology and its relation to physiology, anthropology, sociology, sex, crime, religion, and education (Vols. I & II).* Englewood Cliffs, NJ: Prentice-Hall.
Larson, R. (1989). Beeping children and adolescents: A method for studying time use and daily experience. *Journal of Youth and Adolescence, 18,* 511–530.
Larson, R., & Lampman-Petraitis, C. (1989). Daily emotional states as reported by children and adolescents. *Child Development, 60,* 1250–1260.
Richards, M. H., & Larson, R. (1993). Pubertal development and the daily subjective states of young adolescents. *Journal of Research on Adolescence, 3*(2), 145–169.

3.2 Mary A. Carskadon, Cecilia Vieira, and Christine Acebo, 1993

Association Between Puberty and Delayed Phase Preference

Mary Carskadon, Ph.D., is director of Brown University's E. P. Bradley Sleep and Chronobiology Laboratory. She and her staff examine sleep patterns, circadian rhythms, and related processes in adolescents.

Cecilia Vieira was affiliated with Brown University's E. P. Bradley Hospital Sleep and Chronobiology Laboratory where she examined sleep patterns, circadian rhythms, and related processes in adolescents.

Christine Acebo, Ph.D., is an assistant research professor at Brown University's E. P. Bradley Hospital Sleep and Chronobiology Laboratory. She is also affiliated with Brown's Center for the Study of Human Development. Her research examines sleep patterns, circadian rhythms, and related processes in adolescents.

As children make the transition into early adolescence, they tend to go to bed and wake up at significantly later hours than they did at younger ages. Adolescents are forced to get up on weekdays to meet a school schedule, making their sleep preferences difficult to observe during the school week, but on weekends adolescents' sleep patterns often show a considerable time delay. Mary Carskadon, Cecilia Vieira, and Christine Acebo argue that this *delayed phase preference* may be an important biological factor that plays a role in adolescent storm and stress. The preference for later sleep and waking times places adolescents at odds with the demands of our school systems which start the school day often before 8 A.M., and thus require many high school students to be picked up by school buses before 7 A.M. The demands of extracurricular activities, academic pressures, and work hours that require adolescents to stay up late, and the demands of school schedules that require adolescents to get up early, contribute to adolescents' experiences of daytime sleepiness. Mary Carskadon and her colleagues contend that the storm and stress of adolescence can be attributed in part to the fact that most adolescents are sleep deprived.

The biological changes of puberty are associated with a change in sleep preferences, but the causes of the *delayed phase preference* may be due to social as well as biological variables. Carskadon, Vieira, and Acebo examined a sample of sixth grade students to determine whether the shift in sleep phase on the weekends is attributable to the biological changes of puberty or whether it is a response to social demands and opportunities. They included a variety of measures of sleep preference. In order to determine whether or not sleep preferences are a response to social demands and opportunities, they built in several controls for psychosocial variables including birth order and school type. Finally the researchers assessed physical maturation and pubertal status. The results show that psychosocial factors are less influential than physical maturation in determining late phase preference, and thus provide support for the authors' argument that the biological sleep patterns of adolescents are at odds with the societal demands of early school schedules.

Summary: Many teenagers go to bed and wake up significantly later than younger children, a developmental progression thought to reflect adolescent psychosocial processes. To determine whether biological processes may underlie a delay of phase preference in adolescents, 183 sixth-grade boys and 275 sixth-grade girls completed questionnaires for morningness/eveningness (M/E) and pubertal status. School environment and birth order were also evaluated. A significant relationship of pubertal status to M/E was found in girls, with a similar though nonsignificant trend in boys. No relationship between M/E and psychosocial factors was found. These data support involvement of a biological factor in the adolescent phase preference delay and indicate that our current understanding of adolescent sleep patterns may need revision.

Key Words: Adolescent sleep patterns—Delayed phase preference—Puberty—Circadian rhythms.

The timing of sleep is generally stable during childhood. In children aged 7–9 years, for example, the timing of sleep on weekdays and weekends is quite constant; in particular, morning rising time is generally spontaneous and consistently timed (1). This pattern indicates a stable circadian phase position for this important marker of sleep–wake timing. In adolescents, by contrast, sleep patterns on weekends show a considerable delay versus weekdays, with sleep onset and offset both occurring significantly later on the weekends (2). This shift in sleep phase may be primarily attributed to psychosocial factors that become increasingly salient at the childhood-to-adolescence transition, such as an increase in academic and social demands and opportunities. On the other hand, the shift may result from physiological concomitants of puberty. We have previously identified a midpubertal augmentation of daytime sleepiness (3). When examined using physicians' ratings of pubertal stages, peak daytime sleep tendency also showed a phase delay from mid- to late puberty (4). In the present study, we examined data from a survey designed to evaluate the hypothesis that the adolescent tendency to phase delay may be initiated by a biological process rather than principally as a response to a changing psychosocial milieu. The origins of this behavioral change may have significant implications for understanding adolescent sleep patterns.

Methods

This study was part of a larger survey of fourth through sixth graders and their parents from across the United States. The January 1991, teacher's issue of *SuperScience Blue* (Scholastic, Inc., New York), a science magazine for 4th, 5th and 6th graders, carried a letter to teachers requesting that they write to the senior author if interested in having their students participate in a research project examining physical maturation and body clocks. Of 127 teachers (112 schools) who expressed interest, 93 (78 schools) had their students take part, including 36 schools with 6th graders. Students completed a questionnaire anonymously as a classroom exercise and then took the questionnaire home, along with a letter to parents, forms for parents to complete and a postage-paid return envelope. The letter to parents explained the project, requested that parents complete anonymous questionnaires about their child's patterns and their own and asked parents to decide whether their data and their child's data could be used in the research by choosing whether or not to mail the forms. Forms were sent to teachers of 3,942 students (2,016 boys; 1,926 girls). Student forms were returned for 955 boys (47.4%) and 1,060 girls (55.0%). Of these, 238 boys and 313 girls were 6th-grade students aged 11 or 12 years. Surveys were included in the present analysis if the student completed all the relevant questions about preferred schedule and physical development (final sample: boys n = 183; girls n = 275). Sixth graders were selected for this analysis because they were likely to span pubertal development stages, yet to occupy a narrow age range and psychosocial sphere. The children completing this survey were generally living in single-family dwellings with their parents, largely (85%) Caucasian, and chiefly from small to medium-sized towns or small cities. The sample was neither randomly selected nor is it necessarily a representative sample of 6th graders.

A new morningness/eveningness (M/E) questionnaire for children was used to evaluate M/E preference. M/E is a construct developed to estimate phase tendencies from self-descriptions (5). The child M/E score was derived from responses to 10 questions about preferred timing of such activities as recess, tests, bedtime, rising time and so forth (see Fig. 1). These items were modified from similar questionnaires constructed for use in adults that are valid and reliable (6); we have reported good full-scale reliability for this children's M/E scale, as well as significant relationships of this M/E scale to self-reported sleep variables in pre- and early pubertal 6th graders from this sample (7). M/E scores ranged from 14 to 42, with higher scores indicative of greater morningness. M/E score was the dependent variable used to measure phase preference and scores did not differ between boys and girls (boys mean M/E score = 28.5, SD = 5.6; girls mean M/E score = 28.7, SD = 5.3).

Separate "boys" and "girls" versions of a physical development questionnaire (8) were included in the survey to assess physical maturation and pubertal status. Pubertal development scores were collapsed into three groups for the girls: 1 = no or few signs of pubertal changes (n = 26); 2 = pubertal changes evident (n = 165); 3 = pubertal changes quite marked (n = 84). All girls in group 3 were postmenarchal. Only 2 pubertal categories were derived for boys, because fewer boys rated themselves as showing marked pubertal changes. Therefore, for boys: 1 = no or few signs of pubertal changes (n = 102); 2 = pubertal changes evident, but not completed (n = 81). Pubertal status determined by these scales was an independent variable marking a presumed biological factor that may affect phase preference.

Birth order and a measure of peer groups were used as markers for psychosocial factors that might affect M/E scores. Birth order was used to group children into eldest or only sibling (n = 204) or those with older siblings (n = 254). Peer group was determined by the type of school the children attended: 6th graders in primary schools where 6th grade was the highest grade were designated the Primary School Group (n = 258); 6th graders in middle schools or other school environments that included

Figure 1

Morningness/Eveningness Scale for Children

1*. Imagine: School is canceled! You can get up whenever you want to. When would you get out of bed? Between . . .
   a. 5:00 and 6:30 am
   b. 6:30 and 7:45 am
   c. 7:45 and 9:45 am
   d. 9:45 and 11:00 am
   e. 11:00 am and noon

2. Is it easy for you to get up in the morning?
   a. No way!
   b. Sort of
   c. Pretty easy
   d. It's a cinch

3*. Gym class is set for 7:00 in the morning. How do you think you'll do?
   a. My best!
   b. Okay
   c. Worse than usual
   d. Awful

4*. The bad news: You have to take a two-hour test. The good news: You can take it when you think you'll do your best. What time is that?
   a. 8:00 to 10:00 am
   b. 11:00 am to 1:00pm
   c. 3:00 to 5:00 pm
   d. 7:00 to 9:00 pm

5*. When do you have the most energy to do your favorite things?
   a. Morning! I'm tired in the evening
   b. Morning more than evening
   c. Evening more than morning
   d. Evening! I'm tired in the morning

6*. Guess what? Your parents have decided to let you set your own bedtime. What time would you pick? Between . . .
   a. 8:00 and 9:00 pm
   b. 9:00 and 10:15 pm
   c. 10:15 pm and 12:30 am
   d. 12:30 and 1:45 am
   e. 1:45 and 3:00 am

7. How alert are you in the first half hour you're up?
   a. Out of it
   b. A little dazed
   c. Okay
   d. Ready to take on the world

8*. When does your body start to tell you it's time for bed (even if you ignore it)? Between . . .
   a. 8:00 and 9:00 pm
   b. 9:00 and 10:15 pm
   c. 10:15 pm and 12:30 am
   d. 12:30 and 1:45 am
   e. 1:45 and 3:00 am

9. Say you had to get up at 6:00 am every morning: What would it be like?
   a. Awful!
   b. Not so great
   c. Okay (if I have to)
   d. Fine

10*. When you wake up in the morning how long does it take for you to be totally "with it?"
   a. 0 to 10 minutes
   b. 11 to 20 minutes
   c. 21 to 40 minutes
   d. More than 40 minutes

A score is derived by adding points for each answer: a = 1, b = 2, c = 3, d = 4, e = 5, except as indicated by *, where point values are reversed. The maximum score is 42 (maximal morning preference) and the minimum is 10

older students (e.g. grades 5–8, K–9, 6–12) were designated the Secondary School Group (n = 200).

Evaluations were also performed to examine additional factors that may have been related to the findings, such as parental influence on bedtime, school starting

Table 1

Spearman Rank Order Correlations with M/E Scale Score

Variable	Boys Spearman r	Girls Spearman r
Weekday bedtime	−0.339*	−0.236*
Weekend bedtime	−0.301*	−0.330*
Weekday wake-up time	−0.253*	−0.134
Weekend wake-up time	−0.521*	−0.482*
School start time	−0.009	−0.011

*$p < 0.001$.

time and the students' self-reported bedtimes and wake-up times. Each of these variables was assessed with a question (e.g. What is the *main reason* you usually go to bed . . . ?) followed by categorical choices (e.g. my parents set bedtime; I feel sleepy; my TV shows are over; I finish my homework; my brothers/sisters go to bed; I feel bored; other). Choices for times were offered in 1-hour ranges.

Results

Separate boys and girls contingency tables were prepared for puberty scores versus the items regarding reason for going to bed on weeknights, bedtimes and wake-up times on weekdays and weekend days and school starting time. In both boys and girls, weekday bedtime was significantly related to puberty stage, with later bedtimes reported by students with higher puberty scores (boys chi-square = 8.4, df = 2, p < 0.02; girls chi-square = 15.2, df = 4, p < 0.004). Weekend night bedtimes showed a similar significant relationship in boys (chi-square = 9.7, df = 3, p < 0.05), though in girls the relationship was not significant (chi-square = 6.4, df = 4, p < 0.10). No relationships were found between pubertal stage and reason for going to bed on weekend or weekday nights; thus, parents were equally likely to set bedtime for each group (though consistently less so on weekends than weekdays). The start time of school also did not differ as a function of pubertal stage.

To provide further validation of the M/E scale used in this study, Spearman rank order correlations were performed among the bedtime and wake-up time data. As shown in Table 1, M/E scores were significantly correlated with weekday and weekend bedtimes for girls and boys. Though not highly correlated with weekday wake-up time, a significant correlation was found between M/E and weekend wake-up time.

M/E scores were evaluated separately for girls and boys by analysis of variance with pubertal stage, school type and birth order as independent variables. As illustrated in Fig. 2, pubertal status showed a significant main effect on M/E in girls [$F(2,263)$ = 3.119, p < 0.05], and a similar though nonsignificant trend was found in boys [$F(1,175)$ = 3.461, p < 0.10]. The two psychosocial factors—school type and birth order—were not significantly related to M/E, nor were there any significant interactions.

Figure 2

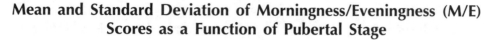

Mean and Standard Deviation of Morningness/Eveningness (M/E) Scores as a Function of Pubertal Stage

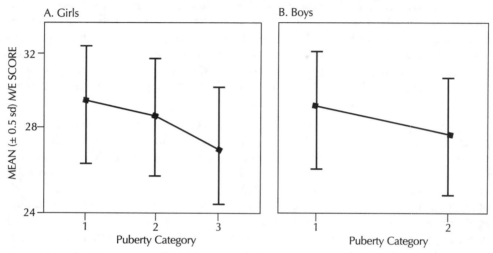

For girls, puberty category 1 = no or few signs of pubertal changes (n = 26); puberty category 2 = pubertal changes evident (n = 165); puberty category 3 = pubertal changes quite marked (n = 84). For boys: puberty category 1 = no or few signs of pubertal changes (n = 102); puberty category 2 = pubertal changes evident, but not completed (n = 81).

Discussion

Although the results of this study are based upon self-reported data, the scales used to measure phase preference and pubertal status have shown quite good psychometric properties (7,8), and these results provide pilot data that favor our hypothesis regarding the influence of puberty on the adolescent phase delay. In this age group, the psychosocial factors were less influential. Thus, if the phase preference delay were influenced by peer-group factors, we expected that children in the Secondary School Group would demonstrate a later phase preference than those in the Primary School Group, predicting that the proximity of older peers would influence preferred timing toward later hours. For example, children with older friends might be influenced or socialized through late-night telephone calls or tastes in late-night television shows. If family influences were involved in the phase preference delay, then 6th graders with older siblings were expected to have a later phase preference than those with no older siblings, since later bedtimes in older children might accelerate a phase delay in younger siblings. On the other hand, if physical maturation were a principal factor related to the adolescent late phase preference, then we expected those children with higher puberty scores to have a preferred later phase than those with lower puberty scores. Our results indicate that pubertal maturation at this transitional phase (age 11/12 years) has a significant influence upon phase preference and that psychosocial factors are less influential than anticipated. This pattern was significant only in girls, perhaps because a higher percentage of our female sample had achieved a more advanced stage of maturation than the boys.

The absence of a significant influence of school type or birth order was surprising and may indicate that our groupings along this dimension were not sensitive or that these peer-group factors do not have a marked effect on sleep/wake cycles and circadian patterns until later in adolescence when youngsters achieve greater capacity to act on available opportunities. In the 6th graders evaluated here, parental influence on bedtime was unrelated to pubertal status. Thus, a "release" of parental control on this sleep behavior did not occur in relationship to puberty and thus did not seem to influence the initiation of a phase preference delay.

Our previous MSLT [multiple sleep latency test] data from youngsters at various pubertal stages showed a midpubertal phase delay in the timing of daytime sleep tendency (4). In isolation, this finding was not thought to be of significance; however, in light of the present result, the pubertal delay of peak sleep tendency provides additional support for a biologically mediated phase delay linked to pubertal development. The source of such a biological process likely involves biological timing mechanisms. A link between the brain mechanisms controlling circadian rhythms and pubertal timing has been suggested principally due to the inverse relationship of melatonin and luteinizing hormone (LH) secretion across pubertal development (9). The potential links of melatonin to circadian as well as maturational processes make it a candidate to mediate a biological influence on a change in sleep phase position, which may influence phase preference.

Many important questions remain about mechanisms that may underlie the adolescent sleep preference delay. Do changes in gonadotropin secretion (associated with the secondary sexual and maturational characteristics used by our subjects in estimating their pubertal status) have a direct impact upon biological timing? Is the putative relationship between melatonin and puberty crucial or central to the change in phase preference? The physical changes of puberty may simply trigger a cascade of changes in the child's family milieu that include a transformation in the way parents control bedtime and secondarily encourage a delay in phase preference, although the present data indicating a lack of relationship between pubertal stage and parental bedtime setting do not favor this hypothesis.

If biological factors in early adolescence initiate a phase preference delay, then certain assumptions about teenagers' sleep patterns may need to be reexamined. For example, we have previously noted that insufficient sleep length may create a significant vulnerability in adolescents and that sleep extension may be a reasonable intervention (10). Behavioral approaches to intervene by altering the psychosocial milieu or the youngster's perception of it—perhaps, by encouraging "early to bed, early to rise"—may be difficult in the presence of a biologically driven delayed phase preference. Furthermore, the widespread practice in U.S. school districts for school buses to run and for the opening bell to ring earlier at high schools than junior high schools, and earlier in junior high schools than primary schools, may run precisely counter to children's biological needs. By the same token, teenagers faced with long school bus rides in addition to early starting time for school may confront incremental challenges in conflict with their biological propensities.

Teenagers' work schedules may need to be reevaluated as well. If an adolescent's phase preference is delayed, he or she may find it quite difficult to fall asleep sufficiently early to obtain adequate sleep before an early morning work shift. Factors such as these may need to be taken into account to provide acceptable lifestyle options for teenagers, options that will limit their exposure to situations that produce insufficient sleep and may interfere with achieving their maximum potential.

Notes

1. Petta D, Carskadon MA, Dement W. Sleep habits in children aged 7–13 years. *Sleep Res* 1984; 13: 86.
2. Carskadon MA. Adolescent sleepiness: increased risk in a high-risk population. *Alcohol Drugs Driving* 1990; 5, 6: 317–28.
3. Carskadon MA, Harvey K, Duke P, Anders TF, Litt IF, Dement WC. Pubertal changes in daytime sleepiness. *Sleep* 1980: 2: 453–60.
4. Carskadon MA. The second decade. In: C. Guilleminault, ed. *Sleeping and waking disorders: indications and techniques.* Menlo Park, CA: Addison Wesley, 1990: 99–125.
5. Horne, J, Östberg O. A self-assessment questionnaire to determine morningness–eveningness in human circadian rhythms. *Int J Chronobiol* 1976; 4: 97–110.
6. Smith CS, Reilly C, Midkiff K. Evaluation of three circadian rhythm questionnaires with suggestions for an improved measure of morningness. *J Appl Psychol* 1989; 74: 728–38.
7. Carskadon MA, Acebo C. Relationship of a morningness/eveningness scale to sleep patterns in children. *Sleep Res* 1992; 21: 367.
8. Carskadon MA, Acebo C. A self-administered rating scale of pubertal development. *J Adolesc Health Care* (in press).
9. Waldhauser F, Steger H. Changes in melatonin secretion with age and pubescence. *J Neural Transm* 1986; 21: 183–97.
10. Carskadon MA. Patterns of sleep and sleepiness in adolescents. *Pediatrician* 1990; 17: 5–12.

Questions

1. What are the dependent variables (measures of delayed phase preference)? On how many of these dependent variables does puberty have a significant effect?
2. Are there other confounding variables (variables other than puberty that might produce changes in sleep preference) that Carskadon and her colleagues do not control for?
3. Based on these data, is it time for a national movement to begin high schools at a later hour?

References and Further Reading

Carskadon, M. A., Harvey, K., Duke, P., Anders, T. F., Litt, I. F., & Dement, W. C. (1980). Pubertal changes in daytime sleepiness. *Sleep, 2,* 453–460.
Wolfson, A. R. (1996). Sleeping patterns of children and adolescents: Developmental trends, disruptions, and adaptations. *Child and Adolescent Psychiatric Clinics of North America, 5*(3), 549–568.

Wolfson, A. R., & Carskadon, M. A. (1998). Sleep schedules and daytime functioning in adolescents. *Child Development, 69* (4), 875–887.

3.3   Laurence Steinberg, 1988

Reciprocal Relation Between Parent–Child Distance and Pubertal Maturation

Laurence Steinberg, Ph.D., is the Distinguished University Professor and Laura H. Carnell Professor of Psychology at Temple University. He is director of the John D. and Catherine T. MacArthur Foundation Research Network on Adolescent Development and Juvenile Justice. Dr. Steinberg is coauthor of numerous books, including *Crossing Paths: How Your Child's Adolescence Triggers Your Own Crisis* (with Wendy Steinberg, 1994), *Beyond the Classroom: Why School Reform Has Failed and What Parents Need to Do* (with B. Bradford Brown and Sanford Dornbusch, 1996), and *You and Your Adolescent: A Parent's Guide for Ages 10 to 20* (with Ann Levine, 1997).

A great deal of evidence demonstrates that changes do occur in the parent–child relationship at adolescence (Reading 10.2). A number of theoretical models have addressed the connection between pubertal maturation and changes in the parent–child relationship (Paikoff & Brooks-Gunn, 1991). The psychoanalytic model contends that with upsurge in sexual energy at puberty, oedipal fantasies come out of repression and take on a more dangerous and threatening reality than in early childhood because they can now, indeed, happen (Freud, 1905/1962). As a consequence, conflict arises as adolescents struggle to disengage from the parental relationship. A second model postulates that hormonal changes may heighten adolescents' emotional lability, making parent–child interactions more volatile and less predictable (Buchanan, Eccles, & Becker, 1992). A third model holds that puberty leads to the development of physical changes, and that these changes serve as a signal to both adolescents and their parents of adolescents' emerging reproductive and social maturity (Brooks-Gunn & Zahaykevich, 1989). The physical changes thus precipitate changed expectations that parents and adolescents hold for one another. A final model, the most complex of the models, holds that pubertal changes act together with cognitive and other developmental changes and with preexisting individual and family characteristics, and together these factors determine the impact of pubertal changes on the parent–child relationship (Collins, 1988).

   The majority of research studies on the impact of puberty on parent–child relationships fit the third model, that pubertal changes serve as signals to parent and child of adolescents' reproductive and social maturation. Laurence Steinberg's research provides an extension to that model. Steinberg surveyed parents and their firstborn adolescents twice over a one-year period and found that pubertal maturation leads to greater parent–child conflict and distance, and that greater parent–child distance accelerates girls' maturation. Steinberg's sample, like the samples found in the majority of the research on parent–adolescent relationships, was based on participants that were predominantly white, middle class, and from two-parent families. The meaning of puberty may vary depending on ethnicity and family structure, and thus consideration needs to be given to whether these results might generalize to nonwhite samples or to adolescents who are not living in traditional two-parent families.

Abstract Previous research on adolescents and their parents has indicated that pubertal maturation, independent of chronological age, is associated with increased distance in the parent–child relationship, but the cross-sectional nature of these studies leaves open questions concerning the direction of effects. Using short-term longitudinal data, this study examines the reciprocal relation between parent–child distance and pubertal maturation in a sample of 157 male and female firstborn adolescents and their parents. Twice over a 1-year period, independent raters assessed each youngster's pubertal status, and parents and adolescents independently completed questionnaire measures of autonomy, conflict, and closeness in the parent–child relationship. Regression analyses indicate that puberty increases adolescent antonomy and parent–child conflict and diminishes parent–child closeness. Analyses also indicate that parent–child distance may, in turn, accelerate pubertal maturation among girls. Both proximal and distal explanations for the relation between parent–child distance and pubertal maturation are discussed.

Previous cross-sectional studies of adolescents and their parents have indicated that pubertal maturation, independent of chronological age, is associated with increased aloofness, dissatisfaction, or conflict in the parent–child relationship (Cantara, 1983; Hill, Holmbeck, Marlow, Green, & Lynch, 1985a, 1985b, Papini & Datan, 1987; Steinberg, 1977, 1981, 1987a, 1987b; Steinberg & Hill, 1978; Sussman, Inoff-Germain, Nottelmann, Cutler, & Chrousos, 1987). This phenomenon appears to be most apparent in relations between adolescents and mothers and during the midpoint of the pubertal cycle, although conflict and dissatisfaction may continue into late puberty, especially in families of girls (e.g., Hill et al., 1985b).[1] Although there are occasional, and generally minor, inconsistencies in the literature on pubertal status and family relations, the association between higher levels of parent–child distance and pubertal maturation has been replicated by several research teams using very different methods to study family relationships—including observational techniques (Papini & Datan, 1987; Steinberg, 1981) and questionnaires (Hill et al., 1985a, 1985b; Steinberg, 1987a; Sussman et al., 1987)—and using different indices of pubertal maturation—including global ratings of secondary sex characteristics made by independent observers (Papini & Sebby, 1987; Steinberg, 1981, 1987a), radioimmunoassays of pubertal hormones from serum (Sussman et al., 1987) or from saliva (Steinberg, 1987b), and questionnaire-derived assessments of menarcheal status (Hill et al., 1985b).

Although the evidence for the distancing impact of puberty on adolescents' relations with their parents is quite compelling, the cross-sectional research cited above still leaves open a question of fundamental importance. Although researchers have assumed that it is puberty that *leads to* distance between adolescents and parents and have interpreted their findings from such a vantage point—using psychoanalytic, social learning, or ethological perspectives on transformations in the family at puberty (e.g., Steinberg, 1981, 1987a)—it is possible that the direction of effect is the other way around. Increased distance between parents and their children may accelerate pubertal maturation, whereas increased closeness between parents and children may slow down the process of maturation. In light of evidence of environmental and social influences on menarcheal timing (Brooks-Gunn & Ruble, 1980; Warren, 1983), menstrual cycling (e.g., McClintock, 1971), and menstrual suppression (McClintock, 1980), and in light of recent findings suggesting that female pubertal timing varies as a function of family structure, with maturation occurring earlier among girls raised in single-parent or stepfamily households than in biologically intact families (M. K. Surbey, personal communication, March 29, 1987), it is entirely plausible that the rate of pubertal maturation may be influenced by the quality of familial relationships.

Data on puberty and social relations among nonhuman primates provide some support for the specific hypothesis that parent–child distance accelerates pubertal maturation. Among many Old World monkeys (e.g., macaques and baboons) and orangutans, the sexual maturation of males is inhibited as long as they remain in the company of dominant males. Among stumptail macaques raised in captivity, for example, it has been observed that the adolescent growth spurt is delayed among males living in the group unless the dominant male is removed; after the dominant male is taken out, the next highest-ranking male of sufficient biological maturity begins sexual development shortly thereafter (R. W. Goy, personal communication, November 1, 1986). Presumably, the psychological intimidation of dominant males over juveniles nearing puberty is great enough to inhibit maturational processes. Similar, and even more dramatic, findings have emerged from studies of monogamous New World monkeys, such as tamarins and marmosets. Here the evidence points to the inhibition of reproduction among female adolescents by the presence of the mother. The established effects are the suppression of ovulation among pubertal female marmosets living in the presence of their mother (Evans & Hodges, 1984); the slowing of sexual maturation among female cotton-top tamarins living in their natal group (Tardif, 1984); and the suppression of fertility among female cotton-top tamarins living in the presence of their mother (Ziegler, Savage, Scheffler, & Snowden, in press). Studies of social influences on pubertal onset in other mammals, including hamsters, wolves, and wild dogs, show similar patterns of effects (Levin & Johnston, 1986).

It is not clear from these studies of other species whether the operating mechanism is pheromonal in nature or related to some sort of stress-mediated behavioral or psychological inhibition. In either case, however, although the inhibitory effect of mothers' presence on daughters' fertility is of considerable duration, it is also very easily and swiftly reversed—suggesting that distance between adolescent females and their mother may accelerate maturation. When young anovulatory female marmosets are removed from their natal group, for example, ovarian cyclicity is established within 4 weeks (Evans & Hodges, 1984). Even more dramatic is evidence provided by Ziegler et al. (in press) of rapid reproductive maturation among female tamarins following their removal from the family environment—ovulation and conception in these monkeys occurred within 8 days of being removed from their mother. Although ovulatory suppression is not the same as maturational inhibition, the possibility that pubertal maturation among human adolescents may be inhibited by maternal closeness (or accelerated by maternal distance) thus is generally consistent with studies of other primates documenting similar patterns of social influence on juveniles' reproductive development and function.

The purpose of the present study was to examine, with short-term longitudinal data, the reciprocal relation between parent–child distance and pubertal maturation among human adolescents. The two hypotheses tested were that pubertal maturation leads to increases in parent–child distance (the *distancing hypothesis*) and that parent–child distance accelerates pubertal maturation (the *accelerating hypothesis*).

Method

Sample

The sample for the study consists of 157 families with a firstborn child between the ages of 11 and 16. Participating families were selected through a three-step process, beginning with a large representative sample of nearly 900 adolescents enrolled in the Madison (Wisconsin) school district, who were surveyed in their classrooms, and ending with a subsample of 157 families with firstborn adolescents, who were surveyed in their homes in 1985 and again in 1986. Participation rates in each phase of the data collection were adequate: Ninety-four percent of all youngsters attending school on the day of the survey participated in the research; 70% of the families contacted by our research staff agreed to participate in the study in 1985; and 75% of these families agreed to participate in the follow-up 1 year later. As a group, the participating families did not differ from the eligible nonparticipants on any of the demographic variables assessed (i.e., socioeconomic status, household composition, maternal employment status). Subsequent comparisons between the demographic characteristics of the study sample and those of the district's student population as a whole (based on information provided by the district) indicated that the school sample and the family subsample were representative of the district population. The sample was evenly divided by sex and was predominantly White (88%), socioeconomically heterogeneous (39% blue-collar, 37% white-collar, 24% professional; as determined by parental oc-

Table 1

Pubertal Status of Study Participants in 1985 and 1986

Status	1985		1986	
	% boys (N = 98)	% girls (N = 106)	% boys (N = 77)	% girls (N = 78)
Prepubertal	11	4	0	0
Early pubertal	23	30	14	3
Apex pubertal	17	14	13	13
Postapex	28	27	38	31
Late pubertal	20	25	35	54

cupation), from a variety of family structures (64% biologically intact, 21% single parent, 15% stepfamily), and with a variety of maternal work patterns (58% employed full time, 31% employed part time, 11% not working).

Measure of Pubertal Maturation

The measure of pubertal maturation derives from a 5-point rating scale, completed by the home visitor, in which the adolescent is rated along three dimensions; facial characteristics, body proportion and shape, and coordination. The interrater reliability of this measure was .81. Earlier work (Steinberg, 1987b) indicated that the measure correlates with hormonal measures in the expected direction. Raters were blind to family scores on the relationship measures, and 1986 raters were blind to pubertal assessments made in 1985. The distribution of youngsters across pubertal maturation categories in 1985 and in 1986 is presented in Table 1.

Measures of Family Relations

Adolescents, mothers, and fathers independently completed a questionnaire battery, which contained, among others, the measures of family relations used to examine the distancing and accelerating hypotheses. The measures of family relations at each point in time included two measures each of *autonomy, conflict* and *closeness* in the family.

Adolescent autonomy   The adolescent's level of *emotional autonomy* was assessed via a scale developed on the basis of Blos's (1979) perspective on individuation (see Steinberg and Silverberg, 1986, for details). The measure was composed of 20 Likert-scale items concerning four components of emotional autonomy: two cognitive components—the extent to which the adolescent perceives his or her parents as people and deidealizes them—and two affective components—an absence of feelings of dependency on parents and feelings of individuation. The internal consistency of the measure as determined by Cronbach's alpha was .75.

Each family member completed a checklist concerning 17 areas of decision making on issues relevant to children in the age range studied (e.g., curfew, spending money, leisure activities, completing school assignments). For each item, individuals indicated whether the parents dictated how the adolescent should behave, asked the youngster's opinion but retained the final say on the matter, or left the decision entirely up to the youngster. A measure of behavioral autonomy, or *parental permissiveness,* was derived by summing the number of items for which each individual reported that the adolescent was given decision-making autonomy. The internal consistency of the measure, as determined by Cronbach's alpha, was .78 for adolescents, .77 for fathers, and .78 for mothers. Adolescents' scores derived from a similar measure have been shown to be significantly related to youngsters' involvement in deviant activities and with youngsters' susceptibility to peer pressure—with adolescent deviance and susceptibility positively correlated with parental permissiveness (Dornbusch et al., 1985; Steinberg, 1987c).

Conflict   The measures of adolescent–parent conflict were derived from adolescents' and parents' responses to a series of questions about the intensity of discussions that may have occurred across 17 different areas of day-to-day decision making (e.g., curfew, clothing, homework) within a particular dyad during the past 2 weeks. Adolescents completed the questions twice, once with regard to their mother and once with regard to their father; each parent completed the questionnaire once with regard to the adolescent. The specific items were chosen in view of previous studies indicating that conflict between teenagers and parents is likely to revolve around mundane issues of day-to-day living (Montemayor, 1986). For each of the 17 items, the respondent was asked whether a discussion took place during the previous 2 weeks, and, if so, to rate the intensity of the discussion on a 5-point scale from *very calm* to *very angry.* The instrument was modeled after the Issues Checklist first developed by Prinz, Foster, Kent, and O'Leary (1979) and subsequently revised by Robin and Foster (1984), who reported that conflict scores derived from the measure significantly discriminate between families with and families without clinical problems. The internal consistency of the measure for adolescents with regard to mothers was .76; for adolescents with regard to fathers, .80; for mothers with regard to adolescents, .75; and for fathers with regard to adolescents, .80. Two scores were generated: *Frequency of conflict* is the number of items discussed for which the respondent reported any anger at all in the discussion (i.e., scores of 2 or more on the scale); *intensity of conflict* is the average level of intensity across all items for which a discussion took place.

Closeness   One measure of family closeness involved the frequency of calm discussions reported between the adolescent and each of his or her parents. The checklist used to derive the measures of conflict was used to derive this measure, and *calm communication* was operationalized as the number of items discussed during the past 2 weeks for which the respondent reported no anger at all (i.e., a score of 1). The second measure of closeness tapped *cohesion* in each of the parent–child dyads, as assessed via the cohesion subscale of the FACES II inventory. The FACES inventory is a widely used measure of family relations during adolescence in both clinical and nonclinical studies (see Olson, Sprenkle, & Russell, 1979, for details). The adolescent completed the inventory with reference to his or her mother and then again with reference to his or her father; each parent completed the inventory in terms of his or her relationship with the adolescent. Recent studies link positive scores on the FACES cohesion scale to positive scores on a measure of parent–adolescent communication

Table 2

Means and Standard Deviations of Family Relationship Measures

Variable	1985		1986	
	M	*SD*	*M*	*SD*
Adolescent's report				
Cohesion with M	56.22	10.25	53.26	9.72
Calm discussions with M	3.08	2.57	2.85	2.71
Cohesion with F	52.51	12.99	51.12	11.61
Calm discussions with F	2.35	2.61	2.86	2.62
Arguments with M	3.83	2.94	3.26	3.12
Intensity of conflict with M	1.90	.69	1.81	.63
Arguments with F	2.70	2.75	2.53	2.91
Intensity of conflict with F	1.95	.88	1.93	.83
Perceived permissiveness	6.43	2.75	6.94	2.93
Emotional autonomy	54.17	8.96	55.24	8.29
Mother's report				
Cohesion with C	59.43	6.37	56.93	6.92
Calm discussions with C	3.69	2.76	3.43	2.89
Arguments with C	4.76	3.22	4.22	3.23
Intensity of conflict with C	1.59	.61	1.94	.67
Perceived permissiveness	5.17	2.50	6.35	3.00
Father's report				
Cohesion with C	55.81	8.33	54.40	7.83
Calm discussions with C	2.88	2.98	2.86	2.62
Arguments with C	5.12	3.72	4.26	3.34
Intensity of conflict with C	2.02	.63	1.93	.66
Perceived permissiveness	4.36	2.66	4.24	3.39

Note. M = mother; F = father; C = child.

and to positive scores on a measure of family satisfaction (Barnes & Olson, 1985). The internal consistency of the measure in the sample discussed here was .87 for adolescents with regard to mother; .87 for adolescents with regard to father; .84 for mothers with regard to adolescent; and .86 for fathers with regard to adolescent. These coefficients are virtually identical to those reported by the developers of the instrument.

Means and standard deviations for all family-relationship variables, assessed at Times 1 and 2, appear in Table 2.

Plan of Analysis

Researchers continue to debate the appropriateness of various approaches to the analysis of longitudinal data in the study of individual development (e.g., Connell & Tanaka, 1987). Despite recent advances in structural equation modeling, it is still generally agreed that the use of multiple regression techniques—in which one predicts scores on a dependent variable at Time 2 while controlling for scores on that same variable at Time 1—is an appropriately conservative strategy. Accordingly, in order to examine the interrelation over time of pubertal maturation and parent–child distance, a series of regression analyses were conducted.

In the first series of analyses, pubertal maturation at Time 1 was used to predict parent–child distance at Time 2 while controlling for parent–child distance at Time 1. In light of previous research indicating that the impact of puberty on family relations may be curvilinear in some respects (e.g., Hill et al., 1985a, 1985b; Steinberg, 1981, 1987a), quadratic trends were tested after controlling for linear effects.

In the second set of analyses, parent–child distance at Time 1 was used to predict pubertal maturation at Time 2 while controlling for pubertal maturation at Time 1. In these latter analyses, youngsters who were rated as postpubertal at Time 1 were excluded because they had already reached the endpoint of the scale and thus could not be used in analyses focused on pubertal change.

These two sets of analyses amount, respectively, to tests of the impact of puberty on changes in parent–child distance and tests of the impact of parent–child distance on changes in pubertal status. Adolescents', mothers', and fathers' reports were examined separately, and analyses were conducted separately for males and females, in view of previous studies indicating both sex-of-child and sex-of-parent differences in the association between puberty and family relations (e.g., Steinberg, 1987a).

Results

Impact of Pubertal Maturation on Parent–Child Distance

Families of girls   The results of analyses concerning the impact of girls' pubertal maturation on their family relationships are presented in Table 3. In general, when girls' reports of family relations are examined, the distancing hypothesis is upheld (5 of the 10 variables examined were significantly predicted at .10 or better by pubertal status). For example, pubertal maturation increases the number of arguments that girls have with their mother, decreases the number of calm discussions that they have with their father, and increases the intensity of father–daughter conflict. Additionally, two quadratic trends reached borderline significance: Around the midpoint of the pubertal cycle, father–daughter cohesion diminished and girls' perceived behavioral autonomy declined. Pubertal maturation had a more modest impact on parents' reports of family relationships (3 of the 10 variables examined were significantly predicted by pubertal status at .10 or better). In each case, the effect was curvilinear. The period surrounding the pubertal apex was one during which the number of calm discussions between daughters and both parents decreased, but, contrary to the distancing hypothesis, one during which the number of arguments between fathers and daughters decreased as well.

Families of boys   The results of analyses concerning the impact of boys' pubertal maturation on their family relationships are presented in Table 4. Once again, when adolescents' reports of family relations were considered, the results provided support for the distancing hypothesis (4 of the 10 relations examined were significant at .05 or better). Specifically, pubertal maturation led to increases in the number of arguments

Table 3

Linear and Curvilinear Impact of Puberty
on Family Relations of Girls

Dependent variable	Linear		Curvilinear	
	b	R^{2a}	b	R^{2b}
Adolescents' reports				
Cohesion with M	.007	ns	.008	ns
Calm discussions with M	−.183	ns	−.589	ns
Arguments with M	.185[d]	.03	.448	ns
Conflict with M	.101	ns	−.191	ns
Cohesion with F	−.017	ns	.979[c]	
Calm discussions with F	−.342[e]	.11	.123	ns
Arguments with F	.019	ns	−.340	ns
Conflict with F	.270[d]	.07	−.045	ns
Emotional autonomy	−.308	ns	.039	ns
Perceived permissiveness	.107	ns	1.090[c]	.03
Mothers' reports				
Cohesion with D	.090	ns	.570	ns
Calm discussions with D	.180	ns	1.190[c]	.03
Arguments with D	−.038	ns	−.133	ns
Conflict with D	−.017	ns	−.550	ns
Permissiveness	.078	ns	.130	ns
Fathers' reports				
Cohesion with D	.045	ns	.109	ns
Calm discussions with D	.040	ns	1.665[d]	.07
Arguments with D	.014	ns	1.680[d]	.07
Conflict with D	−.081	ns	.000	ns
Permissiveness	−.023	ns	.424	ns

Note. M = mother; F = father; D = daughter. Ns range from 65 to 76 for mother–daughter dyads and from 47 to 59 for father–daughter dyads. [a] Additional variance in 1986 family-relations score explained by 1985 pubertal status after controlling for 1985 score on family-relations measure. [b]Additional variance in 1986 family-relations score explained by 1985 quadratic effect of pubertal status after controlling for 1985 score on family-relations measure and for the linear effect of pubertal status. [c]$p < .10$. [d]$p < .05$. [e]$p < .01$.

boys reported having with their mothers, to diminished father–son cohesion, and to increases in sons' reports of emotional and behavioral autonomy. These results were corroborated somewhat by parents' reports (4 of the 10 relations examined are significant at .10 or better). Pubertal maturation led to decreases in mother–son cohesion and, marginally, to increases in mothers' reports of behavioral autonomy. Examination of fathers' reports indicated that the period surrounding the pubertal apex was a time of increases in father–son conflict and, marginally, decreases in the number of calm discussions between father and son.

Impact of Family Relations on Pubertal Maturation

Results of analyses concerning the impact of family relations on adolescent pubertal maturation are presented in Table 5. In contrast to the findings concerning the impact

Table 4

Linear and Curvilinear Impact of Puberty
on Family Relations of Boys

Dependent variable	Linear		Curvilinear	
	b	$R^{2\ a}$	b	$R^{2\ b}$
	Adolescents' reports			
Cohesion with M	−.040	ns	.201	ns
Calm discussions with M	−.077	ns	−.827	ns
Arguments with M	.264 [d]	.07	−.323	ns
Conflict with M	.175	ns	.425	ns
Cohesion with F	−.194[d]	.04	−.277	ns
Calm discussions with F	−.032	ns	−.155	ns
Arguments with F	.151	ns	−.722	ns
Conflict with F	.222	ns	−.103	ns
Emotional autonomy	.222 [d]	.05	−.593	ns
Perceived permissiveness	.276 [e]	.07	−.471	ns
	Mothers' reports			
Cohesion with S	−.238[e]	.06	.723	ns
Calm discussions with S	.048	ns	−.004	ns
Arguments with S	−.109	ns	−.476	ns
Conflict with S	−.137	ns	.803	ns
Permissiveness	.127[c]	.03	.110	ns
	Fathers' reports			
Cohesion with S	−.052	ns	.287	ns
Calm discussions with S	.040	ns	1.024[c]	
Arguments with S	−.155	ns	−.568	ns
Conflict with S	−.140	ns	−1.152[d]	.04
Permissiveness	.000	ns	−.101	ns

Note. M = mother; F = father; S = son. *N*s range from 58 to 73 for mother–son dyads and from 46 to 60 for father–son dyads.
[a]Additional variance in 1986 family-relations factor explained by 1985 pubertal status after controlling for 1985 score on family-relations factor. [b]Additional variance in 1986 family-relations factor explained by 1985 quadratic effect of pubertal status after controlling for 1985 score on family-relations factor and linear effect of pubertal status. [c]$p < .10$.
[d]$p < .05$. [e]$p < .01$.

of pubertal maturation on family relations reported above, indicating that boys' and girls' families were similarly affected by puberty, the impact of family relations on adolescent pubertal maturation appeared to be sex-specific. Whereas boys' rate of maturation was unaffected by their relations with their parents, girls' maturation appeared to be accelerated by parent–child distance, particularly in the mother–daughter dyad. Specifically, when girls' reports were considered, 4 of the 10 relations examined were significant in the hypothesized direction at .10 or better. Girls who report having fewer calm discussions with their mother, more intense conflict with their mother, and more behavioral autonomy matured faster than their counterparts. There was a borderline effect, in the same direction, for the impact of mother–child cohesion on pubertal maturation. This pattern of results, consistent with the accelerating hypothesis, was not consistently corroborated, however, when parents' reports of family rela-

Table 5

Impact of Family Relations on Adolescent Pubertal Development

Independent variable	Boys		Girls	
	b	R^{2a}	b	R^{2a}
Adolescents' reports				
Cohesion with M	−.009	ns	−.183[b]	.03
Calm discussions with M	.000	ns	−.292[d]	.08
Arguments with M	.114	ns	.004	ns
Conflict with M	.101	ns	.232[d]	.05
Cohesion with F	−.044	ns	−.148	ns
Calm discussions with F	.009	ns	−.130	ns
Arguments with F	−.050	ns	.140	ns
Conflict with F	−.135	ns	.178	ns
Emotional autonomy	.058	ns	.146	ns
Perceived permissiveness	.136	ns	.196[c]	.04
Mothers' reports				
Cohesion with A	−.034	ns	−.196[d]	.03
Calm discussions with A	.063	ns	.158	ns
Arguments with A	.096	ns	−.167[b]	.02
Conflict with A	.029	ns	−.016	ns
Permissiveness toward A	−.087	ns	.072	ns
Fathers' reports				
Cohesion with A	.019	ns	−.082	ns
Calm discussions with A	−.116	ns	.093	ns
Arguments with A	.034	ns	−.225[c]	.05
Conflict with A	.116	ns	−.085	ns
Permissiveness toward A	−.134	ns	−.045	ns

Note. M = mother; F = father; A = adolescent. *N*s range from 55 to 59 for mother–son dyads, from 40 to 47 for father–son dyads, from 53 to 59 for mother–daughter dyads, and from 41 to 47 for father–daughter dyads.
[a]Additional variance in 1986 pubertal status explained by 1985 family-relations factor after controlling for 1985 pubertal status. [b]$p < .10$, [c]$p < .05$. [d]$p < .01$.

tions were considered. Although mother–child cohesion tended to slow girls' pubertal maturation (consistent with the accelerating hypothesis), arguments between mothers and daughters and, marginally, between fathers and daughters inhibited maturation as well (contrary to the hypothesis).

Discussion

This short-term longitudinal study provides further support for the notion that pubertal maturation distances youngsters from their parents and suggests, as well, that distance in the parent–child relationship may itself accelerate pubertal maturation among girls. Although students of adolescent psychosocial development have assumed that pubertal maturation is inevitably an independent variable, the pattern of results reported here indicates that the connection between physical development and social relations at adolescence is likely to be reciprocal and bidirectional.

In general, the overall pattern of results provides clear support for the hypothesis that pubertal maturation increases parent–adolescent distance. These results replicate (with longitudinal data) findings that have been reported previously in cross-sectional studies of similar phenomena (e.g., Steinberg, 1987a). Specifically, in families of boys and girls alike, pubertal development leads to increases in conflict between adolescents and their mothers and decreases in closeness between adolescents and their fathers. Among girls, pubertal maturation also leads to increases in father–child conflict; among boys, puberty leads to increases in emotional and behavioral autonomy. In addition to the linear effects of pubertal maturation on parent–child distance, analyses revealed occasional curvilinear effects as well, effects that are generally consistent with the notion that parent–child distance may be especially intense during midpuberty. The combined picture suggests that, whereas pubertal maturation in general exerts an overall distancing effect on the parent–child relationship, the main distancing effects may occur earlier, rather than later, in the pubertal cycle.

As in previous studies of puberty and family relations, this research indicates that the distancing impact of puberty, although clear and consistent, is very modest in magnitude—on average, pubertal status accounts for approximately 5% of the variance in adolescent–parent relations. Thus, although it seems safe to conclude from this and other studies that puberty indeed distances adolescents from their parents, it is important to keep in mind that the amount of increased distance attributable to pubertal maturation is not large. Certainly it would be erroneous to interpret these findings as supportive of the idea that puberty is accompanied by familial "storm and stress."

The findings concerning the impact of parent–child distance on adolescent pubertal development suggest that distance in the mother–child relationship may accelerate pubertal development among girls (or, alternatively, that mother–child closeness may slow girls' pubertal development). No similar effect was found among boys, however. The fact that female reproductive development and functioning are sensitive to environmental factors is not surprising and, indeed, has been documented in studies of delayed menarche and menstrual synchrony in humans (McClintock, 1971; Warren, 1983) and, as noted earlier, in studies of sexual maturation among nonhuman primates (e.g., Tardif, 1984). The specific finding that mother–daughter closeness is associated with slower physical development is consistent with the studies of New World monkeys (cited earlier) indicating that maternal proximity may inhibit pubertal females' ovulation, sexual maturation, or fertility. Although the similarities between the effects noted in this study and those noted in these nonhuman studies are provocative, the results of this research are clearly in need of replication. Again, it is important to keep in mind that the significant effects were small in magnitude (on average, about 5% of the variance in pubertal maturation is explained by any one measure of mother–child distance).

The reader should bear in mind two important caveats in interpreting the findings presented here. First, the relation between pubertal development and family relationships is far more apparent when adolescents' reports of their family relationships are used than when mothers' or fathers' reports are used; indeed, in some instances, significant relations between puberty and parental reports were contrary to hypothesis. The fact that the measure of pubertal maturation derives from an independent rater's assessment, and not from the adolescent's self-report, argues against dismissing the significant findings as mere methodological artifacts. Nevertheless, one must entertain the notion that pubertal maturation is associated with an increase in the adolescent's *subjective* sense of distance from his or her parents, rather than an increase in actual distance—a notion that is certainly consistent with psychoanalytic (e.g., Freud, 1958) and neoanalytic (e.g., Blos, 1979) perspectives on the role of puberty in stimulating adolescent detachment and individuation. These analytic perspectives suggest that much of the impact of puberty on family relations is intrapsychic rather than behavioral. In any event, further longitudinal study using different sorts of measures of family relations (e.g., observational as well as questionnaire) is clearly called for.

A second caveat concerns the issue of causality. Although hypotheses derived from cross-sectional findings were tested with longitudinal data in order to shed light on the direction of effects, even longitudinal data, when nonexperimental in nature, can not demonstrate causality; longitudinal designs of this sort only demonstrate temporal precedence. The possibility that the significant, reciprocal, over-time relation between parent–child distance and pubertal maturation is an artifact of some unmeasured third variable is minimized by the nature of the analyses, however, which control for the concurrent relation between the measures of distance and the measure of pubertal status in predicting their lagged relation. Any such "third variable" arguments, therefore, would have to explain why this variable accounts for the lagged relation between puberty and parent–child distance, but not the contemporaneous relation.

Why might pubertal maturation both provoke and follow from increased parent–child distance? The notion that puberty should *lead to* increased parent–child distance is consistent with both psychoanalytic (e.g., Freud, 1958) and social learning (e.g., McCandless, 1970) perspectives on the family at adolescence and needs little elaboration here. Briefly stated, analytic views suggest that puberty revives adolescent intrapsychic conflicts, ultimately forcing the adolescent to detach from parental objects; social learning models suggest that puberty changes the nature of adolescent social relations, orienting the adolescent toward age mates, and away from parents, as sources of social rewards. In either case, one would expect that it is the adolescent who distances himself or herself from parents, rather than vice versa—an expectation borne out by the observation in this study that adolescents' reports of family relations are more consistently correlated with pubertal maturation than are those of parents. The mechanism underlying the increase in parent–adolescent distance at puberty may involve unconscious psychological processes (cf. Blos, 1979), conscious changes in adolescent self-conceptions or views of family relationships (e.g., Smetana, in press), hormone-mediated changes in behavior or mood (e.g., Steinberg, 1987b; Sussman et al., 1987), or some combination of all three.

Because our understanding of environmental influences on biological processes at adolescence is relatively limited, it is more difficult to account for the inhibiting impact of mother–child closeness on female pubertal maturation. We do know, however, that neuroendocrine processes are sensitive to stress and that stress may interfere with hormonal activity (cf., McClintock, 1980). One hypothesis worthy of future investigation, therefore, is that a high level of maternal closeness at a time when the adolescent may be striving for autonomy is experienced by the adolescent as stressful, and that this stress, in turn, inhibits certain endocrine activity related to pubertal development. Why this process appears to be limited to female adolescents is not clear; in general, less is known about environmental influences on sexual development among male adolescents than among females. An alternative hypothesis, more consistent with a sex-specific effect, suggests a pheromonal mechanism: Chemical and olfactory transducers have been implicated in studies of menstrual synchrony among women (McClintock, 1980) and in studies of fertility suppression among female monkeys (e.g., Epple & Katz, 1984).

It is interesting, in closing, to consider a more distal explanation for the association between pubertal maturation and parent–child distance. Among virtually all group-living nonhuman primates, emigration from the family group takes place around the time of puberty (Caine, 1986). This emigration plays an important role in increasing reproductive fitness, because the process serves to minimize inbreeding and increase genetic diversity. Thus, there may be an evolved basis for individuals to physically distance themselves from their parents sometime shortly after puberty. In fact, historical evidence (e.g., Katz, 1975) and cross-cultural evidence (e.g., Cohen, 1964) suggest that emigration from the family group at puberty has been common at earlier points in time in human history as well. Because the economic dependence of young adolescents on their parents in contemporary society has made leaving the family at puberty virtually impossible, however, a modern analogue of adolescent emigration may well have developed. Psychological distance at puberty—in the form of increased conflict, increased autonomy, and decreased cohesion—may be an atavism related to a pattern of behavior that at one time protected the genetic integrity of the species.

Note

1. This literature should not be confused with that contrasting the family relationships of early and late maturers; studies of pubertal timing and family relations have yielded equivocal findings (see Steinberg, 1987a, for a review).

References

Barnes, H., & Olson, D. (1985). Parent–adolescent communication and the circumplex model. *Child Development, 56,* 438–447.

Blos, P. (1979). *The adolescent passage.* New York: International Universities Press.

Brooks-Gunn, J., & Ruble, D. (1980). Menarche: The interaction of physiological, cultural, and social factors. In A. Dan, E. Graham, & C. Beecher (Eds.), *The menstrual cycle* (Vol., 1, pp. 141–159). New York: Springer.

Caine, N. (1986). Behavior during puberty and adolescence. In G. Mitchell & J. Erwin (Eds.), *Comparative primate biology: Vol. 2A. Behavior, conservation, and ecology* (pp. 327–361). New York: Alan R. Liss.

Cantara, A. (1983). *Pubertal status and assertiveness in family interaction in early adolescent girls.* Unpublished masters thesis, Virginia Commonwealth University, Richmond.

Cohen, Y. (1964). *The transition from childhood into adolescence.* Chicago: Aldine.

Connell, J., & Tanaka, J. (Eds.). (1987). Structural equation modeling. [Special Section of Issue]. *Child Development, 58* (1).

Dornbusch, S., Carlsmith, J., Bushwall, S., Ritter, P., Leiderman, H., Hastorf, A., & Gross, R. (1985). Single parents, extended households, and the control of adolescents. *Child Development, 56,* 326–341.

Epple, G., & Katz, Y. (1984). Social influences on estrogen excretion and ovarian cyclicity in saddleback tamarins (*Saginus fuscicollis*). *American Journal of Primatology, 1,* 171–183.

Evans, S., & Hodges, J. K. (1984). Reproductive status of adult daughters in family groups of common marmosets (*Callithrix jacchus jacchus*). *Folia Primatologica, 42,* 127–133.

Freud, A. (1958). Adolescence. *Psychoanalytic Study of the Child, 13,* 255–278.

Hill, J., Holmbeck, G., Marlow, L., Green, T., & Lynch, M. (1985a). Pubertal status and parent–child relations in families of seventh-grade boys. *Journal of Early Adolescence, 5,* 31–44.

Hill, J., Holmbeck, G., Marlow, L., Green, T., & Lynch, M. (1985b). Menarcheal status and parent–child relations in families of seventh-grade girls. *Journal of Youth and Adolescence, 14,* 301–316.

Katz, M. B. (1975). *The people of Hamilton, Canada West: Family and class in a mid-nineteenth century city.* Cambridge, MA: Harvard University Press.

Levin, R., & Johnston, R. (1986). Social mediation of puberty: An adaptive female strategy? *Behavioral and Neural Biology, 46,* 308–324.

McCandless, B. (1970). *Adolescents.* Hinsdale, IL: Dryden Press.

McClintock, M. (1971). Menstrual synchrony and suppression. *Nature, 229,* 244.

McClintock, M. (1980). Major gaps in menstrual cycle research: Behavioral and physiological controls in a biological context. In P. Komnenich, M. McSweeney, J. Noack, & N. Elder (Eds.), *The menstrual cycle* (Vol. 2, pp. 7–23). New York: Springer.

Montemayor, R. (1986). Family variation in parent–adolescent storm and stress. *Journal of Adolescent Research, 1,* 15–31.

Olson, D., Sprenkle, D., & Russell, C. (1979). Circumplex model of marital and family systems: 1. Cohesion and adaptability dimensions, family types, and clinical applications. *Family Process, 18,* 3–28.

Papini, D., & Datan, N. (1987). *An observational study of affective and identity-oriented family interactions during adolescence.* Manuscript submitted for publication.

Papini, D., & Sebby, R. (1987). Adolescent pubertal status and affective family relationships: A multivariate assessment. *Journal of Youth and Adolescence, 16,* 1–15.

Prinz, R., Foster, S., Kent, R., & O'Leary, K. (1979). Multivariate assessment of conflict in distressed and nondistressed mother–adolescent dyads. *Journal of Applied Behavioral Analysis, 12,* 691–700.

Robin, A., & Foster, S. (1984). Problem-solving communication training: A behavioral–family systems approach to parent–adolescent conflict. In P. Karoly & J. Steffen (Eds.), *Adolescent behavior disorders: Foundations and contemporary concerns* (Vol. 3, pp. 195–240). Lexington, MA: Lexington Books.

Smetana, J. (in press). Concepts of self and social convention: Adolescents' and parents' reasoning about hypothetical and actual family conflicts. In M. R. Gunnar (Ed.), *21st Minnesota symposium on child psychology.* Hillsdale, NJ: Erlbaum.

Steinberg, L. (1977). *A longitudinal study of physical growth, intellectual growth, and family interaction in early adolescence.* Unpublished doctoral dissertation, Cornell University.

Steinberg, L. (1981). Transformations in family relations at puberty. *Developmental Psychology, 17,* 833–840.

Steinberg, L. (1987a). The impact of puberty on family relations: Effects of pubertal status and pubertal timing. *Developmental Psychology, 23,* 451–460.

Steinberg, L. (1987b, April). *Pubertal status, hormone levels, and family relations: The distancing hypothesis.* Paper presented at the biennial meetings of the Society for Research in Child Development, Baltimore, Maryland.

Steinberg, L. (1987c). Single parents, stepparents, and the susceptibility of adolescents to antisocial peer pressure. *Child Development, 58,* 269–275.

Steinberg, L., & Hill, J. (1978). Patterns of family interaction as a function of age, the onset of puberty, and formal thinking. *Developmental Psychology, 14,* 683–684.

Steinberg, L., & Silverberg, S. (1986). The vicissitudes of autonomy in early adolescence. *Child Development, 57,* 841–851.

Sussman, E., Inoff-Germain, G., Nottelmann, E., Cutler, G., Jr., & Chrousos, G. (1987). Hormones, emotional dispositions, and aggressive attributes in early adolescents. *Child Development, 58,* 1114–1134.

Tardif, S. (1984). Social influences on sexual maturation of female *Saquinus oedipus oedipus. American Journal of Primatology, 6,* 199–209.

Warren, M. (1983). Physical and biological aspects of puberty. In J. Brooks-Gunn & A. Peterson (Eds.), *Girls at puberty* (pp. 3–28). New York: Plenum.

Ziegler, T. E., Savage, A., Scheffler, G., & Snowdon, C. T. (in press). The endocrinology of puberty and reproductive function in female cotton-top tamarinds (*Saginus oedipus*) under varying social conditions. *Biology of Reproduction.*

Questions

1. When a child begins pubertal maturation, what feelings does this arouse in parents? In the child?
2. Is there a causal relationship between pubertal maturation and parent–child distance?
3. What is the magnitude of the effect of pubertal maturation on parent–child distance? What is the magnitude of the effect of parent–child distance on pubertal maturation?
4. Why are the results stronger for adolescent reports than for parent reports?
5. Are Steinberg's findings likely to generalize to adolescents who are neither white, middle class, nor from two–parent families?

References and Further Reading

Brooks-Gunn, J., & Zahaykevich, M. (1989). Parent–child relationships in early adolescence: A developmental perspective. In K. Kreppner & R. M. Lerner (Eds.). *Family systems and life-span development* (pp. 223–246). Hillsdale, NJ: Lawrence Erlbaum.

Buchanan, C. M., Eccles, J. S., & Becker, J. B. (1992). Are adolescents the victims of raging hormones: Evidence of activational effects of hormones on moods and behavior at adolescence. *Psychological Bulletin, 111,* 62–107.

Collins, W. A. (1988). Developmental theories in research on the transition to adolescence. In M. R. Gunner, & W. A. Collins (Eds.). *Minnesota symposia on child psychology* (Vol. 21) (pp. 1–15). Hillsdale, NJ: Lawrence Erlbaum.

Collins, W. A., & Laursen, B. (1992). Conflict and the transition to adolescence. In C. U. Shantz & W. W. Hartup (Eds.). *Conflict in child and adolescent development* (pp. 216–241). Cambridge, U.K.: Cambridge University Press.

Freud, S. (1905/1962). Three contributions to the theory of sex. New York: E. P. Dutton.

Laursen, B., Coy, K. C., & Collins, W. A. (1994). Interpersonal conflict during adolescence. *Psychological Bulletin, 115,* 197–209.

Laursen, B., Coy, K. C., & Collins, W. A. (1998). Reconsidering changes in parent–child conflict across adolescence: A meta-analysis. *Child Development, 69*(3), 817–832.

Paikoff, R. L., & Brooks-Gunn, J. (1991). Do parent-child relationships change during puberty? *Psychological Bulletin, 110*(1), 47–66.

Chapter 4

Cognitive Development

Adolescence is marked not only by a period of rapid physical growth and sexual maturation, but also by the development of new cognitive capacities. Whether or not that cognitive growth is attributable to biological maturation is less certain and methodologically very difficult to determine. More is known about *how* thought matures, and the theorist who has made the greatest contribution to our understanding of cognitive development is Jean Piaget. According to Piaget's theory, a transition occurs in early adolescence from the stage of concrete operational thought to the stage of formal operational thought (Piaget, 1932, 1972).

Formal thought enables an individual to think abstractly, to formulate contrary-to-fact hypotheses, and to engage in hypothetico-deductive thought,—to think about all the possibilities inherent in the solution of a problem, to then check out the possibilities one by one, and to understand that the observed is simply one out of a set of logical possibilities. With formal thought, an adolescent comes to understand that a belief is not a truth, but a hypothesis. An adolescent who has attained formal operational thought can deal with many attributes simultaneously and can assume a relativistic view.

The acquisition of formal operational thought has important consequences for the ways that adolescents think about themselves, their peers, their parents, their belief systems, and moral problems. Erik Erikson (Reading 5.1) placed the crisis of identity at this stage in part because of the acquisition of new cognitive capacities that enable adolescents to think differently about the self. Only at this stage do individuals begin to have the capacity to think abstractly about who they were in the past, who they are now, and who they might become or want to become in the future, and to integrate the various identity elements into a coherent whole in accordance with societal roles and opportunities.

Parents are viewed and responded to differently once formal thought is acquired (Reading 10.2). Adolescents move from idealizing parents as omnipotent to conceptualizing them as more complex individuals with strengths and weaknesses. Adolescents have the capacity to engage in more complex and challenging discussions with their parents. When parents tell a 7-year-old to get in bed at 9:00 P.M., the child may protest or complain, but the response is quite different from that of an adolescent told to be home by midnight. From the perspective of a formal thinker, the midnight curfew is seen as totally relative, one of many logical possibilities: one might have an 11 P.M. curfew, a 1 A.M. curfew, or no curfew at all. Adolescents have the capacity to challenge their parents on a new level, demanding that parents defend the logic of their decisions.

Formal thought brings a change in the way individuals think about moral problems. With the acquisition of formal thought comes an awareness that society's definition of right and wrong is relative, only one of many possible definitions. A formal thinker can see that while a society has agreed on a set of laws, society could agree to change those laws. Rather than simply upholding the conventional standards of society, an adolescent begins to question definitions of right and wrong. Research on college students noted extreme relativist responses to moral dilemmas (Kohlberg & Kramer, 1969). Students saw right and wrong as a matter of personal values, and seemed to be caught in a stage of relativism before moving on to a commitment to moral principles that are universal and have validity across situations.

The readings in this chapter address the impact of the development of new cognitive capacities on three areas: adolescent belief systems (Reading 4.1), adolescent egocentrism (Reading 4.2), and adolescents' self-concepts (Reading 4.3).

Additional Resources

References and Suggested Reading

Erikson, E. H. (1968). *Identity: youth and crisis.* New York: W. W. Norton.

Kohlberg, L., & Gilligan, C. (Fall 1971). The adolescent as a philosopher: The discovery of the self in a postconventional world. *Daedalus,* 1051–1086.

Kohlberg, L., & Kramer, R. (1969). Continuities and discontinuities in childhood and adult moral development. *Human Development, 12,* 93–120.

Piaget, J. (1932). *The moral judgment of the child.* London: Routledge & Kegan Paul.

Piaget, J. (1972). Intellectual evolution from adolescence to adulthood. *Human Development, 15,* 1–12.

On the Internet

http://www.personal.psu.edu/faculty/n/x/nxd10/cognition.htm

Adolescence: Change & Continuity—Cognitive Transitions
This site was produced by Pennsylvania State University students taking the following courses: Human Development and Family Studies 433: The Transition to Adulthood, and Human Development and Family Studies 239: Adolescent Development.

4.1   Jerome Kagan, 1971

A Conception of Early Adolescence

Jerome Kagan, Ph.D., is the Daniel and Amy Starch Research Professor Emeritus of Psychology at Harvard University. Dr. Kagan is codirector of Harvard Medical School's Institute of Mind/Brain/Behavior. He is author of many books including *Child Development and Personality* (1969), *Change and Continuity in Infancy* (1971), *Understanding Children* (1971), *Growth of the Child* (1978), *The Nature of the Child* (with Nancy Snidman, Doreen Arcus, and J. Steven Reznick, 1994), *Galen's Prophecy: Temperament in Human Nature* (1998), and *Three Seductive Ideas* (2000).

Researchers have found that normal children across cultures pass through the first three cognitive phases of development that Piaget described in the same fixed order he described. Research has found, however, that the attainment of formal operational thought, the last stage of cognitive development held to be attained at adolescence, does not appear to be universal. Piaget and other cognitive researchers discovered that normal adolescents develop the *potential* for formal operational thought, but whether they actually attain it depends on their environment and whether there is demand for the use of these formal structures. Those with greater educational opportunities are more likely to acquire formal thought. Also, tasks of varying difficulty have been used to measure formal thought, and the number of individuals who display formal thought is influenced by the difficulty of the task that is used in its measurement.

The acquisition of new cognitive capacities at adolescence has far-reaching implications. Formal operational thought gives adolescents the capacity to discover that their own mental constructions may be arbitrary and enables them to formulate their own values and beliefs as separate and different from those they may have internalized during childhood. Jerome Kagan describes a new cognitive competence that comes with the acquisition of formal operational thought, the disposition to examine the logic and consistency of existing beliefs in sets. This new competence enables adolescents to rethink their existing beliefs and to search for inconsistencies between beliefs they have held for many years and beliefs they hold at the moment. Kagan argues that adolescents are induced to rethink existing beliefs because puberty brings sexual thoughts and behaviors that must be addressed to ascendancy. In addition, American society confronts adolescents with many phenomena such as drugs, sex, and school, about which they are likely to feel uncertain and need to resolve their feelings. The re-examination of the logic and consistency of beliefs may be more or less likely to occur depending upon an adolescent's social context and the challenges it poses.

T he Western mind is friendly toward the construction of discrete, abstract categories, each with its special set of defining characteristics, a prejudice best appreciated by comparing the perspective of the West with that of the classical Chinese. The latter preferred to view nature and experience as a contained and continuous whole. Day and night, to the Western eye, are two discrete entities separated by a transitional stage; to the Chinese they are part of one process, each being a diminution of the other. This conceptual posture had profound effects on the early development of physical science in each community. Western science, by celebrating atomism, made extraordinary advances in the physical theory of matter; early Chinese physics, by adhering to a philosophy of wholeness, focused on wave-like phenomena and made discoveries in fluid mechanics and sound that were in advance of the Europeans.

The particularism of the contemporary Western psychologist, perhaps an heir of atomism, leaps naturally to a view of human development as a sequence of discrete stages, each with its own unique attributes, catalyzed into manifest form by a delicate marriage of biological maturation and experience. "Now you see it, now you don't" is the metaphor for growth, and Western psychologists have provided us with a sequence of nodes called infancy, childhood, adolescence, and adulthood. [Sigmund] Freud and [Jean] Piaget invented four more exotic names to mark this journey, while [Erik] Erikson expanded the list to seven by focusing on the changing profile of psychological conflicts, rather than the biological bases of sensuality or complexity of thought. Stage theorists have been enormously attractive to Western intellectuals and Freud, Erikson, and Piaget owe their justly earned popularity to the fact that they chose to describe development in a form that the larger community was prepared, indeed, wanted to believe.

These introductory comments are not intended to negate the simple observation that behavior changes with growth, or the less obvious fact that the rapidity of many of these changes is correlated with particular periods of time. A child's stature increases most rapidly during the first three years and again at puberty, and this knowledge is a sufficient reason to call these time epochs by some name that implies stages of physical development. It is reasonable, therefore, to ask if the period between ten and fifteen years of age should be regarded as a stage of psychological development. Are the changes that occur during this five-year epoch psychologically more coherent than those that occur during the five years that precede or succeed that time. We cannot answer this question easily for dramatically different environmental pressures operate during the successive five-year eras from kindergarten through college. We can tame the equivocation by noting that puberty, which occurs in the middle of this period for the vast majority of children all over the world, supplies a firm platform for further inquiry. This essay poses a simple question—Do the changes that occur around puberty justify the positing of a psychological stage called early adolescence?—and answers that question affirmatively.

The soundest basis for postulating a stage in psychological development occurs when biology has prepared the child for a change in cognitive structure, motive, affect, or behavior, with experience playing the role of inducer. Exquisite, time-locked mechanisms alter the individuals' psychic competence so that he is able to react to events in a new way. An embryological analogy may be helpful. The concept of critical period, which was born in experimental embryology and nurtured in comparative psychology, is appropriately applied whenever there is a delimited period of time when certain events—internal or external—have formative effects on a developing physiological system, organ, or tissue. The biologists conceptualize this process in terms of an inherent biological competence potentiated by external forces. To illustrate, at a particular time in development certain ectodermal cells in the salamander acquire the potentiality to become the lens of the eye, if and only if certain inductive ectodermal tissue is present in the vicinity to alter surface properties of cells and allow that competence to become manifest. The lens will not develop if the inducing tissues and their appropriate chemical substances are introduced before the competence is acquired or after it has been lost. It is possible that biological developments of which we are unaware prepare the child for major psychological changes in early adolescence, if and only if the proper inducing experiences occur. If they occur too early or too late the psychological structures may be aberrant.

How shall this new psychological competence be characterized? Although man has been described as a sensory surface, a collection of responses, a reservoir of affect, or a structure of beliefs, we shall focus on the latter characterization because cognitive functions seem to be central to the changes that occur at puberty.

The essence of the argument is that the twelve-year-old has acquired a new cognitive competence—the disposition to examine the logic and consistency of his existing beliefs. The emergence of this competence, which may be dependent on biological changes in the central nervous system, is catalyzed by experiences that confront the adolescent with phenomena and attitudes that are not easily interpreted with his existing ideology. These intrusions nudge the preadolescent to begin an analytic reexamination of his knowledge.

Biological puberty is the only universal source of conflict inducing information, and it should be appreciated that cultures differ in how many additional inductive catalysts they provide. Since we have insufficient information about the detailed conflicts posed by other cultures, I shall restrict most of the discussion to the American community and consider those experiences that might induce cognitive conflict in

American twelve-year-olds. It seems reasonable to suggest that these experiences are intimately yoked to family, school, religion, and sexuality.

The Nature of the New Cognitive Competence

During the few years prior to puberty the child is gradually acquiring several new and profound intellective capacities. First, he gains an ease in dealing with hypothetical premises that may violate reality. The twelve-year-old will accept and think about the following problem: "All three legged snakes are purple, I am hiding a three legged snake, guess its color?"

The seven-year-old is confused by the fact that the initial premises violate his notion of what is real and he will not cooperate. The younger child, unlike the adolescent, does not appreciate the discontinuity between the self-contained information in a hypothetical problem and the egocentric information he carries with him for more practical challenges. Hence if an adolescent is asked, "There are three schools, Roosevelt, Kennedy, and Lincoln schools, and three girls, Mary, Sue, and Jane, who go to different schools: Mary goes to the Roosevelt school, Jane to the Kennedy school, where does Sue go?" he quickly answers "Lincoln." The seven-year-old may excitedly reply, "Sue goes to the Roosevelt school because my sister has a friend called Sue and that's the school she goes to."

To appreciate that problems can be self-contained entities solved by special rules is a magnificent accomplishment that is not usually attained until early adolescence.

The adolescent is more consistently able to induce rules from events with multiple attributes. Specifically, he is capable of inferring conjunctive and disjunctive concepts from appropriate data. An aunt is both a female and a blood relative; a mammal is an animal who nurses its young. A game is an activity that can be played either alone or with others; a strike is either swinging at a ball and missing it, or failing to swing at a ball thrown in the appropriate area. The adolescent can deal with multiple attributes simultaneously and is not limited to a one-at-a-time analysis. This ability allows the adolescent to think about events as arrangements of multiple dimensions, and to appreciate that an experience is often dependent on events not in the immediate field. He knows that his mother's anger can be provoked by any one of several violations, and realizes that her anger at dinner might be a product of yesterday's report card.

The adolescent can assume a relativistic view and is not troubled by the fact that the acceptability of a lie depends on both the situation and the intentions of the actor. He can excuse a hostile greeting from a friend if he believes the original incentive for the coolness occurred hours earlier in another context. The younger child is more absolute and mechanistic in his inferences. A lie is always bad; a hostile attack is seen as a direct and immediate result of the child's action or existence.

Of special relevance for this essay is the fact that the adolescent is disposed to examine his beliefs in sets, and to search for inconsistencies among them and between the beliefs and related actions. This inclination depends partly on the previous abilities, because critical examination of the logic of a set of related beliefs requires the capacity to consider multiple rules simultaneously. Thus, the fourteen-year-old broods about the inconsistency among the following three propositions:

1. God loves man.

2. The world contains many unhappy people.
3. If God loved man, he would not make so many people unhappy.

The adolescent is troubled by the incompatibility that is immediately sensed when he examines these statements together. He notes the contradiction, and has at least four choices. He can deny the second premise that man is ever unhappy; this is unlikely for its factual basis is too overwhelming. He can deny that God loves man; this is avoided for love of man is one of the definitional qualities of God. He can assume that the unhappiness serves an ulterior purpose God has for man; this possibility is sometimes chosen. Finally, he can deny the hypothesis of God.

The last alternative, which has become the popular form of the resolution in Western society, has profound consequences. This conclusion is a denial of a belief that has been regarded as true for many years, and invites the implication that if this statement is not tenable then all other beliefs held at that moment are also in jeopardy. Suddenly, what was regarded as permanently valid has become tentative.

A fourteen-year-old girl who was asked how her present beliefs differed from those she held several years ago replied, "I had a whole philosophy of how the world worked. I was very religious and I believed that there was unity and harmony and everything had its proper place. I used to imagine rocks in the right places on the right beaches. It was all very neat and God ordained it all, and I made up my own religion, but now it seems absolutely ridiculous."

Consider another inconsistency many adolescents discover and try to resolve.

1. Parents are omnipotent and omniscient.
2. My parent has lost a job, or failed to understand me, or behaved irrationally—or any other liability the reader cares to select.
3. If my parents were omniscient, they would not be tainted with failure and vulnerability.

The statements are examined together and the inconsistency noted. As with the first example, the adolescent can deny the truth of the second premise, but it demands too severe a straining of objectivity and is not usually implemented. The adolescent can invent a statement about parental motivation and excuse the show of incompetence on the basis of willingness, rather than capacity. This alternative is infrequently chosen because its acceptance elicits another troubling notion, for it implies that the parent does not care about the emotional consequences of his motivation for the affect life of the family. Hence, the child is tempted to deny the original hypothesis of parental omniscience. As with the denial of God, the fall of this belief weakens all the others.

A third set of propositions placed under analytic scrutiny involves sexuality:

1. Sexual activity—self-administered or heterosexually experienced—is bad.
2. Sexuality provides pleasure.
3. If sex is pleasant, it should not be bad.

We shall forego the obvious analysis of these propositions and simply note that again the most likely conclusion is that the first assumption is not tenable. The increased masturbation at puberty forces the child to deal with the fact that he is violating, in private, a strong social prohibition. However, the consistent sensory pleasure cannot be denied and this silent violation has to be rationalized. As that rationalization is accomplished, the child is tempted to question a great many other standards and he begins to examine all prohibitions with the same skepticism.

Although the known physiological changes at puberty are not necessary antecedents to the increased sexuality, it is likely that they contribute to the ascendancy of sexual thoughts, feelings, and actions. The adolescent must deal with the temptations of masturbation, petting, intercourse, and homosexuality. The statistics unambiguously indicate that the frequent sexual behavior of the seventeen-year-old is not yet manifest in the eleven-year-old, who may be informed, but not yet active. One reason is that he is afraid; afraid of incompetence, parental discovery, and guilt. It is also likely that the sheer intensity of passion that is so urgent in the older adolescent is attentuated at this earlier age. The tension that is so overpowering in a seventeen-year-old is more like a tickle at eleven and, hence, more easily put aside. However, the eleven-year-old knows that his time is coming and he must prepare for it.

These major ideological conflicts pivot on the fact that old assumptions are challenged by new perceptions and the resulting incompatibility is resolved by delegitimizing the earlier assumption. The inducing perceptions include the acknowledgement of unhappy people, agnostic peers, and the pleasures of sexuality. The sequellae are a questioning of old beliefs and a search for a new start of premises. Each culture presents its children with a different set of beliefs to examine. In our society, standards surrounding family, religion, sexuality, drugs, and school are among the major ideological dragons to be tamed. Partial support for these ideas comes from interviews suggesting that American adolescents begin to wonder about the legitimacy of their belief systems, where, prior to this time, inconsistent propositions were not examined as a structure. Sometimes this analysis leaves the adolescent temporarily without a commitment to any belief. The author asked a fifteen-year-old about the beliefs she was most certain of: "None really. I just take in things and analyze them. Maybe it will change my opinion and maybe it won't. It depends, but I'm not really stuck to anything."

This open wondering produces a state of uncertainty and a need to resolve it. A fundamental principle of human psychological functioning states that child and adult are alerted by events and thoughts inconsistent with their prior understanding. These events provoke the mind to resolve the uncertainty and, through that work, premises are changed. A fourteen-year-old said, "I think religious attitudes change if you go to Sunday school. At that time you just accept it, but when you become older and start thinking about it and try to analyze it, that is, whether there really is a God, then it depends on what your religious beliefs are. I've asked myself this over and over again. I just started thinking about it at that time and I just can't get it off my mind; whether there really is a God. I ask myself questions. Is there a God and I have arguments inside myself. How there might not be, how there might be."

Many of the traditional solutions used to deal with uncertainty have lost their potency because a large portion of the population, including the child's friends, have stopped believing in the effectiveness of these slogans. Young people are confronted with the discrepant experience of knowing large numbers of adults and adolescents to whom they feel similar, but with whom they do not share beliefs about the rituals that heal. This inconsistency weakens the effectiveness of any ideology. As a result, many high school students are caught in a strangling web of apathy. They are confronted with all the major sources of uncertainty—a future that cannot be predicted, bizarre headlines, and persistent doubting of the simple truths their parents made them recite. But they have no effective set of ideas or behaviors to deal with these puzzles.

As hinted earlier, puberty qua puberty makes an important contribution to this process. The child's body changes visibly and there is an accompanying alteration in perceived feeling tone. The psychological accompaniments to this change include the rush of new thoughts, their evaluation, and their arrangement in a fresh structure. The adolescent dimly recognizes that he is capable of fertility and must decide how to handle this power, but many are unclear as to how conception occurs. One thirteen-year-old said, "Up until I was about ten years of age I was told that a seed produced the baby. So we go to this Chinese restaurant and they serve a little piece of candy with seeds all over it, so I said 'Hey, mom, I'm not going to eat this cause I don't want to have a baby.' "

Puberty is also interpreted as a signal that childhood is over, and a reminder that regressive actions and beliefs should be replaced, transformed, or eliminated. This character renovation requires the adolescent to generate a cognitive structure as sturdy as the one being replaced.

A fifteen-year-old girl was asked to recall her thoughts following her first menstrual period: "It was like growing up overnight. I felt that I was not a little kid anymore. I couldn't ride my bicycle anymore; really I'm not kidding you."

Interviewer: "Were you happy?"
Girl: "No, but I just thought I was above riding a bicycle or playing with dolls. I thought I was cool."
Interviewer: "Did you feel that you had to act more grownup?"
Girl: "Yes, that's why I wouldn't ride a bicycle or play with dolls."

A second fifteen-year-old girl noted, "Friends became more important than toys. You had to have a lot of friends, that was more important than anything. And toys were a thing of the past. My mother would say, 'Are you going out to play now?' and I'd say, 'No, I don't play.' I went around to a lot of women and I asked them what it was like to have children. I didn't want to grow up."

Interviewer: "Was there something apprehensive about it, something you didn't like about this new role?"
Girl: "I didn't like it. I remember thinking I'd really hate to be an adult and I started staying in on Saturdays with my mother instead of going out. I didn't want to have to think for myself."

A third fifteen-year-old agreed. "I started thinking that I couldn't ride my bike and couldn't do things that made me look like a baby. I used to think, when are you going to start getting more attention from people. After a few years, I felt that people were treating me like I was older and in a different way from when I was younger. When I went to my grandmother's when I was little, I used to get a glass of milk or tonic, you know, but after I was a certain age I started getting a cup of tea or coffee."

The adolescent knows he must make his own decisions, but must feel free enough to ask adults for advice. He orients toward extrafamilial adults and tries on, with more seriousness than earlier, the beliefs and posturing of teachers and cultural heroes. Closer examination of adult characteristics leads to new insights that have to be assimilated. He notes defect and taint in adults, and he must find a rule that permits him to accept this disappointment, while not turning complete skeptic. He initiates heterosexual relationships, and must rationalize both his exploitative urges toward others, as well as potential or actual rejection by the beloved other. He must preserve the self's integrity in the face of massive, cognitive taunts.

There are also special institutional changes that occur during early adolescence, especially in Western culture, that are influential. In most communities in the United States the child between twelve and fifteen enters junior high or high school. There are two significant consequences of this structural change. First, unlike the elementary school, the junior high and high school contain many more individuals who hold different beliefs. The beliefs concern drugs, sex, authority, the value of study, and attitudes toward parents. Each ideological position has many advocates. The sources of these new views cannot easily be discredited and the adolescent must deal with the dissonance.

Questions

1. How does Kagan characterize the new cognitive capacity that arises at adolescence?
2. What triggers the rethinking of beliefs?
3. How does this new cognitive development influence one's understanding of self, parents, and peers?
4. Why might some adolescents be unlikely to display the kinds of thought that Kagan describes?

References and Further Reading

Kohlberg, L., & Gilligan, C. (1971, Fall). The adolescent as a philosopher: The discovery of the self in a postconventional world. *Daedalus, 1051*–1086.
Piaget, J. (1972). Intellectual evolution from adolescence to adulthood. *Human Development, 15,* 1–12.

Egocentrism in Adolescence

David Elkind, Ph.D., is a professor in the Department of Child Development at Tufts University where he studies cognitive and social development in children and adolescents, and causes and effects of stress on children, youth, and families. He is author of numerous books including *Miseducation* (1987), *Ties that Stress: The New Family Imbalance* (1994), *Reinventing Childhood* (1998), and *All Grown Up and No Place to Go* (1998).

In this classic paper, David Elkind argues that each of Piaget's stages of cognitive development has its own form of egocentrism. The acquisition of new mental structures at each new stage of cognitive development frees a person from a lower form of egocentrism, but at the same time entraps that person in a higher form of egocentrism. Elkind details the nature of adolescent egocentrism, which arises with the acquisition of formal operational thought.

Elkind describes adolescent egocentrism as the inability to differentiate one's own thoughts and feelings from those of others. Adolescent egocentrism gives rise to two mental constructions. The first is the imaginary audience, the belief that others are preoccupied with one's appearance and behavior. The second construction is the personal fable, an unrealistic differentiation of oneself from others and belief that, being so important to so many people, one must be special and unique. Elkind discusses the manifestations of the imaginary audience and personal fable in adolescent behavior and the reasons for the passing of adolescent egocentrism.

The constructs of the imaginary audience and the personal fable have been used to account for a wide variety of adolescent behaviors and experiences and have been the subject of empirical research to the present day. Elkind postulates that adolescent egocentrism arises because of the acquisition of formal thought, yet studies of the relationship between adolescent egocentrism and formal thought have yielded mixed results (Rycek, Stuhr, McDermott, Benker, & Swartz, 1998). While this inconsistency could be due to differences in the particular measures used to assess formal thought across studies, it is also possible that other noncognitive variables contribute to adolescent egocentrism. Some studies have found empirical support for Elkind's contention that adolescent egocentrism arises in early adolescence and then passes. It has been found to increase during early adolescence, to peak at about age 14–16, and then to decline (Elkind & Bowen, 1979). Other studies, however, have found higher levels of egocentrism in female college students than in high school students (Peterson & Roscoe, 1991). Finally, adolescent egocentrism has been found to be more prevalent in females than in males (Elkind & Bowen, 1991; Rycek, Stuhr, McDermott, Benker, & Swartz, 1998).

Abstract This paper describes the different forms of egocentrism characteristic of each of the major stages of cognitive growth outlined by [Jean] Piaget. Particular attention is paid to the egocentrism of adolescence which is here described as the failure to differentiate between the cognitive concerns of others and those of the self. This adolescent egocentrism is said to give rise to 2 mental constructions, the imaginary audience and the personal fable, which help to account for certain forms of adolescent behavior and experience. These considerations suggest, it is concluded, that the cognitive structures peculiar to a given age period can provide insights with respect to the personality characteristics of that age level.

Within the Piagetian theory of intellectual growth, the concept of egocentrism generally refers to a lack of differentiation in some area of subject-object interaction (Piaget, 1962). At each stage of mental development, this lack of differentiation takes a unique form and is manifested in a unique set of behaviors. The transition from one form of egocentrism to another takes place in a dialectic fashion such that the mental structures which free the child from a lower form of egocentrism are the same structures which ensnare him in a higher form of egocentrism. From the developmental point of view, therefore, egocentrism can be regarded as a negative by-product of any emergent mental system in the sense that it corresponds to the fresh cognitive problems engendered by that system.

Although in recent years Piaget has focused his attention more on the positive than on the negative products of mental structures, egocentrism continues to be of interest because of its relation to the affective aspects of child thought and behavior. Indeed, it is possible that the study of egocentrism may provide a bridge between the study of cognitive structure, on the one hand, and the exploration of personality dynamics, on the other (Cowan, 1966; Gourevitch & Feffer, 1962). The purpose of the present paper is to describe, in greater detail than Inhelder and Piaget (1958), what seems to me to be the nature of egocentrism in adolescence and some of its behavioral and experiential correlates. Before doing that, however, it might be well to set the stage for the discussion with a brief review of the forms of egocentrism which precede this mode of thought in adolescence.

Forms of Egocentrism in Infancy and Childhood

In presenting the childhood forms of egocentrism, it is useful to treat each of Piaget's major stages as if it were primarily concerned with resolving one major cognitive task. The egocentrism of a particular stage can then be described with reference to this special problem of cognition. It must be stressed, however, that while the cognitive task characteristic of a particular stage seems to attract the major share of the child's mental energies, it is not the only cognitive problem with which the child is attempting to cope. In mental development there are major battles and minor skirmishes, and if I here ignore the lesser engagements it is for purposes of economy of presentation rather than because I assume that such engagements are insignificant.

Sensori-Motor Egocentrism (0–2 Years)

The major cognitive task of infancy might be regarded as the *conquest of the object*. In the early months of life, the infant deals with objects as if their existence were dependent upon their being present in immediate perception (Charlesworth, 1966; Piaget, 1954). The egocentrism of this stage corresponds, therefore, to a lack of differentiation between the object and the sense impressions occasioned by it. Toward the end of the first year, however, the infant begins to seek the object even when it is hidden, and thus shows that he can now differentiate between the object and the "experience of the object." This breakdown of egocentrism with respect to objects is brought about by mental representation of the absent object.[1] An internal representation of the absent object is the earliest manifestation of the symbolic function which develops gradually during the second year of life and whose activities dominate the next stage of mental growth.

Pre-Operational Egocentrism (2–6 Years)

During the preschool period, the child's major cognitive task can be regarded as the *conquest of the symbol*. It is during the preschool period that the symbolic function becomes fully active, as evidenced by the rapid growth in the acquisition and utilization of language, by the appearance of symbolic play, and by the first reports of dreams. Yet this new capacity for representation, which loosed the infant from his egocentrism with respect to objects, now ensnares the preschool children in a new egocentrism with regard to symbols. At the beginning of this period, the child fails to differentiate between words and their referents (Piaget, 1952b) and between his self-created play and dream symbols and reality (Kohlberg, 1966; Piaget, 1951). Children at this stage believe that the name inheres in the thing and that an object cannot have more than one name (Elkind, 1961a, 1962, 1963).

The egocentrism of this period is particularly evident in children's linguistic behavior. When explaining a piece of apparatus to another child, for example, the youngster at this stage uses many indefinite terms and leaves out important information (Piaget, 1952b). Although this observation is sometimes explained by saying that the child fails to take the other person's point of view, it can also be explained by saying that the child assumes words carry much more information than they actually do.

This results from his belief that even the indefinite "thing" somehow conveys the properties of the object which it is used to represent. In short, the egocentrism of this period consists in a lack of clear differentiation between symbols and their referents.

Toward the end of the pre-operational period, the differentiation between symbols and their referents is gradually brought about by the emergence of concrete operations (internalized actions which are roughly comparable in their activity to the elementary operations of arithmetic). One consequence of concrete operational thought is that it enables the child to deal with two elements, properties, or relations at the same time. A child with concrete operations can, for example, take account of both the height and width of a glass of colored liquid and recognize that, when the liquid is poured into a differently shaped container, the changes in height and width of the liquid compensate one another so that the total quantity of liquid is conserved (Elkind, 1961b; Piaget, 1952a). This ability, to hold two dimensions in mind at the same time, also enables the child to hold both symbol and referent in mind simultaneously, and thus distinguish between them. Concrete operations are, therefore, instrumental in overcoming the egocentrism of the preoperational stage.

Concrete Operational Egocentrism (7–11 Years)

With the emergence of concrete operations, the major cognitive task of the school-age child becomes that of *mastering classes, relations, and quantities*. While the preschool child forms global notions of classes, relations, and quantities, such notions are imprecise and cannot be combined one with the other. The child with concrete operations, on the other hand, can nest classes, seriate relations, and conserve quantities. In addition, concrete operations enable the school-age child to perform elementary syllogistic reasoning and to formulate hypotheses and explanations about concrete matters. This system of concrete operations, however, which lifts the school-age child to new heights of thought, nonetheless lowers him to new depths of egocentrism.

Operations are essentially mental tools whose products, series, class hierarchies, conservations, etc., are not directly derived from experience. At this stage, however, the child nonetheless regards these mental products as being on a par with perceptual phenomena. It is the inability to differentiate clearly between mental constructions and perceptual givens which constitutes the egocentrism of the school-age child. An example may help to clarify the form which egocentrism takes during the concrete operational stage.

In a study reported by Peel (1960), children and adolescents were read a passage about Stonehenge and then asked questions about it. One of the questions had to do with whether Stonehenge was a place for religious worship or a fort. The children (ages 7–10) answered the question with flat statements, as if they were stating a fact. When they were given evidence that contradicted their statements, they rationalized the evidence to make it conform with their initial position. Adolescents, on the other hand, phrased their replies in probabilistic terms and supported their judgments with material gleaned from the passage. Similar differences between children and adolescents have been found by Elkind (1966) and Weir (1964).

What these studies show is that, when a child constructs a hypothesis or formulates a strategy, he assumes that this product is imposed by the data rather than derived from his own mental activity. When his position is challenged, he does not change his stance but, on the contrary, reinterprets the data to fit with his assumption. This observation, however, raises a puzzling question. Why, if the child regards both his thought products and the givens of perception as coming from the environment, does he nonetheless give preference to his own mental constructions? The answer probably lies in the fact that the child's mental constructions are the product of reasoning, and hence are experienced as imbued with a (logical) necessity. This "felt" necessity is absent when the child experiences the products of perception. It is not surprising, then, that the child should give priority to what seems permanent and necessary in perception (the products of his own thought, such as conservation) rather than to what seems transitory and arbitrary in perception (products of environmental stimulation). Only in adolescence do young people differentiate between their own mental constructions and the givens of perception. For the child, there are no problems of epistemology.

Toward the end of childhood, the emergence of formal operational thought (which is analogous to propositional logic) gradually frees the child from his egocentrism with respect to his own mental constructions. As Inhelder and Piaget (1958) have shown, formal operational thought enables the young person to deal with all of the possible combinations and permutations of elements within a given set. Provided with four differently colored pieces of plastic, for example, the adolescent can work out all the possible combinations of colors by taking the pieces one, two, three and four, and none, at a time. Children, on the other hand, cannot formulate these combinations in any systematic way. The ability to conceptualize all of the possible combinations in a system allows the adolescent to construct contrary-to-fact hypotheses and to reason about such propositions "as if" they were true. The adolescent, for example, can accept the statement, "Let's suppose coal is white," whereas the child would reply, "But coal is black." This ability to formulate contrary-to-fact hypotheses is crucial to the overcoming of the egocentrism of the concrete operational period. Through the formulation of such contrary-to-fact hypotheses, the young person discovers the arbitrariness of his own mental constructions and learns to differentiate them from perceptual reality.

Adolescent Egocentrism

From the strictly cognitive point of view (as opposed to the psychoanalytic point of view as represented by Blos [1962] and A. Freud [1946] or the ego psychological point of view as represented by Erikson [1959]), the major task of early adolescence can be regarded as having to do with *the conquest of thought*. Formal operations not only permit the young person to construct all the possibilities in a system and construct contrary-to-fact propositions (Inhelder & Piaget, 1958); they also enable him to conceptualize his own thought to take his mental constructions as objects and reason about them. Only at about the ages of 11–12, for example, do children spontaneously introduce concepts of belief, intelligence, and faith into their definitions of their religious denomination (Elkind, 1961a; 1962; 1963). Once more, however, this new mental system which frees the young person from the egocentrism of childhood entangles him in a new form of egocentrism characteristic of adolescence.

Formal operational thought not only enables the adolescent to conceptualize his thought, it also permits him to conceptualize the thought of other people. It is this capacity to take account of other people's thought, however, which is the crux of adolescent egocentrism. This egocentrism emerges because, while the adolescent can now cognize the thoughts of others, he fails to differentiate between the objects toward which the thoughts of others are directed and those which are the focus of his own concern. Now, it is well known that the young adolescent, because of the psyiological metamorphosis he is undergoing, is primarily concerned with himself. Accordingly, since he fails to differentiate between what others are thinking about and his own mental preoccupations, he assumes that other people are as obsessed with his behavior and appearance as he is himself. *It is this belief that others are preoccupied with his appearance and behavior that constitutes the egocentrism of the adolescent*.

One consequence of adolescent egocentrism is that, in actual or impending social situations, the young person anticipates the reactions of other people to himself. These anticipations, however, are based on the premise that others are as admiring or as critical of him as he is of himself. In a sense, then, the adolescent is continually constructing, or reacting to, *an imaginary audience*. It is an audience because the adolescent believes that he will be the focus of attention; and it is imaginary because, in actual social situations, this is not usually the case (unless he contrives to make it so). The construction of imaginary audiences would seem to account, in part at least, for a wide variety of typical adolescent behaviors and experiences.

The imaginary audience, for example, probably plays a role in the self-consciousness which is so characteristic of early adolescence. When the young person is feeling critical of himself, he anticipates that the audience—of which he is necessarily a part—will be critical too. And, since the audience is his own construction and privy to his own knowledge of himself, it knows just what to look for in the way of cosmetic and behavioral sensitivities. The adolescent's wish for privacy and his reluctance to reveal himself may, to some extent, be a reaction to the feeling of being under the constant critical scrutiny of other people. The notion of an imaginary audience also helps to explain the observation that the affect which most concerns adolescents is not guilt but, rather, shame, that is, the reaction to an audience (Lynd, 1961).

While the adolescent is often self-critical, he is frequently self-admiring too. At such times, the audience takes on the same affective coloration. A good deal of adolescent boorishness, loudness, and faddish dress is probably provoked, partially in any case, by a failure to differentiate between what the young person believes to be attractive and what others admire. It is for this reason that the young person frequently fails to understand why adults disapprove of the way he dresses and behaves. The same sort of egocentrism is often seen in behavior directed toward the opposite sex. The boy who stands in front of the mirror for 2 hours combing his hair is probably imagining the swooning reactions he will produce in the girls. Likewise, the girl applying her makeup is more likely than not imagining the admiring glances that will come her way. When these young people actually meet, each is more concerned with being the observed than with being the observer. Gatherings of young adolescents are unique in the sense that each young person is simultaneously an actor to himself and an audience to others.

One of the most common admiring audience constructions, in the adolescent, is the anticipation of how others will react to his own demise. A certain bittersweet pleasure is derived from anticipating the belated recognition by others of his positive qualities. As often happens with such universal fantasies, the imaginary anticipation of one's own demise has been realized in fiction. Below, for example, is the passage in *Tom Sawyer* where Tom sneaks back to his home, after having run away with Joe and Huck, to discover that he and his friends are thought to have been drowned:

> But this memory was too much for the old lady, and she broke entirely down. Tom was snuffling, now, himself—and more in pity of himself than anybody else. He could hear Mary crying and putting in a kindly word for him from time to time. He began to have a nobler opinion of himself than ever before. Still, he was sufficiently touched by his aunt's grief to long to rush out from under the bed and overwhelm her with joy—and the theatrical gorgeousness of the thing appealed strongly to his nature too—but he resisted and lay still.

Corresponding to the imaginary audience is another mental construction which is its complement. While the adolescent fails to differentiate the concerns of his own thought from those of others, he at the same time over-differentiates his feelings. Perhaps because he believes he is of importance to so many people, the imaginary audience, he comes to regard himself, and particularly his feelings, as something special and unique. Only he can suffer with such agonized intensity, or experience such exquisite rapture. How many parents have been confronted with the typically adolescent phrase, "But you don't know how it feels. . . ." The emotional torments undergone by Goethe's young Werther and by Salinger's Holden Caulfield exemplify the adolescent's belief in the uniqueness of his own emotional experience. At a somewhat different level, this belief in personal uniqueness becomes a conviction that he will not die, that death will happen to others but not to him. This complex of beliefs in the uniqueness of his feelings and of his immortality might be called a *personal fable,* a story which he tells himself and which is not true.

Evidences of the personal fable are particularly prominent in adolescent diaries. Such diaries are often written for posterity in the conviction that the young person's experiences, crushes, and frustrations are of universal significance and importance. Another kind of evidence for the personal fable during this period is the tendency to confide in a personal God. The search for privacy and the belief in personal uniqueness leads to the establish of an I-Thou relationship with God as a personal confidant to whom one no longer looks for gifts but rather for guidance and support (Long, Elkind, & Spilka, 1967).

The concepts of an imaginary audience and a personal fable have proved useful, at least to the writer, in the understanding and treatment of troubled adolescents. The imaginary audience, for example, seems often to play a role in middle-class delinquency (Elkind, 1967). As a case in point, one young man took $1,000 from a golf tournament purse, hid the money, and then promptly revealed himself. It turned out that much of the motivation for this act was derived from the anticipated response of "the audience" to the guttiness of his action. In a similar vein, many young girls become pregnant because, in part at least, their personal fable convinces them that pregnancy will happen to others but never to them and so they need not take precautions. Such examples could be multiplied but will perhaps suffice to illustrate how adolescent egocentrism, as manifested in the imaginary audience and in the personal fable, can help provide a rationale for some adolescent behavior. These concepts can, moreover, be utilized in the treatment of adolescent offenders. It is often helpful to these young people if they can learn to differentiate between the real and the imaginary audience, which often boils down to a discrimination between the real and the imaginary parents.

The Passing of Adolescent Egocentrism

After the appearance of formal operational thought, no new mental systems develop and the mental structures of adolescence must serve for the rest of the life span. The egocentrism of early adolescence nonetheless tends to diminish by the age of 15 or 16, the age at which formal operations become firmly established. What appears to happen is that the imaginary audience, which is primarily an anticipatory audience, is progressively modified in the direction of the reactions of the real audience. In a way, the imaginary audience can be regarded as hypothesis—or better, as a series of hypotheses—which the young person tests against reality. As a consequence of this testing, he gradually comes to recognize the difference between his own preoccupations and the interests and concerns of others.

The personal fable, on the other hand, is probably overcome (although probably never in its entirety) by the gradual establishment of what Erikson (1959) has called "intimacy." Once the young person sees himself in a more realistic light as a function of having adjusted his imaginary audience to the real one, he can establish true rather than self-interested interpersonal relations. Once relations of mutuality are established and confidences are shared, the young person discovers that others have feelings similar to his own and have suffered and been enraptured in the same way.

Adolescent egocentrism is thus overcome by a twofold transformation. On the cognitive plane, it is overcome by the gradual differentiation between his own preoccupations and the thoughts of others; while on the plane of affectivity, it is overcome by a gradual integration of the feelings of others with his own emotions.

Summary and Conclusions

In this paper I have tried to describe the forms which egocentrism takes and the mechanisms by which it is overcome, in the course of mental development. In infancy, egocentrism corresponds to the impression that objects are identical with the perception of them, and this form of egocentrism is overcome with the appearance of representation. During the preschool period, egocentrism appears in the guise of a belief that symbols contain the same information as is provided by the objects which they represent. With the emergence of concrete operations, the child is able to discriminate between symbol and referent, and so overcome this type of egocentrism. The egocentrism of the school-age period can be characterized as the belief that one's own mental constructions correspond to a superior form of perceptual reality. With the advent of formal operations and the ability to construct contrary-to-fact hypotheses, this kind of egocentrism is dissolved because the young person can now recognize the arbitrariness of his own mental constructions. Finally, during early adolescence, egocentrism appears as the belief that the thoughts of others are directed toward the self. This variety of egocentrism is overcome as a consequence of the conflict between the reactions which the young person anticipates and those which actually occur.

Although egocentrism corresponds to a negative product of mental growth, its usefulness would seem to lie in the light which it throws upon the affective reactions characteristic of any particular stage of mental development. In this paper I have dealt primarily with the affective reactions associated with the egocentrism of adolescence. Much of the material, particularly the discussion of the *imaginary audience* and the *personal fable* is speculative in the sense that it is based as much upon my clinical experience with young people as it is upon research data. These constructs are offered, not as the final word on adolescent egocentrism, but rather to illustrate how the cognitive structures peculiar to a particular level of development can be related to the affective experience and behavior characteristic of that stage. Although I have here only considered the correspondence between mental structure and affect in adolescence, it is possible that similar correspondences can be found at the earlier levels of development as well. A consideration of egocentrism, then, would seem to be a useful starting point for any attempt to reconcile cognitive structure and the dynamics of personality.

Note

1. It is characteristic of the dialectic of mental growth that the capacity to represent internally the absent object also enables the infant to cognize the object as externally existent.

References

Blos, P. *On adolescence.* New York: Free Press, 1962.

Charlesworth, W. R. Development of the object concept in infancy: methodological study. *American Psychologist,* 1966, 21, 623. (Abstract)

Cowan, P. A. Cognitive egocentrism and social interaction in children. *American Psychologist,* 1966, 21, 623. (Abstract)

Elkind, D. The child's conception of his religious denomination, I: The Jewish child. *Journal of Genetic Psychology,* 1961, 99, 209–225. (a)

Elkind, D. The development of quantitative thinking. *Journal of genetic Psychology,* 1961, 98, 37–46. (b)

Elkind, D. The child's conception of his religious denomination, II: The Catholic child. *Journal of Genetic Psychology,* 1962, 101, 185–193.

Elkind, D. The child's conception of his religious denomination, III: The Protestant child. *Journal of Genetic Psychology,* 1963, 103, 291–304.

Elkind, D. Conceptual orientation shifts in children and adolescents. *Child Development,* 1966, 37, 493–498.

Elkind, D. Middle-class delinquency. *Mental Hygiene,* 1967, 51, 80–84.

Erikson, E. H. Identity and the life cycle. *Psychological Issues.* Vol. 1, No. 1, New York: International Universities Press, 1959.

Freud, Anna. *The ego and the mechanisms of defense.* New York International Universities Press, 1946.

Gourevitch, Vivian, & Feffer, M. H. A study of motivational development. *Journal of Genetic Psychology,* 1962, 100, 361–375.

Inhelder, Bärbel, & Piaget, J. *The growth of logical thinking from childhood to adolescence.* New York: Basic Books, 1958.

Kohlberg, L. Cognitive stages and preschool education. *Human Development,* 1966, 9, 5–17.

Long, Diane, Elkind, D., & Spilka, B. The child's conception of prayer. *Journal for the Scientific Study of Religion,* 1967, 6, 101–109.

Lynd, Helen M. *On shame and the search for identity.* New York: Science Editions, 1961.

Peel, E. A. *The pupil's thinking.* London: Oldhourne, 1960.

Piaget, J. *The child's conception of the world.* London: Routledge & Kegan Paul, 1951.

Piaget, J. *The child's conception of number.* New York: Humanities Press, 1952. (a)

Piaget, J. *The language and thought of the child.* London: Routledge & Kegan Paul, 1952 (b)

Piaget, J. *The construction of reality in the child.* New York: Basic Books, 1954.

Piaget, J. *Comments on Vygotsky's critical remarks concerning "The language and thought of the child" and "Judgment and reasoning in the child."* Cambridge, Mass.: M.I.T. Press, 1962.

Weir, M. W. Development changes in problem solving strategies. *Psychological Review,* 1964, 71, 473–490.

Questions

1. Why does each of Piaget's stages of cognitive development have its own form of egocentrism?
2. What is adolescent egocentrism and what is its connection to formal operational thought?
3. Why does adolescent egocentrism end?
4. What are the implications of adolescent egocentrism for behavior?
5. What noncognitive variables might produce adolescent egocentrism?

References and Further Reading

Elkind, D., & Bowen, R. (1979). Imaginary audience behavior in children and adolescents. *Developmental Psychology, 15,* 38–44.

Peterson, K. L., & Roscoe, B. (1991). Imaginary audience behavior in older adolescent females. *Adolescence, 26,* 195–200.

Rycek, R. F., Stuhr, S. L., McDermott, J., Benker, J., & Swartz, M. D. (1998). Adolescent egocentrism and cognitive functioning during late adolescence. *Adolescence, 33*(132), 745–749.

4.3   Susan Harter, 1999

The Normative Development of Self-Representations During Adolescence

Susan Harter, Ph.D., is a professor of psychology and head of the Developmental Psychology Program at the University of Denver. She has constructed a widely used battery of self-report instruments to tap dimensions of self-concept and self-esteem. She is author of *The Construction of Self* (1999) and has conducted research on self-concept, self-esteem, and motivational and emotional development.

The acquisition of new cognitive capacities at adolescence leads to considerable shifts in adolescents' self-concepts and understanding of themselves. When asked to describe themselves at early adolescence, subjects provide self-descriptions that are based on external aspects, such as looks, and on concrete observable behaviors, like talking a lot or being sarcastic. By late adolescence their self-descriptions are based on their psychological interiors, on their thoughts and feelings. In addition, adolescents move from describing themselves as multiple and differing selves in different social roles and contexts to describing themselves as an integration of these diverse self-perceptions in a unified, internally consistent, coherent concept of self (Harter, 1999).

Susan Harter looks at the development of the self-concept over the course of adolescence and the impact of cognitive growth on the changes in self-concept using Fischer's (1980) neo-Piagetian theory of cognitive development. Harter finds that in early adolescence the self is experienced as differentiated; early adolescents provide different descriptions of themselves depending upon whether they are describing themselves with their mothers, fathers, close friends, or romantic partners, or whether they are describing themselves in their roles as students, athletes, or workers. Different aspects of the self emerge in different contexts and relationships.

Harter argues that the explanation for why adolescents describe themselves as multiple selves can be found in Fischer's model of the emergence of formal thought. Fischer contends that there are several levels of formal operational thought. While early adolescents have the capacity to form single abstractions, at the first stage of formal thought adolescents cannot yet compare abstractions, so that the single abstractions about self remain fragmented, contradictory, and unintegrated. During middle adolescence, according to Fischer's theory, adolescents acquire the capacity for "abstract mappings," or the cognitive ability to relate single abstractions to one another, to compare and contrast them. The capacity for abstract mappings at this stage helps explain Harter's finding that the awareness of contradictory and opposite selves at this stage becomes a source of intrapsychic conflict and confusion about which is the real self. By late adolescence, according to Fisher, a new cognitive level is attained, characterized by the emergence of "abstract systems." At this stage adolescents are able to integrate single abstractions into higher-order abstractions. When applied to the self, this new capacity enables adolescents to resolve the conflicts between the experience of potentially contradictory characteristics by developing higher-order abstractions about the self. For example, if one is moody then it makes sense that one can be depressed at home around parents and cheerful when socializing with friends. Late adolescents recognize that it is both normal and appropriate to display different aspects of the self in different social contexts.

The period of adolescence represents a dramatic developmental transition, given pubertal and related physical changes, cognitive-developmental advances, and changing social expectations. With regard to cognitive-developmental acquisitions, adolescents develop the ability to think *abstractly* (Case, 1985; Fischer, 1980; Flavell, 1985; Harter, 1983; Higgins, 1991). From a Piagetian (1960) perspective, the capacity to form abstractions emerges with the stage of Formal Operations in early adolescence. These newfound acquisitions, according to [Jean] Piaget, should equip the adolescent with the hypothetico-deductive skills to create a formal theory. This observation is critical to the topic of self-development, given the claims of many (e.g., Epstein, 1973, 1981, 1991; Greenwald, 1980; Kelly, 1955; Markus, 1980; Sarbin, 1962) that the self is a personal epistemology, a cognitive construction, that is, a theory that should possess the characteristics of any formal theory. Therefore, a self-theory should meet those criteria by which any good theory is evaluated, criteria that include the degree to which it is parsimonious, empirically valid, internally consistent, coherently organized, testable, and useful. From a Piagetian perspective, entry into the period of formal operations should make the construction of such a theory possible, be it a theory about elements in the world or a theory about the self.

However, as will become apparent, the self-representations during early and middle adolescence fall far short of these criteria. The self-structure of these periods is not coherently organized, nor are the postulates of the self-portrait internally consistent. Moreover, many self-attributes fail to be subjected to tests of empirical validity; as a result, they can be extremely unrealistic. Nor are self-representations particularly parsimonious. Thus, the Piagetian framework fails to provide an adequate explanation for the dramatic developmental changes in the self-structure that can be observed across the substages of adolescence. Rather, as in our analysis of how self-representations change during childhood, a neo-Piagetian approach is needed to understand how changes in cognitive-developmental I-self processes result in very different Me-self organization and content at each of three age levels: early adolescence, middle adolescence, and late adolescence. As in our examination of self-development during childhood, in addition to describing these changes, the liabilities of each type of self-structure are examined. The major changes are summarized in Table 1.

Early Adolescence

"I'm an extrovert with my friends: I'm talkative, pretty rowdy, and funny. I'm fairly good-looking if I do say so. All in all, around people I know pretty well I'm awesome, at least I think my friends think I am. I'm usually cheerful when I'm with my friends, happy and excited to be doing things with them. I like myself a lot when I'm around my friends. With my parents, I'm more likely to be depressed. I feel sad as well as mad and also hopeless about ever pleasing them. They think I spend too much time at the mall with my friends, and that I don't do enough to help out at home. They tell me I'm lazy and not very responsible, and its hard not to

Table 1

Normative-Developmental Changes in Self-Representations during Adolescence

Age Period	Salient content	Structure/organization	Valence/accuracy	Nature of comparisons	Sensitivity to others
Early adolescence	Social skills, attributes, that influence interactions with others or one's social appeal; differentiation of attributes according to roles	Intercoordination of trait labels into single stractions; abstractions compartmentalized; all-or-none thinking; opposites; don't detect, integrate, opposing abstractions	Positive attributes at one point in time; negative attributes at another; leads to inaccurate overgeneralizations	Social comparison continues although less overt	Compartmentalized attention to internalization of different standards and opinions of those in different relational contexts
Middle adolescence	Further differentiation of attributes associated with different roles and relational contexts	Initial links between single abstractions, often opposing attributes; cognitive conflict caused by seemingly contradictory characteristics; concern over which reflect one's true self	Simultaneous recognition of positive and negative attributes; instability, leading to confusion and inaccuracies	Comparisons with significant others in different relational contexts; personal fable	Awareness that the differing standards and opinions of others represent conflicting self-guides, leading to confusion over self-evaluation and vacillation with regard to behavior; imaginary audience
Late adolescence	Normalization of different role-related attributes; attributes reflecting personal beliefs, values, and moral standards; interest in future selves	Higher-order abstractions that meaningfully integrate single abstractions and resolve inconsistencies, conflict	More balanced, stable view of both positive and negative attributes; great accuracy; acceptance of limitations	Social comparison diminishes as comparisons with one's own ideals increase	Selection among alternative self-guides; construction of one's own self-standards that govern personal choices; creation of one's own ideals toward which the self aspires

believe them. I get real sarcastic when they get on my case. It makes me dislike myself as a person. At school, I'm pretty intelligent. I know that because I'm smart when it comes to how I do in classes, I'm curious about learning new things, and I'm also creative when it comes to solving problems. My teacher says so. I get better grades than most, but I don't brag about it because that's not cool. I can be a real introvert around people I don't know well. I'm shy, uncomfortable, and nervous. Sometimes I'm simply an airhead. I act really dumb and say things that are just plain stupid. Then I worry about what they must think of me, probably that I'm a total dork. I just hate myself when that happens."

With regard to the *content* of the self-portraits of young adolescents, interpersonal attributes and social skills that influence interactions with others or one's social appeal are typically quite salient, as findings by Damon and Hart (1988) reveal. Thus, our prototypical young adolescent admits to being talkative, rowdy, funny, good-looking, and downright awesome. Presumably, these characteristics enhance one's acceptance by peers. In addition to social attributes, self-representations also focus on competencies such as one's scholastic abilities (e.g., "I'm intelligent"), as well as affects (e.g., "I'm cheerful" and "I'm depressed").

From a developmental perspective, there is considerable evidence that the self becomes increasingly differentiated (see Harter, 1998a). During adolescence, there is a proliferation of selves that vary as a function of social context. These include self with father, mother, close friends, romantic partners, peers, as well as the self in the role of student, on the job, and as athlete (Gecas, 1972; Griffin, Chassin, & Young, 1981; Hart, 1988; Harter, Bresnick, et al., 1997; Harter & Monsour, 1992; Smollar & Youniss, 1985). For example, as the cameo reveals, the adolescent may be cheerful and rowdy with friends, depressed and sarcastic with parents, intelligent, curious, and creative as a student, and shy and uncomfortable around people whom one does not know. A critical developmental task, therefore, is the construction of multiple selves that will undoubtedly vary across different roles and relationships, as James (1892) observed over 100 years ago.

. . . [B]oth cognitive and social processes contribute to this proliferation of selves. Cognitive-developmental advances described earlier promote greater differentiation (see Fischer, 1980; Fischer & Canfield, 1986; Harter, 1990a; Harter & Monsour, 1992; Keating, 1990). Moreover, these advances conspire with socialization pressures to develop different selves in different relational contexts (see Erikson, 1968; Grotevant & Cooper, 1986; Hill & Holmbeck, 1986; Rosenberg, 1986). For example, bids for autonomy from parents make it important to define oneself differently with peers in contrast to parents (see also Steinberg & Silverberg, 1986; White, Speisman, & Costos, 1983). Rosenberg points to another component of the differentiation process in observing that as one moves through adolescence, one is more likely to be treated differently by those in different relational contexts. In studies from our own laboratory (see Harter, Bresnick, et al., 1997; Harter & Monsour, 1992), we have found that the percentage of overlap in self-attributes generated for different social contexts ranges from 25% to 30% among seventh and eighth graders and decreases during adolescence, to a low of approximately 10% among older teenagers.

Many (although not all) of the self-descriptions to emerge in early adolescence represent *abstractions* about the self, based upon the newfound cognitive ability to integrate trait labels into higher-order self-concepts (see Case, 1985; Fischer, 1980; Flavell, 1985; Harter, 1993; Higgins, 1991). For example, as the prototypical cameo reveals, one can construct an abstraction of the self as "intelligent" by combining such traits as smart, curious, and creative. Alternatively, one may create an abstraction that the self is an "airhead" given situations where one feels dumb and "just plain stupid." Similarly, an adolescent could construct abstractions that he/she is an "extrovert" (integrating the traits of rowdy, talkative, and funny) as well as that he/she is also an "introvert" in certain situations (when one is shy, uncomfortable, and nervous). With regard to emotion concepts, one can be depressed in some contexts (combining sad, mad, and hopeless) as well as cheerful in others (combining happy and excited). Thus, abstractions represent more cognitively complex concepts about the self in which various trait labels can now be appropriately integrated into even higher-order generalizations.

Although the ability to construct such abstractions reflects a cognitive advance, these representations are highly compartmentalized; that is, they are quite distinct from one another (Case, 1985; Fischer, 1980; Higgins, 1991). For Fischer, these "single abstractions" are overdifferentiated, and therefore the young adolescent can only think about each of them as isolated self-attributes. According to Fischer, structures that were observed in childhood reappear at the abstract level. Thus, just as single *representations* were compartmentalized during early childhood, Fischer argues that when the adolescent first moves to the level of abstract thought, he/she lacks the ability to integrate the many single abstractions that are constructed to define the self in different relational contexts. As a result, adolescents will engage in all-or-none thinking at an abstract level. For Fischer, movement to a qualitatively new level of thought brings with it lack of "cognitive control" and, as a result, adolescents at the level of single abstractions can only think about isolated self-attributes. Thus, contrary to earlier models of mind (Piaget, 1960), in which formal operations usher in newfound cognitive-developmental abilities that should allow one to create an integrated theory of self, fragmentation of self-representations during early adolescence is more the rule than the exception (Fischer & Ayoub, 1994; Harter & Monsour, 1992).

Another manifestation of the compartmentalization of these abstract attributes can be observed in the tendency for the young adolescent to be unconcerned about the fact that across different roles, certain postulates appear inconsistent, as the prototypical self-description implies. (In contrast, at middle adolescence, there is considerable concern.) However, during early adolescence, the inability to integrate seemingly contradictory characteristics of the self (intelligent vs. airhead, extrovert vs. introvert, depressed vs. cheerful) has the psychological advantage of sparing the adolescent conflict over opposing attributes in his/her self-theory (Harter & Monsour, 1992). Moreover, as Higgins observes, the increased differentiation functions as a cognitive buffer, reducing the possibility that negative attributes in one sphere may spread or generalize to other spheres (see also Linville, 1987; Simmons & Blyth, 1987). Thus, although the construction of multiple selves sets the stage for attributes to be contradictory, as James argued in describing the "conflict of the different Me's," most young adolescents do not identify contradictions or experience conflict, given the compartmentalized structure of their abstract self-representations.

Evidence for these claims comes from our own research (see Harter, Bresnick, et. al., 1997; Harter & Monsour, 1992), in which we asked adolescents at three developmental levels, early adolescence (seventh grade), middle adolescence (ninth grade), and late adolescence (11th grade) to generate self-attributes across several roles and then indicate whether any of these attributes represented *opposites* (e.g., cheerful vs. depressed, rowdy vs. calm, studious vs. lazy, at ease vs. self-conscious). After identifying any such opposites, they were asked whether any such pairs caused them *conflict,* namely, were they perceived as clashing within their personality? Across studies, the specific roles have varied. They have included self with a group of friends, with a close friend, with parents (mother vs. father) in romantic relationships, in the classroom, and on the job. Across a number of converging indices (e.g., number of opposites, number of conflicts, percentage of opposites in conflict) the findings revealed that attributes identified as contradictory and experienced as conflicting were infrequent among young adolescents.

An examination of the protocols of young adolescents reveals that there are *potential* opposites that go undetected. Examples *not* identified as opposites included being talkative as well as shy in romantic relationships, being uptight with family but carefree with friends, being caring and insensitive with friends, being a good student as well as troublemaker in school, being self-conscious in romantic relationships but easygoing with friends, being lazy as a student but hardworking on the job. These observations bolster the interpretation, from Fischer's theory, that young adolescents do not yet have the cognitive ability to simultaneously compare these attributes to one another, and therefore they tend not to detect, or be concerned about, self-representations that are potential opposites. As one young adolescent put it, when confronted with the fact that he had indicated that he was both caring and rude, "Well, you are caring with your friends and rude to people who don't treat you nicely. There's no problem, I guess I just think about one thing about myself at a time and don't think about the other until the next day." When another young adolescent was asked why opposite attributes did not bother her, she succinctly exclaimed. "That's a stupid question. I don't fight with myself!" As will become apparent, this pattern changes dramatically during middle adolescence. . . .

Middle Adolescence

"What am I like as a person? You're probably not going to understand. I'm complicated! With my really *close* friends, I am very tolerant. I mean I'm understanding and caring. With a *group* of friends, I'm rowdier. I'm also usually friendly and cheerful but I can get pretty obnoxious and intolerant if I don't like how they're acting. I'd *like* to be friendly and tolerant all of the time, that's the kind of person I *want* to be, and I'm disappointed in myself when I'm not. At school, I'm serious, even studious every now and then, but on the other hand, I'm a goof-off too, because if you're *too* studious, you won't be popular. So I go back and forth, which means I don't do all that well in terms of my grades. But that causes problems at home, where I'm pretty anxious when I'm around my parents. They expect me to get all A's, and get pretty annoyed with me when report cards come out. I care what they think about me, and so then I get down on myself, but it's not fair! I mean I worry about how I probably *should* get better grades, but I'd be mortified in the eyes of my friends if I did too well. So I'm usually pretty stressed-out at home, and can even get very sarcastic, especially when my parents get on my case. But I really don't understand how I can switch so fast from being cheerful with my friends, then coming home and feeling anxious, and then getting frustrated and sarcastic with my parents. Which one is the *real* me? I have the same question when I'm around boys. Sometimes I feel phony. Say I think some guy might be interested in asking me out. I try to act different, like Madonna. I'll be a real extrovert, fun-loving and even flirtatious, and think I am really good-looking. And then everybody, I mean *everybody* else is looking at me like they think I am totally weird! *They* don't act like they think I'm attractive so I end up thinking I look terrible. I just hate myself when that happens! Because it gets worse! Then I get self-conscious and embarrassed and become radically introverted, and I don't know who I really am! Am I just acting like an extrovert, am I just trying to impress them, when really I'm an introvert? But I don't really care what they think, anyway. I mean I don't *want* to care, that is. I just want to know what my close friends think. I can be my true self with my close friends. I can't be my real self with my parents. They don't understand me. What do *they* know about what it's like to be a teenager? They treat me like I'm still a kid. At least at school, people treat you more like you're an adult. That gets confusing, though. I mean, which am I? When you're 15, are you still a kid or an adult? I have a part-time job and the people there treat me like an adult. I want them to approve of me, so I'm very responsible at work, which makes me feel good about myself there. But then I go out with my friends and I get pretty crazy and irresponsible. So which am I, responsible or irresponsible? How can the same person be both? If my parents knew how immature I act sometimes, they would ground me forever, particularly my father. I'm real distant with him. I'm pretty close to my mother though. But its hard being distant with one parent and close to the other, especially if we are all together, like talking at dinner. Even though I am close to my mother, I'm still pretty secretive about some things, particularly the things about myself that confuse me. So I think a lot about who is the real me, and sometimes I try to figure out when I write in my diary, but I can't resolve it. There are days when I wish I could just become immune to myself!"

Self-descriptions are likely to increase in length during this period, as adolescents become increasingly introspective as well as morbidly preoccupied with what others think of them (Broughton, 1978; Elkind, 1967; Erikson, 1959, 1968; Harter, 1990b; Lapsley & Rice, 1988; Rosenberg, 1979). The unreflective self-acceptance of earlier periods of development vanishes, and, as Rosenberg observes, what were formerly unquestioned self-truths now become problematic self-hypotheses. The tortuous search for the self involves a concern with *what* or *who* am I (Broughton, 1978), a task made more difficult given the multiple Me's that crowd the self-landscape. There is typically a further prolif- eration of selves as adolescents come to make finer differentiations; in the cameo, the adolescent describes a self with really close friends (e.g., tolerant) versus with a group of friends (e.g., intolerant), and a self with mother (e.g., close) versus father (e.g., distant). The acquisition of new roles, for example, self at a job, may also require the construction of new context-specific attributes (e.g., responsible).

Moreover, additional cognitive I-self processes emerge that give the self-por- trait a very new look (Case, 1985; Fischer, 1980). Whereas, in the previous stage, single abstractions were isolated from one another, during middle adolescence one acquires the ability to make *comparisons* between single abstractions, namely, be- tween attributes within the same role-related self or across role-related selves. Fis- cher labels these new structures "abstract mappings," in that the adolescent can now "map" constructs about the self onto one another. Therefore mappings force the individual to compare and contrast different attributes. It should be noted that abstract mappings have features in common with the "representational" mappings of childhood, in that the cognitive links that are forged often take the form of *opposites*. During adolescence, these opposites can take the form of seemingly con- tradictory *abstractions* about the self (e.g., tolerant vs. intolerant, extrovert vs. introvert, responsible vs. irresponsible, goodlooking versus unattractive, in the cameo).

However, the abstract mapping structure has limitations as a means of relating two concepts to one another, in that the individual cannot yet truly integrate such self-representations in a manner that would resolve apparent contradictions. Therefore, at the level of abstract mappings, the awareness of these opposites causes considerable intrapsychic conflict, confusion, and distress (Fischer et al., 1984; Harter & Monsour, 1992; Higgins, 1991) given the inability to coordinate these seemingly contradictory self-attributes. For example, our prototypical adolescent agonizes over whether she is an extrovert or an introvert ("Am I just acting like an extrovert, am I just trying to impress them, when really I'm an introvert?" "So which am I, responsible or irrespon- sible? How can the same person be both?"). Such cognitive-developmental limitations contribute to the emergence of what James (1892) identified as the "conflict of the different Me's."

In addition to such confusion, these seeming contradictions lead to very unstable self-representations, which are also cause for concern (e.g., "I don't really understand how I can switch so fast from being cheerful with my friends, then coming home and feeling anxious, and then getting frustrated and sarcastic with my parents. Which one is the *real* me?"). The creation of multiple selves, coupled with the emerging ability to detect potential contradictions between self-attributes displayed in different roles, naturally ushers in concern over which attributes define the true self. . . . How- ever, from a normative perspective, the adolescent at this level is not equipped with the cognitive skills to solve fully the dilemma (e.g., "So I think a lot about who is the real me, and sometimes try to figure it out when I write in my diary, but I can't resolve it"). . . .

Late Adolescence and Early Adulthood

"I'm a pretty conscientious person, particularly when it comes to things like doing my homework. It's important to me because I plan to go to college next year. Eventually I want to go to law school, so developing good study habits and getting top grades are both essential. (My parents don't want me to become a lawyer; they'd rather I go into teaching, but law is what I want to pursue.) Every now and then I get a little lackadaisical and don't complete an assignment as thoroughly or thoughtfully as I could, particularly if our high school has a big football or basketball game that I want to go to with my friends. But that's normal, I mean, you can't just be a total 'grind.' You'd be pretty boring if you were. You have to be flexible. I've also become more religious as I have gotten older, not that I am a saint or anything. Religion gives me a sense of purpose, in the larger scheme of things, and it provides me with personal guidelines for the kind of adult I'd like to be. For example, I'd like to be an ethical person who treats other people fairly. That's the kind of lawyer I'd like to be, too. I don't always live up to that standard; that is, sometimes I do something that doesn't feel that ethical. When that happens, I get a little depressed because I don't like myself as a person. But I tell myself that its natural to make mistakes, so I don't really question the fact that deep down inside, the real me is a moral person. Basically, I like who I am, so I don't stay depressed for long. Usually, I am pretty upbeat and optimistic. I guess you could say that I'm a moody person. I'm not as popular as a lot of other kids. At our school, its the jocks who are looked up to. I've never been very athletic, but you can't be good at everything, let's face it. Being athletic isn't that high on my own list of what is important, even though it is for a lot of the kids in our school. But I don't really care what they think anymore. I *used* to, but now what *I* think is what counts. After all, I have to live with myself as a person and to respect that person, which I do now, more than a few years ago. I'm pretty much being the kind of person I want to be. I'm doing well at things that are important to me like getting good grades. That's what is probably *most* important to me right now. Having a lot of friends isn't that important to me. I wouldn't say I was unpopular, though. While I am basically an introvert, especially on a date when I get pretty self-conscious, in the right social situation, like watching a ball game with my friends, I can be pretty extroverted. You have to be adaptive around other people. It would be weird to be the same kind of person on a date and with my friends at a football game! For example, when our team has a winning season and goes to the playoffs, everyone in the whole school is proud; what the team does reflects on all of us. On a date, the feelings are much more intimate, just between you and the other person. As much as I enjoy my high school friends and activities, I'm looking forward to leaving home and going to college, where I can be more independent, although I'm a little ambivalent. I love my parents, and really want to stay connected to them, plus, what they think about me is still important to how I feel about myself as a person. So leaving home will be bittersweet. But sometimes it's hard to be mature around them, particularly around my mom. I feel a lot more grown-up around my dad; he treats me more like an adult. I like that part of me because it feels more like my true self. My mom wants me to grow up, but another part of her wants me to remain 'her little baby.' I'll probably always be somewhat dependent on my parents. How can you escape it? But I'm also looking forward to being on my own."

With regard to the *content* of the self-representations that begin to emerge in late adolescence and early adulthood, typically, many of the attributes reflect personal beliefs, values, and moral standards that have become internalized or, alternatively, constructed from their own experiences (see findings by Damon & Hart, 1988). These characteristics are exemplified in the prototypical cameo, in that the adolescent expresses the personal desire to go to college, which requires good grades and discipline in the form of study habits. Although classmates tout athletics as the route to popularity, there is less concern at this age with what others think ("I used to care but now what *I* think is important"). In addition, there is a focus on one's *future* selves, for example, not only becoming a lawyer, but also an *ethical* lawyer, as a personal goal. Noteworthy in this narrative is the absence of an explicit reference to the potential origins of these goals, for example, parental encouragement or expectations that one pursue such a career. Moreover, this adolescent's career choice does not conform to the parents' occupational goals for their child.

The failure to acknowledge the socialization influences that might have led to these choices does not necessarily indicate that significant others such as peers and parents had no impact. In fact, findings (see Steinberg, 1990) reveal that the attitudes of adolescents and their parents are quite congruent when it comes to occupational, political, and religious decisions or convictions. Rather, the fact that the impact of significant others is not acknowledged suggests that older adolescents and young adults have come to "own" various values as personal choices, rather than attribute them to the sources from which they may have been derived (Damon & Hart, 1988). In Higgins' (1991) terminology, older adolescents have gone through a process in which they have actively selected among alternative "self-guides" and are no longer merely buffeted about by the expectations of significant others; that is, self-guides become increasingly internalized, namely, less tied to their social origins. Moreover, there is a greater sense of direction as the older adolescent comes to envisage future or "possible" selves (Markus & Nurius, 1986) that function as ideals toward which one aspires.

Another feature of the self-portrait of the older adolescent can be contrasted with the period before, in that many potentially contradictory attributes are no longer described as characteristics in opposition to one another. Thus, being conscientious as a student does not appear to conflict with one's lackadaisical attitude toward schoolwork: "That's normal, I mean, you can't just be a total 'grind.' You'd be pretty boring if you were. You have to be flexible." Similarly, one's perception of the self as ethical does not conflict with the acknowledgment that one also has engaged in some un-ethical behaviors ("It's natural to make mistakes"). Nor does introversion conflict with extroverted behaviors: "You have to be adaptive around other people. It would be weird to be the same kind of person on a date and with my friends at a football game!"

There are cognitive acquisitions that allow the older adolescent to overcome some of the liabilities of the previous period, where potentially opposing attributes were viewed as contradictory and as a cause of internal conflict. The general cognitive advances during this period involve the construction of higher-order abstractions that involve the meaningful intercoordination of single abstractions (see Case, 1985; Fischer, 1980; Fischer & Canfield, 1986). For example, the fact that one is both intro-verted and extroverted can be integrated through the construction of a higher-order abstraction that defines the self as "adaptive." The observation that one is both de-pressed and cheerful or optimistic can be integrated under the personal rubric of "moody." Similarly, "flexible" can allow one to coordinate conscientiousness with the tendency to be lackadaisical. The higher-order concept of "ambivalence" integrates the desire to be independent yet still remain connected to parents. Moreover, "bitter-sweet" reflects a higher-order abstraction combining both excitement over going to college with sadness over leaving one's parents. Such higher-order abstractions provide self-labels that bring meaning and therefore legitimacy to what formerly appeared to be troublesome contradictions within the self.

Neo-Piagetians such as Case (1985), Fischer (1980), and colleagues, observe that developmental acquisitions at these higher levels typically require greater scaffolding by the social environment in the form of support, experiences, instruction, and so on, in order for individuals to function at their optimal level. If these new skills are fostered, they will help the adolescent to integrate opposing attributes in a manner that does not produce conflict or distress. Thus, efforts to assist the adolescent in realizing that it is normal to display seemingly contradictory traits, and perhaps quite appropriate, may al-leviate perceptions of conflict. Moreover, helping teenagers to provide higher-order labels that integrate opposing attributes (e.g., flexible, adaptive, moody, inconsistent) may avert some of the distress that was salient during middle adolescence. These suggestions derive from the observations of Fischer, Case, and others to the effect that these cognitive so-lutions will not necessarily emerge automatically with development. Nor will the potential benefits derived from movement to late adolescence and early adulthood necessarily ac-crue; that is, the levels described [here] represent a normative *sequence* of development. However, the age levels are somewhat arbitrary in that certain individuals may not attain a given level at the designated age period. Development may be delayed or even arrested if there is not sufficient support for the transition to a new level of conceptualization, particularly for the higher stages.

The assertions about how the changing cognitive structures emerge—ideally, in late adolescence to early adulthood—will allow for a potential reduction in the number of contradictory attributes identified in one's self-portrait, as well as diminished conflict, have found partial support in our own findings. For example, in one study (Harter & Monsour, 1992) in which adolescents described their attributes in four roles—with parents, with friends, with romantic others, and as a student—there was a dramatic rise in the number of opposites and conflicts identified as midadolescence, followed by a slight decline among older adolescents. Evidence that older adolescents become better able to consolidate or integrate seeming contradictions within the self-theory come from the comments they made in response to a follow-up interview. As one older adolescent explained, "Sometimes I am really happy, and sometimes I get depressed. I'm just a moody person." Another commented, "I can be talkative, and I can be quiet. I'm flexible, plus they complement each other. It's good to be both ways."

The tendency to *normalize* or find value in seeming inconsistency can also be observed in the comments of other older adolescents, for example, "You wouldn't be the same person on a date as you are with your parents, and you shouldn't be. That would be weird." Another asserted, "It wouldn't be normal to act the same way with everyone. You act one way with your friends and a different way with your parents. That's the way it should be." Others made similar comments, for example, "It's good to be able to be different with different people in your life. You'd be pretty strange and also pretty boring if you weren't." "You can be outgoing with friends and then shy on a date because you are just different with different people; you can't always be the same person and probably shouldn't be." Yet another indicated, "There are situations where you are a good listener and others where you are talkative. It's good to be both." Thus, older adolescents come to the conclusion that it is desirable to be different across relational contexts, and in so doing, they would appear to be cultivating the stance that social psychologists (see Gergen, 1968; Mischel, 1973; Vallacher, 1980) identify as more the rule than the exception for adults.

Questions

1. How does cognitive growth at adolescence impact self-concept?
2. What does Harter mean by multiple selves?
3. How does cognitive development affect the experience of multiple selves?
4. Is there a "real" self and "false" selves? In what contexts or relationships is the "real" self more likely to be experienced? In what contexts or relationships is the "false" self more likely to be experienced?
5. Are there noncognitive reasons that might explain why the experience of multiple selves becomes nonproblematic in late adolescence?

References and Further Reading

Damon, W., & Hart, D. (1982). The development of self-understanding from infancy through adolescence. *Child Development, 53,* 841–864.

Fischer, K. W. (1980). A theory of cognitive development: The control and construction of hierarchies of skills. *Psychological Review, 87,* 477–531.

Harter, S. (1986). Cognitive-developmental processes in the integration of concepts about emotion and the self. *Social Cognition, 4,* 119–151.

Harter, S. (1990). Self and identity development. In S. S. Feldman, & G. R. Elliott (Eds.) *At the threshold: The developing adolescent* (pp. 352–387). Cambridge, MA: Harvard University Press.

Harter, S. (1999). *The construction of the self.* New York: Guilford Press.

Part II

Personal and Social Identity Development

Chapter 5

Theoretical Foundation

One of the major developmental tasks of adolescence is the formation of identity. The adolescent must integrate aspects of the self (physical and psychological traits, abilities, temperament, attitudes, and beliefs) into a coherent whole and find a fit between that self and the adult roles and opportunities that are open in society. Erik Erikson has made a profound contribution to our understanding of the formation of identity, and his theoretical ideas have provided the basis for decades of research on identity development.

Erikson was a prominent figure in the fields of psychoanalysis and human development. His studies of growth in a variety of cultural settings and his clinical work as a psychoanalyst enabled him to create a theory of individual development that was sensitive to the cultural context in which that development unfolds. Erikson described growth as occurring in a series of eight stages of psychosocial development. He believed that each stage of development "comes to its ascendance, meets its crisis, and finds its lasting solution" (Erikson, 1968, p. 95) at a particular moment in the life cycle. Erikson described each stage as a normative crisis centering around a conflict between a positive and negative polarity. By crisis Erikson did not mean catastrophe, but rather, "a turning point, a crucial period of increased vulnerability and heightened potential" (p. 96). Nor did Erikson believe that a nuclear conflict could be completely resolved. Rather, healthy development occurs if the balance of experience is tipped toward the positive polarity. Each stage leaves its marks on personality and contributes to a sense of identity. The eight nuclear crises that Erikson identified were understood to be life issues, to exist from the beginning of life in some form, and to be issues in some form during each of the stages of development. Thus the inadequate resolution of any conflict makes a healthy resolution of the next crisis more difficult to attain.

The first crisis centers around the polarity of Trust versus Mistrust. Infants are wholly reliant on caretakers to meet their needs. In order to overcome their experience of helplessness and dependency, infants need assurance that in some regular way their needs will be met. By *trust* Erikson meant that a baby would develop a trustfulness of others, an inner certainty that there would be outer consistency, continuity, and sameness of experience in its care. If care is consistent and satisfying, infants develop a sense of trust in their caretakers, an inner certainty of an outer predictability. If care is erratic and neglectful, the experience of mistrust predominates, and infants will be unwilling to invest in the world and in relationships.

The second crisis centers around the polarity of Autonomy versus Shame and Doubt. Children at this stage develop a sense of their autonomous wills and want to exert control, to do things by themselves and their way. As yet, however, they do not have the capability to do most things competently by themselves. The struggle at this stage is between a sense of *autonomy,* being able to stand on one's own feet, and a sense of *shame* and *doubt,* a sense of being exposed prematurely as incompetent before one is ready to be exposed. A balance is needed in the care of the child between avoiding excessive control so that a child can exercise autonomy, and offering enough outer control so that a child will maintain a sense of self-esteem and avoid shame and doubt.

The third crisis centers around Initiative versus Guilt. At this stage children are capable of thrusting themselves on the world. *Initiative* involves "undertaking, planning and 'attacking' a task for the sake of being active and on the move" (Erikson, 1950, p. 255). A child punishes his or her own initiative with *guilt.* A sense of guilt can be experienced over acts carried out using one's newly discovered locomotor and mental capacities, and over goals contemplated and not even attempted in actuality. A child must learn to be able to exercise initiative without being constricted by too much guilt.

The fourth stage, which encompasses the years of elementary school in this culture, centers around Industry versus Inferiority. At this stage children develop a sense of themselves as workers. They acquire the skills needed to work within their society, to work with discipline, to do things cooperatively, and to win recognition by producing things. The danger at this stage is *inferiority,* a feeling of inadequacy about whether or not one is competent, can do the work, and can produce things society deems to be valuable.

Erikson placed the crisis of Identity versus Identity Confusion at the stage of adolescence. While a sense of identity begins to accrue during infancy, identity comes to ascendance at adolescence because of the development of adult sexuality and the development of new cognitive capacities that enable an adolescent to weigh many possibilities simultaneously, to imagine who one was, who one is now, and who one might become. *Identity* involves finding a sense of continuity and sameness, an inner unity. The identity crisis also comes at adolescence because of societal demands "to connect the roles and skills cultivated earlier with the occupational prototypes of the day" (Erikson, 1950, p. 261).

Erikson outlined three final stages of development: Intimacy versus Isolation, Generativity versus Stagnation, and Integrity versus Despair. After a firm sense of identity is developed, one is ready for true *intimacy* with another, without fear of loss of identity in the fusion. Fear of intimacy may lead to competitive, combative relations and a readiness to isolate oneself. *Generativity,* the task of adulthood, involves establishing and guiding the next generation by raising children, caring for one's family and beyond, and making the world a better place through one's productivity and creativity. *Stagnation* is a feeling of being locked in by family, children, jobs, and an inability to care. Finally, *integrity* involves an acceptance of one's life, a feeling that one has met the earlier crises with reasonable success and can look back with a sense of satisfaction. *Despair* is a feeling that one should have done things differently, that opportunities were missed, that other choices should have been made, but that time is short and it is too late to do things differently.

Though written fifty years ago, Erikson's theory continues to serve as a theoretical basis for understanding adolescent behavior to this day. Erikson's theory focuses on the development of personal identity, and he gave relatively little attention to a person's social identity, which depends upon the groups to which an individual belongs and how those groups effect self-definition. Sex, race, ethnicity, social class, and sexual orientation are all important in shaping the development of identity and are aspects of identity that have been addressed by more recent researchers discussed below who have drawn upon Erikson's theoretical foundation.

Additional Resources

References and Recommended Reading

Erikson, E. (1950). *Childhood and society.* New York: W. W. Norton.
Erikson, E. (1968). *Identity: Youth and crisis.* New York: W. W. Norton.

On the Internet

http://www.personal.psu.edu/faculty/n/x/nxd10/identity2.htm

Adolescence: Change & Continuity—Identity
This site was produced by Pennsylvania State University students taking Human Development and Family Studies 433: The Transition to Adulthood, and Human Development and Family Studies 239: Adolescent Development.

Identity Confusion in Life History, Case History

Erik Erikson was one of the preeminent psychoanalysts of the twentieth century. He was a professor of human development at Harvard University and served on the senior staff at the Austin Riggs Center in Stockbridge, Massachusetts. He participated in research at the Harvard Psychological Clinic, the Yale Institute for Human Relations, the Institute of Child Welfare at the University of California, and the Western Psychiatric Institute in Pittsburgh. He is author of *Childhood and Society* (1950), *Identity: Youth and Crisis* (1968), *Young Man Luther* (1993), and *Insight and Responsibility* (1994). He died in 1994.

Erik Erikson argues that the major task of adolescence is the formation of identity, and in this selection Erikson describes in some detail many of the dimensions of the process of developing an identity at adolescence. Erikson begins with a discussion of the building blocks of identity, the identifications of childhood. These are components of personality that are developed through the process of internalizing positive and negative aspects of significant others into personality. Erikson goes on to delineate why identity must be based on more than the sum of childhood identifications, and why earlier childhood crystallizations of identity are inadequate as an identity in adulthood. In this chapter, Erikson coins the phrase *psychosocial moratorium* to describe a period of identity exploration that is granted to youth in some societies and enumerates both the potentials and dangers of a moratorium. He discusses the nature of adolescent peer relationships, viewing them as primarily motivated by the need to construct an identity rather than by real intimacy with another. He describes what he labels a "negative identity," a consolidation of an identity in opposition to the values and ideals of one's society, and considers why an adolescent might acquire a negative identity and the function it serves.

Erikson argues that the crisis of identity incorporates elements of all of the other nuclear crises. In the final portion of this selection he looks at the ways the four earlier crises come back and play a role in the crises of identity, how trust, autonomy, initiative, and industry must be renegotiated at adolescence. He also looks at how the crisis of identity anticipates the three nuclear conflicts that will follow in adulthood. To acquire a firm sense of identity, an individual must successfully resolve all of the life crises. Erikson does not lay out these ideas in great detail, making this perhaps the most difficult part of the essay, but it may be the most powerful.

The crisis of Trust versus Mistrust is mirrored in the polarity of *Time perspective versus Time confusion.* Trust arises in infancy out of the repeated experiences of having needs arise, suffering a period of delay of satisfaction of those needs, and finally having caretakers arrive to provide satisfaction. Thus infants build up a storehouse of memories that in some regular way needs will be met in time. They develop a trust in time, a belief that it is worth wanting and waiting because rewards will be forthcoming. The formation of identity requires temporal perspective. To complete an education, for example, involves a trust in time, a belief that working now in school will produce rewards at some future point in time (Readings 1.1 and 7.1).

Autonomy versus Shame and Doubt is reworked in the form of *Self-certainty versus Self-consciousness.* To move beyond childhood identifications and to develop into a unique and separate person with one's own ideology involves the establishment of a sense of autonomy, of individuation and independence from the family, and certainty in oneself (Reading 4.1). *Self-consciousness* arises, as did shame and doubt, from the feeling of being exposed before one is ready and before one's identity is fully formed.

Role experimentation versus Role fixation traces back to Initiative versus Guilt. To achieve an identity it is optimal to experiment freely with available roles. Some youth are granted a moratorium, or period of delay in which to experiment, to participate in apprenticeships and adventure, and to freely exercise initiative. Some adolescents experience *role fixation.* This may take the form of a *negative identity,* an identification with what they are least supposed to be (Readings 13.1 and 13.2). By fixating on roles that may be both undesirable and dangerous, adolescents cut off free experimentation with acceptable roles because these roles are felt to be unattainable.

Finally, *Apprenticeship versus Work paralysis* is a reworking of the crisis of Industry versus Inferiority. Adolescents with a strong sense of industry enjoy a sense of *apprenticeship,* of learning and experimenting, that will pave the way to a future vocation. Some adolescents experience a sense of inferiority and inadequacy that leads to an inability to concentrate and muster the energy necessary for school or work.

The power of Erikson's theory is that it addresses so many aspects of adolescent development. He provides us with conceptual tools useful for the analysis of many adolescent problems such as underachievement (Reading 7.1), delinquency (Readings 13.1 and 13.2), and suicide, and for the analysis of adolescent relationships, belief systems, and occupational striving.

Genetic: Identification and Identity

The autobiographies of extraordinary (and extraordinarily self-perceptive) individuals are one source of insight into the development of identity. In order to describe the universal genetics of identity, one would wish to be able to trace its development through the life histories of "ordinary" individuals. Here I must rely on general impressions from daily life, on guidance work with mildly disturbed young people, and on my participation in one of the rare "longitudinal" studies—a source which excludes the detailed publication of biographic data. In the following genetic sketch, some repetition of what has been said previously is unavoidable.

Adolescence is the last stage of childhood. The adolescent process, however, is conclusively complete only when the individual has subordinated his childhood identifications to a new kind of identification, achieved in absorbing sociability and in competitive apprenticeship with and among his age mates. These new identifications are no longer characterized by the playfulness of childhood and the experimental zest of youth: with dire urgency they force the young individual into choices and decisions which will, with increasing immediacy, lead to commitments "for life." The task to be performed here by the young person and by his society is formidable. It necessitates, in different individuals and in different societies, great variations in the duration, intensity, and ritualization of adolescence. Societies offer, as individuals require, more or less sanctioned intermediary periods between childhood and adulthood, often characterized by a combination of prolonged immaturity and provoked precocity.

In postulating a "latency period" which precedes puberty, psychoanalysis has given recognition to some kind of psychosexual moratorium in human development—a period of delay which permits the future mate and parent first to go to whatever "school" his culture provides and to learn the technical and social rudiments of a work situation. The libido theory, however, offers no adequate account of a second period of delay, namely, prolonged adolescence. Here the sexually matured individual is more or less retarded in his psychosexual capacity for intimacy and in the psychosocial readiness for parenthood. This period can be viewed as a *psychosocial moratorium* during which the young adult through free role experimentation may find a niche in some section of his society, a niche which is firmly defined and yet seems to be uniquely made for him.

If, in the following, we speak of the community's response to the young individual's need to be "recognized" by those around him, we mean something beyond a mere recognition of achievement; for it is of great relevance to the young individual's identity formation that he be responded to and be given function and status as a person whose gradual growth and transformation make sense to those who begin to make sense to him. It has not been sufficiently recognized in psychoanalysis that such recognition provides an entirely indispensable support to the ego in the specific tasks of adolescing, which are: to maintain the most important ego defenses against the vastly growing intensity of impulses (now invested in a matured genital apparatus and a powerful muscle system); to learn to consolidate the most important "conflict-free" achievements in line with work opportunities; and to resynthesize all childhood identifications in some unique way and yet in concordance with the roles offered by some wider section of society—be that section the neighborhood block, an anticipated occupational field, an association of kindred minds, or perhaps (as in Shaw's case) the "mighty dead."

A moratorium is a period of delay granted to somebody who is not ready to meet an obligation or forced on somebody who should give himself time. By psychosocial moratorium, then, we mean a delay of adult commitments, and yet it is not only a delay. It is a period that is characterized by a selective permissiveness on the part of society and of provocative playfulness on the part of youth, and yet it also often leads to deep, if often transitory, commitment on the part of youth, and ends in a more or less ceremonial confirmation of commitment on the part of society. Such moratoria show highly individual variations, which are especially pronounced in very gifted people (gifted for better or for worse), and there are, of course, institutional variations linked with the ways of life of cultures and subcultures.

Each society and each culture institutionalizes a certain moratorium for the majority of its young people. For the most part, these moratoria coincide with apprenticeships and adventures that are in line with the society's values. The moratorium may be a time for horse stealing and vision-quests, a time for *Wanderschaft* or work "out West" or "down under," a time for "lost youth" or academic life, a time for self-sacrifice or for pranks—and today, often a time for patienthood or delinquency. For much of juvenile delinquency, especially in its organized form, must be considered to be an attempt at the creation of a psychosocial moratorium. In fact, I would assume that some delinquency has been a relatively institutionalized moratorium for a long time in parts of our society, and that it forces itself on our awareness now only because it proves too attractive and compelling for too many youngsters at once. In addition to all this, our society seems to be in the process of incorporating psychiatric treatment as one of the few permissible moratoria for young people who otherwise would be crushed by standardization and mechanization. This we must consider carefully, for the label or diagnosis one acquires during the psychosocial moratorium is of the utmost importance for the process of identity formation.

But the moratorium does not need to be consciously experienced as such. On the contrary, the young individual may feel deeply committed and may learn only much later that what he took so seriously was only a period of transition; many "recovered" delinquents probably feel quite estranged about the "foolishness" that has passed. It is clear, however, that any experimentation with identity images means also to play with the inner fire of emotions and drives and to risk the outer danger of ending up in a social "pocket" from which there is no return. Then the moratorium has failed; the individual is defined too early, and he has committed himself because circumstances or, indeed, authorities have committed him.

Linguistically as well as psychologically, identity and identification have common roots. Is identity, then, the mere sum of earlier identifications, or is it merely an additional set of identifications?

The limited usefulness of the mechanism of identification becomes obvious at once if we consider the fact that none of the identifications of childhood (which in our patients stand out in such morbid elaboration and mutual contradiction) could, if merely added up, result in a functioning personality. True, we usually believe that the task of psychotherapy is the replacement of morbid and excessive identifications by more desirable ones. But as every cure attests, "more desirable" identifications at the same time tend to be quietly subordinated to a new, unique Gestalt which is more than the sum of its parts. The fact is that identification as a mechanism is of limited usefulness. Children at different stages of their development identify with those part aspects of people by which they themselves are most immediately affected, whether in reality or fantasy. Their identifications with parents, for example, center in certain overvalued and ill-understood body parts, capacities, and role appearances. These part aspects, furthermore, are favored not because of their social acceptability (they often are everything but the parents' most adjusted attributes) but by the nature of infantile fantasy which only gradually gives way to more realistic judgment.

In later childhood the individual is faced with a comprehensible hierarchy of roles, from the younger siblings to the grandparents and whoever else belongs to the wider family. All through childhood this gives him some kind of a set of expectations as to what he is going to be when he grows older, and very small children identify with a number of people in a number of respects and establish a kind of hierarchy of expectations which then seeks "verification" later in life. That is why cultural and historical change can prove so traumatic to identity formation: it can break up the inner consistency of a child's hierarchy of expectations.

If we consider introjection, identification, and identity formation to be the steps by which the ego grows in ever more mature interplay with the available models, the following psychosocial schedule suggests itself.

The mechanism of *introjection* (the primitive "incorporation" of another's image) depends for its integration on the satisfactory mutuality between the mothering adult(s) and the mothered child. Only the experience of such initial mutuality provides a safe pole of self-feeling from which the child can reach out for the other pole: his first love "objects."

The fate of childhood *identifications*, in turn, depends on the child's satisfactory interaction with trustworthy representatives of a meaningful hierarchy of roles as provided by the generations living together in some form of family.

Identity formation, finally, begins where the usefulness of identification ends. It arises from the selective repudiation and mutual assimilation of childhood identifications and their absorption in a new configuration, which, in turn, is dependent on the process by which a society (often through subsocieties) identifies the young individual, recognizing him as somebody who had to become the way he is and who, being the way he is, is taken for granted. The community, often not without some initial mistrust, gives such recognition with a display of surprise and pleasure in making the acquaintance of a newly emerging individual. For the community in turn feels "recognized" by the individual who cares to ask for recognition; it can, by the same token, feel deeply—and vengefully—rejected by the individual who does not seem to care.

A community's ways of *identifying* the *individual,* then, meet more or less successfully the individual's ways of identifying himself with others. If the young person is "recognized" at a critical moment as one who arouses displeasure and discomfort, the community sometimes seems to suggest to the young person that he change in ways that to him do not add up to anything "identical with himself." To the community, the desirable change is nevertheless conceived of as a mere matter of good will or of will power ("he could if he wanted to") while resistance to such change is perceived as a matter of bad will or, indeed, of inferiority, hereditary or otherwise. Thus the community often underestimates to what extent a long, intricate childhood history has restricted a youth's further choice of identity change, and also to what extent the community could, if it only would, still help to determine a youth's destiny within these choices.

All through childhood tentative crystallizations of identity take place which make the individual feel and believe (to begin with the most conscious aspect of the matter) as if he approximately knew who he was—only to find that such self-certainty ever again falls prey to the discontinuities of development itself. An example would be the discontinuity between the demands made in a given milieu on a little boy and those made on a "big boy" who, in turn, may well wonder why he was first made to believe that to be little is admirable, only to be forced to exchange this more effortless status for the special obligations of one who is "big now." Such discontinuities can, at any time, amount to a crisis and demand a decisive and strategic repatterning of action, leading to compromises which can be compensated for only by a consistently accruing sense of the practicability and feasibility of such increasing commitment. The cute, or ferocious, or good small boy who becomes a studious, or gentlemanly, or tough big boy must be able—and must be enabled—to combine both sets of values in a recognized identity which permits him, in work and play and in official and intimate behavior, to be (and to let others be) a combination of a big boy and a little boy.

The community supports such development to the extent that it permits the child, at each step, to orient himself toward a complete "life plan" with a hierarchical order of roles as represented by individuals of different ages. Family, neighborhood, and school provide contact and experimental identification with younger and older children and with young and old adults. A child, in the multiplicity of successive and tentative identifications, thus begins early to build up expectations of what it will be like to be older and what it will feel like to have been younger—expectations which become part of an identity as they are, step by step, verified in decisive experiences of psychosocial "fittedness."

The final identity, then, as fixed at the end of adolescence, is superordinated to any single identification with individuals of the past: it includes all significant identifications, but it also alters them in order to make a unique and reasonably coherent whole of them.

The critical phases of life have been described in psychoanalysis primarily in terms of instincts and defenses, i.e., as "typical danger situations." Psychoanalysis has concerned itself more with the encroachment of psychosexual crises on psychosocial (and other) functions than with the specific crisis created by the maturation of each function. Take for example a child who is learning to speak: he is acquiring one of the prime functions supporting a sense of individual autonomy and one of the prime techniques for expanding the radius of give-and-take. The mere indication of an ability to give intentional sound-signs soon obligates the child to "say what he wants." It may force him to achieve by proper verbalization the attention which was afforded him previously in response to mere gestures of needfulness. Speech not only increasingly commits him to his own characteristic kind of voice and to the mode of speech he develops, it also defines him as one responded to by those around him with changed diction and attention. They in turn expect henceforth to be understood by him with fewer explanations or gestures. Furthermore, a spoken word is a pact. There is an irrevocably committing aspect to an utterance remembered by others, although the child may have to learn early that certain commitments (adult ones to a child) are subject to change without notice, while others (his to them) are not. This intrinsic relationship of speech not only to the world of communicable facts, but also to the social value of verbal commitment and uttered truth is strategic among the experiences which mark ego development. It is this psychosocial aspect of the matter which we must learn to relate to the by now better known psychosexual aspects represented, for example, in the autoerotic enjoyment of speech; the use of speech as an oral or otherwise erotic "contact"; or in such organ-mode emphases as eliminative or intrusive sounds or uses of speech. Thus the child may come to develop, in the use of voice and word, a particular combination of whining or singing, judging or arguing as part of a new element of the future identity, namely, the element "one who speaks and is spoken to in such-and-such a way." This element in turn will be related to other elements of the child's developing identity (he is clever and/or good-looking and/or tough) and will be compared with other people, alive or dead, judged as ideal or evil.

It is the ego's function to integrate the psychosexual and psychosocial aspects on a given level of development and at the same time to integrate the relation of newly added identity elements with those already in existence—that is, to bridge the inescapable discontinuities between different levels of personality development. For earlier crystalizations of identity can become subject to renewed conflict when changes in the quality and quantity of drive, expansions in mental equipment, and new and often conflicting social demands all make previous adjustments appear insufficient and, in fact, make previous opportunities and rewards suspect. Yet such developmental and normative crises differ from imposed, traumatic, and neurotic crises in that the very process of growth provides new energy even as society offers new and specific opportunities according to its dominant conception of the phases of life. From a genetic point of view, then, the process of identity formation emerges as an evolving configuration—a configuration which is gradually established by successive ego syntheses and resyntheses throughout childhood. It is a configuration gradually integrating constitutional givens, idiosyncratic libidinal needs, favored capacities, significant identifications, effective defenses, successful sublimations, and consistent roles. . . .

Pathographic: The Clinical Picture of Severe Identity Confusion . . .

The Problem of Intimacy

That many of our patients break down at an age which is properly considered more preadult than postadolescent is explained by the fact that often only an attempt to engage in intimate fellowship and competition or in sexual intimacy fully reveals the latent weakness of identity.

True "engagement" with others is the result and the test of firm self-delineation. As the young individual seeks at least tentative forms of playful intimacy in friendship and competition, in sex play and love, in argument and gossip, he is apt to experience a peculiar strain, as if such tentative engagement might turn into an interpersonal fusion amounting to a loss of identity and requiring, therefore, a tense inner reservation, a caution in commitment. Where a youth does not resolve such strain, he may isolate himself and enter, at best, only stereotyped and formalized interpersonal relations; or he may, in repeated hectic attempts and dismal failures, seek intimacy with the most improbable partners. For where an assured sense of identity is missing, even friendships and affairs become desperate attempts at delineating the fuzzy outlines of identity by mutual narcissistic mirroring: to fall in love then often means to fall into one's mirror image, hurting oneself and damaging the mirror. During lovemaking or in sexual fantasies a loosening of sexual identity threatens; it even becomes unclear whether sexual excitement is experienced by the individual or by his partner, and this applies in either heterosexual or homosexual encounters. The ego thus loses its flexible capacity for abandoning itself to sexual and affectual sensations in a fusion with another individual who is both partner to the sensation and guarantor of one's continuing identity: fusion with another becomes identity loss. A sudden collapse of all capacity for mutuality threatens, and a desperate wish ensues to start all over again, with a (quasideliberate) regression to a stage of basic bewilderment and rage such as only the very small child experiences.

It must be remembered that the counterpart of intimacy is distantiation, i.e., the readiness to repudiate, ignore, or destroy those forces and people whose essence seems dangerous to one's own. Intimacy with one set of people and ideas would not be really intimate without an efficient repudiation of another set. Thus, weakness or excess in repudiation is an intrinsic aspect of the inability to gain intimacy because of an incomplete identity: whoever is not sure of his "point of view" cannot repudiate judiciously.

Young persons often indicate in rather pathetic ways the feeling that only by merging with a "leader" can they be saved, the leader being an adult who is able and willing to offer himself as a safe object for experimental surrender and as a guide in the relearning of the very first steps toward an intimate mutuality and a legitimate repudiation. The late adolescent wants to be an apprentice or disciple, a follower, a sexual servant, or patient to such a person. When this fails, as it often must from its very intensity and absoluteness, the young individual recoils to a position of strenuous introspection and self-testing which, given particularly aggravating circumstances or a history of relatively strong autistic trends, can lead him into a paralyzing borderline state. Symptomatically, this state consists of a painfully heightened sense of isolation; a disintegration of the sense of inner continuity and sameness; a sense of over-all ashamedness; an inability to derive a sense of accomplishment from any kind of activity. In these young patients, masturbation and nocturnal emissions, far from being an occasional release of excess pressure, only serve to aggravate tension. They become part of a vicious cycle in which omnipotent narcissism is momentarily heightened only to give way to a sense of physical and mental castration and emptiness. Thus, life is happening to the individual rather than being lived by his initiative; his mistrust leaves it to the world, to society, and indeed to psychiatry to prove that he does exist in a psychosocial sense, i.e., can count on an invitation to become himself. . . .

The Choice of the Negative Identity

The loss of a sense of identity is often expressed in a scornful and snobbish hostility toward the roles offered as proper and desirable in one's family or immediate community. Any aspect of the required role, or all of it—be it masculinity or femininity, nationality or class membership—can become the main focus of the young person's acid disdain. Such excessive contempt for their backgrounds occurs among the oldest Anglo-Saxon and the newest Latin or Jewish families; it can become a general dislike for everything American and an irrational overestimation of everything foreign, or the reverse. Life and strength seem to exist only where one is not, while decay and danger threaten wherever one happens to be. This typical fragment from a case report illustrates the superego's triumph of depreciation over a young man's faltering identity: "A voice within him which was disparaging him began to increase at about this time. It went to the point of intruding into everything he did. He said, 'If I smoke a cigarette, if I tell a girl I like her, if I make a gesture, if I listen to music, if I try to read a book—this third voice is at me all the time—"You're doing this for effect; you're a phony."' This disparaging voice became rather relentless. One day on the way from home to college, his train crossed through the New Jersey swamplands and some poorer sections of cities, and he felt overwhelmingly that he was more congenial with people who lived there than he was with people on the campus or at home. Life seemed to exist only in those places, and the campus, in contrast, was a sheltered, effeminate place."

In this example, it is important to recognize not only an overweening superego, overclearly perceived as a deprecating inner voice (but not integrated enough to lead the young man into an alternative career), but also the acute identity confusion as projected on segments of society. An analogous case is that of a French-American girl from a rather prosperous mining town who felt panicky to the point of paralysis when alone with a boy. It appeared that numerous superego injunctions and identity conflicts had, as it were, short-circuited in the obsessive idea that every boy had a right to expect from her a yielding to sexual practices popularly designated as "French."

Such estrangement from national and ethnic origins rarely leads to a complete denial of *personal identity,* although the angry insistence on being called by a particular given name or nickname is not uncommon among young people who try to find refuge in a new name label. Yet, confabulatory reconstructions of one's origin do occur.

An especially inventive high school girl from Middle-European stock secretly sought the company of Scottish immigrants, carefully studying and easily assimilating their dialect and their social habits. With the help of history books and travel guides she reconstructed for herself a childhood in a given milieu in an actual township in Scotland, which was apparently quite convincing to some descendants of that country throughout long evening talks. She spoke of her American-born parents as "the people who brought me over here," and when sent to me introduced herself as "Lorna" and described her childhood "over there" in impressive detail. I went along with the story, saying that it had more inner truth than reality to it. And indeed the inner truth turned out to be a memory, namely, the girl's erstwhile attachment to a woman neighbor who had come from the British Isles and who had given her more of the kind of love she wanted than her parents did or could. The force behind the near-delusional power of the invented "truth" was in turn a death wish against her parents, which is latent in all severe identity crises. The semideliberateness of the delusion came to the fore when I finally asked the girl how she had managed to marshall all the details of life in Scotland. "Bless you, sir," she said, in a pleading Scottish brogue, "I needed a past." Needless to say, with such gifts for language, histrionics, and personal warmth, a "delusion" is very different in nature and prognosis from a truly psychotic condition.

On the whole, however, our patients' conflicts find expression in a more subtle way than the abrogation of personal identity. They choose instead a *negative identity*, i.e., an identity perversely based on all those identifications and roles which, at critical stages of development, had been presented to them as most undesirable or dangerous and yet also as most real. For example, a mother whose first-born son died and who, because of complicated guilt feelings, had never been able to attach to her later surviving children the same amount of religious devotion that she bestowed on the memory of her dead child, aroused in one of her sons the fateful conviction that to be sick or dead was a better assurance of being "recognized" than to be healthy and about. A mother who was filled with unconscious ambivalence toward a brother who had disintegrated into alcoholism again and again responded selectively only to those traits in her son which seemed to point to a repetition of her brother's fate, with the result that this "negative" identity sometimes seemed to have more reality for the son than all his natural attempts at being good. He worked hard at becoming a drunkard, and, lacking the necessary ingredients, ended up in a state of stubborn paralysis of choice.

In other cases the negative identity is dictated by the necessity of finding and defending a niche of one's own against the excessive ideals either demanded by morbidly ambitious parents or indeed actualized by superior ones. In both cases the parents' weaknesses and unexpressed wishes are recognized by the child with catastrophic clarity. The daughter of a man of brilliant showmanship ran away from college and was arrested as a prostitute in the Negro quarter of a southern city, while the daughter of an influential southern Negro preacher was found among narcotic addicts in Chicago. In such cases it is of utmost importance to recognize the mockery and vindictive pretense in such role playing, for the white girl had not really prostituted herself, and the colored girl had not really become an addict—yet. Needless to say, however, each of them had put herself into a marginal social area, leaving it to law enforcement officers and psychiatric agencies to decide what stamp to put on such behavior. A corresponding case is that of a boy presented to a psychiatric clinic as "the village homosexual" of a small town. On investigation, it appeared that the boy had succeeded in assuming this fame without any actual acts of homosexuality except one, much earlier in his life, when he had been raped by some older boys.

Such vindictive choices of a negative identity represent, of course, a desperate attempt at regaining some mastery in a situation in which the available positive identity elements cancel each other out. The history of such a choice reveals a set of conditions in which it is easier for the patient to derive a sense of identity out of a total identification with that which he is least supposed to be than to struggle for a feeling of reality in acceptable roles which are unattainable with his inner means. The statement of a young man that "I would rather be quite insecure than a little secure" and of a young woman that "at least in the gutter I'm a genius," circumscribe the relief following the total choice of a negative identity. Such relief is, of course, often sought collectively in cliques and gangs of young homosexuals, addicts, and social cynics.

Some forms of upper-class snobbism must be included here because they permit some people to deny their identity confusion through recourse to something they did not earn themselves, such as their parents' wealth, background, or fame, or to some things they did not create, such as styles and art forms. But there is a "lower lower" snobbism too, which is based on the pride of having achieved a semblance of nothingness. At any rate, many a sick or desperate late adolescent, if faced with continuing conflict, would rather be nobody or somebody totally bad or, indeed, dead—and this by free choice—than be not-quite-somebody. The word "total" is not accidental in this connection; we have endeavored to describe [elsewhere] a human proclivity to a "totalistic" reorientation when, at critical stages of development, reintegration into a relative "wholeness" seems impossible. The totalistic solution of a psychotic break cannot be discussed here. . . .

Societal: From Individual Confusion to Social Order

Having offered a picture of the whole condition of acute identity confusion, I would like now to take up each of the part-symptoms described and relate it to two phenomena seemingly remote from one another: the individual's childhood and cultural history. Since we take it for granted that the conflicts we meet in our case histories in vastly aggravated form are, in principle, common to all individuals, so that the picture presented is only a distorted reflection of the normal adolescent state, we may now inquire, first, how this state can be shown to revive old childhood conflicts and, second, what are the various avenues which cultures offer to "normal" youths so that they may overcome the forces that pull them back into infantile regressions and find ways of mobilizing their inner strength for future-oriented pursuits. . . .

Only the *diagonal* of the epigenetic chart [Table 1] has been fully discussed [elsewhere]. It depicts, we said, the ontogenetic unfolding of the main components of psychosocial vitality (I.1–VIII.8). We have also filled in some aspects of the vertical leading from infancy to identity, from I.5 to V.5. These are the specific contributions which previous stages make directly to the development of identity, namely, the primitive

Table 1

	1	2	3	4	5	6	7	8
VIII								INTEGRITY vs. DESPAIR
VII							GENERATIVITY vs. STAGNATION	
VI						INTIMACY vs. ISOLATION		
V	Temporal Perspective vs. Time Confusion	Self-Certainty vs. Self-Consciousness	Role Experimentation vs. Role Fixation	Apprenticeship vs. Work Paralysis	IDENTITY vs. IDENTITY CONFUSION	Sexual Polarization vs. Bisexual Confusion	Leader- and Followership vs. Authority Confusion	Ideological Commitment vs. Confusion of Values
IV				INDUSTRY vs. INFERIORITY	Task Identification vs. Sense of Futility			
III			INITIATIVE vs. GUILT		Anticipation of Roles vs. Role Inhibition			
II		AUTONOMY vs. SHAME, DOUBT			Will to Be Oneself vs. Self-Doubt			
I	TRUST vs. MISTRUST				Mutual Recognition vs. Autistic Isolation			

trust in mutual recognition; the rudiments of a *will* to be oneself; the *anticipation* of what one might become; and the capacity to *learn* how to be, with skill, what one is in the process of becoming. But this also means that each of these stages contributes a particular estrangement to identity confusion: the earliest would come about with an "autistic" inability to establish mutuality. The most radical forms of identity confusion, we have just seen, can be traced back to such early disturbances. Here, a basic confusion of contradictory introjects undermines, as it were, all future identifications and thus also their integration in adolescence. Taking our cues, then, from the clinical picture just described, and experimenting with the chart, we will now distribute the various *part-symptoms* of confusion on horizontal V of the chart, and indicate how we would trace them downward along the "regressive" verticals 1, 2, 3, and 4 to their antecedents in childhood. The reader need only let his eye wander along these verticals to find the location of the numbers which appear after the major items.

Let us begin with the first item of pathology just described, the mistrust of time itself and the dominance of *time confusion* (V.1). A loss of the ego's function of maintaining perspective and expectancy is a clear regression to a time in early infancy when time did not exist. The experience of time arises only from the infant's adaptation to initial cycles of need tension, delay of satisfaction, and satiation. In the infant, as tension increases, future fulfillment is anticipated in a "hallucinatory" way; as fulfillment is delayed, moments of impotent rage occur in which trust seems obliterated; any signs of an approaching satisfaction gives time again a quality of intense hope, while further delay causes redoubled rage. Our patients, as we saw, do not trust time and are not convinced that sufficient satisfaction is sufficiently predictable to make wanting and "working" worth while.

Our most malignantly regressed young people are in fact clearly possessed by general attitudes which represent something of a mistrust of time as such: every delay appears to be a deceit, every wait an experience of impotence, every hope a danger, every plan a catastrophe, every possible provider a potential traitor. Therefore, time must be made to stand still, if necessary by the magic means of catatonic immobility. These are the extremes which are manifest in few but latent in many cases of identity confusion, and every adolescent, I would believe, knows at least fleeting moments of being thus at odds with time itself. In its normal and transitory form, the new kind of mistrust quickly or gradually yields to outlooks permitting and demanding an intense and even fanatic investment in a future, or a rapid succession in a number of possible futures. These, to the elders, often seem quite inconsistent with each other and at any rate quite "utopian," that is, based on expectations which would call for a change in the laws of historical change. But then, again, youth can attach itself to seemingly utopian world images which somehow prove to be realizable in part, given the right leader—and historical luck. Time confusion, then, is more or less typical for all adolescents at one stage or another, although it becomes pathologically marked only in some.

What does the social process do about this, from culture to culture, and from one era to another? I can only offer some suggestive examples. Thus, there was the romantic period, when youth (and artists and writers) were preoccupied with the ruins left by a dead past which seemed more "eternal" than the present. To be emphasized here, however, is not the mere turning to a distant past, but a concomitant change in the whole quality of temporal experience. This, under different cultural or historical conditions, can be acquired in settings as different . . . as a vision-quest in the blinding prairie sun or dancing to drumbeat throughout the night; in utterly passive drug-induced floating in "absolute" time or in goose stepping to blaring trumpets in preparation for the Thousand Year Reich. There is, in fact, an indispensable temporal aspect to all ideology, including the ideological significance which the goals and values of different civilizations have for youth, be they bent on salvation or reform, adventure or conquest, reason or progress, in accordance with newly developing identity potentials. For among the essentials which they provide for youth is a sensually convincing *time perspective* compatible with a coherent world image. It makes supreme sense that today, when the standardization of anticipated futures is at its height, thousands of young people would choose to behave as if the moratorium were a way of life and a separate culture. As they choose to forget about their future, society forgets that theirs is only a modern—that is, more populous and more pub-licized—form of an old phenomenon, as is clearly revealed by the quality of revival in some of our young people's display.

We also diagnosed *identity-consciousness* among the ingredients of identity con-fusion, and we meant by it a special form of painful self-consciousness which dwells on discrepancies between one's self-esteem, the aggrandized self-image as an autono-mous person, and one's appearance in the eyes of others. In our patients an occasional total obliteration of self-esteem contrasts sharply with a narcissistic and snobbish dis-dain of the judgment of others. But again, we see corresponding, if less extreme, phenomena in that sensitivity of adolescents which alternates with defiant shameless-ness in the face of criticism. Again, these are primitive defenses, upholding a shaky self-certainty against the sense of *doubt* and *shame* (II.2). . . . While this is normally a transitory matter, it persists in some character formations and remains characteristic of many creative people who experience, according to their own testimony, repeated adolescences and with them the full cycle of sensitive withdrawal and forceful self-exhibition.

Self-consciousness (V.2) is a new edition of that original doubt which con-cerned the trustworthiness of the parents and of the child himself—only in ado-lescence, such self-conscious doubt concerns the reliability of the whole span of childhood which is now to be left behind and the trustworthiness of the whole social universe now envisaged. The obligation now to commit oneself with a sense of free will to one's autonomous identity can arouse a painful over-all ashamedness somehow comparable to the original shame and rage over being visible all around to all-knowing adults—only such shame now adheres to one's having a public per-sonality exposed to age mates and to be judged by leaders. All of this, in the normal course of events, is outbalanced by that *self-certainty* (V.2) now characterized by a definite sense of independence from the family as the matrix of self-images, and a sureness of anticipation.

Among the societal phenomena corresponding to this second conflict there is a universal trend toward some form of uniformity either in special uniforms or in dis-tinctive clothing through which incomplete self-certainty, for a time, can hide in a group certainty. Such certainty has always been provided by the age-old badges as well as the sacrifices of investitures, confirmations, and initiations, but it can also be temporarily and arbitrarily created by those who care to differ, radically, and yet must evolve a certain uniformity of differing (zoot-suiters, beatniks). These and less obvious uniformities are enforced by comprehensive shaming among peers, a judgmental give-and-take and a cruel banding together which leaves outsiders "holding the bag" in painful, if sometimes creative, isolation.

The display of a total commitment to a *role fixation* (V.3) as against a free *ex-perimentation* with available roles has an obvious connection with earlier conflicts between free initiative and Oedipal guilt in infantile reality, fantasy, and play. Where our patients regress below the Oedipal crisis to a total crisis of trust, the choice of a self-defeating role often remains the only acceptable form of initiative on the way back and up, and this in the form of a complete denial of ambition as the only possible way of totally avoiding guilt. The normal expression of relatively guilt-free and in fact more or less "delinquent" initiative in youth, however, is an experimentation with roles which follows the unwritten codes of adolescent subsocieties and thus is not lacking a discipline of its own.

Of the social institutions which undertake to channel as they encourage such initiative and to provide atonement as they appease guilt, we may point here, again, to initiations and confirmations: they strive within an atmosphere of mythical timelessness to combine some badge of sacrifice or submission with an energetic push toward sanctioned ways of action—a combination which, where it works, assures the development in the novice of an optimum of compliance with a maximum sense of free choice and solidarity. This special proclivity of youth—namely, the achievement of a sense of free choice as the very result of ritual regimentation—is, of course, universally utilized in army life.

Extreme *work paralysis* (V.4) is the logical sequence of a deep sense of the inadequacy of one's general equipment. Such a sense of inadequacy, of course, does not usually reflect a true lack of potential; it may, rather, convey the unrealistic demands made by an ego ideal willing to settle only for omnipotence or omniscience; it may express the fact that the immediate social environment does not have a niche for the individual's true gifts; or it may reflect the paradoxical fact than an individual in early school life was seduced into a specialized precocity which outdistanced his identity development. For all these reasons, then, the individual may be excluded from that experimental competition in play and work through which he learns to find and insist on his own kind of achievement and his work identity. This can become especially relevant in an early turn to delinquency—delinquents being, in many ways, the "positive" counterparts of our patients because at least they act out in company what the isolate suppresses. Some mockery of work and yet a competition with it is obvious in such delinquent phrases as "doing a job" (that is, a burglary) or "making a good job of it" in the sense of completing a destruction. From here it is only one step to another obvious consideration, namely, that young people must have learned to enjoy a sense of *apprenticeship* (IV.4) in order not to need the thrill of destruction. Schizoids and delinquents have in common a mistrust of themselves, a disbelief in the possibility that they could ever complete anything of value. This, of course, is especially marked in those who, for some reason or other, do not feel that they are partaking of the technological identity of their time. The reason may be that their own gifts have not found contact with the productive aims of the machine age or that they themselves belong to a social class (here "upper-upper" is remarkably equal to "lower-lower") that does not partake of the stream of progress.

Social institutions support the strength and distinctiveness of the budding work identity by offering those who are still learning and experimenting a certain status of *apprenticeship,* a moratorium characterized by defined duties and sanctioned competitions as well as by special license.

These, then, are the regressive trends in the identity crisis which are particularly clearly elaborated in the symptoms of identity confusion and some of the social processes which counteract them in daily life. But there are also aspects of identity formation which anticipate future development. The first of these is what we may call a *polarization of sexual differences* (V.6), i.e., the elaboration of a particular ratio of masculinity and femininity in line with identity development. Some of our patients suffer more lastingly and malignantly from a state not uncommon in a milder and transient form in all adolescence: the young person does not feel himself clearly to be a member of one sex or the other, which may make him the easy victim of the pressure emanating, for example, from homosexual cliques, for to some persons it is more bearable to be typed as something, anything, than to endure drawn-out bisexual confusion. Some, of course, decide on an ascetic turning away from sexuality which may result in dramatic breakthroughs of bewildering impulses. For *bisexual confusion* (V.6) in adolescence joins *identity-consciousness* in the establishment of an excessive preoccupation with the question of what kind of man or woman, or what kind of intermediate or deviate, one might become. In his totalistic frame of mind, an adolescent may feel that to be a little less of one sex means to be much more, if not all, of the other. If at such a time something happens that marks him socially as a deviant, he may develop a deep fixation, reinforced by the transvaluation of a negative identity, and true intimacy will then seem dangerous. Here the sexual mores of cultures and classes make for immense differences in the psychosocial differentiation of masculine and feminine and in the age, kind, and ubiquity of genital activity. These differences can obscure the common fact discussed above, namely, that the development of psychosocial intimacy is not possible without a firm sense of identity. Induced by special mores, young people in confusion may foreclose their identity development by concentrating on early genital activity without intimacy; or, on the contrary, they may concentrate on social, artistic, or intellectual aims which underplay the genital element to an extent that there is a permanent weakness of genital polarization with the other sex.

Social institutions here offer ideological rationales for widely different patterns of partial sexual moratoria such as complete sexual abstinence for a specified period, promiscuous genital activity without personal commitment, or sexual play without genital engagement. What a group's or an individual's "libido economy" will stand depends both on the kind of childhood left behind and on the identity gain which accrues from such preferred sexual behavior.

But youth also makes an important step toward parenthood and adult responsibility in learning to take *leadership* as well as to assume *followership* (V.7) among peers and to develop what often amounts to an astonishing foresight in the functions thus assumed. Such foresight can be, as it were, ahead of the individuals' over-all maturity precisely because the prevailing ideology provides a framework for an orientation in leadership. By the same token, the common "cause" permits others to follow and to obey (and the leader himself to obey higher leaders) and thus to replace the parent images set up in the infantile superego with the hierarchy of leader-images inhabiting the available gallery of ideals—a process as typical for delinquent gangs as for any highly motivated group. Where a youth can neither obey nor give orders he must make do with an isolation which can lead to malignant withdrawal but which also, if he is lucky and gifted, will help him respond to guiding voices who speak to him (as if they knew him) over the centuries, through books, pictures, and music.

We now come to that system of ideals which societies present to the young in the explicit or implicit form of an ideology. From what has been said so far we can ascribe to ideology the function of offering youth (1) a simplified perspective of the future which encompasses all foreseeable time and thus counteracts individual "time confusion"; (2) some strongly felt correspondence between the inner world of ideals and evils and the social world with its goals and dangers; (3) an opportunity for exhibiting some uniformity of appearance and behavior counteracting individual identity-consciousness; (4) inducement to a collective experimentation with roles and techniques which help overcome a sense of inhibition and personal guilt; (5) introduction into the ethos of the prevailing technology and thus into sanctioned and regulated competition; (6) a geographic-historical world image as a framework for the young individuals' budding identity; (7) a rationale for a sexual way of life compatible with a convincing system of principles; and (8) submission to leaders who as superhuman figures or "big brothers" are above the ambivalence of the parent-child relation. Without some such *ideological commitment,* however implicit in a "way of life," youth suffers a *confusion of values* (V.8) which can be specifically dangerous to some but which on a large scale is surely dangerous to the fabric of society.

In the conclusion of a pathographic sketch, then, I have also sketched in some phenomena which are the domain of social science. I can justify this only in the belief that clinical work, in trying to arrive at some workable generalities in regard to individual pathology, may well come upon aspects of the social process which the social sciences have by necessity neglected. A psychosocial study of the case history or the life history cannot afford to neglect them.

Questions

1. What does Erikson mean when he says that identity formation begins "where the usefulness of identifications end"?
2. Why are earlier crystallizations of identity inadequate at adolescence?
3. Why does Erikson believe identity must precede intimacy?
4. How does Erikson characterize peer relationships and love relationships at adolescence?
5. Who in this society is granted a moratorium? What are its advantages and disadvantages? Is college a moratorium?
6. Why do some adolescents develop negative identities?
7. What role does society play in identity formation? What cultural factors make finding an identity easy or difficult?
8. Why might time diffusion, identity consciousness, role fixation, and work paralysis come about?

References and Further Reading

Adams, G. R., Gullotta, T. P., & Montemayor, R. (Eds.) (1992). *Adolescent identity formation.* Newbury Park, CA: Sage.
Erikson, E. H. (1950). *Childhood and society.* New York: W. W. Norton.
Erikson, E.H. (1968). *Identity: Youth and crisis.* New York: W. W. Norton.
Kroger, J. (Ed.) (1993). *Discussions on ego identity.* Hillsdale, NJ: Lawrence Erlbaum.

The Empirical Study of Ego Identity

James Marcia, Ph.D., is a professor of psychology at Simon Fraser University in Canada. He has directed psychological clinics at SUNY/Buffalo and Simon Fraser University. In his research, he endeavors to create a model to measure and validate Erik Erikson's theory of psychosocial development. Dr. Marcia also practices clinical psychology.

A number of researchers have attempted to operationalize the construct of identity, that is, to find a way to empirically measure Erikson's construct of ego-identity. Perhaps the most prominent researcher is James Marcia, who devised a semistructured interview based on Erikson's theory to determine an individual's identity status. Numerous research studies have now employed Marcia's methods to investigate various aspects of identity development, thus demonstrating the validity of Erikson's theory and its usefulness empirically.

Marcia conceptualized four concentration points along a continuum from Identity Diffused to Identity Achieved based on two criteria: exploration of chosen alternatives and beliefs, and commitment to chosen alternatives. At one end of the continuum is the person who is *identity diffused,* who has neither gone through a period of exploration, nor made a commitment to occupational goals or ideological beliefs. At the other end of the continuum is the person who is *identity achieved,* who has undergone a period of experimentation, and has committed to an occupation and an ideology. Two concentration points fall intermediate and are labeled *moratorium* and *foreclosure.* A person who is in *moratorium* is in the midst of a crisis or period of exploration, and commitments are still vague. A person who is *foreclosed* has not undergone a period of exploration, but has made commitments to occupational goals, beliefs, and values. In this article Marcia describes his understanding of Erikson's theory, his own research instrument, and his research describing the characteristics of adolescents falling into each of the four identity statuses.

In the Identity Status Interview, individuals are asked about decisions they have made in a number of areas, and they are questioned about how those decisions were arrived at. Interviews are tape-recorded and replayed for judging. Judges evaluate responses in each area in terms of the presence or absence of exploration and of commitment. As originally devised, the interview focused on the areas of occupation and ideology (which included religion and politics). Following Marcia's initial research, criticisms were raised about the limitations of his methodology for studying women. Many argued that women were more concerned with issues of interpersonal relationships and intimacy than men, and that the domains the Identity Status

Interview covered were not those that were important to women. Marcia extended his interview to cover the sexual-interpersonal area, and found that while the ideology area was more predictive of overall identity status for men, the sexual-interpersonal area indeed proved to be more predictive for women (Bilsker, Schiedel, & Marcia, 1988). Marcia's interview has been further extended to cover additional domains such as ethnicity, race, and personal hobbies.

Theoretical Content

The empirical study of ego identity development by means of the identity status paradigm began more than 25 years ago. This model had its origin in Erik Erikson's (1959) ego psychoanalytic theory of psychosocial development. The identity status approach has been extraordinarily productive, yielding more than 300 studies (Marcia, Waterman, Matteson, Archer, & Orlofsky, 1993). In this [selection] I shall describe our way of looking at identity, Erikson's theory from which it proceeded and to which it lends validity, and some of the results of the identity status research.

Erik Erikson, a psychoanalyst whose background in art and education makes him an especially relevant figure for discussion, . . . has described a sequence of eight psychosocial developmental stages, which, at the early ages, parallel [Sigmund] Freud's psychosexual stages but extend beyond them to encompass the whole life cycle (see Table 1). Each stage consists of three components. The first is a physical developmental underpinning, which consists of the individual's needs and abilities, noted on the diagram as psychosexual zones and behavioral modes. The second aspect is those social contexts or institutions that have developed throughout a particular culture's history to be preadapted to individual needs and abilities, providing rewards and demands more or less relevant to them. The third component is the psychological meaning or sense of oneself the individual develops as a result of experience of himself or herself in his or her cultural context.

These eight psychosocial stages represent a sequence of ego growth occurring as the individual meets the challenges of different periods of life and resolves the conflicts that are inherent in those periods. For example, the task of infancy is the development of a balance between a sense of Basic Trust and its inevitably accompanying antithesis: Mistrust. A young adult is confronted with the necessity for coming to terms with Intimacy and its inescapable counterpart: Isolation. Middle-aged adults must deal with Generativity in the face of the alternatives of Self-Absorption and Stagnation. Older adults, approaching the certainty of death and the possibility of overwhelming Despair, have also the opportunity to attain a sense of Integrity.

From both the diagram and this brief delineation of four of the eight psychosocial crises, one may see that they are cast into the form of a dialectic, with a positive thesis, negative antithesis, and presumed resolution in the form of an individually

(continued on page 152)

Table 1

Psychosocial Stages

CHRONOLOGICAL AGE		1	2	3	4	5	6	7	8
OLD AGE	VIII	T-M / Intg.	A-S,D / Intg.	I-G / Intg.	Ind-I / Intg.	Id-ID / Intg.	Int-Is / Intg.	G-S / Intg.	Integrity and Despair
ADULTHOOD	VII	T-M / G	A-S,D / G	I-G / G	Ind-I / G	Id-ID / G	Int-Is / G	Generativity and Stagnation Self-absorption	Inty-D / G
YOUNG ADULTHOOD	VI	T-M / Int.	A-S,D / Int.	I-G / Int.	Ind-I / Int.	Id-ID / Int.	Intimacy and Isolation	G-S / Int.	Inty-D / Int.
ADOLESCENCE o Genital ø Mature intrusion-inclusion	V	T-M / Id.	A-S,D / Id.	I-G / Id.	Ind-I / Id.	Identity and Identity Diffusion	Int-Is / Id.	G-S / Id.	Inty-D / Id.
SCHOOL AGE o Latent	IV	T-M / Ind.	A-S,D / Ind.	I-G / Ind.	Industry and Inferiority	Id-ID / Ind.	Int-Is / Ind.	G-S / Ind.	Inty-D / Ind.
PLAY AGE o Phallic (oedipal) ø Intrusion-inclusion • Individuation	III	T-M / I	A-S, D / I	Initiative and Guilt	Ind-I / I	Id-ID / I	Int-Is / I	G-S / I	Inty-D / I
EARLY CHILDHOOD o Anal ø Eliminative-retentive • Practising	II	T-M / A	Autonomy and Shame, Doubt	I-G / A	Ind-I / A	Id-ID / A	Int-Is / A	G-S / A	Inty-D / A
INFANCY o Oral 1. ø Passive-active Incorporative 2. • Attachment 3.	I	Basic Trust and Basic Mistrust / T	A-S, D / T	I-G / T	Ind-I / T	Id-ID / T	Int-Is / T	G-S / T	Inty-D / T

Identity Issue at Integrity Stage ↓ (above column 5–8 area)

↑ Precursor to Autonomy as Trust Stage (below column 2)

o 1. *Psychosexual zone*
ø 2. *Related behavioral modality*
• 3. *Object relational phase*

Source: Marcia, Waterman, Matteson, Archer, and Orlofsky (1993, Figure 1)

fashioned synthesis whose content is partially determined by the relevant institutions comprised in the person's social context. (The accompanying diagram differs in form from those furnished by Erikson in that the "versus" between alternative stage resolutions [e.g., Intimacy versus Isolation] has been replaced by "and." I feel that this reflects better Erikson's intent, and our experience, that psychosocial stage resolution is not an either-or matter, but that, especially for stages beyond Industry, an individual constructs his other own particular form of resolution incorporating both the positive and negative aspects of the stage. Also, related psychosexual zones and modes, as well as predominant object relational issues, are included along the far right-hand column.) The sequence of stages is assumed to be epigentically prefigured, and the more or less successful resolution of the crises is assumed to be within the capacity of each individual given "an average expectable environment."

Identity as understood within this context is a developmental achievement. It has developmental forerunners at previous psychosocial stages, and it reaches its time of ascendancy about middle to late adolescence. Although there are opportunities for its resolution later in life than adolescence, the pubertal and postpubertal period provides the optimal conditions for its initial resolution. Never again in the life cycle will there be the fortuitous confluence of individual physical, cognitive, and psychosexual changes with relevant social sanctions and expectations. In Western societies, we allow our adolescents (sometimes to their and our distress) a period of time-out so that they may leave the position of being cared for and orient themselves to the imminent roles of caretakers. In more traditional societies, we provide rites of passage to confirm in our adolescents their culturally sanctioned identity (sometimes to their and our psychological rigidity). Neither in liberal nor traditional contexts are we especially tolerant and supportive of identity crises in adulthood. Even the more psychologically sophisticated of us can refer to these somewhat pejoratively as midlife crises.

Let me discuss first this idea of precursors and successors. There are 64 squares in Erikson's diagram, not just 8. The heuristic significance of this is to illustrate that each stage occurs at every other stage. Hence, there is an Identity component in infancy, when the major issue is Trust-Mistrust, and in old age, when the major issue is Integrity-Despair. Identity development at adolescence, therefore, is the heir of the resolution not just of the preceding major stage-specific crises of Trust-Mistrust, Autonomy-Shame/Doubt, Initiative-Guilt, Industry-Inferiority, but also of the Identity components of the resolution of each of these issues. Specifically, with respect to Industry-Inferiority, the identity formed at late adolescence is dependent both upon one's sense that steady work at a project is worthwhile (the Industry component of Industry/Inferiority) and also upon one's sense of oneself as a competent worker (the Identity component of Industry/Inferiority) (Kowaz & Marcia, 1991). In terms of identity resolutions at successive life cycle stages, one can identify in his or her own experience the identity aspects involved in becoming a husband or wife in young adulthood, or in becoming a mother or father in later adulthood, or a grandparent in older age. Interestingly, in some work in progress on developing a measure of Integrity-Despair (Hearn, in progress) we have been able to isolate the Identity component of Integrity and establish its relationship to Integrity (Glenham & Strayer, in progress). It should be clear from the foregoing that in societies that permit some degree of freedom in identity formation, that is, where identities can be individually constructed rather than societally imposed, the identity formed at late adolescence is only the first identity; and it can be expected to change as successive life cycle issues make their claims for resolution.

The definition of identity that we identity status researchers have used springs directly from Erikson's theory. Identity refers to a coherent sense of one's meaning to oneself and to others within that social context. This sense of identity suggests an individual's continuity with the past, a personally meaningful present, and a direction for the future. Identity may also be spoken of in structural terms. That is, once a person forms his or her identity at late adolescence, how he or she views himself or herself in the world and how he or she behaves in that world are given shape by his or her identity. An identity may be expected to be disequilibrated and to undergo an accommodative process when it can no longer assimilate successfully new life experiences occurring later in the life cycle.

To summarize, within the Eriksonian framework, identity is the expectable outcome of a particular developmental period: adolescence. The reason that identity is not assumed to develop fully before middle to late adolescence is because the constituents to be integrated (one's gender, mature physical capacities, sexuality, abilities to reason beyond the concrete operational level, responses to social expectations to become more than a child) do not all exist together until that time. Furthermore, if the initial identity configuration attained at late adolescence is a self-constructed one, rather than one that has been conferred upon the individual, achieved rather than ascribed, successive identity reformulations can be expected throughout the life cycle as the individual meets and resolves the challenges involved in ego growth. Hence, the initial identity, if it is a self-constructed one, is not the last identity (Stephen, Fraser, & Marcia, 1992).

There are two concepts within psychodynamic theory that some may consider similar to identity and from which it should be discriminated. The first is the ego ideal. The ego ideal refers to that aspect of the superego that includes internalized goals and aspirations, as contrasted with the conscience aspect of the superego that embodies internalized prohibitions. It is the ego ideal, in particular, that undergoes significant modification during adolescence, as the individual exchanges parents for rock stars, and, eventually, it is to be hoped, integrates also the values of prized teachers and mentors. An identity, because it includes goals and values, is informed by ego ideal contents, but it goes beyond them to involve the individual's particular style or way of being in the world. Identity also refers to processes closer to the social interface of personality, where the pattern of the person's internal dynamics is expressed in interaction with the environment. Hence, while some ego ideal values are included in one's identity, the ego ideal has an earlier developmental history, lies somewhat deeper in the personality, and is less inclusive than identity.

The other concept to be discriminated is self. The theorists whom I see as having spoken the most clearly in developmental terms about the self are object relational theorists such as Mahler and Kohut (e.g., Kohut, 1971; Mahler et al., 1975). Combining these, perhaps somewhat simplistically, one might say that the self is the outcome of the separation-individuation and rapprochement process undergone by the toddler. This initial self must then be continually responded to and reinforced throughout the lifetime, although the quantity of support needed decreases and the figures qualified to provide it become more selected. Developmentally, the self precedes both the ego ideal and an identity and probably lies the deepest of the three within the personality. A solid sense of self is a necessary, but not a sufficient, condition for an identity.

Research in Identity: The Identity Statuses

Because, as psychologists, we have a commitment to go beyond the theoretical description of a construct and attempt to demonstrate its validity and usefulness in some empirical way, our initial task was to cast Erikson's artistically complex definition of identity into one that could provide a basis for measurement. In doing this, we came to realize, by means of observation, that the original dichotomy of Identity-Identity Diffusion (Confusion) did not capture adequately the variety of styles of identity resolution that our initial research participants described to us about themselves. Specifically, some arrived at an identity by means of an exploratory period; others just became more firmly entrenched in the identities bestowed upon them in childhood. Some seemed to have no firm identity resolution and were relatively unconcerned about this, while others, similarly unresolved, were very concerned and struggling to reach some closure on the issue. This observation of the differing modes with which late adolescents were facing identity formation led us to postulate four identity statuses. These identity statuses are four ways in which any late adolescent (approximately 18–22 years of age) may be expected to be resolving Identity-Identity Diffusion.

The identity statuses are determined by means of a semistructured interview and accompanying rating manual. The interviewer asks individuals about decisions that they may or may not have made, the process by which those decisions were arrived at, and the extent to which they are committed to the directions inherent in those decisions. The topics the interview covers vary from culture to culture and from time to time. However, the areas chosen must be ones that are personally important to the individuals being interviewed and must be ones in which people differ in the decisions that they make.

Almost all identity status interviews contain questions in the domains of occupational or vocational choice; ideology, consisting of religious and political beliefs; and interpersonal values such as sex role attitudes and sexuality. Additional interview domains, varying with specific times and populations, have been ethnicity (Phinney, 1989), hobbies (Bosma, 1985), role of spouse and career-marriage conflict (Waterman & Archer, 1993), and others.

Within a particular interview area, the two crucial processes we are looking for are exploration and commitment. Exploration refers to the extent to which an individual has genuinely looked at and experimented with alternative directions and beliefs. Usually, this involves questioning of childhood positions and some departure from them: ideally, in the form of a unique individual integration. Commitment refers to the choice of one among several alternative paths in the different interview domains. To be acknowledged as a genuine commitment, the choice made has to be one that the individual, at least at the time of the interview, would abandon only with great reluctance. To summarize, the identity status interview typically consists of questions about occupation, ideology, and interpersonal values. An individual is assessed according to the extent of exploration within these interview domains and subsequent commitment to some chosen alternatives.

Based upon the twin criteria of exploration and commitment, four identity statuses have been formulated. These are Identity Achievement, Moratorium, Foreclosure, and Identity Diffusion. Identity Achievement persons have undergone significant exploration and have made commitments in most interview areas. Moratorium individuals are currently in the exploratory period; hence, their commitments are not firm, but they are struggling actively to arrive at them. They may be said to be in an identity crisis. The third identity status is Foreclosure. These persons, while strongly committed, have not arrived at their commitments via the route of exploration; they have retained, virtually unquestioned, the values and occupational directions of their childhood. Hence, having interviewed a Foreclosure, one knows as much about the important figures in the Foreclosure's childhood as one does about the Foreclosure. Identity Diffusion comprises the final identity status. These individuals may have undergone some tentative explorations, but this has actually been more like wandering than exploring. The hallmark of the Diffusion identity status is a lack of commitment. There are subtypes of all of the identity statuses, especially Identity Diffusion (Archer & Waterman, 1990; Marcia, 1989). However, I shall present here only descriptions of the main types.

Foreclosure

This brief discussion begins with Foreclosure, that identity status characterized by commitment with an absence of exploration, because that is the most common identity status and also the one that is usually developmentally prior to the more advanced statuses of Moratorium and Identity Achievement. Foreclosures, in the interview, strike one as well organized, goal-directed, neat, clean, and well behaved. They usually appear well, although conventionally, dressed. Frequently, they live with or near their parents. Some of their experimentally determined characteristics are that they are authoritarian (they prefer to be told what to do by an acceptable authority rather than determining their own direction); set very high goals for themselves, which they maintain rigidly even in the face of failure; are somewhat inflexible in their thought processes; tend to espouse moral values at the level of law and order; report early memories at preoedipal levels of psychosexual development; are generally obedient and conforming; and deal with self-disconfirming information by means of either a facade of acceptance or active resistance. They report, and their families report, a great deal of closeness and warmth. Upon closer examination, this "family love affair" seems to be contingent upon the Foreclosures' continuing subscription to family values; remember, they are the identity status who does not explore. Their relationships with others, as assessed in interviews concerning Intimacy (the psychosocial stage following Identity), appear to be conventional and stereotypic. Because there is no exploration, and hence little attendant interpersonal conflict, their close relationships lack psychological depth.

Also, because Foreclosures have little doubt about what is right, they tend to choose as friends and partners the right people, who are much like themselves. As long as a Foreclosure remains within the context foreclosed upon, this form of resolution of the identity issue is adaptive. It ceases to be adaptive when the context changes.

Moratorium

In describing the Moratorium status, we move from the Foreclosure position of no exploration to one of almost total exploration. The Moratorium status is an in-process position; few persons remain there for a long period of time; most, but not all, move on into Identity Achievement. In the identity status interview, Moratoriums impress one as intense, sometimes active and lively—sometimes internally preoccupied, struggling, engaging, and occasionally exhausting. They tend to use the interview, and the interviewer, as an opportunity for expressing and working out their current dilemmas; hence, many Moratoriums' interviews will go on for as long as the interviewer permits. In studies, we have found them to be the most highly morally sensitive of the statuses as well as being the most anxious. In contrast to the Foreclosures, they are the least authoritarian of the statuses. They vacillate between rebellion and conformity. Frequently, on measures such as the ability to think clearly under stressful conditions, resistance to self-esteem manipulation, and developmental level of moral thought, they perform similarly to Identity Achievements. The family relationships of Moratoriums are marked by ambivalence. They, and their families, alternate between exasperation and appreciation. One has the feeling that both will sigh with relief when "all of this is over." Moratoriums' relationships with others are, as one would expect, intense and relatively brief; while they hold values consistent with Intimacy, they are in motion, and it is difficult for them to maintain a constant commitment to another person. Probably what makes Moratoriums the most engaging of the statuses is just that exploratory process that defines them. Since they are often dealing with fundamental questions to which there is really no one right answer, they arouse those same unanswered questions within ourselves and can set us, once again, to pondering significant issues.

Identity Achievement

Persons who are described as Identity Achievement are those who have undergone the exploratory process and made occupational and ideological commitments, are assumed to have resolved successfully the psychosocial task of Identity-Identity Diffusion. In interviews, they seem solid and settled, able to articulate reasons for their choices and able to describe how those choices were arrived at. They are not as engaging as the Moratoriums nor as certain of their beliefs as the Foreclosures. In the best of them, one senses that a process of identity formation will continue throughout their lives, and one would sometimes like to warn them that this is only the first time around. With others, there is a somewhat dull quality, and one fears that they may lapse into a kind of self-satisfied, quasi-Foreclosure position. On various experimental measures they perform well under stress, reason at high levels of moral development, are relatively resistant to self-esteem manipulation, and appear to have internalized self-regulatory processes. That is, although they are sensitive to external demands, they make their own decisions based upon internalized, self-constructed values. Identity Achievements seem to have made a kind of peace with their families, whereby differences among family members are acknowledged, accepted, and sometimes even appreciated, but they are not all necessarily reconciled. Identity Achievements seem to be the most developed in terms of the next psychosocial stage of Intimacy-Isolation, with a greater number of them than of the other statuses being on their way to establishing intimate relationships. I should like to make quite clear at this point that the initial identity configuration is expected to change at least with every succeeding psychosocial stage resolution, and perhaps even more frequently, as life crises arise. And such crises are more likely to arise for Identity Achievements than for the other statuses, because their greater ego strength permits them to see more alternatives and take more risks.

Identity Diffusion

Persons described as Identity Diffusion are those individuals who may have done some cursory exploring, but who remain uncommitted. Interviews with Identity Diffusions tend to be quite short. They have little to say about the topics in an identity status interview, although they may sometimes try to fill in the gaps with what amounts to chatter. There seem to be two kinds of Diffusion within a normal population: those who are apathetic and socially isolated and those who are like playboys or playgirls. The former try to avoid contact; the latter seek it out almost compulsively. Both are interpersonally shallow. On our experimental measures, Identity Diffusions have the most difficulty thinking under stress, conform the most to external demands, are the most susceptible to self-esteem manipulation, and have the lowest levels of development of moral thought. Their family relationships stand in greatest contrast to the Foreclosures'. Whereas the description of the Foreclosure family could provide material for a full-color government brochure on the happy, healthy family, the description of the Diffusion family is more dismal. Particularly striking is our finding that the adolescent feels that the same-sex parent can never be emulated, even though that parent may be highly admired. It is as if a blessing had been withheld and this is felt keenly by the young person. As one might expect, interpersonal relationships are either sparse or extraordinarily shallow for the Identity Diffusion.

While the foregoing may sound like narrative descriptions, it is important to emphasize . . . that they are based upon numerous experiments involving researchers in North America, Europe, and New Zealand over the past 25 years. Scientific knowledge emerges slowly, the compensation being (it is hoped) its reliability. All of the research findings leading to the above descriptions of the statuses are reported in Marcia, Waterman, Matteson, Archer, and Orlofsky (1993).

Beyond confirming the validity of the identity statuses and telling us something about their antecedents and consequences, our research has also yielded some interesting information bearing on historical change. For example, when we began our research in 1965, it appeared that the identity statuses of Achievement and Moratorium were the most positive ones for men, while those of Achievement and Foreclosure were more positive for women. However, upon reviewing our accumulated findings in 1986, we discovered that this male-female disparity ended around 1976, and most studies after that time showed female patterns to be similar to males'. Our reasoning was that increased social support for women's financial and familial independence made the undergoing of a Moratorium a less threatening event for women, and decreased somewhat the social desirability of a Foreclosure resolution for them.

Another interesting finding has been a possible difference in the relationship between Identity and Intimacy for men and women. Men seem to follow the Eriksonian pattern of Identity being a necessary condition for optimal Intimacy resolution. However, women seem to be distributed among three patterns: the expectable one of Identity preceding Intimacy, more frequently that of Intimacy and Identity codeveloping, and in a few cases, of Intimacy resolution preceding Identity formation.

Finally, in the course of our years of research, we have found differing distributions of identity statuses according to different cultural conditions. For example, during the Vietnam period, we found a resolution pattern we called Alienated Achievement, a pattern not seen these days. However, we are currently finding, at least in our corner of Canada, a preponderance of Identity Diffusions, perhaps due to our recent financial and political situation. That the frequency of the identity statuses and their meaning, in at least narrowly adaptive terms, should change with cultural historical conditions is consistent with Erikson's general psychohistorical emphasis.

Intervention

Because I am a clinical psychologist and psychotherapist, the connection between the identity statuses and psychological intervention is important to me. Although I have spoken and written in other places about psychotherapeutic issues specific to the different identity statuses (e.g., Marcia, 1982, 1986), I think that the most important implications of our research for intervention have to do with addressing the two process variables of exploration and commitment. It may be the case that these two processes underlie all ego growth. At least they, or some form of them, seem appropriate for cognitive development and accompanying development of moral thought, and the attainment of a secure sense of self (Marcia, 1988).

One may consider intervention on societal, educational, and psychotherapeutic levels. If a society can sanction an exploratory period (Erikson's "psychosocial moratorium") and provide multiple valid niches for commitment, then it can contribute greatly to the ego development of its late adolescents. Educational institutions, within which late adolescents will develop a sense of identity, can refrain from requiring too hasty decision making about major areas of study and can support late adolescents in their occupational and ideological experimentation while, at the same time, they can facilitate and reward commitment when it emerges from the individual. One form this might take is allowing university students to switch major areas of study without serious penalty, offering some flexibility in curricular requirements, and providing counseling services geared specifically to identity crises. This would represent a move beyond mere training to true education of our young people. We psychotherapists can aid identity development by providing a safe context within which our patients can engage in exploration, both internally and externally, and provide some support and guidance as they begin to make commitments to new ways of being in the world. To take a specific example with the identity statuses: A safe context is not the same thing for a Foreclosure as it is for a Moratorium. To attack frontally a Foreclosure's rigid defenses and to successfully strip the person of internalized childhood ideals is to leave that person bereft of any internal guarantor of self-esteem and thence to risk an acute depressive episode. What must be done is to establish some connection based upon authentically shared values between therapist and client and then to slowly and gently disequilibrate the existing structure, providing plenty of time for the formation of new ego ideals. While a safe context for a Foreclosure is based upon some alliance with existing ideals, this is not necessarily the case for the Moratorium who is already in a disequilibrated state. What is required here is a validation of the process of struggle itself as an ingredient necessary for psychosocial growth. To make an alliance with either pole of the ambivalences with which the Moratorium is wrestling is to make oneself a participant in that struggle, and not a benevolent and dependable observer. The alliance to be made here is with the Moratorium process itself, and not with any one value.

Summary and Conclusions

I have kept the applied aspect of my description of the identity statuses quite brief because I have been asked to speak here more as a scientist than as a clinician. And as a scientist, I would like to state briefly what I think identity is and is not. Identity is a construct. It is not a thing, any more than an ego is a thing. As a psychological construct, identity is to be evaluated according to its usefulness in summarizing some behaviors and predicting others. The identity statuses are most accurately viewed as intersecting points along the two process dimensions of exploration and commitment. As psychological constructs, they may be expected to eventually become superseded by other constructs accounting for what the identity status constructs once did and entailing phenomena that they did not encompass. Such is the appropriate fate of scientific constructs when they are not kept alive by artificial means.

In closing, even though I have spoken here as to the results of the scientific study of identity, I am well aware that science is not the only validity game in town. There are other aspects to identity that have historical, literary, social, philosophical, and, above all, personal meaning for us that are not encompassed by empirical research. Regarding one author's view of psychological science—Canadian writer Robertson Davies, in his book, *What's Bred in the Bone* (1986)—we read this scathing indictment:

> Well, Science is the theology of our time, and like the old theology, it's a muddle of conflicting assertions. What gripes my guts is that it has such a miserable vocabulary and such a pallid pack of images to offer to us—to the humble laity. It's the most overweening, pompous priesthood mankind has ever endured . . . and its lack of symbol and metaphor and its zeal for abstraction drive mankind to a barren land of starved imagination. (p. 163)

Well, no one ever claimed science to be inspirational—only true to observations and self-correcting.

Questions

1. How do you characterize adolescents who are identity achieved, fore-closed, moratorium, and diffused?
2. Are some identity statuses inherently better than others?
3. How well does Marcia's Identity Status Interview capture Erikson's ideas?
4. Are there dimensions of identity that Marcia does not assess in his interview that are important to identity development?

References and Further Reading

Bilsker, D., Schiedel, D., & Marcia, J. (1988). Sex differences in identity status. *Sex Roles, 18*(3/4), 231–236.

Marcia, J. E. (1966). Development and validation of ego-identity status. *Journal of Personality and Social Psychology, 3,* 551–558.

Marcia, J. E. (1993). The relational roots of identity. In J. Kroger (Ed.) *Discussions on ego identity* (pp. 101–120). Hillsdale, NJ: Lawrence Erlbaum.

Chapter 6

Racial and Ethnic Identity

The proportion of racial and ethnic minorities in the United States is increasing rapidly. In 1980, 75.8% of all 10- to 19-year-olds were non-Latino whites. By 1992 that figure had dropped to 68.8% and according to predictions, non-Latino whites will account for barely half the American population by 2050 (U.S. Bureau of the Census, 1994). The field of adolescent research is slowly shifting to meet the changing demographic realities of adolescents.

Our understanding of the roles that race and ethnicity play in adolescent development has been complicated by the confounding of race and ethnicity with socioeconomic status. Ethnic groups of non-European origin such as African Americans, Native Americans, Latinos, and groups from Asia and the Pacific Islands are overrepresented in lower-income, lower-status positions, making it difficult to distinguish between the ethnic factors that may influence development and the factors associated with lower socioeconomic status that may also influence development. Too often studies comparing adolescents of different racial or ethnic groups have selected groups that differ in social class; for instance, white middle-class youth are compared with nonwhite youth from low-income communities. It is impossible in these studies to untangle the effects of race and ethnicity from the effects due to social class (Doucette-Gates, Brooks-Gunn, & Chase-Lansdale, 1998).

A central problem that arises in trying to study the impact of race and ethnicity on adolescent development is that our understanding of adolescence has been constructed through the lens of the dominant culture, which is white and middle class. Our measures have been developed primarily by researchers who are white to study populations who are white. It is possible that these measures are culturally biased, and as such may not be appropriate for use with ethnic minority populations. Members of minority groups have often been assessed against a standard that characterizes the majority culture, and differences from whites were taken to be evidence of deviance, deficiency, or pathology. Where researchers lack personal contact with research participants, they are vulnerable to bias in what they choose to address, what measures they use, and what they ignore in their research programs. To take an example, if the family is defined as people living in the same household, then African American families will be poorly understood. Persons living in different households may function equally well as a family unit, and the strengths of the African American family were overlooked when using the lens of the traditional model of the two-parent family.

Nonwhite youth face different circumstances in their pathways through adolescence than whites. They are pushed to confront the meaning of race or ethnicity in their lives because they face prejudice and discrimination that whites do not encounter, and because they are caught between two cultures, the traditional culture of their families and the culture of white middle-class America. Thus the process of identity development will include dimensions for minority youth that cannot be understood using models based on whites. When James Marcia's Identity Status Interview (Reading 5.2), developed on white samples, was used to study black high school students, the interview failed to capture significant dimensions of their identities, such as the fact that many of them were parents (Aries & Moorehead, 1989).

The necessity for further research on racial and ethnic minority youth is beginning to be recognized. What is needed, and is beginning to occur in research on adolescence, is an understanding of adolescent development that goes beyond a focus on problem behavior, deviance, and deficiency, and that is based in the experiences of racial and ethnic minority adolescents themselves (Montemayor, Adams, & Gullotta, 2000).

Additional Resources

References and Recommended Reading

Aries, E., & Moorehead, K. (1989). The importance of ethnicity in the development of identity of black adolescents. *Psychological Reports, 65,* 75–82.

Doucette-Gates, A., Brooks-Gunn, J., Chase-Lansdale, P. L. (1998). The role of bias and equivalence in the study of race, class, and ethnicity. In V. C. McLoyd, & L. Steinberg (Eds.) *Studying minority adolescents: Conceptual, methodological, and theoretical issues* (pp. 211–236). Mahwah, NJ: Lawrence Erlbaum.

Montemayor, R., Adams, G. R., & Gullotta, T. P. (Eds.). (2000). *Adolescent diversity in ethnic, economic, and cultural contexts.* Thousand Oaks, CA: Sage.

Phinney, J. S. (1990). Ethnic identity in adolescents and adults: Review of research. *Psychological Bulletin, 108,* 499–514.

Phinney, J. S. (1996). When we talk about American ethnic groups, what do we mean? *American Psychologist, 51* (9), 918–927.

Phinney, J. S., & Landin, J. (1994). Research paradigms for studying ethnic minority families within and across groups. In V. C. McLoyd, & L. Steinberg (Eds.) *Studying minority adolescents: Conceptual, methodological, and theoretical issues* (pp. 89–125). Mahwah, NJ: Lawrence Erlbaum.

U.S. Bureau of the Census. (1994). *Statistical abstract of the United States: 1994.* Washington, DC: U.S. Government Printing Office.

On the Internet

http://eric-web.tc.columbia.edu/digests/dig137.html
ERIC Clearinghouse on Urban Education—The Identity Development
of Multiracial Youth
The Urban Education Web (UEweb) offers manuals, brief articles, annotated
bibliographies, reviews, and summaries of outstanding publications. Many
items in UEweb are published by the Educational Resources Information Center
(ERIC) Clearinghouse on Urban Education. UEweb is presented by the ERIC
Clearinghouse on Urban Education and is funded by the U.S. Department of
Education, Office of Education Research and Improvement.

http://edweb.sdsu.edu/people/cguanipa/ethnic.htm
Ethnic Identity and Adolescence
This essay appears on the Amigos Web site, which is under the direction of
Dr. Carmen Guanipa, director of the Individual and Family Counseling Clinic
at San Diego State University. The site is directed to ethnically diverse middle
school and high school students, parents, and interested adults, and includes
informational essays and resources for locating help.

http://www.med.ucla.edu/cesla/oped/3-28-99.htm
On Being Latino: As American as a Texan
This paper appears on the Web page for the Center for the Study of Latino
Health and Culture, a division of General Internal Medicine at the UCLA
School of Medicine. As a public service the director has been translating his
research into op-ed pieces for the *Los Angeles Times*.

http://www.apa.org/monitor/apr99/fuel.html
Positive Academic Stereotypes Fuel Student Performance
This is the American Psychological Association Web site. The article is from
the American Psychological Association publication, *The Monitor*.

http://lucy.ukc.ac.uk/csacpub/russian/galkina.html
Theoretical Approaches to Ethnic Identity
This is the Web site of the Centre for Social Anthropology and Computing at
the University of Kent at Canterbury, which produces a series of monographs
to make available specialist material in social anthropology.

6.1　　　　　　　　　　　　　　　　William E. Cross Jr., 1995

In Search of Blackness and Afrocentricity: The Psychology of Black Identity Change

William E. Cross Jr., Ph.D. is a professor of education and department chair at the University of Massachusetts's School of Education. His research concentrates on African American and black identity formation. He is author of *Shades of Black: Diversity in African-American Identity* (1991).

The black social movement that occurred in this country from 1954 to 1975 incorporated movements for both civil rights and Black Power and had a profound impact on the identities of many African Americans. In the 1970s scholars began to develop theoretical models of nigrescence to describe the process of identity development that was occurring for African Americans from being Negro toward becoming black. William Cross developed such a model, and in the 1990s extended his original model of the transition from a "Negro-to-Black" identity to a model describing the general process of movement from a non-Afrocentric identity to one that is Afrocentric.

The first stage of Cross's model is the *preencounter* stage, which describes the preexisting identity or the identity to be changed. At the *preencounter* stage, race is given low salience; being black is of little significance to overall identity, due to denial or self-hatred. The first stage includes blacks who are assimilated, who hold a Eurocentric perspective and antiblack attitudes, and blacks who have not been educated about the black experience. An *encounter* stage follows during which a person's identity and worldview are shattered. A single event or multiple encounters with racism or discrimination can trigger one to rethink the meaning of race. The third stage is *immersion-emersion*. This stage is the heart of the process of *nigrescence*. At this stage a person immerses him- or herself in the world of blackness, may adopt a black hairstyle and dress, join black organizations, adopt a black name, read black literature, and listen to black music. For many, this phase is marked by hatred for whites. The fourth stage is *internalization*, a stage at which the emotionality of the previous stage is replaced by a sense of inner peace. Race holds high salience, and there is a sense of black pride and connection to the black community. Uncontrolled rage at whites is transformed into anger at racist institutions. The fifth and final stage is *internalization-commitment*. Blacks who reach this stage have a sustained interest and commitment to black affairs.

Research has shown that the progression through the stages of nigrescence may not be straightforward. Some people may regress to an earlier stage, others become stuck in a transition stage, or others still may recycle back through the stages at a later point in their lives (Parham, 1989). Some researchers have examined the connections between stages of nigrescence and self-esteem, values, and ideology (Goodstein & Ponterotto, 1997; Poindexter-Cameron & Robinson, 1997). Others have extended the model to the understanding of other social groups. For example, Cross's stages have been used to describe the progression for women to a feminist orientation, for gay men and lesbians to coming out, and for people of other ethnicities, such as Native Americans, Hispanics, and Asian Americans, to the acquisition of ethnic pride (Cross, 1994).

Introduction

In this [selection] we are going to discuss the stages of Black identity change. Of course, it is possible for a Black person to be socialized from early childhood through adolescence to have a Black identity. At adulthood, such persons are not likely to be in need of change; that is, they do not need to "discover" their Blackness, for it is already a fully developed aspect of their psyche. Not everyone is so fortunate. Many African-Americans will experience a dramatic shift in their identity *after* they have reached adolescence or *after* they have become adults. We refer to this as the psychology of *Nigrescence*. Nigrescence is a French word that means the process of becoming Black, and over the last twenty years, Black researchers have been able to map out the four or five stages Black people go through when they tear down their "old" identity and replace it with one that is more Black-oriented. Such people grow up with a "non-Black identity," or the identity to be changed (stage one), then they have some sort of experience or *encounter* (stage two) that makes them feel they need to change; next they plunge into an intense period, during which the the old and new identities are at war (stage three), and finally, if all goes well, they grow comfortable with their new sense of self (stage four), and may even dedicate themselves to helping solve problems in the community (stage five). Elsewhere (Cross, 1991), I have labeled these five stages *Preencounter; Encounter; Immersion-Emersion; Internalization;* and *Internalization-Commitment.*

Stage One: Preencounter

Preencounter—low salience attitudes: Persons in the Preencounter Stage hold attitudes toward race that range from low salience, race neutrality, to anti-Black. In the case of persons who hold *low salience* views, they do not deny being physically Black, but this "physical" fact is thought to play an insignificant role in their everyday life. Being Black and knowledge about the Black experience has little to do with their *perceived* sense of happiness and well-being, and it (Blackness) contributes little to their purpose in life. In a sense, preencounter persons place value in things *other* than their Blackness; it may be their religion, their lifestyle, their social status, their profession, and so on. Thus, they *do* have values and they *do* experience meaningful existence, but little emphasis is given to Blackness. As long as their preencounter attitudes bring them a sense of fulfillment, meaningful existence, and an internal sense of stability, order, and harmony, such persons will not likely be in need of any type of identity change, let alone movement toward Afrocentricity.

Some low salience types have not given much thought to race issues, and appear dumbfounded and naïve during such discussions. They often see personal progress as a problem of free will, individual initiative, rugged individualism, and the personal motivation to achieve. Others have taken a more conscious route toward neutrality and see themselves as having reached a higher plane (that is, abstract humanism), beneath which lies what they see as the vulgar world of race and ethnicity. When pressed to give a self-referent, they may respond that they are "human beings who happen to be Black," or, "I am an American who happens to be Black."

Preencounter—social stigma attitudes: A variant of the low salience perspective can be found in the Black person who, while sharing the low salience orientation, also sees race as a problematic or stigma. Thus, race, by default, is attributed some significance, not as a proactive force or cultural issue, but as a social stigma that must be negotiated from time to time. The only "meaning" accorded race is its tie to issues of *social discrimination;* from this perspective, race is a hassle, a problem, a vehicle of imposition. Such people may have a surface interest in Black causes, not as a way of supporting Black culture and the exploration of Black history, but in joining with those who are trying to destroy the social stigma associated with Blackness. The need to defend oneself against Blackness as stigma can be found in preencounter persons who otherwise have very little knowledge of Black history and culture. Consequently, when you ask such people to define their Black identity, they invariably respond by telling you what it is like to be oppressed.

Preencounter—antiblack attitudes: The extreme racial attitude pattern to be found within the Preencounter Stage is anti-Blackness. There are some Blacks for whom being Black is very important, not as a positive force, *but as a negative reference group.* Blackness and Black people define their internal model of what they dislike. They look out upon Black people with a perspective that comes very close to that which one might expect to find in the thinking of White racists. Anti-Black Blacks loath other Blacks, they feel alienated from them and they do not see Blacks or the Black community as a potential or actual source of personal support. Their vision of Blackness is dominated by negative, racist stereotypes, and on the other side of the coin, they may hold positive racial stereotypes of White people and White culture. In viewing Black people to be their own worst enemy, anti-Black Blacks often explain the "race problem" through the prism of some variant of the "victim-blame perspective." When in positions of leadership, anti-Black Blacks can be very effective in weaving an ideology that bashes Black leaders, Black institutions, Black studies, the Black family, and Black culture.

Thus, the first stage, Preencounter, covers a broad range of attitudes from low salience, and Blackness as stigma, to the extreme of anti-Blackness and self-hatred. These preencounter tendencies may be combined with other characteristics, such as varying levels of miseducation; a Eurocentric cultural frame of reference; *Spotlight* or "Race-Image" Anxiety; and assimilationist attitudes.

Miseducation: In being formally educated to embrace a Western cultural-historical perspective, preencounter Blacks cannot help but experience varying degrees of miseducation about the significance of the Black experience. In fact, preencounter Blacks are frequently "average" products of a formal education system that is very White-oriented. One reason the need for Nigrescence is so common in the Black community is that it is very difficult for *any* Black American to progress through the public schools without being miseducated about the role of Africa in the origin of Western civilization and world culture, and the role of Blacks in the evolution of American culture and history in particular. This miseducation does not automatically lead to self-hatred, but it most certainly can distort how Black people discuss Black cultural and historical issues. Preencounter Blacks do not oppose Black Studies because of some "unconscious anti-Black or self-hatred complex"; rather, their *cultural bias* blinds them to the fact that there are other histories besides "American History"; that there are other cultural experiences besides "Western civilization." The most damning aspect of miseducation is not necessarily poor mental health, but the development of a world-view and cultural-historical perspective which can block one's knowledge about, and thus one's capacity to advocate and embrace, the cultural, political, economic, and historical interests of Black people.

Anti-Black Blacks suffer from the type of extreme miseducation which, in fact, *can* result in self-hatred. They tend to have a very distorted interpretation of Black history and thus a very distorted image of the historical, cultural, economic, and political *potential* of Black people. They believe that Black people came from a strange, uncivilized, "dark" continent, and that slavery was a civilizing experience. From their vantage point, there is nothing to be gained from the study of the slavery period—thus, "real" Black history begins at the end of the Civil War. Amongst poor Blacks, anti-Black Blacks actually develop the belief that Blacks somehow deserve the misery that comes with poverty. Extreme miseducation can result in a great deal of skepticism about the abilities and capacities of Black leaders, Black businesses, and Black professionals, and an equal degree of romanticization and near mysticism concerning the capacities and talents of Whites. That is, if Blacks are thought to be intellectually inferior and technologically backward, Whites are seen as intellectually superior and technically mystical.

Eurocentric cultural perspective: As a further extension of the miseducation concept, we note that preencounter persons have frequently been socialized to favor a Euro-centric cultural perspective. It is a perspective in which notions of beauty and art are derived from a White and decidedly Western aesthetic, as reflected in the content, themes, vehicles of emphasis, colorations, and modes of expressions in numerous cultural and academic preferences. Afrocentricists frequently interpret the preencounter person's preference for Western art as an expression of self-hatred, but this is in error. In rare instances, some preencounter Blacks have been raised in a manner that leaves them nearly ignorant of the existence of any other than Eurocentric cultural perspectives. However, most preencounter persons have been socialized to be *bicultural;* that is they know about and sometimes appreciate both Black and White artistic expressions. However, the low salience person, in particular, is more likely to give higher status to Western art. For example, preencounter parents tend to socialize their children to place greater emphasis on "high culture," or "classical art forms" (that is, ballet, classical music, modern dance, and so on), while classes in jazz, African dance, and Black literature are seldom considered. Although they may personally enjoy Black music and art, they may depict Black art as that which is "ethnic," "lowly," "less important," and something to be lost along the way toward acceptance and assimilation into the mainstream. Thus, it is not always the case that preencounter Blacks lack knowledge about or experience with Black art; rather, what separates them from people in more advanced states of Blackness are the *attitudes* they hold toward Black art forms, and the priority and preferences they accord Western versus Black art.

Anti-Black Blacks take the pro-White cultural bias to an extreme and wrongly put White and Black art on the same continuum, with White art defining that which is positive, rational, and highly developed, and Black art connoting that which is exotic, emotional, and primitive. Thus, classical music, ballet and Western theater define "good art," while jazz, the blues, African dance, and so on, are seen as interesting but less well developed, if not primitive and inferior imitations of (White) classical artistic expression. In its more vulgar expression, anti-Black Blacks may even prefer light skin, "flow" hair and European facial features.

Finally, it would be a mistake to think that this is solely a "problem of the Black middle class." Even in the inner city or "ghetto," where purer forms of Black expression can readily be found, one discovers the inner-city resident referring to the blues or jazz as something low, bad, or sexy. Sometimes such descriptions capture the Black urban resident's notion of that which is earthy, funky, and soulful, but at other times the terms suggest a negative perspective toward Black art, Black life, and Black culture. The "White is fine" attitude can be found in preencounter persons of varied socio-economic standings.

Spotlight or race image anxiety: Most Black people, with the exception of those who are anti-Black in perspective, manage to keep from internalizing extremely negative stereotypes that racist Whites have of Black people. But while preencounter Blacks do not believe in these stereotypes, they are often overly sensitive to the fact that many White people *do* accept such images. This can lead to a hypersensitivity toward racial issues in which one is constantly on the lookout for the portrayal of (negative) Black stereotypes. This sensitivity can help the person flush out instances of social discrimination and racism. However, there is also the irony that this "sensitivity" to discrimination and stereotypes can also lead to an anxiety over things being "too Black." Even though a preencounter person may be married to a Black person, and even though he or she may live in a Black community, there are times when the preencounter person feels that a situation is *too Black-oriented,* or "not integrated enough." Things are thought to get out of hand when Blacks act too loud or disorderly. I refer to this anxiety about being too Black as *"Spotlight Anxiety."* It is an anxiety which is often only felt when the person is in the company of Whites, or when the situation is somehow construed as being in the "spotlight." When Whites are around, the person may check him or herself to determine whether he or she, or some other Black who is present, is acting *too* Black, and thus failing to project the best *race image.*

Anti-Black Blacks are beyond any anxiety about the race's image; for them, the negative stereotypes White people hold in reference to Blacks are taken as truth. They feel enslaved in a body and community they hate. They feel nothing but a sense of imposition, alienation, and inferiority, and their sense of Blackness is clearly that of a mark of oppression.

Assimilation-integration: In being socialized to see the system as adequate, in suffering various degrees of miseducation about the origin of Black problems, and in having a basic faith in the system, preencounter Blacks are predisposed to accept a victim-blame analysis of Black problems, and a race-conflict-resolution perspective that stresses assimilationist-integration themes. They feel that if Blacks can "overcome" their own "self-made" problems, and become a part of the system, as they perceive has happened to previously disadvantaged (White ethnic) groups, the race problem could be solved. The message is generally framed with greater sophistication when articulated by well-educated preencounter Blacks, but it can be stated crudely by others. White racism is viewed as a surface-level problem, one that exists alongside the basic strengths and race-neutral opportunity structures and culture of the society. Once one has managed to work through discriminatory obstacles, so their thinking goes, the weight is on Blacks to prepare themselves in a fashion that will lead to their acceptance by Whites. The emphasis is on *one-way change* in which Blacks learn to fit in, while Whites are asked simply to stop discriminating. No real demands are placed on White attitudes, White culture, and White institutions, since, as stated previously, the problem of racism is at the surface level of White institutions and society. Consequently, unlike pluralistic notions of integration or concepts of multiculturalism, the preencounter Black is often wedded to an assimilationist vision of race-conflict-resolution and social mobility.

Summary: Whether of the low salience or anti-Black varieties, the spectrum of preencounter attitudes can be found among poor and well-to-do Blacks. Class status may affect how preencounter attitudes are expressed, but the central messages, priorities, or preferences embedded in both middle- and lower-class Black expressions are generally the same. Thus, low salience can be found in a middle-class Black professional for whom Blackness has little meaning, as it can in an inner-city resident whose primary vehicle for meaning and purpose in life is the Christian church. At the more negative extreme of preencounter, anti-Black Blacks can be the middle-class Black youth who has joined the ranks of a White-dominated, punk street group, or they can be found in the inner-city youth who, as a member of a "Black" street gang, pushes dope on other Black kids. Preencounter-oriented people can be rich or poor, light-skinned or ebony-hued, living in Vermont or in Harlem, attending overwhelmingly White schools or all-Black institutions.

In the past, oppression and miseducation have been the main factors determining the social production of preencounter attitudes. However, today we note that such attitudes are evolving as a result of the *success* of the Black sixties. In other words, Black success, as well as White oppression, can produce preencounter attitudes. Over the last twenty years, some Blacks *have* experienced, as nearly as possible, that which by any standard would be called success within the American system. They are rich, they live in exclusive communities and neighborhoods, they manage in and sometimes head major corporations, and their children attend the finest educational institutions money can buy. They are major contributors to organizations that advocate Western culture, and in the overall scheme of things, they are practically invisible to the Black world. Thus their success, and not experience with oppression, has led them to embrace preencounter attitudes. Of course, not all successful middle-class and wealthy Blacks can be categorized in this fashion. Besides, the point being made here is not the negative stereotyping of the wealthy and the middle class, but to remind the reader that preencounter attitudes in Black people can be caused by a variety of situations and circumstances. As is the case with all the stages, Preencounter is an attitude or perspective, not an inherited or divinely ordained trait, and people who come to share the same preencounter frame of reference do so through a variety of social experiences and circumstances, inclusive of instances of both success and oppression.

It would be a mistake to presume that preencounter is a form of mental illness. While anti-Black Blacks may very well evidence poor mental health, the great majority of preencounter Blacks are probably as mentally healthy as Blacks in the more advanced stages of Nigrescence. The key factors that separate preencounter Blacks from those who are Afrocentric is not mental illness, but value orientation, historical perspective, and worldview. Preencounter Blacks are part of the diversity of the Black experience and must be understood as such. The complexity of the American economy means that there are all sorts of ecological niches within which Blacks are socialized, and each of these niches may support the growth of unique ideas on what it means to be Black, including those which downplay Blackness altogether.

On the other hand, whenever life's circumstances result in the social production of a Black person for whom "race" has limited importance, or, in the case of the anti-Black Blacks, extremely negative meaning, the scene has been set for a possible identity conversion experience. Such people are "sitting ducks" for an encounter that may cause them to rethink their positions in Blackness.

Stage Two: Encounter

In most instances, the preencounter identity is the person's first identity, that is, the identity shaped by one's early development. This socialization has involved years of experiences with one's family, extended family, one's neighborhood and community, and one's schools, covering the periods of childhood, adolescence, and early adulthood. It is a tried and fully tested identity, which serves the person day in and day out. It helps the person feel centered, meaningful, and in control, by making life predictable. The person's identity filters incoming experiences so that the information "fits" into his or her current understanding of him or herself and the world in which he or she lives. Therefore, any fully developed identity, let alone a preencounter identity, is difficult to change.

Since the person's ongoing identity will defend against identity change, the person usually has to experience some sort of *encounter* that has the effect of catching the person off guard. The encounter must work around, slip through, or even *shatter* the relevance of the person's current identity and worldview, and at the same time provide some hint of the new direction the person must now take.

Sometimes the encounter can be a single, dramatic event. In the late 1960s, the death of Martin L. King, Jr., hurled thousands of preencounter Negroes into a search for a deeper understanding of the Black Power movement. Likewise, being personally assaulted, or witnessing a friend being assaulted by the police, televised reports of racial incidents, or discussions with a friend or loved one who is further advanced into his or her Blackness may "turn a person on" to her or his Blackness. Middle-class

Blacks who have somehow managed to avoid or escape racial incidents at an earlier point in their life often begin Nigrescence after an unexpected racial episode in college, or still later, at their place of employment. Having worked so hard at being the "right kind of Negro," racist encounters can completely shatter a preencounter person's conception of him or herself, and his or her understanding of the state of Black America. For lower-class preencounter Blacks, encounters with the law and imprisonment can be a turning point. While on the street, doing his or her "thing," the preencounter Black may be oblivious to discussions about Blackness, but incarceration may so traumatize the person, that he or she becomes receptive to different interpretations of the meaning of his or her life. Malcolm X is the most famous of a long list of Black men and women whose search for Blackness followed on the heels of their imprisonment.

In many instances, it is not a single event that constitutes a person's encounter, but a series of smaller, eye-opening episodes, each of which chips away at the person's ongoing worldview. These small encounters have an accumulative effect, and at a certain point something happens to "break the camel's back," so to speak, and the person feels pushed toward becoming Black.

Looked at more closely, we see that the encounter entails two steps: first, experiencing the encounter, and second, personalizing it. By this two-step analysis, I mean to split a hair. That is to say, one must make the distinction between being in the path or being the object of an encounter event or activity, versus actually personalizing it or being "turned around by it." As a case in point, in April of 1968, not every Black person who first heard about the death of Martin Luther King, Jr., was transformed into a Black Power advocate. They "experienced" the event, but it did not lead to metamorphosis. On the other hand, others, experiencing the same event (that is, hearing the news of King's death), were *personally traumatized* by this encounter, and it became the basis for calling into question the continued embrace of an "integrationist ethos." For them, the void created in doubting their current worldview was simultaneously filled by the increasing credibility of something called Blackness. Using a more contemporaneous example, two Blacks working in different but similar White-dominated corporations may each encounter a potentially powerful, racist situation. One may respond with the attitude that one must learn to "roll with the punches," while the other person may describe the event as having helped him or her see, for the very first time, that racism is still an important obstacle in life. *In effect, an encounter must personally impact the individual in a powerful way.* In the course of a year, let alone a lifetime, just about every Black person is exposed to information or some sort of racist situation which has the potential of an "encounter," but unless the person, for what ever the reason, personalizes the encounter, their ongoing worldview or attitudes about "race" may go unchanged. One last point; the encounter need not be negative, that is, a racist event. It may, instead, revolve around exposure to powerful cultural-historical information about the Black experience, previously unknown to the person. Giving credence to (that is, personalizing) this information may challenge the person to radically rethink his or her conception of Black history and Black culture. Even in such instances, however, a negative flavor of the encounter is often introduced, for it is almost inevitable that the person will quickly become enraged at the thought of having been "previously miseducated by white racist institutions."

While an encounter may eventually steer the person toward Nigrescence, the person's initial reaction may be one of confusion, alarm, and even depression. It can be a very painful experience to discover that one's frame of reference, worldview or value system is "wrong," "incorrect," "dysfunctional," or, more to the point, "not Black or Afrocentric enough." However, such reactions are generally temporary. Somehow the person picks himself or herself up, and he or she begins to cautiously and perhaps even fearfully test the validity of their new perceptions.

The encounter stirs up a great deal of emotionalism, such as *guilt, anger,* and *general anxiety.* On the one hand, the middle-class person feels guilty for having denied the significance of race; the lower-class person feels guilt and shame for having degraded Blackness through street-hustle and exploitation. Simultaneously, the person, regardless of class background, feels angry at those perceived to have "caused" their predicament—White people and all the White world. Furthermore, each person feels anxious at the discovery that there is another level of Blackness to which he or she should aspire. Inner-directed guilt, rage at White people, along with the anxiety about becoming the right kind of Black person, combine to form a psychic fuel or energy that flings the person into a frantic, determined, obsessive, extremely motivated search for Black identity. The preencounter person or "Negro" is dying, and the "Black American" or "Afrocentric" person is beginning to emerge.

Stage Three: Immersion-Emersion

During the first phase of Immersion-Emersion Stage, the person *immerses* him/herself in the world of Blackness. The person attends political or cultural meetings that focus on Black issues, joins new organizations and drops membership in preencounter groups, goes to Black rapping sessions, attends seminars and art shows that focus on Blackness or Afrocentricity. Everything of value must be Black or relevant to Africanity, for the person is being swept along by "a sea of Blackness." The experience is an immersion into Blackness and a liberation from Whiteness. The person perceives him or herself being uprooted from the old self, while drawn into a different experience. This immersion is a strong, powerful, dominating sensation, which is constantly being energized by rage (at White people and culture), guilt (at having once been tricked into thinking Negro ideas) and a third and new fuel, a developing sense of pride (in one's Black self, pride in Black people and pride in Black culture). Superhuman and supernatural expectations are conjured concerning anything Black. The person accepts his or her hair and brown skin, and one's very being is now "beautiful." That the person exists and is Black is an inherently wonderful thing. The person may spend a great deal of time developing an African and/or Black "urban" hairstyle, and such concerns are carried over to one's style of dress. Converts give themselves African names or drop their "American" names, as did Malcolm X; children are named after African heroes. Of course, an intense interest in "Mother Africa" becomes evident, and this is especially true of persons associated with the more contemporary variant of Nigrescence, the "Afrocentricity Movement." The label "Negro" is dropped, as a self-referent, and preference is given to Black, Black-American or African.

Black literature is passionately consumed, and, in some instances, people who never before had an interest in reading, teach themselves to read and write. In fact, their orientation causes them to process all types of information that focus on the Black and African experience (film, press, radio). In a related development, a person or group may decide there is need for a new periodical, journal, newsletter, rap song, television program, and so on, in which case the person may try to produce a new information outlet that does justice to their emerging Black and Afrocentric perspective.

The new convert's attention may be drawn to other than political issues, and during the Immersion-Emersion Stage, some may experience a creative burst in which they feel "driven" to write poetry, essays, plays, rap songs, novels, and literary confessionals. A segment may turn to the plastic arts or painting. People who never before sought or experienced creative activity discover they are able to express themselves in a totally new mode. Established artists speak of a radical shift in the direction of their art, as happened to LeRoi Jones (Imamu Amiri Baraka) or Gwendolyn Brooks or Don L. Lee (Haki Mutabiti). In explaining this change, these artists state that although they were born to a Black situation, their overall socialization and artistic training caused them to look for inspiration and content *outside* the Black experience. For example, some wanted to be "pure" and "free," creating art for art's sake, or others admitted that their artistic sensibility was once decidedly Eurocentric. With the realization of their Blackness, the professional artist is awakened to a vast and new world of rich colors, powerful dramas, irony, rage, oppression, survival, and impossible dreams—and it is all there within reach. The artist (or scholar) has simply to look in the mirror (those familiar with the Black sixties will recall that the Black Arts Movement was one of the most powerful reflectors of Black identity change).

For new converts, confrontation, bluntness, directness, and an either/or mentality may be the primary mode of communications with other people, Black or White. This communication style is associated with the much discussed "Blacker-than-thou" syndrome. As a prelude to passing judgment on whether or not a person has the appropriate level of Blackness, Black people are classified into neat groups or categories such as "Uncle Tom," "militant," non-Afrocentric versus Afrocentric, "together," "soulful," "middle-class," "intellectual snob," and so on. Labeling and passing judgment on others helps the person clarify his or her own identity, but this name-calling, with its attendant ideological fractionation, can produce disastrous results, as in the Californian Black-Panther-versus-US murders of the sixties or the well-documented split between Malcolm X and the Nation of Islam. The more contemporary variant of Blacker-than-thou comes from the Afrocentricity movement, in which some converts see themselves being "more Afrocentric than others." They often describe Blacks who disagree with their perspective as insane, crazy, mentally ill, confused, unreliable, dangerous, and incapable of making a positive contribution to Black life. Often such converts mean well, as they merely seek the means of promoting greater consensus within the Black world, but their zeal for ideological correctness can lead to coercive and even fascist tactics.

The name-calling and Blacker-than-thou propensities are all part of the new convert's anxiety that his Blackness be "pure and acceptable." We can refer to this anxiety as *Weusi Anxiety*. *Weusi* is the Swahili word for Black, and *Weusi* Anxiety is the anxiety the new convert experiences, when one worries about being or becoming Black enough. Should the person be left to his or her own devices to work out all aspects of the identity crisis, such *Weusi* Anxiety could lead to considerable personal chaos. Generally, this is not the case, as most converts will seek and find the social support of others by joining certain organizations and groups. The groups joined provide a counterculture to the identity being replaced (the "Negro" or non-Afrocentric identity), by entangling the person in membership requirements, symbolic dress codes, rites, rituals, obligations, and reward systems that nurture and reinforce the emerging, new (Black or Afrocentric) identity. This can lead to a great deal of conformity on the part of the new recruit. In fact, it is one of the paradoxes of conversion that, while rebelling against the larger society, the new convert may willingly conform to a number of the demands of certain Black organizations. Again, we should keep in mind that the person's new identity is still emerging and has not been internalized; consequently, the person is anxious to be put in a position which allows him or her to demonstrate, in some fashion, that he or she is developing into the "right kind" of Black person.

Much that goes into the demonstration of one's level of Blackness takes place within the confines and privacy of Black organizations, and is part of the overall theme of the Immersion-Emersion Stage, involving the need to turn inward, while simultaneously withdrawing from everything perceived as being or representing the White world. Yet, ironically, there also develops a need to confront the "man" as a means of dramatizing, concretizing, or proving one's Blackness. The confrontation, especially for Black leaders, is a manhood (or womanhood) ritual—a baptismal or purification rite. Carried to its extreme, the impulse is to confront White people in authority, frequently the police, on a life-or-death basis. Such impulses tend not to define reality and action. Brothers and Sisters *dream* about or give a heavy rap about the need for physical combat, but daydreams and rhetoric are about as far as it goes.

Most converts do not get involved with paramilitary activities. Instead, the episodes of hatred they may feel toward Whites during the Immersion-Emersion Stage are worked through as daydreams or fantasies, such as the urge to rip off the first White person one passes on a particular day. During Immersion-Emersion, "kill Whitey" fantasies appear to to be experienced by Blacks—regardless of age, sex, or class background. Persons who fixate or stagnate at this point in their development are said to have a "pseudo"-Black identity because it is based on the hatred and negation of White people, rather than the affirmation of a pro-Black perspective, which *includes* commitment to the destruction of racism, but not the random killing of Whites.

Finally we note that, during this transition period, the person experiences a surge in altruism. A constant theme of selflessness, dedication, and commitment to the (Black) group is evident; the person feels overwhelming *love and attachment* to all that is Black. The person's main focus in life becomes this feeling of togetherness and oneness with the people. It is a religiouslike feeling, and clusters of new converts can create an atmosphere in which Blackness or Africanity has a spiritual and religious quality.

The first part of this transition stage is *immersion* into Blackness, an experience in which the person feels almost driven and compelled to act, think, and feel in a certain way. People are not out of control during immersion, but they often look back upon the episode as something akin to a *happening,* as if Blackness were an outside force or spirit that was permeating, if not invading, their being. The second part of the stage is *emergence* from the emotionality and dead-end, either/or, racist, and over-simplified ideological aspects of the immersion experience. The person begins to level off, and feel in control of his or her emotions and intellect. In fact, the person cannot continue to handle the intense emotional phases and concentrated affect levels associated with conversion, and is predisposed to find ways to level off.

Frequently, this leveling off is facilitated by a combination of the person's own growth, in conjunction with the person's observation that certain role models or heroes appear to be operating from the vantage point of a more advanced state of identity development. The first hint of this advanced state may be discovered during face-to-face interactions with role models who evidence a calmer, more sophisticated quality to their Blackness, or the person may infer it from having read the life and times of a person such as Malcolm X, in which Malcolm depicts moving *beyond* a rigid sense of Blackness, as a consequence of his experiences in Mecca. The story of how one gets over the hump of Immersion is likely to differ from person to person, but however it occurs, it results in the discovery that one's first impressions of Blackness can be romantic and symbolic, rather than substantive, textured, and complex. In fact, the person may find him or herself pulling away from membership in organizations whose activities seem designed to help one feel immersed in Blackness, and toward memberships in and associations with groups or persons who are demonstrating a more serious understanding of Black issues. When the grip of the immersion phase loosens, when the convert begins to comprehend immersion as a period of transition rather than a final point of development, and when the convert seems to understand that continued growth, perhaps of a less emotional nature, lies ahead, the person has reached the end of the transition stage, and is moving toward internalization of the new identity.

Negative consequences of transition: The previous paragraph depicts a person headed toward continued identity development. We should understand, however, that the ups and downs of the transition stage can very well result in regression, fixation, or stagnation, as well as forward movement. The events of the Immersion-Emersion Stage can inspire or frustrate an individual. Consequently, the degree of a person's continued involvement in Black affairs may prove significant or negligible. During the transition stage, the person embraces idealistic, if not superhuman, expectations about anything Black, in which case minimal reinforcement (when you are attracted to something, it does not take a great deal of reinforcement to sustain that interest) may carry the person over into advanced identity development (evolution into the next stage). On the other hand, failure to meet these expectancies may break the person's spirit and desire to change, in which case regression becomes a real possibility. For others, intense and negative encounters with White racists lead to their becoming fixated at Stage Three. They get stuck in a never-ending state of militancy and hatred. In still a third scenario, people may give all the appearance of having grown beyond the boundaries of the Immersion-Emersion Stage, that is, their behavior and attitudes suggest a great deal of internalization of the new identity, but for reasons that are not very clear, they cease involvement in the Black struggle. In effect, they drop out. Keeping in mind that not everyone moves forward, let us examine the experiences of those who are able to sustain growth.

Internalization

Key markers of internalization: If encounter and immersion-emersion usher in confusion and a roller coaster of emotions, then the Internalization Stage marks points of clarity and levelheadedness. The person feels calmer, more relaxed, more at ease. An inner peace is achieved, as *Weusi* Anxiety (tension over being the right kind of Black person) is transformed into *Weusi* Pride (Black Pride) and *Weusi* Self-acceptance (Black self-acceptance). The shift is from concern about how your friends see you ("Am I Black enough?"), to confidence in one's personal standards of Blackness; from uncontrolled rage toward White people, to controlled anger at oppressive systems and racist institutions; from symbolic, boisterous rhetoric, to serious analysis and quiet strength; from unrealistic urgency that can lead to dropping out, to a sense of destiny that enables one to sustain long-term commitment; from anxious, insecure, rigid, pseudo-Blackness based on the hatred of Whites, to proactive Black pride, self-love, and a deep sense of connection to, and acceptance by, the Black community.

In being habituated and internalized, Blackness becomes a backdrop for life's transactions. It can be taken for granted, freeing the person to concentrate on issues that *presuppose a basic identification with Blackness.* One is Black, thus one is free to think about matters beyond the scope of one's personal sense of Blackness (organizational development, community development, problem-solving, conflict resolution, institution building, and so on).

One of the most important consequences of this inner peace is that the person's conception of Blackness tends to become more open, expansive, and sophisticated. As general defensiveness fades, simplistic thinking and simple solutions become transparently inadequate, and the full complexity and inherent texture of the Black condition becomes the point of departure for serious analysis.

The person perceives him or herself to be a totally changed person, with both a new worldview and an equally revitalized personality. However, research findings show that Nigrescence tends to have more of an effect on the group-identity or reference-group component of the Black self-concept than it does the general personality. The person's personality is most certainly put under stress during immersion-emersion, and there is a great deal of emotionality associated with conversion, but with internalization and the easing of internal psychological stress, the basic core of the person's personality is reestablished. For example, if a person was an effective (or ineffective) leader at preencounter, his or her leadership profile will go unchanged at internalization. Likewise, this pattern is likely to be replicated in countless other examples: shy at preencounter, shy at internalization; outgoing and gregarious at preencounter, outgoing and gregarious at internalization; introverted and mildly uncomfortable around large groups at preencounter, introverted and uncomfortable in groups at internalization; calm, rational, and deliberate at preencounter, calm, rational, and deliberate at internalization; anxious and neurotic at preencounter, anxious and neurotic at internalization; relatively normal and happy at preencounter, relatively normal and happy at internalization, and so on. In fact, research suggests that during immersion-emersion one's basic personality strengths act as a *psychological cushion* or relative backdrop of stability for the intense struggle taking place within the group-identity level of the Black self-concept. (Conversely, personality weaknesses may make Nigrescence more stressful to the person, although the point being made here is that successful completion of Nigrescence rides or floats on whatever are the person's extant personality strengths.) At internalization, when the conflict surrounding reference-group and worldview change has been resolved, the person is able to fall back on his or her basic personality traits, which, though greatly stressed, perturbed, and excited during immersion-emersion, helped him or her negotiate the group-identity change in the first place.

For the fraction of people who were anti-Black at preencounter, Nigrescence may enhance their general level of self-esteem, but again, the person's characteristic personality attributes beyond self-esteem are likely to remain the same. As a form of social therapy, Nigrescence is extremely effective at changing the importance of race and culture in a person's life; however, it is not a process that lends itself to the needs of personality therapy.

What makes the person feel completely "new" are the changes experienced at the level of one's group identity. In moving from preencounter to internalization, the person has moved from a frame of reference where race and culture had low salience, to a perspective that places high salience on Blackness in everyday life. With this change in salience comes membership in new organizations, changes in one's social network, changes in one's manner of dress and personal appearance, changes in one's self-referents, changes in what one reads or views on television, changes in how one socializes one's children, changes in one's internal image of the capacity and efficacy of Blacks as a group, changes in one's cultural and artistic preferences, changes in one's historical and cultural perspective, changes in the causes and social problems that engage one's activism, and perhaps even changes in one's name. These types of changes define what is important in *adult life,* and that's why the person feels totally new. Left unnoticed to the person is the fact that his or her basic personality profile is the same as it was during preencounter.

Salience and ideology: While advanced Black identity development results in the person giving high salience to issues of race and culture, not every person in internalization shares the same degree of salience for Blackness, as this is likely to be determined by the nature of one's ideology. Persons who construct a strong nationalistic framework from their immersion-emersion experiences may continue along this ideological path at internalization, while others may derive a far less nationalistic stance. The former can lead to total salience on Blackness, and the latter, less so. For example, *vulgar* nationalists (persons who believe Blacks and Whites are biogenetically different, with Blacks being of "superior" racial stock, and Whites being an "inferior" mutation of Black stock) and traditional nationalists (persons who frame their nationalistic perspective with other than biogenetic constructs) have saliencies about race and culture that in some instances can border on the obsessive. The traditional nationalist presents the most healthy alternative, as his or her high salience and frame of reference are subject to rational analysis and debate, while the vulgar nationalist's reactionary racism, which is usually steeped in an odd mixture of pseudoscientific myths, historical distortions, and outright mysticism, offers a salience and orientation beyond the reach of normal discourse. Although vulgar and traditional nationalists are African-Americans by history and culture, both tend to stress a singularity to their cultural emphasis, and in some instances, they may even *deny* that there is anything American or Eurocentric about their being. In this sense, their internalized Black nationalist identity, though far more sophisticated than the version espoused during immersion-emersion, carries with it, in varying degrees, themes of conflict on how to relate to the other half of their cultural-historical makeup.

Other Blacks reaching internalization derive a *bicultural* reference-group orientation from their Nigrescence experience. From their vantage point, internalization is a time for working through and incorporating into one's self-concept the realities of one's Blackness as well as the enigmatic, paradoxical, advantageous, and supportive aspects of one's Americanness.

Taking this a step further, others may embrace a *multicultural* perspective, in which case their concern for Blackness is shared with a multiplicity of cultural interests and saliencies. Consequently, the cultural identity of the Stage Four person can vary from that of the monocultural orientation of the extreme nationalist to the identity mosaic of the multiculturally oriented Black person. Each ideological stance incorporates certain strengths and weaknesses, and there are times when the holders of one perspective may find themselves at odds with those who share another variant of Blackness. This means that Nigrescence may increase the salience of race and culture for all persons who successfully reach the advanced states of Black identity development, but internalization does not result in ideological unity. One can look upon this variability as ideological fractionation, or as healthy, ideological diversity.

Stage Five: Internalization-Commitment

After developing a Black identity that services their personal needs, some Blacks fail to sustain a long-term interest in Black affairs. Others devote an extended period of time, if not a lifetime, to finding ways to translate their personal sense of Blackness into a plan of action or general sense of commitment. Such people characterize the fifth and final stage of Nigrescence: Internalization-Commitment. Current theory suggests there are few differences between the psychology of Blacks in the fourth and fifth stages, other than the important factor of sustained interest and commitment. Consequently, other than to repeat what has already been said about internalization, a more differentiated look at internalization-commitment awaits the results of future research.

Parham's concept of recycling: A complete Nigrescence cycle involves traversing all four or five stages, and as originally conceived, Nigrescence was thought to be a "one-time event" in the life of a person. Recently, the young, brilliant Nigrescence theorist, Thomas A. Parham, who completed his dissertation under the tutelage of another key figure in the field, Janet E. Helms, has extended the implications of my model across the life span. Parham has noted that, for those who have completed their original Nigrescence cycle at an earlier point in the life span (say, for example, adolescence or early adulthood), the challenges unique to another life span phase (middle age or late adulthood) may induce *recycling* through some of the stages. For example, a young man might go through Nigrescence at the age of twenty, when he is single and a college student. During this first cycle, he is able to successfully address those identity questions that are important to early adult functioning. Subsequently, his marriage may trigger new questions about Blackness, and still later, the raising of his progeny may cause him to discover "gaps" in his thinking about Blackness. These new questions and the discovery of gaps in one's thinking, or a powerful racist incident at work or in the community, represent a new encounter episode, leading to the need to recycle (in all likelihood, recycling does not involve the Preencounter Stage). In recycling, the person searches for new answers and continued growth in his or her thinking about what it means to be Black. Depending on the nature and intensity of the new encounter, recycling may vary from a mild refocusing experience to passage through full-blown Encounter, Immersion-Emersion, and Internalization Stages.

References

Cross, W. E. *Shades of Black*. Philadelphia: Temple University Press. 1991.

Parham, T. A. "Cycles of Psychological Nigrescence." *The Counseling Psychologist*, 17(2): 187–226, 1989.

Questions

1. How do you characterize a person at each of the stages of black identity development: preencounter, encounter, immersion-emersion, and internalization?
2. Do all blacks begin at the preencounter stage?
3. Does being at one stage have advantages over another? Is there an optimal stage?
4. What are the implications of this model for understanding the role of cultural organizations on college campuses?
5. What are the implications of this model for understanding racial tensions or lack of racial mixing on college campuses?

References and Further Reading

Cross, W. E., Jr. (1991). *Shades of Black: Diversity in African American identity*. Philadelphia: Temple University Press.

Cross, W. E., Jr. (1994). Nigrescence theory: Historical and explanatory notes. *Journal of Vocational Behavior, 44*, 119–123.

Goodstein, R., & Ponterotto, J. G. (1997). Racial and ethnic identity: Their relationship and their contribution to self-esteem. *Journal of Black Psychology, 23*(3), 275–292.

Parham, T. A. (1989). Cycles of psychological nigrescence. *Counseling Psychologist, 17*(2), 187–226.

Poindexter-Cameron, J. M., & Robinson, T. L. (1997). Relationships among racial identity attitudes, womanist identity attitudes, and self-esteem in African American college women. *Journal of College Student Development, 38*(3), 288–295.

6.2   Jean S. Phinney and Doreen A. Rosenthal, 1992

Ethnic Identity in Adolescence: Process, Context, and Outcome

Jean S. Phinney, Ph.D., is a professor of psychology at California State University, Los Angeles. She has researched and published articles and book chapters on ethnic identity development, bicultural identity, ethnic attitudes, and intergroup relations during adolescence.

Doreen A. Rosenthal, Ph.D., is director of the Australian Research Centre on Sex, Health, and Society at the University of Melbourne, Australia. She is chair of the Australian National Council on AIDS and Related Diseases Subcommittee on Education. Her research interests include the adaptation and acculturation of ethnic minorities, and the predictors of adolescent sexual risk-taking behavior. She is coauthor (with Susan Moore) of *Sexuality in Adolescence* (1993) and coauthor (with Susan Moore and Anne Mitchell), of *Youth, AIDS, and Sexually Transmitted Diseases* (1996).

Many researchers have documented the importance of ethnic identity in the search for identity at adolescence (Phinney, 1990). Because of the lower power and status accorded to members of ethnic minority groups from non-European backgrounds, the prejudice and discrimination they may confront, and the barriers they face to achieving their aspirations, ethnic identity becomes salient for these minority youth and plays an important role in the development of their self-concepts and in their psychological functioning. Ethnic minority youth are pushed to confront the meaning of ethnicity in their lives, while for whites of European backgrounds, ethnicity tends not to be a salient part of their identity.

Jean Phinney and Doreen Rosenthal review the research on ethnic identity, focusing on the dimensions of ethnic identity, the process of ethnic identity development, the role of social context in shaping ethnic identity, and the relationship between ethnic identity and a variety of psychological outcomes. Phinney and Rosenthal describe ethnic identity as a multidimensional construct comprising a variety of components, such as language, involvement in ethnic traditions and practices, knowledge of ethnic group history, subjective sense of ethnic group membership (feelings of belonging and commitment to the group), self-identification, or self-labeling. They point out that researchers have included different components in their measures of ethnic identity to fit particular ethnic groups, as different components, such as language, may be more salient to one ethnic group than to another.

Phinney and Rosenthal describe a process of ethnic identity development that occurs over time, based on the work of Erikson (Reading 5.1), Marcia (Reading 5.2) and Cross (Reading 6.1). They detail a progression from an unexamined, or foreclosed, ethnic identity, through a moratorium or period of exploration, to an achieved ethnic identity. Individuals may also reexamine their ethnicity at different points throughout their lives. As one moves toward an achieved ethnic identity, research has shown that an accompanying increase in social-psychological well-being occurs.

Phinney and Rosenthal review research focusing on the dynamic quality of ethnic identity, the ways in which the subjective sense of ethnic group membership may change over time and across different social contexts. The meaning and importance of ethnic identity shifts as context changes. Finally, Phinney and Rosenthal examine research on the consequences of having a strong or weak ethnic identity. For members of ethnic minority groups, a high level of ethnic identity helps mitigate the negative effects of discrimination and is associated with self-esteem, self-confidence, and purpose in life, whereas for whites, strength of ethnic identity is unrelated to well-being.

Introduction

The achievement of a positive, coherent identity is a fundamental goal for adolescents (Erikson, 1968). Their critical task is to select and integrate childhood identifications, together with personal inclinations and the opportunities afforded by society, in order to construct a sense of who they are and what they will become. An understanding of this process requires an appreciation of the psychological, social, and cultural web in which the individual grows and changes.

For adolescents from ethnic minority groups, the process of identity formation has an added dimension due to their exposure to alternative sources of identification, their own ethnic group and the mainstream or dominant culture. Growing up in a society where the mainstream culture may differ significantly in values and beliefs from their culture of origin, these youth face the task of achieving a satisfactory and satisfying integration of ethnic identity into a self-identity. The ease, or difficulty, with which this task is accomplished depends on a number of factors, which are the focus of this [selection]. In particular, minority adolescents may have to confront issues of prejudice and discrimination, structural barriers which limit their aspirations and hinder their achievements, and other features of the mainstream society that differentiate them from the majority. If minority youth are to construct a strong, positive, and stable self-identity, then they must be able to incorporate into that sense of self a positively valued ethnic identity.

Ethnic identity has been studied almost exclusively as a phenomenon of relevance to minority groups. Although the concept of ethnic identity can be extended to majority group adolescents, ethnicity is generally not salient for them (Deschamps, 1982; McGuire, McGuire, Child, & Fujioka, 1978), and thus it has little or no importance as an identity issue (Driedger, 1986; Phinney & Alipuria, 1990; Phinney & Tarver, 1988). There is little research on this topic, and this [selection] does not address it.

Our purpose is to examine the process of ethnic identity formation in youth from a variety of ethnic minorities, focusing particularly on the interaction between contextual and developmental factors as this process unfolds. Of course, the experiences of minority youth vary widely. In the United States, the focus of research has been on African-Americans, Hispanics, Asian-Americans, and Native Americans, in large part because of the problems these groups have faced, for both historical and social reasons. Other ethnic minorities, primarily those from European backgrounds, have been subject to fewer negative messages from the mainstream society. For these adolescents the path to acceptance of and pride in their ethnicity may be less problematic.

There is little research that examines the distinction between Caucasian minority groups and minority groups of color; that is, between racial identity and ethnic identity within a racial group. Researchers comparing ethnic identity across groups have generally made comparisons within racial categories (Driedger, 1976; Rosenthal & Hrynevich, 1985) or compared racially different groups with the Caucasian majority (Phinney & Alipuria, 1990). However, there are several obvious differences between ethnic identity based only on culture or country of origin and that based on race. First, racially similar minority groups can eventually assimilate into a dominant society (although this may be difficult for recent immigrants). The option of complete assimilation is not present for racially distinct groups. Therefore, for minorities of color there is less latitude in the ways of establishing an ethnic identity. Second, although prejudice and discrimination have existed against some racially similar groups, such as European immigrants in the United States and Australia, negative attitudes and behaviors have been far less widespread and less virulent than against racially distinct minorities. Phinney, Lochner, and Murphy (1990) suggest that dealing with prejudice and discrimination is a central aspect of ethnic identity formation, especially for minorities of color.

In addition, there are crucial distinctions among various ethnic groups. Each ethnic group has both its own culture and traditions and its own history within a particular society. Ogbu (1987) points out that ethnic groups have become part of another culture for widely differing reasons, including conquest, slavery, political asylum, and economic opportunity. They have brought their own values, attitudes, and practices to the interface with another culture. They have been faced with varying degrees of acceptance and rejection by the dominant group.

It is with differences such as these in mind that we turn to an analysis of the development of ethnic identity in minority youth. We examine the ways in which ethnic identity is conceptualized and the contexts in which ethnic identity formation takes place—the family, the community, and the wider society. The last section reviews evidence regarding the relationships of ethnic identity to self-esteem. The [selection] concludes with an integration of these various strands and implications for future research.

The Conceptualization of Ethnic Identity in Adolescence

Ethnic identity refers to "one's sense of belonging to an ethnic group and the part of one's thinking, perception, feelings, and behavior that is due to ethnic group membership" (Rotheram & Phinney, 1987, p. 13). Most writers agree that the construct includes some or all of the following components: self-identification as member of a group, feelings of belonging and commitment to a group, positive (or negative) attitudes toward the group, a sense of shared attitudes and values, and specific ethnic traditions and practices, such as language, behavior, and customs. Each of these components highlight a different dimension of the construct. Self-identification, or the ethnic label used to describe oneself, is important since it locates the individual within a particular cultural framework. However, an individual may self-identify without feeling strongly committed to the group, so an expressed sense of attachment is also important. The extent to which individuals adopt the ways of their culture is indicated by their participation in activities such as language, friendship networks, religious affiliation, food preference, exogamy, and traditional customs. Finally, since identification with an ethnic group is not necessarily accompanied by positive feelings about that group, the evaluative meaning given to group membership is a critical component.

In studying ethnic identity, researchers have generally selected certain of these components and developed their own measures for application to a particular ethnic group (e.g, Driedger, 1976; Giles, Taylor, Lambert, & Albert, 1976; Rosenthal & Hrynevich, 1985; Taft, 1985; Ting-Toomey, 1981). While this research has yielded rich findings about particular groups, the use of widely differing definitions and measures limits the ability to make comparisons and generalizations across studies (see Phinney, 1990, for a recent review).

A general measure of ethnic identity that can be used with adolescents and young adults from various groups has recently been proposed (Phinney, 1992). The measure focuses on aspects that are common across all groups, assessing attitudes toward the group and feelings of belonging, as well as the process of ethnic identity formation: the extent of exploration of, and commitment to, one's ethnicity. In ethnically diverse high school and college samples, all the components were found to load on a single factor, suggesting a unified construct. This measure, however, does not include other aspects of identification with one's ethnic group, such as language usage or specific cultural knowledge and practices, which many writers have considered to be central to ethnic identity. There is a growing body of research that demonstrates the importance of conceptualizing ethnic identity as a multifaceted, dynamic construct (Garcia, 1982; Giles et al., 1976; Giles, Llado, McKirnan, & Taylor, 1979; Rosenthal & Hrynevich, 1985), with complex and subtle interactions between different elements of ethnic identity and external forces (Rosenthal & Feldman, in press a, in press b).

Nevertheless, most researchers have typically taken a "snapshot" approach to studying ethnic identity, with little attention given to the ways in which it develops. Much research stemming from a social psychological perspective, and in particular social identity theory as elaborated by Tajfel and his colleagues (1978, 1981), focuses on ethnic identity at a given point in the adolescent's history and attempts, for example, to map those elements that are salient for a particular group, or to explore correlates of ethnic identity.

In contrast, a smaller body of work has taken a developmental perspective and has looked at the process of ethnic identity formation. Much of this work has dealt with African-Americans, although other minority groups have been considered from this perspective (Arce, 1981; Atkinson, Morten, & Sue, 1983; Cross, 1978; Parham & Helms, 1981). Ethnic or racial identity is seen in this work as developing from a state of low ethnic awareness, and often preference for the majority culture, to an appreciation for and acceptance of one's ethnicity. In an extension of this process approach, Phinney and her associates (Phinney, 1989, 1990; Phinney & Alipuria, 1990) have drawn on the ego identity literature (Erikson, 1968; Marcia, 1980) as their conceptual framework, placing ethnic identity within the context of ego identity development.

Before turning to work linking ego identity and ethnic identity, it is important to note differences between the two concepts: (a) Ethnic identity is a social identity; its meaning is embedded in the culture to which one belongs. Although ego identity research has given increasing recognition to the impact of the family on identity formation, there has been little attention to the role of the wider context. (b) Ethnic identity deals with a given, one's heritage; it cannot be chosen in the way one can choose a profession or political identity, although the extent or manner of expressing ethnic identity can vary. The ego identity literature has emphasized those aspects of the self where youth can make choices among clear alternatives. (c) The importance and salience of ethnic identity vary among ethnic groups, and between majority and minority group members. The process of ego identity formation is assumed to be comparable for all adolescents, although research has focused on Caucasian youth from Western cultures. (d) Finally, ego identity has been studied primarily by psychologists focusing on adolescence, and by clinical psychologists and psychoanalysts, while ethnic identity has been studied from a wide range of theoretical perspectives, by social and developmental psychologists, sociologists, and anthropologists.

In spite of these differences, the ego identity framework provides important parallels to the study of ethnic identity. It is useful to think of ethnic identity as an additional domain of identity development for minority youth, and, in fact, ethnic identity achievement has been found to be significantly related to high scores on an independent measure of ego identity (Phinney, 1989). The three-stage model of ethnic identity formation proposed by Phinney (1989, 1990) integrates the process models of Arce (1981), Atkinson, Morten, and Sue (1983), Cross (1978), and Parham and Helms (1981), among others, and relates them to the model of ego identity formation proposed by Marcia (1980). Ethnic identity is seen as developing through a series of stages in a manner similar to that described by Waterman (1982) for ego identity.

The first stage is an unexamined ethnic identity. Early adolescents, as a result of negative ethnic images and stereotypes, may express an out-group preference. Alternatively, because of socialization in the family or community, they may have a positive sense of attachment to their ethnic group. In either case, attitudes at this stage have not been arrived at independently, but are derived from others, for example, their parents, community, or the larger society. By analogy with ego identity, ethnic identity at this stage may be thought of as foreclosed. In contrast, some adolescents, perhaps because of the absence of conflicts or salient experiences related to ethnicity, may have given little thought to or have been unconcerned about issues related to ethnicity and can be said to have a diffuse ethnic identity.

At some point, typically during adolescence, an experience that makes ethnicity salient is seen as triggering an exploration of what it means to be a member of a specific minority group in society. It is not clear what initiates the exploration (termed "encounter" by Cross, 1978); it may be a specific instance of prejudice, involvement in a structured ethnic awareness program, identity exploration in other domains, or experiences related to the gradual widening of the adolescent's world through school or work. This period is equivalent to the identity crisis or moratorium described by Erikson (1968) and studied by Marcia (1980) and others. Some of the issues that must be examined at this time are cultural differences between their group and the dominant group, the images and stereotypes of their group held by society, and the experiences of prejudice and discrimination (Phinney, et al., 1990).

The exploration stage is, ideally, followed by a resolution of the conflicts and contradictions posed by minority status in society. At this point, individuals make a commitment to a particular way of being a member of their group; they have an achieved ethnic identity, characterized by a secure sense of themselves as ethnic group members. Cross (1978) has termed this "internalization."

A recent longitudinal study (Phinney & Chavira, in press) showed a significant movement from lower to higher stages of ethnic identity between the ages of 16 and 19. In addition, interview studies of minority youth (Phinney, 1989; Phinney & Tarver, 1988) showed that more African-American 10th graders than 8th graders had explored their ethnicity. College undergraduates scored significantly higher than high school 11th and 12th graders on a questionnaire measure of ethnic identity achievement (Phinney, 1992). It appears that with increasing age, minority youth are more likely to have explored and resolved questions about the meaning of ethnicity as a component of their identity, that is, to have an achieved ethnic identity. However, as with ego identity (Marcia & Kowaz, 1988; Waterman, 1982), there may be regressions and reexaminations at various stages in the process. Even after achieving an ethnic identity, the issues may be reexamined subsequently as new conflicts or contradictions come to the fore (Parham, 1989).

In summary, while ethnic identity has been conceptualized as dynamic and multidimensional, studies have generally addressed only selected aspects of the construct, and relatively few have considered it developmentally. An adequate understanding requires an appreciation of the way developmental and contextual factors interact in the formation of ethnic identity in adolescence.

Ethnic Identity Formation: The Interaction of Development and Context

To understand the task faced by adolescents, we must consider both the early environment in which children first acquire a sense of themselves as ethnic group members and the contextual factors that influence their adolescent years. The family provides the earliest context for a developing sense of ethnicity and is a continuing influence throughout adolescence. Furthermore, the family's effectiveness in socializing a child as an ethnic group member will depend on the supports provided by the ethnic community. But even when the parents present a positive ethnic image and the ethnic community reinforces that image, the developing child is susceptible to society's images of the group, which may differ radically from their own. Young adolescents, then, facing the major task of ego identity achievement, must make sense of the variety of often contradictory knowledge, experience, attitudes, and images relative to their ethnicity that derive from their social context.

Family Influences on Ethnic Identity

There is considerable evidence that family environment shapes the development of minority adolescents in areas as diverse as socio-emotional development and school outcomes (see Spencer & Dornbusch, 1990, for a review). It is reasonable to expect that family influences on the formation and maintenance of ethnic identity in childhood are powerful and pervasive. The family is the source of children's first experiences related to ethnicity, and it is generally with the parents and other family members that children make their first identifications as part of a group. Family and significant others are the principal sources of information and influence providing a cultural context, a lens through which the child views the world. Families that participate with pleasure in their cultural traditions and express positive feelings about their group are likely to lay a basis for a positive ethnic identity.

Research with African-American families suggests that many African-American parents socialize their children to be proud of their race, with the goal of ensuring that the child develops positive feelings and self-confidence as an African-American individual (e.g., Harrison, 1985; Jaynes & Williams, 1989; Nobles, 1973; Peters, 1985; Thornton, Chatters, Taylor, & Allen, 1990). None of these studies actually takes the next step of evaluating whether this parental goal is realized, that is, whether racial socialization does have a significant impact on children's ethnic identity, although Spencer (1983) has shown that Eurocentric (out-group) attitudes are less common among young African-American children whose parents discuss racial discrimination and teach their children about African-American history.

What is clear is that the child brings to adolescence a view of his or her ethnic heritage that has been largely shaped by family influences. But to what extent does this influence extend to adolescence, and how do parental attitudes impact on adolescents' ethnic identity? There is a surprising dearth of research directed at exploring the ways in which parents and family shape an adolescent's sense of belonging to an ethnic group. At a very general level, it appears that parents' involvement in the ethnic community is related to their adolescent's sense of ethnic identity (Rosenthal & Cichello, 1986). However, the same study found that, with Italian adolescents, parental maintenance of traditional customs and norms of behavior was unrelated to adolescents' ethnic identity. A culturally traditional family may even create an environment in which adolescents have difficulty reconciling their ethnicity with their involvement in the mainstream culture (Rosenthal, 1987). Szapozcnik and Kurtines (1980) describe the conflicts that can result when rapidly acculturating adolescents clash with their more traditional parents over values and behaviors. Statements by Asian-American and Mexican-American high school students (Phinney & Chavira, in preparation) illustrate the kinds of family conflicts experienced by some minority youth:

> My parents are sort of old-fashioned, so they tell me that I have to do things. . . . Like, I am a girl so I am always sent to the kitchen to cook. . . . I am more Americanized and I don't believe in that girl thing. We end up in an argument and it does not get solved.

> Mexican culture is more inclined to hold you back as an adolescent. [Parents] try to hold you back and try to protect you more. . . . I try to talk it over with them; they still try to protect me.

Phinney and her colleagues (Phinney & Nakayama, 1991) have demonstrated that parental sensitivity to cultural diversity has positive outcomes for adolescent ethnic identity. Asian-American, African-American, and Mexican-American adolescents who scored high on a measure of ethnic identity (including ethnic practices, attitudes, and commitment) had parents who were significantly more likely than parents of low scorers to state that they have personally tried to prepare their son or daughter for living in a culturally diverse society.

In addition to modeling or discussing ethnic issues specifically, parents may influence adolescents in indirect ways. In a recent study with first- and second-generation Chinese adolescents in two Western cultures, Rosenthal and Feldman (in press a) showed that warm, regulating, autonomy-promoting parenting behaviors which have been shown to lead to positive, well-socialized outcomes in children and adolescents (Maccoby & Martin, 1983; Steinberg, 1990), were predictive of ethnic pride, but not ethnic behaviors or knowledge. They suggest that adolescents whose parents act as positive role models are likely to take on other aspects of parental behaviors and values, specifically the value given by parents to their ethnic heritage.

In other studies of family context, the focus has been on structural factors, such as ethnic intermarriage and transracial adoption, both of which are assumed to result in a weakening of ethnic ties. The sparse evidence available suggests that children of interethnic marriages retain a positive identification with their ethnic origins (Alba

& Chamin, 1983; Salgado de Snyder, Lopez, & Padilla, 1982; Yogev & Jamsky, 1983). Two studies of transracial adoption demonstrated a strong relationship between parents' attitudes and adolescents' self-definition. African-American adolescents who had been raised by Caucasian parents who deemphasized their adoptive children's racial or ethnic origins claimed a mixed (African-American/Caucasian) identity rather than considering themselves African-American (McRoy, Zurcher, Lauderdale, & Anderson, 1984). Similarly, Hispanic adolescents raised by non-Hispanic parents defined themselves as American rather than Mexican-American (Andujo, 1988). It seems that adoptive parents who realistically perceive their child's racial or ethnic identity as different from their own and are accepting of that difference will provide a family environment that is conducive to the development of a positive group identification.

While parents are the primary socializers of their children, they are not the only influence. At adolescence the impact of external forces is likely to be considerably more potent than earlier in the life span. If we are to explain the apparent shifts in various aspects of ethnic identity, we must take account of features of the ethnic community and larger society.

The Ethnic Community

The cultural context provided by the family is reinforced when the ethnic community provides a subculture that allows for many of the activities central to an individual's life (e.g., school, religion, recreation) to be carried out within the group, that is, the group has a high level of institutional completeness (Breton, 1964). The importance for ethnic identity of being part of a group that is cohesive and structured, and whose institutions are central to one's life, is demonstrated in several studies. In Australia, the Greek immigrant community is more cohesive and structured than is the Italian. Rosenthal and Hrynevich (1985) found, not surprisingly, that Greek-Australian adolescents valued their Greek identity, while their Italian peers placed less emphasis on maintaining their cultural heritage and favored assimilation into the host culture. Driedger (1976) found in Canada that status within the society interacted with institutional completeness so that groups high on both status and completeness (French and Jews) had the strongest sense of ethnic identity. Lowest levels of ethnic identity were found among Germans, Ukrainians, and Poles, whose groups have low status and only low to moderate levels of institutional completeness.

When the community lacks cohesiveness and a sense of kinship (Stack, 1974) and also cannot provide role models for ways of being a successful member of a group, adolescents may have little to identify with. Two interview studies of African-American young (Taylor, 1989) contrast the strong parental models, which have influenced college students, with the lack of models for inner-city youth. Among college youth, parental models played a more decisive role than peers. In contrast, many inner-city African-American youth viewed their fathers, if available at all, as unattractive role models and turned more to their peers. Many of these youth lack models whom they regard as resources for knowledge, skills, and social support (Hunt & Hunt, 1977; Silverstein & Krate, 1975). Lack of identification with parents or other adults in the community may leave poor African-American youth at particular risk in the attempt to develop a positive sense of their blackness.

Another characteristic that affects attachment to the ethnic group is whether the ethnic community is present in substantial numbers in a neighborhood or is a small minority (Garcia & Lega, 1979). There are conflicting findings, with low ethnic density related to loss of ethnic identity of Caucasian minorities in one study (Alba & Chamlin, 1983), and to retention of ethnic ties among Mexican-Americans in another (Padilla, 1980). Social identity theory enables us to reconcile these findings in terms of group distinctiveness (McGuire et al., 1978). Members of the Caucasian minorities have more readily available to them the option of blending or "passing" into the mainstream group than do the visibly different Mexican-Americans. This distinctiveness, so social identity theorists argue, results in heightened salience of ethnic identity. However, adolescents who are part of a large minority (Chinese in San Francisco) were found to be similar in terms of levels and nature of ethnic identity to those in a small, dispersed minority, namely Chinese in Melbourne, Australia (Rosenthal & Feldman, in press b).

Furthermore, for immigrant groups, the ethnic community changes over time, as successive generations become more acculturated. While several studies have shown a weakening of ethnic identity among later generations of immigrants, other studies have suggested that ethnic identity remains stable after the second generation or that a resurgence occurs, with stronger identification occurring in third and subsequent generations. Some researchers (e.g., Keefe & Padilla, 1987; Triandis, Kashima, Shimada, & Villareal, 1986) have suggested that elements of the culture that are central (e.g., values) may be more resistant to change than those that are peripheral (e.g., behaviors). Keefe and Padilla (1987), in a study of Mexican-American adults, found that cultural awareness (defined as familiarity with Mexican culture) declined across generations; however, ethnic loyalty, involving an individual's attitudes and feeling about the Mexican culture and people and about discrimination, remained almost constant from the second to the fourth generation. Similarly, in their study of first- and second-generation Chinese-Australian and Chinese-American high school students, Rosenthal and Feldman (in press b) found that ethnic knowledge and behavior decreased over time, but there was no change in the importance accorded to ethnic identity or the positive evaluation of that identity.

Clearly, many characteristics of the ethnic community, including its structure, cohesiveness, density, and the recency of immigration of its members, influence the ethnic identity of its adolescents. Yet the community functions within a broader societal context that strongly affects the developing adolescent.

The Ethnic Group in the Larger Society

The impact on ethnic identity of the position of the minority group in society and the relationship between minority and majority group, at both the individual and group levels, have been the focus of considerably more conceptual and empirical attention than have the family and the community. Social identity theory (Tajfel, 1978, 1981) stresses the dynamic nature of the relationship between the individual and society, explicitly dealing with group belongingness or social identity as a product of individuals' representations of their social world and their place in that world. The outcome of this interaction will be determined by the need individuals have to achieve a positive sense of self-identity via membership in various groups. Tajfel (1978) points out that members of disparaged minority groups face the problem of having to live with negative images of their group. Individuals who accept the negative images of society toward their group face the risk of self-image problems and may show a preference for or identification with another group. Alternatively, individuals may try to leave the group, by assimilation or passing, or they may seek to change the situation, by attempting to re-evaluate and enhance the image of the group.

The tendency to identify with or prefer the majority culture is seen in much research with minority children. Although virtually all minority children can correctly identify their own ethnic group membership by age 8 or 9 (Aboud, 1987; Bernal, Knight, Garza, Ocampo, & Cota, 1990), many continue to show a preference for the majority culture (out-group preference) throughout and beyond childhood (Bernal et al., 1990; Davey, 1983; George & Hoppe, 1979; Semaj, 1980; Spencer, 1982). Thus, there is strong evidence that at least some minority children approach adolescence without a clear preference for their own group. There are fewer studies of preference beyond childhood. Ullah (1985) reports that 9% of second-generation Irish 14- to 18-year-olds in England "sometimes" or "often" hide the fact that they are of Irish descent. Evidence from interviews shows a persistence of out-group preference among some adolescents (Phinney, 1989), although more frequently mentioned are feelings of having wished at a younger age to be a member of the dominant group (Phinney & Chavira, in preparation):

> Before, there was an internal type of conflict. I remember I would not say I was Hispanic. My friends . . . were White and Oriental and I tried so hard to fit in with them.

> I am proud of who I am and I tell people when they ask me; I admit I used to try to hide it.

A preference for mainstream culture, or the wish to be a member of the dominant group, would seem to be incompatible with a secure ethnic identity. As adolescents explore identity options, other strategies suggested by Tajfel may come into play, such as trying to "pass," a strategy used by adolescent Indian boys in Britain (Hogg, Abrams, & Patel, 1987).

Alternatively, minority youth may attempt to change the group's image by stressing positive aspects of their own culture. In contrast to earlier studies showing identification with the Caucasian majority, Milner (1984) found that young British-born West Indians have turned to alternative and positive cultural identities with the emergence of a black British youth culture stressing the positive and unique features of black identity. As with Milner's West Indian adolescents, Ullah (1985, 1987) found that Irish youth in Britain, an ethnic minority that is the target of prejudice and discrimination, are redefining group membership by enhancing their own group characteristics compared with the out-group, in this case the dominant English majority. A similar strategy is evident among Greek-Australian high school students (Gilds, Rosenthal, & Young, 1985), who held exaggerated views of their group's economic and business influence. Movements stressing ethnic pride have likewise developed among African-American and Mexican-American groups in the United States.

The notion of duality, double consciousness, or biculturality is a persistent theme in much research on ethnic minorities (see, for example, Jaynes & Williams, 1989). The description of African-Americans as having "two warring idols in one dark body" (DuBois, 1963, p. 17) is a good example of the commonly expressed view that individuals must choose between two conflicting or competing identities. Yet most studies suggest that ethnic identity is not a bipolar dimension, with ties to the ethnic minority at one end and to the host culture at the other. Rather than considering maintenance of an ethnic identity to be incompatible with identification with the dominant culture, Berry (1980) argues that the two are independent; it is possible to maintain or enhance one's ties with both groups, to varying degrees. Studies of Indians living in Britain (Hutnik, 1986), Armenian-Americans (Der-Karabetian, 1980), Jewish-Americans (Zak, 1973), Chinese-Americans (Ting-Toomey, 1981), and Greek- and Italian-Australians (Rosenthal & Hrynevich, 1985) have all shown two coexisting identities without evidence of conflict between the two.

Nevertheless, other studies report a more complex picture. Elias and Blanton (1987) explored affective, behavioral, and cognitive dimensions of ethnic identity in Israeli-Jewish families living in the United States and found that the relationship between Israeli, Jewish, and American identities differed, depending on the dimension. Other studies using ethnographic methods have shown that the ways in which minority youth relate to the dominant culture involve not just more or less identification with each group but rather qualitatively different ways of relating. Vigil (1979) and Matute-Bianchi (1986) provide descriptions of high school students of Mexican descent, who choose among various ethnic identities: Mexican-oriented, Anglo-oriented, Mexican-American, Chicano, or Cholo. These identities are characterized by varying attitudes toward Mexican culture and toward the mainstream culture of the high school, as well as differing personal styles, academic performance, and proficiency in Spanish. Likewise, Ogbu (1985) reviews studies that identify various types of adaptation to inner-city life among African-American adolescents; the Square or Ivy Leaguer (mainstream oriented), the Regular or the Cool Cat (street-wise), the Jester (prankster), and the Antagonist (fighter). A case study of a West Indian adolescent in Britain (Weinreich, 1979) illustrates the process by which youth examine identity options.

Focusing specifically on African-American youth, several writers discuss extreme choices made by some youth, of either an "oppositional" identity, that is, defining themselves in contrast to the Caucasian culture (Ogbu, 1987), or becoming "raceless," that is, rejecting their blackness (Fordham, 1988, Fordham & Ogbu, 1986). African-American youth who try to achieve success by Caucasian standards face opposition from other African-Americans; "their behaviors tend to be interpreted not only as 'acting White' but also as a betrayal of Black people" (Ogbu, 1987, p. 166). Thus, African-American students have to choose between "acting Black" and "acting White." Those who develop an oppositional identity limit their opportunities in the mainstream culture; those who opt for success in school and in the mainstream do so by "minimizing their relationship to the Black community and to the stigma attached to 'Blackness' " (Fordham, 1988, p. 57).

Yet some minority youth appear to have developed strategies for handling such conflicts (Phinney & Chavira, in preparation). As one Mexican-American male high school student puts it:

> [Some Hispanic friends] say that I am never going to make it. They try and hold me down . . . I get angry but that anger makes me strive for more . . . I don't fight against them, I just leave them alone and try to strive more for myself.

Others feel that they are able to negotiate the demands made on them in differing cultural contexts:

> Being invited to someone's house, I have to change my ways of how I act at home, because of culture differences. I would have to follow what they do . . . I am used to it now, switching off between the two. It is not difficult.

> When I am around my people, I feel more Hispanic. Like at school, it is all English and at my job it is all English . . . I can really be both. I know what to do and what to expect. No problem.

In summary, society presents a range of conflicting messages to minority youth, who adapt to these pressures in many different ways. Ultimately, how they deal with their ethnicity is likely to have important implications for their self-concept.

Ethnic Identity and Self-Concept

In earlier sections of this [selection], we have assumed that achieving a positive sense of ethnic identity is a healthy outcome for minority youth. We can explore this assumption further by investigating the link between ethnic identity and feelings of self-worth in adolescents. There is a good precedent for this strategy since there is evidence from studies of adolescent identity that an achieved ego identity is associated with high self-esteem (e.g., Waterman, 1984). Adolescence is a time of intense preoccupation with self and self-presentation. How they appear to others is a matter of great consequence to adolescents (Elkind, 1967). Imagining the reactions of others to one's self is likely to have a profound effect on one's self-esteem, especially for adolescents who are not part of the mainstream, who are "different" from their peers.

In early research on the self-esteem of ethnic minority children and youth, the underlying expectation was that poor self-esteem would result from factors such as low status, poverty, and perceptions of prejudice and discrimination. In an extended discussion of this question, Tajfel (1978) states that "People who are members of minorities . . . share one difficult psychological problem, which can be described . . . as a conflict between a satisfactory self-realization and the restrictions imposed upon it by the realities of membership in a minority group" (p. 9). However, most recent studies have shown no relationship between ethnicity and self-esteem. A difficulty with much research on this topic has been the lack of a clear distinction between ethnicity and ethnic identity; that is, while purporting to measure ethnic identity, researchers simply use ethnic group membership as the variable of interest, without assessing the adolescent's sense of belonging to the group (self-identification), evaluation of his or her group membership (ethnic pride), or any other aspect of ethnic identity.

In several studies which have examined more closely the effect of levels of ethnic identity on self-esteem, ethnic group membership coupled with a sense of ethnic pride has shown a positive relationship to adolescents' sense of self-worth. Grossman, Wirt, and Davids (1985) found that ethnic esteem mediated between ethnic group and self-esteem in a sample of Chicano adolescents, and racial acceptance was positively correlated with self-esteem in African-Americans (Paul & Fisher, 1980).

Two recent studies of Italian Australian and Anglo-Australian young women (Grieve, Rosenthal, & Cavallo, 1988; Rosenthal & Grieve, 1990) provide insights into the complexity of the relationship between ethnic identity and self-esteem. In a study of high school students, levels of self-esteem were similar in the two groups, but the correlates of self-esteem differed. Unlike the Anglo-Australians, whose self-esteem was associated also with masculine characteristics, the self-esteem of the Italian-Australian girls was associated with stereotypic feminine attributes and preoccupations. In an older sample of college students, those young women who were more highly identified with their Italian culture were both more traditional in their attitudes to the role of women in society (and especially motherhood) and more satisfied with being female than were their more assimilated peers. At the same time, these young women held firmly to a belief in the importance of a career. Rosenthal and Grieve concluded that these contradictory sets of attitudes, especially for those who strongly identified with their ethnic group, may be a source of difficulty should these young women attempt to combine a career with motherhood.

This line of research suggests that the consequences of minority group membership for an individual's sense of self-worth are not due to minority status per se but are mediated by other factors, such as the gender role prescriptions in a society. Research in Australia suggests that minority girls are more likely to be at risk when they come from cultures where sex roles are sharply differentiated and males are accorded greater prestige (Rosenthal, Moore, & Taylor, 1983). Other societal features that have been implicated as mediating the self-esteem of minority adolescents are the presence or absence of a strong and structured ethnic community whose members are involved and committed, and the extent to which adolescents perceive prejudice and discrimination toward the group (Rosenthal & Cichello, 1986; Rosenthal et al., 1983).

Another mediating factor is the process by which adolescents consciously deal with the realities of their ethnic group membership. Some of these strategies have been discussed earlier, in examining the research on social identity. Research that focuses on the issue developmentally provides another perspective. Just as other research indicates that positive psychological outcomes are associated with an achieved identity (Marcia, 1980), Phinney and her colleagues (Phinney, 1989; Phinney & Alipuria, 1990) propose that an achieved ethnic identity (that is, exploration of the issues raised by one's ethnicity, resulting in a resolution of these issues and a commitment to an ethnic identity) contributes positively to self-esteem. They suggest that commitment to an ethnic identity is a critical feature of the self-concept of minority youth and one that mediates the impact of minority status on adjustment (Phinney, Lochner, & Murphy, 1990). This prediction has been supported in a series of studies. Phinney (1989) found that African-American, Asian-American, and Mexican-American adolescents who showed greater resolution of their ethnic identity had significantly higher scores on four measures of psychological adjustment, including self-esteem. This relationship was confirmed in further studies of high school students and college students (Phinney, 1992; Phinney & Alipuria, 1990). Of interest in these studies was the finding that there was generally little relationship between ethnic identity and self-esteem for the Caucasian college students, supporting the conclusions that an achieved ethnic identity is more closely tied to self-esteem for minority youth than majority youth.

The study by Phinney and Alipuria (1990) highlights the complex nature of the interaction between ethnic identity and self-esteem. The results showed consistently higher correlations with self-esteem for ethnic commitment than ethnic search, and fluctuations in these correlations as a function of ethnic group and of gender. Asian-Americans (and females in particular) were more like their Western peers, with only modest correlations between ethnic identity and self-esteem. More substantial correlations were found for African-American and Mexican-American youth. A possible explanation is that the Asian-Americans enjoy special status and prestige as models and high-achieving students, a position not shared by their African-American and Mexican-American peers.

A study of Mexican-American and Japanese American high school students (Matute-Bianchi, 1986) supports this view. For the students of Japanese descent, the issue of their identity as a distinct ethnic group was not relevant to their identity as students, and they tended not to engage in ethnically linked activities; rather, they were active in the mainstream clubs of the school. In contrast, the students of Mexican descent used ethnic identity as a response to their subordinate status in the school community and were more invested in their ethnicity.

The actual process by which minority youth wrestle with and resolve issues associated with cultural conflict, stereotypes, or discrimination, in order to maintain a positive self-concept, is further elucidated in interviews with Asian-American, African-American, and Hispanic high school students (Phinney & Chavira, in preparation). Interviews were conducted with two groups of students, those scoring relatively high or relatively low on ethnic identity. The issues and conflicts about their ethnicity faced by these youth are similar in both groups; for example:

> I am not ashamed of being Hispanic but . . . I am disappointed because I compare the Hispanic race to other races . . . We have not done much.

> I am very proud of my ethnicity, I am very proud of some of the good things my culture has done, and then again, there are certain things like in every culture, there are always some people who have to ruin it for everybody.

Most of the students had experience with both stereotypes and discrimination, and both high and low ethnic identity students felt that it was appropriate at times to ignore ethnic slurs and prejudice. However, significantly more high ethnic identity youth, when asked how they dealt with such incidents, stated that they would respond actively, by pointing out why stereotypes were inaccurate or why discrimination was wrong; for example:

I'm going to let them know, just because you see that on TV, that's not reality.

You talk about it and you try to change things. You try to make people see you not as White, Black, Asian, just see you for who you are and what you can do.

The people I can help, the people I can reach, I try to talk to them.

Furthermore, a high ethnic identity was associated with an understanding that the prejudice was not personally directed at oneself:

A lot of times we have been put down. Before, it used to hurt me a lot emotionally, because I did kind of feel that I was not as good as [the Caucasian students] were. . . . I think I matured. . . . What I saw is how ignorant people could be to think that another person who is of a different color or of a different ethnic group is not as smart.

Adolescents who have achieved a secure, comfortable ethnic identity have dealt with their ambivalence, rejected negative stereotypes, and resolved for themselves conflicts associated with their ethnicity. They feel good about themselves:

I am what I am, and I don't know if that is Asian or if that is American . . . I usually think of myself as totally Americanized, [but] I know I don't want to [be] American [i.e., Caucasian], like brown hair and blue eyes. I am proud to be Japanese American.

I am proud of my heritage and I am also proud that I know how to speak English and that I was born and raised here. I am happy the way I am.

In summary, it is clear that the links between self-esteem, ethnicity, and ethnic identity are not straightforward. The relationship between ethnic identity and psychological well-being varies depending on the particular ethnic group, including the cohesiveness of the group and its status in society; environmental factors, such as family, school, and peers; as well as the adolescent's way of dealing with his or her ethnicity within a particular social context. This complexity highlights the need to go beyond simple correlations between ethnic identity and self-esteem, if we are to "unpackage" the true contributions of ethnic identity to well-being.

Summary and Conclusions

The material presented in this [selection] establishes that ethnic identity is a critical developmental issue for ethnic minority adolescents. In spite of differences among groups, it is clear that the family, community, and societal contexts in which adolescents develop pose a number of conflicts that minority youth must resolve in establishing an ethnic identity. These issues and conflicts do not necessarily result in psychological problems for minority youth, who are no more likely than other adolescents to suffer from low self-esteem. Rather, minority youth, like all adolescents, face a specific range of identity questions, depending on their own particular life experiences and the resources they bring to deal with these questions. As with many issues faced by adolescents, questions about ethnicity are likely to involve competing, often ambivalent feelings. They are not a matter of a simple choice, for example, between close family ties and relationships with members of other groups, or between preference for one's own group and admiration for the mainstream culture. In each instance, elements of contrasting views are likely to coexist to varying degrees. One's ethnicity can provide supportive roots and also limiting stereotypes; it can be a source of pride but also discomfort. The identity task is to integrate these contrasting elements, together with one's own inclinations and options, to achieve a unified sense of self as an ethnic group member.

The research to date has provided only a sketchy, fragmented picture of this process, both because of limitations in the theoretical frameworks used for studying ethnic identity and because of methodological problems in the research itself. Much of the work has been atheoretical, and studies of the same issues have drawn on widely differing theoretical frameworks. The central empirical problem to be dealt with is the multifaceted nature of ethnic identity and the complex and subtle relationships among its components, some of which are specific to particular groups while others apply across all groups. Reliable measures are needed for both specific components, such as particular ethnic practices and attitudes, and general aspects, such as a sense of belonging and commitment (Phinney, 1990). Furthermore, we need to ensure that the study of ethnic identity includes not only members of disparaged minorities (such as African-Americans, Hispanics, and indigenous minorities) but also minority groups that are admired, at least in some respects, by members of the mainstream culture (such as Asians).

A critical task in furthering our understanding is to provide a solid theoretical base by integrating developmental and social psychological perspectives, together with a consideration of contextual factors, as a foundation for future research. Erikson's theory provides a broad developmental view within which ethnic identity can be located. One point of interest is the relationship of ethnic identity to other aspects of ego identity, such as gender, political, and religious identities. Do these develop in synchrony? To what extent are they subject to common influences? What processes enable the minority adolescent to integrate ethnic identity with other identities into a "meta-identity"?

While adolescence is seen as the focal period for ethnic identity formation, a life-span developmental perspective is essential, in order to elucidate the precursors of adolescent ethnic identity and to trace its impact beyond adolescence. We need, for example, to ask what are the antecedents in childhood of a positive ethnic identity at adolescence. What happens to ethnic identity in early and later adulthood, when the relatively sheltered environments of home and school are replaced by work and greater contact with the mainstream society? Questions such as these imply an urgent need for well-planned cross-lagged research designs, by means of which we can obtain information over time and over several cohorts.

The social psychological perspective, especially social identity theory, also has an important contribution to make to our understanding of the ways in which ethnic youth deal with minority status. For example, research is needed to explore why some youth can be comfortable living in, and moving between, two cultures, while others either separate themselves from the mainstream or attempt to assimilate completely. The impact of social class is an important area that has largely been ignored in ethnic identity research. Other broad contextual factors, such as the extent to which the society embraces pluralism, are likely to be critical. What are the consequences for minority youth of living in a mainstream culture that has a "melting pot," assimilationist ethos, versus a multicultural, pluralistic society? How does ethnic identity manifest itself in xenophobic societies where "outsiders" are never truly accepted?

Bronfenbrenner's (1979) ecological model of development provides a valuable framework for addressing contextual influences on ethnic identity development. His work and the research outlined [here] emphasize the need to consider these factors not in isolation but in interaction with each other. It is clear from research cited here that contextual factors, such as parenting practices or community supports, do not exert an influence individually but interact in ways that demand multivariate research designs if we are to do justice to the complexity of family and social influences. We can extend Lerner's goodness-of-fit notion (Lerner, Lerner, & Tubman, 1989) to the important issue of the match between what the environment demands of minority youth, *qua* minority youth, and the special competencies, needs, and attitudes of these youth. When the expectations of the environment and youth match, we can expect positive outcomes for ethnic identity development.

Finally, we need also to consider the conditions under which ethnic identity becomes a salient issue for majority youth. In times of changing demographics and economic uncertainty, when majority group numbers are shrinking relative to those in ethnic minorities, when there is considerable movement between societies, and when there appears to be a resurgence of ethnic pride among many minorities, then majority youth may also be forced to confront the meaning and value that their ethnic group membership has for them.

References

Aboud, F. (1987). The development of ethnic self-identification and attitudes. In J. Phinney & M. Rotheram (Eds.), *Children's ethnic socialization: Pluralism and development.* Newbury Park, CA: Sage.

Alba, R., & Chamin, M. D. (1983). A preliminary examination of ethnic identification among whites. *American Sociological Review, 48,* 240–242.

Andujo, E. (1988). Ethnic identity of transethnically adopted Hispanic adolescents. *Social Work, 33,* 531–535.

Arce, C. (1981). A reconsideration of Chicano culture and identity. *Daedalus, 110* (2), 177–192.

Atkinson, D., Morten, G., & Sue, D. (1983). *Counseling American minorities.* Dubuque, IA: Wm. C. Brown.

Bernal, M., Knight, G., Garza, C., Ocampo, K., & Cota, M. (1990). The development of ethnic identity in Mexican American children. *Hispanic Journal of Behavioral Sciences, 12,* 3–24.

Berry, J. (1980). Acculturation as varieties of adaption. In A. Padilla (Ed.), *Acculturation: Theory, models, and some new findings.* Boulder, CO: Westview.

Breton, R. (1964). Institutional completeness of ethnic communities and the personal relations of immigrants. *American Journal of Sociology, 70,* 193–205.

Bronfenbrenner, U. (1979). *The ecology of human development.* Cambridge, MA: Harvard University Press.

Cross, W. (1978). The Thomas and Cross models of psychological nigrescence: A literature review. *Journal of Black Psychology, 4,* 13–31.

Davey, A. (1983). *Learning to be prejudiced: Growing up in multi-ethnic Britain.* London: Edward Arnold.

Der-Karabetian, A. (1980). Relation of two cultural identities of Armenian-Americans. *Psychological Reports, 47,* 123–128.

Deschamps, J. C. (1982). Social identity and relations of power between groups. In H. Tajfel (Ed.), *Social identity and intergroup relations.* Cambridge: Cambridge University Press.

Driedger, L. (1976). Ethnic self-identity: A comparison of ingroup evaluations. *Sociometry, 39,* 131–141.

DuBois, W. E. B. (1963). *An ABC of color.* Berlin: Seven Seas Books.

Elias, N., & Blanton, J. (1987). Dimensions of ethnic identity in Israeli Jewish families living in the United States. *Psychological Reports, 60,* 367–375.

Elkind, D. (1967). Egocentrism in adolescence. *Child Development, 38,* 1025–1034.

Erikson, E. H. (1968). *Identity: Youth and crisis.* New York: Norton.

Fordham, S. (1988). Racelessness as a factor in black students' school success: Pragmatic strategy or Pyrrhic victory? *Harvard Educational Review, 58,* 54–84.

Fordham, S., & Ogbu, J. (1986). Black students' school success: Coping with the burden of "acting white." *The Urban Review, 18,* 176–206.

Garcia, J. (1982). Ethnicity and Chicanos: Measurement of ethnic identification, identity, and consciousness. *Hispanic Journal of Behavioral Sciences, 4,* 295–314.

Garcia, M., & Lega, L. (1979). Development of Cuban ethnic identity questionnaire. *Hispanic Journal of Behavioral Sciences, 1,* 247–261.

George, R., & Hoppe, R. (1979). Racial identification, preference, and self-concept. *Journal of Cross-Cultural Psychology, 10,* 85–100.

Giles, H., Llado, N., McKirnan, D. H., & Taylor, D. M. (1979). Social identity in Puerto Rico. *International Journal of Psychology, 14,* 185–201.

Giles, H., Rosenthal, D. A., & Young, L. (1985). Perceived ethnolinguistic vitality: The Anglo- and Greek-Australian setting. *Journal of Multilingual and Multicultural Development, 6,* 253–269.

Giles, H., Taylor, D. M., Lambert, W. E., & Albert, G. (1976). Dimensions of ethnic identity: An example from Northern Maine. *Journal of Social Psychology, 100,* 11–19.

Grieve, N. R., Rosenthal, D. A., & Cavallo, A. (1988). Self-esteem and sex-role attitudes: A comparison of Italian- and Anglo-Australian adolescent girls. *Psychology of Women Quarterly, 12,* 175–189.

Grossman, B., Wirt, R., & Davids, A. (1985). Self-esteem, ethnic identity, and behavioral adjustment among Anglo and Chicano adolescents in West Texas. *Journal of Adolescence, 8,* 57–68.

Harrison, A. O. (1985). The black family's socializing environment: Self-esteem and ethnic attitude among black children. In H. P. McAdoo & J. L. McAdoo (Eds.), *Black children* (pp. 174–193). Newbury Park, CA: Sage.

Hogg, A., Abrams, D., & Patel, Y. (1987). Ethnic identity, self esteem and occupational aspirations of Indian and Anglo-Saxon British adolescents. *Genetic, Social and General Psychology Monographs, 113,* 487–508.

Hunt, J., & Hunt, L. (1977). Racial inequality and self-image: Identity maintenance as identity diffusion. *Sociology and Social Research, 61,* 539–559.

Hutnik, N. (1986). Patterns of ethnic minority identification and modes of social adaption. *Ethnic and Racial Studies, 9,* 150–167.

Jaynes, G., & Williams, R. (1989). *A common destiny: Blacks and American society* (Chapter 4). Washington, DC: National Academy Press.

Keefe, S., & Padilla, A. (1987). *Chicano ethnicity.* Albuquerque: University of New Mexico Press.

Lerner, R., Lerner, J., & Tubman, J. (1989). Organismic and contextual biases of development in adolescence: A developmental contextual view. In G. Adams, R. Montemayor, & T. Gullotta (Eds.), *Biology of adolescent behavior and development*. Newbury Park, CA: Sage.

Maccoby, E. E., & Martin, J. (1983). Socialization in the context of the family: Parent-child interaction. In M. E. Hetherington (Ed.), *Handbook of child psychology: Vol. 4. Socialization, personality, and social development* (pp. 1–102). New York: John Wiley.

Marcia, J. (1980). Identity in adolescence. In J. Adelson (Ed.), *Handbook of adolescent psychology* (pp. 159–187). New York: John Wiley.

Marcia, J., & Kowaz, A. (1988, April). *Current research directions in psychological development theory*. Paper presented at the Western Psychological Association meeting, Burlingame, CA.

Matute-Bianchi, M. (1986). Ethnic identities and pattern of school success and failure among Mexican-descent and Japanese-American students in a California high school: An ethnographic analysis. *American Journal of Education, 95,* 233–255.

McGuire, W., McGuire, C., Child, P., & Fujioka, T. (1978). Salience of ethnicity in the spontaneous self-concept as a function of one's ethnic distinctiveness in the social environment. *Journal of Personality and Social Psychology, 36,* 511–520.

McRoy, R., Zurcher, L., Lauderdale, M., & Anderson, R. (1984). The identity of transracial adoptees. *Social Casework, 65,* 34–39.

Milner, D. (1984). The development of ethnic attitudes. In H. Tajfel (Ed.), *The social dimension: European developments in social psychology* (Vol. 1). Cambridge: Cambridge University Press.

Nobles, W. W. (1973). Psychological research and the black self-concept; A critical review. *Journal of Social Issues, 29,* 11–31.

Ogbu, J. (1985). A cultural ecology of competence among inner-city blacks. In M. Spencer, G. Brooks, & W. Allen (Eds.), *Beginnings: The social and affective development of black children*. Hillsdale, NJ: Lawrence Erlbaum.

Ogbu, J. (1987). Opportunity structure, cultural boundaries and literacy. In J. Langer (Ed.), *Language, literacy, and culture: Issues of society and schooling*. Norwood, NJ: Ablex.

Padilla, A. M. (1980). The role of cultural awareness and ethnic loyalty in acculturation. In A. M. Padilla (Ed.), *Acculturation: Theory, models and some new findings,* Boulder, CO: Westview.

Parham, T. (1989). Cycles of psychological nigrescence. *The Counseling Psychologist, 17,* 187–226.

Parham, T., & Helms, J. (1981). Influence of a black student's racial identity attitudes on preference for counselor race. *Journal of Counseling Psychology, 28,* 250–257.

Paul, M., & Fischer, J. (1980). Correlates of self-concept among black early adolescents. *Journal of Youth and Adolescence, 9,* 163–173.

Peters, M. F. (1985). Racial socialization of young black children. In H. P. McAdoo & J. L. McAdoo (Eds.), *Black children* (pp. 159–173). Newbury Park, CA: Sage.

Phinney, J. (1989). Stages of ethnic identity development in minority group adolescents. *Journal of Early Adolescence, 9,* 34–49.

Phinney, J. (1990). Ethnic identity in adolescents and adults: A review of research. *Psychological Bulletin, 180,* 499–514.

Phinney, J. (1992). The multigroup ethnic identity measure: A new scale for use with adolescents and young adults from diverse groups. *Journal of Adolescent Research, 2.*

Phinney, J., & Chavira, V. (in press). Ethnic identity and self-esteem: An exploratory longitudinal study. *Journal of Adolescence.*

Phinney, J., & Chavira, V. (in preparation). Parental ethnic socialization and adolescents' ethnic attitudes.

Phinney, J., & Alipuria, L. (1990). Ethnic identity in college students from four ethnic groups. *Journal of Adolescence, 13,* 171–183.

Phinney, J., Lochner, B. T., & Murphy, R. (1990). Ethnic identity development and psychological adjustment in adolescence. In A. Stiffman & L. Davis (Eds.), *Ethnic issues in adolescent mental health*. Newbury Park, CA: Sage.

Phinney, J., & Nakayama, S. (1991, April). Parental influence on ethnic identity formation in minority adolescents. Paper presented at the biennial meeting of the Society for Research on Child Development, Seattle, WA.

Phinney, J., & Tarver, S. (1988). Ethnic identity search and commitment in black and white eighth graders. *Journal of Early Adolescence, 8,* 265–277.

Rosenthal, D. A. (1987). Ethnic identity development in adolescents. In J. S. Phinney & M. J. Rotheram (Eds.), *Children's ethnic socialization: Pluralism and development.* Newbury Park, CA: Sage.

Rosenthal, D. A., & Chichello, A. (1986). The meeting of two cultures: Ethnic identity and psychological adjustment of Italian-Australian adolescents. *International Journal of Psychology, 21,* 487–501.

Rosenthal, D. A., & Feldman, S. S. (in press a). The nature and stability of ethnic identity in Chinese youth: Effects of length of residence in two cultural contexts. *Journal of Cross-Cultural Psychology.*

Rosenthal, D. A., & Feldman, S. S. (in press b). The relationship between parenting behavior and ethnic identity in Chinese-American and Chinese-Australian adolescents. *International Journal of Psychology.*

Rosenthal, D. A., & Grieve, N. R. (1990). Attitudes to the gender culture: A comparison of Italian-Australian and Anglo-Australian female tertiary students. *Australian Psychologist, 25,* 282–292.

Rosenthal, D. A., & Hrynevich, C. (1985). Ethnicity and ethnic identity: A comparative study of Greek-, Italian-, and Anglo-Australian adolescents. *International Journal of Psychology, 20,* 723–742.

Rosenthal, D. A., Moore, S. M., & Taylor, M. J. (1983). Ethnicity and adjustment: A study of the self-image of Anglo-, Greek-, and Italian-Australian working-class adolescents. *Journal of Youth and Adolescence, 12,* 117–135.

Rotheram, M., & Phinney, J. (1987). Definitions and perspectives in the study of children's ethnic socialization. In J. Phinney & M. Rotheram (Eds.), *Children's ethnic socialization: Pluralism and development.* Newbury Park, CA: Sage.

Salgado de Snyder, N., Lopez, C. M., & Padilla, A. M. (1982). Ethnic identity and cultural awareness among the offspring of Mexican interethnic marriages. *Journal of Early Adolescence, 2,* 277–282.

Semaj, J. (1980). The development of racial evaluation and preference: A cognitive approach. *The Journal of Black Psychology, 6,* 59–79.

Silverstein, B., & Krate, R. (1975). *Children of the dark ghetto.* New York: Praeger.

Spencer, M. (1982). Personal and group identity of black children: An alternative synthesis. *Genetic Psychology Monographs, 106,* 59–84.

Spencer, M. (1983). Children's cultural values and parental child rearing strategies. *Developmental Review, 4,* 351–370.

Spencer, M., & Dornbusch, S. M. (1990). Minority youth in America. In S. S. Feldman & G. R. Elliott (Eds.), *At the threshold: The developing adolescent* (pp. 123–146). Cambridge, MA: Harvard University Press.

Stack, C. B. (1974). *All our kin.* New York: Harper & Row.

Steinberg, L. D. (1990). Interdependency in the family: Autonomy, conflict and harmony in the parent-adolescent relationship. In S. S. Feldman & G. R. Elliott (Eds.), *At the threshold: The developing adolescent* (pp. 255–276). Cambridge, MA: Harvard University Press.

Szapocznik, J., & Kurtines, W. (1980). Acculturation, biculturalism, and adjustment among Cuban Americans. In A. M. Padilla (Ed.), *Acculturation: Theory, models, and some new findings.* Boulder, CO: Westview.

Taft, R. (1985). The psychological study of the adjustment and adaptation of immigrants in Australia. In N. T. Feather (Ed.), *Australian psychology: Review of research.* Sydney: Allen & Unwin.

Tajfel, H. (1978). *The social psychology of minorities.* New York: Minority Rights Group.

Tajfel, H. (1981). *Human groups and social categories: Studies in social psychology.* New York: Cambridge University Press.

Taylor, R. (1989). Black youth, role models, and the social construction of identity. In R. Jones (Ed.), *Black adolescents.* Berkeley, CA: Cobb & Henry.

Thornton, M. C., Chatters, L. M., Taylor, R. J., & Allen, W. R. (1990). Sociodemographic and environmental correlates of racial socialization by black parents. *Child Development, 61,* 401–409.

Ting-Toomey, S. (1981). Ethnic identity and close friendship in Chinese-American college students. *International Journal of Intercultural Relations, 5,* 383–406.

Triandis, H. C., Kashima, Y., Shimada, E., & Villareal, M. (1986). Acculturation indices as a means of confirming cultural differences. *International Journal of Psychology, 21,* 43–70.

Ullah, P. (1985). Second generation Irish youth: Identity and ethnicity. *New Community, 12,* 310–320.

Ullah, P. (1987). Self-definition and psychological group formation in an ethnic minority. *British Journal of Social Psychology, 26,* 17–23.

Vigil, D. (1979). Adaptation strategies and cultural life styles of Mexican-American adolescents. *Hispanic Journal of Behavioral Sciences, 1,* 375–392.

Waterman, A. (1982). Identity development from adolescence to adulthood: An extension of theory and a review of research. *Developmental Psychology, 18,* 341–358.

Waterman, A. (1984). *The psychology of individualism.* New York: Praeger.

Weinreich, P. (1979). Cross-ethnic identification and self-rejection in a black adolescent. In G. Verma & C. Bagley (Eds.), *Race, education, and identity.* New York: St. Martin's Press.

Yogev, A., & Jamsky, H. (1983). Children of ethnic intermarriage in Israeli schools: Are they marginal? *Journal of Marriage and the Family, 45,* 965–973.

Zak, I. (1973). Dimensions of Jewish-American identity. *Psychological Reports, 33,* 891–900.

Questions

1. How are issues of racial identity different from issues of ethnic identity?
2. What are the components of ethnic identity?
3. Can you have a strong ethnic identity if you do not speak the language, engage in ethnic traditions, or know much about your ethnic group's history?
4. How is ethnic identity related to social context?
5. When social context changes, as in the transition from home to college, how is ethnic identity impacted?
6. What is the relationship between ethnic identity and self-esteem?

References and Further Reading

Aries, E., & Moorehead, K. (1989). The importance of ethnicity in the development of identity in Black adolescents. *Psychological Reports, 65,* 75–82.

Martinez, R. O., & Dukes, R. L. (1997). The effects of ethnic identity, ethnicity, and gender on adolescent well-being. *Journal of Youth and Adolescence, 26*(5), 503–516.

Montemayor, R., Adams, G. R., & Gullotta, T. P. (Eds.). (2000). *Adolescent diversity in ethnic, economic, and cultural contexts.* Thousand Oaks, CA: Sage.

Phinney, J. S. (1990). Ethnic identity in adolescents and adults: Review of research. *Psychological Bulletin, 108*(3), 499–514.

Phinney, J. S. (1996). When we talk about American ethnic groups, what do we mean? *American Psychologist, 51*(9), 918–927.

Chapter 7

Social Class

Psychologists have paid relatively little attention to social class as a variable that shapes the lives of adolescents, leaving the understanding of class to the disciplines of sociology and economics. Until recently, psychological studies of adolescence have been based primarily on middle-class individuals. The adolescents from poor neighborhoods who have been studied are often nonwhite, and thus the role of race is impossible to separate from the role of social class. In the past 15 years, however, psychological research interest in how development is affected by economic resources and pressures has grown.

By the age of 2 or 3 children have acquired a gender identity, an understanding that they are male or female. By the age of 3 or 4 children are aware of their race, and by age 6 they have an understanding of its meaning and the denigration of color in our society. The acquisition of an understanding of one's social class has only begun to be studied, but appears to come later in development because it is a more difficult concept to grasp. A person's social class, unlike sex and race, is not based on discernible physical features. In addition, many children are exposed only to people of the same social class as themselves. Working-class students report becoming aware of social class during childhood. Often the awareness came from an incident when they were mocked for wearing a particular piece of clothing, for using a particular form of speech, for their hygiene, or for being unable to pay for a movie (Seider, 1998).

Social class, like sex and race, is a pervasive force shaping the lives of adolescents, and while individuals may not be aware of their social class early on in life, class introduces objective structural constraints into people's lives that they will come to understand and have to cope with in the process of coming of age. The impact of social class shapes the lives of children and adolescents in a variety of ways. First, the impact of social class is transmitted to children through both their families and the characteristics of the neighborhoods and communities in which they live. Economic hardship—unstable employment and/or low income—limits the types of neighborhoods in which one can afford housing and often results in poor families living in neighborhoods plagued by drugs, violence, and crime. Positive role models are not readily available in such neighborhoods, nor are quality schools.

Economic hardship adversely affects the emotional health of parents. Unsteady employment or unemployment poses a threat to parental self-esteem and self-respect, which are tied to being able to provide for the family. Parental stress, worry, and anxiety, in turn, adversely affect parenting behaviors and lead to increased family conflict and child abuse. Parents under economic pressure in dangerous neighborhoods are likely to believe that they cannot control their children's development. Parents who feel ineffectual are less likely to encourage and work with their children.

Social class shapes a person's opportunities for an education. Children bring to school the general cultural background, knowledge, and skills transmitted to them by their families. Most middle-class youngsters enter school with linguistic competence; they have been read to and are exposed to printed material in their homes, have visited museums and seen movies, and have a background that prepares them for academic achievement. Many youngsters growing up poor arrive at school lacking in skills and experiences valued by the dominant society, and are at a decided disadvantage. Working-class children are then blamed for their lower achievement, which is attributed to their flawed character, their lack of effort, ability, and motivation. Teachers hold lower expectations for these children, which further contributes to academic underachievement.

Class shapes one's attitudes and beliefs as well. Children growing up where success is rare, where effort is not linked directly to reward, do not always develop a strong sense of ambition. The decline in manufacturing jobs and the ascendancy of service jobs has led to a drop in wages and job security, and has reduced the possibility for job advancement, increased responsibilities, and wages. Adolescents from low-income neighborhoods are less likely to buy into "the promise" (Reading 1.1) that doing well in school leads to material success.

Much of the research on poor adolescents has focused on understanding negative outcomes, like low school achievement (Reading 7.1), delinquency (Reading 13.1), and teenage pregnancy (Reading 14.1). Research is just beginning to attend to the range of competent outcomes that may be achieved (Reading 7.2; Yoshikawa & Seidman, 2000). In addition, most of the research has been based on traditional developmental models of adolescence that may not be appropriate for understanding adolescents raised in poverty, but the development of new models based on non-middle-class adolescents is beginning to occur (Reading 7.3).

Additional Resources

References and Suggested Reading

Elder, G. H., Eccles, J. S., Ardelt, M., & Lord, S. (1995). Inner-city parents under economic pressure: Perspectives on the strategies of parents. *Journal of Marriage and the Family, 57,* 771–784.

MacLeod, J. (1995). *Ain't no makin' it: Aspirations and attainment in a low-income neighborhood.* Boulder, CO: Westview Press.

Seider, M. (1998). It's a class thing: Biographies of state college students. Unpublished paper, Massachusetts College of Liberal Arts.

Taylor, R. D., Jacobson, L., & Roberts, D. (2000). Ecological correlates of the social and emotional adjustment of African American adolescents. In R. Montemayor, G. R. Adams, & T. P. Gullotta (Eds.), *Adolescent diversity in ethnic, economic, and cultural contexts* (pp. 208–234). Thousand Oaks, CA: Sage.

Yoshikawa, H., & Seidman, E. (2000). Competence among urban adolescents in poverty: Multiple forms, contexts, and developmental processes. In R. Montemayor, G. R. Adams, & T. P. Gullotta (Eds.) *Adolescent diversity in ethnic, economic, and cultural contexts* (pp. 9–42). Thousand Oaks, CA: Sage.

On the Internet

http://www.personal.psu.edu/faculty/n/x/nxd10/teenfamily.htm#kunda

Adolescence: Change and Continuity—Family Changes: Social Class and Social Status

This site was produced by Pennsylvania State University students taking the following courses: Human Development and Family Studies 433: The Transition to Adulthood, and Human Development and Family Studies 239: Adolescent Development.

7.1   Jay MacLeod, 1995

Ain't No Makin' It: Aspirations and Attainment in a Low-Income Neighborhood

Jay MacLeod holds degrees in social studies and theology. He wrote *Minds Stayed on Freedom: The Civil Rights Struggle in the Rural South: An Oral History* with his wife Sally Asher (1991) and *Ain't No Makin' It: Aspirations and Attainment in a Low-Income Neighborhood* (1995). He is an Anglican priest.

Jay MacLeod opens his book with the following statement:

> "Any child can grow up to be president." So says the achievement ideology, the reigning social perspective that sees American society as open and fair and full of opportunity. In this view, success is based on merit, and economic inequality is due to differences in ambition and ability. Individuals do not inherit their social status; they attain it on their own. (MacLeod, 1995, p. 3).

MacLeod cites the myths that Americans are raised on, the legends of men like Andrew Carnegie who rose from rags to riches in the land of opportunity, the stories by Horatio Alger of boys who work tirelessly and are able to rise from poverty to achieve material success.

These myths, however, do not describe the experience of most poor youth who feel their chance for mobility is remote. Decades of quantitative sociological research have shown that the social class structure changes little from one generation to the next, that few who are born poor will attain great wealth (MacLeod, 1995). One of the important questions becomes how social class shapes the experience of coming of age. Bakan (Reading 1.1) suggests that we offer youth "the promise" that if they go to school and do the things they are "supposed to do" they will realize success, status, wealth, and power. Bakan suggests a danger occurs when adolescents perceive that doing what one is supposed to do does not lead to these rewards. When youth realize that they do not achieve status and power from improved academic performance, performance loses its meaning. Such is the case for many working-class youth. Similarly, Erik Erikson (Reading 5.1) suggests that part of the crisis of identity involves reworking the crisis of Trust versus Mistrust. In developing an identity, an adolescent needs a *trust in time,* a belief that it is worth working toward future goals. When youth believe that rewards will not be forthcoming despite the hard work that is put in, when they believe they will never attain a highly remunerative job, then they develop *time diffusion.* They lose a sense of trust in the future and motivation to aspire to middle-class jobs, opting instead to live for the moment.

Jay MacLeod examines the aspirations of working-class adolescent boys. The boys in his study grew up in a housing project whose residents were 65% white, 25% black, and 10% other minorities. Most households in the housing project were female-headed and 70% received some form of public assistance in addition to public housing. MacLeod describes the community as plagued by "overcrowding, unemployment, alcoholism, drug abuse, crime, and racism" (MacLeod, 1995, p. 6). MacLeod began his connection with the boys in his study as part of a summer job to set up a summer youth program while he was an undergraduate student at Harvard University. MacLeod was particularly struck by the fact that so many 12- and 13-year-old boys did not even aspire to middle-class jobs. He decided to write his undergraduate thesis at Harvard on the occupational aspirations of these youth. MacLeod finished his undergraduate thesis in 1984, but returned to the community in 1991 for additional intensive fieldwork to determine how these boys had fared as they moved into adulthood.

MacLeod focused on two groups of boys, one primarily white group called the Hallway Hangers and a second predominantly black group called the Brothers. The families of the Hallway Hangers had lived in public housing for many years. The educational attainments of the boys' parents and older brothers were low; many had not graduated from high school. Their employment histories were unstable, and when they found employment it was in menial, low-paying jobs. Parental authority was absent and parents played a limited role in the Hallway Hangers' lives. The families of the Brothers were marked likewise by low educational achievement and employment. More of the Brothers, however, had male authority figures living with them; their parents exercised a good deal of authority over them; more often their older brothers had finished high school; and their parents had high hopes for them, projecting their unfulfilled occupational aspirations onto their children.

The richness of the reading by MacLeod comes from the opportunity to hear the voices of the boys themselves, and the mix of those voices with an analysis of their experiences based on sociological theory. MacLeod provides insight into the ways in which social class shapes the lives of these adolescents, the development of their identities, and their beliefs and aspirations for the future.

Teenagers in Clarendon Heights: The Hallway Hangers and the Brothers

On any given day, except during the coldest winter months, the evening hours in Clarendon Heights are filled with activity. At one end of the housing development, elderly women sit on wooden benches and chat. In the center of the project, children play street hockey, kickball, stickball, or football, depending on the season. At the other end, teenage boys congregate in the stairwell and on the landing of one of the entries—doorway #13.

The Hallway Hangers: "You Gotta Be Bad"

This doorway and the area immediately outside it are the focus of activity for the Hallway Hangers, one of the two main peer groups of high-school-age boys living in Clarendon Heights. Composed of a core of eight youths, but including up to ten additional people who are loosely attached to the group, the Hallway Hangers are tough, streetwise, individuals who form a distinctive subculture. Except for Boo-Boo, who is black, and Chris, who is of mixed racial parentage, the Hallway Hangers are white boys of Italian or Irish descent. The eight members considered here range in age from sixteen to nineteen. Five have dropped out of school, two graduated last year,[1] and one continues to attend high school. They all smoke cigarettes, drink regularly, and use drugs. All but two have been arrested. Stereotyped as "hoodlums," "punks," or "burnouts" by outsiders, the Hallway Hangers are actually a varied group, and much can be learned from considering each member.

Frankie, the acknowledged leader of the Hallway Hangers, is of only medium height and weight, but his fighting ability is unsurpassed among teenagers in Clarendon Heights. Missing two front teeth from one of his few unsuccessful encounters, Frankie maintains a cool, calculating demeanor that only occasionally gives way to his fiery temper. He commands the respect of the other boys because he is a natural leader and because he comes from a family that is held in high esteem by the city's underworld. His brothers have been involved in organized crime and have spent time in prison; four of them were incarcerated at the time I conducted my research. Although Frankie is the ringleader of the Hallway Hangers, he has never been arrested—no small feat considering the scope of the group's criminal activity.

Whereas Frankie combines physical toughness and mental acuity, Slick, although no weakling, clearly possesses an abundance of the latter attribute. Very articulate and perceptive, Slick scored high on standardized tests and fared well in school when he applied himself (he dropped out last year). Slick gets along well on the street, where his quick wit and sharp tongue are major assets. Although his status falls short of Frankie's, Slick is accorded much respect by the other boys of Clarendon Heights.

As Slick is known for the strength of his intellect, Shorty is known for his physical toughness. When a teacher at the local high school remarked, "What makes someone tough has nothing to do with size or even muscle—it's the fear factor. If someone's fearless, crazy, he'll do anything," he doubtless had Shorty in mind. As his nickname implies, Shorty is small, but well built. His temper is explosive, and under the influence of alcohol or drugs, he has been known to accost strangers, beat up friends, or pull a knife on anyone who challenges him. On one occasion, he repeatedly stabbed himself in the head in a fit of masochistic machismo. Although Frankie and Slick also consider themselves alcoholics, Shorty's drinking problem is more severe. The county court ordered him to a detoxification center—an arrangement Shorty has slyly managed to avoid.

Like the other three boys, Chris is a self-professed alcoholic who also admits to being dependent on marijuana. Chris's father (who does not live at home) is black, and his mother is white, which gives Chris an ethnic heritage that makes his acceptance by the rest of the Hallway Hangers difficult. A tall, very slender youth, Chris is loud and talkative but without the self-confidence and poise of Slick or Frankie. He is often the object of the other boys' abuse, both verbal and physical, but nevertheless has some stature in the group largely because of his loyalty and sense of humor.

Boo-Boo, the other black member of the Hallway Hangers, is a tall, quiet, dark-skinned youth. His serious nature makes him a less frequent target of abuse, which begins as playful racial barbs but often degenerates into downright racial animosity. Like Chris, Boo-Boo is a follower. A sincere and earnest boy, his general demeanor is at odds with the violence and bluster that characterize the group as a whole. Nevertheless, Boo-Boo has been known to fight—and quite effectively—when seriously antagonized and generally is held in moderate esteem by the rest of the boys.

Like Boo-Boo, Stoney is a bit of a loner. The only Hallway Hanger to hold stable employment, Stoney works full time in a pizza shop. His regular income, which he recently used to buy a car, earns him a measure of deference from the other boys, but Stoney lacks the cockiness and bravado necessary for high stature within the group. Skinny and averse to street fights, Stoney perpetually but ineffectively strives to rid himself of the label "pussy." Stoney does share with the other boys an enthusiasm for beer and drugs; he has been arrested for possession of mescaline and is psychologically dependent on marijuana. He has a steady girlfriend (another anomaly for the Hallway Hangers, who generally reject serious relationships in favor of more casual romantic encounters) with whom he spends much of his time, but Stoney still values the friendship of the Hallway Hangers and remains an integral member of the group.

Steve, Slick's younger brother, is the stereotypical project youth. Constantly on the lookout for a free ride, Steve is insolent and loud but lacks his brother's sophistication. He is courageous, full of energy, and fights well, but Steve is not particularly popular with the other boys, who tolerate him as Slick's brother and as a person who can be counted on for support and loyalty in the most trying situations. Steve is the only Hallway Hanger still in school; he expects to graduate in two years (1986).

In contrast to Steve, Jinks is a sensitive, shy boy who shares with Stoney and Chris a psychological dependence on marijuana. Although he is considered immature and is taunted as a "mamma's boy" by some of the Hallway Hangers, Jinks seems to have inner reserves of confidence and self-esteem that protect his ego from such assaults. Lighthearted and understanding of others, Jinks is the only white member of the Hallway Hangers who is not overtly racist. Although he takes a good deal of abuse from the others, especially Frankie and Shorty, Jinks's acceptance as a bona fide member of the group is beyond question.

These boys come together in the late afternoon or early evening after dinner and "hang" in doorway #13 until late at night. They come to "see what's up," to "find out what's goin' down," to "shoot the shit," and, generally, to just pass the time. Smelling of urine, lined with graffiti, and littered with trash and broken glass, this hallway is the setting for much playful banter, some not so playful "capping" (exchange of insults), and an occasional fight. The odors of cigarette smoke, beer, and marijuana are nearly always present. During the weekend, there may be a case or two of beer, a nearly constant circulation of joints, and some cocaine, mescaline, or "angel dust" (PCP). Late at night, one occasionally stumbles upon a lone figure shooting up heroin.

In an inversion of the dominant culture's vocabulary and value scheme, the subculture of the Hallway Hangers is a world in which to be "bad" is literally to be good. A common characteristic of lower-class[2] teenage peer cultures, this emphasis on being bad is inextricably bound up with the premium put on masculinity, physical toughness, and street wisdom in lower-class culture. Slick, in articulating the prominence of this value for the Hallway Hangers, states in definite terms what being bad often involves.

(*in an individual talk*)

SLICK: You hafta make a name for yourself, to be bad, tough, whatever. You hafta be, y'know, be with the "in" crowd. Know what I mean? You hafta—it's just all part of growing up around here—you hafta do certain things. Some of the things you hafta do is, y'know, once in awhile you hafta, if you haven't gotten into a fight, if you have a fight up the high school, you're considered bad. Y'know what I mean? If you beat someone up up there, especially if he's black, around this way . . . if you're to be bad, you hafta be arrested. You hafta at least know what being' in a cell is like.

(*in a group discussion*)

JM: So how is it that to be what's good down here, to be respected . . .
SLICK: You gotta be bad.
FRANKIE: Yeah, if you're a straight A student, you get razzed.
SLICK: Then you're a fucking weirdo, and you shouldn't be living here in the first place.
SHORTY: No, you got people down here who don't drink and don't smoke.
SLICK: Who? Name one.
SHORTY: Crane, Bruce Crane.
FRANKIE: Yeah, but like he's sayin', whadda we think of Bruce Crane?
SHORTY: Fucking shithead (*all laugh*).

Thus, good grades in school can lead to ostracism, whereas time spent in prison earns respect. To be bad is the main criterion for status in this subculture; its primacy cannot be overemphasized, and its importance is implied continually by the boys.

Frankie carries the notion of being bad to the extreme, despite its offensiveness to conventional American values. In June 1983, John Grace, a bartender in a pub across the city, shot two police officers and was himself wounded in a gunfight in Clarendon Heights. All three survived, and at the time of this interview, Grace was awaiting trial in a county jail where two of Frankie's brothers were also serving time. "Fucking Grace, he's my man. He's taken care of. My brother says he'll have a fucking joint when he see him in his cell. He's in lock-up, but they take care of him. He's a big fucking dude. He's respected up there, man. He's the baddest. He shot a fucking cop. He's golden, he's there. That's the best you can fucking do."

Although such a drastic view is seldom voiced or acted upon by the Hallway Hangers, success for members of the peer group does involve physical and emotional toughness. In addition, a quick wit is essential, for much time is spent capping on one another.

(*in the hallway late one afternoon*)

SHORTY: (*drunk*) Hey Steve, what are you doing tonight?
STEVE: Nuttin'. Why?
SHORTY: You wanna suck my dick?
STEVE: You're the only gay motherfucker around here.
SHORTY: Yeah? Ask your girlfriend if I'm gay.
STEVE: Yeah, well, you ask your mother if I'm gay.

This type of sportive banter is common, a diversion to interrupt the boredom inherent in hanging in hallways for a good portion of the day.

JINKS: Everyone gets ragged on out there. It's just when you're high, y'know, you're drunk—you start ragging on people. Helps the time go by.

Sometimes, of course, real venom lies behind the words. In that case, size and strength are the crucial elements for success in an altercation. For behind all the posturing lies the reality of the pecking order, which is determined primarily by physical toughness. Fighting ability is the deciding factor for status demarcation within the group; those lacking in physical stature must compensate for it with aggressiveness and tenacity or learn to live with a lot of abuse, both verbal and physical.

For the Hallway Hangers, being bad entails the consumption of alcohol and the use of drugs on a regular basis. The boys are intoxicated for a good portion of almost every weekend and drink heavily during the week. During the summer, the level of drinking reaches staggering proportions, often involving the consumption of two or more "beer balls" (the equivalent of two and half cases of beer pressurized into a plastic ball about two feet in diameter) a day for a group of eight or ten boys. Although none of the Hallway Hangers is drunk constantly, Frankie, Shorty, Slick, and Chris all consider themselves alcoholics.

FRANKIE: See, the way we are right now, technically we are alcoholics. Y'know, I can go days without drinking alcohol. It ain't like I need it, but right now I want it, y'know; it helps me get through. Y'know, get through problems, whatever; it helps me get through. Take away all the fucking problems down here, and there would be no problems with alcohol.

Shorty is honest about the debilitating effects of his dependence on alcohol.

(*in a group discussion*)

SHORTY: I think when you're an alcoholic like me, man, you ain't gonna be able to hold no fucking job. You say things you fucking forget.
FRANKIE: Yeah, yeah. I hear ya.
SHORTY: I mean, I don't remember trying to stab my own brother in the back; my other brother caught me. That's when I knew I was dead-up an alcoholic. Then I stabbed myself and three other people.
JM: How'd you get to be an alcoholic in the first place?
SHORTY: Being with these motherfuckers (*all laugh*). These got me going. Frankie always used to drink before me. I only used to drink about a beer a night, and I used to get buzzed every night. It's like this now: six pack—Monday through Friday. Friday, it's a case, and when summer comes, it's . . .
ALL: Beer balls!

Most of these boys began drinking beer regularly at the age of thirteen or fourteen; their preferences now include whiskey and Peppermint Schnapps.

The Hallway Hangers also began smoking marijuana when they were twelve or thirteen years old, a tendency that has led many to use an assortment of heavier drugs as well. Most of them describe stages in their adolescence during which they used PCP, mescaline, valium, or THC (the chief intoxicant in marijuana). Only Chris admits to having used heroin; Frankie's experience is more typical of these boys.

(in a group interview)

FRANKIE: My drug was, my freshman and sophomore year, I was into THC, right?
   And you get a tolerance and shit, and you start doing three and four hits.
SLICK: Frankie was a junkie.
FRANKIE: Well, yeah, I didn't boot it [shoot it up], but I was addicted to it, definitely.

Having moderated what they now see as their youthful enthusiasm for different drugs, the Hallway Hangers generally limit themselves to marijuana and cocaine. All the Hallway Hangers smoke a great deal of marijuana; Chris, Jinks, and Stoney acknowledge their dependence on the drug. Marijuana joints circulate in doorway #13 almost as often as cans of beer, and all admit they get high before and during school.

(in an individual interview, before he dropped out of school)

JM: Chris, you get high a lot in school?
CHRIS: Oh, yeah. I'm high every time I go to school. I gotta be. Sometimes I even
   drink before I go—I'll have a few beers. It's too much if you don't. I'm a fucking
   alcoholic. I do a lot of cocaine. I'll do up cocaine whenever I can get it. Fucking
   expensive though.

Despite their own widespread use of marijuana and occasional consumption of cocaine, the Hallway Hangers have no respect for junkies or "dustheads," those who are addicted to heroin or angel dust.

(in an interview with Shorty and Slick)

SHORTY: Little Tony and them, fuckin' ten, twelve years old, smoking pot, taking
   drugs. And that ain't good, at that age, cuz me and him don't do drugs, maybe
   coke, y'know? Coke and pot. But a lot of other dudes out here, they'll be taking;
   they'll be shooting up and everything. We don't even bother with them.

Obviously, underage drinking and drug use are illegal, and the Hallway Hangers have made their share of trips to the police station and the courthouse. Stoney has three convictions, twice for possession of narcotics and once for passing stolen property. Boo-Boo has been arrested for "hot boxes" (stolen cars). Chris has assault with a deadly weapon in addition to some less serious convictions on his record. Shorty has been to court for larceny, assault with a deadly weapon, and other less substantial crimes. One of the older teenagers on the fringes of the Hallway Hangers was convicted of rape and sentenced to eighteen months in the maximum security state prison after his sophomore year in high school.

These, of course, represent only the crimes at which the Hallway Hangers have been caught. Their criminal activity is actually much more widespread. Those trusted by the Hallway Hangers are occasionally approached with offers for good deals on bicycles, stereo equipment, or musical instruments, all of which have been stolen. Chris makes serious money dealing drugs. Other Hallway Hangers make small amounts of cash selling drugs to friends and acquaintances.

JINKS: We all know how to make a fast buck on the street. Buy the pot, roll up joints, sell 'em for two bucks a joint. Pay thirty for a bag; get twenty-five bones out of a bag—there's fifty bucks for thirty bucks.

Jimmy Sullivan, an experienced and perceptive teacher of the adjustment class in which Frankie, Shorty, and Steve are, or were at one time, enrolled, gives a good description of the Hallway Hangers' criminal careers.

JS: One thing about these kids: Crime pays, and they know it. . . . It's so easy to go over to the hallowed halls across the street there [a large university] and pick up a bike. I know three or four stores in the city that will pay thirty to forty dollars for a good bike, no questions asked. They'll turn it over for a hundred fifty or two hundred bucks. What do these kids need money for? What do they care about? Beer, sneakers, joints. They're not going to work when they can make easy money through virtually riskless criminal enterprises. Only suckers are gonna work for that. As long as their expectations stay low and they only need a hundred bucks a week—as Steven said, "All I want is my beer money"—they're all set. Up to when they're seventeen years old there's no risk. But when they turn about eighteen, the peer group doesn't accept that anymore. If they could go on stealing bikes for the rest of their lives, I think they would. But when you're seventeen or eighteen and someone says, "Hey man, where'd you get the cash?" it's unacceptable to say, "Oh, stealing bikes, man." You've got to be into cars, dealing drugs, or holding people up. That's when the risk and fear start coming into it. For many of them, the easiest route is to get a job. Of course, some of them don't, and they end up in jail.

Although this dynamic certainly plays a role in the Hallway Hangers' rationale, the legal system's distinction between a juvenile and an adult is more important in their determination of whether or not crime pays.

(*in a group interview*)

JM: Most of you are seventeen or over now?

SLICK: Only Chris is sixteen.

JM: Doesn't that make a big difference in terms of what you're doing to get money?

SHORTY: Hey, I'm doin' good. I don't deal no more, Jay. I got a good job coming at the weapons lab; most likely I'm gonna get my brother one there.

FRANKIE: Yeah, you slow down. Seventeen—you're an adult.

SLICK: Yeah, at seventeen you start slowing down.

SHORTY: You gotta start thinking.

(*in a separate interview*)

FRANKIE: Now that I think about it, I should've did more crime when I was a juvenile cuz when you're a juvenile you get arrested a good eight or nine times before they put you away. So I could've did a lot more crime, but I don't really mind. It was all right. But yeah, that's what most people do is once they go to seventeen, they smarten up and say that's big-time prison. And I've had many good examples of what not to do. I know jail ain't no place for nobody, even though some of my brothers make a living out of it.

Like many urban slums, the teenage underworld of Clarendon Heights is characterized by predatory theft, and some of the Hallway Hangers specialize in "cuffing" drugs, stolen merchandise, and money off those who themselves are involved in illegal activity. Shorty and Frankie have sold hundreds of fake joints, robbed other drug pushers, and forced younger or less tough boys to give them a share of their illegal income. The consensus among the Hallway Hangers is that this type of thievery is morally more defensible than conventional theft. More importantly, there is less risk of detection, for the authorities are unlikely to become involved.

(*in a group discussion*)

SLICK: You chump off thieves, and then you're like a hero. At least you got him back, y'know? You steal off a fucking thief who makes his life off stealing off other people, then its like you're fucking . . .

FRANKIE: You rip off illegal people, y'know? You rip off dealers.

SHORTY: That's why if you deal, you gotta be able to kill.

FRANKIE: Yeah, sometimes it could mean your life if you get caught. But you can't get put in jail.

For those raised with a strong sense of law and order, these attitudes are difficult to fathom. The Hallway Hangers, for their part, however, cannot understand the contempt and disdain the upper classes display for their lifestyle and launch a counterattack of their own.

(*in a group interview*)

SLICK: All right, you get people making fucking over fifty thousand dollars, and they fucking ask us why do we hang there? What the fuck, man?

CHRIS: What else are we gonna do?

JINKS: They can go fuck themselves.

CHRIS: They want us to deal the drugs so they can buy them.

SLICK: See, they don't know what the deal is. See, they're just doing what we're doing, except they're doing it in a more respectable way. They're ripping off each other up there. That's all they're doing. They're all ripping each other off up there. But they're doing it in a fucking legal way.

FRANKIE: Yeah, check this out.

SHORTY: We ain't doin' it behind anybody's back.

FRANKIE: All them fucking businessmen, man. All them stockbrokers and shit in New York. All them motherfuckers are out to rip people off. There's more fucking scamming going on up there. They're like legally ripping everyone off.

SLICK: We're just doing it illegally.

This is an insightful, if incomplete, critique of the social order, but not one about which the Hallway Hangers get particularly upset. Rather, they accept it as a simple fact of life with an acquiescent attitude that is typical of their outlook.

An important characteristic of the subculture of the Hallway Hangers is group solidarity. Membership in the Hallway Hangers involves a serious commitment to the group: a willingness to put out for others and to look out for the rest of the group's well-being as well as one's own. This loyalty is the glue that holds the group together, and honoring it is essential. The requirements and limits of this commitment to the group are seldom expressed, but are such that Slick would not leave Shorty "hanging with the cops," even though to stay with Shorty resulted in his own arrest.

SHORTY: See, that's how Slick was that day we were ripping off the sneakers [from a nearby factory]. He figured that if he left me that would be rude, y'know? If he just let me get busted by myself and he knew I had a lot of shit on my head, that's what I call a brother. He could've. I could've pushed him right through that fence, and he coulda been *gone*. But no, he waited for me, and we both got arrested. I was stuck. My belly couldn't get through the fucking hole in the fence.

This cohesion between members of the Hallway Hangers is a striking characteristic of their subculture and one to which they constantly draw attention. Not only are they proud of their adoption of communitarian values, but they also see their "brotherhood" as inconsistent with conventional middle- and upper-class attitudes.

(*in a group discussion*)

SLICK: What it is, it's a brotherhood down here. We're all fucking brothers. There's a lot of backstabbing going on down here, down in the streets. But we're always there for each other. No shit. There's not a guy in here that wouldn't put out for one of the rest of us. If he needs something and I got it, I'll give it to him. Period. That's the way it works. It's a brotherhood. We're not like them up there—the rich little boys from the suburbs or wherever. There's a line there. On this side of the line we don't fuck with each other; we're tight.

FRANKIE: We'd chump them off [rob] on the other side, though.

SLICK: Fucking right. If he's got four hundred bucks in his pocket, there's more where that came from. Fuck him. But they also chump each other off; only they do it legally. How do you think they got rich—by fucking people over. We don't do that to each other. We're too fucking tight. We're a group. We don't think like them; we think for all of us.

FRANKIE: That's the fucking truth. If you don't have your fucking buddies, where are you? You're fucking no one. Nuttin'.

SLICK: If I had the choice, and this isn't just me but probably everyone in here, if I had the choice between being a good person and making it, I'd be a good person. That's just the way I am. If I had my bar exam tomorrow and these guys needed me, I'd go with them. That's just the way it is down here.

SHORTY: Yeah, you wanna be here with your family, with your friends; they're good people. You're comfortable with them. You don't feel right with these other people. I dunno. . . . You wanna be like them, y'know? You see they're rich; you wanna be rich. You can't be the poor one out of the crowd. You got all the crowd, and places like that—the suburbs—they're all rich. Y'know, a lot of places, they say quiet places; around here, you'll just be able to hang together, and nobody has that much money.

SLICK: But I'll tell you right now, you cannot find better friends because everybody's in the same boat. You'll find a few assholes, rats, whatever, but mostly when you have all of us, we all know everybody's poor. You're not better than me; I'm not better than him, y'know? Like, say if I have a hundred dollars or he has a hundred dollars, y'know, it's not just his or mine—it's *our* money. It goes between us, y'know what I mean? Like up there, it's not as tight. People aren't tight up there. I just came back from Fort Lauderdale, and I seen it up there. Real rich people, it's not like this at all.

These comments bear ample testimony to the solidarity that characterizes the subculture of the Hallway Hangers. This solidarity is not an ideal to which they only pay lip service; shared money, shared drugs, and shared risks in criminal activity are all facts of life in doorway #13.

At the same time that these boys affirm the lifestyle and values of people in their neighborhood, they assert with peculiar constancy their deeply felt desire to move with their families out of Clarendon Heights. Many of them want to make enough money to get their families out of the projects forever.

(all in separate discussions, unsolicited by me)

SLICK: Most of the kids down here, most of 'em wanna make money so they can help their families and help themselves to get out of this place. . . . My main concern is to get my family out of the projects.
CHRIS: I just wanna get my mother out of the projects, that's all.
SHORTY: All's I'm doing, I'm gonna get enough money, save enough money to get my mother the fuck out of here.

These statements are evidence of the stigma the Hallway Hangers, as public housing tenants, feel as a matter of course. Their pride in their lifestyle is pierced by the dominant culture's negative judgments. One implication of the culture's achievement ideology is that those of low socioeconomic stature are personally deficient. This negative evaluation and the inability of the Hallway Hangers to shield themselves completely from it combine to produce the deep ambivalence the boys feel toward themselves and their community.

Daily life for the Hallway Hangers is marked by unrelieved boredom and monotony. The boys are generally out of work, out of school, and out of money. In search of employment or a "fast buck on the street," high or drunk a good deal of the time, many are preoccupied with staying out of prison—a struggle some already have lost—and with surviving from one day to the next.

(in a discussion with Shorty and Slick)

SLICK: All through the teenage years around here, you hafta learn to survive, before you learn to do anything else.
SHORTY: Nobody learns anything from school around here. All it is is how to survive and have money in your pocket.
SLICK: You hafta learn how to survive first.
SHORTY: This is the little ghetto.

SLICK: Y'know, you hafta learn how to survive; if you can't survive, especially around here, that's why you see so many people who are just down and out. It's tough. That's what it is. It's tough. . . .

The Brothers: Conspicuous by Their Conventionality

In contrast to the Hallway Hangers, the Brothers accommodate themselves to accepted standards of behavior and strive to fulfill socially approved roles. It is the white peer group from Clarendon Heights that is at odds with mainstream American culture. Nonconformity fascinates the sociologist, and if in this [selection] undue attention is given to the distinctive cultural novelty of the Hallway Hangers, it should be borne in mind that the Brothers also pose an interesting and in many ways exceptional case. However, because my primary interest is the role that aspirations play in social reproduction, and because the Hallway Hangers undergo the process of social reproduction in a unique fashion, my emphasis in both the presentation of ethnographic material and in its analysis inevitably falls on the Hallway Hangers.

The most obvious difference between the two peer groups is in racial composition: The Brothers have only one white member. When one considers that this peer group emerges from the same social setting as do the Hallway Hangers, other striking differences become apparent. Composed of a nucleus of seven teenagers and expanding to twelve at times, this peer group is not a distinctive subculture with its own set of values defined in opposition to the dominant culture. The Brothers attend high school on a regular basis. None of them smokes cigarettes, drinks regularly, or uses drugs. None has been arrested.

Craig is a quiet, tall, dark-skinned youth with a reserved manner and easy smile, except on the basketball court. A graceful athlete, he is on the varsity basketball team at the high school. He moved to the projects six years ago and was one of a few black children to attend the neighborhood grammar school. His family is tightly knit; he lives with his parents, four brothers and sisters, and two stepsiblings. Self-assured and agreeable, Craig maintains a leadership role in the peer group, although such status demarcations are much less clearly defined among the Brothers than among the Hallway Hangers.

In contrast to Craig, Super is a fiery, loud, yet often introspective lad who, despite his medium size, never backs down from a fight. Hesitant in speech and uncomfortable with written material, Super struggles in the classroom. He is, however, a natural athlete. His speed, quickness, and agility lend themselves to football and basketball but his carefree attitude toward sport and his flare for flashy moves do not sit well with high school coaches and have prevented success in these areas at the varsity level. Super's home life is turbulent; his temper, apparently, is matched by his father's, and the confrontations between father and son have prompted Super to leave home for safer environs for a week or two on at least three occasions.

Originally from the Dominican Republic, Juan is the only Brother to have finished school, but he currently is unemployed. He is slight of build, a sincere and sensitive youth. Juan speaks in somewhat broken English, was not particularly successful in school, and is not a good athlete. His loyalty, kind manner, and sense of fair play, however, are attributes that have earned him respect. Such remarks as these are typical of him: "Yup," he said, as he left one evening to meet his girlfriend, "there's the three things everyone needs—a job, a car, and a girl. And the girl's the most important. Because otherwise you'd be lonely. You need someone to talk to and somebody to love." In a neighborhood notorious for its toughness, such a comment is remarkable for its honesty and tenderness.

Mokey is a quick-tempered boy whose impatience with others often borders on insolence. Stocky and of medium height, Mokey commits himself with vigor and enthusiasm to whatever he is pursuing but has difficulty sustaining this drive for an extended period of time. One week he is enthused about his prospects on the school football team, but two weeks later he has quit the squad and exhibits a newfound zeal for track and field. Full of energy and constantly on the move, Mokey chafes against the tight rein his mother keeps on him but generally accedes to her wishes. When necessary, his father, who does not live with the family, is called in to straighten out any problems.

James, a junior at the high school, is very small for his age. He manages to compensate for his diminutive size, however, with a quick and caustic tongue. He is not as well integrated into the group as the other boys, perhaps because of a long, involved relationship with a girl that recently ended. A year ago, James was a fixture in one of the city's video arcades during school hours; now he attends school every day as well as on Thursday evenings to make up for failed subjects. This turnabout resulted from a serious talk with his father, whose presence in the household is sporadic. James's wit, sense of humor, and toughness have earned him the esteem of the Brothers.

Derek is Boo-Boo's half brother. The two boys have different friends, interests, and attitudes and are not particularly close, but they do maintain an amiable cordiality outside their home, which is a considerable achievement in view of the animosity between the Brothers and Hallway Hangers. . . . Their paths parted when, as a third grader, Derek's scholastic achievements enabled him to secure a government scholarship to a prestigious private school. Derek attended Barnes Academy through the eighth grade with great success; his grades were good, and he had many friends. Nevertheless, he decided to attend the city high school, where he has continued his academic achievement. Although lacking in athletic prowess, Derek is admired by the other boys for his scholastic success and personal motivation.

Mike is the sole white member of the Brothers. He lives with his mother and grandmother and rules the household. His large frame and strength have made him a valuable asset to the high school's football, wrestling, and track and field squads. His athletic ability and an aversion to drugs and alcohol inculcated by his mother as well as a strong and lasting friendship with Super all account for Mike's allegiance to the Brothers. He is subject to some abuse from his white peers on this account but seems to take their ribbing in stride.

The Brothers, in contrast to the Hallway Hangers, are not a distinctive subculture with its own set of shared values. The Brothers accept the dominant culture's definitions of success and judge themselves by these criteria. A night in the city jail would permanently tarnish a Brother's reputation rather than build it up. In the eyes of the

Brothers, John Grace, the bartender who was involved in the shootout in Clarendon Heights, only would be worthy of disdain, and perhaps pity, rather than the respect Frankie accords him. While the Hallway Hangers have little concern for the judgments of the dominant culture, the Brothers become uncomfortable and embarrassed when recounting disciplinary problems they have had at home or in school. Such a "confession" for a member of the Hallway Hangers, on the other hand, might be accompanied by laughter and a sense of triumph.

Just as the Brothers accept the values of the dominant culture, their behavior generally conforms to societal expectations. Whereas the Hallway Hangers are conspicuous in their consumption of cigarettes and beer, the Brothers reject both. Although many of the Brothers drink beer in moderation every once in a while at a party or on a similar occasion, their consumption of alcohol is very limited. Likewise, although most of the Brothers have tried marijuana, they rarely smoke it, and they never use other drugs.

The Brothers are uncomfortable with simply "hanging"; they cannot tolerate such inactivity. They often can be found playing basketball in the park or the gym. If a pick-up game of basketball cannot be mustered in the immediate neighborhood, they often will walk a half mile to the Salvation Army gym or another housing project. Energetic and spirited, the Brothers dislike the idleness of the Hallway Hangers.

DEREK: I would never hang with them. I'm not interested in drinking, getting high, or making trouble. That's about all they do. . . . I don't like to just sit around.

Although the Brothers do not adopt those practices that symbolize rejection of authority or basic societal values, their peer group does have its own distinctive attributes. The Brothers carry themselves in ways familiar to most urban black Americans, although somewhat scaled down. Their style of dress, mode of speech, and form of greeting clearly set them apart from other residents of Clarendon Heights. However, the caps, neck chains, and open shirts so prevalent among teenagers in the predominantly black sections of the city are lacking among the Brothers, whose residency in a white neighborhood has important implications for much more than their dress.

Athletics is one activity into which the Brothers channel their energies. Many excel in organized youth, church, and school basketball leagues as well as in regular pick-up games. Mike, Super, and Mokey also play on the school football team. Only Juan and Derek are not good athletes, and even they maintain an interest in sports, often rounding out the teams for a pick-up game of basketball.

Girls also claim much of the Brothers' time. A frequent topic of conversation, their interest in girls seems much more widespread than is the case for the Hallway Hangers. While the Hangers tend to go out with girls on a casual basis (typically for a weekend), the Brothers often have steady girlfriends, with whom they are constantly speaking on the phone, to whose house they are forever headed, and about whom they always are boasting. Whereas the Hallway Hangers focus on their beer and drugs, the Brothers have their basketball and girlfriends.

Since Juan bought an old worn-out Vega for two hundred dollars and fixed it up complete with paint job and functioning engine, cruising the streets also has become a favorite pastime for the Brothers. It gives them access to the "Port" and the

"Coast," the black sections of the city. Considering the tense racial atmosphere of the Clarendon Heights community, it is no wonder that the Brothers do not spend as much time in the vicinity of the Heights as the Hallway Hangers do and instead prefer the black neighborhoods.

In addition to being the objects of many of the Hallway Hangers' racist slurs and insults, the Brothers suffer from even more substantive racial abuse. Super tells how the windows in his family's car have been broken year after year and how one morning last spring he awoke to find "KKK" drawn in spray paint on the side of the car. Juan recounts with anger accompanied by matter-of-fact acceptance how his mother was taunted by some members of the Hallway Hangers, which led his father into a confrontation with them. His father was lucky to escape unharmed from the ensuing argument. Juan has a measure of understanding for the Hallway Hangers: "When they call me a nigger, I usually don't let it bother me none. They drunk or high, y'know. They don't know what they're doing." In his freshman year of high school, however, Juan was beaten up by Shorty for no apparent reason; he still bears the scar on his lip from the fight, and the memory of it burns in his mind, fueling the resentment he feels toward the Hallway Hangers.

Although the Brothers are not submissive in the face of racial animosity from the Hallway Hangers, they are outnumbered and outmatched, and they usually find it expedient to walk away before a confrontation explodes into a street fight. They are accustomed to the violent racial prejudice of the Hallway Hangers. In fact, Craig, instead of being upset that a simple basketball game threatened to erupt into a racial brawl, merely commented, "That was good of Shorty to come over and tell us we better leave before his friends start all sorts of trouble." Although the Brothers are hesitant to answer openly the insults of the Hallway Hangers, they do vent their contempt for the Hallway Hangers in private discussions.

(all in separate interviews)

JUAN: I don't like their attitude, their gig, what they do. . . . They'll be there, hanging in front of the Heights, fighting and arguing and stuff like that. . . . It wasn't until I moved here that I heard the word "nigger." I had heard about people in the projects; I knew they'd be a pain in the ass sometimes. . . . I swear, if I ever see one of them touching my mother or doing something to my car, I don't care, I'll kill them. Cuz I don't like none of them. I'm afraid I'm gonna hurt one of them real bad. Every time I hear them call me nigger, I just don't say anything, but I can't take the pressure of people getting on my case every time, y'know?

CRAIG: I don't know why they just hang out there being crazy and getting drunk and bothering people. Maybe cuz they need attention or something. They got nuttin' better to do so they might as well cause trouble so people will think they're bad and stuff. They're just lazy. They wanna take the easy way out—that is, hang around outside all day.

JAMES: They're not gonna get anywhere except for standing at that same corner going *(imitating someone who is very benumbed)*, "Hey man, got some pot, man? Hey Frank, let's get high."

DEREK: We just have different attitudes. We like to stay away from the projects as much as possible, or they'll give us trouble. That's about all they do; make trouble.

SUPER: They smoke reefer; they drink. They ain't friendly like people, y'know what I'm sayin? They go around the street laughing at people, ragging them out, y'know what I mean? They just disrespect people.

MIKE: They're just a bunch of fuck-ups.

Such perceptions are often voiced by the Brothers. The situation between the two peer groups, however, is not one of constant strife. Rather, there is a constant underlying tension that surfaces occasionally—often during basketball games or when the Hallway Hangers have been drinking excessively—but that threatens to erupt into considerable violence.

Aside from racial factors, the character of the two peer groups differs markedly in other ways. The Brothers have no pecking order based on fighting ability. Although Craig is generally respected most, there is no hierarchy in the group, hidden or otherwise; the Brothers do not playfully abuse each other, physically or verbally. Loose and shifting cliques develop among the members and sometimes encompass outsiders. Friendships wax and wane according to the season and the extracurricular activities and responsibilities of the boys. During the winter, for example, Craig is so tied up with the basketball team that he effectively drops out of the group, and his best friend, Super, becomes closer to Derek and Mokey. During the school day, the Brothers often see little of each other and, once out, invariably break up into smaller friendship groups, coming all together only once in awhile. In short, the Brothers are no more than a peer group, whereas the Hallway Hangers are a much more cohesive unit with its own subculture.

The Hallway Hangers, who reject the values of the dominant culture and subscribe to their own distinctive cultural norms, have a sense of solidarity that is noticeably absent from the Brothers' peer group. Internal cohesion and the adoption of communitarian values, in which the Hallway Hangers take pride, are missing among the Brothers. Although all the Brothers would support each other in a fight, the ties that bind them are not as strong and are not as strongly affirmed as those that bind the Hallway Hangers.

The Brothers do not compare themselves to members of the upper classes, nor do they feel as keenly the stigma or shame associated with life in public housing. . . .

Daily life for the Brothers is far less circumscribed than it is for the Hallway Hangers. Active, enthusiastic, and still in school, the Brothers are not preoccupied with mere survival on the street. Their world extends into the classroom and onto the basketball court, and it extends into the home a great deal more than does the world of the Hallway Hangers, as we shall see. . . .

School . . .

The Underlying Logic of Student Behavior

As with many urban high schools, Lincoln High School is preoccupied with maintaining discipline. The team of security guards policing the hallways is ample evidence of this fact. Aside from specific sanctions (suspensions, detentions, parent notifications), teachers attempt to secure discipline by reinforcing the achievement ideology: "Behave yourself, work hard, earn good grades, get a good job, and make a lot of money." This line of reasoning rests on two assumptions: what I shall term the efficacy of schooling—the notion that academic performance is the crucial link to economic success—and the existence of equality of opportunity. Although used primarily to ensure proper behavior by highlighting its eventual rewards, the ideology has more than a disciplinary function.

Before we move on to consider the implications of this line of reasoning, we must address the question of how commonly it is used in the school. This task is not difficult, for both students and teachers draw attention to its prominence. Karen Wallace, the career counselor, in an unsolicited remark, mentioned that this argument is constantly reinforced by teachers: "We tell them that if they try hard enough, work hard enough, and get good grades, then anything is possible." On another occasion, Mike, excited about the prospects of securing a lucrative computer job, recounted the computer teacher's remark about a friend who makes two thousand dollars a week working with computers. The teacher assured his students that comparable jobs are available in the computer industry "for those who don't fool around and really learn the trade." In another unsolicited remark, Chris drew attention to this tendency of teachers to forge a secure link between success in school and success on the job market: "They tell you they'll get you a job when you're done. They say that to you right at the beginning. They say it to you all the time." The difference between Mike and Chris, and more generally, as we shall see, between the Brothers and the Hallway Hangers, is that Mike believes this line of reasoning, whereas Chris reacts to it with: "That's *bullshit*. They don't fucking give you shit."

Swallowing the Achievement Ideology

[Elsewhere] I noted the Brothers' widespread belief in the reality of equality of opportunity. Like most Americans, they view this society as an open one. Crucial to this widely held notion is a belief in the efficacy of schooling. As the achievement ideology propagated in school implies, education is viewed as the remedy for the problem of social inequality; schooling makes the race for prestigious jobs and wealth an even one. The Brothers have a good deal of faith in the worth of schooling.

The Brothers' belief in the equality of opportunity and the efficacy of schooling emerges very strongly from their responses to particular interview questions. When asked whether they feel they have an equal chance to do as well in school as would a wealthy boy from an affluent part of the city, the nearly unanimous response is "yes," as it is when they are asked if they have an equal chance to get as good a job as the same hypothetical wealthy boy would. With respect to their views on the efficacy of schooling, the Brothers' responses to the question of why they work hard in school are illustrative.

(*all in separate interviews*)

DEREK: I know I want a good job when I get out. I know that I have to work hard in school. I mean, I want a good future. I don't wanna be doing nothing for the rest of my life.

CRAIG: Because I know by working hard it'll all pay off in the end. I'll be getting a good job.

MIKE: Get ahead in life; get a good job.

When asked whether their academic achievement will influence the type of job they will be able to secure, the Brothers all agree that it will.

This viewpoint explains the Brothers' commitment to their school work and the relatively high level of effort that characterizes their academic participation. But whereas their acceptance of the achievement ideology accounts for the ease with which the Brothers are integrated into the school, their mediocre academic performance requires further explanation.

One cannot attribute the Brothers' lack of scholastic success to lack of effort; as we have seen, they try hard in school. Moreover, the Brothers generally are intelligent and able. Although their scores on I.Q. tests, which purport to measure intelligence, are not available, three years of acquaintance with the boys leaves me assured that, on average, they are not substantially less "gifted" or "clever" than my university classmates. What, then, accounts for the academic mediocrity of the Brothers?

In attempting to answer this question, we find ourselves in the company of many eminent sociologists who have tackled the problem of the "educability" of the lower classes. The consistent tendency of working-class children to perform less well in school than their middle-class counterparts is demonstrated by a wealth of empirical evidence, but the actual processes and mechanisms by which this comes about remain almost completely obscured.

Many conventional sociologists look to the working-class family to explain differential academic performance by social class, an approach that has yielded little in the way of concrete results. As Olive Banks admits in *The Sociology of Education:*

> The consistent tendency of working-class or manual workers' children to perform less well in school, and to leave school sooner than the children of non-manual workers, calls for explanation, and it has seemed reasonable to look for that explanation in the working-class family.
>
> It would, however, be far from the truth to conclude that the attention paid by sociologists in recent years to this problem has taken us very far towards a solution. We have many studies into the relationship between social-class background and educational achievement, and many different aspects of that background have been suggested as causal factors in the link between home and school, but up to now we have very little knowledge of the precise way in which these different factors interrelate to depress intellectual performance.

In addition to the inability of this approach to account for the problem of differential academic achievement, this emphasis on the family, in its extreme form, has produced some very dubious conclusions and destructive results. Propagated in the United States since the 1960s in an attempt to explain the low educational attainment of black and lower-class white children, the concept of cultural deprivation attributes their problems solely to the cultural deficiencies of their families. The view that the problem resides almost exclusively with the children and their families, and that some sort of cultural injection is needed to compensate for what they are missing, is not only intellectually bankrupt but also has contributed to the widespread popular notion that the plight of poor whites and minorities is entirely their own fault.

To understand the problems lower-class children face in the American educational system demands that attention be paid not just to their families but also to the school. Theories that give primacy to the family inhibit critical scrutiny of the nation's schools. The problem is not that lower-class children are inferior in some way; the problem is that *by the definitions and standards of the school,* they consistently are evaluated as deficient. The assumption of some mainstream sociologists that the problem must lie with the contestants, rather than with the judge, is simply unfounded.

Conventional sociologists as well as Marxist theorists have been singularly unable to put forth a convincing explanation of lower-class "educability." As [Jerome] Karabel and [A. H.] Halsey point out, the only explanation Bowles can muster is the vague assertion that the "rules of the game" favor the upper classes. Although this sentiment undoubtedly is true, he offers us no explanation of how the rules are biased and reproduced. Clearly, what is needed is a comprehensive analysis of how the educational system's curricula, pedagogy, and evaluative criteria favor the interests of the upper classes.

Although such a formidable task has yet to be undertaken, the guiding theoretical concept for the endeavor has been provided by [Pierre] Bourdieu—the notion of cultural capital. To recapitulate: Bourdieu's theory maintains that the cultural capital of the lower classes—their manners, norms, dress, style of interaction, and linguistic facility—is devalued by the school, while the cultural capital of the upper classes is rewarded. As Halsey, [A. F.] Heath, and [J. M.] Ridge put it, "The ones who can receive what the school has to give are the ones who are already endowed with the requisite cultural attributes—with the appropriate cultural capital." Although Bourdieu is primarily a theorist, Paul Dimaggio has substantiated Bourdieu's concept by analyzing data sets with measures for cultural attitudes, information, and activities for more than 2,900 eleventh grade boys and girls. He found that the impact of cultural capital on high school grades is "very significant," which confirms "rather dramatically the utility of the perspective advanced here [by Bourdieu]."

Although neither Bernstein nor Nell Keddie self-consciously situates his or her empirical work within Bourdieu's theoretical framework, both provide analyses of actual classroom processes that enforce class-linked differences in educational achievement. These analyses fit nicely into Bourdieu's theoretical perspective. . . . Bernstein actually demonstrates how class-based differences in speech patterns affect academic achievement and place working-class students like Frankie and Craig at a disadvantage with respect to their middle-class counterparts. Keddie's study also demonstrates how observed classroom phenomena—the different expectations teachers hold for students of different social origins, the determination of what counts as knowledge, teacher-student interaction, the tracking of courses—serve to handicap the performance of the lower classes. As Karabel and Halsey remind us, because dominant social groups determine what is valued in the educational system, it should not surprise us that subordinate social groups are judged deficient by the criteria set by the powerful.

These complex mechanisms of social reproduction are embedded deeply in the American educational system; they are well hidden, and thus the Brothers are unaware of the processes that work to hinder their performance. The Brothers believe in equality of opportunity and reject the idea that they have less of a chance to succeed in school than do middle- or upper-class students. Instead, the Brothers attribute their mediocre academic performance to personal inadequacy—laziness, stupidity, or lack of self-discipline.

(all in separate interviews)

SUPER: I would try—if I had more study skills, I bet you I'd be trying my hardest. I bet I'd be getting good grades. . . . I dunno; I just can't seem to do it.

MOKEY: I try my best to do as good as anyone else. But there's some real smart people up there, plus I can't seem to get myself to work, especially during football. It's hard.

MIKE: I did horrible [my freshman year in high school]. I used to do good. I got all A's in grammar school. Now I'm doing shitty. I guess I started out smart and got stupider.

If one accepts the equality of opportunity line of reasoning, those who are not "making it" have only themselves to blame.

Clearly, the self-esteem of the Brothers suffers as a result of their inferior academic performance. A careful review of the literature on the effects of academic achievement and particularly track placement on students' sense of self, undertaken by Maureen Scully in a 1982 unpublished essay, reveals that although we can expect academic self-esteem to vary according to scholastic performance, students' general self-esteem is often more resilient. Because some high school students do not value academic achievement very highly and instead emphasize nonacademic activities and values, their general sense of self-esteem is sheltered from the negative onslaughts of academic failure. The Brothers, however, care a great deal about their academic performance, and thus their general self-esteem is sensitive to academic failure.

In summary, the Brothers believe that American society is an open one; equality of opportunity is perceived as a reality. Moreover, schooling is regarded by the Brothers as the means to economic success; consequently, they care about school, accept its norms and standards, and conform to its rules. As black lower-class students, however, the Brothers are lacking in the cultural capital rewarded by the school system—hence their poor academic achievement and placement into low tracks. The Brothers blame themselves for the mediocrity of their scholastic performance. The implications of this dynamic are important to an understanding of the overall process of social reproduction. . . .

Spurning the Achievement Ideology

The school experiences of the Hallway Hangers suggest that they are a group of disaffected, rebellious, undisciplined boys who have been labeled "emotionally disturbed," "learning impaired," and "slow." Beneath their uncooperative conduct and resistance, however, lies a logic that makes sense to these boys and informs their attitudes toward school.

The Hallway Hangers do not "buy" the achievement ideology because they foresee substantial barriers to their economic success, barriers this ideology fails to mention. It is important to note that the Hallway Hangers could reject the notion that equality of opportunity exists but accept the reasoning that school can still help them. Just because one does not have the same chance to succeed in school or on the job market as a middle- or upper-class student does not mean necessarily that achievement in school will be of no use in securing a job. Indeed, the connection between schooling and occupational achievement is so deeply ingrained in the minds of most Americans that it is difficult to imagine people completely rejecting it.

The Hallway Hangers, however, challenge the conventional wisdom that educational achievement translates into economic success. In their view of the opportunity structure, educational attainment is of little importance. Convinced that they are headed into jobs for which they do not need an education, the Hallway Hangers see little value in schooling. Jinks perfectly summarizes this view: "Even if you get a high school diploma, that don't mean shit. A lot of people say, 'Oh, you need it for that job.' You get a high school diploma, and they're still gonna give you a shitty job. So it's just a waste of time to get it."

Because this point of view runs counter to a deeply rooted, collective belief, it offends our sensibilities. In fact, however, it is a rational outlook based on experience. Jinks looks at his four older brothers, one of whom graduated from high school, and observes that the one with the diploma is no better off than the rest of them. The brother who struggled through the four years of high school is in the navy, as was another who did not graduate.

Stoney feels the same way. He insists that school performance has no effect on what kind of job one will get. He argues instead that "fucking experience, man, it comes in handy," particularly in the case of his current job in a pizza shop.

STONEY: So the very next day, I went looking for another job. Went into this place, told him my experience, made a few pies. That was it; he hired me on the spot. No application or nothing.

JM: No high school diploma.

STONEY: That's right. He didn't want one.

JM: For your goals, how would it help you to have a diploma?

STONEY: (*immediately*) It won't, cuz I don't need no diploma to open a store. Like I said, if you know how to do something, you do it. If you don't, you don't.

JM: Do you think it would help you at all if you got fired tomorrow, and you went up to another pizza shop somewhere? Do you think it would help you if you could show them a diploma?

STONEY: No, it wouldn't help me. They wanna see what you got, what you can do. If you can do the job. I used to always get hired on the spot. They'd look at me and be real surprised a young kid can make pizza this good.

Relevant job experience is much more important than educational attainment for landing a job in food preparation, at least in Stoney's experience. The same logic holds true for a prospective construction worker or auto mechanic.

Shorty draws on the experiences of his brothers, much like Jinks, to reach a similar conclusion regarding the efficacy of schooling. Two of Shorty's brothers have graduated from high school; one of these apparently graduated from college as well. Nevertheless, neither has been able to secure desired employment. The college graduate is working security at a local research firm. Despite relatively high educational achievement, "they don't seem to be getting anywhere," comments Shorty.

Frankie need only look at his own experience to assert that schooling is generally incapable of doing much for the Hallway Hangers. In interviews, he constantly reiterates this theme.

JM: Okay, so why is it that some kids, even coming from down here, will go to school, and they'll work real hard, go to all their classes, and do all the work? Why do some kids take that route?

FRANKIE: Well none of my friends take that route. But I dunno. I never took that route. But I guess, I dunno, they're dopes. I dunno, I guess, y'know, they fuckin' think if they go through high school and go through college, they think they're gonna get a job that's gonna pay fifty grand a year. Y'know, a white-collar job. I don't think that's true.

JM: Do you think how you do in school is gonna affect what kinda job you get?

FRANKIE: I got my diploma, and you don't even need that. Y'know, my diploma ain't doing me no good. It's sitting in my bottom drawer. Y'know, it ain't gonna help me. I got my diploma, and you don't even need that. . . . All those Portegi [Portuguese] kids, they never went the fuck to school. Now they fuckin' got good jobs, cars—y'know, they fucking made it. They went out and fuckin' worked machinery and mechanics. So a high school diploma really isn't fucking shit.

(*in a separate interview*)

FRANKIE: They dropped out of school, and they got better fucking jobs than we do. I got my fuckin' diploma, and I ain't got jack shit. So it wasn't worth it for me to get my high school diploma. If I dropped out when I was sixteen—that was two years ago—I prob'ly would've already been through a job training program, and I'd already have a fucking job, saving me fucking money.

(*following an assertion by me that schooling is of some use on the labor market*)

FRANKIE: (*angrily*) But, but (*stuttering because he is upset*), still, I *did,* I did, I *did* the fucking, I did my school program, I went to school, I fuckin', I got my diploma, I went what you're s'posed to do. 'Cept you're s'posed to further your education— college and many more thousands of fucking dollars. Look how many fucking college graduates ain't got jobs. You know how fucking hard it is. They got educations. What the fuck they doin' with it? They ain't doin' shit. So fucking school ain't paying off for no one.

This last assertion—that school does not pay off for anybody—is not one to which all the Hallway Hangers would give their support. Even Frankie, in a less tense moment, would agree that some kids do "make it" and that success in school is a crucial ingredient for economic and social advancement, Nevertheless, although exaggerated in this case, Frankie's comment is indicative of the general attitude of the Hallway Hangers.

The Hallway Hangers do not maintain that schooling is incapable of doing anything for anyone because they all know Billy. Billy used to hang with the Hallway Hangers, getting high every day before, during, and after school, drinking excessively, and stealing cars. During his freshman year and the early part of his sophomore year, however, Billy underwent a number of personal crises out of which he emerged a much different person. Part of a large family, Billy had a father who was an alcoholic and has a mother who is mentally ill. In the span of a year and a half, Billy's mother was deemed unfit by the Department of Social Services to have custody of her children, so Billy moved in with his father, who died shortly thereafter. At about the same time, Billy's best friend was murdered brutally in an abandoned building a few blocks from Clarendon Heights. Billy, who currently lives in a three bedroom apartment in Clarendon Heights with his aunt and uncle, three cousins, and a baby nephew, is a senior at Lincoln High School. Goalie of the varsity hockey team and recipient of a special college scholarship for "individuals of extraordinary ability and need," Billy has switched from Oc. Ed. to the Fundamental School in preparation for college.

The view among the Hallway Hangers is that Billy is "making it." He is living testimony to the fact that schooling can work, that it can pay off. So the Hallway Hangers are not of the view that success in school is irrelevant but rather that the odds of "making it" are simply too slim to bet on. In what can be likened to a cost-benefit analysis, the Hallway Hangers, much like Willis's lads, conclude that the possibility of upward social mobility is not worth the price of obedience, conformity, and investment of substantial amounts of time, energy, and work in school.

For the Hallway Hangers, perhaps the biggest cost of going to school every day is the deferred income from full-time work. As [Henry A.] Giroux reminds us, the economic issue often plays the crucial role in a working-class student's decision whether to attend school full-time, part-time, or not at all. The issue of potential work earnings entered into all the boys' decisions to drop out of school. Chris and Jinks comment on the tension between school and employment directly.

(*in a joint interview*)

CHRIS: Jay, lemme tell you how I feel about school. I wanna go to school; I'd like to go til like 11:30 and then at about twelve o'clock work until about five. Y'know, so I could go to school plus make some money.

JINKS: You won't like that brother, cuz that's what I do. That's what I do. He'll start going to work, getting a little money in his pocket, and he'll always want more.

(*later in the same interview*)

CHRIS: So Jay, people should fucking give us a break, y'know? (*laughing*) Pay us to go to school y'know?

JM: How would that work?

CHRIS: Give us forty bucks a week to go to school 'til twelve o'clock. At twelve we go to work and make about fifty bucks.

JM: What would be in it for them?

CHRIS: They'd get a lot of people to go (*laughing*). They'd get a helluva lot more than they got now, I'm tellin' ya.

CHRIS: On Friday, I'd say, "Oh *yeah!* Got my job."

JINKS: Got my ounce all paid for.

This last comment is revealing. The world that the Hallway Hangers inhabit, with its preponderance of drugs and alcohol, demands financial resources. The pressure to come up with money is keenly felt by all these boys, a pressure to which Slick alludes often.

SLICK: (*motioning to doorway #13*) Hey, everyone out there has a goal. Their goal is one thing and that's money. You hafta have money, to make it. . . . That's what depresses them. That's what puts them into the pressure situation. They hafta make money; they know they hafta do it. The name of the game is money. You hafta get it. If you don't get it, there's no way you're gonna be able to do anything. You hafta make it.

Locked into the present by the pressing need for money, the Hallway Hangers, in contrast to middle-class teenagers, do not have the resources to bide their time while long-range educational or occupational plans come to fruition. Moreover, believing they have missed out on the indulgences of American consumerism, they are starved for immediate financial success.

(*in a group interview*)

SLICK: Y'know what it is, Jay? All of us down here, we just don't wanna make a buck; we wanna make a fast buck. We want it *now*. Right fucking now. And you know why? Not cuz we're stupid and can't wait for anything, but because we've never had it.

SHORTY: Fuckin' right. We're all poor as shit.

SLICK: No one in this room has thirty bucks in his pocket. Fuckin' right we want it. We've never had it.

The desire of these boys to go for the fast buck, to focus only on the present, becomes understandable in light of the uncertainty of the future and their bona fide belief that they may be in prison or dead.

In considering the experiences of the Brothers in school, we have seen that the effects of schooling on their self-esteem are significant. The Hallway Hangers also feel a measure of personal inadequacy with respect to their dismal educational attainment, but for them schooling is merely tangential to the overall experience of being a lower-class teenager in an urban setting. Hence, little of their self-esteem is tied up in school; academic performance has less effect on their sense of self. It is possible, however, that this apparent indifference toward school is itself in part a defense mechanism that protects the boys from assaults on their self-respect. Evidence for this type of failure-avoidance strategy has been documented in a number of quantitative studies of students' self-esteem. For the Hallway Hangers, the prospects of failure in school and the accompanying feelings of inadequacy are further reasons not to invest themselves in education; the potential threat to self-esteem is another item on the cost side of the equation.

The cost of deferred work earnings, the price of obedience and conformity to rules and authority that run counter to the peer group's ethos, the risk of failure, and the investment of time and energy all make up the costs of school involvement for the Hallway Hangers. On the benefit side are improved prospects for social mobility resulting from educational achievement. For the Hallway Hangers, who see through the achievement ideology and have little faith in the efficacy of schooling, the improved prospects for social mobility are not worth the price that schooling exacts. Although their approach to school assuredly is not based on a rational cost-benefit analysis, these considerations do underlie their orientation toward education.

This logic dictates that the Hallway Hangers drop out of school or at least minimize their involvement with it. That most of the Hallway Hangers pursue this latter course is evident from their paths into the less demanding programs at Lincoln High School, such as BTS, the Adjustment Class, Enterprise Co-op, and the after-school program. With teachers for whom they have more respect, fewer rules, and lighter academic workloads, entry into these alternative programs sometimes minimizes the costs to the point where schooling becomes worthwhile. Both high school graduates (Boo-Boo and Frankie) and the one boy currently enrolled in school (Steve) are or were in such alternative programs. Even for the boys in these programs, however, schooling often is not worth the price that must be paid, and thus most have dropped out. For Frankie to stay in school, for instance, the added benefit of "keeping my moms happy" was necessary to swing the balance in favor of schooling.

Whereas at first glance the rebellious behavior, low academic achievement, and high dropout rate of the Hallway Hangers seem to stem from lack of self-discipline, dullness of wit, laziness, or an inability to project themselves into the future, the actual causes of their rejection of school are quite different. Their unwillingness to partake of the educational system stems from an assessment of the costs and benefits of playing the game. Their view is not that schooling is incapable of propelling them up the ladder of social mobility, but that the chances are too slim to warrant the attempt. The Hallway Hangers' alienation from school rests not so much on a perceived lack of the means to succeed in school as of the means to convert that success into success on the labor market. Convinced that they are headed into dead-end jobs regardless of their educational attainment, the Hallway Hangers dismiss school as irrelevant.

Given this logic, the oppositional behavior of the Hallway Hangers is a form of resistance to an institution that cannot deliver on its promise of upward social mobility for all students. Furthermore, Lincoln High School, like almost all American schools, is essentially a middle-class institution. Its curriculum, grading system, and disciplinary code all reward middle-class traits, values, and skills. In coping with the difficulties of growing up poor in America, the Hallway Hangers have developed a set of survival skills of which they are very proud. These skills, however, are accorded little or no recognition in the school setting; instead, students must relinquish their street identities and move beyond their neighborhood ties. The Hallway Hangers resent the fact that the school, because of its middle-class orientation, ignores the skills they have picked up on the street. Thus, they do anything they can to express themselves in an institution that denies and violates their cultural identities.

Notes

1. All temporal citations in Part One have as their reference point February 1984, when the first draft of the book was written. Thus, "presently" and "currently" refer to the winter of 1984 and "last year" means June 1983. The present tense is used throughout the book, and no developments after February 1984 are included in Part One.
2. *Lower-class*, as the term applies to public housing residents, is not used in this book as an analytical construct but as a descriptive term that captures their position at the lower end of the socioeconomic spectrum. Similarly, the term *upper classes* is used to refer to all those whose position is higher on the socioeconomic scale; *middle class* refers more specifically to salaried white-collar workers, including professional and managerial personnel.

Questions

1. How do you characterize the values, aspirations, and characteristics of the Hallway Hangers and the Brothers?
2. How do you account for the differences between the Hallway Hangers and the Brothers, two groups that are similar in social class, and grow up in the same housing project in the same neighborhood?
3. How do Erikson's concepts of negative identity, psychosocial moratorium, time diffusion, and work paralysis apply to these youth?
4. What are the costs to members of both groups of believing and not believing in "the promise"?
5. What is cultural capital? How does it play a role in the development of a sense of industry?
6. What is the involvement of the Brothers and the Hallway Hangers in social institutions?
7. What do you think the future held for members of each of these groups?

References and Further Reading

Bronfenbrenner, U. (1986). Ecology of the family as a context for human development: Research perspectives. *Developmental Psychology, 22,* 723–742.

MacLeod, J. (1995). *Ain't no makin' it: Aspirations and attainment in a low-income neighborhood.* Boulder, CO: Westview Press.

Montemayor, R., Adams, G. R., & Gullotta, T. P. (Eds.). (2000). Adolescent diversity in ethnic, economic, and cultural contexts. Thousand Oaks, CA: Sage.

Our America: Life and Death on the South Side of Chicago

LeAlan Jones graduated from Martin Luther King High School in Chicago. He was the national junior spokesperson for No Dope Express. He contributed to two of National Public Radio's *All Things Considered* documentaries: "Ghetto Life 101" and "Remorse: The 14 Stories of Eric Morse". He is coauthor of *Our America: Life and Death on the South Side of Chicago* (with Lloyd Newman, David Isay, and John Anthony Brooks, 1997).

Lloyd Newman attended Future Commons High School in Chicago. He contributed to two National Public Radio's *All Things Considered* documentaries, "Ghetto Life 101" and "Remorse: The 14 Stories of Eric Morse." He is coauthor of *Our America: Life and Death on the South Side of Chicago* (with LeAlan Jones, David Isay, and John Anthony Brooks, 1997).

Psychological studies of minority youth growing up in the inner city are rare, and it is even rarer to hear the voices of ghetto youth directly. Our knowledge of inner-city youth derives from statistics on broken homes, on high rates of unemployment for teens in the inner city, on violence and gangs, on incarceration. We get only the briefest of glimpses into the actual lives shaped by the vastly unequal distribution of wealth in this country. One poignant and moving account of inner-city youth has been written by Alex Kotlowitz (1992), *There Are No Children Here.* In his book, Kotlowitz followed the lives of two brothers coming of age in the Henry Horner Homes in Chicago. Such accounts are rare.

In the following excerpt from *Our America: Life and Death on the South Side of Chicago* we have the unique opportunity to hear the voices of two remarkable and articulate ghetto youth, LeAlan Jones and Lloyd Newman, describing their world and adolescent experiences. While in Kotlowitz's work we get an account of the lives of ghetto youth abstracted through the experience of an outside writer, in this case we get the account directly from the boys themselves. In 1993 David Isay, a regular contributor to National Public Radio's *All Things Considered,* was asked to produce a documentary for a series on the Chicago public radio station WBEZ examining issues of race and ethnicity. He decided to equip two boys from the inner city with tape recorders to interview friends, family, adults at school—whomever they wished—to create a diary telling the story of their lives. Of all the kids David Isay interviewed to work on this documentary, he was most taken with 13-year-old LeAlan Jones, who was referred to him by the Chicago

231

antigang program No Dope Express. LeAlan in turn selected his best friend, Lloyd Newman, then 14 years old, to work with him. The documentary they put together was titled "Ghetto Life 101" and after being aired on WBEZ, the documentary was broadcast nationally on *All Things Considered,* winning over a dozen national and international awards.

David Isay was left with a wealth of material that never made it into "Ghetto Life 101" that he felt needed to be heard. This led to the publication of *Our America,* which draws from the original interviews, monologues, and conversations that LeAlan and Lloyd conducted for "Ghetto Life 101." LeAlan and Lloyd added an epilogue, revisiting some of the same people, and conducting some new interviews.

In 1993 when the original interviews were done, LeAlan lived around the corner from the Ida B. Wells housing project with his grandparents, his mother, his older sister Janell (age 17) and her baby, his younger sister, and his cousin. LeAlan's mother suffered from bipolar disorder, and his grandmother had legal custody of LeAlan and his sisters. LeAlan had no knowledge of who his father was. LeAlan's friend Lloyd Newman lived in the Ida B. Wells with two older sisters, Sophia and Precious, an older brother, and two younger siblings. His mother had suffered from alcoholism and had died 2 years previously, and since then Lloyd had been raised by his two older sisters. His father was an alcoholic and was in and out of rehabilitation programs. Lloyd saw him on occasion.

The imagery used by LeAlan and Lloyd and their insightfulness about their lives and those around them provide a foundation for understanding the experience of coming of age in the inner city and the effects of poverty, transmitted through family, neighborhoods, and schools, on development. Both social class and race impact the lives of LeAlan, Lloyd, and the adolescents they describe, and thought needs to be given to the separate effects of these two factors.

The Maze

LeAlan: It's Thursday, the twelfth of September 1996. It's me and my partner in crime, Lloyd Newman, catching you up on some things that have happened since we told you about our lives in 1993. Talk about yourself, Lloyd.

Lloyd: I'm seventeen, a junior at Future Commons High School. Could be doing better, but I'm gonna get it together.

LeAlan: And I'm seventeen years old and a senior at Martin Luther King High School. Varsity football and baseball captain, on my way to college just a few months from now. So one thing I want to talk about is the neighborhood and how it has changed. It *has* changed.

Lloyd: The fighting, the violence.

LeAlan: It was a lot cooler back in '93.

Lloyd: In school I wrote a story about how living in the projects is like being in a big maze that you almost can't get out of.

LeAlan: That's the truth. It's like you're in this maze, and you either die in it or you escape. Right now I'm probably close to getting out. But you never know—it could be a trap. I might take that wrong turn and be right back at the beginning again. I don't know. But I sit here, you know, and a lot of people might look at our situation as being terrible, but the terrible thing about it is I can't say it's all bad.

Lloyd: It ain't all bad. You have some people out here who are good. But I think that if people keep messing up, by the year 2000 everybody will be either dead or out on the corner.

LeAlan: True, I mean with them cutting off welfare, a lot of these shorties [young ones] are going to be even more messed up.

Lloyd: That's the worst thing you could do—cut off aid round the projects!

LeAlan: Shorties are going to be out here starving, and they're going to want to eat. It's going to be hell out here!

Lloyd: It's going to be war.

LeAlan: An apocalypse!

Lloyd: Shorties are going to be sticking up.

LeAlan: It's going to be unreal! But I've been thinking about this: Why are we dependent on other folks to take care of us? Why can't we be independent instead of dependent? I know I just couldn't sit around all month waiting for a check. I mean, if you're a grown, able-bodied adult you should be working. So I think of that—but then I think of these little shorties when welfare gets cut off. . . .

Lloyd: And all the mothers who have little children. It ain't right.

LeAlan: But think of this: If I was hungry, would you feed me a fish?

Lloyd: Yeah. . . .

LeAlan: Or would you teach me how to fish so I wouldn't be hungry anymore?

Lloyd: I'd teach you how to fish.

LeAlan: Right. Because if I'm used to you giving me this fish, when you're gone I can't eat.

Lloyd: But you can't just let people starve. . . .

LeAlan: True. So I'd feed them that first day, but then teach them so they could do if for themselves.

Lloyd: Right. People out here want to learn, they're just getting taught the wrong things. Yesterday I caught this six-year-old boy smoking a cigarette—I wanted to smack him!

LeAlan: But the sad thing is that these shorties out here are *smart*. That's what kills me.

Lloyd: They're smart!

LeAlan: But it's like crabs in a crab barrel—you got one crab trying to get out, and the others pull him down. Around here, when someone tries to make it out, everyone tries to pull him back in, and he's not strong enough to fight them off. Just think of our eighth-grade class—all the people that were smart back then are out here dealing now.

Lloyd: Every last one of them.

LeAlan: Every last one of them. It's only about . . . let me see . . . fifteen percent of us who are doing something with our lives: me, you, your brother Mike—that's it.

Everybody else is messing up. And I'm not saying this just to scare people—it's the truth.

Lloyd: Sure is.

LeAlan: But I *still* can't say living around here is all bad. If I say that the community I live in is sad, that means my life is sad—and that's not true. I have a prosperous life—have a car, play ball . . .

Lloyd: But no matter what you accomplish, you're going to die.

LeAlan: That's true—I can sit out here and be a thug and die or I could be a lawyer and die. Either way I'm going to die. But the point is how fast and how quick.

Lloyd: The point is how you live your life.

LeAlan: Just think how many people have died out here since '93. There is nothing here that's permanent. We're all temporary. It's like we're working a part-time job—because life isn't full-time.

Lloyd: I wish it was, though. Would you want to live forever?

LeAlan: No, I wouldn't. And I know I'm not coming back either.

Lloyd: You're not coming back, so you better have fun while you're here. Hey, LeAlan, how would this world be with nothing?

LeAlan: Be like it was before.

Lloyd: I'm talking about nothing. No buildings, nobody—nothing!

LeAlan: It would be a peaceful place—that's all I can say.

Lloyd: That's the most peaceful place you can get.

LeAlan: True. . . . Hey, kid, I'm sleepy now, so we'll leave on that note. I'm out.

The 'Hood

Our neighborhood has changed for the worse since we did *Ghetto Life 101* in '93—for the *ultimate* worse. The violence and killing are out of control. In the summer of '96, we had our first major gang war in The Wells in years. Everyone around here was scared.

To find out more about the situation, we talked to Helen Finner, who's been president of the Ida B. Wells tenant organization for twenty-three years and has lived in The Wells since 1968.

LeAlan: *Mrs. Finner, how has The Wells changed since you moved here?*
From good to bad. When I came here, The Wells was the prettiest place I ever moved to in my life—I thought I had moved into heaven. All the kids played, you could sit out on your porch all night long. Now it's almost like living in hell. Especially with the gang war that's going on now. Last week I was standing on my front porch and got shot. I could have been killed but I was lucky—the bullet just skinned my ankle. So the community is running scared, but now it's too late. We've let this war get a grip on us.

Lloyd: *What problems have made Wells what it is now?*
Gangs. Drugs. And the main thing is no jobs. All the young men standing around that are involved in gangs wouldn't be a problem if they had jobs. Once a young man gets involved in gangs there is no returning—there's no way out but death. And I've seen it happen. I went to two funerals yesterday. Just *yesterday*. And these

were good kids. You know, sometimes I get so angry when I'm talking, because I look at all these kids and I wonder, "How many are going to grow up into men and women?" Lives are snatched just like that around here. I fear for these children every day. Every day.

And the parents are afraid of their children. If you would just come to my office and sit with me for one day, you'd see how many mothers bring their kids over. "Can you talk to my child?" Because they are afraid of them. They are afraid of their *own children.* I'm not afraid of any kids. I don't have sense enough to be afraid.

LeAlan: *How did you feel about the incident in 3833?*
It was the most horrible thing I ever witnessed in my life. I could not believe it when I saw that baby laying on the ground dead. And everybody made such a big commotion—you saw so many TV cameras here that week, running all around the Darrow Homes taking pictures, interviewing everybody. But who's in here interviewing the ones that have been killed lately? Nobody. Nobody comes here now. The people that got shot on Saturday weren't even in the newspapers. It's ridiculous! See, Eric became a martyr. He became a symbol. But even then, nothing's been done for him. Some kind of memorial should have been set up to remember that this little boy's life was taken from him before his time. They should rename the Darrow Homes for him.

Lloyd: *They named a basketball hoop in the Darrow Homes for him.*
What good is it? Who's playing on it? Is anybody playing basketball over there? No. Why? 'Cause they can't. It's too dangerous. It's ridiculous.

LeAlan: *How does it make you feel when you know that the building where he was thrown from . . .*
Is gonna get torn down at long last? You know what? If I had my way, I would empty the buildings out right now and hurry up and knock all four of 'em down and start a new beginning. That's what it's gonna take—a new beginning.

To tell you the truth, I'm sick of it. I'm on the verge of giving up and moving out—it's gotten *that bad* with me. It's like fighting a losing battle every day. We need help. Someone needs to hear our cry.

School

In the summer of '96 we also went back to Donoghue Elementary School to see how things were going. We found our principal, Ms. Margaret A. Tolson, still in charge at the school.

LeAlan: *How have the last three years been since the class of '93 left Donoghue?*
Ms. Tolson: The last three years have been exciting but difficult. There have been a lot of changes in the community and a lot of changes with the students. Not all for the best. There's a lot more violence now than there was in '93. In '93 it was not the case of police coming to school to take you out. This school year we have had the police coming into the building on several occasions to take children out, and it's been a matter of talking to them and saying, "This is how you act when the police pick you up. No, you will not give them lip and you will not give them resistance."

And parents have begun to understand the need to keep our records current so that when those children are taken we can contact someone. We've also had a couple of stabbings. And the difficult thing about it has been when you return the child who was stabbed to the same classroom with the child who did the stabbing, it's difficult to ask them to concentrate on what they need to concentrate on.

Lloyd: *What do you remember about our class?*
What do I remember about your class? I remember that you were a group of very creative individuals. And I do mean *individuals*. Each one of you was distinctly different. You didn't believe that you really needed all of the education that we were trying to give you. You were convinced that you knew it all, and that you could have taught the class, run the building, and gotten it all done better than we could.

Your class had a lot of private and personal battles. I remember a lot of students who worked hard at Donoghue, but for whom their freshman year of high school was a very bad year. I recall seeing some late at night on the street with police officers and stopping to say, "Are you all right?" And them saying, "I can handle it." So I think your class had to grow up fast.

LeAlan: *It's now 1996. You said in '93 that only about five or six percent of our class would not make it. Right now where do you think that percentage is?*
That's difficult, and it's difficult because it takes time with some of you. What I like to emphasize is that learning is a lifelong process. And I would say the percentage of students who will end up making it from your class is probably fifty percent. A good half of them are going to make it and do well. They won't all make it at the same time—some of those who are now dealing drugs and fighting with the law need to learn their lessons, and as they learn those life lessons, they'll make changes and turn themselves around. It may take them until they're twenty-five or thirty before they make that decision, but they will make it.

LeAlan: *Is there anyone who you can look at now who you felt was very bleak back then but has changed around?*
I can look at Lloyd, because he was very quiet until you two started doing the interviews. He didn't have a lot to say in classes. He was the little person people would push in corners and say, "As long as he doesn't cause a problem we can pass him along." Lloyd is one of the children I would have had a question mark about. But at this point I think he's going to make it. I have no problem saying he's going to make it. He's definitely going to make it.

LeAlan: *How does it make you feel when you see that the violence is increasing? How does it make you feel as a principal and a person that's trying to help kids in life but you can't be around them twenty-four hours a day to shelter them from what they see?*
It makes me feel as if I need to convince parents that they've got to take some time with their children. The majority of my children are more satisfied with a hug than they are with a buck. They want the closeness. They want somebody who cares about them.

Donoghue is in a war zone. Our children here have some of the same symptoms that you see if you look at children who live in war zones in Africa. When my children have heard shooting all night and they come here in the morning and they're tired and sleepy—that's living in a war zone. When they're dodging bullets—that's living in a war zone. When they know they'll be beaten going from one gang area to the next when they walk to school—that's living in a war zone. It's that kind of thing that should not be. It simply shouldn't be. But it's there. And somehow we have to get the children who live in this war zone to feel that life is worthwhile. But I'm here to fight the battle. I'm here with teachers who are willing to fight the battle. We won't give up on you. We can't give up.

You see, if nothing else, the children of Donoghue are survivors. They may go through trials and they may go through tribulations, but they survive. And once they have survived, watch out—there's no telling where they can go! They will be strong and they will be able to meet the future—whatever it brings. I'm very proud of you two. Tell the world to watch out, because I may be talking to the next President of the United States and his Secretary of State.

Lloyd: *Thank you very much, Ms. Tolson.*

✳ ✳ ✳

In 1996, the Chicago Board of Education enforced new rules saying that students had to make at least a 6.8 grade level in reading and math to move on to high school. This past year, only eleven out of the forty kids in the eighth-grade class at Donoghue had high enough scores to graduate. Now the school has been put on probation. If the test scores don't come up, the Board might remove Ms. Tolson and all of the teachers, or even close Donoghue down completely.

But whatever happens, I will never forget Donoghue or our eighth-grade class. We did a lot of stuff together—we climbed through ceilings, we trashed classrooms— we were wild! We were wild, and we were smart. And now most of us are just doing what society wants us to do—contributing to the jail population, selling drugs, having babies, living on welfare. But I know I'll never turn my back on the kids I grew up with. We went through a lot together!

LeAlan

What's up? LeAlan Jones here. Almost four years have passed since you first heard my voice. When we made *Ghetto Life 101* I was thirteen years old, about four foot two and 115 pounds. I was in eighth grade then—a little man. I don't consider myself a little guy anymore. One thing that makes me older is my mental state—I listen to jazz, read, try to educate my mind. I'm seventeen now, doing well, and everybody tells me, "You're gonna be this!" and "You're gonna be that!" But that's scary in a way. It's a lot of stress thinking about the possibility of not making it. So I still work constantly. It's like swimming. While you're working you're going to stay afloat, but the minute you stop moving is the minute you start sinking. When you think you're comfortable is when you drown. I'm never going to drown!

My family is doing well too. Since '93 my mom hasn't had a mental relapse and my sister, Janell, has calmed down. In September 1996, my grandmother and my grandfather celebrated their fiftieth wedding anniversary. They had a big party and renewed their vows to each other at church. My grandfather is now almost completely recovered from the strokes he had back in '89, and has a much easier time talking. I interviewed both my grandparents one Saturday night in their bedroom.

Hello. Today I'm here with . . .

June: June Marie Jones, your grandmother, and your grandfather Gussie Lee Jones.

What are we going to talk about?
June: About the neighborhood and how it's changed since 1993.

How has it changed?
June: The most significant change that I have seen is the gang-wars. There's more drug activity, more drive-by shootings, and more innocent people being killed. I see no improvement. I only see negative things happening now. And with the cutting off of people's public aid and SSI, basically I don't see any hope for the people around here.

What are some of the improvements that you have seen in the last three years?
June: Well. . . . They're tearing down some of the developments that need to be torn down. . . . And with the Democratic Convention this summer they redid King Drive and put little golden plaques with different black people's names on them, and they have new shrubbery and cute little benches for people to sit on while they are waiting for the bus. So that's an improvement.

What good experiences have you had in the last few years?
June: Oh, that's a tough question. Just being alive is good. Our family having good health and no major sicknesses. And my fiftieth wedding anniversary—that was a beautiful occasion.

How did you and Granddaddy stay together for fifty years?
June: Hell if I know. [She laughs]
Gus: I always let her have her way. I never interfered in her having her way. I never judged her in no form or fashion.
June: He knew it wasn't going to do no good to tell me what to do anyway, because I have a mind of my own.

Granddaddy, what changes have you seen in me since I was young?
Gus: Well, LeAlan, you never did appear like no other boys to me. When you were about eleven I would sit on the porch and listen to you talk, and you would say things that were just amazing to me. I couldn't do nothing but sit there and look at you. You are a smart boy. You are smart!

How does it make you feel that I'll be going away to college?
Gus: It makes me feel ten feet tall, LeAlan. And I'm still growing! Everything you do, every attempt you make to climb higher, I feel taller. Every time I see you going higher, I go higher. It makes me grow a little bit every day.

How did it make you feel bringing me on the airplane to go down to Orlando to give that speech a while back?

Gus: That made me feel good. Made me feel good! How many miles to get to Orlando?

Five or six hundred miles.
Gus: Five or six hundred miles? That whole trip was a joy. In the airport you walked so fast I couldn't keep up with you. I knew where you were going but I couldn't keep up with you, you were walking so fast. You were going out of sight. Out of sight. But then I knew you had been taught right when you slowed down to wait for me. You didn't walk off from me. I knew then that you were going the right way.

What advice would you give me for next year when I'm at college and I don't have you around?
June: I feel that wherever you are, I'll be there. Not in body, but I'll be there. And the things that I have tried to teach you have caught hold of you. I know looking at how you are now that my efforts were not in vain. Like Martin Luther King said, "I've been to the top of the mountain with you." So you have to carry on from here by yourself. And I know that you can make it.

What advice can you give me, Granddaddy?
Gus: The same advice I've always given you, LeAlan, is the advice I would give you now. Do not stop learning. Learning is the greatest form of happiness known to man. If you learn one thing, let that be a stepping-stone to learn some more. Every book you can find—read it. Keep on studying and keep on learning.

What do you see in my future?
June: I see very good things for you. I don't know if you will continue with this kind of work or not, but as I've said before: No matter what you do you will be running your mouth. You've come far, and I believe that you will continue to do good work— whatever you choose to do with your life.

Are there any concluding thoughts that you would like to talk about here?
June: Not really—just to take life one day at a time. Because tomorrow is not promised to you. Tomorrow may never come, so just ask for the strength to do what you can on *this* day. One day at a time.

Thank you.

✳ ✳ ✳ ✳

What's up, y'all? This is LeAlan Jones and I just feel like talking tonight. I got a lot of energy. Thinking about my life. I mean, it's ironic. Here I am, seventeen years old, and I take business trips for the weekend, speak on the same stage as Hillary Clinton, fly back home, and go to school the next day. I grew up in the ghetto, got an uncle and a cousin who are career criminals, no father, a mother who was pronounced mentally ill, a grandmother who raised damn near twenty children, a sister who had a baby at fifteen—but yet, I'm still making it. That's a testament to giving a person an opportunity and letting them make something of it. And the sad thing about it is that there's a lot more people out here just like me. But it's like they're in shallow quicksand and don't realize that it's not too deep to survive. All they've got to do is stand up. But people get scared and give up. The streets just suck them in like a Hoover vacuum cleaner and spit them back out.

I'm five foot seven and 147 pounds. I live in the ghetto. I'm supposed to be a loser. I'm supposed to be on the six o'clock news shooting people's heads off. I'm supposed to be the one that you grab for your purse when I walk by. I'm the person that doesn't vote. I'm the person that is supposed to drink. I'm the person that is supposed to smoke weed. I'm the [person] that is supposed to fill your jails. I'm the person that you make examples to your kid of what not to be like. I'm supposed to be a basketball player. I'm supposed to make it only because of affirmative action. I'm not supposed to be positive. I'm not supposed to be educated. I'm not supposed to know what I know. But I do.

I just sit back and contemplate: Why did things turn out this way? Why have I been given these opportunities? Why will I probably make it out of here while others won't? Why? I don't know. This world is a funny, perplexing place. I'm going to leave on that thought. Peace.

✳ ✳ ✳ ✳

A few words with my mother, Tootchie:

So, what have you been doing in the last three years? Any relapses?
No, because I'm on my medication. I take my medication and I feel better and I think better.

What are some of your greatest experiences in the last three years?
Two years ago I flew to New York to get an award with you. Flying is something I said I'd never do, but we flew to New York and I wasn't afraid—I just wanted to try it. They had salmon at the awards ceremony, but I didn't eat it.

How did being a reporter change me?
I think we were closer before. We used to talk about your homework, and we don't do that anymore. I'm not as close to you as I'd like to be. But I think you are growing. You are seventeen now, a young man, and I think you are doing great academically and spiritually.

What type of person do you think I am overall?
I think you should have your blood pressure checked because you got a lot of stress and your nose bleeds. You need to stop getting so hyper and take things more calmly. You are not calm.

If I don't make it, will you be disappointed?
No, I wouldn't be disappointed. I know that you did all you can do. If you don't make it, I'm going to still love you and keep encouraging you to go farther.

How do you feel about me going to college?
I hope you don't call home collect.

That's my mother. Peace.

* * * *

My sister, Janell, is doing better too, even though it took her a little while. In '94 she moved out of our house and got her own place in a project near us called Stateway Gardens. It's not a great apartment—on the top floor with rats running through it—but she's done her best to make it a home. There's a lot of holes in the walls from a violent boyfriend she had staying with her—he used to beat her pretty bad. And a year ago Janell was seriously assaulted by another ex-boyfriend who had just gotten out of prison. So it hasn't been an easy time for here. But somehow Janell has begun to turn her life around. In the past year she got herself a job at McDonald's and started taking computer classes at a technical institute. Now she's getting ready to take the test for the GED. I'm very proud of her.

Since 1993 what are some of things that have changed in your life?
Janell: I think I'm doing a little bit better. I don't drink as much as I used to. I've been doing more thinking than I was a couple of years ago. I try to spend more time with my son and help him read. I try to help my grandmomma and do other little things to help keep me busy so I won't have to be out there in the street—because it ain't nice out there.

Who do you think helped change your life around?
I did it myself mostly. I mean, I had encouragement from a lot of people, but mostly I had to put my mind to it and do it myself—because can't nobody change me but me.

How do you think your son changed you?
He stopped me from lying. He asks me questions about everything—like my drinking—and if I lie he always figures it out. He's big enough now to know when stuff ain't right and how people should act. So I can't be acting like I used to act—because I don't want him to start acting like that.

What do you think the future holds for him?
My baby is going to be great. He's going to get a good education and my baby is *not* going to be sitting around here selling drugs or holding a gun on anybody. He is *not* going to be like that—if I have to move out of this whole country and go somewhere else to keep him away from it!

If you could tell the President of the United States about your community, what would you tell him?
Well, let me see. . . . I think if people didn't feel like they were behind bars when they were walking outside at night, a lot of things would be different. I think what we need is to get people together and clean up around here so they can feel that they're doing something good at least for once in their life. See, there are a lot of bad people around here but there are a lot of good people too. It's just that it's hard to find anybody doing good—I guess because they feel ashamed that they aren't doing what everybody else is doing.
What do you think has happened to most of the guys in this community since 1993?
Most of them are dead—killing each other for no reason. There's been a lot of people that got killed, girls and boys, and that's a shame.

What do you think the reason is behind that?
Jealousy. People sell drugs and make their fast money, and other people get jealous and just shoot them for the hell of it. They really don't have any reason to be doing what they are doing—it's all stupid.

What do you see yourself doing in the next three or four years?
I plan by January to have my GED, and then start working at the post office. Maybe within the next eight to ten months I should be moving out of Stateway and finding an apartment somewhere better.

From running in the streets like you used to do to what you are doing now, what advice could you give a young female teenager?
Don't do it. Believe me. It seems like it's fun at the time, but you have to think about what's going to happen after you get through. I just wish that I would have stayed in school. It ain't no fun waiting once a month for that little check that the government gives you, and then you try to get a job and you can't. Just do what your parents tell you. My mistake is that I started listening too late.

Take your time—you will get there. If people want to help you—as long as they aren't doing anything to hurt you or your baby—listen to them. Take everything slow. Don't rush anything, especially if you aren't sure about something. The more that you rush, the more you are going to have to end up going back and repeating what you've already done. Just take your time.

What is the one single thing that you would like to let everybody know about people who live in the situation that we do?
It's hard living around here. It is. Because if you're trying to make honest money and not just dealing drugs, people are always trying to take what you've got. And you get judged differently by living around here. Like me, if I try to apply for a job and I use my address, they will not hire me. I can't really explain how it is, because you'd have to be here. I can't say, "Come visit," because it wouldn't be no good to visit. You'd have to live here to see how it really is, and you wouldn't want to do that either. So I'll just say it ain't easy.

Thank you.

Lloyd

Let me see. . . . Since 1993, we moved into a better apartment in The Wells. My sister Precious got a job working in the little corner store and had her second baby—Rockell. My sister Sophia is doing the same as she was. Right now both of them are pregnant. My father, Chill—he's the same. And me myself—I'm doing much better. I got dreams—go to college, move my family away from here, be rich and famous, maybe own a hardware store. I'll be anything that I can be to help me stay off the streets and take care of myself and my family.

But I got to go to school. I haven't been doing good in school—it just seems like I'm too tired to do anything. I have to get my mind focused and stop listening to myself—because I send myself the wrong way sometimes. But now I'm going to start doing my homework and pay more attention to what people are trying to tell me. It isn't hopeless. I'll go to summer school and regular school and night school—I'll never drop out. I don't care how long it takes, I'm going to make it!

I interviewed my sister Sophia about how her life has changed over the last four years.

Hello, this is Lloyd Newman interviewing Sophia Newman. What's happened since 1993?
Sophia: Things seem to be the same. I'm still not happy like I'm supposed to be. I just get through the days. Mostly I just wake up every day and do the same thing: get out of bed, put on clean clothes, and stay in the house. I never go outside. There's nowhere to go. Sometimes people say, "You never leave the house!" And I'm like, "For what? There ain't nothing to do."

Let me see. . . . Precious had another baby—Rere. Now she's got another one on the way. And I just found out that I'm pregnant with my first child. It took me by shock at first, but now I'm O.K. with it. What else?. . . . A couple of years ago our best friends died. Mark and Marvin. They were gunned down in front of their house on Christmas Day. They were twins, and their birthday is February 19—the same day as Rere was born.

What's happened with Chill?
He's the same. I can't say he's doing better, because he's still drinking. . . .

Been in and out of rehab . . .
Chill's always going to be the same. I don't think he's ever going to change. Seems like he wants to drink himself to death. He says he wants to be with Momma, so I guess that's what he's doing.

What about me?
I don't know. You're doing bad in school, but I ain't worried. One day you're going to realize that acting up in school isn't worth it and get yourself together. You've always been hardheaded, even when Momma was living. You always say to us, "You're not my mother!" We know we're not your mother. We're not trying to take the place of Momma. We're just trying to help lead you in the right way. You don't realize that, but you're going to wake up. And I don't care if it takes an extra year, you're going to pull through school. So I ain't too much worried about you. I don't got time to be worried about you—I have enough headache as it is.

Do you think you've been a good mother to us?
Yes. I was only seventeen when Momma died. Most teenagers wouldn't have done what me and Precious did, so I think we did real good. I remember I was in the hospital with my sickle cell and I was telling a nurse about us, and she said, "I'm real proud of you because most people wouldn't have done what you did. Things probably aren't going too good for you-all now, but God is looking after you and he likes what you've done. Your day will come sometime, and you all will be blessed." I like to think about that.

What are your feelings about the future?
I want to go back to school. I want to get a good job. But my main thing is to move away from these projects. I don't care what it takes. I don't know how I'm going to do it, but I'm getting away from here! I hate it—this neighborhood, the people shooting each other, killing each other. I'm going to be twenty-three next month and I just want to do something with my life before it's over.

Thank you.

* * * *

I talked to my five-year-old nephew, Mookie—my sister Precious's son—in my room.

Lloyd: Mookie, what do you want to be when you grow up?
Mookie: Superman.
Lloyd: You can't be Superman.
Mookie: Than I'm gonna get a job.
Lloyd: What do you have to do first? First you got to go to . . .
Mookie: Uhhh . . . School!
Lloyd: Then you got to go to . . .
Mookie: Uhhh . . .
Lloyd: College.
Mookie: Ain't nobody in college!
Lloyd: Yeah, there's a whole bunch of people in college.
Mookie: What happens when they get out of college?
Lloyd: They get a job.
Mookie: Where they stay?
Lloyd: They can live anywhere they want to. They can buy big houses, cars—anything they want.
Mookie: You got to be big to go to college?
Lloyd: Yup. Got to be my size or a little shorter. If you are not my size or a little shorter and you're in college, something's wrong. Mookie, do you know what it means not to be able to get out of something?
Mookie: You'll be stuck?
Lloyd: Yeah, you'll be stuck in it. That's how the projects are.
Mookie: What's the projects?
Lloyd: These are the projects. That's where black people live who get aid checks. You're living in the projects. It ain't easy.
Mookie: What ain't easy?
Lloyd: Trying to get out of the projects. It's hard to get out of them. You got to be a hundred percent confident to make it out.
Mookie: What's that?
Lloyd: Confident? To have faith in yourself. Now it's 1996. We got four more years to go till the year 2000. . . .
Mookie: We learn how to count in school—1996, one, two, three, four, five . . .
Lloyd: You smart, man.
Mookie: What you mean?

Lloyd: You don't know what smart is?

Mookie: I got a smart mouth?

Lloyd: No, you're smart. You know a lot of stuff. . . . Hey, Mookie?

Mookie: What?

Lloyd: You know what?

Mookie: What?

Lloyd: No matter what happens, I won't let you turn out to be wild. You're gonna go to school, get an education, and get out of here. You got to believe in yourself. You're gonna make it.

* * * *

My father, Chill, is still not doing too good. I spent a couple of days looking for him around The Wells to do an interview, but I couldn't find him anywhere. Finally I called my grandmother, and she told me that he was at Doctors Hospital in Hyde Park.

Why are you here?

Chill: Well, by my drinking so much, I have seizures. I used to drink two and three pints of wine every day, and the alcohol ate my brain cells. So last week I was cooking, heating up a pot with grease in it, and all of a sudden I had a seizure and fell on the floor. I tried to grab the pot with my hand and I burned it real bad. Lucky I woke up out of my seizure or the house would have caught on fire and I would have been dead.

How has your life changed since 1993?

It hasn't changed. Not really. I'm not able to work now because of my liver—I only have about thirty percent of my liver left from drinking. I used to get drunk every day, but I have slowed down. I had been clean in an alcoholic program for two months—I got a diploma for that—but I relapsed when I got out again. Really, my life has been up and down. I'm up one day and down the next day. That's all I can say.

How have I changed?

Well, Lloyd, you have changed a lot. You are getting very intelligent and learning real well. But what I want you to do is to go to school every day. I'm worried about your grades. I'm worried about you in the streets. I know you game a lot. You used to watch me shoot pool and think you could do it. You always used to say, "There's a pool table in there, Daddy!" 'Cause you loved to watch me beat people. But I don't like gambling anymore—I've seen people get killed over that. I know about that part of life, and I don't ever want you to be like that—because it's a dirty, rotten, low-down life. Quit listening to people on the streets and grow up to be a man. That's all I want out of you.

Why are you still drinking?

I have a lot on my mind—mostly about my children and what's happening on the streets. I go out and I see killings, and I think about my kids and start drinking. It's like I'm running away from my thoughts.

Do you still think about my mother?

Oh yes. I dream about her because I love her a lot. When she died is when I started really going on the drinking spells. We had been together seventeen years. She was young and pretty and she had a good mind. But she died from drinking, just like I am dying from it.

When you die, do you want to be buried next to Mom?

Yes, I would like to be buried next to Lynn. If I don't stop drinking, I may not have more than six months to live, 'cause my liver is down to about thirty percent. I have been trying awful hard to clean myself up. Trying the best I can. That's all I can do—give it my best and maybe one day it'll turn around. Just hoping that one day I'll wake up and it'll just turn around.

Parting Words

LeAlan: What's up? It's LeAlan and Lloyd coming at you one last time, going to say good-bye and give you our parting words. We're seventeen now, almost eighteen. We were only what in '93—thirteen?

Lloyd: We came a long way!

LeAlan: A long way. We've done three major things in our life now: [our] book and our two documentaries. What do you think about this?

Lloyd: It's one of the best things that ever happened to me. Without this I don't know what I'd be doing. It helped me out a lot.

LeAlan: What are some of the things that we did that stay in your mind?

Lloyd: Everything. Everything.

LeAlan: Like what?

Lloyd: Walking around, interviewing people, going to the lake, riding buses, going out of town to win awards. Everything.

LeAlan: I guess we found an oasis. Our little oasis in the ghetto.

Lloyd: Now I just can't wait to get out of here.

LeAlan: I'll be gone in August. What's that—seven months: It seems like eternity, but I've almost made it. . . .

Lloyd: You ain't made it until you're out of here. The other day they were shooting right outside my house and I thought I was fixing to get shot. I didn't know where to run, so I just ran into somebody's hallway and closed the door. I was spooked.

LeAlan: I bet you woke up and went to school the next morning, though, didn't you?

Lloyd: Heck yeah!

LeAlan: People forget about stuff like that. Man, I think if we make it out of here we deserve a Medal of Honor or a Purple Heart. Because if you aren't wounded physically, you're wounded spiritually. We deserve a Purple Heart coming out of this [place]. I believe we've been in a damn war.

Lloyd: It has been a war. . . .

LeAlan: And now we're grown almost. No more kiddy games, no more wishing on a star. Things have changed. And things have changed with me and you.

Lloyd: I guess we're not as close as we used to be.

LeAlan: You still got a little more child in you, and I've grown up a little more. Like the jokes we told then are just not as funny now. . . .

Lloyd: We're still friends, but we just don't kick it like we used to—like going on bus rides—because we got older. We had to separate—we couldn't be together all our life.

LeAlan: But you're still my best friend. . . .

Lloyd: That hasn't changed.

LeAlan: It's just that as you get older . . . over time . . . things change. . . .

Lloyd: We grew up.

LeAlan: And you went through a few problems, but that ain't going to stop you.

Lloyd: I know.

LeAlan: But you should be graduating with us, man.

Lloyd: I know—I just start crying sometimes thinking about that. But I'm going to make it.

LeAlan: Got to make it, man. Got to.

Lloyd: I just can't see myself staying here. I can't see it.

LeAlan: We got to make it.

Lloyd: I just can't fall. I went up too high. All these things that we've accomplished—I just can't fall down.

LeAlan: But with God on our side, we're going to make it.

Lloyd: It's hard, though. It ain't easy.

LeAlan: It ain't easy, but we're going to make it. I'll be out of this place in a heartbeat—literally a heartbeat.

Lloyd: What college are you going to?

LeAlan: Howard. I hope Howard. So next year you're going to be here by yourself, man.

Lloyd: But I'm coming right up out of it too, right behind you. Might take another year, but I'm getting out of here. I just think about that every night.

LeAlan: So if you go next year, what's going to happen to Mookie and Rere?

Lloyd: I'm going to move us all up out of here!

LeAlan: Me too. I'm gonna get my grandmother a home. When I do that, I'll be happy to the day I die!

Lloyd: Yup.

LeAlan: So now it's over. We go our separate ways. It's kind of sad, but I guess some way or another we both made it. I believe we wouldn't have let each other fail. We got to sign off now, so is there anything else you would like to say about the end of our partnership?

Lloyd: I wish it wasn't the end. That's all.

LeAlan: Peace.

Lloyd: Peace.

Our America

Hello. This is LeAlan Jones with the last chapter. It's November 19, 1996, and I want to leave you with some final words about our America.

We live in two different Americas. In the ghetto, our laws are totally different, our language is totally different, and our lives are totally different. I've never felt American, I've only felt African-American. An American is supposed to have life, liberty, prosperity, and happiness. But an African-American is due pain, poverty, stress, and anxiety. As an African-American I have experienced beautiful things, but the majority of the things I've experienced are not beautiful. And I don't even have it as bad as most—there are millions of young men and women living the struggle even harder than me. As children, they have to make day-to-day decisions about whether to go to school or whether to go on the corner and sell drugs. As children, they know that there may not be a tomorrow. Why are African-American children faced with this dilemma at such an early age? Why must they look down the road to a future that they might never see? What have my people done to this country to deserve this?

And yet I am supposed to feel American. I am supposed to be patriotic. I am supposed to love this system that has been detrimental to the lives of my people. It's hard for me to say how I'm an American when I live in a second America—an America that doesn't wave the red, white, and blue flag with fifty stars for fifty states. I live in a community that waves a white flag because we have almost given up. I live in a community where on the walls are the names of fallen comrades of war. I live in a second America. I live here not because I chose to, but because I have to. I hate to sound militant, but this is the way I feel.

I wonder sometimes, "Why am I alive? What is my purpose?" And I can always find a reason. But for a kid whose mother is a crack addict and who doesn't have a father and doesn't have a meal at night and has holes in his shoes when he walks the streets and can barely read and can barely communicate his feelings (which is almost the usual characteristics of a child from the ghetto), when he asks himself the question "What is my reason for being? What is my purpose?" what can he tell himself? These are the thoughts that go on in my mind and really mesmerize me.

Some people might look at me and say, "He's just some little nigger from the ghetto that knows some big words." Well, true. That might be. But listen to what I'm saying. I know you don't want to hear about the pain and suffering that goes on in "that" part of the city. I know you don't want to hear about the kids getting shot in "that" part of the city. But little do you know that "that" part of the city is your part of the city too. This is our neighborhood, this is our city, and this is our America. And we must somehow find a way to help one another. We must come together—no matter what you believe in, no matter how you look—and find some concrete solutions to the problems of the ghetto. Right now we are at the point of no return. We've got to make a change, because if we don't we'll go into the millennium in total disarray. But I believe it's going to be all right. Somehow, some way, I believe in my heart that we can make this happen. Not me by myself. Not you by yourself. I'm talking about all of us as one, living together in our America.

This is LeAlan Jones on November 19, 1996. I hope I survive. I hope I survive. I hope I survive. Signing off. Peace.

Questions

1. What kinds of imagery do LeAlan and Lloyd use to describe their neighborhood?
2. How does growing up in this neighborhood affect coming of age?
3. What is the impact of race versus class in shaping the lives of these boys?
4. Can you apply Erikson's theory to LeAlan and Lloyd's adolescent experience?
5. Why haven't LeAlan and Lloyd developed a negative identity?
6. How are these kids recognized or viewed by society? How does this impact their self-concepts?
7. What is the role of family versus environmental variables in shaping adolescent experience?

References and Further Reading

Jones, L., & Newman, L. (1997). *Our America: Life and death on the south side of Chicago.* New York: Scribner.

Kotlowitz, A. (1992). *There are no children here: The story of two boys growing up in the other America.* New York: Anchor Books.

Suskind, R. (1998). *A hope in the unseen: An American odyssey from the inner city to the Ivy League.* New York: Broadway Books.

7.3   Linda M. Burton, 1997

Ethnography and the Meaning of Adolescence in High-Risk Neighborhoods

Linda Burton, Ph.D. is a professor of sociology, human development, and family studies at Pennsylvania State University. Her research concerns families and adolescents, and the public policies that affect them.

The parameters of development that have been identified for middle-class youth may not be relevant for economically disadvantaged youth. The markers of entry into and exit from adolescence may differ, as well as the behavioral practices and role expectations that occur during this transition. In a very informative study on this topic, Linda Burton examines the relationship between socioeconomic context and development through an ethnographic investigation of adolescents and families in nine high-risk neighborhoods. Burton identified patterns operating in these contexts that make development during adolescence markedly different from the middle-class experience. She suggests that the stage of adolescence is more ambiguously defined for inner-city African American teens and provides new ways to conceptualize adolescence as a developmental experience.

Burton found that adolescents in inner-city neighborhoods perceived that they had an accelerated life course. Poignant illustrations of this phenomenon are provided in *Our America: Life and Death on the South Side of Chicago* (Reading 7.2). When LeAlan Jones asked his 17-year-old sister how many of her close friends have been killed over the years, she answered that somewhere between 30 or 40 of her friends were now dead. LeAlan spoke with George, a 12-year-old boy hanging out on the street corner selling drugs, and told him that because he was not going to school George would be begging for money for a drink in 25 years. George answered, "I ain't gonna be alive in 10 years because I'll be selling my drugs and they're gonna pop my ass. No one's going to be alive in 20 more years!" (Jones & Newman, p. 45). LeAlan himself at age 17 reflected on the number of people in the neighborhood who had died in the past 4 years and said, "There is nothing here that's permanent. We're all temporary. It's like we're working a part-time job—because life isn't full-time" (p. 161). In Erikson's framework (Reading 5.1) adolescents growing up in such high-risk neighborhoods suffer from time diffusion, brought on by a lack of trust in the future. Many adolescents lack the belief that it is worth working for a future and waiting for the rewards of one's efforts.

Burton discusses other structural differences in the adolescent experience that arise for youth growing up in poor neighborhoods. They tend to grow up in age-condensed families where the distance between the generations is typically 13 to 17 years, where the work worlds of adults and teens overlap, and where there are few positive images of adulthood. They experience inconsistent role expectations between families and other social institutions. At home these adolescents have responsibility for the care of the household as well as younger siblings, while at school they are treated as children. Each of these phenomena has a psychological impact on the nature of the adolescent experience.

The importance of Burton's study is that it demonstrates that existing developmental frameworks based on middle-class youth cannot be imposed on the study of teens in diverse environments. An important limitation, however, is that Burton's focus on inner-city African American teens makes it difficult to disentangle the effects of social class from the effects of race in her study.

Abstract: In this commentary it is argued that ethnography is the "most important method" for studying development among ethnic minority teens growing up in high-risk neighborhoods. Data from a five-year ethnographic study of inner-city African American families and their adolescent children illustrates the utility of ethnography in identifying contextual issues that are critical for understanding development among urban minority teens, but have yet to be systematically "uncovered" and explored in studies that use traditional survey methods. The implications of ethnographic approaches for developing future research on context and adolescent development in ethnic minority populations is discussed in the conclusion.

The principal focus of the NIMH [National Institute of Mental Health] workshop was to discuss the use of ethnographic methods in the study of culture, context, and human development. In line with this focus, I have addressed a specific question: How does ethnography help us to understand adolescent development among ethnic minority teens growing up in high-risk neighborhoods?

I believe, as do others, that currently ethnography is the most important method for studying development among ethnic minority teens in high-risk neighborhoods (Bronfenbrenner 1986; Spencer and Dornbush 1990; Weisner 1996). Why? Because human development researchers have not systematically examined the meanings, patterns, rules, and behaviors comprising development for ethnic/racial minorities growing up in high-risk environments (Anderson 1990; Bell-Scott and Taylor, 1989; Edelman and Ladner 1991; Jessor 1993). Consequently, to establish relevant conceptual and methodological starting points in the study of adolescence and neighborhoods in ethnic/racial minority populations, fine-grained assessments of context, culture, and "everyday understandings" of development processes are required (Allison and Takei 1993; Ogbu 1985; Seidman 1991). Ethnography provides both the conceptual and methodological grounding to identify and evaluate the impact of culture, context, and "everyday understandings" on urban teens' developmental processes (Becker 1996; Schulz 1962).

My commitment to ethnography as "the most important method" is simultaneously guided by prevailing ethnographic observations that suggest that teens growing up in high-risk environments may attach different meanings to adolescence than teens growing up in mainstream contexts (Burton et al. 1996; Myers 1989). Several ethnographic accounts of the lives of ethnic/racial minority families in high-risk environments suggest that, in these contexts, adolescence is an ambiguously defined life stage comprising mixed directives about appropriate roles, behaviors, and rites of passage (Anderson 1990; Burton et al. 1996; Jarrett 1990; Sullivan 1989; Williams and Kornblum 1985). For example, several ethnographic accounts of the lives of economically disadvantaged teen parents living in inner-city "ghettos" indicate that in adapting certain skills to survive in their environments many adolescent parents move from childhood to adulthood without experiencing the "illusive" stage of adolescence (Burton 1991; Hamburg 1974; Hembry 1988; Ladner 1971; MacLeod 1987; Stack 1974).

In support of my contention of the importance of ethnography for studying development in context, I will share several important insights about the meaning of adolescence in high-risk neighborhoods that emerged in my five-year ethnographic study of urban African American teens (ages 11 to 18) and their families. These insights reflect the taken-for-granted understandings that families in high-risk neighborhoods share concerning adolescence (Becker 1996; Schutz 1962). I am convinced that I would not have captured these important insights without the conceptual and methodological tools of ethnography.

Insights on Adolescence in High-Risk Neighborhoods

I began my ethnographic study in June 1989 in nine high-risk neighborhoods in a Northeastern city. High-risk neighborhoods were defined as residential communities characterized by high crime and poverty rates, environmental hazards, geographic isolation, residential instability, inadequate housing, low-quality schooling, and scarce social service and economic resources (Garbarino et al. 1991).

Data collection involved the systematic use of multiple qualitative strategies to identify prevailing contextual norms concerning stages of life-course development in high-risk neighborhoods. Strategies included: field observations (community ethnography); focus groups; life-history interviews with 186 African American teens and their families; participant-observation in family activities; content analysis of local newspapers; and in-depth interviews with ministers, school officials, health care providers, school counselors, grass-roots political activists, and informal community leaders (see Burton 1995 for a detailed description of the data-collection strategies).

Seven African American field researchers collected data using these six strategies. The data generated using the multiple strategies were transcribed and then analyzed using the grounded theory approach (Glaser and Strauss 1967). The grounded theory approach is a style of analyzing qualitative data using a specific coding scheme to generate a profile of conceptual themes and relationships among variables that emerge in the data (Strauss 1987). Several themes emerged from the data concerning the meaning of adolescence as a developmental stage for teens in high-risk neighborhoods. The themes reflected three forces that together suggested that adolescence was an ambiguously defined life-course stage for teens in these neighborhoods. These items included (1) *the accelerated life course,* (2) *diffuse age hierarchies,* and (3) *inconsistent role expectations within families and other social institutions.*

Accelerated Life Course

The first theme, the *accelerated life course,* is based on an individual's perception that he/she has a foreshortened life expectancy. A truncated view of the length of one's life reflects both the perceptions and realities of mortality and incarceration rates of minority teens residing in high-risk communities (Gibbs 1985). For example, at age 15, the mortality rates for urban African American males is twice that of their White counterparts. Moreover, urban African American male teens disproportionately experience high rates of incarceration (Myers 1989; Staples 1985).

Consistent with prevailing mortality and incarceration rates for young African American males, families involved in the ethnographic study reported high numbers of deaths and "jailings" of teenage and young-adult relatives and friends. In each of the 186 families interviewed, at least one male relative or friend under age 21 had either been incarcerated or killed during the course of the study. While most of the incarcerations involved minor offenses, and a number of the deaths, unexplained accidents, or illnesses, a significant percentage (86 percent) of the teen males inter-viewed did not expect to either stay out of prison or live past the age of 21. Conse-quently, when asked to reflect on adolescence as part of their life course, most of the young men replied, as did Stephon, a 19-year-old father:

> I can't even imagine what you mean when you ask about being a teenager. In this neighborhood boys grow up to be men before they are five. There is no such thing as being a teenager. You're a child, then a man, and then you die. Most of my friends that stayed around here are dead or near dead in prison. If I make it past 25 I will consider myself lucky. Most people who don't live here wouldn't under-stand. You have to live it to understand.

Age Hierarchies

A second theme that emerged in the data concerned *age hierarchies*. Age hierarchies are characterized by a stratification system in which the distribution of leadership responsibilities, power, authority, decision making, respect, and access to resources are determined on the basis of an individual's age and stage in the life course (Linton 1942). In some contexts and families, age hierarchies are clearly delineated with lead-ership responsibilities and power being distributed among midlife and older individu-als. However, when there is ambiguity within a context or family concerning what age hierarchies exist, delineations of life-course stages and the incumbent roles are not necessarily clear. It is likely, under these circumstances, that adolescence can be perceived as an ambiguous life stage.

Data from this study indicated that age hierarchies in the high-risk neighbor-hoods studied were not clearly defined. Three factors appeared to be related to the ambiguity of age hierarchies: (1) age-condensed families, (2) the overlapping work worlds of adults and teens, and (3) the limited visibility of midlife as a viable life-course stage.

Over half of the families studied represented an age-condensed family struc-ture. Age-condensed families are characterized by a relatively narrow age distance between generations, typically 13 to 17 years old (Bengtson et al. 1990). The mean age distance between generations in families involved in the ethnographic study reported here was 16 years. The narrow age distance between generations in these families often resulted in the blurring of developmental role boundaries and ex-pectations, particularly between parents and their children. For example, daughters and mothers in several of the families studied behaved like siblings toward each other rather than like parents and adolescent children. The slight age distance between generations also created some dissonance with respect to how the parents and the teens thought about themselves developmentally. Desiree, a 14-year-old 8th grader, remarked:

> I'm just as grown as my momma and grand momma. We hang tough together. They can't tell me what to do cause I'm always tellin' them what to do.

Overall, findings from this study indicated that a lack of clarity in family roles and developmental boundaries contributed to the ambiguity of families identifying adolescence as a distinct life-course stage. The ambiguity was further exacerbated by the overlapping work worlds of parents and children in the high-risk neighborhoods studied.

For many of the families participating in the study the work worlds of parents and their adolescent children overlapped. These overlapping work worlds were directly related to limited neighborhood job opportunities for parents and teenagers. Thus teenage daughters and sons and their adult mothers and fathers often competed for the same low-wage labor jobs. For example, Devon, a 17-year-old 11th grader, noted:

> I can get a job around here when my father can't. We fight about that sometime. He gets mad because they hire me and not him. One man told him he was too old and beat up to get a job. He wanted a young blood.

According to Bronfenbrenner (1986) the lack of distinction between the work worlds of parents and their adolescent children may create difficulties for families in establishing mutually exclusive developmental life stages among its members. One implication of blurring developmental stages for adolescents is that youths such as Devon may have a less clear notion of behavioral expectations regarding their roles as teenagers. This lack of clarity may also have implications for teens' sense of role placement in other social contexts.

The third theme concerning age hierarchies is the visibility of midlife as a "viable" developmental stage in high-risk neighborhoods. Traditional developmental theory suggests that successful midlife is a distinct period in the life course characterized by generativity, competence, and personal and financial security (Baruch and Brooks-Gunn 1984). In concert with this characterization, images created and promoted in the media, workplace, and other social arenas portray midlifers as individuals at the height of their careers and in control of the distribution of power and resources in their environments. While this image of midlife is often fostered in mainstream context, it is not necessarily promoted in economically disadvantaged high-risk neighborhoods. In fact, in some high-risk environments, teens are believed to have more power and resources than their midlife parents or grandparents (Silverstein and Krate 1975; Sullivan 1989).

Data from this study indicated that midlife was perceived by the majority of teens interviewed as a stage in the life course characterized by little success and limited access to power and financial resources. The images that teens had of midlife as a life-course stage involved unemployment, poverty, illness, and despair. Shawna, an 18-year-old mother, commented:

> You ask a lot of questions about people lives. When you ask about what being middle-aged means I have to laugh. Being middle-aged seems like a depressing time to me. I don't know anyone who is happy and 45. Everyone is stressed, sick, broke, and broken-hearted. I'm not looking forward to that time in my life. I'll just move right on pass it.

Shawna's perceptions were consistent with images of how African Americans in midlife were portrayed by the media in this community. While clearly there were successful African American midlifers in the neighborhoods studied, over the entire course of the study less than 10 percent of the articles that appeared in local newspapers spotlighted the accomplishments of midlife African Americans who were doing well. This finding is striking given that over 51 percent of the population in this city was African American.

Positive images of later life-course stages give teens a sense of age hierarchies, life-course continuity, and expectations for the future. When these images are not consistently visible for teens they may develop ambiguous perceptions about what the future holds for them. A number of studies support this contention, noting the importance of positive midlife role models in the lives of teens (see Jarrett 1990, 1995 for a review).

Inconsistent Role Expectations within Families and Other Social Institutions

Recent reviews of the ethnographic literature indicate that a prevalent pattern in high-risk communities concerns inconsistent expectations between parents and social institutions regarding the roles of children and teens (Burton et al. 1996; Jarrett 1990). Although some researchers believe that inconsistencies in adolescents' experiences across different social settings are common, these inconsistencies are often exacerbated for teens growing up in economically deprived high-risk environments (Davis and Dollard 1964; Lerner 1987).

A common inconsistency in the developmental expectations of teens in low-resource neighborhoods involves divergent role expectations in school and at home (Clark 1983). School systems generally expect adolescents to adhere to mainstream educational aspirations, adult-monitored activities, and academic protocols. In school, adolescents are often treated like "older children." At home, however, some adolescents are treated like "grown folks" and are often saddled with adult responsibilities that are in direct conflict with the "older child" treatment and adult monitoring they receive in school. Most of the teens involved in the study were members of families who were barely surviving economically and, as such, often took on adult roles in their families. These roles involved assuming primary care of the household as well as the assumption of surrogate parent responsibilities for younger siblings. Many of the teens had engaged in these roles since the age of eight.

While most of the teens involved in this study were expected to behave as adults in their families and their neighborhoods, they were often treated, as one respondent states, "as stupid, irresponsible, incompetent white teenagers" in school. Kenya, a 13-year-old, pronounced:

> This is a bunch of crap. These teachers treat me like I'm some stupid-ass kid. I take care of all my brothers and sisters and my momma too plus my baby. Please, please, I ain't hardly no jive-ass kid.

This example suggests that the "adult" expectations of families, and the "older child" behavior expectations of schools, send adolescents mixed messages concerning their life stage. These mixed messages may result in adolescence being considered an abridged or ambiguous developmental stage among teens who are struggling to survive in challenging environments. The implications of mixed messages and the ambiguity of adolescence as a developmental stage are far-reaching in terms of how teens may interpret their own behaviors. While "older child" behavior is rewarded in one context, it may be a liability in another. Thus teens may be forced to choose one behavioral style over the other. For many teens in high-risk neighborhoods, that choice results in a premature transition to adulthood.

Concluding Comments

My primary objective in sharing these ethnographic insights on the meaning of adolescence in high-risk neighborhoods was to stress the importance of ethnography in studying a phenomenon that we know very little about. In this example, ethnography provided unique and important perspectives on the development of teens in high-risk neighborhoods—perspectives that have escaped traditional mainstream assessments of adolescent development.

Overall, participation in this workshop has provided scholars with various substantive interests the opportunity to visit and revisit the strengths and weakness of ethnographic methods. In visiting these strengths and weaknesses one important issue has been reified for me. Ethnography is the "most important method" for elucidating phenomena that other approaches typically cannot. It empowers researchers to "get inside the black box." For me that black box involves understanding the meaning of adolescence in high-risk neighborhoods.

References

Allison, Kevin, and Yoshi Takei. 1994. Diversity: The Cultural Contexts of Adolescents and Their Families. *In* Adolescence: Perspectives on Research, Policy, and Intervention. R. M. Lerner, ed. 51–69. Hillsdale, NJ: Lawrence Erlbaum Associates.

Anderson, Elijah. 1990. Streetwise: Race, Class, and Change in an Urban Community. Chicago: University of Chicago Press.

Baruch, Grace, and Jeanne Brooks-Gunn, eds. 1984. Women in Midlife. New York: Plenum Press.

Becker, Howard. 1996. The Epistemology of Qualitative Research. *In* Ethnography and Human Development. Richard Jessor, A. Colby, and Richard A. Shweder, eds. Pp. 53–71. Chicago: University of Chicago Press.

Bell-Scott, Patricia, and Ronald Taylor. 1989. The Multiple Ecologies of Black Adolescent Development. Journal of Adolescence Research 4:119–124.

Bengston, Vern L., Carolyn Rosenthal, and Linda M. Burton. 1990. Families and Aging. *In* Handbook of Aging and the Social Sciences. R. Binstock, L. George, eds. Pp. 263–287. New York: Academic Press.

Bronfenbrenner, Urie. 1986. Ecology of the Family as a Context for Human Development: Research Perspectives in Developmental Psychology 22(6): 723–742.

Burton, Linda M. 1991. Caring for Children. The American Enterprise 34–37.

_____ 1995. Intergenerational Patterns of Providing Care in African-American Families with Teenage Childbearers: Emergent Patterns in an Ethnographic Study. *In* Intergenerational Issues in Aging. K. Warner Schaie, Vern L. Bengtson, and Linda M. Burton, eds. Pp. 79–96. New York: Springer Publishing.

Burton, Linda M., Dawn Obeidallah, and Kevin Allison, 1996. Ethnographic Insights on Social Context and Adolescent Development among Inner-City African-American Teens. *In* Essays on Ethnography and Human Development. Richard Jessor, A. Colby, and Richard A. Shweder, eds. Pp. 397–418. Chicago: University of Chicago Press.

Clark, Reginald, M. 1983. Family Life and School Achievement: Why Poor Black Children Succeed or Fail. Chicago: University of Chicago Press.

Davis, A., and J. Dollard. 1964. Children of Bondage: The Personality Development of Negro Youth in the Urban South. New York: Harper Row.

Edelman, P., and Joyce Ladner, eds. 1991. Adolescence and Poverty. Washington DC: Center for National Policy Press.

Feldman, Shirley S., and Glen R. Elliott, eds. 1990. At the Threshold: The Developing Adolescent. Cambridge, MA: Harvard University Press.

Garbarino, James, Kathy Kostelny, and Nancy Dubrow. 1991. What Children Can Tell Us about Living in Danger. American Psychology 46:376–383.

Gibbs, Jewelle T. 1985. Black Adolescents and Youth: An Endangered Species. American Journal of Orthopsychiatry 54:6–21.

Glaser, Bernard, and Anselm Strauss. 1967. The Discovery of Grounded Theory. Chicago: Aldine.

Hamburg, Beatrice A. 1974. Early Adolescence: A Specific and Stressful Stage of the Life Cycle. In Coping and Adaptation. G. V. Coelho, D. A. Hamburg, and J. E. Adams, eds. Pp. 102–124. New York: Basic Books.

Hembry, Karen F. 1988. Little Women: Repeat Childbearing among Black, Never-Married Adolescent Mothers. Ph.D. dissertation, Department of Sociology, University of California, Berkeley.

Jarrett, Robin L. 1990. A Comparative Examination and Socialization Patterns among Low-Income African-Americans, Chicanos, Puerto Ricans, and Whites: A Review of the Ethnographic Literature. New York: Social Science Research Council.

_____ 1995. Growing up Poor: The Family Experiences of Socially Mobile Youth in Low-Income African-American Neighborhoods. Journal of Adolescent Research 10: 111–135.

Jessor, Richard. 1993. Successful Adolescent Development among Youth in High-Risk Settings. American Psychologist 48:117–126.

Ladner, Joyce A. 1971. Tomorrow's Tomorrow: The Black Woman. New York: Anchor Books.

Lerner, Richard M. 1987. A Life-Span Perspective for Early Adolescence. In Biological-Psychological Interactions in Early Adolescence. Richard M. Lerner and Teri T. Foch, eds. Pp. 9–34. Hillsdale, NJ: Erlbaum.

Linton, Ralph. 1942. Age and Sex Categories. American Sociological Review 7:589–603.

Macleod, Jay. 1987. "Ain't No Makin' It: Leveled Aspirations in a Low-Income Community. Boulder, CO: Westview Press.

Myers, Hector F. 1989. Urban Stress and the Mental Health of Afro-American Youth: An Epidemiologic and Conceptual Update. In Black Adolescents. R. L. Jones, ed. Pp. 123–152. Berkeley, CA: Cobb and Henry.

Ogbu, John. 1974. The Next Generation: An Ethnography of Education in an Urban Neighborhood. New York: Academic Press.

_____ 1985. A Cultural Ecology of Competence among Inner-City Blacks. In Beginnings: Social and Affective Development of Black Children. Margaret Beale Spencer, Geraldine K. Brookings, and Walter R. Allen, eds. Pp. 45–66. Hillsdale, NJ: Erlbaum.

Schulz, Alfred. 1962. The Problem of Social Reality. Vol. 1 of Collected Papers. The Hague: M. Nijhoff.

Seidman, Edward. 1991. Growing Up the Hard Way: Pathways of Urban Adolescents. American Journal of Community Psychology 19: 173–205.

Silverstein, Barry, and Ronald Krate. 1975. Children of the Dark Ghetto: A Developmental Psychology. New York: Praeger.

Spencer, Margaret, and Sanford Dornbusch. 1990. Challenges in Studying Minority Youth. In At the Threshold: The Developing Adolescent. S. S. Feldman and G. R. Elliott, eds. Pp. 123–145. Cambridge, MA: Harvard University Press.

Stack, Carol B. 1974. All Our Kin: Strategies for Survival in a Black Community. New York: Harper & Row.

Staples, Robert. 1985. Changes in Black Family Structure: The Conflict between Family Ideology and Structural Conditions. Journal of Marriage and the Family 47:1005–1013.

Strauss, Anselm. 1987. Qualitative Analysis for Social Scientists. Cambridge: Cambridge University Press.

Sullivan, Mercer. 1989. Getting Paid: Youth Crime and Work in the Inner-City. Ithaca, NY: Cornell University Press.

Weisner, Thomas S. 1996. Why Ethnography Should Be the Most Important Method in the Study of Human Development. Ethnography and Human Development. *In* Richard Jessor, A. Colby, Richard Shweder, eds. Pp. 305–324. Chicago: University of Chicago Press.

Williams, Terry, and William Kornblum. 1985. Growing Up Poor. Lexington, MA: Lexington Books.

Questions

1. What difficulties are encountered in studying adolescents from high-risk neighborhoods?
2. Do teenagers growing up in the inner cities have an adolescence? If so, what are its developmental tasks?
3. What are the consequences of growing up in age-condensed families?
4. What is the effect of the high rate of incarceration and mortality on adolescent development?
5. What are the impacts of high unemployment and perceiving no legitimate means of making it on adolescent development?
6. What is the impact of the discontinuity in expectations between home and school?

References and Further Reading

Burton, L. M., Allison, K. W., & Obeidallah, D. (1995). Social context and adolescence: Perspectives on development among inner-city African-American teens. In L. J. Crockett, & A. C. Crouter (Eds.), *Pathways through adolescence: Individual development in relation to social contexts* (pp. 119–138). Mahwah, NJ: Lawrence Erlbaum.

Gibbs, J. T. (1985). Black adolescents and youth: An endangered species. *American Journal of Orthopsychiatry, 54,* 6–21.

Jarrett, R. L. (1995). Growing up poor: The family experiences of socially mobile youth in low-income African-American neighborhoods. *Journal of Adolescent Research, 10,* 111–135.

Chapter 8

Gender Role Identity

Societal definitions of masculinity and femininity provide prescriptions for behavior, dictating how males and females ought to behave to be socially acceptable. Males are expected to acquire instrumental traits, like leadership, competence, dominance, independence, and assertiveness. Females are expected to acquire affective traits, like warmth, sympathy, tact, expressiveness, nurturance, and awareness of the feelings of others. Those who deviate from societal gender role norms may pay a price in terms of social rejection and discrimination, but those who fulfill societal gender role expectations pay a price as well.

Adolescence marks a time of coming to terms with gender role prescriptions for behavior; for determining the extent to which one will identify with societal definitions of masculinity and femininity. Research has focused on how identification with the female gender role may adversely affect the development of girls (Brown & Gilligan, 1992; Gilligan, Lyons, & Hanmer, 1990). Girls attempting to acquire the trappings of womanhood are confronted with contradictory expectations. Sexual attractiveness becomes salient, yet while girls are expected to be sexy, if they are sexually active they are viewed negatively. Girls are expected to be physically attractive, but definitions of attractiveness place pressures on girls to be unrealistically thin, and to fit images promoted in the media that put them at risk for disordered eating. Girls are expected to put the needs and feelings of others first, at the cost of attending to their own needs. Girls are expected to be highly achieving, but not so achievement oriented as to be smarter than boys. Based on her observation of girls seen in psychotherapy, Mary Pipher (1994) argues that in an attempt to fulfill societal definitions of the female gender role, girls develop false selves; they start to disown their true selves in order to avoid expressing unacceptable feelings and to avoid unacceptable behavior. Further research is needed to test Pipher's claims.

One of the adverse effects that has been attributed to the endorsement of the feminine role is lowered self-esteem. Researchers have reported a drop in self-esteem for adolescent girls as they enter adolescence. The American Association of University Women (AAUW, 1992) carried out a nationwide study and found that 69% of elementary school boys and 60% of girls reported being, "happy the way I am," but these percentages dropped to 46% and 29% respectively by high

259

school. The report did note, however, that the drop in self-esteem for girls occurred primarily among white girls and not among girls who were African American. Unlike whites, African Americans consider masculine characteristics to be no more desirable for a man than they are for a woman (Harris, 1994). African American women describe themselves as androgynous, as possessing both masculine and feminine traits, more often than white women do (Binion, 1990). Thus cultural variations exist in definitions of masculinity and femininity and gender roles.

The AAUW report found a more dramatic drop in self-esteem for adolescent girls than for adolescent boys, and it paid little attention to the drop in self-esteem that occurred for boys. Male psychologists and psychiatrists are focusing now on the drop in self-esteem that occurs for boys at adolescence, and on the costs to men of meeting male gender role expectations (Reading 8.2). Many researchers argue that the fulfillment of male gender role expectations is equally if not more costly to men, and that the consequences of violating sex role norms may have more severe consequences for men than for women (Pollock, 1998; Thompson & Kindlon, 1999). Males who display behavior remotely considered to be "feminine" are the targets of discrimination. Males are pressed into extreme daring, toughness, bravado, violence, and risky behavior. Males are cut off from experiencing their emotions, as the male gender role does not allow boys to admit weakness, fear, uncertainty, and need. They must be stable, show no pain or weakness, and repress feelings of failure or unhappiness.

Part of the process of identity formation involves coming to terms with gender role pressures and finding healthy ways to be masculine, feminine, or some combination of both. Taken as a whole, the research on gender roles reveals that conformity to either the female or male role has both costs and benefits.

Additional Resources

References and Suggested Reading

American Association of University Women. (1992). *The AAUW report: How schools shortchange girls.* Washington, DC: American Association of University Women.

Basow, S. A., & Rubin, L. R. (1999). Gender influences on adolescent development. In N. G. Johnson, M. C. Roberts, & J. Worell (Eds.), *Beyond Appearance: A new look at adolescent girls* (pp. 25–52). Washington, DC: American Psychological Association.

Binion, V. J. (1990). Psychological androgyny: A black female perspective. *Sex Roles, 22,* 487–507.

Brown, L., & Gilligan, C. (1992). *Meeting at the crossroads: Women's psychology and girls' development.* Cambridge, MA: Harvard University Press.

Gilligan, C., Lyons, N., & Hanmer, T. J. (1990). *Making connections: The relational worlds of adolescent girls at Emma Willard School.* Cambridge, MA: Harvard University Press.

Harris, A. (1994). Ethnicity as a determinant of sex role identity: A replication study of item selection for the Bem Sex Role Inventory. *Sex Roles, 31* (3/4), 241–273.

Pipher, M. (1994). *Reviving Ophelia: Saving the selves of adolescent girls.* New York: Ballantine Books.

Pollock, W. (1998). *Real Boys.* New York: Henry Holt.

Thompson, M., & Kindlon, D. (1999). *Raising Cain.* New York: Ballantine.

On the Internet

http://www.apa.org/monitor/julaug99/youth.html

APA Monitor—Boys to Men: Emotional Miseducation
This is the Web site of the American Psychological Association. This article is from the monthly publication of the American Psychological Association, *The Monitor.*

http://www.cmwf.org/programs/women/adoleshl.asp

The Commonwealth Fund Survey of the Health of Adolescent Girls
This is the Web site of the Commonwealth Fund, a private foundation in New York City supporting independent research on health and social issues.

http://wizard.ucr.edu/~kmcneill/gender.htm

Gender Roles
This paper on gender roles is on the Web site of Kevin McNeill, a Ph.D. candidate at the University of California, Riverside.

http://gozips.uakron.edu/~susan8/parinf.htm

Parental Influence on Children's Socialization to Gender Roles
This paper, published in *Adolescence,* Summer, 1997, is on the Web site of Susan D. Witt, Ph.D., an assistant professor at the University of Akron.

8.1   Susan Harter, et al., 1998

Level of Voice Among Female and Male High School Students: Relational Context, Support, and Gender Orientation

Susan Harter, Ph.D., is a professor of psychology and head of the Developmental Psychology Program at the University of Denver. She has constructed a widely used battery of self-report instruments to tap dimensions of self-concept and self-esteem. She is author of *The Construction of Self* (1999). She has conducted research on self-concept, self-esteem, and motivational and emotional development.

Based on her in-depth interviews with preadolescent and adolescent girls, Carol Gilligan claimed that as girls enter adolescence they find that speaking up and speaking honestly becomes dangerous. If girls say what they truly think and feel directly, they risk losing their relationships and finding themselves all alone. Gilligan argued that as girls move toward adulthood they become increasingly aware of the cultural stereotypes of the good and bad woman. They are aware that a woman must be nice, smile, be interested, be too-good-to-be-true—and they are hindered by the image of the "perfect girl." To fulfill the cultural expectations for women, girls feel they must mask their true feelings; to speak honestly would be to say things that were not nice, and that might hurt others. In her interviews, Gilligan found that girls constantly interrupted themselves to say, "I don't know," which Gilligan interpreted to be their attempt to cover up what they did know. Girls were "dissociating their voice from their feelings and thoughts so that others would not know what they were experiencing, taking themselves out of relationships so that they could better approximate what others want and desire, or look more like some ideal image of what a woman or what a person should be" (Brown & Gilligan, 1992, pp. 217–218). Young girls at adolescence face a crisis, according to Gilligan, which many respond to by devaluing themselves.

Gilligan's work has been widely popularized. She has made claims about characteristics of adolescent girls and the crisis they face at adolescence, yet she has no comparison group of adolescent boys to provide a basis for determining whether the characteristics she describes are unique to girls. It is impossible to know whether or not she would have found the same pattern of behavior if she had done similar interviews with adolescent boys. In addition, Gilligan's research is based on in-depth interviews; further credence could be given to her findings if they were replicated using more standard measures and larger samples of adolescents.

The research by Susan Harter, Patricia Waters, Nancy Whitesell, and Diana Kastelic tests Gilligan's claims that girls lose their voice at adolescence. Harter and her colleagues developed an empirical measure of "voice" and used a sizeable sample of both males and females in their study. The authors conceptualized voice to be more complicated than Gilligan did, believing that level of voice would vary across relationships. They looked at level of voice across five relationships: voice with teachers, parents, male classmates, female classmates, and close friends. Harter and her colleagues found no evidence that voice declines at adolescence. They found no gender differences in level of voice with teachers, parents, or male classmates, but they did find that level of voice was higher for girls than for boys with female classmates and close friends. These results do not support Gilligan's claims. They also hypothesized, however, that gender orientation—endorsement of a masculine, feminine, or androgynous sex role—might be predictive of level of voice. Indeed, the girls most likely to experience a suppression of voice at adolescence were also most likely to endorse the societal ideal of femininity and to display a feminine gender role orientation.

Abstract: Adolescence brings with it displays of false self-behavior, including the suppression of opinions. C. Gilligan (1993) argued that lack of "voice" is problematic for girls when they enter adolescence. In the present study, the authors examined level of self-reported voice with parents, teachers, male classmates, female classmates, and close friends among both female and male high school students. Findings revealed no gender differences nor evidence that voice declines in female adolescents. For both genders, perceived support for voice was predictive of level of voice. Moreover, feminine girls reported lower levels of voice than did androgynous girls in public (but not private) relational contexts. Lower levels of voice were associated with more negative evaluations of self-worth. Discussion focused on the need to understand the causes of individual differences in voice within each gender, cautioning against generalizations about either gender as a group.

The period of adolescence presents critical challenges to the development of a coherent, consolidated sense of self, given the need to create multiple selves in different roles, for example, with parents, teachers, classmates, close friends, and romantic partners (see Erikson, 1950; Griffin, Chassin, & Young, 1981; Grotevant & Cooper, 1983; Harter & Monsour, 1992; Hill & Holmbeck, 1986; Kolligian, 1990; Rosenberg, 1986; Smollar & Youniss, 1985). This proliferation of selves naturally introduces concern over which is "the real me," particularly if attributes in different roles appear contradictory or conflicting. Thus, adolescents begin to express concern over which attributes represent the true self and which represent false self-behavior (see also Broughton, 1981; Harter, Marold, Whitesell, & Cobbs, 1996; Selman, 1980). The true self is described as the "real me inside," "what I really think and feel," whereas the false self includes "being phony" and "putting on an act" (Harter et al., 1996).

One vehicle through which false self-behaviors are typically communicated by adolescents is *verbal* behavior. Adolescents' more specific definitions of true self-behavior include "saying what you really think," "expressing your true opinion," and "telling people what you really feel or believe inside." In contrast, false self-behaviors are described as "not saying what you think," "expressing things you don't really believe or feel," "not stating your true opinion," "saying what you think other people want to hear."

These observations converge with what Gilligan and colleagues (Gilligan, 1982, 1993; Gilligan, Lyons, & Hanmer, 1989) have referred to as "loss of voice"—namely, the suppression of one's thoughts and opinions. However, our analysis of the determinants of lack of voice differs from that of Gilligan. From a developmental perspective, Gilligan found loss of voice to be particularly problematic for *female* adolescents. She contended that prior to adolescence, girls seem to be clear about what they know, and most are able to express their opinions forcefully. However, with the onset of adolescence, many cover over what they knew as children, suppressing their voices, diminishing themselves, and hiding their feelings in a "cartography of lies." Gilligan and colleagues cited a number of motives for why adolescent girls' voices should go underground.

They noted that during the developmental transition to adolescence, girls begin to identify with the cultural role of the "good woman" because the onset of puberty makes this impending role more salient. Gilligan argued that teenage girls quickly perceive that the desirable stereotype is being nice, polite, pleasing to others, unassertive, and quiet. This juncture creates a conflict for female adolescents because to remain faithful to themselves, girls must resist the conventions of feminine goodness. However, to remain responsive to others, the good woman must put others' needs and desires ahead of her own, a powerful motive for suppressing one's voice. According to Gilligan, many girls observe these stereotypic behaviors in their own mothers, who serve as role models for how women in this culture should act; thus, in emulating their mothers, adolescent girls come to not speak their minds. At a more societal level, Gilligan contended that in what is still largely a patriarchy, girls observe that women's opinions are typically not sought, not valued, and not supported. The message is to keep quiet, notice the absence of women, and say nothing.

In addition, Gilligan (1982) described a more proximal motive that derives from the relational impasse in which many adolescent girls find themselves. Given the importance for girls and women of connectedness to others (see Belenky, Clinchy, Goldberger, & Tarule, 1986; Chodorow, 1989; Miller, 1986; Rubin, 1985), behaviors that threaten relationships are to be avoided at all costs. Beginning in adolescence, many females compromise their authenticity; they take themselves out of "true" relationships to preserve connectedness in some lesser form. If they were to speak their minds or express their true voices, it may well cause tension or conflict in the relationship, may anger the other person, may hurt the other's feelings, and, at worst, may lead to abandonment. Thus, according to Gilligan, adolescent girls opt not to risk potential rejection by masking their true selves, a solution that for many is accompanied by conflict and distress.

Gilligan's (1993) analysis is quite provocative, and her observations, including extensive interviews, dialogues, sentence completion data, and intense focus group interactions reveal that for many female adolescents, suppression of voice becomes the only path through which they can preserve relationships. However, Gilligan's efforts have not, to date, resulted in any systematic empirical demonstration of the prevalence of loss of voice among adolescent girls. Undoubtedly, there are adolescent girls who fit these patterns; however, of critical interest is how extensive the patterns identified by Gilligan actually are. In the present study, we challenged the assumption that the level of voice would decline for most girls as they moved through adolescence.

Moreover, Gilligan (1993) has not yet addressed these issues in adolescent boys. Rather, she and her colleagues have committed themselves to understanding voice processes among female adolescents only. However, any compelling analysis must address the question of whether the processes that Gilligan feels are specific to adolescent girls in our culture do or do not characterize the development of adolescent boys. Furthermore, there has been little attention given to potential individual differences in level of voice within each gender, differences that our work has revealed to be much more powerful than gender effects (Harter, Waters, & Whitesell, 1997; Waters & Gonzales, 1995). In addition, voice has been treated as a relatively global construct, with little consideration of how it may vary across different interpersonal contexts.

Thus, we offer an alternative approach to understanding the level of voice among adolescents, focusing on particular processes that can explain individual differences in voice among both female and male adolescents across five relational contexts: parents, teachers, male classmates, female classmates, and close friends. We anticipated that an adolescent may be more comfortable sharing his or her thoughts in some interpersonal arenas than in others. For adolescents as a group, we predicted that level of voice would be highest with close friends, given that an important function of close friendships is the sharing of intimate thoughts and feelings, particularly during adolescence (see Brown, 1990; Gilligan et al., 1989; Savin-Williams & Berndt, 1990). Level of voice should be somewhat lower with peers in the classroom, given concerns such as appearing stupid or alienating others, and with teachers and parents, given the extent to which adolescents often feel that adults do not understand or validate their opinions, thoughts, and feelings (see Elkind, 1967, 1984).

However, more critical to our framework was the hypothesis that there would be individual differences in the level of voice that adolescent boys and girls reported across the five contexts. Adolescence is a period of heightened self-consciousness for both genders (see Harter, 1990), particularly as it becomes increasingly apparent that one is the object of other's evaluations. Thus, as Elkind (1967, 1984) also observed, adolescents may attempt to obscure their true selves if they feel that they do not measure up to the standards set by others whose opinions are critical and therefore may not meet with their approval (see also Broughton, 1981; Selman, 1980). The level of such support may well vary across relational contexts, leading to corresponding differences in the level of voice displayed within each context.

We focused specifically on the support that individual adolescents receive for *voice*—namely, the encouragement and validation they receive for expressing their opinions. As previous analyses have suggested (see Bleiberg, 1984; Horney, 1950; Sullivan, 1953; Winnicott, 1965), if significant others do not validate the child's authentic experiences and attributes, the true self goes into hiding, as the child increasingly feels compelled to suppress its expression (see also Deci & Ryan, 1995). In a previous study, we examined the relationship between level of validation from parents and peers and adolescents' displays of true versus false self-behavior, more generally defined (Harter et al., 1996). Perceived support was highly predictive of self-reported levels of true versus false self-behavior. Adolescents who acknowledged that parents and peers respected who they were as a person reported high levels of true self-behavior, whereas those who experienced lack of approval reported high levels of false self-behavior. In that study, we obtained no gender differences. Rather, support from significant others predicted marked individual differences in true self-behavior for both genders.

Thus, in the present study, we did not anticipate major gender differences. Rather, we hypothesized that those adolescents of both genders reporting high levels of support for voice—namely, that others listened with respect to their opinions— would report high levels of voice; in contrast, those experiencing low levels of support for voice should report low levels of voice. Our predictions are consistent with findings in the adult communication literature revealing that men and women are more similar than different in their self-presentational styles and that individual differences in self-disclosure and self-assertiveness within each gender are far more salient than gender differences per se (see Pearson, Turner, & Todd-Mancillas, 1991). Consistent with the communications literature, we view the predicted relationship between support for voice and level of voice within each gender as a transactional, reciprocal process. Thus, support, in the form of encouraging and listening to the expression of opinions, should provide an incentive leading to higher levels of adolescent voice. To the extent that adolescents' expressions of voice are then rewarded through positive responses to what adolescents have to say, high levels of voice should be further promoted or maintained.

Although our voice construct bears some similarity to constructs such as self-discourse and self-assertion, there are differences. Self-disclosure is typically defined as "intentional sharing of intimate information about oneself," whereas self-assertion is defined as "communication of one's needs and wants in an effort to gain another's volitional understanding and/or compliance" (Pearson et al., 1991, p. 162). The voice construct refers to the expression of one's opinions or what one is thinking rather than to intimate information or the expression of needs and wants. Moreover, the voice construct is different in that it is embedded within the larger framework of true versus false self-behavior. The presence of voice is viewed as an honest expression of one's true opinions (i.e., saying what one really believes), whereas its absence is viewed as false self-behavior—namely, the suppression of one's true self. To document these assumptions, we included questions that directly asked adolescents whether failure to express their opinions reflected false or true behavior. Initial support for this assumption came from a study (Buddin & Harter, 1997) in which the majority of adolescents indicated that failure to say what they thought was considered false or phony.

Gender Orientation

Although we did not anticipate overall gender differences per se, we hypothesized that gender *orientation* among female adolescents would be predictive of level of voice. One of Gilligan's (1993) arguments is that female adolescents attempt to emulate the "good woman stereotype" in the culture. Part of this ideal involves an ethic of caring, in which female adolescents are encouraged to be more sensitive to the needs and desires of others than to their own. With regard to the voice construct, the "good woman" listens empathically to others, often at the expense of speaking her own mind. Yet what percentage of female adolescents in the 1990s are buying into this stereotype, accepting it as their ideal? We anticipated that there would be a subgroup of girls who would endorse this ideal, although others would not. Thus, we hypothesized that those adolescent girls who display a feminine gender orientation, endorsing feminine sex role attributes that reflect features of the "good woman" stereotype and eschewing masculine attributes, should report lack of voice. In contrast, androgynous adolescent girls, who endorse a combination of feminine and masculine attributes, were predicted to report relatively high levels of voice. Pilot studies have supported these general predictions (Waters & Gonzales, 1995; Johnson, 1995).

We further hypothesized that feminine girls may be particularly vulnerable to low levels of voice in some contexts but not in others. We reasoned that they would feel more compelled to display the "good woman stereotype" in the public social context of school—around teachers and classmates. However, in more private interpersonal relationships with close friends or parents, feminine girls should be more comfortable expressing their opinions. In contrast, androgynous adolescent girls should be able to express themselves equally well in both situations. We also hypothesized that differing levels of support for voice may contribute to the gender orientation effects anticipated. That is, adolescent girls endorsing a feminine orientation were expected to report lower levels of support for voice in the public arena of school (from teachers and classmates) than were those endorsing an androgynous orientation.

Among adolescent boys, we anticipated that we could identify both masculine and androgynous subgroups in sufficient numbers (on the basis of previous samples). However, we had no clear basis for predicting that level of voice might differ as a function of these two gender orientations. Thus, it was simply of empirical interest to determine whether any differences in voice would be obtained across the relational contexts included.

The Liabilities of Lack of Voice

Scholars who have examined the consequences of inauthenticity (Chodorow, 1989; Gilligan, 1982; Gilligan et al., 1989; Jordan, 1991; Jordan, Kaplan, Miller, Stiver, & Surrey, 1991; Lerner, 1993; Miller, 1986; Stiver & Miller, 1988) concurred that there are definite liabilities to suppressing oneself within relationships. In addition to displays of depressive affect, global self-worth, a correlate of depression, is also negatively affected. Thus, feelings of personal worth and confidence become eroded if individuals compromise or disown their true selves. In our own work, we have empirically demonstrated with both adolescents (Harter et al., 1996) and adults (Harter, Waters, Pettitt, Whitesell, Kofkin, & Jordan, 1997) that those who acknowledge high levels of false self-behavior also report a constellation of reactions that includes depressed affect, hopelessness, and low global self-worth. We have also found global self-worth to be related to level of voice (Johnson, 1995).

In this study, we sought to examine the relationship between voice and a new construct that we have labeled *relational self-worth*—namely, how much an individual values oneself within particular relational contexts. Findings (Harter, Waters, & Whitesell, in press) have revealed that adolescents assess their worth differently across interpersonal contexts as shown by a clear, context-related factor pattern and by the magnitude of the discrepancies in individuals' self-worth scores across relationships. Thus, we hypothesized that level of voice within a given relational arena would be more predictive of self-worth in that particular relationship than in all others. Therefore, the liabilities of suppressing one's voice were also hypothesized to be context specific.

In summary, our major goals were (a) to demonstrate that level of voice varies across contexts, (b) to document that context-specific levels of voice were more highly related to support for voice within each context than to gender per se, (c) to test the prediction that girls with a feminine gender orientation will be particularly vulnerable to low levels of voice in more public and social situations, and (d) to assess the hypothesis that level of voice within a given relationship will be associated with low self-worth in that particular relational context.

Method

Participants

Participants were 307 high school students (165 girls, 142 boys) at three grade levels: 9th ($n = 138$), 10th ($n = 85$), and 11th ($n = 84$). Students were drawn from a school district in a middle-class neighborhood ranging from lower- to upper-middle-class socioeconomic status. Seventy-five percent of the students were Caucasian, 9% were Asian, 5% were Hispanic, 1% were African American, and 7% were "other" or non-classifiable. However, there were insufficient numbers of minority participants to include ethnicity as a factor in the analyses. The questionnaires were group-administered in students' Language Arts classes.

Measures

Level of voice   Self-reported level of voice was assessed with questionnaire items that tapped the extent to which respondents were able to "express their opinions," "share what they are really thinking," "let others know what is important to them," "say what is on their mind," and "express their points of view." Items tapping this content were constructed for each of five contexts: voice with parents, voice with teachers in the classroom, voice with male classmates, voice with female classmates, and voice with close friends. The order of items was randomized across contexts. Questions were written in a "structured alternative format" designed to reduce the tendency to give socially desirable responses (Harter, 1988). A sample item reads as follows: "Some teenagers share what they are really thinking with [particular other]" but "Other teenagers find it hard to share what they are really thinking with [particular other]." The respondent is first asked to decide whether he or she is more like the teenagers described in the first or the second part of the statement. The participant is then asked to check one of two boxes at the side of each statement, indicating whether that description is only "sort of true for me" or "really true for me." Items are counterbalanced such that approximately half of the five items per subscale are worded to begin with a description of the presence of voice, whereas the others are worded to express lack of voice. Items are scored on a 4-point scale in which a 4 represents the *highest* level of voice and a 1 represents the *lowest* level of voice. The internal consistency reliabilities across the five relational contexts were .86 (parents), .86 (teachers), .86 (male classmates), .89 (female classmates), and .89 (close friends).

In a previous study (Johnson, 1995), the convergent validity of our voice measure has been established, tapping voice with parents, male friends, female friends, classmates, and teachers. On a separate task designed to tap multiple selves, participants were asked to generate six attributes for each of the same five roles (reflecting any characteristics that the adolescent felt were displayed in each context). A subset of attributes could be scored as *high voice* (e.g., talkative, open, argumentative, assertive, speak my opinion, truthful, say how I feel, being myself) and as *low voice* (e.g., quiet, keep thoughts to myself, closed off, withdrawn, not completely honest, not truthful, not being "me"). Participants were selected as either high voice or low voice if at least two of the six attributes per role fell into one of these categories (with none in the other category). For purposes of validity, we then compared the voice scores from our questionnaire for these high and low voice groups. Across the five roles, low voice participants' questionnaire scores ranged from 1.83 to 2.56, whereas high voice participants' scores ranged from 3.27 to 3.50. For every role, t tests revealed that the differences were highly significant (ps of .0001 for all but one role, which was significant at .01).

In the present study, we addressed the issue of construct validity by asking whether lack of voice is actually perceived by adolescents to be false self-behavior. In our initial studies of voice, we simply assumed that lack of voice represents false self-behavior, in large part because adolescents cite the inability to express their opinions as one manifestation of the false self. However, one can imagine other motives for lack of voice that do not imply lack of authenticity. For example, (a) one may be shy temperamentally, (b) it may seem socially inappropriate to express one's opinions in certain contexts, or (c) one may not share opinions that are considered private. Thus, we created items to determine whether adolescents perceive lack of voice as false or true self-behavior (e.g., "When I don't say what I am thinking around [particular persons], I feel like I am not being the 'real me' " vs. "When I don't say what I am thinking around [particular persons], it feels like I am being the 'real me' "). These subscales were highly reliable (αs = .84, .92, .92, and .92, for the contexts of parents, teachers, male classmates, and female classmates, respectively).

Mean scores for each context were 2.06, 2.14, 2.21, and 2.09, where these low scores (on a 1- to 4-point scale) reflect judgments that lack of voice is considered to be false self-behavior. There were no significant gender differences. Participants were further divided at the midpoint into those who judged lack of voice to be false self and those who judged absence of voice to be true self-behavior. Across the four contexts, the percentages reporting that suppression of opinions reflects false self-behavior were 78%, 69%, 70%, and 76%, respectively. Thus, approximately three fourths of all adolescents view suppression of voice as a manifestation of false self-behavior.

Support for voice   To examine the role of perceived support, we developed questions that tapped the extent to which others (a) listen to one's opinions and take them seriously, (b) show that they want to hear what one has to say, (c) respect one's ideas even if they don't agree, (d) are interested in what is on one's mind, and (e) try to understand one's point of view. A sample item is "My [particular others] show that they want to hear what I have to say" or "My [particular others] usually don't show that they want to hear what I have to say." As with the level of voice measure, participants first decide which statement is more like them and then indicate whether this statement is *sort of true* for them or *really true* for them. A score of 4 represents the highest level of support for voice, whereas a score of 1 reflects the lowest level of perceived support. For the present sample, internal consistency reliabilities were .92, .88, .88, .89, and .89, for parents, teachers, male classmates, female classmates, and close friends, respectively.

Gender orientation   To assess gender orientation, we drew items from several instruments in the literature, including the Personality Attributes Questionnaire (Spence, Helmreich, & Stapp, 1975), the Sex Role Inventory developed by Bem (1981), and Boldizar's (1991) adaptation for children and adolescents. Feminine items tap themes that include sensitivity, warmth, empathy, expressions of affection, enjoyment of babies and children, gentleness, and concern for others who are in distress. Masculine items tap dimensions such as competitiveness, ability to make decisions, independence, risk taking, confidence, athleticism, mechanical aptitude, individualism, leadership, and enjoyment of math and science. (Across these instruments, there are a few items that tap voicelike constructs, e.g., assertive vs. shy. However, we did not include these items in our analyses because they represent potential confounds between the independent variable, gender orientation, and the dependent variable, level of voice.)

Items were worded as statements (e.g., "I am willing to take risks." "I care about other people's feelings."), and respondents rated them on a 4-point scale (*very true for me, sort of true for me, not very true for me, not at all true for me*). There were 19 masculine and 12 feminine items. Reliabilities were .82 and .91 for masculine and feminine items, respectively. Participants were identified as having a feminine orientation if their feminine score was 3.4 or greater and their masculine score was 2.9 or lower. Masculine participants had the opposite pattern. Participants were identified as androgynous if both their masculine and feminine scores were 3.4 or greater. On the basis of these criteria, we identified 24 feminine girls and 34 androgynous girls as well as 21 masculine boys and 27 androgynous boys. (There were insufficient numbers of masculine girls and feminine boys to include in the analyses.)

Relational self-worth   The Relational Self-Worth Scale (see Harter, Waters, & Whitesell, in press) represents an adaptation of the Global Self-Worth subscale on the Self-Perception Profile for Adolescents (Harter, 1988). In each relational context, item content taps the extent to which adolescents like or don't like the kind of person they are, are pleased or disappointed with themselves, and are happy or unhappy with the way they are. A sample item from the Parents scale is "Some teenagers *don't* like the kind of person they are around their parents" but "Other teenagers do like the kind of person they are around their parents." There were four items per Contextual subscale. As with the other instruments, respondents select the type of teenager they are most like and then indicate how true that choice is for them. Items are scored on a 4-point scale in which a 4 represents the *most positive* sense of self-worth in that context and a score of 1 represents the *most negative* self-evaluation. Internal consistency reliabilities were .91, .88, .88, and .87 for parents, teachers, male classmates, and female classmates, respectively. Factor analysis, with an oblique rotation, has revealed a very clean four-factor solution with extremely high loadings on designated factors and only one cross-loading (of .21) above .20. The average cross-loadings of the items defining each factor were .79 (teachers), .86 (parents), .80 (male classmates), and .79 (female classmates).

(Close friends, not included in the instrument in this study, has been included in a previous study and was not only highly reliable but also defined its own, clear factor.)

Results

Framework With Regard to Significance Levels and Effect Sizes

As scholars (see Eagly, 1995) have noted, most gender differences are not large, and of those that are statistically significant, effect sizes may be relatively small, given the tremendous overlap in the distributions for males and females. Therefore, we interpreted only those differences significant at the .01 level or better associated with moderate to large effect sizes, using Cohen's (1977) guidelines (large effect sizes are .15 or better, moderate effect sizes are between .06 and .14, and small effect sizes are between .01 and .04, as indicated by their eta-square value).

Level of Voice Across Relationships

To examine the prediction that level of voice would vary across relationships, we factor-analyzed voice scores across the five contexts (with teachers, parents, male classmates, female classmates, and close friends), using an oblique rotation. As Table 1 reveals, we obtained a very clean factor pattern with very high loadings on the designated factors, with no cross-loadings greater than .20. Thus, individuals displayed different levels of voice across contexts.

For the group as a whole, we anticipated that voice would be higher with close friends than with teachers, parents, and classmates. A grade (3) × gender (2) × context (5) multivariate analysis of variance (MANOVA) was performed on the voice scores. The significant main effect for context, $F(4, 1092) = 59.72$, $p < .001$ ($\eta^2 = .18$), provides general support for this pattern (see Table 2, grades combined). The main effect for gender, $F(1, 1092) = 31.29$, $p < .001$ ($\eta^2 = .10$), reflecting higher levels of voice for girls compared with boys, was qualified by the Gender × Context interaction, $F(4, 1092) = 8.51$, $p < .001$ ($\eta^2 = .03$). Contrasts revealed that level of voice with both female classmates and close friends was significantly higher ($ps < .001$, $\eta^2 = .15$

Table 1

Factor Pattern for Level of Voice Scores

Scale Item	Factor 1	Factor 2	Factor 3	Factor 4	Factor 5
Teacher 1	.86				
Teacher 2	.84				
Teacher 3	.83				
Teacher 4	.71				
Teacher 5	.70				
Parent 1		.87			
Parent 2		.77			
Parent 3		.86			
Parent 4		.79			
Parent 5		.62			
Male classmate 1			.85		
Male classmate 2			.86		
Male classmate 3			.82		
Male classmate 4			.69		
Male classmate 5			.69		
Female classmate 1				.83	
Female classmate 2				.79	
Female classmate 3				.86	
Female classmate 4				.77	
Female classmate 5				.82	
Close friend 1					.87
Close friend 2					.90
Close friend 3					.90

Note. For clarity, only factor loadings greater than .20 are included. Only three items were administered for close friend.

and .11, respectively) for female participants than for male participants, whereas levels of voice were comparable for the two genders with teachers, parents, and male classmates. Additional contrasts within gender revealed that for *male* adolescents, voice with a close friend was significantly ($ps < .001$) higher than in all other relationships. Voice with male classmates was also significantly higher ($ps < .01$) than with female classmates, parents, and teachers. For *female* adolescents, a similar pattern emerged in that voice with close friends was significantly ($ps < .001$) higher than in all other contexts. Voice with female classmates was also significantly ($ps < .001$) higher than with male classmates, parents, and teachers.

Grade and Gender Effects

A major purpose of the present study was to determine whether there was any cross-sectional evidence among a high school sample that levels of voice declined for female adolescents as a function of grade level, but did not for male adolescents. As can be

Table 2

Mean Level of Voice by Grade and Gender

Relational context	9th graders Female	Male	10th graders Female	Male	11th graders Female	Male	Grades combined Female	Male
Teachers								
M	2.80	2.60	2.99	2.64	3.01	2.76	2.93	2.66
SD	0.66	0.70	0.77	0.63	0.78	0.79	0.72	0.70
Parents								
M	2.77	2.66	2.99	2.71	3.19	2.89	2.98	2.75
SD	0.82	0.70	0.69	0.68	0.76	0.74	0.78	0.71
Male classmates								
M	2.96	2.95	3.01	2.87	2.96	3.03	2.98	2.95
SD	0.66	0.66	0.63	0.64	0.70	0.68	0.66	0.65
Female classmates								
M	3.40	2.71	3.36	2.80	3.32	2.88	3.36	2.79
SD	0.51	0.81	0.57	0.68	0.63	0.74	0.55	0.74
Close friends								
M	3.73	3.23	3.63	3.35	3.74	3.23	3.70	3.27
SD	0.44	0.77	0.55	0.66	0.49	0.79	0.48	0.74

seen in Table 2, voice scores do not decline as a function of grade for female adolescents. In the Grade × Gender × Context MANOVA described above, there was no significant main effect for grade, $F (2, 273) = 1.68$, $p = .19$ ($\eta^2 = .01$), nor was there a significant Grade × Gender interaction, $F (2, 273) = .03$, $p = .97$ ($\eta^2 = .00$). As observed above, in two contexts, with female classmates and with close friends, the adolescent girls reported significantly higher levels of voice than did the adolescent boys. Thus, using this particular methodology, there is neither evidence for a decline in voice among high school girls nor reports from girls at any grade levels of lower levels of voice than boys.

Support for Voice

It was our expectation that individual differences in level of voice *within* each gender would be predicted by the level of support for voice that adolescents experienced in each relational context. The correlations between support for voice and level of self-reported voice confirmed this expectation ($rs = .48, .59, .46,$ and $.51,$ for voice with

Figure 1

Level of Voice as a Function of Support for Voice Within Each Relational Context

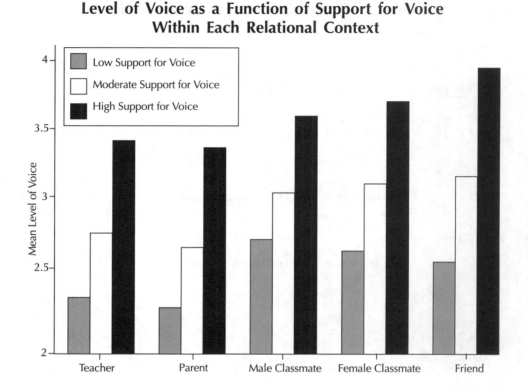

teachers, parents, male classmates, and female classmates, respectively). All are significant (*p*s between .01–.0001). Moreover, as can be seen in Table 3, support within a given context is more highly correlated with level of voice in that same context compared with other relational arenas. An examination of the significance of the difference between those correlations on the diagonal and all others in the same row or column revealed that each was significantly different (*p*s ranging from .01–.001).

To examine the absolute levels of support and voice contributing to these correlations, we divided participants into one of three levels of support: *low* (1.0–1.9), *moderate* (2.5–3.0), and *high* (3.5–4.0). As can be seen in Figure 1, within each context, there was a strong effect for level of support for voice, with highly significant main effects and large effect sizes: teachers, F (2, 266) = 36.90, $p <: .001$ ($\eta^2 = .22$); parents, F (2, 266) = 72.40, $p < .001$ ($\eta^2 = .35$); male classmates, F (2, 266) = 25.30, $p < .001$ ($\eta^2 = .16$); female classmates, F (2, 266) = 22.68, $p < .001$ ($\eta^2 = .15$); and close friends, F (2, 266) = 87.94, $p < .001$ ($\eta^2 = .40$). Contrasts revealed that within each context, those with low support reported significantly lower levels of voice than did those with moderate support (all *p*s < .001, η^2s .06–.30), and those with moderate support reported lower levels of voice than did those with higher support (all *p*s < .001, η^2s .07–.24). There were no significant Level of Support × Gender interactions,

Table 3

Correlations Between Level of Support and Voice in Each Context

	Level of voice				
Support for voice	Teachers	Parents	Male classmates	Female classmates	Close friends
Teachers	.49	.37	.14	.26	.26
Parents	.18	.59	.11	.12	.23
Male classmates	.27	.27	.46	.35	.25
Female class-mates	.25	.22	.32	.51	.29
Close friends	.24	.29	.25	.38	.70

indicating that the effects of support are highly similar for both male and female adolescents.

Gender Orientation

Specific predictions were advanced with regard to the effects of gender orientation on voice for female adolescents only. It was predicted that those who endorsed a feminine orientation would report lower levels of voice in the public arena of school (with teachers and male classmates, in particular) than they would in private, interpersonal relationships with parents or close friends. We hypothesized that androgynous female participants would report equally high levels of voice in public and private contexts. (Voice with female classmates was excluded from the particular analysis because of confounds between female classmate and friend status; that is, friends were very likely to be a subset of female classmates, such that we could not classify the pool of female classmates as either public or private relationships.)

Figure 2 presents the comparison of voice means for feminine and androgynous females in public versus private contexts. As can be observed, our hypothesis was supported, as revealed by a significant Gender Orientation × Type of Context interaction, $F(1, 52) = 6.78$, $p < .01$ ($\eta^2 = .07$). Contrasts revealed that the feminine girls reported significantly ($p < .001$, $\eta^2 = .34$) lower levels of voice in the public, as compared to private, contexts, whereas there were no context effects for the androgynous girls. This interaction also reflects the finding that, as predicted, feminine girls reported significantly ($p < .001$, $\eta^2 = .19$) lower levels of voice than did androgynous girls in the public contexts, whereas the two groups of girls did not differ in their level of voice in private contexts. Thus, as we hypothesized, feminine girls are particularly at risk for lack of voice in the public arena.

Figure 2

Level of Voice for Feminine and Androgynous Female Adolescents as a Function of Public and Private Relational Contexts

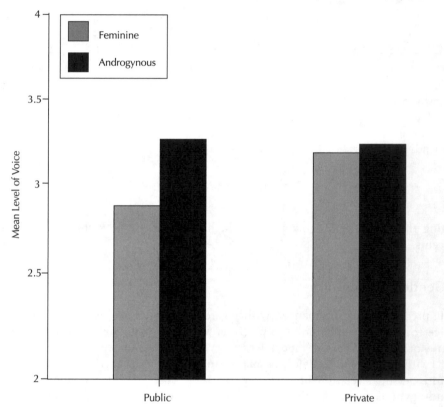

It was also of interest to determine whether feminine girls reported lower levels of support for voice from those explicitly in the public school arena—namely, teachers and male classmates. Examination of the support scores revealed that feminine girls did report receiving lower levels of support for voice from both teachers ($M = 2.9$) and male classmates ($M = 2.5$) compared with the androgynous girls (Ms = 3.2) for both teacher and male classmate support). To determine whether these differential levels of support may contribute to the lowered levels of voice among feminine girls, voice scores in the public arenas for the two groups were analyzed, with support for voice covaried out. The results revealed that the significance of the difference between feminine and androgynous girls in public contexts ($p < .001$, $\eta^2 = .19$) was reduced when support was partialed out ($p < .14$, $\eta^2 = .04$), suggesting that the lower levels of support experienced by feminine girls contributed to their lower levels of voice.

Table 4

Correlations Between Voice and Relational Self-Worth in Each Context

	Relational self-worth			
Level of voice	Teachers	Parents	Male classmates	Female classmates
Teachers	.43	.28	.38	.33
Parents	.34	.55	.27	.24
Male classmates	.31	.17	.44	.23
Female classmates	.23	.09	.23	.44

In comparison to the public contexts, feminine girls reported significantly ($ps = .01$) higher levels of support in the two private contexts with friends ($M = 3.40$) and with parents ($M = 3.32$). As anticipated, these support levels were comparable to those of the androgynous girls with friends ($M = 3.69$) and with parents ($M = 3.25$).

Among male adolescents, we did not have any basis for making clear predictions about how relational context might affect levels of voice. Both masculine and androgynous males could be identified in sufficient numbers for the purpose of analyses. A context (5) × gender orientation (2) analysis of variance (ANOVA) revealed a significant main effect for context, $F(4, 168) = 7.86$, $p < .002$ ($\eta^2 = .16$), favoring androgynous boys. However, this main effect was qualified by a significant Context × Gender Orientation interaction, $F(4, 168) = 3.65$, $p < .01$ ($\eta^2 = .08$). The public–private distinction did not contribute to these effects. Rather, contrasts revealed no significant differences between masculine and androgynous boys in three contexts—namely, with parents ($Ms = 2.62$ and 2.92, respectively), with teachers (Ms of 2.86 and 2.93), or with female classmates ($Ms = 2.91$ and 3.15). However, masculine boys reported significantly ($p < .02$, $\eta^2 = .12$) higher levels of voice with male classmates ($M = 3.41$) than did androgynous boys ($M = 2.99$). The direction of effects was just the reverse with close friends, where masculine boys reported significantly ($p < .01$, $\eta^2 = .10$) lower levels of voice ($M = 3.19$) than did androgynous boys $M = 3.64$). Thus, masculinity itself may empower male adolescents to speak their mind with male classmates; however, masculinity combined with feminine attributes would appear to better facilitate adolescent boys' expressions of thoughts and feelings with close friends.

Relationship Between Voice and Relational Self-Worth

It was hypothesized that level of voice within a context would be related to relational self-worth in that context. Correlations between voice and self-worth within each context were moderately high, as can be seen on the diagonal of Table 4, and significant (*p*s from .01–.001). Moreover, support was obtained for the hypothesis that voice within a relationship should be more highly predictive of self-worth within that same context than within other contexts. The correlations of voice and self-worth within a given context were significantly higher (*p*s between .03–.001) than those correlations that are off of the diagonal. (Of the 24 relevant comparisons, there was only one exception—namely, *r* = .43 vs. *r* = .38.)

Discussion

A major goal of the present study was to determine whether there was any evidence that levels of voice decline for adolescent girls as they move through the high school years. Our alternative framework specified that social processes occurring in each relational context would better predict individual differences in level of voice within each gender. The findings of the present study did not support a general decline among adolescent girls as a group, and there were no gender differences in level of voice that favored boys. To the contrary, girls reported higher levels of voice than did boys in two interpersonal contexts, with female classmates and with close friends who are most likely to be girls. Thus, in these two relationships, 15- to 17-year-old female adolescents appear quite comfortable expressing their opinions. It could be argued that the decline in level of voice that Gilligan (1993) described for girls has already occurred prior to high school. However, the absolute level of voice scores ranged from moderate to high across contexts and was virtually identical to the scores we have obtained among younger female adolescents, aged 12 to 15 years, in a previous study (see Harter, Waters, & Whitesell, 1997). Thus, in our cross-sectional work, there appears to be no general decline for female adolescents across the 12- to 17-year age range.

In previous analyses, voice has been treated as a relatively global construct. In the present study, we demonstrated that the ability to share one's opinions is context specific. For the sample as a whole, voice was strongest with close friends, as anticipated, because close friends provide an interpersonal arena in which thoughts, opinions, and feelings can be safely shared (see Brown, 1990; Buhrmester & Furman, 1987; Gilligan et al., 1989; Savin-Williams & Berndt, 1990). Voice was next highest with same-gender classmates and was lowest for opposite-gender classmates, parents, and teachers, as predicted. However, a major goal was to document the marked differences in voice levels that individual adolescents reported across the five contexts. Most participants reported moderate variation in voice across relationships. In the extreme, some participants reported the lowest possible level of voice in one context and the highest level in another context. These differences were documented in the factor analysis of voice scores, where each context defined a discrete factor with high item loadings and negligible cross loadings.

The Role of Support for Voice

We hypothesized that the individual differences in level of voice would be predicted by the perceived support from significant others within each context, anticipating that this process would apply to both male and female adolescents. Correlational findings as well as mean differences in level of voice reported for those experiencing low, moderate, and high levels of support confirmed this expectation. Thus, if adolescents of either gender perceive that significant others in a particular context do not take their opinions seriously, their voices will be compromised in that context. It was also documented that the correlations between support for voice in a given context and level of voice in that same context were higher than level of support in a given context with voice in all other contexts, providing further evidence for the usefulness of a context-specific framework in examining these processes.

The Contribution of Gender Orientation

Although the findings of the present study revealed that girls, as a group, did not lack voice, we hypothesized that a particular subset of girls—namely those who endorsed a feminine gender orientation—would be more vulnerable in certain relational contexts. Specifically, we predicted that feminine girls would report lower levels of voice within the public arena of school than they would in more private, interpersonal contexts with close friends and parents. In contrast, we hypothesized that there should be no such difference for adolescent girls reporting an androgynous gender orientation. The findings confirmed these predictions.

This pattern suggests a refinement of Gilligan's position. First, it would appear to be gender orientation rather than gender, per se, that contributes to lack of voice. Second, our evidence suggests that a feminine gender orientation is only a liability in certain situations—namely, more public contexts. It is in these contexts that one might expect highly feminine adolescent girls to display behaviors consistent with the "good woman" societal stereotype, leading to their suppression of voice. Within the public arena, such girls would appear to feel that certain stereotypic feminine behaviors (e.g., being unassertive and a good listener) are appropriate or demanded to be socially acceptable. In the present study, the finding that feminine girls reported that they receive less support for expressing their opinions within the school setting is consistent with this interpretation.

Gilligan's argument hinges on changes as girls move through adolescence in that she contended that many lose the strong voices that they possessed as children. In the present study, we do not know if the feminine adolescent girls have actually lost their voice in the public arena; we only know that they lack voice as teenagers. For those who have embraced a stereotypically feminine orientation from childhood, their voices may have been muted from a much earlier age, leading to continuity in level of voice across childhood and adolescence. Thus, longitudinal designs, in which researchers assess voice as a function of gender orientation beginning in childhood, would allow us to address issues of whether voice is actually lost or whether for some girls as well as some boys, socialization factors contribute to lack of voice at earlier periods of development.

The Liabilities of Lack of Voice

The suppression of self within interpersonal relationships has been related to a number of liabilities, including correlates of depression such as low self-worth (Chodorow, 1989; Gilligan, 1982; Gilligan et al., 1989; Jordan et al., 1991; Lerner, 1993; Miller, 1986; Stiver & Miller, 1988). In the present study, we documented the strong relationship between level of voice and relational self-worth within each interpersonal context (see Harter, Waters, & Whitesell, in press). Those with low levels of voice reported low self-worth in the corresponding context, whereas those with high levels of voice reported correspondingly high self-worth. Moreover, level of voice was more predictive of self-worth within the same relationship than in other relationships, providing additional support for a context-specific framework.

Low self-worth has been viewed as a potential liability of lack of voice, implying directionality—namely, that if an individual is suppressing his or her opinions, this will lead to negative evaluations of one's worth as a person. However, it is possible that the opposite may also be true; that is, if an individual evaluates the self negatively in a given context, his or her voice is suppressed. In the present study, we could not determine which interpretation best describes the relationship between level of voice and relational self-worth. It is likely that the relationship becomes reciprocal in that lack of voice may lead one to question one's worth as a person; however, the more one questions one's worth, the more one feels that there is little to say.

Analyses implying that suppression of the self will erode positive evaluations of self-worth hinge on the assumption that low levels of voice represent false self-behavior. In the present study, it was determined that approximately 75% of adolescents reported that suppression of their opinions did indeed reflect their being false or phony, lending credence to our assumptions. We know less about the 25% who feel that withholding their points of view reflects true self-behavior. Are these individuals temperamentally shy? Do they feel it is socially inappropriate to express their opinions? Might it be disrespectful in some contexts, for example, with adults? These are possible interpretations that await further research.

Conclusion

The present study suggests that researchers need to move beyond predictors such as gender and age to consider the particular psychological processes that predict individual differences in level of voice within each gender. The findings revealed that context-specific support for making one's opinions known is highly predictive of voice for both male and female adolescents. The results also documented that among female adolescents, gender orientation is critical, given that those with a feminine orientation reported lower levels of voice in the public context of school compared with androgynous female adolescents. However, the feminine style was not found to be a liability in the more private contexts with close friends and parents. It is likely that those with a feminine orientation may be compelled to act in accordance with the good woman stereotype in more public, compared with private, relational contexts. Thus, the dynamics that Gilligan (1993) articulated appear to apply to only a subset of female adolescents in certain contexts. Moreover, future research needs to address whether this pattern appears prior to adolescence.

It should be noted that the failure to find evidence for a decline in voice for females, as a group, was demonstrated with a questionnaire measure tapping self-reported levels of voice assessed within a cross-sectional design. In future work, it is urged that this methodology be broadened to include observational procedures as well as semistructured interview techniques, ideally using longitudinal designs. Such designs will be especially important in determining whether particular adolescents actually lose their voices or whether many simply lack the ability to express their opinion. Still others may find their voices. Moreover, it will be important to examine the ability to voice one's opinions across different content areas because some topics (e.g., dating, sexuality) may be more difficult to discuss in certain relational contexts compared with others.

Other dynamics of the voice process also require elucidation. For example, Gilligan et al. (1989) found that their interview techniques revealed the active struggle that many girls consciously experience as they face the conflict between remaining faithful to their authentic selves versus silently capitulating to the desires of significant others. Thus, female and male adolescents at comparably low levels of voice may well differ in the extent to which such suppression causes conflict, with female adolescents reporting greater conflict, another potential liability. Our ultimate goal should be to identify prevention and intervention strategies that allow adolescent boys as well as girls to confidently display their authentic selves rather than to experience the liabilities of suppressing the self.

References

Belenky, M., Clinchy, N. G., Goldberger, N. R., & Tarule, J. M. (1986). *Women's ways of knowing: The development of self, voice, and mind.* New York: Basic Books.

Bem, S. (1981). Gender schema theory: A cognitive account of sex typing. *Psychological Review, 88,* 354–364.

Bleiberg, E. (1984). Narcissistic disorders in children. *Bulletin of the Menninger Clinic, 48,* 501–517.

Boldizar, J. P. (1991). Assessing sex-typing and androgyny in children: The children's sex role inventory. *Developmental Psychology, 27,* 505–515.

Broughton, J. (1981). The divided self in adolescence. *Human Development, 24,* 13–32.

Brown, B. B. (1990). Peer groups and peer cultures. In S. S. Feldman & G. Elliot (Eds.), *At the threshold: The developing adolescent* (pp. 171–196). Cambridge, MA: Harvard University Press.

Buddin, B., & Harter, S. (1997). *Level of voice in adolescents as a function of parental modeling and support.* Unpublished manuscript, University of Denver.

Buhrmester, D., & Furman, W. (1987). The development of companionship and intimacy. *Child Development, 58,* 1101–1113.

Chodorow, N. (1989). *Feminism and psychoanalytic theory.* New Haven, CT: Yale University Press.

Cohen, J. (1977). *Statistical power analysis for the behavioral sciences.* New York: Academic Press.

Deci, E. L., & Ryan, R. M. (1995). Human autonomy: The basis for true self-esteem. In M. H. Kernis (Eds.), *Efficacy, agency, and self-esteem* (pp. 31–46). New York: Plenum Press.

Eagly, A. H. (1995). The science and politics of comparing women and men. *American Psychologist, 50,* 145–158.

Elkind, D. (1967). Egocentrism in adolescence. *Child Development, 38,* 1025–1031.

Elkind, D. (1984). *All grown up and no place to go: Teenagers in crisis.* Reading, MA: Addison-Wesley.

Erikson, E. (1950). *Childhood and society.* New York: Norton.

Gilligan, C. (1982). *In a different voice.* Cambridge, MA: Harvard University Press.

Gilligan, C. (1993). Joining the resistance: Psychology, politics, girls, and women. In L. Weis & M. Fine (Eds.), *Beyond silenced voices* (pp. 143–168). Albany: State University of New York Press.

Gilligan, C., Lyons, N., & Hanmer, T. J. (1989). *Making connections.* Cambridge, MA: Harvard University Press.

Griffin, N., Chassin, L., & Young, R. D. (1981). Measurement of global self-concept versus multiple role-specific self-concepts in adolescents. *Adolescence, 16,* 49–56.

Grotevant, H. D., & Cooper, C. R. (1983). *Adolescent development in the family: New directions for child development.* San Francisco: Jossey-Bass.

Harter, S. (1988). *The Self-Perception Profile for Adolescents.* Unpublished manual, University of Denver.

Harter, S. (1990). Adolescent self and identity development. In S. S. Feldman & G. Elliot (Eds.), *At the threshold: The developing adolescent* (pp. 352–387). Cambridge, MA: Harvard University Press.

Harter, S., Bresnick, S., Bouchey, H., & Whitesell, N. R. (in press). The development of multiple role-related selves during adolescence. *Development and Psychopathology.*

Harter, S., Marold, D. B., Whitesell, N. R., & Cobbs, G. (1996). A model of the effects of parent and peer support on adolescent false self behavior. *Child Development, 67,* 160–174.

Harter, S., & Monsour, A. (1992). Developmental analysis of opposing self-attributes in the adolescent self-portrait. *Developmental Psychology, 28,* 251–260.

Harter, S., Waters, P. L., Pettitt, L., Whitesell, N. R., Kofkin, J., & Jordan, J. (1997). Autonomy and connectedness as dimensions of adult relationship styles. *Journal of Social and Personal Relationships, 14,* 147–164.

Harter, S., Waters, P. L., & Whitesell, N. R. (1997). Lack of voice as a manifestation of false self behavior among adolescents: The school setting as a stage upon which the drama of authenticity is enacted. *Educational Psychologist, 32,* 153–173.

Harter, S., Waters, P. L., & Whitesell, N. R. (in press). Relational self-worth: Adolescents perceptions of their worth as a person in different relational contexts. *Child Development.*

Hill, J. P., & Holmbeck, G. N. (1986). Attachment theory and autonomy during adolescence. *Annals of Child Development, 3,* 145–189.

Horney, K. (1950). *Neurosis and human growth.* New York: Norton.

Johnson, E. (1995). *The role of social support and gender orientation in adolescent female development.* Unpublished doctoral dissertation, University of Denver, CO.

Jordan, J. V. (1991). The relational self: A new perspective for understanding women's development. In J. Strauss & G. Goethals (Eds.), *The self: Interdisciplinary approaches* (pp. 136–149). New York: Springer-Verlag.

Jordan, J. V., Kaplan, A. G., Miller, J. B., Stiver, L. P., & Surrey, J. L. (Eds.). (1991). *Women's growth in connection.* New York: Guilford Press.

Kolligian, J., Jr. (1990). Perceived fraudulence as a dimension of perceived incompetence. In R. J. Sternberg & J. Kolligian, Jr. (Eds.), *Competence reconsidered* (pp. 261–285). New Haven, CT: Yale University Press.

Lerner, H. G. (1993). *The dance of deception.* New York: Harper Collins.

Miller, J. B. (1986). *Toward a new psychology of women* (2nd ed.). Boston: Beacon Press.

Pearson, J. C., Turner, L. H., & Todd-Mancillas, W. (1991). *Gender and communication* (2nd ed.). Dubuque, IA: William C. Brown.

Rosenberg, M. (1986). Self-concept from middle childhood through adolescence. In J. Suls & A. Greenwald (Eds.), *Psychological perspectives on the self* (pp. 107–135). Hillsdale, NJ: Erlbaum.

Rubin, L. (1985). *Just friends: The role of friendship in our lives.* New York: Harper & Row.

Savin-Williams, R. C., & Berndt, T. J. (1990). Friendship and peer relations. In S. S. Feldman & G. Elliot (Eds.), *At the threshold: The developing adolescent* (pp. 277–307). Cambridge, MA: Harvard University Press.

Selman, R. (1980). *The growth of interpersonal understanding.* New York: Academic Press.

Smollar, J., & Youniss, J. (1985). Adolescent self-concept development. In R. L. Leahy (Ed.), *The development of self* (pp. 247–266). New York: Academic Press.

Spence, J. T., Helmreich, R., & Stapp, J. (1975). The Personal Attributes Questionnaire: A measure of sex role stereotypes and masculinity–femininity. *JSAS Catalog of Selected Documents in Psychology, 4,* 43–44.

Stiver, I. P., & Miller, J. B. (1988). From depression to sadness in the psychotherapy of women (Work in Progress No. 36). Wellesley, MA: Stone Center Working Paper Series.

Sullivan, H. (1953). *The interpersonal theory of psychiatry.* New York: Norton.

Waters, P. L., & Gonzales, R. (1995, March). *Level of voice among young adolescent males and females.* Paper presented at the meeting of the Society for Research in Child Development, Indianapolis, IN.

Winnicott, D. W. (1965). *The maturational processes and the facilitating environment.* New York: International Universities Press.

Questions

1. According to Carol Gilligan, what negative changes occur for girls at adolescence? Why do they occur?

2. In what ways does Harter's research extend our understanding of voice beyond Gilligan's claims that women lose their voice at adolescence?

3. What are the costs and benefits of endorsing a feminine sex role?

4. How do you reconcile the differences between the portrait of girls at adolescence promoted by Gilligan in the popular press and the findings of Harter and her colleagues?

References and Further Reading

Brown, L. M., & Gilligan, C. (1992). *Meeting at the Crossroads: Women's psychology and girls' development.* Cambridge, MA: Harvard University Press.

Gilligan, C., Lyons, N., & Hanmer, T. J. (1990). *Making connections: The relational worlds of adolescent girls at Emma Willard School.* Cambridge, MA: Harvard University Press.

Gilligan, C. (1991). Women's psychological development: Implications for psychotherapy. In C. Gilligan, A. Rogers, and D. Tolman (Eds.) *Women, girls and psychotherapy: Reframing resistance* (pp. 5–31). New York: Harrington Park Press.

Jason and His Brothers: What It's *Really* Like for Adolescent Boys in America

Michael Gurian is a therapist and educator who works with families, school districts, churches, and criminal justice agencies. He is author of *The Wonder of Boys: What Parents, Mentors, and Educators Can Do to Shape Boys into Exceptional Men* (1996), *A Fine Young Man: What Parents, Mentors, and Educators Can Do to Shape Adolescent Boys into Fine Young Men* (1998), and *The Good Son: Shaping the Moral Development of Our Boys and Young Men* (1999).

While research attention has been given in recent years to the drop in self-esteem that occurs for girls at adolescence, the self-esteem of adolescent males at this stage has been largely unexamined. Michael Gurian, who has devoted much of his professional life to working with and studying boys, is one of a number of therapists who have written for the popular press claiming that adolescent boys are at equal, if not greater, risk at adolescence than girls due to gender role prescriptions for behavior. Gurian focuses on the issue of self-esteem in adolescent males, arguing that low self-esteem for males has gone unrecognized due to their posturing and bravado, their attempts to fulfill male role expectations. Gurian presents statistics demonstrating that more boys than girls are diagnosed with Attention Deficit Hyperactive Disorder (ADHD), have learning problems, and drop out of school. Boys are at greater risk than girls are for being diagnosed and hospitalized for being mentally disturbed, for becoming addicted to drugs and alcohol, for committing suicide, and for harming themselves and others.

Gurian's argument that self-esteem is problematic for both boys and girls at adolescence is supported by three large-scale studies carried out by the National Center for Educational Statistics, covering approximately 50,000 adolescents (reported in Kling, Hyde, Showers, & Buswell, 1999). These studies found gender differences in self-esteem to be small to very small in magnitude in early adolescence. Similarly, a recent meta-analysis reveals that the magnitude of gender difference in self-esteem among 11-to-14-year-olds is small in magnitude, and much smaller than the difference between the self-esteem of males and females reported by the AAUW (Kling et al., 1999). Thus, if self-esteem drops at adolescence, it is at comparable levels for males and females. Problems of self-esteem are not unique to girls at adolescence, and the costs of acquiring the male role at adolescence, as Gurian suggests, merit further research attention.

"We cannot rescue America's families unless we make up our minds to save the boys."

—William Raspberry

I met Jason when he was twelve years old. His grades had been falling since he was nine. He had a problem with anger, as his mother put it. In fact, he had broken his wrist once from smashing it into the wall. He had been diagnosed with attention deficit disorder at ten by his teacher, and was on Ritalin. There was some improvement but now also a kind of blankness in him—his father's words. He had difficulty in athletics, mainly because he was a discipline problem, yet he wanted to play soccer.

He was a hard shell of a boy already at twelve. Though he and I lived in a middle-sized American city in the Pacific Northwest, he reminded me of urban youth who feel they have nothing going for them at all, trapped in inner cities, dangerous schools, and more dangerous streets. Jason dressed in the hip-hop style, and he had a buzz cut, his baseball cap on backwards, baggy jeans, and a flapping belt. He liked to talk about music, rap music, of course. He liked to show off.

Jason, his family, and I met a few times, with little progress. But one day Jason came in enraged. His mother apologized as she dropped him off and scooted out of my office, leaving him to me. I worked with him for a few minutes, until he started to cry. I listened, and pieces of a story came out. I found out he had been sexually abused by the father of a friend when he was ten, for a period of three months. He confessed, as his tears dried, that he couldn't get along with anyone, and he hated himself for it. He couldn't stay focused. He thought he should kill himself.

He had been enraged today, he said, because he'd just found out his parents were divorcing. He hated them, he hated himself, he hated life. Jason opened up to me, a man whom he barely knew, because he had no one else.

The activity that gave him the most solace, I knew, was playing violent video games. When our time was up, I knew he would return to them, soothe himself with them and whatever other distraction he could muster.

Jason's Brothers

Jason represents a "difficult" case. His is among those in our adolescent male population who are considered high risk. They are the adolescent males who are hurting most obviously and will hurt others most obviously. In my experience, no adolescent boy is immune to the pressures that can, over his decade of adolescence, put him at risk. Jason and his brothers are not so different from any mother's son.

Brian was seventeen when he killed himself. He was a high achiever, an A student, a lacrosse player. His father was a physician, and Brian planned on going to law school. Brian's girlfriend left him. He became depressed. "He wore his Walkman all the time," his mother said, "listening to bands I'd never heard of." He hanged himself, leaving a note: "I'm not worth loving and it's not worth living."

Kellen had very little fathering, no real relationship with grandparents; he was a quiet, inactive thirteen-year-old. His mother worried about his love of video games and TV in general. His grades were in the Cs, though he was naturally bright. His mother felt he was constantly unhappy. He smoked marijuana and cigarettes; what else, she didn't know and he wouldn't say.

"There's nothing wrong with me," he told me. His intelligence was wonderfully expressed in his ability to analyze games and media. He knew the computer games Myst and Riven very well. He loved the TV series "Men Behaving Badly." He confessed once that he felt he would never amount to much, so he had stopped trying. He was on Ritalin and Prozac both, a kind of typical media-linked and medicated youngster whose mom just prayed he would get through adolescence with a high school degree or G.E.D.

Max, fourteen, reminded me of a bird—he was six feet tall, with a pointed nose and chin, and filmy blue eyes. He had already tried cocaine. He too was on Ritalin. He had been kicked off the football team. He got into fights. He had been to three junior high schools. One day he said, "I'm gonna live hard, die young, and leave a pretty corpse," a strange statement of self-esteem he had learned from an old movie he couldn't name. "I'm gonna freak everyone out!" he said proudly.

He meant something else, too, in the end. After a number of weeks, he finally really opened up, cried, and said, "I'm like a top; I try to keep spinning and spinning so no one will notice how fucked up I am."

None of these weeping or stoically hard boys wanted me to hold him in the kind of physical embrace he truly needed, but what heart cannot go out to him?

The State of Male Adolescence Today

Statistics and stories about our homicidal adolescent males are dramatic enough to garner most of the headlines: the fourteen-year-old in Mississippi who killed two children and wounded seven; the fourteen-year-old in Kentucky who shot three dead; the thirteen-year-old in Washington who opened fire in his school and killed three; the eleven- and thirteen-year-olds who killed five in Jonesboro, Arkansas. But they don't describe the whole picture. It seems impossible for us to fully comprehend the state of male adolescence in our culture, yet it is essential we do so. There is hardly any social or personal health indicator in which adolescent boys do not show the lion's share of risk today. Decades ago, our females suffered more in more high-risk areas, and now our adolescent males are suffering privation we have not fully understood. I will take a moment here to lay out statistics for you, statistics that present just some of the areas of distress experienced by our adolescent males as a group. If you do not find your son fitting into one of these, you can be nearly assured that he knows boys who do. You yourself will know such boys. Your family life, your business, your neighborhood, your school has met them and been affected by them for years.

The Declining Safety of Our Adolescent Boys

- Adolescent boys are significantly more likely than adolescent girls to die before the age of eighteen, not just from violent causes but also from accidental death and disease.

- Adolescent boys are significantly more likely than adolescent girls to die at the hands of their caregivers. Two out of three juveniles killed at the hands of their parents or stepparents are male.
- Adolescent boys are fifteen times as likely as peer females to be victims of violent crime.
- One-third of adolescent male students nationwide carry a gun or other weapon to school.
- Gunshot wounds are now the second leading cause of accidental death among ten- to fourteen-year-old males.

The Mental Health of Adolescent Boys

- Adolescent boys are four times more likely than adolescent girls to be diagnosed as emotionally disturbed.
- The majority of juvenile mental patients nationwide are male. Depending on the state, most often between two-thirds and three-fourths of patients at juvenile mental facilities are male.
- Most of the deadliest and longest lasting mental problems experienced by children are experienced by adolescent males. For example, there are six male adolescent schizophrenics for every one female. Adolescent autistic males outnumber females two to one.
- Adolescent males significantly outnumber females in diagnoses of most conduct disorders, thought disorders, and brain disorders.

Drugs, Alcohol, and the Depression Link

The majority of adolescent alcoholics and drug addicts are male.

Terrence Real, a Cambridge, Massachusetts, psychotherapist, uses this statistic, among others, to point out the obvious: Although females are popularly considered to suffer more depression than males, in fact it is "overt depression" that our adolescent females experience two to four times more often than males. "Covert depression"—evidenced in drug and alcohol use, criminal activity, avoidance of intimacy, and isolation from others, especially family—brings the male/female depression ratio at least to par.

Terrence Real makes another important observation about male depression. Depression in males often has been overlooked because we don't recognize the male's way of being depressed. We measure depression by the female's model of overt depression. She talks about suicide, expresses feelings of worthlessness, shows her fatigue. Unaware of the male's less expressive, more stoic way of being, we miss the young depressed man who, in a town in Washington, walked into his high school and opened fire on his classroom, killing his classmates.

Suicide

- Adolescent males are four times more likely than adolescent females to commit suicide. Suicide success statistics (i.e., death actually occurs) for adolescent males are rising; suicide success statistics for adolescent females are not.

This suicide statistic is one of the most startling to health professionals not just because lives are lost but because it indicates dramatically how much trouble adolescent males are in and the degree to which male psychiatric illness is increasing.

- One of the most important findings of youth suicide studies is that adolescent males seem to have so much more trouble than their female peers in reaching out for help when they are in deep trouble, except through violence against others, society, or self.

Body Image

Steroid use among adolescent boys is now on par with their use of crack cocaine. Consequences of steroid use range from increased rage to early death.

Attention Deficit Hyperactive Disorder (ADHD)

This brain disorder, like so many others, is almost exclusively a male malady. Only one out of six adolescents diagnosed with ADHD is female.

ADHD is one of the reasons for the high rate of adolescent male vehicle accidents and fatalities. Adolescents with a history of ADHD (or, in fact, any conduct disorder) are significantly more likely to commit traffic offenses and be in accidents.

While many adolescent males do need Ritalin, many are misdiagnosed and do not. Misdiagnosis is dangerous. The social labeling of an ADHD kid in the school stretches into national interests—children who are diagnosed with ADHD at twelve or older will not be allowed in the military. Ironically, many of the kids who have ADHD or are active enough to be misdiagnosed with ADHD would find the military one of the *best* environments for their particular way of being—well structured, well led, well focused.

Sexual Abuse

One out of five males has been sexually abused by the age of eighteen. Most of our sexual offenders are heterosexual males who have been physically and/or sexually abused as boys themselves. In this area, adolescent females suffer at a higher rate: at least one in four. However, male sexual abuse has only recently been studied and some researchers have found that as many as two out of five male children are sexually abused—comparable to the rate of female sexual abuse.

These numbers should frighten us terribly. A sexually abused adolescent male is more likely than his female counterpart to act out against someone else, generally someone younger and weaker than himself, through rape, physical violence, and sexual molestation.

Adolescent Males in the Educational System

Although well-publicized studies by the American Association of University Women, David and Myra Sadker, and the Wellesley Report on Women have done much to pave the way for a better educational atmosphere for my own daughters and millions of other girls, unfortunately, we have neglected the problems of our boys. Our boys are not in better shape than our girls in schools. Not only are they the primary victims of violence in schools, and not only do they comprise the majority of dead, injured, mentally ill, and substance-abusing adolescents in the schools, but they exhibit the majority of *academic problems* as well. Statistically, there is only one area of healthy activity where males outnumber females: sports.

Adolescent boys are twice as likely as adolescent girls to be diagnosed as learning disabled. Two-thirds of high school special-education and handicapped students are male. One colleague of mine, a teacher of speech pathology and a consultant on student-disability curricula, put the situation this way: "When I walk into a classroom of learning-disabled students, I know I'll face a sea of boys." She has further pointed out to me that adolescent male adaptability is a problem as well. Adolescent male learning disabilities are more intractable, on average, than those of adolescent females. When teachers and consultants face a roomful of learning-disabled adolescents, they know that they'll have greater impact on females than on males.

Adolescent males drop out of high school at four times the rate of adolescent females (this includes females who drop out to have babies).

Ninety percent of adolescent discipline problems in schools are male, as are most expulsions and suspensions.

Adolescent males are significantly more likely than adolescent females to be left back a grade.

Adolescent males on average get worse grades than adolescent females. The majority of salutatorians and valedictorians now are female.

Adolescent females now dominate school clubs, yearbooks, and student government.

Often we will hear in the media that before middle school, girls and boys are on par academically, but then by the end of high school, boys end up academically ahead. While this statement may be true for some girls, most of the time it is in fact the boy who ends up behind. The boys finish their education less frequently, they finish high school with lower average grades, and fewer go to college.

More college students are female (55 percent) than male (45 percent). More graduate students are female (59 percent) than male (41 percent). The discrepancies that did exist thirty years ago—the gender gap that put female school attendance lower than male—have more than reversed. This reversal began more than sixteen years ago. Since 1981, more women than men have been enrolling in college. The problem regarding low male college attendance prompted an article devoted to that subject in a recent issue of *Chronicle of Higher Education:* "Where Have All the Men Gone?"

Only our public consciousness has not caught up to the changes that have occurred in the many gender gaps, including the educational ones that statistically favor the adolescent female rather than the adolescent male. The area where males still are favored is in SAT scores. Females are slightly behind males in the college-application test scores. The Educational Testing Service has offered to change the SAT test, most likely to include a more developed essay format—girls generally test better than boys in essay writing—in order to make the test more fair.

According to the National Center for Education Statistics of the U.S. Department of Education, *fewer* boys than girls now study advanced algebra and geometry, about the same number study trigonometry and calculus, and *more* girls than boys study chemistry. What was true about gender gaps in these math/science areas twenty years ago is not true now.

Even more dramatic is the gender gap in reading/writing. Adolescent males are outscored by adolescent females by twelve points in reading and seventeen points in writing. The U.S. Department of Education recently pointed out that this gender gap in reading/writing is equivalent to about one and a half years of school! That is how far behind our adolescent males have fallen. While some boys read far better than some girls, the average high school freshman girl is reading as well as the average high school junior boy.

According to the U.S. Department of Education, eighth-grade girls are twice as likely as eighth-grade boys to aspire to a professional, business, or managerial career. When twelfth-graders are surveyed, the results are nearly similar. Twelfth-grade females are more likely to aspire to a college or graduate degree, on top of their professional aspirations. . . .

Adolescent Male Self-Esteem

My understanding of adolescent male self-esteem has been something of a journey. I hope it will reflect in some ways the journey that you may have had to make toward seeing adolescent male self-esteem issues in your own family.

While I knew, as a professional, that much of what our adolescents face is rooted in general in the transitional disturbance in self-esteem that they experience during the second decade of their lives, and while I knew that by most psychological measures not only our females but also our males encounter the adolescent drop in self-esteem, I couldn't see how it worked in males as well as in females. In this I was like most people—parents or professionals or in between—who find it hard to reach behind the toughness and isolationism of so many adolescent males to the emotional life hidden inside. But as a parent in the 1990s, I had another problem. Seeing males clearly meant noticing how most of our self-esteem research concerns only adolescent girls and grown women. We haven't spent much time as a culture focusing on self-esteem issues in our adolescent boys. Unfortunately too, much of our research into female self-esteem has pitted females against males, or shown males to be tough and females to be the only fragile ones.

When the Ms. Foundation for Women launched the Take Our Daughters to Work® Day, it provided as rationale the "fact" that "adolescence takes a greater toll on the self-esteem and school performance of girls than boys." This kind of blanket statement was echoed by reports such as that of the American Association of University Women (AAUW) in 1991, the Wellesley Report on Women, and the David and Myra Sadker research. These studies came out in the early to mid-1990s.

Some of them mentioned boys, mainly as problems. If the boys could be taught to calm down, be less aggressive, and "have less of a sense of entitlement" in the classroom, the playground, and the home, then girls' self-esteem would not be destroyed.

During this time, a study came out showing that black adolescent males have the highest self-esteem of any demographic group, far higher than white females. I knew from experience that this was absolutely false, and I noticed that the press and some researchers as well had mistaken bravado and compensatory grandiosity for self-esteem. For them, self-esteem was measured by the aggressive show, the mask, of self-esteem. Boys, of course, would show higher self-esteem, especially the boys who had perfected the business of posturing. Press and researchers thought posturing showed a healthy core self. When I realized that this kind of study was being used to bolster the cause of adolescent girls, I became disappointed. Self-esteem research obviously needed to move to the next level.

Fortunately, that next level is available to us.

Just after the AAUW study came out, *Science News* asked leading scholars and researchers to evaluate the AAUW report. Their conclusion was that *both* adolescent males and females experience significant drops in self-esteem during adolescence. Researchers Tim Blankenhorn, Michael Reichert, and Joseph Healey, in their study of Philadelphia boys, concluded that all boys, even privileged ones, go through male versions of what Mary Pipher describes in *Reviving Ophelia:* a drop in self-esteem during middle-school years and soon after. Says Blankenhorn, "Boys lose themselves at just about exactly the same time."

Even more startling, since 1991, further research has suggested that in many circumstances, adolescent males experience a *worse* self-esteem drop than females. Under pressure to check their findings, the AAUW commissioned an independent study, conducted by Valerie E. Lee of the University of Michigan. Her study of 9,000 eighth-grade males and females showed no significant difference in self-esteem drops between males and females, but concluded that in many academic categories where self-esteem might be measurable—for instance, study habits, grades, engagement in school activities—the females were, quite simply, doing better than the males. The Michigan study is consistent with similar research on eighth-graders and twelfth-graders by the U.S. Department of Education.

Researcher Diane Ravitch, in *Forbes* magazine in 1996, summed up the self-esteem research this way:

> If there is a crisis in self-esteem, it is not among young women. Girls are doing very well indeed. Boys, in the meantime, are killing themselves and each other at alarming rates. If either sex is in trouble in our society, it is the males.

If we could view every statistic and anecdote, we would find that there is no reason to argue about who "has it worse." Both our adolescent females and males need our help. We would also find, however, that paying attention to adolescent male fragility is absolutely essential, and we must reeducate ourselves in order to learn how to do it. Research into self-esteem has developed along the standards of how *females* show self-esteem drops—talking less often in class, letting others talk for them, becoming more passive, become overtly depressed, becoming body-image obsessed to the point of anorexia.

Boys often will show their fragility in different ways.

Bravado and Beyond

Many times, boys will show their fragility not through increased passivity but through increased bravado. When compared to adolescent girls, adolescent boys experiencing an average drop in self-esteem will pretend more self-confidence, will admit less weakness, will posture more, will pursue more overt attention, and will appear more aggressive. A teacher at a workshop once said something very powerful about who she calls on in class.

> *When I went to a gender-fairness workshop I was shocked to notice that I, like so many teachers, called on my eighth-grade boys more than my girls. I've worked hard to be more fair. But at the same time what the trainers don't tell you is that a lot of the quiet girls just need a lot less attention in school than the loud boys. Truthfully, I don't worry as much about them as some of these boys who seem to live on the edge of failure so much.*

The bravado, the aggression among the males, in her experience, was hardly a show of high self-esteem. I have heard her words echoed all over the country.

Another high school teacher told me, "In my classroom, all the kids do a certain amount of posturing, but it's mainly the boys who lose their focus to the posturing. Their self-concept is so easily shaken. The girls seem more able to 'be cool,' but still keep their minds on what they have to do."

About her fourteen-year-old son, a mother, who was also a teacher, said:

> *He was doing great in elementary school, but by the time he finished junior high I felt like we lost him. No matter what we do, he just seems to think he's never okay, never good enough, never cool enough. He won't talk about it. He just tries to walk around now like he's tough enough to handle anything.*

In the next century, as we expand our self-esteem research, both personal and cultural, we will be better able to decipher fully the self-esteem picture our boys and girls are painting. Researchers will have to see beyond bravado and posturing—something the AAUW study, based on a questionnaire given to students about self-image, was not able to do. Questionnaires that require self-reflection by children are answered by boys and girls in some very different ways. Generally, boys will posture higher self-esteem than girls, will practice more bravado, will have access to their innermost feelings less instantaneously than girls, and will, on average, have weaker verbal skills in answering questions involving emotive data. When the 1991 AAUW report found slightly higher self-esteem results for the males than the females, it did not inform the media or anyone else of the vast limitations of a questionnaire format as a measurement of self-esteem among boys and girls.

Now we are challenged to look beyond bravado in our assessments of how fragile boys really are. Recall how you may have watched your three-year-old boy so aggressively playing with sticks or forming guns or tearing heads off dolls with his hands and yet you knew that behind that aggression lay a fragile self that could lose control in an instant and lie weeping in a puddle. An adolescent male will probably not weep in a puddle, but he is fragile indeed, and his mask of bravado is sometimes a greater clue to his fragility than a lesser one. His increased aggression or stoic bravado often is a sign of armoring against fragility.

From Posturing to Trauma Responses

Because we have paid little attention to male fragility, we certainly have not connected that fragility with the social dangers males create. Let us make that connection in earnest now. Much adolescent male posturing may not lead to any significant danger. Much male armoring is necessary and healthy for the male at a given time in his life. Much of it can transpire with emotional development taking place as well. Much of it can soothe a self-esteem drop—for instance, in that difficult year, the high school freshman year, when male self-esteem is very much at risk.

Simultaneously, much of the posturing and armoring can move from the safe to the dangerous. It does so when adolescent male self-esteem drops so low and the fragile self's resources are so minimal that the adolescent male feels *traumatized*. The majority of adolescent male suicides, violent deaths, and violent activity grow from what we call *endangering trauma responses*—triggered responses to threats within the fragile male self that create behavior and physical action that endanger the self, others, or property. Interestingly, not just among human adolescent males, but among the other primates, *when an adolescent male is most fragile we often can expect him to cause others and himself the most, not the least, crisis and distress*.

An adolescent male's despair at the loss of his father or mother through divorce, the loss of a girlfriend, lack of age-appropriate social and economic opportunity, a failure of small or large proportion, an inability to compete—each and all may translate into emotional and social withdrawal or increased bravado and posturing until the point at which an action is taken that is more physically and socially violent than the female peer, in equal distress, would entertain. In addition, an adolescent male may respond to his stress either immediately or a year or two after the situation has passed. For example, in a Southern state recently, two adolescent males, both fifteen, committed suicide. Just before killing themselves, they held up a gas station and traveled by car illegally for three days. The boys' intention to take their own lives was precipitated by a girl's not choosing one of them as a boyfriend, at a time when the boys' self-esteem was very low. Specialists called in on the case have noted that the boys did not respond to their long-term stress—stored-up trauma—until *much later*, when a new stress factor—the girls' rejection—was introduced. Similarly, a thirteen-year-old boy in Washington state who walked into his school and shot three classmates dead was responding not only to his present psychiatric illness but to a history of family traumas and stresses, including his parents' fights.

The basic fragility of the male self becomes increasingly clear when we see beyond the terrible and reprehensible acts and the internal histories that led up to them. We are dealing with adolescent males who broke down internally and had no resources to repair internal damage to fragile psychological structures.

Questions

1. What are the criteria for masculinity that adolescent boys are expected to meet?
2. What price do adolescent boys pay for adherence to male gender roles?
3. Compare the attainment of masculinity for boys with the attainment of femininity for girls. Which has more advantages? More adverse outcomes?
4. Why have we overlooked the drop in self-esteem that occurs for boys at adolescence, and focused on raising the self-esteem of girls?
5. Are males as vulnerable as Gurian makes them out to be?

References and Further Reading

American Association of University Women. (1992). *The AAUW report: How schools shortchange girls.* Washington, DC: American Association of University Women.

Kling, K. C., Hyde, J. S., Showers, C. J., & Buswell, B. N. (1999). Gender differences in self-esteem: A meta-analysis. *Psychological Bulletin, 125*(4), 470–500.

Pollock, W. (1998). *Real boys.* New York: Henry Holt.

Thompson, M., & Kindlon, D. (1999). *Raising Cain.* New York: Ballantine.

8.3   Peggy Orenstein, 1994

Striking Back: Sexual Harassment at Weston

Peggy Orenstein is a familiar name in the world of magazine publishing. She served as the managing editor of *Mother Jones* and the founding editor of *7 Days.* Her work has appeared in the *New York Times Magazine, Vogue, Glamour, New Yorker, New York Woman,* and *Mirabella.* She has been on the editorial staffs of *Manhattan, Inc.,* and *Esquire.* In *School Girls: Young Women, Self-Esteem, and the Confidence Gap* (1994) and *Flux: Women on Sex, Work, Kids, Love, and Life in a Half-Changed World* (2000), she writes about the challenges facing women in a modern world.

The most common environment where adolescents spend their time is school, a setting in which young people across the country are reporting a high degree of sexual harassment. Students report being sexually harassed in school not only by fellow students, but also by teachers and administrators. Sexual harassment influences the way adolescents experience their developing sexuality, and it carries important messages about what it means to be male and female in this society. When middle school girls report to guidance counselors that boys have been grabbing at their breasts in the hall, they are often told that no boy would do that, or that "boys will be boys." When girls speak up for themselves to boys who sexually harass them, boys often say they didn't do anything, and further disparage these girls. Girls learn through these experiences that it is the male version of reality and not their own that is heard and respected. Girls learn that they are sexual objects and that they do not have rights over their own bodies. Girls learn that men have power over women. They learn that they will not be supported if they do speak up, that they will be put down by the very males whose attention is so important to them.

Sexual harassment has serious academic, emotional, and behavioral consequences. Many adolescents feel unsafe in school. Rather than feeling pride and pleasure in their developing sexuality, many are made to feel ashamed, embarrassed, afraid, and unprotected in school. They may grow to dislike school and disengage from learning. The AAUW (1993) found that girls who had been sexually harassed in school showed a decrease in desire to attend school or to participate in classroom discussion, and a decrease in grades. Sexual harassment contributed to their inability to take full advantage of the learning opportunities offered to them.

Peggy Orenstein describes the sexual harassment to which adolescent girls are subjected by boys in middle school, girls' silence in response, and the lessons that sexual harassment teaches. In the reading we see one principal's attempt to end sexual harassment in her school by suspending the instigators, and by forming a discussion group for girls to empower them to speak up for themselves and let boys know when their behavior was offensive. Orenstein details the obstacles this school principal encounters in trying to change the status quo. Parents are angry and unsupportive and file complaints with the district superintendent. The superintendent, in turn, is displeased and unsupportive of this principal's efforts. The reading highlights the difficulties involved in trying to stop sexual harassment in the context of a larger culture that tolerates it.

P rincipal Andrea Murray is on the phone when I enter her office. She motions me into a battered oversized chair and swivels away from me to continue her conversation, tapping the long, red-painted nails of one hand impatiently against her cluttered desk. Ms. Murray's office is small and, on this January day, overheated; there's barely room in it for her file cabinets, her computer terminal, and the two empty chairs that lay in wait for errant children. The walls are an unforgiving shade of institutional green, but on the corner of her desk nearest me, Ms. Murray has placed an enormous jar of hard candy, a gesture of warmth and approachability from the person whose position usually fills students with dread.

Ms. Murray completes her call and turns toward me. A small, amiable woman with carefully styled brown hair wearing a flower-sprigged dress and sensible shoes, she folds her hands in her lap and looks at me expectantly.

An eighth-grade girl, she informs me, is being sexually harassed.

Laying Down the New Law

Jeanie Mayes, a quiet, somewhat mousy girl, has lodged a formal complaint against a group of boys in her gym class who have been taunting her about the size of her breasts. The gym teacher, who is male, has largely ignored the remarks, although he has occasionally punished the most insolent boys by making them run a lap around the school track. For the most part, though, Jeanie silently endured the heckling until last week, when a new, more physically developed girl moved to Weston and the harassment escalated. The boys began to walk by Jeanie, their hands cupped a few inches away from their chests, smirking, saying, "You're got competition, Jeanie. Connie is bigger than you are, but we'll always remember that you're second!" A few days later, one of the boys reached out and grabbed Jeanie's breasts.

"The thing is," says Ms. Murray, "this girl is actually not large-chested, this isn't happening because she's Dolly Parton. I suspect it's because they know they're getting to her. She doesn't have a lot of friends, and she's very nonassertive. She wouldn't even come in here on her own. Her mother told me what was going on and asked me to call her out of class."

Ms. Murray tells me she has been concerned about the level of sexual harassment on campus since she arrived at Weston last year. She describes incidences of boys insulting girls; boys restraining girls; boys grabbing girls' breasts, buttocks, and crotches. She's been mystified and frankly exasperated over why, in the face of such ill-treatment, the girls remain silent. They even remain deferential to some of the harassers who are "popular" boys.

"They won't see this as something boys do to girls as one group to another, like racism," Ms. Murray says. "If they could just see themselves as a group, as powerful, if they just agreed to look at those boys as if they had leprosy, the boys would correct their behavior immediately."

But January 1, 1993, brought an opportunity for change at Weston, and that's why Ms. Murray has called me in here, that's why she looks oddly energized by this unhappy situation. On that day a new, innovative law took effect in California. Every school in the state is now required to develop a written sexual harassment policy for staff and students, to display it prominently on campus, and to distribute a copy to each teacher and parent. More to the point, a principal may suspend or even expel students as young as fourth graders who engaged in sexual harassment.

Ms. Murray informed the students of the new law at a school-wide assembly just after winter break, in which she also discussed a number of other issues, such as the dates for upcoming standardized tests and the rising incidents of spitting on campus. The message was reinforced several days later in the school bulletin, which is read aloud in each class during first period.

Jeanie's Mayes's complaint, Ms. Murray says, will be Weston's first test of the new law.

Ms. Murray has already transferred Jeanie to another gym class, and her science class has been switched as well, since most of the boys who harass her go directly there with her after gym, where they continue their behavior. The next challenge is to confirm her allegations, so it won't be just her word against the boys'. At Ms. Murray's request, Jeanie has compiled a list of girls who have witnessed the harassment; one of the school counselors has been assigned to convene that group after lunch today. The hope is that the girls will not only identify the perpetrators but begin to build a sense of cohesion and power among themselves.

"I'd like Jeanie to see that she's not the sole victim of abusive talk," Ms. Murray says. "That's part of why she's been so distressed. I even want her to see, maybe, why other kids don't take it as hard." Ms. Murray also suggested to the counselor that the girls might want to write an anonymous open letter to the Weston boys about harassment that would be placed in the school bulletin.

Once she's built her case, Ms. Murray plans to suspend the instigators of the harassment, using the new law—there will be no expulsions unless the boys persist—then she'll call their *fathers* with the news. "No man wants to hear from a woman that his parenting hasn't been too good," Ms. Murray explains. "Let alone hear it in graphic terms. I'll just say, 'It's not my job to train your child to be civil in public. You need to take him home and tell him not to make references to girls' bouncing boobs at school.' " She smiles impishly. "If I were a man I'd be so mad at my son for getting me in this humiliating situation!"

If she meets with any resistance, Ms. Murray says, she'll take her crusade into the community. "It's one thing for *me* to say I find it despicable when boys call girls 'ho's' and "sluts,' " she says, "but it's not as meaningful as if our PTA supports the idea that certain behavior—including certain comments and language used consistently on campus—has adverse effects on the psyche of the girls and affects their academic performance.

"I see this as an evolution of standards," she continues. "We used to tolerate people saying nigger, we used to tolerate physical abuse of children, we used to tolerate slaves at one point if you go back far enough. We've evolved. We don't tolerate those things anymore, and now we won't tolerate sexual harassment."

Sexual Harassment: Who Decides?

Ms. Murray's fervor on this issue is unusual among school principals, to say the least. Technically speaking, students have been protected from sexual harassment since 1972, when Title IX of the Education Amendments banned discrimination based on sex and required school districts to designate an employee to handle complaints. Up until recently, few administrators have enforced those regulations and students have remained ignorant of their rights. But just about the time that the Anita Hill–Clarence

Thomas hearings riveted national attention on sexual harassment among adults, a series of lawsuits brought it roiling to the surface in public schools. In 1991, in what may be the most celebrated of those cases, nineteen-year-old Katy Lyle won a $15,000 settlement from the Duluth, Minnesota, school district, which, while she was a high school student there, had failed to remove explicit graffiti about her from the walls of a boy's bathroom even after her parents' numerous complaints. The following year, in Petaluma, California, Tawnya Brawdy won a $20,000 out-of-court settlement from Kenilworth Junior High School, which did not stop boys who mooed at her and jeered about the size of her breasts. In a third significant case, Christine Franklin took her $6 million claim against the Gwinnett County, Georgia, school district all the way to the Supreme Court after a lower court held that Title IX violations were not subject to suit for punitive damages. In February 1992, the Justices unanimously sided with Franklin—even Clarence Thomas agreed. By the spring of 1993, nearly half of the forty sexual harassment cases that were being investigated by the U.S. Department of Education's Office of Civil Rights involved elementary and secondary schools.

In spite of the Supreme Court verdict, it has remained contentious to suggest that sexual harassment is possible—even has its behavioral roots—among young children. Media outlets from the daily papers to the afternoon television gab shows to such *éminces grises* as *60 Minutes* have served up reports on sexual harassment among schoolchildren. Yet, oddly, no matter how many times the issue is raised, and regardless of the growing hostility toward girls exhibited in such disparate incidents as Lakewood, California's "Spur Posse" sex-for-points scandal and the recent mob assaults on girls in New York City swimming pools, the media remain piously skeptical, hinting that this "teasing," this normal adolescent rite of passage, is being taken too seriously.

Perhaps if sexual harassment—which includes unwelcome sexual remarks that create a hostile learning environment—happened in equal measure between boys and girls (or men and women) that argument might have merit. But it doesn't: overwhelmingly boys harass and girls (or other boys) are harassed, indicating that the behavior is less a statement about sexuality than an assertion of dominance. The prevalence of sexual harassment reminds us that boys learn at a very young age to see girls as less capable and less worthy of respect. One need only consider that the most shameful insult that one boy can hurl at another is still *"girl!"* (or "pussy" or "faggot," which has similar connotations) to understand how aware children are of female powerlessness, how important it is for boys to distance themselves from that weakness in order to feel like men.

Ms. Murray is right about the girls, too: middle-class and affluent girls in particular tend to accept sexual harassment as inevitable. And why not? The sexual teasing, stalking, and grabbing merely reinforces other, more subtle lessons: it reminds them that they are defined by their bodies; it underscores their lack of entitlement in the classroom (in fact, the harassment frequently *happens* in the classroom); it confirms their belief that boys' sexuality is uncontrollable while their own must remain in check. Without encouragement and proper information, these girls, who already feel diminished, have little reason to believe that they could have recourse against boys' ridicule.

Certainly, middle school children are exploring their sexual identity; but, as we've seen, from the outset those explorations are mired in inequity, and that, too, serves to silence girls when they are harassed. If boys wield the power to ruin girls' reputations, speaking out against boys who offend becomes too risky. Meanwhile, since girls look to boys for confirmation of their desirability (which they've learned is central to their self-esteem), they are left in a muddle: like adult women, they are expected to draw the line between flattery and harassment. Like adult women, they judge one another by where and how they draw that line.

Ideally, the new California law would help redress the power inequities between boys and girls. And the legislation does take a step in that direction: by requiring a sexual harassment policy it admits to the existence of a problem. By stipulating a punishment, it offers girls a measure of the institutional support that they've been sorely lacking, and puts the burden of change squarely on boys. Those shifts in perception alone could have a profound impact on girls' self-esteem. Yet in spite of its good intentions, the law, which may well become a model nationwide, is essentially toothless. Gender equity specialist Nan Stein has pointed out that the state offers no guidance for the development of these new sexual harassment policies and, more importantly, its approach is solely punitive: there are no provisions either for staff training or for a curriculum that would help students define the boundaries of appropriate behavior and dissect power relations. In fact, since the state has no means of enforcing the law, principals are free to soft-pedal it. Those administrators who are concerned about sexual harassment, such as Ms. Murray, are forced to improvise their own plans. They are also left with the fallout if those plans fail.

Strength in Numbers: The Girl Group

Just after lunch, Edie Deloria, a half-time counselor at Weston, convenes the group of girls whose names Jeanie Mayes submitted on her list. Mrs. Deloria is a heavyset woman in her late forties, with heavily moussed hair and bright pink nails; she wears olive stretch pants with a matching sequined shirt and suede ankle boots. As we wait in her office for the girls to assemble, she confides, "I've never done anything like this before, so I don't really know what I'm supposed to do. Andrea kind of booted this onto me."

Seven girls file in and perch uncomfortably on the chairs that Mrs. Deloria has arranged in a circle. Some of them look familiar: I recognize Emily and Samantha from Evie's math class. Amanda is in Becca's English class. Jeanie is among the last to arrive, trailing on the heels of her best friend, a compact girl with flowing red hair named Angie. Jeanie has ruddy skin with a patch of acne on one cheek. She's wearing a baggy sweatshirt that makes her upper body appear formless, and she lets her blond hair, which is limp and a little dirty, hang across her eyes. She looks around nervously and takes a seat under a poster that reads: "Make It Happen!"

The group gets off to a crashingly slow start.

"There've been some things happening in gym class," Mrs. Deloria begins. "Some boys saying some sexual things to girls, and some of you know about it and some of you don't."

A few of the girls stare straight ahead; others look baffled. Jeanie blushes deeply.

"How many of you are aware of this problem?"

There is no response for several seconds, then, one by one, five of the girls raise their hands. Mrs. Deloria looks heartened.

"You may have some feelings about this," she says, "Would anyone like to comment?" Several of the girls shrug. Some study the ground.

Mrs. Deloria glances at me, then tries another tack. "We want to make the school safe," she says. "We want to be free from remarks and other things that keep you from feeling comfortable learning here. Do you agree that this needs to be stopped?"

The girls shift in their seats. Jeanie darts her eyes back and forth. Seeing only disinterest, she sinks back into her chair. The meeting appears to be a flop. Then Emily, who is tiny and brooding, winces and says, "Sometimes guys say to other people that they're sluts."

At that, Samantha, who has been staring resolutely at the linoleum while wrapping her hair into a bun, begins to speak. "Something happened today in another class," she says reluctantly. "This guy called this girl a slut and . . . things like that . . . " She trails off and the other girls appear even more uneasy.

"That was my brother," Emily says. Emily, it turns out, skipped a year in elementary school; she is now in the same grade as her older brother Sid, who is a ringleader among the boys.

"And sometimes guys say to girls that they're half guy if they like sports," Samantha continues, then adds, squirming, "but they don't use those words . . . exactly."

"Jeanie's too scared to talk," says Angie, who wears a floppy T-shirt and oversized jeans. Jeanie drops her eyes. "But boys talk about her breasts. And today when we were playing hockey, they'd take the stick and make this motion." She holds her hand near her crotch and pumps it up and down.

"Like masturbating?" Mrs. Deloria asks.

Several of the girls nod.

"Who does that?"

Angie names several names, then adds, "But a lot of the guys do it."

"Guys are just immature," says Samantha.

"It doesn't bother me," says Angie. "But it bothers Jeanie. They come up to her and say, 'Can I have some skim milk?' and stare at her breasts."

Amanda, who has been chewing her fingernails assiduously since the meeting began, snaps her head up. "Are you talking about all our classes?" she asks. "Because Robbie Jordan says he had sex with my mom and that . . . and other stuff."

"Can you say it?" Mrs. Deloria asks.

"Well, that my mom gave him a blow job."

The girls are loosening up now, and a tone of exasperation is replacing their initial reluctance. They begin recounting boys' remarks in detail: they talk about boys who say, "Suck my fat Peter, you slut," who call them "skank" and "ho' " (a variation on "whore" popularized by male rap artists). They talk about boys who pinch their bottoms in the hallways, or grab their breasts and shout, "Let me tune in Tokyo!" They insist that it isn't just "bad" boys who badger them: it's boys with good grades, boys who are athletes, boys who are paragons of the school. And, they all agree, their fear of reprisal is much too acute to allow them to confront their harassers.

Nonetheless, here in the safety of the counselor's office, the girls do name names, many of which are familiar to me: they are the same boys who interrupt and belittle girls in the classroom. They are often the very same boys whom I've seen demand—and get—the most teacher attention in the least productive ways.

During a brief pause in the girls' litany, Mrs. Deloria breaks in. "Girls think that guys 'just say these things,' " she says. "And after a while you think that this is the way that guys are supposed to talk to girls. But it doesn't have to be that way. Your feelings are important and you have to remember that. If you girls want them to stop, you have to tell them what's going to happen if they do it; and then you have to follow through. We take this very seriously at Weston."

"After assembly, the boys acted like it was a big joke," says Katie, a cherub-faced Asian girl. "Now they walk down the hall and touch you on the arm and say, 'Ooooh! Sexual harassment!' Like that's funny."

"I'm not saying it's easy," the counselor says. "But you have to be role models. I know it's just words, but you have to make it happen."

"Jeff Bellamy grabbed my breasts," Jeanie says softly, her eyes misting.

"How did you feel, Jeanie?" asks Mrs. Deloria.

"Jeanie was upset," Angie says. "I know, because I was sitting beside her and . . ."

"Let *Jeanie* finish," Mrs. Deloria interrupts.

"I'm finished," says Jeanie, who appears unaccustomed to speaking for herself.

Amanda, who has gone back to her fingernails, looks up thoughtfully. "I like guys who are your friends," she says. "Guys who talk to you for your personality, not just to get things from you."

The girls ponder this comment in silence; Jeanie looks morose.

"Would you girls like to meet again next week?" Mrs. Deloria asks. All seven girls raise their hands, as if they're in class; they decide, at that time, to work on a letter for the school bulletin.

As the girls get up to leave, Mrs.Deloria cautions, "This conversation is confidential, girls, it's between us. If anyone finds out about it, it was one of you who said something."

The girls nod solemnly; they won't tell a soul.

"Okay," the counselor continues, reaching for a jar of candy, "everyone have a piece of chocolate before you go. Like we need to add to our rear ends—that's where it goes on us!"

Mrs. Deloria shuts the door after the girls leave, leans back in her chair, and offers me the candy jar, apparently seeing no irony in her final remark. "I think that went pretty well," she says, relieved. "You know, a lot of these girls think they have to take this. They're taking it now, and by sixteen years old it will be so ingrained in them that they'll just accept it. Some of them, the girls who don't think they can fight back, they'll grow up and become depressed or battered, you can see it."

Mrs. Deloria's speech is cut short by Andrea Murray, who rushes into the room. "The group went very well," Mrs. Deloria begins to say, but Ms. Murray brushes her aside.

"You won't believe this," she says, turning to me. "Two eighth-grade girls just came into my office and they are livid about something that happened in *their* gym class—a different class. Sid Connelly called one of them a hooker, and another boy said, 'She can't be a hooker because she gives it away for free.' "

Ms. Murray shakes her head. "This girl was raped two years ago by a family member," she says, "so she's taking the remark pretty hard. Her friend brought her in to see me. I promised them I'd suspend Sid first thing tomorrow."

I Did It; So What?

At nine o'clock the next morning, Ms. Murray, wearing a "Distinguished California School" T-shirt, sits in her office with Gary Sanchez, the police officer who is assigned to work with her at the school.

"Are we going for tears here?" Officer Sanchez asks Ms. Murray. The principal nods.

Sid Connelly saunters in the door and, barely glancing at Officer Sanchez, sprawls in the chair next to Ms. Murray's desk. He's a tall, skeletal boy with dewy skin and crooked teeth. Like many boys at Weston, he's shaved the sides of his head and wears a baseball cap over the remaining thatch, giving the impression of total baldness. Since he's also wearing his jeans a fashionable three sizes too big and a huge T-shirt, the baldness makes him look vulnerable rather than tough, as fragile as an egg. He truly looks like a little boy dressed up in a bigger man's clothes, and the words he's been hurling at girls show just how important it is for him to convey that virile impression. Sid's eyes snap with defiance. He's been in here twice already this year for racial slurs and a number of times for other infractions, so he knows the drill.

Ms. Murray looks at him sharply. "We hear you've been talking about girls, Sid," she says.

"You mean Lisanne?"

"Yes, I mean Lisanne."

"So what, she calls me names and I called her one. I called her a hooker, so what?"

"What's a hooker, Sid?" Officer Sanchez asks. He's a big man, too big for the chairs in the office, which are the largest in the school. His graying hair is ridged around his head where his cap usually sits.

"A prostitute." Sid leans back in his chair and folds his arms.

"So you've been calling girls prostitutes," says Andrea.

"Sure," Sid says, shrugging. "She called *me* an asshole."

"Other girls say that's not all you call them."

Sid looks away. "I just did it once."

That's when Ms. Murray slips up, unwittingly identifying one of the girls. "Your sister and other girls say that's not true. They say you call them slut, ho', a lot of names. Are you calling them liars?"

"No," Sid says, kicking his feet against his chair.

Officer Sanchez turns to Sid, shaking his head. "Sid, Sid, Sid. Society doesn't accept boys calling girls sexual names anymore. It's illegal. You can be expelled for it. You can go to jail for it."

"Well, if they want people to know that, why don't they tell them," Sid says sullenly.

"We did, Sid," Ms. Murray says. "Weren't you at the assembly Friday?"

"I was absent."

"Well, didn't your first-period teacher read the note in the bulletin and discuss it this week?"

"I don't listen to him," Sid says.

The cop and Ms. Murray exchange a look.

"Expulsion means you're out of school for the rest of the year," Officer Sanchez continues. "You don't go on to high school next year either. And the parents of those girls? They can sue you, Sid. But since you're a minor . . . you live in . . ."

"Redwood Estates."

"Redwood Estates. There's a lot of nice homes up there," Officer Sanchez says, nodding appreciatively. He leans in toward the boy. Since you're a minor," he says, "your mom could be sued by those girls' parents for what you did. And then you couldn't live in Redwood Estates anymore. Instead of your nice, comfortable house, you'd be down here in town living in a little apartment. Your mom wouldn't be too happy with you then, would she, Sid?"

Sid's eyes are getting a little glassy.

Ms. Murray interjects. "Do you see your dad on weekends?" she asks.

Sid nods.

"Do you live with him during the week at all?"

Sid shakes his head.

"Well, I'm going to call him right now and tell him to talk to you about how a man acts." She spins her chair around and places the call. "Will? This is Andrea Murray at the middle school. I have your son here. I'm calling you rather than his mother because we have a serious problem. I have girls complaining that he's making sexually harassing remarks to them." She recounts the incident. "I need your support in talking to him to say it's inappropriate to call girls sluts and hookers."

Sid's jaw tightens. He fights back tears as Ms. Murray goes on to explain the new law to his father.

"If you'd talk to him and explain how girls feel . . . "

She is interrupted as the father speaks. She tries to reiterate her point but is interrupted again. Sid looks, in addition to unhappy, uncomfortable. Something else is being exposed here.

"Well, the information really needs to come from you, Will," Ms. Murray says. "He needs to hear it from a father figure, he needs to identify with your values, to learn his behavior from you. You can help him if you can have that conversation with him. If you tell him . . . "

There is another long pause.

"Yes, I'll notify her, but if you could talk to him from a male perspective maybe you can have a greater influence . . . "

By now, Ms. Murray is fairly begging Will Connelly to talk to his son, and the father is clearly refusing. Sid runs a finger under his eyes. His face is pink.

Ms. Murray hangs up the phone. "You know what your dad tells me, Sid?"

Sid shakes his head.

"He says this might not do any good. He says suspension might not get the message to you. He says he's surprised this hasn't happened before."

Sid looks rigidly ahead, his eyes brimming, his lips full and moist. Ms. Murray ceremoniously fills out a suspension form and hands it to him. He snatches it from her hand and runs out the door, just as the bell signals the end of second period.

After he leaves, Ms. Murray rolls her eyes. "Well, that's where he gets it. You can tell that vulgarity is that man's main way of communicating. He says that it's all his ex-wife's fault, that she doesn't know how to raise them. He probably usually uses those words that Sid used to describe his ex-wife." She lets out a long breath. "Well," she says grimly, "I can't fix his family, but I'm going to stop his behavior."

She begins to brief Officer Sanchez on the next boy who is coming in today, the one who said Lisanne "gives it away for free." This boy is a good student, from a solid family with a mother whom Ms. Murray describes as a feminist; the principal believes he was motivated less by malice than peer pressure, so she plans to go easy on him, just giving him a Saturday detention. But just as she locates his third-period class on the computer, the secretary slips in with a note from Sid's sister. Emily is panicked; she was promised anonymity in the counseling group, but suddenly Sid is blaming her for his suspension. He's told some of his friends, too, and they're starting to come up to her calling her "a big fat ho'." According to Emily, the other girls from the group are terrified; what if their names were used, too? What will the boys do to them?

"They are so scared," Ms. Murray says, shaking her head, "it's unreal."

Ms. Murray calls both Sid and Emily into her office. Emily sits in a chair and folds her hands in her lap. Sid stands next to her.

"Did you see your sister after we talked?" she asks. "Did you say anything to her?"

"Yeah," Sid says. "You said it was my sister who came in here and said I call girls hookers."

"I said what?" Ms. Murray sputters. "Sid, you don't listen too well. I said, 'Even your sister knows what you do.'"

Sid shifts from foot to foot, his lips tight and his eyes wet with anger.

"Your suspension is now *two* days," Ms. Murray says. "And if any girl comes in here and says you're harassing her, I'll just keep adding the days. And I'm calling your mother right now." Sid sniffles. Emily casts her eyes downward. Ms. Murray dials the phone.

When Ms. Murray reaches Sid's mother, Mrs. Connelly tries to dismiss her son's behavior, making excuses for it. Then Ms. Murray hands the phone to Emily, who tells her mother exactly what Sid has been doing. When she hears her own daughter's frightened voice, the excuses stop.

"She just said, 'I'll take care of it, and it *won't* happen again,'" Ms. Murray says after the children leave. "She became completely supportive. I wish every boy had a sister in the same grade."

The More Things Change . . .

Over the next several weeks, Ms. Murray suspends five boys for sexual harassment, including two of the boys who were hounding Jeanie Mayes. She gives several other boys, whom she views as "followers," detention or Saturday school. Her thoroughness buoys the Weston girls' spirits; they believe that Ms. Murray is on their side and will protect them from harm. But this seismic shift toward equality leaves the boys confused and hostile. For the first time, they cannot do or say anything they want. Some of the boys are philosophical about the change, but most are unsure of—or unwilling to consider—what, exactly, constitutes inappropriate behavior. A few of the boys suggest that sexual harassment is too subtle to define, but if girls let them know that they're being offensive, they'll stop. Others are like Carl Ross, who was suspended for making masturbatory motions at Jeanie Mayes and asserting that several other girls "suck dick," and now complains, "The principal says it's degrading gossip, but you can't even say a girl's fine anymore, and how's that degrading?" Rather than try to work through the dilemma, Carl has simply decided to avoid girls for the rest of the year. "I'll just wait until high school," he says, "and talk to the girls then."

Even Jeff Bellamy, the boy who grabbed Jeanie's breasts, seems to have difficulty understanding the charges against him. I stop to chat with him the day after his suspension, while he is running an errand for his math teacher. "I was puzzled by the punishment," he tells me, stroking the few downy hairs on his chin. "I don't remember doing it, but maybe I did. All the guys do that stuff, it's no big deal. The girls don't mind. I mean, they don't do anything about it. I'd beat the crap out of someone if they touched me like that. But girls are different, they don't really do anything, so I guess it's okay to do."

✳ ✳ ✳ ✳

On February 4, less than a month since her campaign to eradicate sexual harassment at Weston began, Ms. Murray calls me back into her office. Her sexual harassment policy, she announces glumly, has "all . . . come back to bite me."

First, she says the father of one of the girls in the counseling group called her. At home. He wanted to know why the word "masturbating" had been used in front of his daughter without his consent. Apparently, she had yet to learn what the word meant and he wasn't anxious to fill her in.

"I tried to explain that boys in this school are talking about girls' mothers giving them blow jobs," she says. "I told him there's no underestimating the depth of these kids' knowledge or their misinformation. But he wouldn't listen."

Worse still, Jeanie Mayes's case has collapsed. Ms. Murray had told Jeanie's mother in confidence that according to one of the other girls in the class (who happened to be Lisa Duffy), Jeanie was not forceful enough toward her harassers; Lisa and Jeanie sent "mixed signals," and that the boys as well as some of the girls thought she invited the problem. Mrs. Mayes did not find this well-intentioned critique illuminating. She informed her daughter that a girl was spreading rumors about her, and the next day Jeanie retaliated, persuading the other girls in her former gym class to ostracize Lisa (something she never tried against the boys). At that point, Jeanie stopped being the "victim" and Ms. Murray called home again, to request that the mother have a talk with the daughter about her aggressive behavior. Mrs. Mayes exploded.

"She was happy as long as I met the agenda, as long as I suspended boys who misbehaved," Ms. Murray says. "But when her own daughter was held accountable she didn't like it. Now she's pulled Jeanie out of the school."

Before she did, though, Mrs. Mayes called the district superintendent to complain about the principal's mismanagement of her daughter's case. The superintendent agreed that Ms. Murray had botched the proceedings, but not because she hadn't attended to Jeanie. Her complaint was that the principal had failed to protect the boys. "The superintendent was upset that Mrs. Mayes had the names of the boys who had perpetrated this," Ms. Murray says. "But if one kid was hitting another, the parent would know that so-and-so hit his kid, so why is this different? She was also concerned that I'd allowed a group of girls to discuss what had happened. She said the girls could spread it around and stigmatize the boys. But individually, girls are afraid to speak out, and I thought that the group empowered them. And part of the point was supposed to be that these girls would identify boys who were doing this and make them stop by not accepting the behavior.

"I guess I misread the situation," she says. "I thought I should be applauded for this, I thought I was doing something for girls, and that I was developing a culture where girls stood up for their rights. But I guess it's more important to keep a lid on it."

Ms. Murray says the superintendent's reprimand has made her feel "burned" and "gun-shy," so she's not going to confront the remaining boys on her list of chronic harassers. And since she's met with outrage from the parents of both boys and girls, she is dropping her initial plan to rally community support at a PTA meeting. She has already told Edie Deloria to discontinue the girls' group, which, in spite of the counselor's promises, had yet to meet again anyway. That means the open letter for the school bulletin will be abandoned as well.

Maybe she folded without much of a fight, but, Ms. Murray claims, she can't effect broad-based change in her school without the backing of the superintendent. And, practically speaking, Ms. Murray says she has her own reputation to protect; if she crosses too many people, she could endanger her job. So instead of spearheading Weston's sexual harassment policy herself, Ms. Murray has decided to follow her boss's lead.

"There's still no procedure in place for dealing with this in the district," she says, "and no one seems to have any plans to develop one. There's been no discussion among the administrators, no talk about staff training, nothing. There's just the law, no way to carry it out . . . and I guess, looking back, I wouldn't try something like this again."

✳ ✳ ✳ ✳

After leaving Ms. Murray's office that morning, I stop by the school gym. It is a rainy day, and the students are inside playing basketball. The boys dash back and forth, chiding one another for mistakes and slapping high fives over their triumphs. The girls, for the most part, hover on the periphery of the game, halfheartedly guarding one another. This is Lindsay's class, and at one point, when she is the only person on her team who is both near the basket and open, a boy passes her the ball. She purses her lips and shoots.

As the ball leaves her hands, I turn away. I don't want to know whether Lindsay makes the basket or not. I like to imagine that she does, that the ball arcs through the air and swishes perfectly through the hoop, that she embraces her friends, jumping up and down with glee. But perhaps that's not what happens. Perhaps the ball goes wild, and the boys in the class roll their eyes in disgust before continuing the game. Either way, I hope she tries again.

Questions

1. Why do boys sexually harass girls in middle school?
2. Why do girls remain silent?
3. What does this behavior tell us about the female sex role? The male sex role?
4. Why don't adults stop this behavior in schools? Can they?

References and Further Reading

American Association of University Women. (1992). *The AAUW report: How schools shortchange girls.* Washington, DC: American Association of University Women Educational Foundation.

American Association of University Women. (1993). *Hostile hallways: AAUW survey on sexual harassment in American schools.* Washington, DC: American Association of University Women Educational Foundation.

DeZolt, D., & Henning-Stout, M. (1999). Adolescent girls' experiences in school and community settings. In N. G. Johnson, M. C. Roberts, & J. Worell (Eds.), *Beyond appearance: A new look at adolescent girls* (pp. 253–275). Washington, DC: American Psychological Association.

Lee, V. E., Croninger, R. G., Linn, E., & Chen, X. (1996). The culture of sexual harassment in secondary schools. *American Educational Research Journal, 34,* 485–511.

Sadker, M., & Sadker, D. (1994). *Failing at fairness. How America's schools cheat girls.* New York: Scribner.

Chapter 9

Sexual Identity

Relatively little research attention has been given to sexuality as an aspect of the self and of adolescent relationships. Sexual identity involves developing a sense of the self as a sexual being, understanding one's sexual desires and sexual preferences, and making decisions about how to respond to them. Sexual identity becomes salient as puberty increases sexual arousal and triggers interest in sexual intimacy and as an adolescent grapples with the transition to being sexually active. Integrating sexuality into one's identity is a process. Adolescents may engage in identity exploration, experimenting with different ways to be a sexual person before coming to a final resolution.

For all theorists who have written about adolescent development, integrating adult sexuality into one's personality and interpersonal life is an important developmental task of adolescence. For most theorists, the implicit assumption is made that the course of normal development involves becoming heterosexual. Freud (1905/1962), for example, evoked the poetic fable of the person divided into two halves, male and female, who strives for reunion through love. Erikson (1963) described the utopia of genitality as including mutuality of orgasm with a loved partner of the opposite sex. For both Freud and Erikson attraction to—and union with—a member of the opposite sex was the normal form of sexual development.

Growing up in a culture where negative stereotypes of homosexuality are prevalent, recognizing that one is gay or lesbian, and determining how to fit that aspect of self into one's life while achieving a sense of interpersonal security or self-esteem is a daunting task.

> Most youths are raised in heterosexual families, associate in heterosexual peer groups, and are educated in heterosexual institutions. Youth who are not heterosexual often feel they have little option except to pass as "heterosexually normal." The fact that they must hide their sexual orientation makes it assume a global significance to them considerably beyond necessary proportions. (Savin-Williams, 1990, p. 1)

Gay and lesbian youth find themselves faced with hostile peers, are labeled "fag" and "dyke," and may face unsympathetic parents who cannot tolerate the fact that their child has turned out differently from what they and societal norms deem acceptable. Thus the task of establishing a positive sense of oneself as a sexual being can be extremely difficult for gay and lesbian youth.

Even for youth who are heterosexual, the task of becoming sexual is not an easy one. Adolescents need to develop confidence in their sexual attractiveness and in their understanding of the practical aspects of sexual activity in order to maintain a sense of security or self-esteem in their sexual relationships. Adolescents face the risk of HIV and AIDS and of sexually transmitted disease in becoming sexually active. In trying to become sexual, adolescent girls face a conflict between the desires they may experience and societal norms which imply that only men may be expressive sexual agents. Women's desires can get them into trouble, and a bad reputation is the price paid for being sexually active. In addition, women fear male violence. They fear being unable to say no to unwanted sex and being able to assert their desires. Thus the task of integrating sexuality into one's identity and interpersonal relationships poses complexities for all adolescents, and remains an important topic for future research. We know relatively little about the childhood, individual, or social-contextual factors that make this transition easy or difficult.

Additional Resources

References and Suggested Reading

Brooks-Gunn, J., & Paikoff, R. (1997). Sexuality and developmental transitions during adolescence. In J. Schulenberg, J. L. Maggs, & K. Hurrelmann (Eds.), *Health risks and developmental transitions during adolescence* (pp. 190–219). Cambridge: Cambridge University Press.

Erikson, E. H. (1963). *Childhood and Society.* New York: W. W. Norton.

Freud, S. (1905/1962). *Three contributions to the theory of sex.* New York: E. P. Dutton.

Savin-Williams, R. C. (1990). *Gay and lesbian youth: Expressions of identity.* New York: Hemisphere Publishing.

Sullivan, H. S. (1953). *The interpersonal theory of psychiatry.* New York: W. W. Norton.

On the Internet

http://parentingteens.about.com/parenting/parentingteens/msubmenu3.htm

About.com: Parenting of Adolescents—Teen Sexuality
The About.com Network consists of over 700 Guide sites covering more than 50,000 subjects with over 1 million links to resources on the Net and a fast-growing archive of original content. The About.com Network provides links to issues of teenage sexuality.

http://www.siecus.org/teen/index.html

SEICUS—For Teens: Let's Talk about Sex
This site is part of the Sexuality Information and Education Council of the United States (SEICUS) Web site, which is a starting place for teens to learn about sexuality issues.

Adolescent Girls, Women and Sexuality: Discerning the Dilemmas of Desire

Deborah L. Tolman, Ed.D., is a senior research scientist and director of the Adolescent Sexuality Project at Wellesley College's Center for Research on Women. Formerly, she served as assistant project director of the research study "Understanding Adolescents at Risk" and is a member of the Harvard Project on the Psychology of Women and the Development of Girls. She is author of *Dilemma of Desire: Portraits of Adolescent Girls' Struggle for/with Sexuality* (in press).

Most of the research on adolescent sexuality looks at adolescents' sexual behavior: rates of contraceptive use, intercourse, pregnancy, sexually transmitted diseases, AIDS; the age at which first intercourse takes place; and how all these patterns differ by sex, race, and social class. The research focus has been primarily on problems that are associated with adolescent sexual behavior, while less attention has been given to the psychological experience of sexuality or to the development of sexual identity.

One source of learning about sexuality is through health education classes in schools. Michelle Fine (1988), in a study of how teachers and administrators discuss sexuality in school, identified three forms of discourse about sexuality that are prevalent in health classes and argued that these discourses shape the ways girls come to experience their own sexuality. Fine found the discourse about female sexuality centered around victimization by males, exposure to disease, and the imperative to uphold moral standards. What was missing, Fine observed, was a discourse of desire.

Tolman's research with adolescent girls follows from the work of Michelle Fine. Tolman studied the acceptable discourses that exist for girls about sexual desire. She found that girls struggle with wanting others to know them to be good and acceptable, yet wanting to act on their own sexual desire. Girls find themselves in a difficult situation because to become sexually active for a girl is to incur the risk of developing a bad reputation. Tolman found that girls were aware of having strong sexual feelings, but while they could speak of their embodied sexual feelings, these feelings were at odds with cultural conventions that limit girls' desires to a desire for relationships. Girls were aware of the double standard for adolescent males and females: males are expected to be turned on and sexually active, girls to be virgins and obedient to men. The consequence for some adolescent girls is to disconnect from their sexual desires. Thus the development of a sexual identity, which requires the ability to understand and respond to sexual feelings, is a complicated process for adolescent girls.

I. Female Adolescent Sexual Desire: A Conundrum

In her 1987 paper "Clarity in Connection: Empathic Knowing, Desire and Sexuality," Judith Jordan has taken the lead in grappling with some troubling questions about female sexuality. She has engaged in a risky and admirable struggle to explain her own and other clinicians' pervasive observation that women have trouble knowing their own sexual desire. In this paper, she suggests that women's lack of clarity about their own desire may be rooted in a developmental difference between girls and boys that occurs in adolescence. She outlines two developmental paths in adolescence, the emergence in boys of "sexual entitlement" and in girls of "sexual accommodation" which leads to a lack of clarity for females about their own desire. Jordan says that she has not heard her women patients speak about an "explosion of sexual impulses in adolescence" (p. 14). In her view, the central dynamic of female sexuality is the relational context; in sexual terms, the "primary needs" of females are "the need not to be used, and to be emphatically validated and 'emotionally held'" (p. 15). She posits an alternative conception of desire that highlights the experience of women, a relational model of desire, "contextual desire," which is the "desire for the experience of joining toward and joining in something that thereby becomes greater than the separate selves" (p. 11) and is "informed by empathic knowing of the other" (p. 18). Jordan suggests that women's lack of clarity about their own desire emerges out of the failure of a woman's male sexual partner to be empathically aware of her desire as an aspect of his own desire; this absence of empathy thus makes it difficult for a woman to have clarity about her own desire.

I am interested specifically in the tension which runs through this paper. Jordan makes the observation that the sexual activity in which adolescent girls and women engage is physically exciting to them: "I am not suggesting that girls don't become powerfully aroused in the early adolescent explorations of kissing and fondling . . . and women are clearly capable of powerful, intense orgasms" (p. 16). Jordan has stated her knowledge that adolescent girls can and do experience intense embodied sexual desire, yet she leaves out this bodily fact in how she speaks about the adolescent girl as centrally "interested in closeness, tenderness, being loved" (p. 16) when it comes to sex. Despite Jordan's knowledge that sexual desire, excitement and pleasure occur in female bodies, embodied sexual hunger is curiously missing as a fundamental aspect of female sexuality in the relational model she is exploring. An ambivalence seems to run through this paper, as Jordan speaks about the importance of "attunement to our bodies" (p. 17) yet emphasizes only the relational aspects of female sexual experience, focusing on women's lack of clarity about sexual desire.

Jordan concludes that little is known about the development of female sexuality and that "the picture of adolescent sexuality is still heavily colored by the male experience" (p. 16). But she does have some knowledge about adolescent female sexual desire—that girls can "become powerfully aroused." By discounting her own knowledge of embodied female sexual feelings, she overlooks the tensions between what she knows and what is missing in what she hears her clients say about their adolescent experience. Jordan honors her client's experiences and tries to understand what they have told her through a relational model of female sexuality. But when she leaves aside their bodies in framing and understanding their experience as essentially relational, she loses what might be an important question: If I know that adolescent girls can experience sexual excitement in their bodies, why don't I hear about embodied sexual desire when adolescent girls talk of their sexual experience or in women's recollections of their adolescent sexual experience? I am struck that Jordan knows that adolescent girls have embodied sexual feelings and yet she does not wonder about the absence of physical sexual desire in what women and adolescent girls say about their adolescent sexual experience.

II. The Missing Discourse of Desire: A Dilemma for Adolescent Girls

Jordan's willingness to think out loud about the conundrum of sexual desire in female adolescence is, as Irene Stiver observes in the discussion summary of the paper, deserving of congratulations. She is, in fact, speaking into a deafening silence within the psychological literature. Outside of the domain of psychology, however, feminist writers have been naming and exploring the absence of female sexual desire in Western patriarchal culture's conceptions of female sexuality for the past fifteen years (i.e., Hite, 1976; Snitow, Stansell and Thompson, 1983; Vance, 1984). Having revealed the silencing, denigration and obscuring of female sexual desire that androcentric notions of female sexuality served, feminists are now exploring what female sexual desire is. A number of feminist scholars have built on Foucault's (1978) analysis that discourse about sexuality—the terms, tenor and tone in which sexuality is talked about—shapes sexual experience and that discourse is controlled and deployed by those in power (Duggan, 1990; Rubin, 1984; Snitow, Stansell and Thompson, 1983; Vance, 1984); a number of French feminists are engaged in creating a way of speaking about female sexual desire, ecriture feminine—writing the body—that they suggest does not exist in "phallocentric" language (Cixous, 1981; Irigaray, 1981, 1985; see also Dallery, 1989). These writers emphasize that what we do and do not say, what we do and do not hear, about sexual desire is a critical shaping force of our capacity to acknowledge, understand and respond to the feelings in our bodies. It is interesting to note that few feminist scholars consider specifically the experience of adolescent girls in their analyses of female sexual desire (Tolman, 1990). Jordan senses that the lack of clarity about desire she hears from women may have something to do with the development of sexuality in adolescence. The silence about adolescent girls' sexual desire has only recently been acknowledged and broken.

In her 1988 article "Sexuality, Schooling, and Adolescent Females: The Missing Discourse of Desire," feminist psychologist Michelle Fine reports her observation that a discourse of desire is missing from the ways in which adolescent female sexuality is conceived of and discussed by teachers and administrators in schools. Girls' sexuality was a topic of discussion but only spoken about in the condoned sexuality discourses, each of which discourages girls' sexual exploration: the discourse of victimization, that girls are taken advantage of by boys; the discourse of disease, that girls need to avoid being infected by sexually transmitted diseases and AIDS; and the discourse of morality, that girls need to behave in a moral fashion that does not include sexual activity. I have searched the literature on adolescent sexuality and female development for theoretical or empirical work on girls' sexual desire (Tolman, 1990). There has been no research by psychologists on female adolescent sexual desire; the major developmental theories since Freud have not only left out girls' experience (Gilligan, 1977, 1982), they have also muted sexual desire as a central dynamic in adolescent development, moving development out of the body, first into society and then into the mind.[1] Even feminist theories of female development have been silent about adolescent girls' sexual desire (i.e., Chodorow, 1974, 1989; Gilligan, 1977, 1982; Miller, 1976, 1984; Surrey, 1984). The glossing over of adolescent girls' sexual desire that Fine encountered in schools and that I discovered in the literature of developmental psychology reflects the missing discourse of adolescent girls' sexual desire in society at large.

From the perspective of feminist analyses of female sexual desire, Michelle Fine began to hear a discourse of adolescent girls' desire in schools when she started to listen to girls themselves; she heard it as "a whisper . . . an interruption of the ongoing conversation" (Fine, 1988, p. 33) articulated by girls themselves. By listening carefully to what girls said in schools when they spoke about their sexuality in bathrooms, classrooms and in conversations with her, Michelle Fine discerned some girls weaving a discourse of desire, a naming of their own embodied longing for sexual pleasure, through the ways in which they talked about their sexual experience. Because this discourse of desire was missing in the condoned discourses of adolescent female sexuality in schools, girls' sexual desire was neither audible nor knowable to most of the adults, however. In Fine's view, the absence of an acknowledgement of girls' embodied sexual feelings is a problem. She suggests that this missing discourse may result in girls' failure to know themselves as the subjects of their own sexuality. If girls could conceive of themselves as sexual subjects, they could then potentially make decisions about their sexual behavior and experience that would be healthy for them.

Coming of age in a culture in which their embodied sexual desire is silenced, obscured and denigrated poses a problem for girls. Adolescent girls get a clear message that they are not supposed to become aroused; they hear what the discourses spoken within dominant culture frame for them as their sexual experience—the discourses of victimization, disease and morality that Fine heard spoken in schools. Yet as Judith Jordan (1987) points out, girls' bodies "become powerfully aroused" (p. 16). The tension that I perceive running through Jordan's paper may in fact be the struggle that adolescent girls themselves are engaged in. If girls know about their sexual desire from their experience of their own bodies but encounter a disembodied way of speaking, hearing, and knowing about their sexuality, then a central dilemma is posed for adolescent girls: In what relationship can an adolescent girl be with her sexual desire, with her own body, with her own experience? How do girls both take in the messages from the culture (Gilligan, 1990; Gilligan, Brown and Rogers, 1990) that encourage them not to know their sexual desire and also stay connected to their own bodily experience?

If I tune my ears to listening for dilemmas which can arise when girls do speak about their own sexual feelings, these feelings that no one names, in what girls say when they speak about their sexuality, I can hear some girls struggling with this problem. Listen to the words of Anne Frank, writing to Kitty, the persona of her diary, about her conundrum:

> Once more there is a question which gives me no peace: 'Is it right? Is it right that I should have yielded so soon, that I am so ardent, just as ardent and eager as Peter himself? May I, a girl, let myself go to this extent?' . . . I am afraid of myself, I am afraid that in my longing I am giving myself too quickly. (cited in Dalsimer, 1986, p. 67)

Anne knows and names the feelings of sexual desire in her body—she is "ardent and eager;" she experiences "longing." But she understands also that she, "a girl," should not "let herself go" and be "giving [her]self too quickly." Coming up against what she has learned is appropriate for a girl in the 1944 culture of Western Europe to feel and to do, Anne ponders "a question which gives [her] no peace." I can hear Anne struggling with the dilemma that emerges, precisely because she is keenly aware of both her own sexual desire and the cultural prohibition against her feeling or responding to her sexual feelings. Carol Gilligan has observed that, elsewhere in her diary, Anne Frank raises questions about how this culture dismisses women, and how women do not fight to be known in ways that reflect the reality of their experience (Gilligan, 1990); Gilligan observes that Anne resists taking in what the culture says about women and female experience when it runs counter to her own experience. Here too, I think Anne has painted a self-portrait of resistance to messages about her sexuality, but the dilemma that results from her resistance is obvious: If she knows that she has sexual feelings and, at the same time, she knows that she is not supposed to feel this way as a girl, how can she both have these feelings and be an acceptable girl?

Now I listen to the words of a 16-year-old girl, speaking fifty years later, in a note written to her psychiatrist. After the sexual revolution and the enormous changes that have taken place in how society responds to female sexuality, this girl is caught in the same dilemma in which Anne found herself, struggling between her experience of sexual desire and knowing that she's "not supposed to get excited."

> I don't know how to bring up the subject of these feelings I get. Girls aren't sup- posed to—they're not supposed to get excited . . . It's hard to know what to think about this subject. I wake up, and I've had a dream and I'm all excited because of the dream, I think. So then my body starts moving on me. Do you know what I mean? I'm not sure I do, myself! I'm sorry I can't write better. I mean, express myself. That's the worst part of being a teenager, there's so much going on inside you, but you can't talk to anyone about it, even to your closest friend . . . I saw this movie 'Cat on a Hot Tin Roof,' and I thought to myself, that's you, and when will you get off the roof, or when will the roof quiet down? (Coles, 1985, pp. 4–5)

Coles pronounces her "forthright" (p. 5) but does not notice that she is speaking about how she is not supposed to notice sexual feelings in her body or talk about these feelings, *because* she is a girl: "Girls aren't supposed to—they're not supposed to get excited." Confused by the contradiction that her own experience makes visible, she knows that she has these feelings but says she does not know—"Do you know what I mean? I'm not sure I do myself"—and in this way starts to "undo" what she has said about her knowledge of her own sexual excitement and the cultural ban on those feelings. She is articulate and "forthright," yet she says she "can't write" or "express herself." Coles concludes that her struggle is a typical adolescent concern about normality, missing entirely that her conflict is about being a girl who gets sexually excited in the context of a culture that says she is not supposed to feel this way. He does not hear that she is trying to resist messages that run counter to her own bodily feelings.

Both Anne Frank and Coles' patient seem to be in a process of resistance against taking in the message that they do not and cannot have sexual desire. As resisters, these girls are probably more the exception than the rule; because adolescent girls live in a culture which obscures, denigrates, silences and is silent about their desire, I think that most girls can and will speak in the voice of the culture. If no one around them speaks about girls' desire, then girls may have trouble speaking directly them-selves. The missing discourse of desire that pervades Western culture then creates a problem both for girls and for therapists, as well as other adult women working with adolescent girls: how can we hear and speak to girls about the feelings they have in their bodies, if we hear and speak in the socially condoned missing discourse of their desire—which girls themselves may have taken in?

III. Responsive/Resisting Listening: Hearing/ Exploring Girls' Missing Discourse of Desire

Even when we as women begin to listen to girls with a clear understanding both of their potential to feel sexual desire and the knowledge that this desire is not talked about in dominant Western culture, it can still be hard to hear adolescent girls speak about their desire. While Michelle Fine writes eloquently about girls' discourse of desire, in the few examples of girls speaking about desire that pepper her text, their discourse of desire is difficult to discern. For instance, an example in the article which illustrates girls' discourse of desire is one girl's explanation for not showing up for an interview: "my boyfriend came home from the Navy and I wanted to spend the night with him, we don't get to see each other much" (p. 33). This reference to desire is almost like a code; it is hard to pick up unless one has a key. Another feminist scholar, Sharon Thompson, struggles to hear girls speak about their sexual desire and pleasure in the 400 narratives about sexuality, reproduction and romance she has collected (Thompson, 1984; 1990). She was dismayed to hear most girls speaking not of their own desire but of "the quest romance," not of the sexual excitement and pleasure of initial experiences of intercourse but of pain and boredom. These efforts to hear girls speak about their sexual desire illustrate how hard it may be both for girls to speak and how hard it may be for women to hear a discourse of desire. Girls' discourse of desire may be subtle, encoded in the constricted ways which the culture makes available for them to speak about an unspeakable topic. Or girls may describe their experiences consciously in a missing discourse of desire, knowing full well that they should not name their sexual hunger. Many girls may in fact solve the dilemma of their own sexual desire in the face of a culture that does not acknowledge their bodies by not feeling those feelings. Women who have been sexually abused as adolescents often have difficulty with their sexual desire (Kaplan, 1990; Llera, 1991). They may actually have experienced a doubled disconnection in protecting themselves psychologically by dissociating from their bodies and also in astutely picking up a cultural message not to speak about sexual feelings. Lesbian women, who often report not feeling their sexual feelings until adolescence (de-Monteflores and Schultz, 1978), may come up against a doubled resistance as well; in addition to the missing discourse of desire that all adolescent girls must negotiate, they encounter silence about their sexual desire for women as well.

In order for women to hear girls speak about desire, it may be helpful for women to become responsive/resisting listeners of girls (Brown and Gilligan, 1990). This approach builds on the Reading Guide, a strategy for analyzing girls' narratives about their experience that has been developed by researchers at the Harvard Project for the Psychology of Women and the Development of Girls (see Brown, 1988). It may also be used as a form of clinical listening. Acknowledging that female voice and experience are muffled and silenced in the context of Western culture, this approach enables the reader or listener to "bring to the surface the 'undercurrent' of female voices and visions as it filters through an androcentric culture" (Brown and Gilligan, 1990, p. 4). It is an explicitly psychological method, which encourages the reader to consider the meaning of what is said and what is not said by girls about aspects of their experience that are silenced by the culture and about which girls are encouraged to be silent (Brown et al., in press; Gilligan, Brown and Rogers, 1990; Rogers and Gilligan, 1988). A responsive/resisting listener struggles to connect with what girls do and do not say about their experience by being explicitly grounded in her own experience as female in this culture.

I suggest that we, as therapists and other women working with girls, can use our knowledge that adolescent girls can feel sexual desire, and our awareness of the missing discourse of this desire, in the dominant culture to begin to be responsive/resisting listeners to girls when they speak about their sexuality and sexual experiences, as well as to women recollecting their adolescence. I will present a narrative told by Pamela, a 15-year-old Hispanic girl in a longitudinal study of female development.[2] While this narrative was told to an adult woman in a research interview, this story about girls' sexual experience might also be shared in therapy. Pamela tells this narrative in response to the question: "Can you tell me about a time when you were considering a decision about sex and you had to work something out?"

> I liked this kid in February and . . . I got to know him and I like him but I don't like him as a boyfriend. I like him as a real good friend. Everyone here thinks that we go out, but we are just real good friends . . . For now, I'd say definitely no [to having sex], because I don't want my husband to be like, you are already leftovers you know, so I would want to be, I want to wear white when I get married . . . I know one of my friends, she, I asked her because I knew the kid, . . . I told her, if he asks you are you gonna and she said no, because I used to go out with I don't know who for a year or something and it never came it, well, it did and I said no, I didn't have to do that just to be his girlfriend and all that. So then she's been going out with him for seven months and I know she's already had sex with him about three times or something. So I guess, I guess you can't really say nuthin

until the time happens, because she was sure, she was like I'm just going to be like no, Derek, I don't want to do it right now but she said when it came up, it just happened and half of her was like go for it, and the other was like no, you know, your mother. So she said that, she couldn't really say no, it was just was happening and it happened before she even thought about it.

Pamela begins the story by speaking obliquely about how she does not experience desire—"I don't like him as a boyfriend. I like him as a real good friend" translates that she is not sexually interested in him. Pamela explains her very good reasons for "definitely saying no" to sex: She wants to avoid being branded as a girl who desires sex, because she is under enormous pressure, particularly in her context in a traditional Hispanic family (see Espin, 1984), to "wear white when [she] gets married" and to avoid being "leftovers" to her husband. If I listen for how she speaks about herself, I begin to consider how she may be speaking in a missing discourse of desire. I begin to wonder if she may be having physical feelings and how she may be responding to them. Because Pamela speaks clearly in the voice of the culture which will not name her own bodily feelings, it is difficult to know what feelings she may have for the boy who is "just a friend." Is she struggling not to know or feel her own desire? Is she not sexually interested in him, introducing him into the narrative in order to fortify a portrait of herself as a girl who does not feel desire? Is there someone whom she desires who goes unnamed when she speaks in this missing discourse? Or, more simply, does she experience no sexual desire for this particular boy?

Then a tension arises in her story between this description of herself told in missing discourse—"I'd definitely say no . . . I want to wear white"—and her knowledge that girls do experience sexual desire and can end up having sex without intending to. Pamela goes on to tell a story about "Sally," her friend, who, in the face of the dilemma posed by her own desire and her knowledge that she "should" say no, ends up having sex "happen" to her. As responsive/resisting listener, I can pose the question: What is Pamela saying about her knowledge and questions about her own sexual desire by telling this story about another girl? It would be very easy and quite tempting as women in this culture to align with Pamela's circumvented ways of speaking about herself and to remain silent about her missing discourse of desire. It would be so simple to applaud and support her firm claim that she "wants to wear white" when she gets married; after all, this stance would protect her from pregnancy, sexually transmitted diseases and AIDS, and she sounds so clear and confident about this position. So why would I want to identify and explore with Pamela her ways of speaking about sexual feelings and to engage with her in an embodied discourse of desire? While Pamela does not ever name explicitly her own sexual desire or any struggle with it, by telling the story about Sally's sexual experience, she may be cueing me that the picture she has drawn of herself may not be so neat.

As a responsive/resisting listener, I am drawn to how Pamela describes Sally's struggle: "half of her was like go for it and the other was like no, you know, your mother." Pamela lets the listener know that she is aware that girls can have sexual feelings in their bodies—girls may want to "go for it"—and that girls know that they are not supposed to respond to these feelings—"no, you know, your mother," which makes Sally's sexual longing problematic. Pamela signals the listener that she may understand that this experience could happen to her as well, despite her clear statement that she "wants to wear white;" she shifts out of the story about Sally, making a more general aside: "I guess you can't really say nuthin until the time happens, because she was sure, she was like 'I'm just going to be like no, Derek, I don't want to do it right now.' " Pamela, too, appears to be sure. But Pamela is under real pressure to take on, live and speak as the image of the bride in white. What purpose does Pamela serve by telling this story about Sally? Does Pamela wonder herself, behind her firm resolve, if she too would want "to go for it?" If Pamela continues to speak in a missing discourse of desire, might she find herself in the same position as Sally? If Pamela can move out of a missing discourse of desire, to know and respond to her own desire, may she be less likely to find sex "just happening" to her and more likely to make responsible choices about what she will and will not do?

In noticing that Pamela is not speaking about her own desire, yet she is letting her listener in on her awareness of other girls' sexual desire, I become curious about Pamela's own sexual feelings and struggles with her body and the messages about it she has taken in. I think the unspoken questions that Pamela seems to be raising in this complicated narrative could go unrecognized quite easily. It would be very easy for me to misalign with the missing discourse she knows so well and, I would imagine, hears from many women in her life. I might miss her struggle, the clues she has laid out that can be picked up by listening for a missing discourse of desire.

IV. Implications for Psychotherapy

Sharon Thompson made an observation about a small group of adolescent girls among the 400 she has interviewed whom she calls "pleasure narrators" (Thompson, 1990), who describe their own desire and pleasure as key aspects of their first experiences of sexual intercourse. Unlike the majority of the girls with whom she spoke, these girls had talked with their mothers about female sexual desire and pleasure. These mothers interrupted the culture's missing discourse of desire and shared with their daughters what they knew about the sexual feelings their daughters would be experiencing, and in that way validated and celebrated this embodied knowledge. As an adult woman in a relationship with Pamela, listening to her story, I might ask her about her own bodily feelings. Should I wonder with her about the conundrum in which she may find herself: How is it possible for her to know, respond to or speak about her sexual feelings? Should I speak to her about the embodied sexual feelings I experienced when I was her age? Should I introduce to her the possibility of resisting the cultural messages that deny these feelings, the possibility of an embodied discourse of desire? Should I acknowledge that this missing discourse is problematic and engage in resistance against it with her? Would it be possible for me to engage in this same resistance myself? If I could, she and I could try to move toward a way of talking about adolescent girls' and women's sexuality together that takes as central strong sexual feelings, and we might begin to work through the dilemma that these feelings create.

I realize that when girls know, experience and speak about those fabulous feelings in their bodies, trouble follows—for them and for their parents, teachers and therapists. Girls' sexual desire upsets people, because it challenges and might upset the cultural mandate which requires that girls (and women) not be connected to their bodies in general, and to their sexual hunger in particular. Girls' sexual desire is an interruption of the condoned version of what happens in girls' bodies. If girls know their desire, what else might they begin to know about themselves and their situation in the culture?

Notes

1. See Miller and Simon (1980) for a summary of Erikson's, Piaget's and Kohlberg's disembodied descriptions of sexuality in adolescence.
2. This young woman was a participant in a study of adolescents considered at-risk for school leaving and early pregnancy or parenting funded by the Boston Foundation, with additional support from the Mailman Foundation.

References

Brown, L. (Ed.). (1988). *A guide to reading narratives of moral conflict and choice for self and moral orientation.* (Monograph No. 2). Cambridge, MA: Harvard Project on the Psychology of Women and the Development of Girls, Harvard Graduate School of Education.

Brown, L., Debold, E., Tappan, M. & Gilligan, C. (in press). Reading narratives of conflict for self and moral voice: A relational method. In W. Kurtines and J. Gewirtz (Eds.), *Handbook of moral behavior and development: Theory, research and application.* Hillsdale, NJ: Lawrence Erlbaum.

Brown, L. M. & Gilligan, C. (1990, August). *Listening for self and relational voices: A responsive/resisting reader's guide.* Paper presented at the annual meeting of the American Psychological Association, Boston, MA.

Cixous, H. (1981). The laugh of the Medusa. In E. Marks and I. de Courtivron (Eds.), *New French Feminisms.* New York: Schocken.

Chodorow, N. (1974). *The reproduction of mothering: Psychoanalysis and the psychology of gender.* Berkeley, CA: University of California Press.

Chodorow, N. (1989). *Feminism and psychoanalytic theory.* New Haven, CT: Yale University Press.

Coles, R. (1985). Introduction. In R. Coles & G. Stokes. *Sex and the American teenager.* New York: Harper Colophon Books.

Dallery, A. (1989). The politics of writing (the) body: *Ecriture feminine.* In A. Jaggar and S. Bordo (Eds.), *Gender/Body/Knowledge.* New Brunswick, NJ: Rutgers University Press.

Dalsimer, K. (1986). *Female adolescence: Psychoanalytic reflections on works of literature.* New Haven: Yale University Press.

deMonteflores, C. & Schultz, S. J. (1978). Coming out: Similarities and differences for lesbians and gay men. *Journal of Social Issues, 34* (3), 59–72.

Duggan, L. (1990). From instincts to politics: Writing the history of sexuality in the U.S. *Journal of Sex Research, 27* (1), 95–112.

Espin, O. (1984). Cultural and historical influences on sexuality in Hispanic/Latin women: Implications for psychotherapy. In C. Vance (Ed.), *Pleasure and danger: Exploring female sexuality.* Boston: Routledge and Kegan Paul.

Fine, M. (1988). Sexuality, schooling and adolescent females: The missing discourse of desire. *Harvard Educational Review, 58*(1), 29–53.

Foucault, M. (1978). *The history of sexuality, Volume 1: An introduction.* New York: Vintage.

Gilligan, C. (1977). Woman's place in man's lifecycle. *Harvard Educational Review, 49*(4), 431–446.

Gilligan, C. (1982). *In a different voice: Psychological theory and women's development.* Cambridge: Harvard University Press.

Gilligan, C. (1990). Joining the resistance: Psychology, politics, girls and women. *Michigan Quarterly Review, 29* (4), 501–536.

Gilligan, C. Brown, L., & Rogers, A. (1990). Psyche embedded: A place for body, relationships and culture in personality theory. In A. Rabin et al. (Eds.), *Studying persons and lives.* New York: Springer.

Hite, S. (1976). *The Hite report: A nationwide study of female sexuality.* New York: Dell Publishing Company.

Irigaray, L. (1981). This sex which is not one. In E. Marks and I. de Courtivron (Eds.), *New French Feminisms.* New York: Schocken.

Irigaray, L. (1985). *This sex which is not one.* Ithaca, NY: Cornell University Press.

Jordan, J. (1987). Clarity in connection: Empathic knowing, desire and sexuality. *Work in progress* No. 29. Wellesley, MA: Stone Center Working Papers Series.

Kaplan, L. (1990). *The dynamics of desire: Early sexual abuse and adult sexual desire.* Unpublished doctoral dissertation, Massachusetts School of Professional Psychology, Dedham, MA.

Llera, D. (1991). *Sexually abused adolescent females: Preventing victimization by introducing desire.* Unpublished manuscript, Harvard University.

Miller, J. B. (1976). *Toward a new psychology of women.* Boston: Beacon Press.

Miller, P. and Simon, W. (1980). The development of sexuality in adolescence. In J. Adelsen, (Ed.), *Handbook of adolescent psychology.* New York: J. Wiley and Sons.

Miller, J. B. (1984). The development of women's sense of self. *Work in progress,* No. 12. Wellesley, MA: Stone Center Working Papers Series.

Rogers, A. & Gilligan, C. (1988). *The language of adolescent girls: Themes of moral voice and stages of ego development.* (Monograph No. 6). Cambridge, MA: Harvard Project on the Psychology of Women and The Development of Girls, Harvard Graduate School of Education.

Rubin, G. (1984). Thinking sex: Notes for a radical theory of the politics of sexuality. In C. Vance (Ed.), *Pleasure and danger: Exploring female sexuality.* Boston: Routledge and Kegan Paul.

Snitow, A., Stansell, C. & Thompson, S. (Eds.). (1983). *Powers of desire: The politics of sexuality.* New York: Monthly Review Press.

Surrey, J. (1984). The "self-in-relation:" A theory of women's development. *Work in progress,* No. 13. Wellesley, MA: Stone Center Working Papers Series.

Thompson, S. (1984). Search for tomorrow: On feminism and the reconstruction of teen romance. In C. Vance (Ed.), *Pleasure and anger: Exploring female sexuality.* Boston: Routledge and Kegan Paul.

Thompson, S. (1990). Putting a big thing in a little hole: Teenage girls' accounts of sexual initiation. *Journal of Sex Research, 27* (3), 341–351.

Tolman, D. (1990). *Discourses of adolescent girls' sexual desire in developmental psychology and feminist scholarship.* Unpublished manuscript, Harvard University.

Vance, C. (Ed.). (1984). *Pleasure and danger: Exploring female sexuality.* Boston: Routledge and Kegan Paul.

Questions

1. What type of discourse prevailed in your own sex education courses about female sexuality?
2. What type of discourse exists for males about sexuality?
3. What type of discourse is missing for males?
4. How does the discourse about sexuality shape adolescents' understanding of themselves sexually and their sexual experiences?

References and Further Reading

Fine, M. (1988). Sexuality, schooling and adolescent females: The missing discourse of desire. *Harvard Educational Review, 58,* 29–53.

Tolman, D. H. (1999). Female adolescent sexuality in relational context: Beyond sexual decision making. In N. G. Johnson, M. C. Roberts, & J. Worell (Eds.), *Beyond appearance: A new look at adolescent girls* (pp. 227–246). Washington, DC: American Psychological Association.

Tolman, D. H., & Szalacha, L. (1999). Dimensions of desire: Bridging qualitative and quantitative methods in a study of female adolescent sexuality. *Psychology of Women Quarterly, 23,* 9–41.

9.2   Ritch C. Savin-Williams, 1998

Labeling Self as Gay or Bisexual

Ritch C. Savin-Williams, Ph.D., is a professor of developmental psychology in the Department of Human Development at Cornell University. He is a clinical psychologist whose clinical work and research has focused on gay and lesbian youth. He is author of *Adolescence: An Ethological Perspective* (1987), *Gay and Lesbian Youth: Expressions of Identity* (1990) and " . . . And Then I Became Gay": Young Men's Stories (1998). He is coeditor with (K. M. Cohen) of *The Lives of Lesbians, Gays, and Bisexuals: Children to Adults* (1996).

Just as race is not a salient aspect of identity for those who are white and members of the majority culture, so sexual orientation is not a salient aspect of identity for those who are heterosexual and whose sexuality is normative and judged to be normal by society. While the task of integrating adult sexuality into one's personality and interpersonal life poses difficulties for all adolescents, an additional component exists to the process of establishing a sexual identity for those who are not heterosexual. The application of the term gay or lesbian to oneself is a complex and often costly process.

How does one know whether the label gay or lesbian applies to oneself or to others? Some gay and lesbian youths who are still virgins are certain of their sexual orientation, and some heterosexual youth engage in extensive same-gender sexual behavior. Carla Golden, in a study of lesbians, found that women's sexuality was an aspect of identity that was "fluid and dynamic as opposed to fixed and invariant" (Golden, 1987, p. 19). Some lesbians Golden interviewed viewed their sexual attraction to women as an unchanging aspect of who they were, while other lesbian women saw no contradiction between the fact that at one point in their lives they were heterosexual and at a later point came to define themselves as lesbian. Thus adolescents must struggle to make sense of their sexual attractions, feelings, thoughts, and fantasies about members of the same and the opposite sex, as well as their sexual behavior over time, in determining whether to label themselves as gay, lesbian, bisexual, or heterosexual.

The reading by Ritch Savin-Williams is drawn from an interview study of gay and bisexual male youth who were asked to, "recall their developmental progression from first memories of being attracted to other males—which for some was as early as their first memories of life—to a subsequent integration of their sexual identity with their personal identity" (p. 1). Given the paucity of research on gay and bisexual youth, Savin-Williams felt the best place to begin to understand the issues faced by sexual-minority youth was through the use of personal narratives of the youths themselves, by listening to their voices. Savin-Williams takes up the issue of labeling or identifying one's sexuality as gay or bisexual. He looks at the age at which this self-identification occurs, the length of the time period over which this recognition occurs, and the feelings that it engenders. He discusses the difference between recognizing that one's attractions are to people of the same sex and actually understanding the implications of this for one's own identity. He then goes on to discuss the complex process of identifying oneself as gay or bisexual, developing an acceptance of a self-identity as gay or bisexual, and disclosing that identity to others.

Labeling one's sexuality is generally a process unknown to heterosexual youths, who appear to naturally flow into the abyss of "normal sexuality"—that is, heterosexuality. For sexual-minority youths, however, the means by which they come to recognize that their sexuality has been named by their culture as an "other" is a vivid, memorable process that can never be forgotten. It alters interpretations of the past, current conceptions of the self, and future life trajectories.

Although the internal process of naming a sexuality is seldom an isolated event but is embedded within a progressive series of milestones for gay and bisexual youths, the critical developmental "crises" of self-labeling and first disclosing this information to others frequently occur in today's cohort of youths during the adolescent and young adult years. Both have been subsumed by the popular term "coming out"; however, labeling of self is distinct, both conceptually and temporarily, from the disclosure process. . . . The first often begins from earliest memories of feeling different and an awareness that one's attractions to males are sexual and homoerotic and resolves in an act of self-disclosure; the second is a process that begins with one's first disclosure of same-sex attractions and identity to another and ultimately concludes at one's deathbed, for one is constantly coming out to new others. The two are neither identical nor separate but "exist in a dialectic relationship: coming out to others constantly redefines one's notion of self, and the development of a self-identity drives the process of disclosure" (p. 76).

The application of a sexual-identity label to oneself provides not only an explanation for formerly vague and misunderstood feelings but also affords a context in which future thoughts and emotions can be understood. Most youths ultimately navigate these terrains with difficulty but with success, becoming healthy, well-functioning adults. However, for a significant number of youths the self-recognition process is not an easy journey. Published reports lament the fact that all too many do not survive, ending their lives distraught because of their willingness to listen to the lies of family, friends, religion, and culture. . . . Others are left with permanent scars that may be physical, such as HIV infection; emotional, such as depression; cognitive, such as self-depreciation; or social, such as being rejected by friends and family. In its most benign form, internalizing particular negative cultural values and beliefs regarding homosexuality lead some youths to postpone their self-labeling process several years or decades.

Indeed, nonheterosexual labels are still beyond the reach of many youths. In a comprehensive study of sexual orientation among nearly thirty-five thousand Minnesota youths, about 1 percent of junior and senior high-school students defined themselves as gay, lesbian, or bisexual. More youths were willing to report that they had same-sex attractions (5 percent), fantasies (3 percent), and behavior (1 percent). Furthermore, relatively few of those who reported same-sex attractions or fantasies or who engaged in same-sex behavior labeled themselves as anything other than heterosexual. These numbers correspond with the reports of adult men in which far more "confessed" during face-to-face interviews with a research stranger to having experienced desire for sex with a person of the same sex (8 percent) than having had sex with another man (5 percent) or having identified self as a gay or bisexual (3 percent).

Despite these numbers, an *increasing* number of gay/bisexual youths are self-defining their sexual identity at *increasingly* younger ages, largely because of the recent visibility of homosexuality in the macro culture (such as in the media), the reality of a very vocal and extensive gay and lesbian culture, and the presence of homosexuality in their immediate social world. For example, one student in my sexual minorities class reported that her high school had seven "out" teachers. Thus, defenses are shattered because now homoerotically inclined adolescents have available to them a construct of homosexuality and gay role models (bisexual models are still scarce) that increase the likelihood of recognizing and labeling their same-sex attractions. Facilitative factors that ease the transition from an assumed but frequently unexamined heterosexual identity to a gay/bisexual identity have seldom been adequately explored and are thus largely unknown.

Youths also now have available a number of support, advocacy, and recreational groups that can facilitate the transition from feelings of nonheterosexuality to a tentative identification as gay or bisexual. For example, the National Advocacy Coalition on Youth and Sexual Orientation, whose mission is to end discrimination against lesbian, gay, bisexual, and transgendered youths and to secure their physical and emotional well-being, lists nearly eighty participating organizations located in all regions of the United States. This public focus on sexual-minority youth further weakens the defenses of adolescents who try to deny or ignore their sexuality.

All too often, however, attempts are made to homogenize the developmental processes by which youths come to an understanding about their sexual identity. What is new and is perhaps the key development for many youths is the visibility and hence possibility of multiple ways of being gay, many of which break traditional images and stereotypes of how one must act, think, and feel if one is gay. Across individuals, sufficient variability is now apparent to warrant an expanded discussion of the broad outlines that are the essential developmental features of many gays and bisexuals during their childhood and adolescence.

Self-Identifying as Gay or Bisexual

The internal process of identifying as gay or bisexual is a very personal, private affair. As opposed to other developmental milestones, such as first gay or heterosexual sex or disclosure to another, in which an identifiable event marks the occasion, many youths consider the identity process to be an abstraction that is difficult to specify as an exact moment in time. Many notable exceptions, however, are apparent in the narratives cited in this section. For example, some youths recalled a very specific instant in which they said clearly and discreetly, "I'm gay/bisexual."

Youths identified their sexuality as early as third or fourth grade or as late as graduate school. The largest number self-identified during their high-school years or while in college—about 40 percent each. A much smaller number, approximately 20 percent, labeled themselves during childhood and early adolescence.

Nearly one in four recognized their homoerotic attractions and sexual identity simultaneously. One youth described this process as, "I really didn't make the distinction. The attractions just happened, and I didn't question them." The absence of a boundary between the two was much more likely to characterize early adolescence than any other time. Another quarter labeled their identity within one to three years after recognizing that they had gay attractions. A third quarter connected their attractions and identity within four to five years; the final quarter, from six to eleven years.

Excluding bisexual youths, nearly 25 percent of gay youths reported that they went through a "bisexual stage" on their way to labeling themselves gay. What prevented these "bisexual" youths from immediately embracing a gay identity was the same as that which prevented many other youths who also delayed naming themselves from moving beyond their heterosexual identity—they felt that their attractions to males would go away. When this temporary aberration did not abate, youths became confused, frightened, and anxious. Many had been taught, especially by their religious or cultural group, that being gay is wrong and they should make all efforts possible to change. Others had more secular fears—that they would be stigmatized by family members, peers, and the culture at large, or verbally and physically harassed.

This should not, however, be construed as a monolithic portrait of these gay/bisexual youths. Although much smaller in number than the previously described group, other youths were relieved that they had finally come to terms with their feelings. Being gay/bisexual was not a handicap or a disability but an extension of living a new life filled with exhilarating prospects for homoeroticism and romantic relationships with those compelling, passionate objects known as men.

When asked what led to their decision to identify as gay or bisexual, the most frequent response was, "I just knew." That is, something just "clicked" in their head, and everything made sense. It could be a sudden event or a gradual process. The second most common response was expressed by those who knew their identity based on the strength of homoerotic feelings that just would not go away. Masturbatory fantasies remained centered on males and sex with girls was just not changing anything.

Friends, both gay and liberal heterosexuals, were the third most frequent contributors to a youth's decision to "come out" to himself. To these individuals, a youth was able to verbalize, "I'm gay/bisexual," and in the process say the same to himself for the first time. The following youth secured the greatest gift a pregay could receive from a friend—someone who would become an even better friend in the process.

> I got very excited and nervous when we talked about gay people and I didn't know why. My friend was very confident and sure of himself and I was not. I'm asking him questions about gays and he was very positive. I remember I got upset with something he said. Somehow he knew that I was gay, which was something I didn't even know then. He tried to calm me down as I muttered, "I'm a faggot! I'm a queer!" He was very supportive. He said he figured it out a long time ago and that he was my friend regardless. He liked me as me. I said that I feared for what my life would be like and what my parents would be like because I was gay. He said he'd be there for me and we became great friends.
>
> So I was crying and very relieved. Part of me should have been developed much earlier but it never was. I missed out on normal development because I didn't even know myself. I was afraid what my parents would think, what my life would be like, no family, alone for the rest of my life. So I feared for the worst. But I had my friend.

Contrary to what many may presuppose, relatively few youths depended on their first sexual experience with a male to label themselves as gay or bisexual. . . . More commonly, youths self-identified as gay after they fell in love with a man or after they accepted their undeniable emotional feelings for a friend. These strong emotional attractions provided the necessary fodder for what their feelings for another man meant, including exiting their "bisexual stage" of development.

> I was just sort of hanging out my senior year of high school at a cafe. I met this guy who turned out to be a male prostitute, and I told him that I had a female friend and he said that he was bisexual. I said that I was too. We drew closer and closer and I said that I loved him; then I told him that I was gay which was telling myself in my mind that I was gay, but I didn't really tell anyone else except him at this point.

Some, but not many, youths made the transition from straight to gay with the emotional support of a therapist, gay peer counselor, or gay hotline. After falling in love with a friend and not understanding what was happening to him, one youth told his therapist about his feelings. She gave him the encouragement he needed to realize that he was gay. Not all, however, received support from their mental-health provider.

During my junior year of high school the feelings began to come back and I seriously thought that I must be gay, although I was not yet ready to call myself gay. During the summer before my senior year I knew I had to do something about it, so I told my psychiatrist, and he gave me that old spiel about how do I really know that I am since I had no experience sexually. He encouraged me to get a girlfriend and have sex. But I just knew that this is what I was but I didn't get very much good feedback from the psychiatrist. He just sat there a lot.

What eventually helped a relatively small number of youths make sense of their blocked feelings was living in an enlightened community or being exposed to gay images in the mass media. Several youths had an openly lesbian or gay relative, and that helped; others attributed their self-recognition to reading a gay-positive book or article or seeing a gay-positive movie or television show.

At thirteen I felt I was my own person, and I can't recall any major concerns with my sexual identification. A year later I was gay. Before this I didn't have a name for it. Just sort of happened and then I had to deal with it. Which I did, probably because Ithaca is such an enlightened place that I knew what it meant to be gay.

The nature and influence of these factors and the reactions that youths had in making the transition in self-perception from someone with same-sex attractions to a gay or bisexual identity are presented [here]. The narratives are organized based on the age at which the transition occurred.

Childhood and Early Adolescence

Twenty percent of the youths first recognized their gay or bisexual status during late childhood or early adolescence. Compared with other youths, reaching this developmental milestone uncommonly early had particular perils. Although this precarious theme dominates the narratives in this section, several youths were extremely happy to have this aspect of their lives resolved at such an early age.

Over one-half who knew their sexual identity at a relatively early age named their sexual identity within a year of labeling their attractions as "homosexual." For the following two youths, no gap separated labeling feelings and self. Disclosing this information to others, however, was an altogether different matter.

I never went through a period when my feelings and attractions and my identification were separate. I knew that I was gay but certainly what I was not going to do was come out or advertise it. I spent a lot of my childhood denying what I was but certainly by the age of fourteen I couldn't deny it. But I didn't tell anyone.

I never did have the real split. I realize that the behavior and feelings and attractions were all labeled gay and that I then was as well. In sixth grade I was really wondering. I still denied it to others but there was a certainty by seventh grade that I knew I was gay.

Similar to these two, most of the other boys who identified themselves as not heterosexual at this age knew instinctively that it would be a mistake to disclose their sexual identity to anyone else. To cope, they played a game—they pretended. One said he knew, "even then that if anyone were to ask me I would have to pretend to be straight." Another reported, "I really wanted my feelings and myself to be heterosexual but I just knew that they really never were. I said to others that I was straight even though I knew within myself that that was not true." Nearly all youths kept their secret close to them and pretended to their families and social world that they were not gay or bisexual. . . .

One motive to hide one's homoerotic identity was provided by religion. God did not come to one youth's rescue, although be beseeched Him to come to his aid through fervent prayers.

> Around eleven years old, I began to label my attractions and myself as gay. I said to myself even then that I was gay, but I wasn't going to tell anyone because I knew that I would have to change. My aunt and uncle are born-again Christians and I went on a massive prayer crusade to sort of get rid of these feelings. I felt that I just had to find the right girl.

Others who struggled believed that their feelings for other boys were only temporary and would disappear with time. Other youths must surely have the same problem, they reasoned.

> At one point I thought maybe that it was just a stage that I was going through. If it was a stage, then it was probably no problem. In junior high I knew I had gay feelings but I was really only out about this to myself. I remember using sort of a Kinsey idea that everyone has had homosexual experiences, although I certainly knew that it was more fun for me.

Although not a common practice, some early adolescents sought refuge in the arms of bisexuality. To understand his feelings, the following youth took the "middle ground," labeling his "temporary" attractions to males as bisexual. Being bisexual was not perceived as so bad or as so permanent as being gay.

> At first I thought that maybe I was bisexual. I had the feelings but thought that I would probably grow out of it and get married. This is probably when I was in middle school. I would never had said to myself at that point that I was gay. But I really wasn't sure; I think I was just trying to take the middle ground. It was very much of a gradual process, not just one moment. By sixth grade I pretty well knew for sure that I certainly was attracted to guys. But I certainly could never have shared that with anyone.

After the hope of temporality vanished, these early adolescents expressed a number of fears that delayed naming their identity. Among these included one who said: "I was crushed because of what I had hoped to be, I wasn't going to be. I was not straight, not normal."

Given the struggle these youths had in naming their identity and placing themselves in a socially despised class of individuals, an interesting question emerges: What
convinced a young adolescent that he was gay or bisexual? The overwhelming response was simply, "I just knew. Something clicked inside." Several had difficulty
identifying a moment in time. The following youth expressed these themes.

> I can remember knowing that I had homosexual feelings but I really felt that these
> would wear off, that I could make the decision as an adult not to be gay. By eighth
> grade I knew in the back of my mind that I was attracted to males but I never
> really said it to others or to myself. I hoped that I would change, so I really never
> directly thought about it. It was about that time that I think I began to realize or
> at least that I began to remember that I had forgotten all about those feelings, then
> I began to put two and two together and began to realize what I was.

Other young adolescents named particular assets that they believed helped them
make the transition from gay attractions to gay identity. The following three had the
assistance of a family member.

> My parents split very early on and my father moved to New York City so I spent
> a lot of time there with him and by the age of twelve I was going to gay bars with
> my older brother. So I was certainly familiar with the gay lifestyle.

> Why so early? I'm not really sure. But certainly by the beginning of high school
> I knew. I certainly knew what it meant and I certainly knew I was attracted to
> boys. Maybe in part this was helpful because I had a gay cousin who sort of helped
> prepare me.

> My parents always provided me with sexually explicit education so I knew what ho-
> mosexuality was. So by thirteen I could consciously say to myself that I was gay.

Although relatively few in number, other youths relied on their sexual feelings
to guide them in identifying their gay/bisexual identity. When comparing their attractions to boys versus girls, they came to the inevitable conclusion that they must be
gay or bisexual.

> I was going out with this girl but we like never did anything. We would hang out
> and then we broke up and it sort of hit me like a lightning bolt that I really was
> into girls only in terms of spiritual and emotional intimacy. But with males they
> were the object of my sexual fantasies. I knew that my sexual fantasies were of
> males and this told me that I was gay. It was very liberating to finally figure this
> out; it was a real positive experience.

One early adolescent came to realize his gayness because of his emotional attachments to other males. A new friend in school became something more than a
"regular guy friend" to him, and as eighth grade closed he knew that his "love" had
significance for who he was as a person. "I knew I wanted to be with him. It's sort
of like the T-shirt that says, 'I'm not gay, but my boyfriend is.' That's sort of the way

that I felt at that time." Another youth moved from hell to heaven during the course of early adolescence.

> In junior high school I was confused as hell. I was in a Catholic school, an all-male school and I was going through confirmation class and at one point in the confirmation class it was very clear that homosexuality was bad and that everyone was going to hell. I just felt very confused because I had the feelings. I recognized that my feelings were homosexual but I decided that I could purge the feelings from me.
>
> The second semester of the eighth grade I developed a serious crush on my [male] English teacher. At the time I said that I was bisexual because I had a girlfriend. At this point everything just clicked; it all made sense. I had to basically leave the church, and then labeling myself gay felt exciting yet scary. I knew that I would have to be closeted during my high-school career because I knew that if I was not I would get beat up on because gay bashing was a popular sport in my high school. But inside I felt blessed, a state of nirvana after the years of hell.

The 20 percent of youths who identified themselves as gay or bisexual during childhood or early adolescence were also considerably advanced of their gay peers regarding when they reported awareness of same-sex attractions, labeling those attractions as homoerotic, disclosing their sexual identity to others, and evolving a positive gay/bisexual identity. They were not, however, more or less likely to have gay sex, heterosexual sex, or same-sex romantic relationships or to do so at an earlier age. Although these youths appeared to be advanced in their cognitive awareness of their sexuality, they did not thus act on it in their sexual behavior or romantic relationships.

In summary, youths who made an important and nearly instantaneous connection at pubertal onset knew that their attractions to males implied something about their sexual identity. Others, however, waited a year or more, hoping that their homoeroticism was merely a temporary aberration, perhaps reflecting a bisexual phase. Some youths had a gay role model within their family; still others labeled themselves as the result of having stronger gay than heterosexual feelings or after having an emotional attachment to another male. For most, however, something just "clicked" in their minds and they knew they were gay or bisexual. The teachings of social institutions, such as their religious or ethnic community, frightened them from disclosing that which they knew was true about their sexuality. Despite these handicaps, . . . these youths were on their way to an early and long gay career.

The High-School Years

Nearly 40 percent of the youths came to the conclusion during their high-school years that they were gay or bisexual. For these youths, an average of three and one half years transpired after labeling their attractions as homoerotic before they labeled themselves as gay or bisexual. The range of time between these two, however, is more informative. The interval was either nonexistent, for 20 percent, or was extended to between three and five years for over half of the youths. Several delayed the identity process more than six years. One youth knew immediately during his senior year of high school when suddenly "a light switched on." Another "wasted" six years of his life.

> I spent a lot of time reading in the library about homosexuality. This was in the sixth and seventh grade. I still didn't identify as gay even after that because I was not like those that I read about. Then early in high school I was very, very devoted to my academic work and I just put all this on the back burner. By my senior year I started to have very strong emotional feelings towards male friends. This was six years after I should have known; six wasted years.

Twenty percent of youths who became aware of their sexual identity during their high-school years were delayed in labeling their sexual identity because, according to one, "I spent all this time hiding myself in this bisexual stage." This bisexual transition—distinct from true bisexuality—could take several years and perhaps a broken relationship with a girl before a boy could finally say to himself that he was not bisexual but gay.

> I sort of went through a bisexual stage, but then doesn't everybody? In middle school I would have said that I was straight with bi tendencies. In high school I would have said bisexual and by eleventh grade, definitely gay. I felt pretty bad, but it's not easy given the rural, Republican community I grew up in. It was definitely not gay positive. I did have a girlfriend and I felt like I was using her because when I entered into the relationship I should have known that I was gay.

Other youths perceived that they delayed the naming process because they feared what their lives would be like if they were to be gay/bisexual. As such, several reported that they were under the strong, irresistible, and oppressive influence of religious dogma. Once they had thrown off the confines of religion and other institutions that oppress gay people, they felt liberated to name their sexuality.

> At age sixteen I said to myself that I was gay. I was in the hospital away from Thomas (youth minister] and all of his religious beliefs that led to this suicide attempt in the first place so that I could indeed think about it. It was at this time, in fact, that I was struggling with all the religious issues Thomas kept reminding me of, that I would go to hell and stuff like that.

Many youths simply hoped that they would outgrow their attractions to other boys. They had heard or read that such a phase during adolescence was not uncommon and so they decided to put all such thoughts out of their minds. This sometimes worked for a year or two, but seldom lasted beyond three or four. Eventually, they could not deny their reality.

> The feelings were not passing as they were supposed to. They were staying and I was beginning to get scared. At first, the label was very negative. This was when I was fifteen years old. I tried to engage in behavior that would encourage heterosexuality, such as looking at girls, imagining their breasts, and trying to date them.

> I read my Bible six times that one year to find a way out of my predicament. My senior year I gave up outgrowing it.

Extensive soul-searching, journal writing, or taking long walks could also be helpful. The contribution of sex was powerful for a few. One youth could not deny to himself that "at fifteen I wasn't dating girls and I was having sex with guys." Because first gay sex was most likely to occur between the ages of thirteen and fifteen years, the consequence for some youths of having this experience was that they concluded that it must mean they were gay/bisexual. That is, having the attractions was one thing but to actually act on them made these youths strikingly aware of their sexual identity.

The persistence of homoerotic fantasies and feelings was sufficient information for some to conclude that they were gay or bisexual. When one sixteen year old's sexual fantasies consisted exclusively of male images, despite his attempts to alter them, he looked in the mirror one day and said to himself, at first tentatively and then louder, "Gay! Gay! Gay!" This was not, however, a happy revelation: "For the next year or two I was depressed on and off." However, another youth was much relieved once the mystery was solved. "I remember that I had been fantasizing about men and at some point I just finally said to myself, 'Why am I denying this?' I had such relief that this was finally settled!"

For several youths, more important than sexual fantasies was the development of a strong emotional attachment for another male. This was initially experienced as a crush or an infatuation that just would not go away.

> There's this guy in my class I developed a crush on and yet I was still seeing a woman. I knew what my feelings for him were and that was what I was supposed to feel for her. I think this is sort of the beginning of my realization. I had concluded before that I must be bi because I had an emotional bond to women and I never really had that with guys. Then I discovered that one can have both an emotional bond and a sexual attraction to a guy.

Friends often helped a gay/bisexual youth make the jump from pregay to gay. Some were themselves gay, while others were understanding girlfriends or accepting heterosexuals. The following youth did not initially recognize that he wanted to walk across the "continental divide into the unknown abyss of homosexuality."

> I went to an all-Catholic military school and in my senior year I was friends with this guy who was obviously gay. You could tell by his handshake and his mannerisms. We were friends and then at one point I was freaking out because he was fucking with my mind. I had just broken up with this girlfriend and I was crying and he said that I needed to face the fact that I was gay and over the phone he got me to admit that I was. I hung up on him and then he called me back and we talked more. He practically outed me, asking me rather than me telling him. Even though he tried to be supportive, it was not something that I wanted to accept at the time. I am grateful now, but I wasn't then. Our friendship suffered for several years but we are okay now.

It was apparent to everyone, especially his friends, that the following youth was gay. They were not sure how to help him except to be honest with him about themselves.

> I was close to a lot of people and in particular, five of my very best friends, including my girlfriend, brought the whole issue of homosexuality to the forefront. These five included two who were gay, my very closest friends including my very best friend and he's the one who told me all about the gay lifestyle, and it was through this that I came to see that it was certainly something that I was all about. They actually suspected that I might be gay but it was not that they were trying to make me gay but it was just that we had the kind of relationship in which they confided in me these kinds of things.

Books, educational materials, and the media were occasionally helpful for gay/bisexual youths in understanding the meaning of their homoerotic attractions. This was not always the case, as the following narrative illustrates.

> I was wondering about homosexuality so I went and did some research in medical books on what it meant to be gay. Most of the stories were about young boys in boarding schools and the approach was either that it was temporary and something that would go away or that it was permanent, a lifestyle. This did not help me come out.

More common was the experience of the following high-school senior who found what he needed to make the transition to a gay identity.

> I was reading sort of all this educational stuff about homosexuality and it portrayed it in a positive way and that is, that they have their own culture and their own heroes and models. So at this point then I was able to say to myself that I am gay myself.

In some cases, an accumulation of knowledge proved beneficial when a decision needed to be made regarding the meaning of strongly felt attractions.

> I wasn't sure what homosexual meant but by the age of fifteen I had enough information to know. I'd always assumed that my attractions were shared by everyone else. What was helpful for me was having sex education in junior high. I knew that males could be attracted to other males and that this was normal and so I didn't really worry much about it.

One youth went to a movie with several of his female friends who were enamored with several of the male movie stars appearing in the picture. The event had a far-reaching effect on him.

> I had fooled around and then I saw "Making Love," and I realized at that point that it was me and that I could relate to it. I remember lying awake all night and I said to myself, what am I going to do? The next day I told the two close female

friends that I had seen the movie with that I was gay. They has suspected it, and I guess maybe the entire town as well. I really never dated and I really made no attempt to date.

As was true for this youth, many felt a sense of great relief that they had solved their life mystery. Although they knew that their daily routine would now be more difficult, the persistence of low-level anxiety and alienation was now over. Once he had named himself, one sophomore found "the answer to all of my struggles. I knew that my life would be difficult but at least I had my answer. I could now stop trying to be straight."

The following narrative illustrates several factors that helped a high-school youth name his sexual identity. It took an accumulation of "too much evidence not to be gay" before he understood the implications for himself.

> I began to explore the whole issue of my sexuality. Like I would call 900 numbers and see if that turned me on or I would buy magazines or go to porno movies. It took me awhile to say that I'm gay. In fact, it took me a year until my senior year. I think I just gave up, not being gay. I never had dreams of sex with females; they were all of males. My friends kept hinting by saying they like gay people. I knew that it would be hard being gay but I knew that I also had to be out to myself.

The decisive event of self-liberation varied considerably across the high-school youths. For some it was gay or heterosexual sex while for others it was introspection, a friend, a support group, a book, a television show, or an infatuation. Feelings of emancipation followed, offering a name for their feelings and attractions. An equal number, however, delayed this liberation until their college years.

The College Years

Forty percent of the interviewed youths did not name their sexuality until they had graduated from high school. Most were in college at the time. Less than one-quarter of these youths simultaneously recognized their attractions and identity as gay or bisexual. The majority waited at least four years, including one-third who had a gap of seven or more years between realizing their attractions were homoerotic and understanding the implications of them for their identity. One youth "had an inkling" when he was twelve; ten years later he finally believed it sufficiently to accept his homoeroticism.

> I remember feeling guilty when I read about how bad it was, as a Catholic, to have thoughts about sex. This bothered me and I felt real guilty because I knew it was negative. In my junior year I said to myself, "I might be gay," but then I just shut off all feelings. It was not until my junior year of college that I was able to say "gay" and to accept it, if only for a minute. A year later I finally said it to myself and I accepted it. This was a little bit less than a year ago.

Unlike those who named their sexual identity at earlier ages, relatively few of these youths believed that their gay feelings constituted a phase to be outgrown. Also, few reported that they felt frightened, believed that their homosexuality was wrong, or were confused about their feelings. Most simply could not explain why it took them so long. Typical was the youth who modestly stated, "I felt I really was not being honest with myself."

This dual sense of having strong erotic attractions for males that did not disappear, even when involved with a woman, and of feeling an increased need to be honest with oneself characterized many stories. A mirror again proved critical for one youth to reflect on his true self.

> Always before because I was interested in females, as least as friends, I could not consider myself gay, but by this time I had to honestly say to myself that it was not going to go away. In high school I knew I was attracted to guys but I was not yet ready to deal with it. One day I said to myself in the mirror, "You are gay!" over and over until I believed it.

Another had to graduate from college to finally understand that his sexual feelings did not disappear once he left his liberal college campus.

The external factor that was most responsible for promoting an end to the charade of heterosexuality was coming into contact with friends who were gay. The chances of this occurring were considerably enhanced once away from the high-school closet and enrolled in a college where gay instructors, courses, and organizations existed. Such contact induced one youth to reconsider his previous assumed understandings and to conclude that he too was gay.

> In the dorm I met this guy who came out and he was very comfortable with it. He encouraged me to give up my act on a camp out I went with him. We talked and actually fooled around. I really didn't like this because I had never fooled around with a gay guy, which was different than just fooling around with guys. But he kept saying to relax, to relax, and by the third night I had come to accept these feelings. We fooled around all week while I was up there and so by this point I knew that gay actually had some positive dimensions as well. He wasn't all the negative things that I had heard about.

The friend need not be gay to be effective in helping a young adult recognize his sexual identity. Several youths noted that a liberal heterosexual friend "pulled it out of me." Another youth said to a straight friend that he was bisexual. "That was my way of saying it to myself. I had to say it out loud to someone I knew would be supportive."

One relatively common instigating factor combined internal and external components—becoming infatuated with another male. These youths were suddenly and unexpectedly startled into self-awareness; denial of their sexuality became less possible or desirable.

> Well this happened two summers ago when I was dating a female, as I have all my life, yet I always knew I was attracted to males. Then it all came together. I had a crush on a fellow student who was a bisexual male. Like him, I called myself

bisexual at that point. I knew what bisexual meant since the age of sixteen because I have friends who were bisexual, including dating a female who was bisexual.

Identifying as bisexual posed particular difficulties not encountered by those who reached the conclusion that they had exclusive attractions to males. One youth who had feelings for both sexes tried to gauge which were stronger because he felt that he had to figure out if he was gay or heterosexual: "I was trying to understand how I should grapple with this and to make a *final* decision." Another with dual attractions wanted definitely to land on the heterosexual side. It was not so simple.

> I wanted desperately to be straight and the label implied some level of commitment. I dated females and realized that I was attracted to females and so I thought of myself as straight. I sort of let all of this go for awhile and then in the early months of my sophomore year I realized that my feelings for guys must mean something, and it must mean that I'm bisexual. Or, maybe what I was, was just sexual.
>
> I've lived with it as if it were a part of me but not that it was real important. With males I'm finding I'm very attracted to them and want to be close to them but really not have sex, and that's still sort of what I'm looking for, even now. I don't want to go out and just have sex but I want to find emotional attractiveness with males like I have with females. Now I know that I prefer males, though I'm probably more bi than most gays.

Struggles among competing sexual identities frequently lasted for many years for those who did not identify as gay or bisexual until after high-school graduation. Denial continued until self-revelation would no longer allow it, when sexual feelings for men intruded into their daily lives. Occasionally, falling in love with another male was the instigating factor; other times it was having gay or liberal friends who either presented a positive image of being gay or who helped end the charade of heterosexuality. Youths who desperately wanted to be heterosexual and had the sexual and emotional feelings to give credence to their desires often struggled with their attractions to males before they labeled themselves bisexual.

Reflections on Self-Identifying as Gay or Bisexual

In his review of the various coming-out models that were proposed during the 1970s, McDonald notes that the process of revelation to self is complex and highly significant.

> A developmental process through which gay persons become aware of their affectional and sexual preferences and choose to integrate this knowledge into their personal and social lives, coming out involves adopting a nontraditional identity, restructuring one's self-concept, reorganizing one's personal sense of history, and altering one's relations with others and with society . . . all of which reflects a complex series of cognitive and affective transformations as well as changes in behavior. (p. 47)

The youths' narratives remind us that identifying as gay/bisexual was often an extremely complex process. Seldom understood but keenly felt attractions to males early in life could eventuate as early as childhood or as late as young adulthood in self-identifying as gay or bisexual. This could be an instantaneous event or a very long, protracted affair; a relatively easy process, or a feature of oneself that is denied or actively suppressed for years, perhaps decades. If the former, feelings were often long-standing and had evolved during childhood and adolescence as a natural aspect of the self. If the latter, youths tried to not think about their sexuality as anything other than heterosexual and a tone of fear dominated their stories. In some cases a youth was not aware that homosexuality was an option until eventually the evidence, consisting of recurrent same-sex fantasies or, less frequently, same-sex encounters, convinced him that he must be gay or bisexual. To combat overwhelming homoerotic feelings without taking on the mantle of the real thing—gayness—other youths claimed a temporary or transitory bisexual identity, remained "heterosexual," or decided not to decide.

Although many forces impact a youth's process of coming out to self, it is abundantly clear from the youths' stories that external agents neither created nor destroyed their desires, at least for long. Many youths related how macro-level forces such as family values and institutional heterosexism handicapped their understanding of what their same-sex attractions meant. To overcome these forces, layer upon layer of internalized homophobia—the incorporation of the hatred and fears that are readily apparent in our cultural biases and attitudes—had to be penetrated. The closer, more intimate aspects of their social world, such as best friends, as well as larger, more distant cultural customs, including gay positive media presentations of homosexuality and living in a liberal, often collegiate, community helped many of these youths overcome these barriers.

What had to be mastered internally was the stereotype many youths had of what it meant to be gay or bisexual and the kind of life they would have if they accepted "the gay lifestyle." The process was very individualized but most youths could point to some event, experience, or person that helped them make this leap to self-recognition. It was the rare but fortunate youth who had the guidance of an older gay or lesbian mentor who helped him see an alternate way of being gay that did not mean conforming to stereotypes. He need not be queer, transgendered, promiscuous, radical, or HIV positive; he need only be who he was before "becoming gay."

Yet, one factor, often ignored, that has increasingly assisted gay and bisexual teens to come to terms with their sexuality is the visibility of gay issues in our culture—a visibility that has sometimes been fostered by those very queer, radical activists whom these youths desired not to be. Counterbalancing this presentation of being a modern gay are other forces such as the gay-positive, famous heterosexuals who grace the covers of gay/lesbian national newsmagazines and the multiple images of homosexuality tendered in the media of renowned athletes, rock singers, artists, movie stars, and politicians who are declaring their gay, lesbian, or bisexual identities. This diversity has given young pregays the opportunity to better understand their experiences, regardless of their physical appearance, private thoughts, and public behavior, and not to think or feel poorly of themselves because of the experiences.

Although these external factors are critical, they may not be the most important catalyst for a youth to reach the decision to self-identify as gay or bisexual. Many of the narratives recounted intense self-reflections, an inner voice, that pushed youths to place honesty with self above the negative conceptions they had of being gay. Something clicked, and all became clarified. One fifteen-year-old never wrote one word in his daily journal about what was most on his mind. Then he began to write about "it" and his identification followed. "I kept it out of my journal but finally had to admit it if this journal was going to be an accurate reflection of my life." Another kept repeating to himself, "I'm gay," practicing, even trying on the concept, until it began to feel comfortable and right.

Thus, a single coming-out-to-self pattern did not emerge among the interviewed youths. The range was from one of ease and tranquillity to one of torture and disgust. At some point during their childhood, adolescence, or young adulthood, many youths felt threatened by their sexual fantasies, which did not, as planned, go away but in fact increased over time, especially after pubertal onset. The "homosexual" label was initially viewed as unacceptable by most, but not all, until high school or college, even though nearly all had strong suspicions before this point. Their willingness to label themselves as something other than heterosexual ranged from "absolutely" to "most likely" to "might be," and their comfort level from "feeling great" to "feeling ambivalent" to "feeling awful."

Some youths become more or less resigned to the inevitable, although they remained wary of the potential consequences of being gay for their future careers, pessimistic of the possibilities for finding a romantic relationship with a man, and racked with guilt for possibly destroying interpersonal relations with friends and family. The very clarity of their sexual identity frightened them immensely, and thus they developed elaborate defenses to protect themselves against that which they knew to be true, long-standing, and petrifying. They wanted to reject it but the evidence simply would not disappear, even with girlfriends, sex with girls, and a heterosexual persona in the eyes of peers. Once away from family and the home-town community, self-recognition of sexual identity for some was swift—most of those who identified as gay or bisexual in college did so during their first two years.

Others felt relieved that mysteries had been solved, sexual and romantic feelings could be freely expressed, and a basic sense of self could be experienced and expressed. One interviewee said, "I wanted to shout it to everybody. I really talked for the first time with my friends." Another said, "The fact that men found me attractive did wonders for my self-image in ways no female ever had." Of course, these timelines and the accompanying developmental milestones apply only to the interviewed youths. Many others, perhaps far exceeding in number those who disclosed prior to young adulthood, may never reach the point in their developmental trajectory at which they identify as gay or bisexual, or do so only in adulthood or old age.

Bisexual youths often experienced unique difficulties sorting through the complexities of their attractions. One reflected about his future, "Maybe I'll marry and deal with guys on the side." One began a gay relationship during his senior year of high school but was still disturbed by his continuing heterosexuality: "My 'Perfect Life Guard' wanted me, but I had Sally for so long, so why continue with him which would make my life so hard?" Some were not comfortable with the resolution of heterosexuality but it seemed the best compromise given the multitude of sexual feelings, confusions, and expectations from family and friends. One youth noted, "I was too scared to do anything or go to anyone. Was it really true? A phase? How could I possibly accept these gay feelings?" Another youth had sex with sixteen males and two females by the age of twenty-two and felt equally bisexual, which did not make sense to him. His homoerotic attractions came late, at age sixteen, when he was in the process of breaking up with his girlfriend since seventh grade. His working-class Catholic heritage still loomed powerful for him. Youths with emotional, romantic relationships with girls often tried to find opportunities to experiment with their male erotic feelings without disclosing their homoeroticism to their girlfriends. How many will be able to maintain this balance in adulthood is unknown.

Indeed, some youths reflected a theme of sexual fluidity in their longitudinal assessment of their sexuality. They may have understood themselves as bisexual but perhaps did not feel totally comfortable with the label or the absence of certainty. Whether these males are fluid in their sexual identity or momentarily uncertain is difficult to discern. The following youth represents a third alternative—confused and fluid; he wanted the best of both worlds.

> Well last summer I decided to tell my friends that I "might" be gay and that I "might" want to go to gay clubs. Sort of a couple of years before that I knew I wasn't straight and I was dealing with this issue in therapy a lot. I'm still today questioning myself as a gay person. Sometimes I want to say that I'm bisexual and then at times I wonder well maybe I'm straight, and this is when I contemplate marrying and having kids and having the pictures and all, but would this ever be meaningful for me? I'd have to have my own mister mistress.

Cultivating an acceptance of this self-identity and then disclosing this information to others are separable processes. The youths themselves made this distinction. Openly declaring their sexuality was seldom a high-school event. Many too much feared that they would be battered and insufficiently supported to make the declaration to their hometown community. Given the complexity of the coming-out-to-self process, it is not surprising that sharing this information with others was often delayed until youths left home.

Questions

1. "Homosexual" is an imprecisely used term. When people use the term homosexual, are they basing this on a person's behavior at one point in time, behavior over time, a person's fantasies, attractions, or self-identification? Are these different criteria correlated?
2. When do people come to the realization of a gay, lesbian, or bisexual identity?
3. What is involved in accepting a gay, lesbian, or bisexual identity?
4. What are the issues involved in coming out or not coming out?
5. Can you apply Cross' stages of *pre-encounter, encounter, immersion-emersion, internalization, internalization-commitment* to the process of self-identification as gay, lesbian, or bisexual?

References and Further Reading

Golden, C. (1987). Diversity and variability in women's sexual identities. In Boston Lesbian Psychologies Collective (Eds.), *Lesbian Psychologies* (pp. 19–34). Chicago: University of Illinois Press.

Savin-Williams, R. C. (1990). *Gay and lesbian youth: expressions of identity.* New York: Hemisphere Publishing.

Savin-Williams, R. C. (1998). " . . . *And then I became gay": Young men's stories.* New York: Routledge.

Part III

Social Contexts and Contemporary Social Issues

Chapter 10

Family Relationships

While popular beliefs hold that adolescents' relationships with parents are marked by detachment, disengagement and conflict, the research literature does not support this view (Reading 10.2). A transformation occurs in the parent-child relationship during adolescence toward greater symmetry and mutuality, but throughout this transformation the relationship is marked by harmony, closeness, and warmth (Reading 10.2). Conflict does arise between parents and adolescents, but it tends to be centered on mundane matters of everyday life, such as curfew, homework, and household chores. A recent meta-analysis of the literature on parent-child conflict found that both conflict rate and total conflict decrease with adolescent age (Laursen, Coy, & Collins, 1998).

Researchers have approached family relationships from a variety of perspectives. Some researchers have focused on how parents may be struggling with issues at midlife, and this factor interacts with and impacts their responses to their adolescent children (Reading 10.1). Other researchers have focused on identifying parenting styles and examining how parenting styles affect adolescent personality development and well-being (Reading 10.2). The nature of family interaction has also been examined for the role it plays in putting adolescents at risk for involvement with gangs and violence (Readings 13.1 and 13.2), for teenage pregnancy (Reading 14.1), and for the development of eating disorders (Reading 15.2).

Research has been directed to understanding how changes in the structure of the family impact adolescent development (Hetherington, Bridges, & Insabella, 1998). Two-parent families are becoming less prevalent as almost half of all marriages end in divorce. By the time they are 16, half of all adolescents will see their parents' marriages dissolve. Remarriage rates are high (75% for men, 66% for women); therefore, many adolescents will make the transition from living in a single-family household to living in stepfamilies. Some adolescents are likely to experience the dissolution of a second marriage because rates of divorce in remarriages are 10% higher than in first marriages. Thus many adolescents are likely to be impacted both by parental divorce and by a number of marital transitions (Hetherington, Bridges, & Insabella, 1998).

Finally, research attention has been directed to understanding how parenting style itself is impacted by demographics. The functioning of the family is shaped by its economic circumstances. Families that struggle with unstable work, low income, or periodic loss of income are at higher risk for marital breakdown, child abuse, and neglect. Studies have documented the impact of economic hardship on the emotional health and parenting effectiveness of inner-city parents. Parents who are depressed and overly stressed are less able to offer encouragement to their children, to monitor them, and to engage in joint activity. In addition, neighborhood influences are problematic for inner-city families. "High levels of negative and risky opportunities for youth in African American neighborhoods add appreciably to the challenge encountered by family efforts to minimize risk and promote opportunity for children" (Elder, Eccles, Ardelt, & Lord, p. 783).

The studies in this chapter offer two approaches to the parent-child relationship and its effect on adolescent development. The first reading examines the parent-child relationship from the perspective of parents' struggles with midlife issues (Reading 10.1). The second reading addresses the transformation of the parent-child relationship during adolescence, the nature of adolescent-parent conflict, and the impact of parenting style on adolescent behavior (Reading 10.2).

Additional Resources

References and Recommended Reading

Elder, G. H., Eccles, J. S., Ardelt, M., & Lord, S. (1995). Inner-city parents under economic pressure: Perspectives on the strategies of parenting. *Journal of Marriage and the Family, 57,* 771–784.

Furstenberg, F. F. (1990). Coming of age in a changing family system. In S. S. Feldman & G. R. Elliott (Eds.) *At the threshold: The developing adolescent* (pp. 147–170). Cambridge, MA: Harvard University Press.

Hetherington, E. M., Bridges, M., & Insabella, G. M. (1998). What matters? What does not? Five perspectives on the association between marital transitions and children's adjustment. *American Psychologist,* 53(2), 167–184.

Laursen, B., Coy, K. C., & Collins, A. (1998). Reconsidering changes in parent-child conflict across adolescence: A meta-analysis. *Child Development,* 69 (3), 817–832.

On the Internet

http://www.personal.psu.edu/faculty/n/x/nxd10/teenfamily.htm
Adolescence: Change & Continuity—Family Changes

http://www.personal.psu.edu/faculty/n/x/nxd10/teenfamilyb.htm
Adolescence: Change & Continuity—Family Influences
These two Web sites were produced by Pennsylvania State University students taking Human Development and Family Studies 433: The Transition to Adulthood; and Human Development and Family Studies 239: Adolescent Development.

http://education.indiana.edu/cas/adol/development.html
Adolescent Directory On-Line—Normal Adolescent Development
Adolescence Directory On-Line (ADOL) is an electronic guide to information on adolescent issues. It is a service of the Center for Adolescent Studies at Indiana University. The information about changing family relationships at adolescence comes from the American Academy of Child and Adolescent Psychology.

http://www.aacap.org/publications/factsfam/divorce.htm
American Academy of Child and Adolescent Psychiatry—Children and Divorce

http://www.aacap.org/publications/factsfam/stepfmly.htm
American Academy of Child and Adolescent Psychiatry—Stepfamily Problems

http://www.aacap.org/publications/factsfam/adolescence.htm
American Academy of Child and Adolescent Psychiatry—Parenting: Preparing for Adolescence
These three Web sites are fact sheets produced by the American Academy of Child and Adolescent Psychiatry. The AACAP developed Facts for Families as a public service to provide concise and up-to-date information on issues that affect children, teenagers, and their families.

http://www.vix.com/men/mitch/needless.html
Men's Issues Page: How Divorce Affects Children
The goals of the Men's Issue Page Mission is to maintain comprehensive reference lists of men's movement organizations, books, periodicals, Web links, and other related resources, and to serve as an online reference source for statistics, studies, and bibliographies of interest to the men's movements.

10.1   Harry Prosen, John Toews,
                                            and Robert Martin, 1981

The Life Cycle of the Family: Parental Midlife Crisis and Adolescent Rebellion

Harry Prosen, M.D., M.S., is chairman of the Department of Psychiatry and Mental Health Sciences at the Medical College of Wisconsin. He is also an adjunct professor in the Department of Cultural and Social Sciences at Marquette University. He has researched the life cycle, intergenerational conflicts, and psychotherapy.

John Toews, M.D., FRCPC, is the associate dean of continuing medical education at the University of Calgary, Canada. Dr. Toews is author of *No Longer Alone: Mental Health and the Church* (with Eleanor Loewen, 1995).

Robert Martin, Ph.D., is a senior scholar and intern adviser at the University of Manitoba, Canada Health Sciences Centre, Department of Clinical Health Psychology.

As children make their transition into adolescence, their parents are often in midlife. In an ideal world, early adolescents making their way through the stresses of adolescence would be fully supported by loving and unconflicted parents. But in reality, the situation is more complex. Parents are at a stage of their lives when they are undergoing a midlife transition, a stage that has been characterized by pervasive dissatisfaction (Gould, 1978; Levinson, 1978; Valliant, 1977). In his study of adult men, Daniel Levinson found this to be a stage of reappraisal of the meaning, value, and direction of one's life. For some men this questioning led to a divorce or love affair, or to a change of occupation; for others it involved an internal change in one's commitment to one's job or marriage. The studies of midlife issues however, have focused on white, middle-class individuals, and thus their results may not generalize to many parents of adolescents from poor neighborhoods where the life course is accelerated, the distance between generations is foreshortened, and midlife issues may be strikingly different (Reading 7.3).

A few studies address how the issues parents are facing influence their relationships with their adolescent children. Studies of the interplay of adult and adolescent issues have found, for example, that the idea of a child leaving home signals the death of the nuclear family as it has existed for many years and causes some parents to try to slow down time, putting parents at odds with the adolescent's thrust toward independence (Prosen, Toews, & Martin, 1981). The presence of a teenager in the home may trigger feelings such as jealousy, abandonment, loss, powerlessness, and regret for parents, which in turn influence parents' responses to their adolescents (Steinberg, 1994).

Harry Prosen, John Toews, and Robert Martin examine the way an adolescent's developmental crisis interacts with the developmental crisis faced by his or her parents. Both parent and child are reworking identities and planning for the future. Prosen and his colleagues discuss the issues that adults may struggle with at midlife, feelings of marital dissatisfaction, recognition that one's early ambitions may not have been fully met and that time has become short, and the shift from "alloplastic mastery," or an attempt to control the world through active mastery and achievement, to a stage of "autoplastic mastery," where the emphasis is on changing the self and adapting the self rather than changing the external world. The authors go on to discuss how these parental issues relate to the developmental issues of adolescence.

I̤t has become increasingly common in recent years for conceptualizations of the human life span to be organized into systems based on a recognition of a series of life stages, each with its own age-related developmental tasks and its characteristic conflicts. Basically these conceptualizations stem from the life-cycle model popularized by [Erik] Erikson (1959). While the major focus of the literature related to the life cycle is on specific developmental stages, in our studies we are reexamining Erikson's original concept of the life cycle as an entity which, despite discrete stages, has a certain sense of wholeness.

The emphasis of life-cycle theory so far has been more on an individual's experience of his or her own life cycle than on the interaction of an individual's life cycle with that of others, particularly in a family setting. Family members are at different developmental stages which interplay and interrelate. The maturational tasks of different family members are continuously at variance, and the conflicts are often clearly evident, although perhaps not recognized in developmental terms. The purpose of these chapters, therefore, is to discuss life-stage interrelationships with particular reference to some of the problems encountered by middle-aged parents and their adolescent children.

Midlife Crisis and Adolescence

Because of the demands for reevaluation and change brought about by the maturational transitions that are required of both adolescents and their middle-aged parents, the upset and turmoil of a life crisis may occur. A life crisis can be defined as a critical problem that disrupts the life style of the individual or family and threatens their physical, emotional, or economic well-being.

Our particular interest in life-span psychology arose from several clinical issues relating to the midlife crisis specifically. The first significant clinical issue was our noting that a number of our middle-aged male patients suddenly and unpredictably became promiscuous, even though they had seemed to have lived rather stable and happily married lives. What we explored originally as a concern about a sexual matter became an exploration of normative ego aspects of midlife.

Self-examination includes a review of one's attainments in life, the awareness that early ambitions and plans embodied in the ego ideal may never be totally met, and the recognition that aging occurs without enough opportunity to achieve a sense of true ego mastery. This sense of frustration and disappointment provides a background for sexual acting out as well as the many impulsive characteristics of the midlife period.

An adult, now struggling with a midlife crisis, may make sudden changes in direction in order to make up for lost time and to realize as much achievement as possible. While impulsivity is characteristic of the adolescent stage of development, basic to both an understanding of midlife and adolescence is a sense of the use of time. Midlife is characterized by a realization that time has become short. There is a change in time perspective that comes with aging and is described by Neugarten (1970) as "a particularly conspicuous feature of middle age. Life is restructured in terms of time left to live rather than time since birth. Not only is there a reversal in directionality but an awareness that time is finite."

Another view of the transition in midlife has been described by Gutmann (1971). This begins with the transition from the stage of "alloplastic mastery," in which the emphasis is on control of outer world affairs and on pursuit of achievement through independence, to the stage of "autoplastic" or internal mastery, where the emphasis is on accommodation to the outer world and on changing the self rather than the external domain. In this stage thought is said to substitute for action, and philosophic resignation begins to substitute for drive toward achievement and autonomy. A later stage, more related to the shift toward older age, is "omniplastic" or magical mastery. This stage involves the maintenance of security and self-esteem by regressive, defensive strategies of denial and projection rather than through action against the external world or accommodation.

Characteristic of midlife is the life review (Butler 1963). The life review stems partly from the realization of the shortness of time left to live, and it is made possible by the shift to thought and reflection rather than action as a dominant mode of mastery. It is difficult to achieve change even through the expenditure of forceful energy, and it is therefore natural to become more contemplative and thoughtful. The need to take a more passive and reflective stance usually comes into conflict with the aggressive seeking for mastery of adolescents in the same family, although there are also times when the contemplative motive of a parent might complement the temporary contemplative moments of an adolescent child.

In those originally described midaged males who resorted to action in order to find an idealized younger mate, there was evidence of marked midlife crises and difficulties in midlife transition. Our theoretical explanation of this onset of promiscuity was based on the concept of the "remembered mother and the fantasized mother" (Prosen, Martin, and Prosen 1972). The essential hypothesis was that as the wife ages, the husband is reminded increasingly of his own mother. We suggested that he may start off in a quest to find a person embodying the younger more attractive image of his earlier and more erotically interesting mother, that is, the mother of his childhood. This quest usually ends disastrously because the middle-aged man is distorting time by attempting to turn it back to regain, through active mastery, that which is already long past. Promiscuity in this case is a reaction to the aging, a defense mechanism which also includes another important dynamic force, the reawakening of the oedipal conflict.

While it is well recognized that the adolescent must deal with the resurgence of the oedipal conflict at the time of puberty (Blos 1962, 1972), yet another resurgence of the conflict can be conceptualized to occur in middle age, particularly when it was inadequately resolved in adolescence. Possible stimuli for this resurgence are the retreat from the aging mate; having sexually stimulating adolescent children who once again awaken the incestuous strivings characteristic of the oedipal conflict; the memory of the younger mother; the subjective sense of the shortness of time; the pressure to act and to risk before it is too late; as well as the reawakening of the oedipal conflict through jealousy by fathers of daughters and by mothers of sons.

As with the earlier oedipal awakenings, in this rekindling there may be renewed pressure to prove one's role, one's competence and prowess. When this occurs in the family setting, the ordinary issues of control and family leadership become distorted by issues of jealousy and competition. There results much opportunity for misidentification of the adolescent by the adult and the adult by the adolescent. There arises also the opportunity for a fluctuating variety of age-related roles adopted by the parents and adolescents in the family. These roles may switch on a momentary basis, ranging from adult-parent and adolescent-child to adolescent-parent and adult-child.

To come to terms with midlife and to arrange a realistic accommodation with one's ego ideal, to take responsibility for living the way one has lived until midlife, and to take power over the rest of one's life means that one must accept passivity and helplessness in certain situations by using autoplastic mastery. It may be impossible by this time of life to make fundamental changes in a work situation or to make major changes in a family situation that would not ultimately be destructive. Of course, in some cases, dramatic and good changes can be made, but the prospect of making such changes is often frightening and risky.

While much of the early consideration of midlife issues involves clinical descriptions of men, it is now apparent that the same issues apply to women as well and are evident in the family context. In older midlife, the woman's reactions are made more complex by the fact that the impending cessation of menstrual function and reproductive capability add a definite pronounced reminder of aging. The effects are many and may vary from a feeling of decreased sexuality and more limited feminine identity to a sense of freedom, an explosion of oedipal feelings, and a resurgence of adolescent sexuality. The latter, in some cases, leads to a syndrome called "post-menopausal promiscuity" (Prosen and Martin 1979). In these situations one sees the concerns of mothers about their daughter's sexuality in adolescence, the possibility of fostering daughter's sexual acting out, or the creation of inhibitions and conflict about the expression of sexuality in adolescent female children.

Adolescence and Midlife Crisis

While the middle-aged parent may experience a certain passivity and helplessness, their adolescent children tend to experience opposite feelings. They are in rebellion, actively questing for their own identity and the right to control and determine their own future in line with their own goals and dreams. They resent parental authority and control and indicate to the parents that the parents are helpless. As a result, the midlife feelings of helplessness and passivity experienced by the parent are intensified. Added to the passivity of not being able to control one's own life is the distress of not being able to control one's own children; added to the anxiety about the uncertainty of one's own future now is the anxiety about the uncertainty of the adolescent's future.

It is evident then that some of the life-stage tasks and conflicts of the adolescent complement those of the parents. Both the youth and parent are involved in working through issues of identity. The youth's task is to form an identity that is secure enough to carry through to adulthood. The parent is concerned with the examination of his or her own identity and achievements in light of their own ego ideals. The adolescent experiences concerns about sexual intimacy and sexual adequacy. Both adolescent and parent may experience the fear of impotence or of sexual failure. Youths' fear is based on uncertainty at the beginning of a new and vulnerable aspect of their lives, but the parents' (particularly the father's) fear is based on the realization of declining sexuality and on the apprehension that sexuality as it represents and symbolizes youth will be sacrificed to advancing age.

In addition to these particular fears there is also a curiosity about the other's sexual life. The adolescent may often deny that the parent has a sex life. By the same token, parents may attempt to prepare themselves for the sexuality of their adolescents but may find it difficult to accept. There may well be a reciprocal relationship between the strength of the incestuous impulse that has existed between the adolescent and the parent of the opposite sex and the strength of their own sexual drives. The parents, in reaction formation to the blossoming sexuality of their teenage child, may become jealous of the sexual relationships of their adolescent children and attempt in various ways to interfere with their friendships, an interference that is often difficult to see and not readily admitted.

Since identity formation in the adolescent occurs usually against the backdrop of the parents' midlife crisis, parents and adolescents are both engaged in modifying their views of themselves and each other. Adolescents struggle with deidealizaton of their parents, and parents often attempt to force their adolescents to behave in such a way that the idealization of the younger child can continue. Part of the modification that is required has to do with the idealization, each of the other, that may have existed relatively unchecked by reality until this period of family life. The adolescent is expected by parents to conform to an idealized expectancy while, at the same time, this is the period during which the adolescent is often most ashamed and disappointed in his parents and sees them as least understanding. Both parents and adolescents find themselves in conflict, sometimes to the point of death wishes or suicidal thoughts. We see expression in families of desires to separate; and through fighting and threats of separation sometimes actual separation does occur. The more subtle loss, however, is that of the deidealizaton. The parent in midlife, already suffering from the damaging effects of deteriorating self-esteem, due to the loss of active ego mastery, is especially vulnerable to disappointment.

Ambivalence has long been recognized as a keynote in the feelings of adolescents toward their parents. We should also acknowledge that the parents' ambivalence toward their adolescent children is just as unpredictable and tumultuous. One would wish to see a healthy admiration available between adolescent and parent at the end of the adolescent turmoil and its complimentary midlife phase in the parent, but the opposite of admiration is too often present.

Adolescents often rebel against gratifying parental wishes but play out the rejected parental wishes with their own friends. In our clinical work with families of professionals it is common to see the adolescent who rejects learning, fails in school, and drops out in an effort to avoid compliance with parental wishes, an example of Erikson's (1962) concept of negative identity. In other situations, where the adolescent appears to be completely rejecting and different from the parent, one may actually see that the teenager, rather than express a negative identity, is hostilely identifying with the parent and is participating in a microsociety which replicates in parody the society of the parent. The society discovered and created by the teenager is reinforcing and protective, making it most difficult for the parents to make inroads on the adolescent's defenses. At the same time, it produces struggles within the family context that can be particularly reflected with other children who are directed to turn out differently from the disappointing adolescent. This produces further rejection of the adolescent, who then forms a greater tie to his or her own peer group. This type of identification is illustrated in the following case example.

Jane, age seventeen, was seen at the request of her parents, who had become concerned when she precipitously dropped out of senior high school. Jane's grades had been deteriorating for some time, although previously she had performed well in school. Despite coming from a home where alcohol was used in strict moderation, Jane had taken to returning home grossly intoxicated most weekends. The parents were concerned and confused by her actions. She refused all attempts to talk about her behavior and angrily accused her parents of not understanding her and of trying to live her life for her.

Jane's father, a high school principal, placed great value on education. He and Jane's social worker mother had been encouraging Jane to get a university education leading to a profession. During the initial interviews Jane described feeling parental pressure to perform up to their expectations. She felt pushed toward a university education, but was confused about her own plans for the future. She saw her failure at school as a statement of her disinterest in continuing her education and her use of alcohol as acceptable and usual by the standard of her friends, She realized her behavior worried her parents, but she protested that she had to determine her own future.

During the interviews she talked of many conversations with her friends, who also were failures of various sorts. In effect Jane related to these friends as though she were a high school counselor who encouraged education and future planning. She had rejected her parents' encouragement, but had at the same time taken a parental role with her peers.

Other conflicts are the ambivalence and resentment of the teenager toward the parents' material resources. The teenager, in rejecting the values of the parents, often denounces the desire and need for material wants and, as a result, is derisive of parental possessions or values. This is the use of the ascetic defense as described by Freud (1966). Parents, on the other hand, examine their own resources as they approach older age and use the counting of resources as some sign of success.

To this description of parallel and complementary conflicts between parent and youth we would also like to add some thoughts about the timing of maturational events as they occur in both the youth and the parent. The basic conflicts tend to involve an idea of the fullness of time for the youth as compared to the increasing shortness of time for the parent. In these situations, it is natural for the parent and the child to become out of phase with each other in their approach to the timing of maturational trends and events. The obvious example is the situation in which the midaged parent attempts to deny and retard the progression of the life cycle of their adolescent, who at the same time is attempting to accelerate his or her own progress. The parents wish to slow the child down, to keep him dependent, under control, and in what they see as a secure family environment; whereas the adolescent wants the freedom to have his or her own experiences. As one would expect, the families in which this happens experience sharp and continued conflict.

Another pattern occurs in families in which both parents and children collude in an attempt to delay the progression of the life cycle. In this case we see a dependent child afraid of the demands of independence in adulthood and dependent parents concerned about the implications of their own aging in terms of their roles as parents. On the surface in these families everything appears agreeable and there is often little conflict. However, close scrutiny of these families often shows neurotic and sometimes even psychotic symptomatology.

Discussion

The various developmental tasks of the middle-aged parent and adolescent child are of a magnitude that demand the utmost in accommodation and resiliency. Families in which parents are in midlife crisis and in which a parent is acting out in some way may find the destruction and chaos worsened by the adolescent's rebelling and acting out at the same time. The helplessness of the parents may only reinforce the adolescent turmoil, and it is not infrequent that the expression of this turmoil is ego alien to the parents. A previous example noted that parents often find their children responding negatively to the parental wishes and yet creating or living in a microsociety in which they take on their own parents' role. Parents with a strong academic achievement orientation often find their bright children failing academically. When reputation is important to the family, the adolescent may threaten its loss through some form of antisocial behavior. When parents are concerned about social propriety, the adolescent may act out sexually or through drugs. These reactions can arise developmentally, but there is often a direct connection between the unconscious impulses and fantasies of the parents and the acting out of the teenager (Johnson and Szurek 1952).

In the same way we may see parents acting out their own conflicts engendered by the reactions of their adolescent children. The helpless anger arising from the midlife changes and the action of the children may be projected upon the marital partner with further deterioration of a suffering marriage. Promiscuity of a parent may have as one of its etiological components erotic feelings for an attractive child. In these instances, and others, family members may foster the acting out of others in order to hide or avoid the real developmental issues and tasks. That these should be played out in the family is no surprise when one considers that collectively within the family a major threat results from the transitions required of its members. This threat is the threat to the continued existence of the family itself.

Conclusions

How then, can we help the midage parent and the adolescent child, caught as they are in their life-stage clashes? As clinicians we are all familiar with how difficult it is to give parents wise counsel in dealing with the issues they face with their struggling adolescent children. Similarly, those of us interested in the treatment of adolescents know how difficult it is to help the adolescent child to understand the reactions of the parent struggling with his or her own life tasks.

Perhaps the best approach to these problems is a combination of individual and family therapeutic interviews focused on the tasks and reviews necessary for both parent and youth to make the transitions required of them at their own particular ages. The concept of life stages and life tasks helps to give some understanding and strength in dealing with these issues, particularly in terms of the helplessness we so often encounter in these parents and families.

In order to help with these problems it is necessary to diagnose accurately the situation not just from an individual perspective, but from a family perspective as well. Both parents and youth should be assessed from the point of view of their own life tasks and the difficulties that they each encounter with them. One must then assess how the life tasks of the parent and youth complement each other and where their attempts at the solution of their life-stage problems bring them into inevitable conflict. In opening up the family to the review of what it is like to be the other family members at their life stage and with their life tasks one also hopes to open up an awareness and appreciation within the family each for the other. If this can be done, life tasks can be encountered in an open and supportive environment, in which, ideally, both parents and adolescents will be more tolerant of one another and will demonstrate more understanding with less recourse to panic reactions which are on the parents' part calculated to demonstrate authority, control, and degree of active mastery and on the youth's part to demonstrate autonomy and independence from the parents.

One would then summarize by saying that the solution involves describing and discussing the maladaptive attempts to both the midlife parent and the adolescent to solve their individual problems as well as to show them the way in which they have negatively reinforced and yet paradoxically mimicked the other's solution.

References

Blos, P. 1962. *On Adolescence.* New York: Free Press.

Blos, P. 1972. The epigenesis of the adult neurosis. *Psychoanalytic Study of the Child* 27: 106–135.

Butler, R. N. 1963. The life review: an interpretation of reminiscence in the aged. *Psychiatry* 26:65–76.

Erikson, E. H. 1959. Identity and the life cycle. *Psychological Issues.* Vol. 1. New York: International Universities Press.

Erikson, E. H. 1962. *Young Man Luther.* New York: Norton.

Freud, A. 1966. *The Ego and the Mechanisms of Defense.* New York: International Universities Press.

Gutmann, D. L. 1971. Cross-cultural research on human behavior: a comparative study of the life cycle in the middle and later years. In N. Kretchmer and D. N. Walcher, eds. *Environmental Influence on Genetic Expression.* Fogarty International Center Proceedings, no. 2. Washington, D.C.: Government Printing Office.

Johnson, A., and Szurek, S. 1952. Genesis of antisocial acting out. *Psychoanalytic Quarterly* 21:323–343.

Neugarten,B. 1970. Dynamics of transition of middle age to old age. *Journal of Geriatric Psychiatry* 4:71–87.

Prosen, H., and Martin, R. 1979. Postmenopausal promiscuity. *Medical Aspects of Human Sexuality* 13(6):26–34.

Prosen, H.; Martin, R.; and Prosen, M. 1972. The remembered mother and the fantasized mother. *Archives of General Psychiatry* 12:791–794.

Questions

1. What issues do parents face at midlife?
2. What feelings are aroused for parents about their own lives when their children reach adolescence?
3. How do parents' midlife issues (about identity, work, marriage, sexuality, mortality, control) affect their relationships with their adolescents?
4. Why would a parent want to slow down time?
5. How might the ideas raised in this article be extended to families living in poverty as described by Burton?

References and Further Reading

Gould, R. (1978). *Transformations.* New York: Simon & Schuster.
Levinson, D. L., with Darrow, C. N., Klein, E., Levinson, M., & McKee, B. (1978). *Seasons of a man's life.* New York: Ballantine.
Steinberg, L., with Steinberg, W. (1994). *Crossing Paths: How your child's adolescence triggers your own crisis.* New York: Simon & Schuster.
Toews, J., Prosen, H., & Martin, R. (1981). II. The life cycle of the family: The adolescent's sense of time. *Adolescent Psychiatry, 9,* 180–188.
Valliant, G. (1977). *Adaptation to life.* Boston: Little, Brown.

10.2   Laurence Steinberg, 1990

Autonomy, Conflict, and Harmony in the Family Relationship

Laurence Steinberg, Ph.D., is the Distinguished University Professor and Laura H. Carnell Professor of Psychology at Temple University. He is director of the John D. and Catherine T. MacArthur Foundation Research Network on Adolescent Development and Juvenile Justice. Dr. Steinberg is author of numerous books including *Crossing Paths: How Your Child's Adolescence Triggers Your Own Crisis* (with Wendy Steinberg, 1994), *Beyond the Classroom: Why School Reform Has Failed and What Parents Need to Do* (with B. Bradford Brown and Sanford Dornbusch, 1996), and *You and Your Adolescent: A Parent's Guide for Ages 10 to 20* (with Ann Levine, 1997).

For decades, the psychoanalytic perspective on the parent-child relationship at adolescence has had a profound impact on our understanding of parent-child relationships at adolescence. The psychoanalytic position holds that with the advent of pubertal maturation and genital sexuality, repressed oedipal feelings are reawakened toward parents, and to cope with these feelings, adolescents employ a number of defensive measures

(Freud, 1958). Anna Freud described displacement as a defense by which adolescents withdraw their loving feelings abruptly and altogether from parents and direct those feelings to persons outside the family. A second defense Freud noted was reversal of affect, by which adolescents turn their "love into hate, dependence into revolt, respect and admiration into contempt and derision" (Freud, 1958, p. 270). Freud argued that the parent-child relationship becomes marked by hostility and aggressiveness. Thus from the psychoanalytic perspective, the turn away from parents to other relationships, and hostility and conflict with parents, are a normal part of the adolescent process.

Laurence Steinberg reviews the more recent empirical work on the parent-child relationship at adolescence and argues that the classical psychoanalytic view of parent-child relationships is not correct. Conflict between parents and adolescents is not the norm. The reading by Steinberg reveals that the conflict that does exist between parents and adolescents is over mundane matters of everyday life, and serves a positive function, facilitating individuation, and helping adolescents relinquish childhood dependencies and come to terms with parental fallibility. While adolescents spend less time with their parents than they did as children and become more autonomous, the emotional bond is in no way severed. Steinberg reviews research that shows that detachment from family ties, in fact, is not desirable. Adolescents who break ties with parents score lower on psychological measures of well-being, and higher on social problems.

Steinberg discusses the transformations that occur in the parent-child relationship. A shift occurs from parents having unilateral authority to a more cooperative relationship. Adolescents engage more in cooperative decision making with parents, discuss differences, and seek compromises. A shift occurs from an idealized view of parents (Reading 4.1), to seeing parents more as persons, as more complex individuals. Finally, Steinberg examines research on parenting styles and the impact of parenting style on the psychological development and well-being of adolescents.

Although the popular and clinically influenced stereotype of the adolescent's family as a crucible of intrafamilial tension and hostility has not been confirmed in empirical studies of teenagers and their parents, research has shown that the second decade of a child's life—and, in particular, the first few years of this decade—is a critical time for the realignment and redefinition of family ties. Parent-child relations do not seem to be reconstituted in any dramatic way during the transition from childhood into adolescence, but they nevertheless are transformed in subtle yet significant respects. The purpose of this [selection] is to examine the nature of and influences on this set of relational transformations.

It is important to note at the outset what this [selection] will *not* cover. Although I will consider the ways in which various demographic factors—especially household composition—may moderate patterns of relational change during adolescence, studies of the impact of these demographic factors in their own right are reviewed by Furstenberg. . . . [B]ecause this [selection] emphasizes research and theory about the developing youth as an individual, I do not focus on the family as a system, nor do I examine marital or sibling relationships in families with adolescent children. Although crucial transformations in these relationships may occur during the teenage years, space considerations preclude coverage of these topics.

Theoretical Considerations

The Psychoanalytic Legacy

I want to note at the outset the profound influence that psychoanalytic models have had in shaping and defining the empirical agenda in this area. The work of A. Freud, in particular, has directed the attention of students of adolescent family relations to describing and understanding the process through which adolescents detach themselves from their parents. According to this view, the process of detachment, triggered by the biological changes of puberty and their sexual sequelae, is characterized by intrafamilial storm and stress, and adolescent rebellion is viewed as both an inevitable and normative response to this "second oedipal" event. From the analytic vantage point, the development of autonomy during adolescence is conceptualized as autonomy *from* parents; parent-adolescent conflict is seen as both a normative manifestation of the detachment process and as a necessary stimulus to the process; and parent-adolescent harmony, at least in the extreme, is viewed as developmentally stunting and symptomatic of intrapsychic immaturity. Indeed, as Freud wrote:

> We all know individual children who as late as the ages of fourteen, fifteen, or sixteen show no . . . outer evidence of inner unrest. They remain, as they have been during the latency period, "good" children, wrapped up in their family relationships, considerate sons of their mothers, submissive to their fathers, in accord with the atmosphere, ideas, and ideals of their childhood background. Convenient as they may be, it signifies a delay of normal development and is, as such, a sign to be taken seriously.

The implications of the psychoanalytic view of adolescence for the study of family relationships have been many. The chief legacy is the notion that conflict and detachment, rather than harmony and attachment, characterize normal family life during this period of development. As a result, most research has been biased toward the study of the extent to which, the ways in which, and the reasons why adolescents and their parents grow apart, to the exclusion of research on the ways in which close family ties are maintained (or perhaps become even closer). Far more is known about the nature of parent-adolescent conflict and ideological differences between the generations than about the nature of parent-adolescent closeness or intergenerational similarity. As will be evident, this imbalance is especially ironic in light of research on representative populations of young people and parents which indicates that harmony is a far more pervasive feature of family life during this period than is contentiousness, and that the values and attitudes of adults and youth are more alike than different.

(2) A second influence of the psychoanalytic view concerns the issue of discontinuity. The theory holds that detachment abruptly terminates the latency, or preadolescent, period. In response to the resurgence of latent drives—mainly, but not exclusively, sexual drives—the formerly obedient and respectful young adolescent "regresses" to a more psychologically primitive state and turns spiteful, vengeful, oppositional, and unpredictable. As Adelson and Doehrman note: "The boy may suddenly turn surly or sullen or cocky or competitive or scornful vis-a-vis his father; the girl may treat her mother with withering scorn or her most patronizing, brittle 'friendliness,' or may be overcome with dark, inexplicable rages." An important implication of this disjunctive view of adolescence is the belief that a prior history of parent-child harmony is more or less irrelevant to the development of parent-child relations in adolescence; the overpowering libidinal forces of puberty are believed to imperil even the most sturdy of relational foundations. This emphasis on adolescent upheaval and its unpredictability has steered researchers away from studying the continuities between family relations in childhood and those in adolescence. Perhaps as a consequence of this view, no studies exist of the ways in which earlier family characteristics (for example, levels of harmony or conflict) moderate the nature of the family's transition into adolescence.

Neoanalytic Revisions and Extensions

Orthodox analytic views of the detachment process have given way to more tempered neoanalytic theories that emphasize the process of adolescent individuation rather than detachment. The primary proponent of this theoretical orientation is Blos, who has written extensively about the "second individuation process"[1] of adolescence. Individuation occurs as the young person develops a clearer sense of self as psychologically separate from his or her parents. Neoanalytic perspectives generally minimize the behavioral storminess of the adolescent's movement toward emotional and behavioral emancipation and emphasize instead the somewhat more pacific process through which the adolescent develops a new view of himself or herself and parental figures. In Blos's view, the individuation process is marked by the repudiation of parents; but much of the process is cognitive, not behavioral, and successful individuation is not necessarily accompanied by overt rebellion or oppositionalism.

Recent Theoretical Developments

Since the middle 1970s a new look has appeared in the literature on family relations during adolescence, one that for the most part disavows the orthodox analytic view and further transforms the neoanalytic perspective espoused by Blos and others. This new look, which is mainly empirical and somewhat less theoretical (or at least less grandly theoretical) begins with the premise that major realignments in family relations occur during the adolescent years, but it challenges the view that these realignments necessarily occur against a backdrop of distantiation or emotional detachment. Rather, the thrust of these more recent writings has been to emphasize, first, that most adolescents develop responsible autonomy without severing their emotional bond to their parents; second, that differences between families resulting from demographic and individual factors influence the way in which family relations are transformed; third, that changes in family relations must be understood in light of the psychological development of the parents as well as the adolescent; and fourth, that the family must be viewed as a system of intertwining relationships rather than a collection of independent dyads.

Much of the recent empirical work on transformations in family relations at adolescence has examined parents' and adolescents' behavior toward one another either through studies of interaction patterns or through self-reports. The neoanalytic perspective on family relations, however, draws attention to the fact that much of the readjustment in family relations at adolescence is intrapsychic, not only interpersonal. Changes in the teenager's and parent's conscious and unconscious images of each other, therefore, may be just as significant as changes in their behavior toward each other. Accordingly, students of family relations during adolescence must attend to subjective and subtle, as well as objective and overt, indications of changes in parent-adolescent conflict, harmony, and autonomy. Unfortunately, empirical research has rarely addressed this issue systematically, and researchers have seldom examined the relation between subjective and objective indexes of transformations in family relations.[2]

Central Issues

Consider the following excerpt of an interview with a 12-year-old girl, conducted as part of my own program of research:

I WAS WONDERING ABOUT THE WAY THAT YOU AND YOUR MOM TREAT EACH OTHER NOW. IS IT THE SAME AS IT WAS A FEW YEARS AGO, OR DO YOU NOTICE ANY DIFFERENCE IN THE WAY SHE TREATS YOU?

Yeah, she treats me—she seems to trust me more with things. Like leaving me alone with my sister at night when they're away.

WHAT ABOUT THE ARGUMENTS OR FIGHTS THAT YOU HAVE? HAVE THOSE CHANGED AT ALL?

I guess I argue more with her.

WHY DO YOU THINK THAT IS?

I'm not sure.

WHAT KINDS OF THINGS DO YOU ARGUE ABOUT?

When I'm supposed to go to bed. She tells me to clean up my room and I don't want to. I want to read a book or play with my friends.

DO YOU TREAT YOUR MOM DIFFERENTLY?

Yeah, I guess so. I guess I used to not yell at her back. But now I do.

SO WHEN SHE YELLS AT YOU, YOU YELL BACK. DOES SHE YELL AT YOU MORE THAN SHE USED TO?
I don't think so . . . We don't really have more arguments; it's just that I yell back at her when we do have arguments.

HAVE YOU NOTICED ANY CHANGES IN YOUR OPINION OF HER, WHAT YOU THINK OF HER? HAS THAT CHANGED SINCE YOU WERE LITTLE?
Maybe. When I was little, she was just my mother. Now she's more of a real person. I don't know. She still seems like she did when I was little, but now besides being the one who takes care of me and stuff like that, she's like everybody else. She has a career and all that kind of stuff too.

Is this passage best understood in terms of the development of autonomy, changes in the nature of parent-child conflict, or in the manifestation of parent-adolescent harmony? In my view the interchange has implications for understanding all three. Accordingly, the review that follows is organized not around the separate topics of autonomy, conflict, and harmony but rather around several fundamental issues that cut across all three domains. I begin with an examination of the view that storm and stress is normative.

Storm and Stress

I noted earlier that a key legacy of the psychoanalytic view of adolescent development is the belief that family relationships deteriorate during this period and that adolescent rebellion, conflict with parents, and detachment are all normative. A careful examination of the evidence on this issue is critical, because policy makers, practitioners, and parents need to know whether and to what extent familial stress is predictable and normal. Insofar as the public believes that adolescence is a time of normative disturbance in the family, families in distress will be less likely to seek professional help. And insofar as policy makers and personnel in funding agencies subscribe to this view, organizations will be less inclined to support programs and research aimed at preventing difficulties that are erroneously believed to be inevitable or at ameliorating problems that are mistakenly thought to remit spontaneously after adolescence.

The weight of the evidence to date indicates that the portrait of family storm and stress painted by early analytic writers is unduly pessimistic. Several large-scale surveys of adolescents and parents indicate that approximately three-fourths of families enjoy warm and pleasant relations during these adolescent years. The vast majority of teenagers are likely to report admiring their parents, turning to them for advice and counsel, and feeling loved and appreciated by them. Of the one-fourth of families who report less-than-happy relations, a large majority have experienced prior family problems.

It appears, therefore, that only a very small proportion of families—somewhere between 5% and 10%—experience a dramatic deterioration in the quality of the parent-child relationship during adolescence. Not surprisingly, family relations are more likely to be strained (both prior to and during adolescence) in households of delinquent or psychologically disturbed youth. The view that adolescent detachment and family stress are inherent features of domestic life may thus accurately describe families of teenagers with problems but may not apply to the normal population of young people and their parents. There is reason to believe, therefore, that families who experience a marked worsening in the quality of their relationships are likely to be in need of professional attention.

It is not known whether these estimates of the prevalence of family problems, derived almost exclusively from studies of firstborn adolescents from white, middle-class families, can be generalized to other populations, but there is little reason to assume a priori that family relations are inherently more strained in nonwhite, non–middle-class households. Although research on these populations is needed, it would be prudent to begin from the premise that neither storm nor stress is normative for them either.

While we can confidently say that conflict is not the norm in white, middle-class, intact households, it does appear that strained or distant parent-adolescent relationships may be more prevalent among single-parent households and stepfamilies than in biologically intact households. Even in these populations, however, parent-adolescent discord is not the norm; it is more accurate to say that the proportion of families who report difficulties at adolescence is simply smaller in biologically intact two-parent homes than in others. More to the point, variations within family-structure groups are likely to be more substantial than are differences between groups.

Current information on how parent-adolescent relations may vary as a function of household composition is limited in several respects, in part as a consequence of the excessive use of the "social address" research design, which merely contrasts adolescents raised in different family structures without examining intrafamilial processes. First, although the popular press often makes sweeping comparisons between two-parent, intact households and all other groups combined, there is considerable diversity within the population of nonintact families that is all too often overlooked. For example, the category of adolescents in single-mother households includes some living with a divorced or separated single mother; some living with a widowed mother; some living with a mother who has never married; some living with a mother and an unrelated adult male; and some living with a mother and a member of the extended family. These variations in household composition are likely to affect the nature of parent-adolescent relations, but they seldom are examined systematically.

Second, cross-sectional comparisons of families that differ in household composition do not tell us whether the nature of the relational transformations that occur at adolescence differs as a function of family structure. For example, studies indicate that familial discord and adolescent detachment are greater in single-parent homes and stepfamilies than in biologically intact two-parent homes; and that parental permissiveness is greater in single-parent than two-parent homes. But these studies do not tell us whether these differences arise from, or are related in any systematic way to, features of the adolescent transition. Parent-child discord and distance and parental permissiveness may be greater at all points in the family life cycle in nonintact households.

Several researchers have followed families with adolescents through the process of divorce or remarriage, a more difficult, but likely more fruitful, approach. Generally these studies suggest that teenagers have less difficulty coping with parental divorce than do younger children but more difficulty coping with parental remarriage.

Remarriage appears to be especially hard on adolescent girls; several studies suggest that adolescent-stepfather relations are more strained among daughters than sons. Even these studies, however, do not examine how divorced or reconstituted families negotiate the transition into adolescence, or whether the pattern of relational transformation experienced in these households at adolescence differs from that observed among biologically intact two-parent families. Given the continued high rate of divorce and remarriage among parents of school-aged children, it is imperative that social scientists interested in transformations in family relations at adolescence initiate longitudinal research that begins prior to the teenage years and follows families of different structures through the transition. They must ask whether detachment is more likely to occur in these households at adolescence, or, alternatively, whether youngsters growing up in nonintact homes enter their teens with more distant relationships with parents.

There is some suggestion in the literature that familial strain may be more characteristic of relations between firstborn children and their parents. The reasons remain unclear, although studies of parental images of adolescence suggest that parents may have different expectations before their firstborn reaches adolescence than they do as their subsequent children become teenagers. One hypothesis worthy of investigation is that a self-fulfilling prophecy may operate whereby novice parents of teenagers expect, provoke, and find more oppositional behavior in their youngsters than do parents who have already experienced an older child's adolescence. Whether a similar process helps account for the family-structure differences discussed earlier (that is, whether single parents or stepparents may have different expectations for adolescence) is another interesting but unresearched question.

Far less is known about whether family relations in adolescence vary systematically across ethnic groups. The little research that exists, mainly on African-American teenagers, suggests that researchers must attend to the ways in which the prevalence of households headed by the mother, the relatively more matrifocal orientation in general, and the widespread use of extended family networks among African-American families may moderate patterns of relational change in adolescence. Because most studies of African-American adolescents have not systematically separated the effects of ethnicity and socioeconomic status, however, we must be cautious about generalizing findings derived from studies of low-income minority youth to more affluent minority populations. This caveat notwithstanding, it is important to note that theories about "normal" interpersonal development based on an image of the relatively isolated two-parent nuclear household may not apply to young people growing up under other circumstances.

Is Detachment Desirable? no

There is a strong evidence against the view that detachment from family ties during adolescence is desirable. The prediction derived from analytic models, of course, is that adolescents with close relations to parents should show stunted psychological development. Yet the empirical evidence is directly antithetical to this prediction: Teenagers who report feeling relatively close to their parents score higher than their peers on measures of psychosocial development, including self-reliance and other indicators of responsible independence; behavioral competence, including school performance; and psychological well-being, including self-esteem. Not surprisingly, they score lower on measures of psychological and social problems, including drug use, depression, and deviant behavior. This finding is robust across socioeconomic and ethnic groups. Although the argument has been made in clinical circles that a moderate degree of closeness is preferable to too much or too little, studies of nonclinical populations do not support the hypothesis that the parent-adolescent relationship can be so cohesive as to be enmeshing. There is some evidence, however, that teenagers whose parents are excessive in their use of guilt-inducing and other psychologically controlling techniques may suffer developmentally as a result.

In view of the clear and consistent evidence that detachment from family ties during adolescence is neither normative nor desirable, we must ask why this notion persists. A quick pass through the child-development section of most bookstores indicates that this viewpoint is indeed alive and well; most of the titles of books aimed at parents of teenagers suggest that adolescence is something for parents to survive rather than enjoy.[3] In view of the very reasonable hypothesis suggesting that parental expectations may influence the quality and nature of parent-adolescent relations, more research on the sources of information sought and used by parents, as well as the impact of this information on parenting practices, is needed. It would also be fruitful to examine whether and in what ways the mass media continue to promote the view that adolescence is an inherently difficult time during which detachment from parental ties is the norm.

It is impossible to discuss expectations about adolescence (whether held by parents, practitioners, scientists, or adolescents themselves) without acknowledging the role of the broader social context in shaping these beliefs. We know from the work of the many cultural anthropologists who have studied adolescence that expectations and beliefs about "normal" adolescence, and about "normal" parent-child relations in particular, are highly variable across cultures. We know less about variations among ethnic groups within contemporary American society, but we do know, for instance, that expectations concerning the appropriate ages at which various "autonomies" should be granted vary considerably across ethnic groups. It is likely that expectations concerning the expression of harmony and conflict vary as well.

Historical forces also shape attitudes and beliefs about adolescence. During the late 1960s, for example, it is likely that the attention given by the mass media to the "generation gap" contributed to parents' anxieties about their ability to influence their children's values; stereotypes of adolescents as rebellious and oppositional were probably strengthened during this era. Today, concerns over crack, AIDS, and school crime create different anxieties, with their own implications for understanding the genesis of parental belief systems. My intent in challenging the storm-and-stress model of adolescence is not to imply that contemporary parents' worries about their youngsters' exposure to drugs, sexually transmitted diseases, and violence are unwarranted or unjustified. There is a crucial difference, however, between portraying the world in which adolescents currently live as a potentially dangerous place (which is accurate) and portraying adolescence as an inherently stressful time for the individual or the family (which is not). It is essential that we understand how best to keep these two messages distinct.

Alternatives to the Detachment Model

Part of the difficulty we encounter in debunking the myth of storm and stress is that a suitable substitute has yet to be completely articulated. Virtually all scholars writing about family relations in adolescence agree that transformations in the present-child relationship do occur during this period, that families vary in the ways in which their relationships are transformed, and that these variations are likely to influence the young person's mental health and behavior. Several writers have attempted to describe these transformations in terms other than of storm and stress or detachment, and their work offers promising leads for a new theory of normative transformations in the parent-child relationships.

Moving toward an interdependent relationship   Youniss and his colleagues have argued that transformations in family relations at adolescence reflect the adolescent's growing understanding of his or her *interdependence* within the family and the parents' willingness to engage in a process through which close ties are maintained but the young person's individuality is not threatened. Both parent and adolescent actively participate in the mutual and reciprocal process of redefining the relationships. Transformation of the relationship from one of unilateral authority to one of cooperative negotiation is necessary for the adolescent's social and psychological development to proceed on course; a severing of the parent-child bond jeopardizes this process. In healthy families adolescents remain responsive to parental authority and continue to seek parents' advice, but they do so in a context of greater freedom. The parents, at the same time, retain their authority through "giving more freedom to adolescents by recognizing their personal needs and capabilities . . . It is clear that parental relationships have not been discarded nor have they lost their binding power. In fact, the adolescents said that the transformation helped to bring them and their parents closer."

This suggests that, if emancipation does occur at adolescence, it is more likely to be manifested in subtle changes in parents' and adolescents' conscious and unconscious images of one another than in dramatic changes in behavior. According to several studies adolescence is a time for the shedding of childhood (and childish) conceptions of parental omniscience and omnipotence, a finding consistent with the work of Blos and other neoanalytic theorists. As children get older, for instance, the gap between their description of an "ideal" parent and their characterization of their own parents widens. But as Smollar and Youniss point out—and in contrast to neoanalytic theory—the realization that one's parents are far from ideal does not necessarily lead to a rejection of their authority or a repudiation of their wisdom. Instead, once the relationship has been transformed, parental authority and wisdom are seen in more balanced, and probably more accurate, terms.

A handful of studies point to the very different roles played by mothers and fathers in their relations with adolescent sons and daughters. The overall picture suggests that the four parent-adolescent dyads may be characterized by quite different types of relations and may undergo quite different sorts of transformations in adolescence. Mother-daughter relations are the most affectively charged, characterized by high levels of both closeness and discord, and by a high level of shared activities. Mothers' relations with sons are also high in conflict and harmony but are not characterized by the same level of joint activities. Fathers appear to have emotionally "flat" relations with their teenagers in comparison to mothers, and share few activities with daughters. In general, the father-daughter relationship appears to be the outlier, distinguished by its affective blandness and relatively low level of interaction. An investigation by Gjerde reminds us, however, that assessments of maternal and paternal behavior must take into account the context of the interaction. In families with adolescent boys, for example, the adolescent's interaction with his mother is more positive when the father is present, while his interaction with his father is more positive when the two are alone. We do not yet understand the reason for this difference.

Temporary "perturbations" in the family system　Youniss and Smollar's work on mutuality in the parent-adolescent relationship does not fully address the emotional and behavioral aspects of the process of relational transformation. Although the end result of the transformation may be a happier and more mature parent-child relationship in which cooperative negotiation and mutual respect is the norm, the road traveled toward this destination may have its share of bumps and potholes. A different group of writers, including Collins, Hill, and Steinberg, have focused on the emotional and behavioral manifestations of the process through which family relationships are transformed, especially during the critical early adolescent years. According to these writers, early adolescence in particular is a period of temporary perturbation in the family, characterized by heightened bickering and squabbling (especially between mothers and teenagers) and diminished levels of positive interaction (between teenagers and both parents). The nattering is generally over mundane issues of daily life; the lessening of positive interaction typically takes the form of fewer shared activities and less frequently expressed affection.

Several researchers have shown that temporary periods of perturbation in the family system occur at around the onset of puberty. These researchers interpret transformations in family relations in terms of the family's adaptation to the adolescent's physical development. Generally speaking, pubertal maturation leads to a modest increase in distance in the parent-adolescent relationship, a finding that supports the psychoanalytic proposition that the somatic and hormonal changes of puberty set in motion a series of intrapsychic and interpersonal processes that culminate in the adolescent's successful individuation from parental objects and engagement in intimate relationships with age-mates.[4] Although the distancing effect of puberty on parent-adolescent relations is observed in several studies, the magnitude of the effect is modest, and the studies in no way suggests that puberty provokes familial storm and stress.

Collins has written about the perturbations that occur in the family system in early adolescence as well, but from a cognitive-mediational perspective. Here the focus is on understanding the expectations that parents and children have for one another's behavior, the ways in which these expectations may (or may not) change during adolescence, and the impact of violations of expectations on parent-adolescent interactions. Violations of expectations take two forms. First, patterns of behavior established prior to adolescence engender expectations (typically on the part of the parent) that may be violated as the child becomes older. Second, new expectations may be formed by both parent and child, but they may be discordant. Perturbations in the family system result, he argues, when expectations are violated, and violations are more likely to occur during periods of rapid development. As I noted earlier, more research on the nature of, and bases for, parents' expectations of adolescence is needed.

Because perturbation in family relations typically do not threaten the emotional cohesion of the parent-child bond, the fact that families pass through such periods should not be taken as evidence of adolescent detachment. Indeed, we must ask whether and how periods of realignment—even when accompanied by conflict—may contribute in *positive* ways to the psychosocial development of the adolescent. As Cooper correctly points out: "Although conflict is often considered an indicator of incompatibility, current research provides evidence that conflict can function constructively when it co-occurs with the subjective conditions of trust and closeness and their behavioral expressions."

It is all well and good to discuss the positive function of conflict in the parent-adolescent relationship, but we must not lose sight of the fact that the important question is not whether conflict is functional or dysfunctional but under what circumstances conflict is likely to be one or the other. There undoubtedly are families in which conflict is unhealthy, either because it is pervasive, because it does not occur against a backdrop of emotional closeness, or because it escalates regularly into angry fighting or physical violence. But research suggests that these families are in the minority. Most parents and children who enter adolescence with a sturdy foundation of trust and a strong bond in all likelihood negotiate the transition with relatively little cost (albeit with some increase in daily hassling), and youngsters may actually benefit from the interchange and dialogue that accompany disagreement. This process may facilitate movement toward the more mutual, reciprocal relations described by Youniss and Smollar. Families whose emotional foundation is shaky to begin with, however, may find the period of perturbation too much to bear and may fall into deeper levels of disengagement and detachment. Future research on perturbations in the family system and their consequences for adolescent development should examine preadolescent variations in parent-child closeness as a factor that may moderate the impact of conflict on individuals and the family system.

The enduring attachment bond A third set of writers has attempted to cast the parent-adolescent relationship in terms derived from attachment theorists such as Bowlby. These writers, including Greenberg, and Kobak and Sceery, have suggested that early attachment relationships help foster working models of interpersonal relations that are carried, albeit in modified form, over the life span. If this view is correct, variations in the security of youngsters' attachment to their parents prior to adolescence should influence the way in which family relations are transformed during the adolescent passage. Thus far, with one exception, attempts to extend the attachment paradigm to adolescence have focused on assessing individual differences in attachment security and examining the implications of these differences for mental health and psychological functioning, rather than on developmental changes in the meaning or manifestations of the attachment bond. It remains to be seen whether the working model of relationships that the young person brings to adolescence influences the pattern of relational transformation experienced by the family. A reasonable (but untested) hypothesis is that the successful movement toward healthy interdependence and the negotiation of temporary periods of perturbation are more likely to occur in families in which teenager and parents are securely attached.

Positive Functions of Parent-Adolescent Conflict

I noted earlier that disagreements over family rules and other mundane features of everyday life may become more frequent during early adolescence than before or after, but that in most families this discord does not diminish the emotional attachment between adolescents and their parents. The frequency of disagreements increases between childhood and early adolescence, remains stable through middle adolescence, and declines somewhat thereafter. Although studies employing different methodologies yield different estimates, it appears that the typical teenager and parent quarrel about two times weekly, or about twice as often as the typical husband and wife.

An examination of the sources of disagreement between parents and adolescents casts doubt on many widely held notions about the nature of intergenerational conflict. It is widely believed that adolescents and parents hold conflicting views about political and social matters, and that this divergence in values and attitudes is a primary source of intergenerational tension. This is not the case today, nor was it the case during the height of the political and social turbulence of the 1960s and 1970s. The clarity of hindsight indicates that the nature and existence of a generation gap was grossly overstated by the popular media, and that calls of alarm from blue-ribbon commissions writing in the 1970s about the pervasiveness of a counterculture and the widespread rejection of adult values by American youth were exaggerated. Indeed, as Montemayor points out, the topics that adolescents and parents argue about have changed little since researchers began examining this issue over sixty years ago. Squabbles about curfew, household chores, and school responsibilities are the most commonly mentioned sources of argument, even in studies conducted during historical periods in which adolescents and adults were alleged to argue frequently over more lofty concerns than dirty laundry.

Despite the banality of most family disagreements, several writers have suggested that this sort of low-level quarreling serves an important purpose in the adolescent's development. Steinberg, arguing from a sociobiological perspective, has suggested that this bickering and squabbling at puberty is an atavism that ensures that adolescents will spend time away from the family of origin and mate outside the natal group. Parent-offspring conflict intensifies at puberty in most other species of primates, and it is possible that the tension experienced by humans has an evolved basis. Because the squabbling occurs within the context of a close emotional relationship, it may force the adolescent to look outside the family for intimate companionship without breaking ties to parents.

Holmbeck and Hill have offered a complementary perspective on the adaptive significance of parent-adolescent conflict that draws on both psychoanalytic and social learning theory. They argue that conflict promotes adjustment to developmental change through intrapsychic as well as interpersonal processes. At an intrapsychic level, the conflict may facilitate individuation. Recalling the work of Youniss and Smollar, one might argue that the intrapsychic emancipation that permits the adolescent to develop a more mature and more realistic appraisal of his or her parents—and ultimately a more mature and more mutual relationship with them—is helped along by a temporary period of heightened squabbling. These frequent disagreements, in the context of a strong attachment, force the adolescent to come to terms with parental fallibility and, consequently, relinquish childish dependence on mother and father. At an interpersonal level, the conflict arising between adolescents and parents at puberty may serve an informational function. Disagreement may be a mechanism through which the adolescent informs his or her parents about changing self-conceptions and expectations.

Smetana has offered a cognitive-developmental perspective that is also instructive. She contends that parent-adolescent conflict is best understood in terms of the different ways in which parents and their children understand and define family rules, events, and regulations. Using the results of an extensive series of interviews, Smetana demonstrates that the growing frequency of conflict in early and middle adolescence is related to the development of advanced levels of social reasoning. She cites two reasons. First, as young people develop, they are increasingly likely to view issues that they and their parents had once defined as matters of social convention (for example, "In this family we all make our beds every morning") as matters of personal choice ("Since it's my bed, I'll decide how often to make it"). Because parents are likely to maintain a conventional stance toward these issues, conflict ensures. The conflict is not so much over the issue as it is over the *definition* of the issue (that is, a matter of personal taste versus one of social convention).

Second, during early and middle adolescence young people pass through a period of cognitive development in which they cast social conventions as arbitrary—including social conventions that regulate the sundry matters that parents and teenagers squabble about. Thus, even when both the adolescent and the parent define an issue of contention in conventional terms (that is, there are "rules" that govern one's behavior), the adolescent may be unlikely to adopt the parent's convention (for example, "Your friends may dress that way, but mine don't"). The following excerpt of one of Smetana's interviews, with a tenth-grader, will sound annoyingly familiar to most parents of teenagers:

WHEN CLEANING YOUR ROOM COMES UP, IS IT THAT YOU DON'T WANT TO CLEAN YOUR ROOM?

I don't care whether I clean it up or not, it's just that, it's a big issue with my mother, she gets really upset about it.

WHY?

It's just that way, because I'll go, "I don't care," and she says, "Well I do," and then it keeps going.

WHY DO YOU THINK SHE MAKES YOU CLEAN IT THEN?

I don't know . . . I don't know, she keeps saying, "All little kids have to clean their room."

[Handwritten margin notes: "conflict helps adjustment to developmental change →"; "Intrapsychic level - facilitates individuation - promotes mature + realistic view of parents + more mutual relationship w/ them - parents aren't perfect"; "Interpersonal level - serves informational function - way to have adolescent inform parent about changing expectations"; "personal taste vs. social convention"]

WHAT DO YOU THINK ABOUT THAT?
She's probably right, but I don't think I should have to, I don't think I should have to like make sure there's nothing gross in there . . . and have to clean up an entire room.

Frequent disagreements, however minor, are understandably sources of tension and stress to many parents of teenagers. Studies have found that parents of adolescents are likely to feel less adequate and more anxious about parenting than parents of younger children. Reports of parental stress are highest in early adolescence and are related to youngsters' demands for more independence and, presumably, to conflicts that arise over issues of autonomy. In addition, distance between parents and adolescents may diminish marital satisfaction and provoke midlife reappraisal and self-evaluation, especially among parents with a teenager of the same sex, and especially among parents without a strong orientation toward work outside the home.

As Cooper points out, however, the process of disagreeing—so long as it takes place in the context of a close parent-child relationship—may contribute in important ways to the adolescent's psychosocial development, despite its impact on parents' peace of mind. For example, adolescents' identity development and interpersonal skills are more advanced in families in which members are willing to express their own points of view and tolerate disagreements with one another. Similarly, adolescent ego development is greater in families in which discussions are characterized by relatively frequent discourse that reflects problem solving, empathy, and acceptance, and relatively little interchange that is devaluing, judgmental, or constraining. These studies recall the finding, noted earlier, that adolescents whose parents use excessive amounts of psychological control may suffer somewhat in the development of competence.

Tolerance of disagreement and the discord that may ensure is apparently a key feature of parent-child interaction in families with psychosocially healthy adolescents. The combination of conflict and cohesion is critical, however: "When family conflict is hostile, impulsive, and inconsistent, and prone to escalation to high intensity, children feel neglect and lack of love, and avoid interaction with their parents. Thus, contentiousness alone may not be the distinctive feature of dysfunctional conflict, but whether or not conflict occurs within a context of relational cohesion." This notion is consistent with available data on the disproportionate prevalence of abusive relations between adolescents and stepparents. Although the level of squabbling in these dyads may be no greater than that between adolescents and biological parents, stepparents and adolescents may lack the affective cohesiveness that prevents low-level bickering from escalating into dysfunctional discord and abuse. More research is needed on identifying families predisposed toward dysfunctional conflict, and on the processes through which functional disagreement escalates into dysfunctional discord. Patterson's work on the escalation of family conflict from simple problems of noncompliance to serious problems of physical violence serves as a useful starting point for the study of adolescent-parent conflict and its vicissitudes.

Cooper's contention that it is not the presence of conflict per se that is the issue but the context in which conflict occurs suggests that researchers should focus more on the study of conflict resolution than on conflict genesis. Unfortunately, researchers have spent far more time and energy on the latter than on the former. The limited available data on conflict resolution suggest that if negotiation and discussion are essential components of functional conflict, most parents and teenagers are missing opportunities to facilitate the adolescent's development. According to a telephone survey by Montemayor and Hanson, nearly half of all adolescent-parent conflicts are "resolved" by one or both parties withdrawing from the incident, nearly 40% by one person simply telling the other what to do, and only 15% through negotiation.

Studies of conflict resolution would appear to be indicated, but it is not clear how to overcome some inherent methodological difficulties. Laboratory studies of family interaction processes in which family members are asked to discuss an issue or plan an event yield rich information on the processes of discourse, but they typically force artificial conflict resolution and do not permit withdrawal. These tasks probably tell us very little, therefore, about the extent and nature of conflict resolution in everyday situations. Researchers may want to consider alternatives to laboratory studies of interaction processes, as well as ways of revising interaction task instructions to permit irreconcilability and allow for parties to withdraw without reaching agreement.

The Power of Authoritative Parenting

Thus far I have suggested that adolescents thrive developmentally when the family environment is characterized by warm relationships in which individuals are permitted to express their opinions and assert their individuality. (One might label these characteristics *warmth* and *psychological autonomy*). A third component of functional parenting, *demandingness,* has also been identified. Demanding parents expect mature behavior from their adolescent, set and consistently enforce reasonable rules and standards for behavior, and when necessary discipline their youngster firmly yet fairly. The constellation of warmth, psychological autonomy, and demandingness, first identified and described by Baumrind, has been labeled *authoritative*. Adolescents who grow up in authoritative homes score higher on indexes of psychological development and mental health, however they are defined. Although most studies of parenting practices and their outcomes do not disentangle the effects of warmth, psychological autonomy, and demandingness from one another, it appears that the absence of parental warmth is associated mainly with deficits in the domains of social skills and self-conceptions; the absence of psychological autonomy with deficits in the domains of self-reliance and competence; and the absence of demandingness with deficits in the domains of impulse control and social responsibility.

The authoritative pattern may be contrasted with three other prototypes: the *autocratic* or *authoritarian* pattern, characterized by high levels of demandingness but low levels of warmth and psychological autonomy; the *indulgent* pattern, characterized by low levels of demandingness, high levels of warmth, and a laissez-faire attitude toward decision making; and the *indifferent* or *uninvolved* pattern, characterized by laissez-faire decision making and low levels of demandingness, but low levels of warmth as well.[5] Research on developmental differences among adolescents growing up in these four types of family environments is summarized in

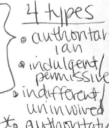

authoritative
authoritarian
indulgent
indifferent

which is worse:
authoritarian or
indulgent?

Maccoby and Martin and will not be reviewed here. Suffice it to say that youngsters raised in indifferent households are at greatest risk for psychological dysfunction and involvement in various problem behaviors (drug and alcohol use, delinquency, sexual precocity), and that youngsters raised in either autocratic or indulgent households are likely to score somewhere between those raised in authoritative and those raised in indifferent households on measures of social competence, self-reliance, self-esteem, and other indicators of psychosocial development.[6]

Much of the work on the benefits of authoritative parenting has been conducted on samples of white, middle-class youngsters growing up in two-parent households. Given the consistency, over time and across studies, with which youngsters from this population who are raised in warm, democratic, and demanding environments outscore their peers on measures of psychosocial development and prosocial behavior, it does not appear that further research on the consequences of authoritative parenting *in this population* is necessary or warranted. It would seem timely to initiate research on the *determinants,* rather than the *consequences,* of authoritative parenting practices.

Whether these same principles apply to other populations of adolescents and parents is an exceedingly important question, and one that must be answered before large-scale attempts are made to alter parenting practices in an authoritative direction. The recent work of Dornbusch and his colleagues demonstrates that the deleterious consequences of autocratic parenting for adolescent school performance appear to cut across ethnic boundaries. The positive consequences of authoritative parenting and the negative consequences of indifferent parenting hold up across socioeconomic groups and family structures as well. More research in this vein, with different outcome variables, is certainly needed. Such research should adopt a longitudinal design, beginning prior to the child's entry into adolescence and following the family through the critical early adolescent transition. There is ample reason to hypothesize that many of the benefits of growing up in an authoritative family environment—at least in contemporary America—transcend the boundaries of socioeconomic status, ethnicity, and family structure, but we must keep in mind that this remains a hypothesis.

can!
authoritative
style be taught?

In view of the apparent power of authoritative parenting, several researchers have asked whether the parenting practices that make up this style can be taught. The most critical work in this area comes from Patterson and his associates, who have developed an effective treatment program for distressed families with an aggressive, delinquent, or noncompliant child. The program focuses on the training of demandingness—supervision, monitoring, limit setting, and the like. Patterson's program is unlike conventional family therapy, because it emphasizes the tuition of constructive child-management practices rather than the analysis of underlying interpersonal dynamics. Specifically, the program is designed to teach parents how to convey to their children clear expectations for acceptable and unacceptable behavior, how to monitor their children's behavior, how to respond consistently and swiftly to noncompliance, and how to reward prosocial behavior. One of the most encouraging findings reported by Patterson's team is that participation in this training program leads not only to a decrease in problem behavior among the target children but to significant improvements in the behavior of their siblings as well. To date the long-term effectiveness of this program is unknown, as is its effectiveness in inner-city communities. Research on the efficacy of this and related approaches is urgently needed.

Future Directions *Recap*

Conventional models of familial storm and stress and adolescent detachment are being replaced, however slowly, by a number of promising perspectives that are more tempered and optimistic. As research from these new perspectives continues to develop, researchers should explore ways of disseminating findings of these studies to parents and practitioners, whose views of adolescence are likely to be somewhat anachronistic and unduly pessimistic.

Although empirical research has not supported the view that adolescence is an inherently contentious period for the family, recent studies of young people and their parents indicate that major transformations in the parent-child relationship occur during the second decade of life. While these transformations do not threaten the integrity of the emotional bond between young people and their parents, they may be associated with a temporary period of perturbation or realignment in the parent-adolescent relationship, especially during the early adolescent years.

The period of disequilibrium, likely triggered by the biological and cognitive changes of adolescence, is characterized by a somewhat diminished level of positive interaction between teenagers and their parents and a concomitant increase in bickering and squabbling. Although this period of perturbation may take a temporary toll on the psychological well-being of parents, for most families it leads within a few years to a redefinition of the parent-child relationship from one of unilateral parental authority to one that is more cooperative and reciprocal. Among the factors most likely to moderate the pattern of this relational transformation are the affective quality of the parent-child relationship prior to adolescence, the structure of the family (whether intact, divorced, or remarried), and the expectations about adolescence held by parents, teenagers, and the society in which they live. Unfortunately we know very little about the ways in which childhood attachments, family structure, and individual expectations affect the family's transitions into adolescence, nor has research examined the nature and sources of these expectations. Research on these issues is much needed.

In general, healthy adolescent development is facilitated by a parent-child relationship that maintains a strong affective bond while tolerating disagreement and the expression of the young person's growing sense of individuality. A style of parenting that has been labeled authoritative, characterized by parental warmth, democratic parent-child interaction, and parental demandingness, is consistently associated with positive developmental outcomes in young people. Conclusions about transformations in the parent-adolescent relationship and the implications of variations in this process for adolescent development, however, are limited by the restricted range of populations included in most research. Although there is good reason to suspect that authoritative parenting has positive consequences for most adolescents, research on nonwhite and nonintact families is urgently needed.

As we look to the future and to the changing demography of the United States, it becomes essential to study the new models of the parent-adolescent relationship in more heterogeneous samples of families. The next generation of research must examine whether and how variations in socioeconomic status, family structure, and ethnicity influence the ways in which families adapt to adolescence, and it must explore the ways in which these demographic factors moderate the developmental outcomes of familial adaptation. This is not to say that the current literature, with its foundation in studies of white, middle-class families, is too compromised to be of value; nor is it to suggest that studies of group differences in family processes should replace studies of family process and its developmental outcomes. As research on families with adolescent children proceeds, however, we must not lose sight of the changing social context in which families live and the implications of this change for the study of family relations.

Notes

1. The first individuation process is held to occur during infancy.

2. Some of the more insightful treatments of the issue of cognitive realignment may be found in Collins, Youniss and Smollar, and Hill and Holmbeck. Also, Smetana . . . has provided a cognitive-developmental perspective on transformations in family relations that may serve as a basis for rapprochement between the cognitive and analytic viewpoints.

3. For example, an examination of titles turned up the following: S. Hayman, *Adolescence: A survival guide to the teenage years* (New York: Gower, 1986); R. Kolodny et al., *How to survive your adolescent's adolescence* (Boston: Little, Brown, 1984); P. Buntman & E. Saris, *How to live with your teenager: A survivor's handbook for parents* (New York: Ballantine, 1982); and D. Powell, *Teenagers: When to worry, what to do* (New York: Doubleday, 1986).

4. Interestingly, at least one study has shown that distance in the parent-adolescent relationship may itself accelerate pubertal maturation in girls.

5. In many discussions of Baumrind's perspective, the "indulgent" and "neglectful" groups are combined and discussed under the label "permissive." But because the effects of permissiveness vary as a function of the level of parental warmth, grouping these two together leads to confusing and inconsistent findings. It is recommended that "permissive" be used only as the antithesis of "demanding" and not as a label for a constellation of parenting practices.

6. A word or two is in order on the difference between psychological and behavioral control and their respective effects on the developing adolescent. Some readers may find it inconsistent, or perhaps confusing, that the two forms of control appear to have opposite effects on the adolescent. (Many researchers do not distinguish between these different forms of control, which is clearly a mistake.) Adolescents appear to be adversely affected by psychological control—the absence of "psychological autonomy"—but positively influenced by behavioral control—the presence of "demandingness." Too little behavioral control may leave the youngster without adequate guidance and supervision and may, as a consequence, expose him or her, especially in contemporary society, to an array of developmentally risky temptations and dangers. Too much psychological control, in contrast, may facilitate dependency and impede the development of psychological competence and self-direction. The challenge for parents—and it may be a difficult one—is to grant sufficient psychological autonomy to their child without being behaviorally permissive.

Questions

1. How do you characterize the changes that occur in the parent-child relationship during adolescence?
2. What is the nature of parent-adolescent conflict?
3. Why do stereotypes persist about parent-adolescent relationships being marked by conflict and detachment?
4. What are the consequences of holding these stereotypes?
5. Is there a generation gap?
6. What qualities in parenting style are advantageous to positive outcomes at adolescence?

References and Further Reading

Freud, A. (1958). Adolescence. *Psychoanalytic Study of the Child, 13,* 255–278.

Laursen, B., Coy, K. C., & Collins, W. A. (1998). Reconsidering changes in parent-child conflict across adolescence: A meta-analysis. *Child Development, 69*(3), 817–832.

Maccoby, E., & Martin, J. (1983). Socialization in the context of the family: Parent-child interaction. In E. M. Heatherington (Ed.) *Handbook of child psychology,* Vol. 4 (pp. 1–101). New York: John Wiley.

Offer, D., Ostrov, E., & Howard, K. (1981). *The adolescent: A psychological self-portrait.* New York: Basic Books.

Steinberg, L., & Silverberg, S. (1986). The vicissitudes of autonomy in early adolescence. *Child Development, 57,* 841–851.

Youniss, J., & Smollar, J. (1985). *Adolescent relations with mothers, fathers, and friends.* Chicago: University of Chicago Press.

Chapter 11

Peers and Peer Groups

Peer groups and peer relationships play a large role in the lives of adolescents and make an important contribution to their social and psychological development. Adolescents' activities center around peers, who exert increasing influence over their lives. Adolescents turn to their peers for advice about issues that confront them in their daily lives, for example, problems regarding dating and relationships, personal experiences, and sexuality. Adolescents are more likely to be self-disclosing to their peers than to their parents and feel better understood by their peers than by their parents. Peers become a major source of emotional support.

Peer relationships have been understood from a number of different theoretical perspectives. Anna Freud (1958) argued that adolescents are struggling to detach from parents, and in coping with that enormous loss, adolescents attach to new people. They form friendships and have crushes and love affairs. From the psychoanalytic perspective, the importance of peer relationships derives from the need to relinquish the depth of emotional ties to one's parents and to divert that emotional energy into other relationships. From a psychosocial perspective, Erik Erikson (1968) argued that peer relationships play an important role in the formation of identity. Adolescents will temporarily overidentify with peers because they lack an assured sense of identity and individuality. Conformity to peers provides a temporary identity and sense of self-certainty. Through peer relationships adolescents come to know themselves through the eyes of another. From an interpersonal perspective, Harry Stack Sullivan (1953) argued that the need for intimacy begins at birth and becomes increasingly complex as a child matures. Peer relationships from Sullivan's perspective derive from a basic inborn need for intimacy, which takes the form at this stage of a need for a chum or friend of the same sex, with whom one can be intimate. The intolerable emotion of loneliness is now experienced for the first time, and Sullivan contends that loneliness will drive early adolescents to seek out intimacy with a peer of the same sex.

Research has been directed to various aspects of peer relationships, from peer groups and peer cultures to close friendships and romantic relationships. Peer groups have often been viewed as a negative force due to their cruelty and intolerance of difference. Years ago Erikson noted that adolescents can become "remarkably clannish, intolerant, and cruel in their exclusion of others who are 'different,' in skin color or cultural background, in tastes and gifts, and often in entirely petty aspects of dress and gesture arbitrarily selected as the signs of an in-grouper or out-grouper" (Erikson, 1968, p. 132). He understood this intolerance to be motivated by adolescents' lack of a firm sense of individuality. Peer groups were also seen as a negative force due to their pressures for conformity to value systems and behavior patterns that were at odds with those endorsed by parents and that would put adolescents at risk.

More recently the view of cross-pressures between parents and peers has been modified. Parents and peers, both, are now seen as having an important influence on adolescents, and the positive aspects of membership in peer crowds for development have been noted (Brown, 1990). When close friendships have been studied as relationships in themselves, apart from peer groups, a positive picture has emerged. Close friendships are seen as making an important contribution to social development. The majority of close friendships at adolescence are marked by "mutual intimacy, mutual understanding, acceptance of and respect for differences of opinions, a wide range of topics for discussion; and a perception of self as relaxed, open, natural, outgoing, accepted, and accepting" (Youniss & Smollar, 1985, p. 109).

While considerable growth occurs in peer relationships and friendships during adolescence, romantic relationships emerge for the first time. Pubertal maturation contributes to the awakening of sexual desires and interests, and leads to interest in the formation of romantic and sexual relationships. Romantic relationships are not static, but show an evolution over the course of adolescence and into adulthood as adolescents gain a surer sense of identity, of themselves as sexual beings, and a deeper capacity for intimacy.

The readings in this section cover several dimensions of peer relationships. They examine the nature and importance of adolescent friendships (Reading 11.1), the role of peer crowds in shaping the quality and nature of peer relationships (Reading 11.2), and the nature of early romantic experiences (Reading 11.3).

Additional Resources

References and Suggested Readings

Brown, B. B. (1990). Peer groups and peer cultures. In S. S. Feldman, & G. R. Elliott (Eds.) *At the Threshold* (pp. 171–196). Cambridge, MA: Harvard University Press.

Erikson, E. H. (1968). *Identity: Youth and crisis.* New York: W. W. Norton.

Freud, A. (1958) Adolescence. *Psychoanalytic Study of the Child, 13,* 255–278.

Savin-Williams, R. C., & Berndt, T. J. (1990). Friendship and peer relations. In S. S. Feldman, & G. R. Elliott (Eds.) *At the Threshold* (pp. 277–307). Cambridge, MA: Harvard University Press.

Sullivan, H. S. (1953). *The interpersonal theory of psychiatry*. New York: W. W. Norton.

Youniss, J., & Haynie, D. L. (1992). Friendship in adolescence. *Developmental and Behavioral Pediatrics, 13*(1), 59–66.

Youniss, J., & Smollar, J. (1985). *Adolescent relations with mothers, fathers, and friends.* Chicago: University of Chicago Press.

On the Internet

http://www.personal.psu.edu/faculty/n/x/nxd10/social2.htm#friendship

Adolescence: Change & Continuity—Adolescent Friendship in the Context of Social Change

http://www.personal.psu.edu/faculty/n/x/nxd10/peers2.htm

Adolescence: Change & Continuity—Peer Groups
These two Web sites were produced by Pennsylvania State University students taking Human Development and Family Studies 433: The Transition to Adulthood; and Human Development, and Family Studies 239: Adolescent Development.

http://allkids.org/Epstein/Articles/Peer_Pressure.html

All Children's Hospital—The Doctor's Office: The Importance of Peer Pressure! Located in St. Petersburg, Florida, All Children's Hospital is a regional referral center for children with medical problems. The Doctor's Office is a collection of articles written by Bruce A. Epstein, M.D.

http://www.apa.org/monitor/jun96/friends.html

APA Monitor—Adolescent Friends Not Always a Bad Influence
This is the Web site of the American Psychological Association. The article was published in the American Psychological Association journal, *The Monitor.*

11.1   Willard W. Hartup, 1993

Adolescents and Their Friends

Willard W. Hartup, Ph.D., is the Regents' Professor Emeritus of Child Psychology at the Institute of Child Development, University of Minnesota, Minneapolis. He has written extensively and edited books on the subjects of child and adolescent development and child and adolescent relationships.

Relationships with friends make an important contribution to adolescent development. By the early 1980s researchers began to study friendship seriously, drawing on the work of Harry Stack Sullivan (1953), one of the first theorists to stress the importance of friendship to personality development at adolescence. Sullivan argued that friendship offers the opportunity for the validation of one's sense of self-worth. Friendship also offers the opportunity for consensual validation, a process by which two people seek to understand their experiences through mutual exchange of thoughts and perceptions, each offering his or her unique perceptions, receiving comments on those perceptions, and continuing the exchange until agreement is reached. The process of consensual validation can be very helpful in correcting distorted conceptions of self and of others, and contributing to a more accurate understanding of oneself and of others. Research has provided support for Sullivan's contention that friendships are important to the development of social maturity (Youniss & Smollar, 1985).

Hartup examines the nature and significance of adolescent friendships. His review of the research findings suggests that adolescents tend to seek out friends who are similar to themselves in terms of demographic characteristics, such as age, race, and class, as well as attitudes toward school, drugs, drinking, and dating, and that these similarities increase over the course of the friendship. Friendships vary significantly in their stability and in their degree of supportiveness and intimacy. Sex differences in friendship have been identified, with girls' friendships being marked by greater intimacy and self-disclosure. Friendships contribute to social adjustment, to feeling good about oneself, to being socially connected, and to being successful in subsequent relationships.

Hartup raises questions about the relative influences of parenting style and friendship on antisocial behavior, drug use, and academic achievement, and how these influences vary according to race. For example, research has shown that for whites, firm discipline, warmth, and high standards by parents disposed adolescents toward friendship networks that in turn encouraged academic achievement, whereas for African Americans, weak support for academic achievement from friends offset the positive effects of authoritative parenting. Finally, Hartup points to future directions for research on adolescent friendship.

Considerable evidence now shows that peer relations contribute substantially to both social and cognitive development, and to the effectiveness with which we function as adults. Indeed, the best early predictor of adult adaptation is not IQ, or school grades, or classroom behavior but rather the adequacy with which children and adolescents get along with their contemporaries (Parker and Asher, 1987). Adolescents who are generally disliked, who are aggressive and disruptive, and who cannot establish a place for themselves in the peer culture are developmentally at risk. In this [selection], the significance of adolescent friendships is examined. Questions addressed include the following: How ubiquitous are these relationships? How similar are friends? How stable are these relationships? Does having a friend make a difference in social and emotional development? New directions in research dealing with adolescents and their friends are also discussed.

Ubiquity of Friendships

Friendships can be identified among toddlers (Howes, 1989) and obtain ubiquity by middle childhood. Friendship networks or clusters are also evident in childhood and become highly significant in adolescence.

Best Friends   Most adolescents have one or two "best friends" and several "close friends" or "good friends," the exact number depending on the manner in which best friends, close friends, and good friends are identified and distinguished (Crockett, Losoff, and Petersen, 1984). Best friends are usually assumed by adolescents to involve mutual attraction, and almost no one admits to not having a best friend, even on anonymous questionnaires. Self-reported best friends are most numerous in early adolescence, averaging between four and five, with this number gradually declining thereafter (Reisman and Shorr, 1978). But stable, reciprocated friendships (mutual choices lasting a year or more) are rarer, characterizing only about one-third of high school students according to one account (Epstein, 1983). Friendships are thus ubiquitous in the teenage culture, although we must recognize that more individuals report that they are involved in reciprocated friendships than actually are.

Contact among best friends usually occurs on a daily basis, and, among American teenagers, these contacts consume several hours each day (Csikzentmihalyi and Larson, 1984). Fewer than 10 percent of American adolescents have no regular contact with their friends outside school. Behavior with friends varies enormously, consisting mostly of "socializing," that is, talking on the telephone (girls more than boys), hanging out, cruising, and having fun. Among adolescents in other cultures (for example, Japan), contacts among friends are not as frequent or as time-consuming as they are among American teenagers (Savin-Williams and Berndt, 1990).

Cliques and Crowds   Friendships are dyadic. Adolescents use the phrase "my friends" to refer to a superordinate entity consisting of more than one of these relationships. Actually, "my friends" refers to an aggregate that includes one's best friends, close friends, and good friends (and perhaps *their* friends as well). These aggregates, sometimes called *cliques* or *networks,* are important structural elements in the adolescent social world and are as ubiquitous as friendships (Brown, 1989). Sometimes normative pressure from a best friend is concordant with normative pressure extending across the social network, but sometimes not. For this reason, what "my friends" think is not a proxy for what "my best friend" thinks, and the research literature must be read in this light.

Larger and looser aggregates, called *crowds,* are also evident in adolescent social relations. Sometimes crowds are regarded as collections of cliques (Dunphy, 1963), sometimes as aggregations of individuals from overlapping cliques who share certain norms (Brown, 1989) such as investment in athletics (the sporties), school achievement (the debaters), or antisocial behavior (the toughs). Even though consensus is not evident concerning the best way to describe these higher-order aggregates, one point is certain: Neither friendship functioning nor social networks can be understood without reference to them.

Cliques and crowds characterize nearly all adolescent societies (at least in the West), but their specific contours vary according to community, ethnic, and historical contexts. Generally, the peer pressure associated with both cliques and crowds is multidimensional (encompasses more than a single social norm) and multidirectional (encompasses both socially sanctioned and unsanctioned norms). Pressure varies, too, with age and crowd affiliation (Brown, 1989).

At present, investigators do not have very good models with which to represent the individual adolescent within a hierarchical structure consisting of dyads, cliques, and crowds. Accordingly, we rarely consider adolescent behavior simultaneously in relation to these three contexts. Friendship relations receive more attention than either cliques or crowds probably because dyadic entities seem easier to study than polyadic ones and because most adolescents seem more invested in proximal than in distal social relations. But friendships and their significance in adolescent development cannot be appreciated out of context. Moreover, significant variation among teenagers can be traced to each of these contexts separately. For example, concordance in antisocial attitudes exists between two adolescent best friends (Kandel, 1978b), but similar concordance also exists among adolescents who "hang around together" (Cairns and others, 1988; Dishion, 1990b).

Summary   Friendships are among the most prominent features of the social landscape during adolescence. Although most teenagers consider themselves to have best friends, reciprocated friendship choices are not as common as adolescents claim. What it means to "have a friend," or, conversely, to be "friendless," varies according to the method used to identify these relationships. Cliques and crowds are other features of adolescent socialization that affect the manner in which friendships function. Currently, the interconnections among friendships, clique membership, and crowd membership are not well specified.

Friendship Stability

Friendships vary considerably in their stability. Some last for a long time, others for much shorter periods.

Beginnings, Middles, and Ends   Most friendships have beginnings, middles, and ends. Relatively little is known about the progression from one "stage" to another except that tremendous variation exists across relationships. Some friendships move quickly from beginning to end, others undergo lengthy "buildups"; some are short-lived and others long-lived. These variations are well recognized but seldom studied. Friendship dissolution occurs for myriad reasons. Personal characteristics (for example, emotional difficulties) are sometimes accompanied by friendship instability or friendlessness (Rutter and Garmezy, 1983). Relationship conditions (for example, a decreased sense of "common ground" or emotional support) may lead to friendship dissolution (Bukowski, Newcomb, and Hoza, 1987). Dissimilar attitudes toward important issues in the teenage culture also dispose toward breakup. Finally, exogenous factors may bring about friendship terminations, for example, school transitions (Berndt and Hawkins, 1991) and high school graduations (Shaver, Furman, and Buhrmester, 1985). Sometimes, the breakup is foreseeable: Unstable friends (who will eventually terminate their relationships) talk more frequently about disloyalty and lack of intimacy than do stable friends; they also report fewer contacts with one another (Berndt, Hawkins, and Hoyle, 1986).

How Stable?   Although some adolescent friendships terminate, most are relatively stable across time—clearly more stable than the friendships of elementary school children. Some investigators have found that both stability and reciprocity increase from early to late adolescence (Epstein, 1983), whereas others have reported that stability reaches a peak in preadolescence, increasing only a small amount thereafter (Berndt, 1982). Most adolescents in reciprocated friendships, however, report that their relationships have lasted for substantial lengths of time (Crockett, Losoff, and Petersen, 1984); various studies show that the percentage of these relationships that last at least a year range upward to 70 percent (Berndt, Hawkins, and Hoyle, 1986). These data suggest that adolescent friendships are far from ephemeral entities.

Since numerous conditions bring about friendship dissolution, it is not surprising to discover that friendship stability is multidetermined. For example, adolescents who have both positive attitudes about their relationships and frequent contacts prior to school transitions are likely to remain friends afterward (Berndt and Hawkins, 1991). Friendship stability thus reflects both how well the relationship "works" and whether or not the two individuals continue to spend time with one another.

Summary   Adolescent friendships are relatively stable. When they fail, friendships are terminated for both endogenous and exogenous reasons. In some instances, the common ground supporting the relationship simply dissolves; in other instances, school or family transitions lead to the termination. In most cases, the stability or instability of these relationships is determined by more than one condition.

Conditions of Friendship

Friendships are based on reciprocity and commitment between individuals who see themselves more or less as equals. In this context, reciprocity implies mutuality in orientations and feelings. But "being friends" also implies a special sensitivity and responsibility for one another; in this sense, friendships are committed or communal relationships (Clark, Mills, and Corcoran, 1989; Collins and Repinski, in press). And friends interact on an equal power base; friendships are thus egalitarian relationships. These three friendship conditions—reciprocity, commitment, and egalitarianism—are first fully understood and appreciated during the adolescent years.

Reciprocity   Among young children, friendship expectations center on common activities and concrete reciprocities. Preschool children, for example, understand that friends share food with one another, whereas this norm does not extend to those who are not friends (Birch and Billman, 1986). Among young children, friendship expectations center on common activities and concrete reciprocities. Common activities also undergird friendship relations in middle childhood, and adolescents expect to spend time with their friends and share activities too. But between middle childhood and middle adolescence, psychological sharing (intimacy) begins to assume significance in friendship relations (Bigelow and LaGaipa, 1980).

Intimacy differentiates middle childhood from adolescence more sharply than any other aspect of friendship relations. Indeed, the emergence of a need for intimacy (sharing thoughts and feelings with someone else) has long been regarded as the social threshold of adolescence (Sullivan, 1953). Empirical studies show that comments about shared feelings and self-disclosure appear initially in descriptions of friends during the transition to adolescence and increase steadily thereafter (Berndt, 1982; Bigelow and LaGaipa, 1980; Furman and Bierman, 1984; Furman and Buhrmester, 1992). When asked, in one investigation, to describe their relationships with their best friends in terms of self-disclosure and exchange of intimate information (for example, "I know how she feels about things without her telling me"), agreement with such statements increased between the ages of eleven and seventeen among both girls and boys (Sharabany, Gershoni, and Hofman, 1981). Manifestations of intimacy showing the greatest change with age were frankness and spontaneity, knowing and sensitivity, attachment, exclusiveness, and giving and sharing. Adolescents also expect friends, more frequently than anyone else, to meet their intimacy needs (Furman and Buhrmester, 1985).

Boys and girls both recognize that girls' relationships are more intimate than boys' (Bukowski and Kramer, 1986). Girls' assessments of their friendships show greater increases in intimacy from early to late adolescence (Sharabany, Gershoni, and Hofman, 1981); they report more frequent occurrences of self-disclosure (Rivenbark, 1971) and spend more time with their friends, on average, than do boys (Wong and Csikzentmihalyi, 1991). Some researchers have suggested that these differences may be more a matter of style than substance (Buhrmester and Furman, 1987); others have reported that the differences may reflect the greater variability of intimate behavior among boys than among girls. Youniss and Smollar (1985), for example, found that most girls describe their friendships in terms of shared activities, mutual intimacy, and understanding, whereas about 40 percent of boys describe their friendships similarly. Only about 30 percent of male relationships with friends, though, were described as guarded in communication and lacking in mutual understanding. Thus, developmental changes in intimacy must be considered against a background of sex and gender.

Adolescents and their friends thus clearly interact on the basis of reciprocity. Common interests and activities are important; intimacy is expected. Friendship expectations undergo considerable change across the transition to adolescence, but whether these changes represent cognitive elaborations of one core construct such as reciprocity (Youniss, 1980), structural transformations in the child's understanding of social relationships (Selman, 1980), or increased differentiation among relationships (Berndt and Perry, 1986; Collins and Repinski, in press) is not clear. The evidence suggests, however, that reciprocity undergirds friendship relations throughout childhood and adolescence, at the same time that the specific friendship expectations of adolescents differ from those characterizing children.

Commitment   When asked to describe their best friends (or ideal friends), both younger and older adolescents almost always mention loyalty and commitment: "A friend is a person that sticks by you when all the troubles come," and "Friends don't drop you as soon as something goes wrong" (Goodnow and Burns, 1988). Commitment is also cited by adolescents as a condition for friendship, and disloyalty is commonly the reason given for termination of a friendship. Children, in contrast, seldom mention commitment in their descriptions of best friends and seldom mention commitment issues in relation to either the strengthening or weakening of these relationships (Bigelow and LaGaipa, 1980).

Relatively little is known about the origins of social commitment, but its importance is apparent in the extent to which related constructs such as genuineness, loyalty, trust, and "being real" appear among friendship expectations. Collins and Repinski (in press) suggest that trust is one condition that attracts individuals to one another and enhances commitment. But where does trust come from? Theoretically, trust can be both a determinant and an outcome of social interaction. On the one hand, an individual's consistency and sensitivity elicit attributions by others of sincerity, truthfulness, and constancy. On the other hand, trust emerges when two individuals discover through cooperation that they can depend and rely on each other according to consensual norms (Youniss, 1980; Rotenberg and Pilipenko, 1983–1984). Trust is correlated with the quality of communication existing between adolescent friends (Armsden and Greenberg, 1987), and its appearance in adolescent friendship expectations has been linked to the greater stability of friendships among adolescents than among children (Hartup, 1992). Relatively little else, however, is known about this important friendship condition.

Conflict management is salient in the commitments of adolescent friends. Conflicts between friends are recognized as inevitable, but adolescents believe that friends have a special commitment to each other in managing conflicts: "A good friend is someone you fight with, but not forever" (Goodnow and Burns, 1988). Once again, effective conflict management is more than a friendship by-product: Effective management seems to be necessary to the continuation of these relationships and to the satisfaction that one receives from them. Accordingly, adolescents use negotiation rather than power assertion in managing their disagreements with friends, an ordering that differs from the ordering of strategies employed with parents (Laursen, 1993).

Conflicts and conflict resolutions are recognized by adolescents as events that sometimes strengthen friendships (Selman, 1980), but, generally, these relationships are seen as delicate balances of exchange in which self-interest must be weighed against consideration for the other, and conflict weighed against cooperation. Conflict management also differs between friends and nonfriends among younger children; age differences have not been directly assessed except in children's understanding of rules and responsibilities in conflicts with friends (Selman, 1980).

Equality   Peer relations are generally understood by children and adolescents to be structured horizontally rather than vertically; socializing is egalitarian, in contrast to the complementary interaction that marks relations with adults (Youniss, 1980). Consequently, both school-aged children and adolescents perceive themselves as having more power in relationships with same-sex friends than in relationships with adults (Furman, 1989). At the same time, the power base existing between same-sex friends is *not* regarded as exactly equal until midadolescence. Ratings, obtained using 5-point scales ranging from "they always [have the most power]" to "I always [have the most power]," showed that ten- and thirteen-year-olds perceived themselves as having a bit *less* power than their friends, whereas exact equivalence was evidenced only among sixteen- and nineteen-year-olds. This age difference was relatively small, but significant nevertheless. These results suggest that children and younger adolescents perceive themselves as yielding to their friends more than vice versa, whereas older adolescents do not. This interpretation is consistent with earlier results showing that conformity to peer pressure generally declines across the adolescent years (Costanzo and Shaw, 1966).

Power imbalances have important implications within relationships in that strategies for conflict resolution are related directly to them. For example, Cowan, Drinkard, and MacGavin (1984) showed that preferred modes of resolving conflicts varied according to perceived differences in relative power between competitors: With friends, both children and adolescents preferred negotiation and bargaining (strategies that always predominate when competitors are equally powerful), whereas, with adults, submission was more likely (the usual strategy when one competitor perceives himself or herself to be less powerful than the other).

Summary   The main conditions that support friendships among adolescents are reciprocity, commitment, and equality. Similar conditions support friendships among younger children, but specific manifestations differ from those supporting these relationships among adolescents.

Similarities Among Friends

Friends are similar to one another in many respects. These similarities, however, occur for several reasons.

Demographic Concordances   Adolescent friends are similar in age, race, sex, and social class. Within school grades, age concordances are not especially noteworthy, but, within schools, they are very evident. Racial concordances are also strong, and more extensive in adolescence than in middle childhood (Asher, Singleton, and Taylor, 1988). Concordances in social class are relatively constant from early to late adolescence (Epstein, 1983).

The most clear-cut concordance among adolescent friends relates to sex (see Hartup, 1983). Friendships (especially best friends) are same-sex relationships virtually by definition, so cross-sex friendships are rare. Actually, cross-sex friendships, as distinguished from romantic relationships, account for only about 5 percent of friendships in early to middle adolescence. Romantic relationships, of course, become increasingly common, but the frequency of boy-girl best friendships remains about the same as in middle childhood. Only by late adolescence does this concordance decline; Epstein (1983) reported gender concordances to be a bit more than .90 between grades six and nine, falling to about .70 among high school seniors.

Behavioral Concordances   Behavioral concordances between friends are not as strong as demographic concordances but are nevertheless appreciable. Adolescents are most similar to their friends in two general areas: (1) school-related attitudes, aspirations, and achievement (Epstein, 1983; Kandel, 1978b), and (2) attitudes and behaviors that are significant in the contemporary teenage culture, such as smoking, drinking, drug use, dating, and church attendance (Kandel, 1978b; Epstein, 1983; Karweit, 1983; Urberg, Halliday-Scher, and Tolson, 1991). Personality characteristics and social attitudes are not very concordant; friends are generally dissimilar in self-esteem, sociability, and closeness to parents. Concordances in intelligence are also not strong (Kandel, 1978b).

Similarities among friends are not greatly different for boys and girls. Boys are somewhat more likely than girls to be discordant in social class (Epstein, 1983), but, otherwise, male-female differences in these concordances occur mainly in sexual activity. Among eighth-, ninth-, and tenth-grade girls (both black and white) in the United States, friends were found to be similar in sexual behavior and attitudes, even when age and antisocial attitudes were taken into account. Among boys in these same grades, however, sexual activity (especially sexual intercourse) was not strongly concordant (Billy, Rodgers, and Udry, 1984). The reasons for this sex difference are not clear, although sexual intercourse is more directly related to social reputation among girls than it is among boys. Reputational differences, together with the greater readiness of females to engage in self-disclosure, may account for this sex difference.

Homophiletic Processes   Similarities among friends derive from three main sources: demographic homophilies, selective homophilies, and mutual socialization. Certain similarities result, first, from the manner in which the adolescent social world is organized. Demographic forces, for example, determine the segregation of neighborhoods and schools by social class and race, attitudes and abilities, norms and values. Schools are also age-graded. These demographic realities mean that adolescents have more opportunities for contact with other adolescents who are similar rather than dissimilar to themselves in age, sex, race, and social class. But social class concordances in friendship choice are somewhat reduced when schools are "highly participatory" (that is, when students all know one another and engage in many different activities) (Epstein, 1983). Racial concordances are also somewhat reduced in desegregated as compared to segregated schools (Schofield, 1982).

Similarities among friends also derive from the well-known human tendency for choosing close associates who resemble oneself (Berscheid and Walster, 1969). Socializing with a similar individual is more stimulating and rewarding than socializing with someone whose interests are vastly different; equity and reciprocity in social interaction are more likely; emotional support and consensual validation are more forthcoming; conflict and contention are minimized. Friends are never completely homomorphic, of course, and the importance of differences in friendship functioning should not be ignored, even though there is substantial evidence that friends are similar to one another.

Similarities among friends do not tell us whether adolescents select one another on the basis of similarity or whether they become similar through mutual socialization; cross-sectional data do not disentangle selection and socialization effects. Longitudinal studies reveal, however, that similarities among friends derive from both sources. Kandel (1978a), for example, found that changes in behavior over the course of a school year (in drug use, educational aspirations, involvement in delinquency) stemmed from both selection and socialization, in approximately equal amounts. Other studies have shown that friends socialize one another in their attitudes toward school and academic achievement (Epstein, 1983), sexual behavior (Billy and Udry, 1985), and use of alcohol and cigarettes (Fisher and Baumann, 1988). Relative contributions of selection and socialization to similarities among friends, however, are not always clear in these studies. One exception is that selection seems to be more important than socialization in cigarette and alcohol use (Fisher and Baumann, 1988). Such variations mean that the relative contribution of selection and socialization to friendship relations must be estimated separately for each attribute.

Summary   Friends are notably similar in sex, age, race, and social class. Behavioral similarities are most evident in educational and other normative attitudes. Friends select one another on the basis of these similarities but also socialize one another so as to become even more similar over time.

Friendships and Social Adaptation

The significance of adolescent friendships extends beyond their ubiquity. Many investigators have argued that "having friends" amounts to a developmental imperative: Good developmental outcomes depend on having friends and keeping them, friendships furnish the individual with socialization opportunities not easily obtained elsewhere (including experiences in intimacy and conflict management), and these relationships are important in emotion regulation, in self-understanding, and in formation and functioning of subsequent relationships (including romantic relationships). Folk wisdom, however, argues that people are known by the company they keep, suggesting that one's friends may exert negative as well as positive influences. There is also considerable research evidence of these influences. Consequently, *having friends,* the *identity of one's friends,* and the *quality of one's friendships* must be regarded as different variables with different developmental implications. These dimensions in friendship relations are addressed separately in the following sections.

Having Friends   Children who are disliked by other children are at risk in general, mostly for antisocial behavior in adolescence and early adulthood and for early school leaving (Parker and Asher, 1987). Being disliked and being without friends, however, are different attributes, even though rejected children have fewer friends than do popular children (Bukowski and Hoza, 1989). Estimates vary, but between 10 percent and 20 percent of rejected children and adolescents actually have friends (Hartup, 1992).

Correlational studies demonstrate that children who have reciprocated friendships are more socially competent than are children who do not. They evidence more mature perspective taking (Jones and Bowling, 1988), enter groups more easily, engage in more cooperative play, are more sociable, and have fewer difficulties with other children (Howes, 1989). School-aged children who have been referred to guidance clinics are more likely to be friendless than are nonreferred children, and, when they have them, their friendships are less stable over time (Rutter and Garmezy, 1983). Among adolescents, those with stable friendships are more altruistic than those without them (Mannarino, 1976); self-esteem is also greater (Mannarino, 1978; Bukowski, Newcomb, and Hoza, 1987). Friendless children and adolescents, in contrast, report loneliness and depression (Asher, Hymel, and Renshaw, 1984).

Correlational results are difficult to interpret. Having friends may enhance social adaptation, but the reverse may also be true. Alternatively, being sociable and having friends may derive from a common source, such as good social relationships in early childhood. Longitudinal studies assist in disentangling these effects, and research with both children and adolescents suggests that having friends contributes constructively to social adjustment. With data collected from fourth and fifth graders over a one-year interval, Bukowski, Hoza, and Newcomb (1991) showed that having friends was causally related to self-esteem but not to the children's attributions about their own social skills. Being liked (being popular), however, was causally related to self-reports about social competence but not to self-esteem. Self-worth thus appears to depend on having friends, while self-perceptions of social competence depend on being popular. Concordantly, disturbances in self-concept and social adjustment that are generally associated with school transitions during adolescence are reduced when school changes occur in the company of good friends (Simmons, Burgeson, and Reef, 1988).

Having friends may also contribute to romantic and sexual socialization. First, "having friends" as well as "having a friend to confide in" between the ages of nine and twelve were reported significantly more often by undergraduate students who had a sexual experience in childhood *with another child* than by students who did not report an experience of this kind (Haugaard and Tilly, 1988). Since most of these friendships were same-sex and most of the sexual encounters were cross-sex, these data suggest that friendships are significant in sexual socialization. But "having friends" and "having a childhood sexual experience" may both reflect some common source of variance such as self-esteem or social attractiveness, so a causal connection between them cannot be inferred. Longitudinal data, however, show that having friends between eight and twelve years of age forecasts romantic relationships between fourteen and seventeen years of age, and having a same-sex friend between fourteen and seventeen forecasts having a romantic relationship between eighteen and twenty-three (Neeman, Hubbard, and Kojetin, 1991). Note that significant correlations occurred in only one direction; same-sex friendships forecast romantic relationships, but not the reverse. Consequently, Sullivan's (1953) notions that same-sex relationships facilitate the formation and functioning of cross-sex relationships may be correct. Whether or not friendships are stepping-stones to gay and lesbian relationships is not known.

Research data suggest, then, that having a best friend is causally linked to a good developmental outcome. Friendship quality, however, was not differentiated in the studies cited above. Most likely, in these investigations, having a friend amounted to having a *good, supportive* friend, a confounding that makes it difficult to tell whether the sheer existence of these relationships or their qualities account for the outcomes noted. Friendships are not all alike, and other studies have demonstrated that who one's friends are and what these relationships are like also determine developmental outcomes.

The Company They Keep   Similarities among adolescent friends increase over time, which suggests that the company one keeps bears directly on social adjustment. Socialization effects have been demonstrated for smoking and drinking, drug use, and delinquency, as well as for educational aspirations and achievement. Taken together, these results suggest that children and adolescents who behave more-or-less normatively contribute positively to the socialization of their friends, whereas others may contribute negatively.

Several data sets reveal these dynamics clearly: Ball (1981) reported that among teenagers in lower-ranking academic streams in British schools, many individuals contributed negatively to the school success of their friends through their disruptiveness and general disinterest in school. Friends were more positive influences in higher-ranking streams, given that they were more likely to discourage disruptive, distracting behaviors and to encourage achievement. Actually, these results highlight two friendship issues: First, friends contribute either positively or negatively to adolescent socialization. Second, societal forces (for example, streaming) frequently restrict friendship opportunities to individuals who resemble one another. As mentioned earlier, friendships derive only partly from choice: Whether two individuals become friends depends on their opportunity to meet, and which individuals meet depends on the organization of the social world.

Friendship networks as well as friendship dyads demonstrate the importance of the company that one keeps. For example, aggressiveness distinguishes children who "hang around together," beginning among boys in middle childhood and becoming evident among both sexes by early adolescence (Cairns and others, 1988). Antisocial behavior (and its more deviant forms) increases among network members who are attracted to one another originally because of shared interests in antisocial activities. Actually, antisocial adolescents originate in families in which parents do not use discipline effectively or monitor their children closely (Dishion, 1990a). Such family circumstances establish children as "troublesome," which, in turn, reduces their attractiveness to others and increases the likelihood that their friends will be antisocial (Snyder, Dishion, and Patterson, 1986). Marijuana use among adolescents also seems to derive from a causal chain that begins with poor parenting, extends to the selection of friends who engage in marijuana use and other delinquent behaviors, and then involves further socialization in deviant behavior (Kandel and Andrews, 1987). Conversely, among adolescents who are at risk for antisocial behavior, "desisting" is predicted more strongly by a turning away from antisocial friends than by any other variable (Mulvey and Aber, 1988). Network socialization among adolescent friends thus resembles "shopping" or "foraging" for companions with whom there is common ground and mutual reinforcement that will sustain the network and the normative behaviors that bind its members together (Patterson and Bank, 1989).

This "shopping" model may not apply in the same way in every circumstance. In Steinberg, Dornbusch, and Brown's (1992) investigation, the academic performance of white, African American, Asian American, and Hispanic American adolescents was studied in relation to support for achievement provided by parents and friends. Students in every group whose families and friends supported academic achievement performed better than those who received support from only one source. But cultural variations were evident in the manner in which family relations and peer pressure were correlated with achievement. Among white youngsters, "authoritative" parent-child relations (that is, firm discipline, warmth, high standards) were common, disposing the children toward friendship networks that, in turn, encouraged academic success. For reasons not completely understood, however, no correlation existed between parenting practices and network affiliation among the minority students. Dynamics differed across ethnic groups: Among Asian American students, generally strong support for achievement from friends tended to offset generally negative consequences of authoritarian parenting; among African American students, generally weak support for academic achievement from friends undermined the positive effects of authoritative parenting; and Hispanic American students suffered from a combination of both parenting and friendship influences, neither of which disposed the students toward academic achievement.

The company they keep, then, has major significance in adolescents' socialization. One's friends are determined on the basis of a synergy involving both family and peer experiences as well as the organization of the adolescent social world. Different causal models may be needed, however, to describe this synergy across different cultures and for different norms.

Friendship Qualities   Some friendships are secure and smooth-sailing; others are rocky with disagreement and contention. Some friends describe their relationships as supportive and intimate; others describe theirs as rivalrous and absent of intimacy. Qualitative differences such as these are closely related to social and emotional adjustment during the teenage years: The belief that one's friends are not supportive is associated with depression and other symptomatology, especially among girls (Compas, Slavin, Wagner, and Cannatta, 1986; Feldman, Rubenstein, and Rubin, 1988), psychological and school-related problems (Kurdek and Sinclair, 1988), negative perceptions by classmates (Berndt and Hawkins, 1991), lower self-esteem (Mannarino, 1976; McGuire and Weisz, 1982), and less favorable self-perceptions of scholastic, athletic, and social competence than found when friends are considered supportive (Perry, 1987). Adolescents who perceive their friendships as supportive are more likely to be popular and considered socially competent than are adolescents with less supportive friendships (Cauce, 1986); they are also more strongly motivated to achieve, are more involved in school, have higher achievement test scores, receive higher grades, and exhibit fewer behavioral problems (Berndt and Hawkins, 1991; Cauce, 1986).

Once again, correlational findings are difficult to interpret. Satisfying friendships, for example, may constitute rose-colored glasses through which the entire world seems beautiful, as opposed to the darker glasses constituted by unsatisfying friendships. Alternatively, supportive relationships may assist adolescents in stress management and problem solving, thereby enhancing social adjustment. Or good social relations and good social adjustment may simply both be manifestations of general sociability.

Here, too, longitudinal studies assist the disentangling of effects: Berndt and Keefe (1992) asked teenagers in the fall and the spring of a school year about positive and negative qualities in their friendships (for example, emotional support and intimacy, as well as conflicts and rivalry). School involvement and conduct were rated by both the children and their teachers; grades were also studied. Correlations between friendship quality and school adjustment were calculated separately during the fall and the spring and showed again that good friendships and good school adjustment go hand in hand. Most important, regression analyses showed that students whose friendships were most intimate and supportive in the fall became increasingly involved in school, whereas those whose friendships were marred by conflict and rivalry became more disruptive and progressively less involved in school. Qualitative features of these relationships thus forecast *changes* in school adjustment. So, while supportive friendships and good school adjustment may each reflect adolescent adaptation separately, the evidence suggests that friendship quality also directly affects academic attitudes. Whether these effects extend to areas other than school adjustment is not known; additional studies are required before more can be said about friendships and their developmental significance.

Summary   Existing evidence suggests that having friends and having supportive friends are associated with two outcome clusters: (1) feeling good about oneself, feeling socially connected, and being positive (nondepressed) in outlook, and (2) being successful in subsequent relationships, especially romantic ones. The mechanisms responsible for the correlation between having friends and behavioral outcome have not been clearly established, so the findings may mean little more than that good self-attitudes are reflected in good relationships, and vice versa. But other interpretations are plausible; for example, supportive interactions with friends probably furnish adolescents with the kind of feedback and reinforcement needed for generating self-esteem. At the same time, these transactions can serve as exemplars for other relationships, with members of both the same and the opposite sex. According to this interpretation, friendship experience contributes mainly to self-attitudes and "relationship potential" rather than to general sociability or social competence.

The company one keeps (who one's friends are) contributes to adolescent socialization, too, but mainly to the kinds of norms that one internalizes, not to self-esteem or capacities for forming and maintaining relationships. Antisocial friends are likely to be antisocial influences; prosocial friends are likely to be prosocial influences. Both antisocial and prosocial friends can thus contribute positively to social adaptation as long as friendships are supportive and smooth-running. But this state of affairs also means that adolescent friendships may be both "protective" and "risk" factors—at one and the same time.

New Directions

Current research extends beyond the interest of adolescents in their friends and beyond what they expect of them. There are at least four cutting-edge issues to which investigators need to turn their attention: models for demonstrating developmental significance, processes by which friends socialize one another, qualitative differentiation among adolescent friendships, and cultural diversity in their dynamics and implications.

Developmental Models   One of the most promising new directions in research on children and adolescents is the increased effort to understand the concatenations within families and within friendship relations that together determine the course of social and emotional development. Until recently, family relations and friendship relations were regarded as nearly separate sources of variation in developmental outcome, and friendships were believed to carry relatively little weight. New models and methods, however, are challenging these notions. On the one hand, investigators are specifying the affective and cognitive processes that tie family and friendship experiences together in adolescent development. On the other hand, investigators are examining the causal chains in which family socialization constrains friendship relations, which, in turn, affect the behavior of the individual adolescent. Research in behavioral genetics is also part of this investigative effort, since individual differences in both cooperation and aggression do not seem to be completely determined by environmental variations. Different developmental models, compared and contrasted using complex quantitative methods, are being used. The work thus far indicates that having friends, the company one keeps, and friendship quality each belong in these equations, but much more needs to be done.

Modes of Social Influence   Most theories accounting for the socialization that occurs among friends are little more than theories of conformity, that is, theories dealing with group pressures and the individual's reactions to them (Berndt and Savin-Williams, in press). Social influences among friends are seldom examined as mutual, dyadic, dynamic entities. We must give greater attention to coercion, compliance, and conflict resolution, as well as to reinforcement and support in friendship interaction, considering always that these processes are dyadically regulated and occur in a time series. Finally, we seldom recognize that friends interact within higher-order social structures in which group decision making and other group interactions occur (Berndt and Savin-Williams, in press; Hinde, 1992). We still lack good models to account for the manner in which dyadic interaction between friends is moderated by the social networks to which each individual belongs, and this deficiency must be corrected. Distinctions also must be made between social influences deriving from "my best friend" and those deriving from "my friends." Relatively little is known about this entire range of processes, and relevant studies have not yet been conducted.

Friendship Qualities   One of the most significant recent advances in research dealing with adolescent friendships is the discovery that these relationships are not all alike. Considerable progress has been made in differentiating among them. Using factor analysis, Berndt and Perry (1986) discovered that the simple differentiation of "positive" and "negative" relationship features greatly assists the study of the correlates and developmental significance of friendships, among both children and adolescents. Scales are also available for differentiating among these relationships in terms of intimacy (Sharabany, Gershoni, and Hofman, 1981) and closeness (Repinski, 1992). Distinctions have also been drawn between interdependent and disengaged relationships. But these are preliminary refinements. Friendships vary along many other dimensions, including security, diversity, the balance of power within them, and commitment (Hinde, 1979; Hartup and Sancilio, 1986). More thorough descriptions of friendships thus remain an important research objective.

Cultural Diversity   The research community still does not fully recognize that friendship processes may vary in terms of cultural and ethnic contexts. Studies have already shown that the combined influences of families and friends on academic achievement during adolescence are different across ethnic groups (Steinberg, Dornbusch, and Brown, 1992). Whatever our progress in race relations over the past forty years in the United States, adolescent societies remain segregated; the vast majority of adolescent friendships involve youngsters of the same race. Social attraction, social influence, and the social implications of adolescent friendships may be similar across ethnic groups in some ways but are undoubtedly different in other ways. At present, what we know about friendships and their developmental significance derives mainly from studies of white children and adolescents. But now that we are aware of the central role of friendship relations in social development and adaptation, some of the newly available federal funds for normative research on minority children and adolescents should be committed to the investigation of cultural diversity.

Conclusion

Current data suggest that the developmental significance of adolescent friendships extends beyond their ubiquity. The conditions giving rise to these relationships—reciprocity, commitment, and equality—are understood differently by children and by adolescents, and the stability of these relationships varies accordingly. Recent studies indicate that three dimensions of adolescent friendships affect the course of the individuals' development: having friends, who one's friends are, and the quality of the friendship. The influences of family and friends combine to determine developmental outcomes, but much remains to be learned about these synergies, especially as they are played out during adolescence. Dyadic processes, through which friends influence each other, must be better conceptualized, friendship qualities must be more precisely differentiated, and cultural differences in friendship dynamics must be better documented. The active pursuit of these objectives in the years ahead promises to be fruitful.

References

Armsden, G. C., and Greenberg, M. T. "The Inventory of Parent and Peer Attachment: Individual Differences and Their Relationship to Psychological Well-being in Adolescence." *Journal of Youth and Adolescence,* 1987, *16,* 427–454.

Asher, S. R., Hymel, S., and Renshaw, P. D. "Loneliness in Children." *Child Development,* 1984, *55,* 1456–1464.

Asher, S. R., Singleton, L. C., and Taylor, A. R. "Acceptance Versus Friendship: A Longitudinal Study of Racial Integration." Unpublished manuscript, Bureau of Educational Research, University of Illinois, 1988.

Ball, S. J. *Beachside Comprehensive.* Cambridge, England: Cambridge University Press, 1981.

Berndt, T. J. "The Features and Effects of Friendship in Early Adolescence." *Child Development,* 1982, *53,* 1447–1460.

Berndt, T. J., and Hawkins, J. A. "Effects of Friendship on Adolescents' Adjustment to Junior High School." Unpublished manuscript, Psychological Sciences, Purdue University, 1991.

Berndt, T. J., Hawkins, J. A., and Hoyle, S. G. "Changes in Friendship During a School Year: Effects on Children's and Adolescents' Impressions of Friendship and Sharing with Friends." *Child Development,* 1986, *57,* 1284–1297.

Berndt, T. J., and Keefe, K. "Friends' Influence on Adolescents' Perceptions of Themselves at School." In D. H. Schunk and J. L. Meece (eds.), *Student Perceptions in the Classroom.* Hillsdale, N.J.: Erlbaum, 1992.

Berndt, T. J., and Perry, T. B. "Children's Perceptions of Friendships as Supportive Relationships." *Developmental Psychology,* 1986, *22,* 640–648.

Berndt, T. J., and Savin-Williams, R. C. "Variations in Friendships and Peer-Group Relationships in Adolescence." In P. Tolan and B. Cohler (eds.), *Handbook of Clinical Research and Practice with Adolescents.* New York: Wiley, in press.

Berscheid, E., and Walster, E. *Interpersonal Attraction.* Reading, Mass.: Addison-Wesley, 1969.

Bigelow, B. J., and LaGaipa, J. J. "The Development of Friendship Values and Choice." In H. C. Foot, A. J. Chapman, and J. R. Smith (eds.), *Friendship and Social Relations in Children.* New York: Wiley, 1980.

Billy, J. O. G., Rodgers, J. L., and Udry, J. R. "Adolescent Sexual Behavior and Friendship Choice." *Social Forces,* 1984, *62,* 653–678.

Billy, J. O. G., and Udry, J. R. "The Influence of Male and Female Best Friends on Adolescent Sexual Behavior." *Adolescence,* 1985, *20,* 21–32.

Birch, L. L., and Billman, J. "Preschool Children's Food Sharing with Friends and Acquaintances." *Child Development,* 1986, *57,* 387–395.

Brown, B. B. "The Role of Peer Groups in Adolescents' Adjustment to Secondary School." In T. J. Berndt and G. W. Ladd (eds.), *Peer Relationships in Child Development.* New York: Wiley, 1989.

Buhrmester, D., and Furman, W. "The Development of Companionship and Intimacy." *Child Development,* 1987, *58,* 1101–1113.

Bukowski, W. M., and Hoza, B. "Popularity and Friendship: Issues in Theory, Measurement, and Outcome." In T. J. Berndt and G. W. Ladd (eds.), *Peer Relationships in Child Development.* New York: Wiley, 1989.

Bukowski, W. M., Hoza, B., and Newcomb, A. F. "Friendship, Popularity, and the 'Self' during Early Adolescence." Unpublished manuscript, Department of Psychology, Concordia University, 1991.

Bukowski, W. M., and Kramer, T. L. "Judgments of the Features of Friendship Among Early Adolescent Boys and Girls." *Journal of Early Adolescence,* 1986, *6,* 331–338.

Bukowski, W. M., Newcomb, A. F., and Hoza, B. "Friendship Conceptions Among Early Adolescents: A. Longitudinal Study of Stability and Change." *Journal of Early Adolescence,* 1987, *7,* 143–152.

Cairns, R. B., Cairns, B. D., Neckerman, H. J., Gest, S., and Garieppy, J. L. "Peer Networks and Aggressive Behavior: Peer Support or Peer Rejection?" *Developmental Psychology,* 1988, *24,* 815–823.

Cauce, A. M. "Social Networks and Social Competence: Exploring the Effects of Early Adolescent Friendships." *American Journal of Community Psychology,* 1986, *14,* 607–628.

Clark, M. S., Mills, J. R., and Corcoran, D. M. "Keeping Track of Needs and Inputs of Friends and Strangers." *Personality and Social Psychology Bulletin,* 1989, *15,* 533–542.

Collins, W. A. and Repinski, D. J. "Relationships During Adolescence: Continuity and Change in Interpersonal Perspective." In R. Montemayor, G. R. Adams, and T. P. Gullotta (eds.), *Advances in Adolescent Development.* Vol. 5: *Personal Relationships During Adolescence.* Newbury Park, Calif.: Sage, in press.

Compas, B. E., Slavin, L. A., Wagner, B. M., and Cannatta, K. "Relationship of Life Events and Social Support with Psychological Dysfunction Among Adolescents." *Journal of Youth and Adolescence,* 1986, *15,* 205–221.

Costanzo, P. R., and Shaw, M. E. "Conformity as a Function of Age Level." *Child Development,* 1966, *37,* 967–975.

Cowan, G., Drinkard, J., and MacGavin, L. "The Effects of Target, Age, and Gender on Use of Power Strategies." *Journal of Personality and Social Psychology,* 1984, *47,* 1391–1398.

Crockett, L., Losoff, M., and Petersen, A. C. "Perceptions of the Peer Group and Friendship in Early Adolescence." *Journal of Early Adolescence,* 1984, *4,* 155–181.

Csikzentmihalyi, M., and Larson, R. *Being Adolescent.* New York: Basic Books, 1984.

Dishion, T. J. "The Family Ecology of Boys' Peer Relations in Middle Childhood." *Child Development,* 1990a, *61,* 874–892.

Dishion, T. J. "The Peer Context of Troublesome Child and Adolescent Behavior." In P. Leone (ed.), *Understanding Troubled and Troublesome Youth.* Newbury Park, Calif.: Sage, 1990b.

Dunphy, D. C. "The Social Structure of Urban Adolescent Peer Groups." *Sociometry,* 1963, *26,* 230–246.

Epstein, J. L. "Examining Theories of Adolescent Friendship." In J. L. Epstein and N. L. Karweit (eds.), *Friends in School.* San Diego: Academic Press, 1983.

Feldman, S. S., Rubenstein, J. L., and Rubin, C. "Depressive Affect and Restraint in Early Adolescence: Relationships with Family Structure, Family Process, and Friendship Support." *Journal of Early Adolescence,* 1988, *8,* 279–296.

Fisher, L. A., and Baumann, K. E. "Influence and Selection in the Friend-Adolescent Relationship: Findings from Studies of Adolescent Smoking and Drinking." *Journal of Applied Social Psychology,* 1988, *18,* 289–314.

Furman, W. "The Development of Children's Social Networks." In D. Belle (ed.), *Children's Social Networks and Social Supports.* New York: Wiley, 1989.

Furman, W., and Bierman, K. L. "Children's Conceptions of Friendship: A Multi-Method Study of Developmental Changes." *Developmental Psychology,* 1984, *20,* 925–931.

Furman, W., and Buhrmester, D. "Children's Perceptions of the Personal Relationships in Their Social Networks." *Developmental Psychology,* 1985, *21,* 1016–1024.

Furman, W., and Buhrmester, D. "Age and Sex Differences in Perceptions of Networks of Personal Relationships." *Child Development,* 1992, *63,* 103–115.

Goodnow, J. J., and Burns, A. *Home and School: Child's Eye View.* Sydney: Allen & Unwin, 1988.

Hartup, W. W. "Peer Relations." In E. M. Hetherington (ed.), *Handbook of Child Psychology.* Vol. 4: *Socialization, Personality, and Social Development.* New York: Wiley, 1983.

Hartup, W. W. "Friendships and Their Developmental Significance." In H. McGurk (ed.), *Childhood Social Development.* Hove, England: Erlbaum, 1992.

Hartup, W. W., and Sancilio, M. F. "Children's Friendships." In E. Schopler and G. B. Mesibov (eds.), *Social Behavior in Autism.* New York: Plenum, 1986.

Haugaard, J. J., and Tilly, C. "Characteristics Predicting Children's Responses to Sexual Encounters with Other Children." *Child Abuse and Neglect,* 1988, *12,* 209–218.

Hinde, R. A. *Towards Understanding Relationships.* London: Academic Press, 1979.

Hinde, R. A. "Developmental Psychology in the Context of Other Behavioral Sciences." *Developmental Psychology,* 1992, *28,* 1018–1029.

Howes, C. *Peer Interaction of Young Children.* Monographs of the Society for Research in Child Development, vol. 53 (serial no. 217). Chicago: University of Chicago Press, 1989.

Jones, D. C., and Bowling, B. "Preschool Friends and Affective Knowledge: A Comparison of Mutual and Unilateral Friends." Paper presented at the Conference on Human Development, Charleston, South Carolina, Mar. 1988.

Kandel, D. B. "Homophily, Selection, and Socialization in Adolescent Friendships." *American Journal of Sociology,* 1978a, *84,* 427–436.

Kandel, D. B. "Similarity in Real-life Adolescent Pairs." *Journal of Personality and Social Psychology,* 1978b, *36,* 306–312.

Kandel, D. B., and Andrews, K. "Processes of Adolescent Socialization by Parents and Peers." *International Journal of the Addictions,* 1987, *22,* 319–342.

Karweit, N. "Extracurricular Activities and Friendship Selection." In J. L. Epstein and N. Karweit (eds.), *Friends in School.* San Diego: Academic Press, 1983.

Kurdek, L. A., and Sinclair, R. J. "Adjustment of Young Adolescents in Two-Parent Nuclear, Stepfather, and Mother-Custody Families." *Journal of Consulting and Clinical Psychology,* 1988, *56,* 91–96.

Laursen, B., *Close Friendships in Adolescence.* San Francisco: Jossey-Bass, 1993.

McGuire, K. D., and Weisz, J. R. "Social Cognition and Behavior Correlates of Preadolescent Chumships." *Child Development,* 1982, *53,* 1478–1484.

Mannarino, A. P. "Friendship Patterns and Altruistic Behavior in Preadolescent Males." *Developmental Psychology,* 1976, *12,* 555–556.

Mannarino, A. P. "Friendship Patterns and Self-Concept Development in Preadolescent Males." *Journal of Genetic Psychology,* 1978, *133,* 105–110.

Mulvey, E. P., and Aber, M. S. "Growing Out of Delinquency: Development and Desistance." In R. Jenkins and W. Brown (eds.), *The Abandonment of Delinquent Behavior: Promoting the Turn-Around.* New York: Praeger, 1988.

Neeman, J. D., Hubbard, J., and Kojetin, B. A. "Continuity in Quality of Friendships and Romantic Relationships from Childhood to Adolescence." Poster presented at the biennial meeting of the Society for Research in Child Development, Seattle, Apr. 1991.

Parker, J. G., and Asher, S. R. "Peer Relations and Later Personal Adjustment: Are Low-Accepted Children at Risk?" *Psychological Bulletin,* 1987, *102,* 357–389.

Patterson, G. R., and Bank, L. "Some Amplifier and Dampening Mechanisms for Pathologic Processes in Families." In M. Gunnar and E. Thelen (eds.), *Minnesota Symposia on Child Psychology.* Vol. 22. Hillsdale, N.J.: Erlbaum, 1989.

Perry, T. B. "The Relation of Adolescent Self-Perceptions to Their Social Relationships." Unpublished doctoral dissertation, Department of Psychology, University of Oklahoma, 1987.

Reisman, J. M., and Shorr, S. I. "Friendship Claims and Expectations Among Children and Adults." *Child Development,* 1978, *49,* 913–916.

Repinski, D. J. "Closeness in Parent-Adolescent Relationships: Contrasting Interdependence, Emotional Tone, and a Subjective Rating." Unpublished manuscript, Institute of Child Development, University of Minnesota, 1992.

Rivenbark, W. H. "Self-Disclosure Patterns Among Adolescents." *Psychological Reports,* 1971, *28,* 35–42.

Rotenberg, K. J., and Pilipenko, T. A. "Mutuality, Temporal Consistency, and Helpfulness in Children's Trust in Peers." *Social Cognition,* 1983–1984, *2,* 235–255.

Rutter, M., and Garmezy, N. "Developmental Psychopathology." In E. M. Hetherington (ed.), *Handbook of Child Psychology,* Vol. 4: *Socialization, Social Development, and Personality.* New York: Wiley, 1983.

Savin-Williams, R. C., and Berndt, T. J. "Friendship and Peer Relations." In S. S. Feldman and G. R. Elliott (eds.), *At the Threshold: The Developing Adolescent*. Cambridge, Mass.: Harvard University Press, 1990.

Schofield, J. W. *Black and White in School: Trust, Tension, or Tolerance?* New York: Praeger, 1982.

Selman, R. L. *The Growth of Interpersonal Understanding: Developmental and Clinical Analyses*. San Diego: Academic Press, 1980.

Sharabany, R., Gershoni, R., and Hofman, J. E. "Girlfriend, Boyfriend: Age and Sex Differences in Intimate Friendship." *Developmental Psychology*, 1981, *17*, 800–808.

Shaver, P., Furman, W., and Buhrmester, D. "Transition to College; Network Changes, Social Skills, and Loneliness." In S. Duck and D. Perlman (eds.), *Understanding Personal Relationships: An Interdisciplinary Approach*. London: Sage, 1985.

Simmons, R. G., Burgeson, R., and Reef, M. J. "Cumulative Change at Entry to Adolescence." In M. Gunnar and W. A. Collins (eds.), *Minnesota Symposia on Child Psychology*. Vol. 21. Hillsdale, N.J.: Erlbaum, 1988.

Snyder, J., Dishion, T. J., and Patterson, G. R. "Determinants and Consequences of Associating with Deviant Peers During Preadolescence and Adolescence." *Journal of Early Adolescence*, 1986, *6*, 29–43.

Steinberg, L., Dornbusch, S. M., and Brown, B. B. "Ethnic Differences in Adolescent Achievement: An Ecological Perspective." *American Psychologist*, 1992, *47*, 723–729.

Sullivan, H. S. *The Interpersonal Theory of Psychiatry*. New York: Norton, 1953.

Urberg, K. A., Halliday-Scher, K., and Tolson, J. M. "Similarity Between Adolescent Best Friends." Paper presented at the biennial meeting of the Society for Research in Child Development, Seattle, Apr. 1991.

Wong, M. M., and Csikzentmihalyi, M. "Affiliation Motivation and Daily Experience: Some Issues on Gender Differences." *Journal of Personality and Social Psychology*, 1991, *60*, 154–164.

Youniss, J. *Parents and Peers in Social Development: A Piaget-Sullivan Perspective*. Chicago: University of Chicago Press, 1980.

Youniss, J., and Smollar, J. *Adolescent Relations with Mothers, Fathers, and Friends*. Chicago: University of Chicago Press, 1985.

Questions

1. What are the costs and benefits of forming friendships with people similar to oneself?

2. What are the differences between male and female friendships? Is it fair to characterize male friendships as lacking in intimacy?

3. What is the contribution of parenting style to the nature of adolescent friendships?

4. What contribution does friendship make to the developmental tasks of identity, intimacy, and autonomy from parents?

References and Further Reading

Bukowski, W. M., Hoza, B., & Boivin, M. (1993). Popularity, friendship, and emotional adjustment during early adolescence. *New Directions for Child Development, 60*, 23–37.

Keefe, K., & Berndt, T. J. (1996). Relations of friendship quality to self-esteem in early adolescence. *Journal of Early Adolescence, 16* (1), 110–129.

Sullivan, H. S. (1953). *The interpersonal theory of psychiatry.* New York: W.W. Norton.

Youniss, J., & Haynie, D. L. (1992). Friendship in adolescence. *Developmental and Behavioral Pediatrics, 13*(1), 59–66.

Youniss, J., & Smollar, J. (1985). *Adolescent relations with others, fathers, and friends.* Chicago: University of Chicago Press.

11.2   B. Bradford Brown, Margaret S. Mory,
                                                    and David Kinney, 1994

Casting Adolescent Crowds in a Relational Perspective: Caricature, Channel, and Context

B. Bradford Brown, Ph.D., is a professor of human development with the University of Wisconsin-Madison's Department of Educational Psychology and Wisconsin Center for Education Research. He is coauthor (with Laurence Steinberg, 1997) of *Beyond the Classroom: Why School Reform Has Failed and What Parents Need to Do* and *Contemporary Perspectives on Adolescent Romantic Relationships* (with Wyndol Furman and Candace Feiring, 1999). His research has focused on the formation and operation of peer cultures and crowds and the effect of peer pressure on school achievement and deviant behavior.

Margaret S. Mory, Ph.D., is an educational psychologist at the University of Wisconsin, Madison. In her research, she seeks to understand how adolescents use peer crowds to interpret their peer world and their own social identities.

David Kinney, Ph.D., is an associate professor of sociology at Central Michigan University. His ethnographic research has focused on peer culture and identity formation at inner city schools in Philadelphia and Chicago. He is a faculty affiliate at the University of Michigan's Center for Ethnography of Everyday Life.

Research has shown that among adolescents there is not a monolithic peer culture with values discrepant from those of adults. Rather there are multiple peer cultures that encompass a diversity of value systems and behavior patterns (Brown, 1990). In addition, research has also found that peer groups do not necessarily draw adolescents away from parental influence into deviant activities. Rather, adolescents may be driven to these crowds by ineffective child-rearing practices (Brown, 1990).

The research of B. Bradford Brown has made an enormous contribution to the understanding of the role of peer groups in the development of social identity and social support. Peer crowds are reputation-based collections of adolescents characterized by interests, abilities, and personal characteristics. Peer crowds provide provisional identities through which an adolescent can be known while struggling to work out a more personal sense of identity. Peer groups also help structure social interactions and social relationships.

In the following reading, B. Bradford Brown, Margaret S. Mory, and David Kinney examine the ways in which peer crowds shape the quality and nature of peer relationships. Stark contrasts have been identified between relationships in crowds at different ends of the status hierarchy, with relationships among members of high status crowds of populars or jocks being quite different from relationships between members of greaser, burnout, or druggie crowds. Brown and his colleagues also note that crowds are dynamic. Adolescents move from one crowd to another, a more diverse set of crowds develops over time, the popular crowd loses its attractiveness, and belonging to a crowd decreases in importance as the development of personal identity increases.

F or most individuals in our society, the transition from childhood to adolescence, often heralded by entry into middle school or junior high school, is accompanied by major transformations in peer relationships. Not only does the new school feature a much larger population of peers (by combining students from several elementary schools), but the daily routine of moving from class to class brings students into contact with a greater number of peers than they typically saw in the self-contained classrooms of elementary school. What is more, youngsters soon discover that the adolescent social world is a heterosexual world, so that opposite-sex peers, who have been largely ignored in middle childhood (Hartup, 1983), must become part of their social network—and they must become proficient at interacting with both sexes. At the same time, adult supervision of peer relationships recedes, leaving the young person to negotiate this expanded peer context with its new relational demands without the guiding or controlling hand that adults provided in earlier years.

Such momentous transformations in the peer social system could easily overwhelm a young person if programs, institutions, and cultural forms did not evolve to help adolescents adjust to them. One such "evolution" is the emergence of peer "crowds." Crowds refer to collections of adolescents identified by the interests, attitudes, abilities, and/or personal characteristics they have in common. They differ from other groupings of adolescents, such as friendship groups or "cliques," in that they are based on a person's reputation rather than interaction patterns (Brown, 1990). A crowd defines what a person is like more than who she or he "hangs around with." Of course, because "birds of a feather flock together" it is common for adolescents to interact with peers from the same crowd and avoid relationships with peers from other crowds with markedly different reputations. Yet such interaction patterns are not a prerequisite of crowd affiliation.

For many decades, social scientists have debated the functions that crowds serve without reaching clear consensus. From our perspective, however, crowds have two major functions: They foster individuals' development of identity or self-concept, and they structure social interactions. In this [selection] we are concerned primarily with the second function, the ways in which crowds serve to regulate social relationships among adolescents. Some investigators have regarded this as the major organizing principle of adolescent crowds. For example, several authors have argued that high school crowds cluster adolescents into the socioeconomic strata (Buff, 1970; Eckert, 1989; Hollingshead, 1949) or the racial and ethnic groupings (Ianni, 1989; Matute-Bianchi, 1986) that structure social interactions in the surrounding (adult) community. Others have portrayed crowds as a major mechanism for socializing young people into adult social roles. The most classic example is Dunphy's (1963) portrait of how crowds evolve across adolescence to facilitate heterosexual orientations and dating patterns.

In much of this work, authors cast their depictions of crowds in relational perspective: How do various crowds get along with each other? What is the quality of relationships within each crowd? Rarely, however, are these relational issues the focus of analysis. Rather, they are a mechanism by which researchers can address the larger sociological or social psychological issues with which they are concerned: socioeconomic stratification, generational conflict, socialization into adult roles, and so on. As a result, our understanding of adolescent crowds from a relational perspective is rather fragmented.

Our intent [here] is to provide a more systematic analysis of how relational principles reveal the structure and function of adolescent crowds. We perceive three major ways in which crowds may be cast in relational perspective. First, adolescents construct an image, or *caricature,* of each crowd that reflects their perceptions of the typical or stereotypical traits of its members. These caricatures trace the symbolic relationships that exist among crowds: How crowds are different from one another and how well crowds get along with each other. This helps teenagers to understand the alternative "social identities" that are available, as well as to appreciate the norms governing relationships and peer interactions within their social milieu. Second, in a more concrete fashion, crowd affiliation serves to *channel* teenagers toward forming relationships with certain peers rather than others. Crowds are arranged in "social space" in such a way that relationships between teenagers in different crowds are facilitated in some cases and inhibited in others. Finally, crowds serve as *contexts* for peer relationships in which systematic variations in the quality of relationships can be observed as a function of the group's norms, orientations, and status position. Thus whereas adolescents in one crowd may form lasting and caring friendships, adolescents in another crowd may display superficial and competitive relationships.

. . . Our commentary is intended to be more suggestive and provocative than definitive. . . . [I]t seems wise to clarify our perspective on the nature or essence of adolescent crowds.

The Nature of Adolescent Crowds

From ethnographic depictions one often gets the impression that adolescent crowds are very concrete entities (e.g., Cusick, 1973; Eckert, 1989; Eder, 1985). They have widely acknowledged labels and readily identifiable memberships. They lay claim to a particular hangout at school or in the neighborhood—a lunchroom table or hallway or street corner. They have implicit control of certain school activities: The politicos preside over the student council, while the burnouts dominate the auto shop. To be sure, such depictions reflect a concrete and visible reality in most American high schools, namely, cliques that embody the attitudes, behaviors, and lifestyles that define a particular crowd.

Yet such depictions have perplexed other ethnographers, who witness blatant contradictions between the spoken norms of a crowd and crowd members' observable behavior. Varenne (1982), for example, was bemused that members of two crowds routinely depicted as archrivals could often be observed interacting with each other, or that a student widely regarded as a member of the popular crowd, known for its trendy style of dress, often came to school in blue jeans and a work shirt—the signature apparel of a very different crowd. Such contradictions led Varenne to propose that crowds seemed to exist much more "in teenagers' heads" than in reality.

How visible and distinctive are adolescent crowds? Certainly, individuals or cliques that are widely acknowledged representatives of a particular crowd can be easily located in most schools. They also can easily become the target of ethnographic or participant observer studies. But to a certain degree, adolescent crowds exist more profoundly at the cultural and symbolic level than at the level of definitive individual behaviors (Lesko, 1988). Crowds stipulate (in stereotypic ways) a set of alternative value systems, lifestyles, and behavioral repertoires that are readily recognizable within the adolescent social system. In other words, each crowd represents a different prescriptive identity or identity prototype. Thus teenagers may feel quite comfortable characterizing jocks as individuals who are "out for" sports teams, out for a good time on the weekend, into the latest styles, and only moderately concerned with academic achievement, even though they recognize that several peers associated with the jock crowd do not manifest all of these characteristics.

In fact, a teenager's *actual* attitudes and behaviors are unlikely to jibe perfectly with the normative image of *any* single crowd in his or her social milieu. If a teenager's characteristics are highly similar to the prototypic attitudes and behaviors of a specific crowd, he or she is likely to be associated with that crowd by most peers. But for many, if not most, adolescents, the fit between personal attitudes and behaviors and the prototypic characteristics of a given crowd is an imperfect one. As a result, a certain teenager may be viewed as a member of crowd X by some peers, a member of crowd Y by other peers, and a member of *both* crowds by still other peers. In other words, although some adolescents fit neatly into a specific crowd, many others seem to have multiple or partial crowd affiliations, often of varying intensities.

This helps to define adolescent crowds as distinctive in several ways from most other groups that social scientists study. In the first place, membership in adolescent crowds is not as obvious and exclusive. By occupation, one is a lawyer or a hairdresser or a physician or a construction worker or whatever. By religious affiliation, one is an Orthodox Jew or an Episcopalian or a Roman Catholic or an atheist, and so on. But by crowd, an adolescent can easily be both a "jock" and a "Mexican."

Second, exclusive membership in a particular crowd is readily disavowed by adolescents. Few adults would deny their occupation or their neighborhood of residence. They might "waffle" a bit about their political party affiliation or their socioeconomic status. Rarely, however, do social scientists encounter the sort of reluctance or denial that we and others (Lesko, 1988; Varenne, 1982) have observed when asking adolescents, "What crowd do *you* belong to?" "I really don't belong to any crowd" or "I mix with several crowds" are common responses. There are several reasons for such responses. One is that students are reluctant to appear close-minded and exclusionary, as if they only interact with peers in one particular crowd. Another is that because they mix with several crowds during the school day (even if they tend to hang out with one specific group after school or on weekends) it is difficult for them to see themselves as belonging to just one crowd. What's more, because crowds are meant to depict one's global identity, or basic reputation with peers, rather than just one facet of self (as occupation or religious affiliation or political party membership do for adults), being "typecast" too rigidly into one crowd violates the American emphasis on individuality, autonomy, and personal uniqueness.

Finally, some crowds are legitimate, meaningful categories but are—almost by definition—unobservable. The "loners," for example, comprise a crowd of adolescents who are described as having no friends, no hangouts, no group activities; yet they possess (in the minds of adolescents) as clear a prototypic identity as any other group (Brown, Lohr, & Trujillo, 1990).

Such characteristics give teenage crowds a different dynamic than other groupings of adolescents or adults. They also affect the effort to examine and understand the relational characteristics of crowds. For one thing, they encourage analyses on a symbolic as well as a behavioral level. That is, researchers must attend to adolescents' "social construction" of peer crowds, to the way that teenagers employ crowd labels, and to crowd characterizations to explain and understand their social world. . . .

Crowds as Contexts for Social Relationships

The relational feature of crowds that has attracted the most attention from researchers—primarily ethnographers—is the manner in which crowds provide a context for peer interactions. Ethnographers are fond of contrasting the quality and character of relationships that are displayed by members of different crowds. They have considered relationships with adults (particularly school personnel) as well as peers, and relationships with members outside one's crowd as well as with fellow crowd members. Indeed, the implicit message of these studies often has been that it is through probing members' *relationships* that one can come to understand the motivations and behavior patterns that typify a crowd.

. . . [M]any ethnographies have been organized to contrast two rival crowds in a school—usually a group high in peer status that draws from the ranks of the middle class or upper middle class in the community, and a lower status crowd that is often populated by students from lower socioeconomic strata. These studies have spanned more than a decade and have addressed adolescents in a variety of communities. The labels ascribed to the high- and low-status crowds are not consistent across studies. Yet descriptions of the quality of relationships within each crowd have been surprisingly similar.

Within the high-status group—populars, jocks, trendies, preppies, politicos, and so on—relationships are usually characterized as superficial and competitive, more "instrumental" than "expressive." Adolescents in this crowd often use friendships to establish and maintain their social position, which means that one must be prepared to cast aside friends (or be cast aside as a friend) when a better candidate comes along. Eder (1985) found populars to be rather wary in their friendships, especially with peers outside their own crowd. They were conscious of and concerned about how associations would affect their image and standing in the popular crowd. Lesko (1988) noted that populars were so status conscious that they even jockeyed for position within their own crowd, which made for unstable friendships. Our own interviews with adolescents reflect this instrumental orientation. One boy explained that to be popular one must "learn how to score points with every group." The objective is to develop a large network of friendships across crowds that can be exploited to extend or maintain one's status—an interesting twist on Granovetter's (1973) conception of the "strength of weak ties." Such an orientation discourages relationships based on loyalty, trust, and self-disclosure.

What accounts for the superficial nature of peer relationships among members of the elite crowd? Eckert (1989) linked it to their socialization into middle-class culture. Parents and teachers, she argued, had trained these youth to adopt a hierarchical, corporate orientation to relationships—an awareness of power and status differentials among interactants. One must be aware of who is above and below oneself in the corporate hierarchy and how these individuals should be treated to enhance one's own success in the corporate structure. In effect, interpersonal relationships were to be viewed as a social means to personal ends. Friendships were secondary to students' academic or extracurricular objectives, so it was reasonable to keep them superficial. Yet it is also possible that the superficiality that ethnographers have observed is a response to the intense relational pressures that confront youth in high-status crowds (Eder, 1985). Perhaps the only rational way—or at least the most expedient way—to cope with the steady barrage of friendship overtures is to settle for short-term, superficial relationships that allow one to be wary of one's partner's motives.

Whatever the reason is for the superficial quality of populars' peer relationships, they are a stark contrast to ethnographers' impressions of friendships among the "contrast" crowd—greasers, burnouts, headbangers, druggies, or whatever. In these crowd contexts, relationships are usually characterized by depth, stability, loyalty, commitment, and honesty. Lesko (1988) portrayed burnouts' peer relationships as blunt and undiplomatic, but egalitarian and enduring. These students did not cultivate a large network of friends and usually drew friendships exclusively from within their own crowd.

Eckert (1989), again, found an explanation for these friendship patterns in the class culture of the lower status crowd. The emotionally distant relationships that working-class parents cultivate with their teenage offspring encourage young people to rely more upon peers than family for emotional and instrumental support and gratification. As a result there is a strong sense of solidarity with peers and an inclination to pool resources within the friendship group. One's friendship network becomes a surrogate family, linking individuals across grade levels and even across schools to a much greater extent than is observed among members of high-status crowds. This familial organization of peer networks is reminiscent of relational styles in deviant gangs (e.g., Campbell, 1984), which, of course, draw a considerable portion of their membership from these lower status crowds.

In sum, ethnographers have argued that crowds at different ends of the status hierarchy provide sharply different contexts for peer relationships, contexts that tend to foster friendships of markedly different character. The different relational styles that typify youth in these two contexts are partly the result of the demands or expectations of their status position and partly the consequence of family interaction patterns or socialization strategies.

We suspect, however, that the different styles also stem from discrepancies in the level of social skills that characterize one crowd or another, discrepancies that may actually be nurtured by the structure of elementary school education. Schwartz (1981) observed classroom interactions in several elementary and junior high schools that "tracked" students into academic ability groups. She noted that students could be differentiated not only by their academic behaviors (their ability, concentration, motivation to do well in school, etc.) but also by their styles of interacting with peers. High-ability students had the capacity to remain "on task" and to appear to be attentive to and compliant with the teacher even when engaging in secretive interactions with peers. They also worked effectively in groups and carried their work-group identity into noninstructional time. Low-ability students, on the other hand, were openly noncompliant, if not hostile, to teachers and squandered much of the class time reserved for individual or group work by socializing with peers. During free time, they displayed an antagonistic interaction style with peers, in which they belittled classmates' academic abilities or efforts and exaggerated their own aptitude and skills (academic or otherwise). The separation of these students into ability groups served to isolate low ability students from peers who might otherwise have served as role models of more effective social skills. This helped reinforce the social interaction patterns that teachers obviously attended to in making tracking assignments. By adolescence, the different ability groups had developed incompatible interactional styles, creating as much of a social as an intellectual chasm between groups.

Although Schwartz did not follow her samples into adolescent crowds, the low ability students that she observed seem to have much in common with the greasers and burnouts that Eckert (1989) and others have described—except in terms of their social skills. Schwartz, however, provides a much less flattering portrait of this group than Eckert does.

Others who have observed the emergence of deviantly oriented peer groups in preadolescence have noted relational skill deficits among members of this group. Cairns et al. (1988), for example, found a tendency for aggressive youngsters who are low in peer status (classified as "rejected" by sociometric ratings) to coalesce into cliques that are characterized not only by deviant activity but also by unstable and antagonistic relationships among group members. Giordano, Cernkovich, & Pugh (1986) found that both deviant and nondeviant youth manifest a number of positive features in their friendships, but these are complemented by negative characteristics only among deviant youth. Dishion (1993) confirmed this distinction, but also found that the positive features of deviant youths' friendships were often in the service of negative behaviors. That is, delinquents are most cordial and accepting, in conversations with their friend, when the friend is discussing deviant behavior! Discourse focusing on prosocial behaviors goes unrewarded by the dyad.

In any event, the roots of the contrasting interactional styles that characterize different adolescent crowds seem to lie in the social skills and interpersonal orientations that crowd members develop well before adolescence. This helps explain why some adolescents will actually "defect" from a particular crowd when its interactional norms become too onerous to the individuals' own sensibilities. Kinney (1992) traced several such defectors in his ethnographic study. He describes one group of females who became disenchanted with the pressures of being a trendy—the need to "look perfect every day and have the right friends" (Kinney, 1992, p. 16). They were attracted to the headbangers (similar to Eckert's burnouts) because of the loyalty, intimacy, and trust that seemed to characterize their friendships. But they became disaffected by the crowd's negative attitudes toward outsiders and disaffection from academics. So, they developed a new crowd, based on the "hippie" culture of the 1960s, which featured a genuine openness to individuals in all crowds. In this context, and with support of the prototypic hippie identity ("do your own thing," etc.), they were able to nurture a different sort of friendship relationship than they found possible to pursue in other crowds in their school.

Certainly, these studies provide fascinating accounts of the different patterns of peer and adult relationships that characterize adolescents from different crowds. But our understanding of crowds as contexts for interpersonal relationships is constrained by the restricted range of crowds and relationships that they have considered. In this regard, three factors are especially worrisome. First, in most cases, investigators have focused on members of the most socially prominent crowd in a school (populars, jocks, etc.) and their alienated and deviantly oriented counterparts at the other end of the status hierarchy (burnouts, headbangers, greasers, and so on). In such studies, comparisons of crowds are confounded (often rather intentionally) by the distinctive class cultures from which the crowds draw, and this serves to obscure the contribution that crowds make to teenagers' interpersonal orientations. Like Larkin (1979) and Kinney (1992), investigators need to consider the broader array of crowds that exist in most schools. Researchers also need to venture into multiethnic schools to discover how crowd affiliation and ethnicity interact to shape the relational styles that adolescents display.

Second, researchers have relied upon relatively small samples of students—one or two prominent cliques from each crowd—to form their impression of the crowd. A well-established and widely recognized clique of populars may not truly reflect the norms and interactional styles of the broader membership of the popular crowd. We have found, for example, that students often view the popular crowd as consisting of two factions: "stuck-ups" or "snobs," who form the sort of tight-knit cliques on which ethnographies tend to focus, and the "nice populars," who remain friendly, approachable, and relatively humble for their high station. It would be wise, then, to complement ethnographic work with methodologies that can reach a broader representation of crowd members.

Finally, few investigators have ventured beyond the study of intracrowd friendships and what might be called intercrowd "acquaintanceships" (the treatment of outsiders); other types of relationships, most notably romantic relationships, have been virtually ignored. Because crowds have been proposed as the primary socializing agent of adolescent heterosexual relationships (Dunphy, 1963), this is a glaring deficiency for future research to address.

As a modest step in this direction, we offer findings from our own self-report survey of a sample of over 800 adolescents (Grades 7–12) in two midwestern communities. The sample was drawn primarily from five of the most prominent crowds in these schools: brains, druggies, jocks, populars, and outcasts (a combination of loners and nerds); participants' crowd affiliation were ascertained by peer ratings (Brown, 1989a). The survey included several basic questions about best friends and romantic (boyfriend/girlfriend) relationships. It also contained scales to assess the importance that respondents attached to socializing with peers, the amount of peer pressure they felt to socialize with peers, and the degree to which they actually engaged in socializing behaviors (going out with friends, conversing with friends on the phone, attending school dances and sporting events, etc.). Respondents also indicated, on a 4-point Likert scale (1 = none; 4 = a great deal), how much time on weekends they spent with different categories of associates. Finally, they noted how often in the past month they had gone out with someone of the opposite sex, both in the company of other peers and just as a couple; scores on these items ranged from 1 (never) to 5 (almost every day).

Whereas ethnographers have highlighted the different relational styles of groups that in our schools were called populars and druggies, we found these crowds to be strikingly similar on the questions we asked. We found the most consistent differences between populars and druggies on the one hand and brains and outcasts on the other. Crowd members did not differ significantly in whether they had a best friend (80% to 90% of each crowd did) or how long this person had been their best friend (from 3 to 3.5 years), but there were significant differences in time spent with one's best friend. The average for druggies (13 hours per week) was over 50% higher than that for brains (8 hours); the other groups averaged between 9.5 and 11 hours per week.

The contrast was even sharper with regard to romantic relationships (see Table 1). Nearly two-thirds of the druggies claimed to have a boyfriend or girlfriend at the time of the survey, compared to just over one-quarter of the brains. Among those with a boyfriend or girlfriend, the relationship had lasted twice as long for druggies as for brains, and occupied considerably more of druggies' free time each week. The incidence of dating, whether with a group of peers or just as a couple, was considerably higher among druggies than brains. On all of these items, responses of brains and outcasts did not differ significantly, nor did the responses of druggies and populars. The only indications of superficiality in the relationships of elites was in the slightly

Table 1

Crowd Differences in Self-Reported Characteristics of Romantic Relationships

Characteristic	Brains	Druggies	Jocks	Outcasts	Populars	Others
% who have had a boy/ girlfriend this year	58	94	84	60	88	73
% who currently have a boy/ girlfriend	28	64	46	33	55	40
Duration of relationship (in months)	5	10	7	6	8	5
Hours per week spent with boy/ girlfriend	8.85	13.64	9.23	11.03	13.58	10.78
Frequency of dating:						
with a group	1.86	2.97	2.57	1.97	2.90	2.44
just as a couple	1.63	2.89	2.36	1.91	2.49	2.17

(but nonsignificantly) lower duration of best friendships among jocks and populars (just over 3 years, compared to at least $3\frac{1}{3}$ years in other crowds).

These contrasts carried over to respondents' allocation of time among social network members on weekends (Table 2). Brains and outcasts appeared to balance their time more evenly between family and peers (lovers and close friends), whereas druggies and populars tipped the balance more clearly in favor of peers. In the scale scores, although brains accorded comparatively low importance to peer interactions and reported a low incidence of socializing with peers, the pressure they felt from friends to spend time with peers was relatively high. On these scales, outcasts reflected their image as social isolates, reporting comparatively little pressure from friends to socialize with peers and a lower incidence of peer social activities than other groups. It also appeared as if jocks were more oriented toward group relationships than other crowds. Unlike other respondents with a boyfriend or girlfriend, jocks devoted almost as much time on weekends to their friendship group as their romantic relationship.

Of course, these data lack the depth of insight that is provided by ethnographic work. Yet they broaden the perspective of ethnographies to indicate that each crowd has a distinct profile of characteristics in peer relationships. These distinctions undoubtedly affect the ease with which adolescents can move among crowds. A teenager whose lack of interest in romantic relationships caused little concern among fellow brains would probably feel very uncomfortable amidst the more intense dating pressures of the druggies or populars. A loner, accustomed to focusing interaction on a few close friends, might find membership in the jock crowd, with its emphasis on group interactions, to be a major adjustment. If future studies can integrate the more qualitative

Table 2

Crowd Differences in Allocation of Weekend Time and Peer Socializing Scale Scores

Item or Scale Score	Brains	Druggies	Jocks	Outcasts	Populars	Others
Time on weekend spent with:						
Closest friends	2.78	3.09	2.91	2.61	2.97	2.78
Boyfriend/girlfriend	2.73	3.20	2.82	2.81	3.01	2.85
Friendship group	2.20	2.66	2.71	2.21	2.67	2.31
Peer crowd	1.64	2.30	1.99	1.76	2.20	1.95
Family members	2.71	2.22	2.46	2.63	2.36	2.50
Alone	2.38	2.03	2.11	2.29	2.03	2.20
Scale scores:						
Importance of socializing	3.61	4.04	3.84	3.70	3.95	3.81
Peer pressure to socialize	2.10	1.85	2.10	1.87	2.00	1.93
Peer socializing behavior	2.64	3.06	3.04	2.58	3.16	2.84

Note: Scores for items reflecting time on weekends spent with various portions of the social network ranged from 1.00 ("none") to 4.00 ("a whole lot"). Scale scores ranged from 1.00 ("not at all important") to 5.00 ("extremely important") for the importance of socializing with peers, 1.00 ("no pressure from friends") to 4.00 ("strong pressure") for peer pressure, and 1.00 ("never") to 5.00 ("almost every day") for peer socializing behavior.

relational focus on ethnography with the broader sampling of survey research, they can provide a more comprehensive portrait of the distinctive contexts for social relationships that are inherent in the peer group system within a particular community.

In sum, we are beginning to understand how adolescent crowds nurture different patterns of social relationships among their members. These differences are not simply a function of crowd norms, but a consequence of a variety of factors: the level of social skills and socializing interests of crowd members, the expectations and orientations of other members of their social network (especially family members), the attractiveness of crowd members as partners in relationships, and so on. We have barely begun to explore the factors that shape the nature of social relationships in the diverse array of crowds that comprise adolescents' social system. It is clear, however, that crowd affiliation is a significant factor in the quality of adolescents' social relationships. It would be difficult to fully appreciate the nature of adolescents' relationships with peers and adults without taking their crowd affiliation into consideration.

The Dynamic Nature of Crowds

One of the special challenges for those who study adolescent crowds is that they are chasing a moving target. Crowds are a dynamic, not a stable and static feature of adolescence. The structure of the crowd system and an individual's place within it change from one year to the next, especially, it seems, when individuals make the transition from one school to another. Few investigators have taken a dynamic perspective on crowds; fewer still have attempted longitudinal studies. Yet the data from these few, along with findings from cross-sectional and retrospective analyses, are sufficient to give us some understanding of the dynamic features of crowds. In particular, four such features should be borne in mind by those attempting a relational analysis of adolescent crowds.

First, *peer group structures change* across adolescence. One of us (Kinney, 1993), for example, discovered a marked transformation in the crowd structure between middle school and high school in one midwestern community. From a two-crowd system in middle school (the populars and the dweebs), the structure blossomed into a more diverse array of crowds in high school: normals, punkers, headbangers, grits, and so on. This permitted those who had not "made it" into the popular crowd in early adolescence to find a more self-enhancing crowd identification than their default middle school classification as dweebs. One consequence of the broadening array of crowds was that over time the popular crowd lost exclusive rights to the top rung of the status hierarchy. By senior year, the status differential between populars, normals, and headbangers was barely noticeable.

There are too few studies of the structure of crowds across middle school and high school to determine how common this sort of diversification really is. In other middle schools we have studied, students seem to be aware of a more diverse set of crowds. Yet we have also found that the number of crowds students name increases across adolescence. Also, the proportion of crowds named that fit into what might be called "major" crowds (groups that are common to a number of studies: populars, jocks, brains, drug-oriented youth, and so on) peaks around eighth or ninth grade, the point of transition between junior and senior high school (Brown & Clasen, 1986). Thus there seem to be changes across adolescence in the number and types of crowds that are available to adolescence—or at least in the salience of these groups in the minds of teenagers—as well as in the status ranking of crowds.

A second dynamic feature that investigators have described involves *changes in relational characteristics* of crowds. We have already noted shifts in the status hierarchy (Brown & Clasen, 1986; Kinney, 1993). Yet even during middle school, when populars retain undisputed possession of top rung on the status ladder, individuals' feelings toward and treatment of the populars seems to change (Eder, 1985; Schofield, 1981). Envy and ingratiation turn to resentment and avoidance as young people become disenchanted with populars' snobbery and cliquishness.

Several researchers have noted an increase with age in the permeability of crowds. As one of Larkin's (1979) high school respondents explained:

> It's not so tight that you feel uncomfortable when you go into somebody else's group if you know someone there. You know, there are floaters—people who go around to just any particular group they feel like that particular day. And you just go in and you start talking and it doesn't matter. Nobody really cares. I think that's really good. It's quite an improvement over junior high. (p. 88)

Gavin and Furman (1989), who examined students' perceptions of same-sex cliques between Grades 7 and 12, attributed this to the fact that, with age, adolescents tended to treat "out-group" members in a more positive fashion. This is also reflected in sociometric data suggesting that the tightly bounded cliques of early adolescence give way to a looser pattern of interaction, with more individuals acting as "liaisons" between several friendship groups (Shrum & Cheek, 1987). Kinney (1992), however, cautioned that the increasing permeability may be selective; the boundaries between certain crowds (e.g., populars and headbangers in his study) may start to diminish while the boundaries between other crowds (e.g., punkers and "grits") remain strong.

These structural and relational changes in the crowd system are accompanied by developmental changes in adolescents' orientations toward crowds. One of these (the third dynamic feature) is a *shift in the salience of crowd affiliation.* Both Coleman (1974) and Brown, Eicher and Petrie (1986) found an age-related decline in the importance of belonging to a crowd. According to Brown et al. (1986), early adolescents found reassurance in a crowd's norms and conformity demands, whereas older adolescents felt that crowds frustrated their efforts to express their own personal attitudes and interests. Such a drive toward individuality helps explain the age-related decline in conformity pressures from peers that Clasen and Brown (1985) reported.

Finally, *crowd affiliation itself changes,* that is, it appears as if individuals do not remain attached to the same crowd across adolescence. In one recent longitudinal study (Brown, Freeman, Huang, & Mounts, 1992), over half of a sample of 7th- through 12th-graders changed the crowd with which they claimed affiliation over a two-year period. Interestingly, the likelihood of changing crowds not only varied substantially by initial crowd affiliation but also diminished steadily across grade levels. Perhaps this was because, as crowd boundaries became more permeable, older youth felt less of a need to change affiliations in order to broaden their circle of associates or express an identity that commingled the norms of several crowds.

Developmental analyses are still very much the exception rather than the rule in studies of adolescent peer groups. Yet the need to approach relational features of crowds from a developmental perspective is absolutely clear. Generalizing to adolescence as a whole on the basis of a study of middle school students or, worse, yet, high school seniors, is simply not tenable. What is more, the dynamic nature of crowd structures and crowd affiliations is one of the strongest indicators of the relational nature of adolescent peer groups. Just as dyadic relationships evolve over time, so does the adolescent crowd system.

Conclusions

Some people regard adolescent crowds as a curiously amusing feature of the rather obscure world of American teenagers. Others consider them to be a potent and dangerous force, mandating conformity to teen culture at a time when individuals should be striving for an autonomous identity and integration into adult society. From our perspective, crowds are an important and usually very effective mechanism by which teenagers structure social interactions and forge meaningful social relationships within the new and sometimes confusing social system of adolescence. There are, we believe, four important lessons to be learned from the review that we have undertaken in this [selection].

First, *crowds are an inherently relational construct.* In defining crowds as reputation- rather than interaction-based entities, we seem to be distancing ourselves from a relational perspective. We argue that crowds categorize adolescents by *individual* interests, abilities, attitudes, or ethnic heritage—*not* by social interaction patterns. Yet the label applied to a crowd and the caricatures that accompany it take on meaning only when compared to another crowd. A jock or a druggie or a Korean is not someone with a rigid and absolute set of characteristics, but someone with more of this and less of that than members of some other crowd. What is more, adolescents come to understand crowds through social interaction; crowd images are crafted through mutual consensus, not individual insights. As Lesko (1988, p. 74) has remarked, "Through groups, that is, through associations with people similar to oneself and those who are different, personal and social identities are wrestled with and visualized." Adolescents perceive crowds in relational terms, so for researchers and practitioners to understand the function of crowds, a relational perspective must be adopted.

This brings us to the second lesson, that *adolescents use crowds to construct a symbolic road map of prototypic peer relationships.* Most teenagers recognize the limitations of responding to peers simply as crowd caricatures rather than as unique individuals. Yet they find that the crowd system gives them a language by which to understand and express the complicated and sometimes confusing patterns of social relationships with peers (Schwartz & Merten, 1967; Varenne, 1982). Crowds create abstract models of peer relationships that can provide order and predictability—and therefore a sense of personal control—to actual interactions with friends, acquaintances, and strangers. The symbolic road map of crowds stipulates the ease or difficulty of interacting with certain peers, and what is risked, gained, or lost by nurturing particular peer relationships. These are valuable commodities among individuals whose world is filled with uncertainties. Thus whereas adults may decry the tendency of crowds to compel conformity, reinforce prejudices, and restrict exploration in social interaction patterns, teenagers seem to find that crowds nurture social skills and foster satisfying peer relationships.

A third lesson is that, despite their abstract nature, crowds do affect teenagers' actual social relationships. That is, *a teenager's crowd affiliation and understanding of the crowd system affect the choice of peer associates and the features of peer relationships.* Particularly in the early adolescent years, one's allegiance to or interest in a particular crowd and one's awareness of the social distance among crowds effectively channel a teenager toward particular peers and away from others as candidates for friendship and romance. Teenagers use their symbolic road map of crowds not only to understand peer relationships in general, but also to help decide which peers to pursue for relationships, and which offers of affiliation to accept or ignore. We pointed to proximity, permeability, and desirability as three factors by which adolescents use the crowd system to make choices about peer associates.

What is more, crowd affiliation affects the quality or character of social relationships. The distinguishing features of friendship and romance—and even relationships with adults—are not consistent across adolescents, but contingent upon the norms and social pressures within their crowd. Friendships may be superficial or intense and enduring. Romantic attachments may be instrumental or altruistic. Such variability can be explained, in large measure, by the context that one's crowd affiliation(s) supplies for social relationships.

A final lesson is that crowds are not universal and enduring features of adolescents. Rather, *the crowd system is a dynamic phenomenon that is sensitive to contextual features of a social milieu.* The structure and interrelationships of crowds can change dramatically across the adolescent years. So, too, can a particular teenager's pattern of affiliation with crowds. For example, an adolescent may negotiate middle school as a dedicated member of the populars, become disaffected in early high school and transfer affiliation to the druggies, then drift toward the end of high school into marginal memberships with several groups. The forces that prompt a teenager to remain loyal to a particular crowd or to be constantly seeking new affiliations are not well understood. Yet the flexibility of crowd affiliation and the developmental nature of crowd structure are undoubtedly essential to the capacity of crowds to nurture teenagers' social skills and social relationships (see, e.g., Dunphy, 1963).

By the same token, crowds are sensitive to their social and historical milieu. Coleman (1961) found substantial variation among communities in the capacity of academic achievement to propel someone into or away from membership in the popular crowd. Larkin (1979) reported a remarkable transformation in the character of the politicos that corresponded to historical shifts in the American political climate across a 10-year period. Brown and Mounts (1989) discovered significant differences across communities in adolescents' descriptions of the number, types, and size of crowds in their school. There are even contexts in which adolescent crowds simply do not exist: small, stable, rural populations, for example, in which classmates have grown up together and know each other so well that crowds are unnecessary. Certainly, such contextual variation should make researchers cautious about generalizing from observations of crowds in one particular school or community, just as the developmental nature of crowds limits generalizations from studies of one age group.

For most teenagers, crowds are an important component of negotiating the social world of adolescence. They transform strangers and acquaintances into recognizable types. They channel individuals toward engaging certain peers in social relationships and not others. They provide a context that influences the quality and character of these relationships. They change developmentally and respond to contextual cues in ways that, hopefully, better nurture teenagers' relational skills and interpersonal experiences. Approaching crowds from this relational perspective will not only help researchers to understand the place of crowds in adolescent development, but also provide insights about the character of young people's social relationships.

References

Brown, B. B. (1989a). *Social type rating manual.* Madison, WI: University of Wisconsin-Madison, National Center on Effective Secondary Schools.

Brown, B. B. (1990). Peer groups and peer cultures. In S. S. Feldman and G. R. Elliott (Eds.), *At the threshold: The developing adolescent* (pp. 171–196). Cambridge, MA: Harvard University Press.

Brown, B. B., & Clasen, D. R. (1986, March). *Developmental changes in adolescents' conceptions of peer groups.* Paper presented at the biennial meetings of the Society for Research in Adolescence, Madison, WI.

Brown, B. B., Eicher, S. A., & Petrie, S. (1986). The importance of peer group ("crowd") affiliation in adolescence. *Journal of Adolescence, 9,* 73–96.

Brown, B. B., Freeman, H., Huang, G. H., & Mounts, N. S. (1992, March). *"Crowd hopping": Incidents, correlates, and consequences of change in crowd affiliation during adolescence.* Paper presented at the biennial meeting of the Society for Research in Adolescence, Washington, DC.

Brown, B. B., Lohr, M. J., & Trujillo, C. M. (1990). Multiple crowds and multiple lifestyles: Adolescents' perceptions of peer group characteristics. In R. E. Muss (Ed.), *Adolescent behavior and society: A book of readings* (pp. 30–36). New York: Random House.

Brown, B. B., & Mounts, N. (1989, April). *Peer group structures in single versus multi-ethnic high schools.* Paper presented at the biennial meetings of the Society for Research in Child Development, Kansas City.

Buff, S. A. (1970). Greasers, dupers, and hippies: Three responses to the adult world. In L. Howe (Ed.), *The white majority* (pp. 60–77). New York: Random House.

Cairns, R. B., Cairns, B. D., Neckerman, H. J., Gest, S. D., & Gariepy, J. L. (1988). Social networks and aggressive behavior: Peer support or peer rejection? *Developmental Psychology, 24,* 815–823.

Campbell, A. (1984). *The girls in the gang.* New York: Basil Blackwell.

Clasen, D. R., & Brown, B. B. (1985). The multidimensionality of peer pressure in adolescence. *Journal of Youth and Adolescence, 14,* 451–468.

Coleman, J. C. (1974). *Relationships in adolescence.* Boston: Routledge & Kegan Paul.

Coleman, J. S. (1961). *The adolescent society.* New York: Free Press.

Cusick, P. A. (1973). *Inside high school.* New York: Holt, Rinehart & Winston.

Dishion, T. J. (1993, March). Boys' close friendships and early adolescent problem behavior: Geographic and parenting contexts. In L. Steinberg (Chair), *Interactive influences of parents and peers on adolescent misbehavior.* Symposium conducted at the biennial meetings of the Society for Research in Child Development, New Orleans.

Dunphy, D. (1963). The social structure of urban adolescent peer groups. *Sociometry, 26,* 230–246.

Eckert, P. (1989). *Jocks and burnouts: Social categories and identity in the high school.* New York: Teachers College Press.

Eder, D. (1985). The cycle of popularity: Interpersonal relations among female adolescents. *Sociology of Education, 58,* 154–165.

Gavin, L. A., & Furman, W. (1989). Age differences in adolescents' perceptions of their peer groups. *Developmental Psychology, 25,* 827–834.

Giordano, P. C., Cernkovich, S. A., & Pugh, M. D. (1986). Friendships and delinquency. *American Journal of Sociology, 91,* 1170–1202.

Granovetter, M. (1973). The strength of weak ties. *American Journal of Sociology, 78,* 1360–1381.

Hartup, W. W. (1983). Peer relations. In P. H. Mussen (Ed.), *Handbook of child psychology: Vol 4. Socialization, personality and social development* (pp. 103–196). New York: John Wiley.

Hollingshead, A. B. (1949). *Elmtown's youth.* New York: John Wiley.

Ianni, F. A. J. (1989). *The search for structure.* New York: Free Press.

Kinney, D. A. (1992, March). Coming together and going your own way: Delineating diversity and change in adolescent crowd associations. in B. Brown (Chair), *Stability and change in adolescent peer relations: Characteristics and consequences.* Symposium conducted at the biennial meetings of the Society for Research in Adolescence, Washington, DC.

Kinney, D. A. (1993). From "nerds" to "normals": Adolescent identity recovery within a changing social system. *Sociology of Education, 66,* 21–40.

Larkin, R. W. (1979). *Suburban youth in cultural crisis.* New York: Oxford University Press.

Lesko, N. (1988). *Symbolizing society: Stories, rites, and structure in a Catholic high school.* Philadelphia: Falmer.

Matute-Bianchi, M. E. (1986). Ethnic identities and patterns of school success and failure among Mexican-descent and Japanese-American students in a California high school: An ethnographic analysis. *American Journal of Education, 95,* 233–255.

Schofield, J. W. (1981). *Black and white in school: Trust, tension, or tolerance?* New York: Praeger.

Schwartz, F. (1981). Supporting or subverting learning: Peer group patterns in four tracked schools. *Anthropology and Education Quarterly, 12,* 99–121.

Schwartz, G., & Merten, D. (1967). The language of adolescence: An anthropological approach to youth culture. *American Journal of Sociology, 72,* 453–468.

Shrum, W., & Cheek, N. H. (1987). Social structure during the school years: Onset of the degrouping process. *American Sociological Review, 52,* 218–223.

Varenne, H. (1982). Jocks and freaks: The symbolic structure of the expression of social interaction among American senior high school students. In G. Spindler (Ed.), *Doing the ethnography of schooling* (pp. 213–235). New York: Holt, Rinehart & Winston.

Questions

1. Why do members of high-status crowds tend to develop relationships that are competitive and superficial?
2. Why do members of lower-status crowds tend to develop relationships that have loyalty, commitment, and honesty?
3. What gives one crowd more status than another?
4. What makes it easy or difficult for an adolescent to move between crowds?
5. Why does a more diverse array of crowds develop in high school?
6. What accounts for the diversity of crowds that exists in a given school?

References and Further Reading

Brown, B. B. (1990). Peer groups and peer cultures. In S. S. Feldman, & G. R. Elliott (Eds.), *At the threshold: The developing adolescent* (pp. 171–197). Cambridge, MA: Harvard University Press.

Brown, B. B., Eicher, S. A., & Petrie, S. (1986). The importance of peer group ("crowd") affiliation in adolescence. *Journal of Adolescence, 9,* 73–96.

Stone, M. R., & Brown, B. B. (1999). Identity claims and projections: Descriptions of self and crowds in secondary schools. *New Directions for Child and Adolescent Development, 84,* 7–20.

Urberg, K. A., Degirmencioglu, S. M., Tolson, J. M., & Halliday-Scher, K. (1995). The structure of adolescent peer networks. *Developmental Psychology, 31*(4), 540–547.

Concepts of Romance in 15-Year-Old Adolescents

Candice Feiring, Ph.D., is a professor in the Department of Psychiatry at the University of Medicine and Dentistry, New Jersey. Her research covers several areas: adolescents' experiences of romantic relationships; the role of shame and self-blame in children's, adolescents', and young adults' adaptation to sexual abuse; social networks; and developmental psychopathology.

Romantic relationships have been seen to have two central functions: to foster identity development and to foster the capacity for intimacy. Erik Erikson viewed adolescent love as an attempt to arrive at self-definition, "by projecting one's diffused self-image on another and by seeing it thus reflected and gradually clarified." (Erikson, 1968, p. 132). Romantic relationships, from Erikson's perspective, may be problematic during adolescence before a firm sense of identity is established because they tend to be "the self-seeking, identity-hungry kind; each partner is really trying only to reach himself" (p. 137). Harry Stack Sullivan has argued that the intimacy skills learned in the development and maintenance of same-sex friendships are further developed in romantic relationships. Therefore, from Sullivan's perspective, romantic relationships provide an important context in which adolescents explore issues of sexuality and intimacy and play an important role in the social development of adolescents.

Relatively little research has been done on the interpersonal aspects of romantic relationships. Candice Feiring examines concepts of romance in a sample of white middle-class 15-year-olds. She found dating relationships to be brief in duration, lasting on average for four months. While relatively brief, these relationships were intense and marked by frequent contact. Daily contact occurred either in person or by phone. Feiring analyzed the qualities adolescents use to describe their romantic attachments and reported that adolescents view the positive aspects of romance in terms of companionship, intimacy, and support. Feiring also found sex differences in those descriptions: boys focused more on physical attraction, while girls focused on interpersonal qualities. Because the study by Feiring is based on a white, middle-class, heterosexual sample, the results may not generalize to romantic relationships between adolescents who differ by race, ethnicity, social class, or sexual orientation. Further research is needed on how romantic relationships are characterized for members of these diverse groups.

Abstract: Early romantic experiences are believed to play a central role in the development of the self and intimacy, although little work exists on the nature of romance in early to middle adolescence. This study examines White, middle class 15-year-olds' descriptions of their dating partners and romance. As expected, the majority of the sample had dating experiences that were brief in duration, although they were intense in terms of frequency of contact. Affiliative more than attachment qualities characterized these adolescents' conscious views of romance. Girls were more likely to mention interpersonal qualities, and boys were more likely to mention physical attraction when describing romantic relationships.

Early romantic experiences are believed to play a central role in the development of the self and the ability to be intimate with significant others. Interaction and relationships with the other sex are believed to influence the course of subsequent romantic involvements and marriage in adulthood (Erikson, 1968; Sullivan, 1953). Although romantic relationships presumably involve more than sexual encounters, the adolescent literature emphasizes the sexual aspects of emerging heterosexual relationships and patterns of dating.

Dating is viewed as the social processes through which adolescents practice and experiment with heterosexual relationships. In early adolescence, interest in other-sex friends increases and they become more likely partners for interaction and companionship (Blyth & Foster-Clark, 1987; Buhrmester & Furman, 1987; Epstein, 1986; Feiring & Lewis, 1991; Hallinan, 1978–79; Schofield, 1981). This process appears to follow a progression from being in situations in which other-sex peers are likely to be present, to participation in mixed-sex group activities, to group dating in which couples see each other in a group context, to individual dyads going out alone (Blyth & Padgham, 1987; Dunphy, 1963). By 15 years of age, most teenagers have had some experience dating (Blyth, Hill, & Thiel, 1982; Buhrmester & Furman; Csikszentmihalyi, Larson, & Prescott, 1977; Hansen, 1977; Wright, 1982). For many adolescents, sexual activity takes place as part of dating. By 15 years of age, most girls and boys from the White middle class report having had at least some sexual experience (Smith & Udry, 1985; Zelnik & Shah, 1983).

Theories of dating focus on the development of sexual identity rather than the attachment, friendship, or caregiving aspects of heterosexual relationships (Feinstein & Ardon, 1973; McCabe, 1984). The earliest stages of adolescent sexual identity development involve first directing attention to, but minimal interaction with, other-sex peers. This is followed by numerous short-term relationships in which the practice of basic sexual relations and comfort with the other sex are achieved.

It is generally believed that social skills learned in maintaining and developing same-sex friendships, such as companionship and intimacy, are further developed in romantic relationships. Dating has been observed to serve diverse purposes, some of which overlap with friendship. These functions include recreation, autonomy seeking, status seeking, sexual experimentation, social skills practice, and courtship (Grinder,

1966; Hansen & Hicks, 1980; Husbands, 1970; McDaniel, 1969; Rice, 1975; Skipper & Nass, 1966; Smith, 1962).

The interpersonal nature of romantic relationships in early to middle adolescence has received limited attention (Furman & Wehner, 1994; Katchadourian, 1990; Savin-Williams & Berndt, 1990). The conceptualization of the qualitative, interpersonal nature of romance in this time period is problematic because most work on romantic relationships has been done in late adolescence or adulthood (e.g., Ainsworth, 1989; Hazan & Shaver, 1994; Lee, 1977, 1988; Sternberg, 1986). Some work on adult romance has focused on characterizing its components and functions. Sternberg's (1988) triangular theory of love emphasizes the structure of romance. He believes love comprises three components—intimacy, passion, and decision/commitment. Love is seen as derived from genetically transmitted instincts and socially learned role modeling (Sternberg, 1986). Lee (1988) proposed a typology of love with three love styles: Eros (powerful physical attraction), Storage (affection that develops slowly), and Ludus (multiple casual relationships).

The attachment view of adult heterosexual love relationships offers a developmental perspective of love relationships. As a result of hormone changes, adolescents shift the focus and nature of primary attachment relationships (Ainsworth, 1989). Typically, an other-sex partner becomes the new principal attachment figure, replacing the parental figures as primary in the attachment hierarchy. In contrast to infant attachment, which is typically complementary in caregiving, adult attachment relationships are usually reciprocal, with each partner being both a provider and recipient of care (Weiss, 1982). Adult romantic relationships are seen as an integration of the attachment, caregiving, and sexual reproductive behavioral systems (Hazan & Shaver, 1994). Differences in how romantic love is experienced and manifested are related to differences in past attachment histories, resulting in three types of adult love: secure, preoccupied, and dismissing (Hazan & Shaver, 1987; Shaver & Hazan, 1988). Although the attachment approach is appealing in terms of understanding the different types and origins of adult love relationships, it lacks sufficient explanation and emphasis on the nature and course of romance in adolescence.

The work of Sullivan (1953) and, more recently, Furman and Wehner (1994) suggests that peer relationships and the affiliative behavioral system are more critical for the development of adolescent romance than is indicated in the adult attachment approach. Sullivan asserted that intimacy experiences with friends provide the adolescent with consensual validation of self-worth and create the opportunity for learning sensitivity and caregiving. During adolescence, the mature type of intimacy is increasingly sought in heterosexual relationships. Sullivan proposed that the need for security, intimacy, and lustful satisfaction must all be coordinated in order for the adolescent to achieve satisfactory relations with the other sex. Close friendships with same-sex friends and romantic relationships share common attributes in adulthood (Davis & Todd, 1982). Intimacy, understanding, and enjoyment of each other's company are common attributes; fascination and exclusiveness distinguish romantic relationships from friendships. Essential features of romantic relationships, such as collaboration, affiliation, and reciprocal intimacy, are developed in friendships with peers (Berndt &

Hoyle, 1985; Furman & Wehner, 1994; Sharabany, Gershoni, & Hofman, 1981; Youniss & Smollar, 1985).

In the theory of adolescent romantic relationships offered by Furman and Wehner (1992), close relationships involve the integration of affiliative, attachment, caregiving, and sexual reproductive behavioral systems. Mature attachments to romantic partners are seen as unlikely to emerge early on in romantic life when relationships are casual and short-lived. Rather, a number of short-term relationships may serve as the context for the development of affiliative and sexual behavioral systems in romantic encounters. It is not until the onset of more stable or committed relationships, usually in late adolescence or young adulthood, that the attachment and caregiving behavioral systems emerge as a central part of romantic relationships.

This study examines 15-year-olds' descriptions of their dating partners as well as romance in general. Of central concern is an understanding of these adolescents' conscious views of the benefits and costs of romantic relationships. Two major issues are addressed. The first issue involves the extent to which descriptions of dating partners and romance resemble characteristics of attachment and affiliative behavioral systems. Affiliative more than attachment qualities were expected to characterize descriptions of dating partners and romance. Contact with the other sex and dating appears to most often emerge within a group context of friends and peers (Blyth & Padgham, 1987; Dunphy, 1963; Feinstein & Ardon, 1973). Within this context, affiliative qualities and skills should be most important. In addition, as suggested by Furman and Wehner (1994), the attachment system should not become central until stable or committed relationships emerge. Because 15-year-old adolescents are more likely to be engaged in casual short-term relationships (Feinstein & Ardon, 1973), attachments to partners are less likely to develop.

The second issue of interest involves the nature of gender differences in descriptions of dating partners and romance. Society encourages women and men to have somewhat different attitudes toward the desire for intimacy, love, and sex. Women are socialized to be more relationship and caregiving oriented and expressive of love (Hatfield & Rapson, 1987b; Hazan & Shaver, 1994). Weak gender differences have been found in the frequency and intensity of adult passionate love, with women reporting higher scores than men (DeLamater, 1982; Hatfield & Rapson, 1987a; Peplau, 1983). Women also may be more anxious about being unloved and rejected (Bartholomew, 1991; Brennan, Shaver, & Tobey, 1991).

Research on the development of same-sex and other-sex friendships indicates that intimacy is more important and emerges earlier for girls than boys (Belle, 1989; Berndt, 1982; Bigelow & LaGaipa, 1975; Blyth & Foster-Clark, 1987; Buhrmester & Furman, 1987; Furman & Buhrmester, 1985; Rivenbark, 1971; Sharabany et al., 1981). Girls are more likely to base their friendships on mutual support and self-disclosure than are boys, who rely on joint activities and companionship. Work on older adolescents suggests that girls initially emphasize the interpersonal aspects of romantic relationships such as commitment and self-disclosure, whereas boys focus more on their partners' physical attractiveness and sexual relations (Maddock, 1973; McCabe, 1984). Consequently, girls were expected to emphasize intimacy more than boys. Boys were expected to emphasize physical attraction more than girls.

In summary, although romantic relationships are known to emerge in early to middle adolescence, little is known about the interpersonal nature of romantic involvements as they begin to develop. This study provides new information on the relationship qualities of romantic involvements as described by a sample of White, middle class 15-year-olds. The extent to which affiliative and attachment qualities characterize romantic relationships in this age group and the nature of gender differences are of primary interest.

Method

Study Participants

The sample consisted of 117 White, middle class 15-year-olds who have been participating in a longitudinal study from infancy.[1] Sixty of the adolescents were girls and 57 were boys. Fifty-nine were from upper middle and 58 were from middle socioeconomic status families (Feiring & Lewis, 1981). The large majority of adolescents were from two-parent families (94%), and all were White, of European descent, and residing in suburban communities.

Procedure

The participants were interviewed in their homes by a same-sex young adult concerning dating, volunteer and prosocial behavior, and friendships. Interviewers were trained to provide nonevaluative feedback to make the adolescents feel comfortable and encourage them to talk. Following the adolescents' initial responses to the interview questions, the interviewer probed for additional information without pressuring the participant to talk. In regard to dating, the participants were administered a structured interview with specific questions that allowed for open-ended responses about these topics:

1. The duration of the relationship and frequency of contact (in person and on the phone) with their current or most recent girlfriend or boyfriend.
2. When going on dates, the type and frequency of activities they engaged in as part of a group and alone as a couple.
3. Their likes and dislikes about their current or most recent girlfriend or boyfriend.
4. The advantages and disadvantages of having a girlfriend or boyfriend.

The interviews were audiotaped, and the adolescents' comments transcribed for coding.

Coding, Reliability, and Limitations of Dating Data

For the interview questions concerning likes and dislikes and advantages and disadvantages of having a girlfriend or boyfriend, the transcripts were reviewed to determine what categories best described the data. The categories derived were as follows:

Likes about girlfriend or boyfriend: (a) positive personality (e.g., funny, outgoing, nice), (b) intimacy (e.g., open about feelings, can talk to each other about problems), (c) support (helps me, cares about me, there for me), (d) companionship (enjoy each other's company, have fun to together), (e) physical attraction (e.g., cute, pretty), and (f) common interest (e.g., like same activities, have same attitudes)

Dislikes about girl- or boyfriend: (a) negative personality traits (e.g., stubborn, obnoxious, bossy), (b) negative interpersonal relations (e.g., fights, hassles, breaks dates, nags), (c) jealousy, and (d) nothing (could not think of anything negative).

Advantages of having a girl- or boyfriend: (a) intimacy, (b) support, (c) companionship, (d) friendship (e.g., having a good, close friend), (e) social status (e.g., image, being status quo), and (f) learn about the other sex (e.g., finding out how to be with girls or boys).

Disadvantages of having a girl- or boyfriend: (a) too much commitment (e.g., cuts down on freedom, always tied down, not much time together), (b) negative interpersonal relations, (c) jealousy, (d) costs money, (e) worry about other's feelings, and (f) nothing (could not think of any disadvantages).

Using these categories, each participant's answers were coded according to whether they mentioned a given category in response to a particular question (e.g., likes about girlfriend or boyfriend). In order to establish interrater reliability on these categories, 20 transcripts (10 girls, 10 boys) were coded independently by two raters. Interrater reliability for each category was calculated using Cohen's Kappa [measure of agreement based on a contingency table]. On all but three categories, agreement was perfect. The exceptions were companionship (for likes, $\kappa = .77$), negative personality traits (dislikes, $\kappa = .88$), and jealousy (dislikes, $\kappa = .77$).

The interview data used in this study are thus highly reliable and provide adolescents' own descriptions of romantic relationships rather than investigator-imposed ratings. Nevertheless, the data do not provide in-depth information about adolescents' feelings and thoughts about romantic relationships. The majority of adolescents did not answer each interview question with more than several sentences. The limited nature of adolescents' discussion is not unusual when they are interviewed by an unfamiliar friendly adult (W. Furman, personal communication, 1993; R. Kobak, personal communication, 1993). There also is the tendency to present socially desirable information and inhibit the discussion of negative or highly personal feelings or thoughts. This suggests that adolescents would be less likely to mention characteristics of relationships such as fights, jealousy, or sexual behavior.

Results

This section begins with a discussion of the structure of dating in this adolescent sample, followed by a report of the positive (likes about partner and advantages of having a girlfriend or boyfriend) and negative (dislikes about partner and disadvantages of having a girlfriend or boyfriend) aspects of romantic relationships.

Structure of Dating

Table 1 presents data on the occurrence of dating, duration and frequency of contact, context of dates, and type of dating activities. Although the majority of the sample reports having had a girlfriend or boyfriend in the past 3 years, most of the teenagers interviewed were not currently dating. Girls and boys did not differ on whether they had dated.[2]

As expected, short-term relationship, averaging 4 months, characterized the majority of the sample. Only 8% of those adolescents with dating experience had a relationship for 1 year or longer. As a point of comparison, 97% of the adolescents have known their current same-sex best friend for 1 year or more.

Although the length of dating relationships is relatively brief, contact is very frequent. The adolescents report seeing each other in person and talking on the phone almost daily. There were no gender differences in length or frequency of contact.

Context   A repeated-measures analysis of variance was performed on the number of times per month that adolescents dated their partners in a group compared to a couples-alone context (between-subjects factor = sex; within-subject factor = context). Dating occurs more in a group than in a couples-alone context, context effect, $F(1, 103) = 7.9$, $p = .01$, and girls report a greater number of dates in a group context than boys, Sex × Context interaction, $F(1, 103) = 7.6$, $p = .01$. There are no gender differences in number of dates in a couples-alone context.

Activities   Adolescents were asked to describe what activities they engaged in with their dating partners and whether they had done this activity a part of a group or as a couple alone. Going out to movies, dinner, and hanging out at the mall or school are activities adolescents are equally as likely to report having done in a group or as a couple alone. Parties are more often reported as a group activity, whereas visiting each others' homes was only reported as a couples-alone activity.

Positive Aspects of Romantic Relationships

Likes about dating partner   Table 2 shows the types of qualities most often mentioned by the adolescents when asked to describe what they liked about their dating partners. Data are given for the total sample and by sex of adolescent. Chi-square analyses by sex of adolescent were performed to determine if there were gender differences in types of likes mentioned. Descriptions of positive personality traits (e.g., nice, funny) is the type of response most often given by the large majority of the sample. Physical attractiveness also is frequently mentioned, followed by intimacy, support, and companionship. Common interest is not mentioned very often. As expected, boys are more likely to mention physical attraction, whereas girls are more likely to mention support and intimacy when describing dating partners.

Table 1

The Structure of Dating

Occurrence of Dating			Total
Have dated			88%
Currently dating			21%
Never dated			12%

Duration and Frequency	*M*	*SD*	Median
Length of relationships (weeks)	16.7	18.8	12
Frequency of contact (days per week)			
In person	5.6	2.1	7
By phone	5.5	2.2	7
Context (number of times per week)			
Group			
Total	7.5	7.5	4
Boys	5.4	4.9	4
Girls	9.4	8.7	8
Alone			
Total	4.9	4.9	4
Boys	5.4	5.9	4
Girls	4.6	3.8	4

Type of Date	Group %	Alone %
Activities		
Movies	74	72
Dinner	18	20
Hang out	32	35
Parties	30	6
Home visits	0	30

Advantages of having a dating partner   Table 2 also shows the types of qualities mentioned by the adolescents when asked to describe advantages of having a dating partner. Companionship was the advantage most frequently mentioned by the sample. Intimacy and support also were mentioned fairly frequently, followed by friendship, social status, and learning about the opposite sex. Chi-square analyses by sex of adolescent revealed that girls mentioned intimacy and social status more than boys as advantages.

Negative Aspects of Romantic Relationships

Dislikes about dating partner   Table 3 shows the types of qualities mentioned by the adolescents when asked to describe dislikes about dating partners. These data are given for the total sample and by sex of adolescent. Negative personality traits (e.g., boring, stubborn) are mentioned most frequently as dislikes, followed by negative interpersonal relations (e.g., fights). Approximately one third of the sample had nothing

Table 2

Positive Aspects of Romantic Relationships

Qualities	Girls %	Boys %	Total %
Likes about dating partner			
Positive personality traits	85	88	86
Physical attraction[a]	46	68	57
Intimacy[b]	42	26	34
Support[c]	44	14	29
Companionship	27	24	26
Common interests	6	10	8
Advantages of having a dating partner			
Companionship	71	60	66
Intimacy[d]	54	32	43
Support	36	23	30
Friendship	18	16	17
Social status[e]	18	7	12
Learn about opposite sex	9	16	12

[a] $\chi^2 = 4.11$, $p = .04$. [b] $\chi^2 = 3.01$, $p = .08$. [c] $\chi^2 = 9.51$, $p = .001$. [d] $\chi^2 = 4.73$, $p = .03$. [e] $\chi^2 = 3.05$, $p = .08$.

negative to say about their dating partners. Jealousy was a dislike mentioned only by girls.

Disadvantages of having a dating partner   Table 3 also shows the types of characteristics mentioned by the adolescents as disadvantages of having a dating partner. Too much commitment (the adolescents often used this phrase), especially in terms of time, was mentioned by the majority of the sample. Negative interpersonal relations were mentioned fairly frequently, followed to a lesser extent by worried about other's feelings, jealousy, and costs money. A small percentage of the adolescents could not think of any disadvantages to having a dating partner. Only boys mentioned the disadvantage of having to spend money on dates.

Number of Comments About Romantic Relationships

In conducting the interviews, we noticed that girls appeared to have more to say than boys about positive and negative aspects of romantic relationships. Consequently, a multivariate analysis of variance was conducted on the number of different types of comments (likes, dislikes, advantages, disadvantages) made by the adolescents. Sex of adolescent was the between-subjects factor and type of comment (i.e., categories of likes, dislikes, advantages, and disadvantages) was the within-subject factor. Table 4 shows the mean number of comments for each type of comment by sex of adolescent. For each type of comment, girls had significantly more to say than boys. These findings cannot be explained by verbal fluency because covarying verbal IQ from the Wechsler Intelligence Scale for Children–Revised (Wechsler, 1974; available

TABLE 3

Negative Aspects of Romantic Relationships

Qualities	Girls %	Boys %	Total %
Dislikes about dating partner			
Negative personality	43	40	42
Negative interpersonal relations	25	26	25
Nothing	30	44	37
Jealousy[a]	19	0	10
Disadvantages of having a dating partner			
Too much commitment	79	65	72
Negative interpersonal relations	34	21	17
Worried about other's feelings and well being	9	11	10
Jealousy	7	5	6
Costs money[b]	0	9	4
Nothing	9	11	10

[a]$\chi^2 = 8.41$, $p = .01$. [b]$\chi^2 = 5.14$, $p = .02$.

from the 13-year assessment of participants) did not change the results. For both sexes, there was also a significantly higher number of positive compared to negative comments.

Discussion

Structure and Context of Early Romantic Relationships

Consistent with other findings, most 15-year-old adolescents from this study have had some experience with dating (Hansen, 1977; Offer, 1969; Wehner, 1992; Wright, 1982). For all but a small minority, these adolescents are in what has been described as the casual stage of dating, in which the duration of relationships is brief, lasting on average only a few months (Feinstein & Ardon, 1973; Furman & Wehner, 1992; McCabe, 1984). This is in contrast to best same-sex friendships, which are relatively stable during this period, with most adolescents maintaining friendships for 1 year or more (Berndt, 1982; Crockett, Losoff, & Petersen, 1984). Although stability in same-sex friendships is evident by preadolescence (Berndt, 1982, 1989), it is not common in romantic relationships until late adolescence (Blyth & Padgham, 1987; Feinstein & Ardon; Wright, 1982). Stable, supportive, same-sex friendships in early to middle adolescence are related to good social adjustment, especially during times of transition or environmental change (Berndt, 1989; Berndt & Hawkins, 1987). In contrast, stable romantic relationships in this period have been associated with subsequent emotional and school problems (Neeman, Kojetin, & Hubbard, 1991). Premature stability in romantic relationships may preclude healthy development of self-identity (Erikson, 1968).

Table 4

Number of Comments About Partners by Type of Comment and Sex of Participant

Type of Comment	Girls		Boys		F	p
	M	SD	M	SD		
Likes	3.9	(2.3)	2.7	(1.3)	11.5	.001
Dislikes	1.6	(1.2)	.9	(1.8)	11.9	.001
Advantages	2.8	(1.4)	1.9	(.9)	13.4	.0001
Disadvantages	2.2	(1.2)	1.7	(1.1)	4.3	.04

Note. The F tests given are for sex differences. Also note, a significant measure effect with more positive than negative comments $F(1, 103) = 83.98$, $p = .001$.

The short-term nature of these adolescents' romantic relationships may merit the label *casual*, but this term does not capture the daily involvement with boyfriends and girlfriends. When dating, these 15-year-olds report seeing and talking to their partners on the phone almost daily. The average length of a phone conversation is reported to be 60 min! The quality of fascination has been used to differentiate romantic from friendship relationships in adolescents and adults (Davis & Todd, 1982; Hatfield & Rapson, 1987b). One adolescent used the expression "like a candle in the wind" to describe his current dating experiences. This statement captures the brief but intense nature of adolescent romance in this sample. Given the amount of attention focused on the dating partner, *short-term fascination* might best describe the initial stage of romance in adolescence.

Consistent with the work of Dunphy (1963) and Sullivan (1953), this study finds that adolescent romance emerges in a peer-group context. Group activities are much more frequent than activities engaged in alone as a couple. Both group and couple-alone activities are more likely to occur in public than in private settings. These findings indicate that it is the peer group that sets the stage to facilitate the transition to interactions and relationships with the other sex. It is not until late adolescence to young adulthood that dyadic dating is the norm (Dunphy, 1963, 1969; Padgham & Blyth, 1991). Dating in a group context appears to be more characteristic of girls than boys. For girls beginning to date, a group context may have the advantage of providing constraints on sexual activity with one's dating partner. It is interesting to note that the dyadic pairing more frequently observed in girls' friendships from childhood onward may prepare them for greater comfort in the dyadic romantic interactions more characteristic of late adolescence (Berndt, 1982; Hartup, 1983).

Characteristics of Romance in 15-Year-Olds

Models of dating and mate selection in late adolescence and early adulthood propose that partners are initially selected on the basis of stimulus characteristics (e.g., desirable personality and physical attractiveness). If the relationship continues, common interests and values, and then interpersonal compatibility, become important (Kerckhoff & Davis, 1962; Murstein, 1976). These results indicate that stimulus characteristics of the partner are particularly important for adolescents' newly formed relationships with the other sex. Positive personality traits and physical attractiveness are the most frequently reported likes about the dating partner. Physical attraction is obviously a distinctive characteristic of romantic relationships (Hatfield & Rapson, 1987b; Sternberg, 1988). In the adolescents' reports, it is most often described in general terms, such as cute, pretty, or handsome, rather than in terms of sexuality (e.g., a good kisser).

The failure to explicitly discuss sexual attraction was more than likely due to the adolescents' discomfort in talking about such personal feelings and behavior in a face-to-face interview with an unfamiliar adult. Because adolescents were not asked directly about the importance of sexuality, failure to mention it does not mean it was not important for romantic relationships. Research suggests that most of this sample would be expected to have experience with precoital sexual behavior (Katchadourian, 1990; Smith & Udry, 1985).

Interpersonal qualities of the relationship also play a central role in adolescents' conscious views of romance. Given the casual nature and group context of romance in early to middle adolescence, affiliative qualities were expected to characterize descriptions more than attachment qualities. Consistent with this prediction and the work of Furman and Wehner (1994), the affiliative qualities of companionship, intimacy, and support were frequently mentioned as positive aspects of romantic relationships, whereas love and security were not. Companionship, a fundamental characteristic of friendship, is reported most frequently as an advantage of having a dating partner. Close same-sex friendships in adolescence also are characterized by intimacy, support, and extensive companionship (Youniss & Smollar, 1985). Developmentally, the emphasis on these characteristics in same-sex friendships emerges in early adolescence (Berndt, 1982; Bigelow & LaGaipa, 1975; Buhrmester & Furman, 1987). The results here indicate that these qualities—important for same-sex friendships—appear to provide the foundation for romantic relationships as well.

In general, adolescents were less likely to mention negative aspects compared to positive aspects of romantic relationships. Typical negative characteristics of close relationships, such as jealousy and fights, were not frequently mentioned. This may have been due to the adolescents' desire to make a positive impression during the interview or a tendency to conceptualize romantic relationships as being more of a positive than negative experience. The most frequently mentioned disadvantage of romantic relationships was too much commitment. The view of commitment as a negative characteristic rather than positive one by the majority of the sample suggests that the attachment system does not predominate for these adolescents engaged in casual relationships with the other sex. This finding is in direct contrast to research showing the central importance of loyalty and commitment in adolescents' same-sex friendships (Berndt, 1981; Bigelow & LaGaipa, 1975, 1980; Douvan & Adelson, 1966; Hartup & Overhauser, 1991; Youniss & Smollar, 1985).

The data presented here are obviously limited in their ability to capture attachment attributes, because the interview questions and analyses were not designed to assess working models of attachment expectations in describing dating partners. Nevertheless, the results do indicate that the affiliative system needs to be incorporated into any theory of adolescent romance (Furman & Wehner, 1994). Recent research has shown that, for 14-year-old to 18-year-old adolescents, the security of relationship style with romantic partners is more highly correlated with the security style for close friends compared with parents (Wehner, 1992). Furthermore, only relationship style with friends predicted relationship style with romantic partners. Adult attachment theory has focused on the association between parent–child and romantic relationships. The importance attributed to friendship relationships for newly forming romantic relationships has been limited. These results, and those of others, suggest that friendships may provide the most proximal basis for evolving romantic relationships.

Gender Differences

Girls' development of intimacy skills in same-sex friendships appears to accelerate in adolescence. Girls are more likely than boys to report sharing feelings, acceptance, and understanding of each other as the basis for same-sex friendships (Berndt, 1982; Bigelow & LaGaipa, 1975; Blyth & Foster-Clark, 1987; Buhrmester & Furman, 1987; Hill, Thiel, & Blyth, 1981). Girls have been found to value intimate conversations and intimate knowledge of friends as part of friendship more than boys (Berndt, 1982). This study finds that girls are more likely than boys to mention intimacy and support when describing romantic relationships. This suggests some degree of continuity in girls' perceptions of the importance of intimacy and support for close relationships with the same and other sex.

During adolescence, boys do not show strong developmental increases in intimacy with same-sex friends and they do not report reaching as high a level of disclosure as girls (Blyth & Foster-Clark, 1987; Buhrmester & Furman, 1987). It may be that shared activities, more so than interpersonal disclosure, are the means by which boys achieve intimacy in same-sex friendships (Buhrmester & Furman, 1987). This may be the case for newly emerging romantic relationships as well. However, research on adults indicates that men are more likely to use opposite-sex rather than same-sex friends or lovers as primary confidants (Antonucci & Akiyama, 1987; Wheeler, Reis, & Nezlek, 1983). Thus, intimacy as self-disclosure is probably more important to men's views of romance in late adolescence or early adulthood (Feiring, 1993; Sharabany et al., 1981). Fifteen-year-old boys also may be more reluctant to mention intimacy and support because traditional masculine stereotypes do not stress expressivity and disclosure. On the other hand, they do mention physical attraction more than girls, which is consistent with masculine stereotypes and research on how men decide who to date (Hinde, 1984; Huston & Ashmore, 1986; McCabe, 1984).

This study also finds that girls have more to say about the positive and negative aspects of romantic relationships than boys. Girls express interest in the other sex earlier than do boys (Blyth & Foster-Clark, 1987; Blyth et al., 1982; Feiring & Lewis, 1991, 1993). It has been argued that women's sense of self, to a greater extent than men's, is organized around being able to make and maintain affiliations and relationships (Archer, 1985; Gilligan, 1982; Miller, 1976). During adolescence, girls spend a significant amount of dyadic interaction time with their close same-sex friends analyzing interpersonal events and relationships. A topic that receives considerable attention is relationships and events with the other sex, including current or potential romantic partners (Parker & Gottman, 1989). Thus, girls may have more to say than boys because the interview questions focus on relationships, a topic of central concern and one that girls have had more practice thinking and talking about.

In interpreting these gender differences, it is important to remember that self-assessed tendencies by female and male participants often show stronger differences than observational measures (Deaux, 1987). Self-reported gender differences such as these may reflect the operation of demand characteristics, with participants describing gender stereotypes rather than accurately assessing their own behavior. Future research that includes observation of interactions as well as self-report techniques will help clarify this issue. It also is important to realize that the differences reported are relative ones with considerable agreement between girls and boys in their views of romantic relationships.

Early adolescence is believed to be a period of accelerated gender differential socialization (Hill & Lynch, 1983). Although socialization pressure from same-sex peers and parents, as well as the role of puberty, have been discussed as mechanisms for gender role development in adolescence, little work has focused on romantic relationships (Hill & Lynch; Simmons, Blyth, & McKinney, 1983; Steinberg, 1981). Examination of self-report and observational measures of romantic relationships in early to middle adolescence, as they are related to the development of gender related role expectations, behavior, and self-concept, is needed.

In conclusion, this study represents an initial step in understanding adolescents' conscious views of romance as they begin to date. Although theory and research on adult love provide a point of departure, they do not sufficiently address issues of importance during the adolescent period. Most notable is the importance of friendship and affiliative qualities in these adolescents' conceptions of romance. The challenge of adolescence is to integrate the sexual and social aspects of romantic relationships (Damon, 1983; Erikson, 1968; Sullivan, 1953). The sexual aspects of romantic relationships are, for the most part, first experienced in interactions with dating partners. Social aspects of romantic relationships should have a basis in relationships with parents and close friends. How skills and expectations learned in close relationships with family and friends influence the nature of romance in adolescence is an important topic for future investigation.

Notes

1. Of 120 possible participants, only 3 completed questionnaire data and declined to be interviewed, citing lack of time or interest. The 117 adolescents on whom dating information is available at 15 years do not differ significantly from the original sample in the distribution of gender, socioeconomic status, family size, or development of secondary

gender characteristics. It should also be noted that self-reported stage of secondary gender characteristics (using Petersen, Crockett, Richards, & Boxer, 1988) was not related to dating status or description of dating partners.

2. Eighty-eight percent of the sample answered the questions about dating partners because they had current or recent (past 3 years) experience dating. Of this sample, 53 were girls and 50 were boys; 49 were upper middle and 54 were of middle socioeconomic status.

References

Ainsworth, M. D. S. (1989). Attachments beyond infancy. *American Psychologist, 44,* 709–716.

Antonucci, T. C., & Akiyama, H. (1987). An examination of sex differences in social support among older men and women. *Sex Role: A Journal of Research, 17* (11/12), 737–749.

Archer, S. L. (1985). Identity and choice of social roles. In A. S. Waterman (Ed.), *Identity in adolescence: Processes and contents* (pp. 79–100). San Francisco, CA: Jossey-Bass.

Bartholomew, K. (1991). Attachment styles among young adults: A test of a four-category model. *Journal of Personality and Social Psychology, 61,* 226–244.

Belle, D. (1989). Gender differences in children's social networks and supports. In D. Belle (Ed.), *Children's social networks and social supports* (pp. 173–188). New York: Wiley.

Berndt, T. J. (1981). Age changes and changes over time in prosocial intentions and behavior between friends. *Developmental Psychology, 17,* 408–416.

Berndt, T. J. (1982). The features and effects of friendship in early adolescence. *Child Development, 53,* 1447–1460.

Berndt, T. J. (1989). Obtaining support from friends during childhood and adolescence. In D. Belle (Ed.), *Children's social networks and social supports* (pp. 308–331). New York: Wiley.

Berndt, T. J., & Hawkins, J. A. (1987). *The contribution of supportive friendships to adjustment after the transition to junior high school.* Unpublished manuscript, Purdue University.

Berndt, T. J., & Hoyle, S. G. (1985). Stability and change in childhood and adolescent friendships. *Developmental Psychology, 21,* 1007–1015.

Bigelow, B. J., & LaGaipa, J. J. (1975). Children's written descriptions of friendship: A multidimensional analysis. *Developmental Psychology, 11,* 857–858.

Bigelow, B. J. & LaGaipa, J. J. (1980). The development of friendship values and choice. In H. G. Foot, A. J. Chapman, & J. R. Smith (Eds.), *Friendship and social relations in children* (pp. 15–44). New York: Wiley.

Blyth, D. A., & Foster-Clark, F. S. (1987). Gender differences in perceived intimacy with different members of adolescents' social networks. *Sex Roles: A Journal of Research, 17* (11/12), 689–718.

Blyth, D. A., Hill, J. P., & Thiel, K. S. (1982). Early adolescents' significant others: Grade and gender differences with familial and non-familial adults and young people. *Journal of Youth and Adolescence, 11,* 425–450.

Blyth, D. A., & Padgham, J. J. (1987, August). *Stages of adolescent same- and other-sex peer relations.* Poster session presented at the meeting of the American Psychological Association, New York.

Brennan, K. A., Shaver, P. R., & Tobey, A. E. (1991). Attachment styles, gender, and parental problem drinking. *Journal of Social and Personal Relationships, 8,* 451–466.

Buhrmester, D., & Furman, W. (1987). The development of companionship and intimacy. *Child Development, 58,* 1101–1113.

Crockett, L., Losoff, M., & Petersen, A. C. (1984). Perceptions of the peer group and friendship in early adolescence. *Journal of Early Adolescence, 4,* 155–181.

Csikzentmihalyi, M., Larson, R., & Prescott, S. (1977). The ecology of adolescent activity and experience. *Journal of Youth and Adolescence, 6,* 181–194.

Damon, W. (1983). *Social and personality development.* New York: Norton.

Davis, K. E., & Todd, M. J. (1982). Friendship and love relations. In K. E. Davis & M. J. Todd (Eds.), *Advances in descriptive psychology, Vol. 2* (pp. 79–122). Greenwich, CT: JAI.

Deaux, K. (1987). Psychological constructions of masculinity and femininity. In J. M. Reinisch, L. A. Rosenblum, & S. A. Sanders (Eds.), *Masculinity/Femininity* (pp. 289–303). New York: Oxford University Press.

DeLamater, J. (1982, March). *Gender differences in sexual scenarios.* Paper presented at the meeting of the American Sociological Association, San Francisco, CA.

Douvan, E., & Adelson, J. (1966). *The adolescent experience.* New York: Wiley.

Dunphy, D. C. (1963). The social structure of urban adolescent peer groups. *Sociometry, 26,* 230–246.

Dunphy, D. C. (1969). *Cliques, crowds, and gangs.* Melbourne, Australia: Chesire.

Epstein, J. L. (1986). Friendship selection: Developmental and environmental influences. In R. C. Mueller & C. R. Cooper (Eds.), *Process and outcome in peer relationships* (pp. 129–160). New York: Academic.

Erikson, E. H. (1968). *Identity: Youth and crisis.* New York: Norton.

Feinstein, S. C., & Ardon, M. S. (1973). Trends in dating patterns and adolescent development. *Journal of Youth and Adolescence, 2* (2), 157–166.

Feiring, C. (1993, March). Developing concepts of romance from 15 to 18 years. In W. Furman (Chair), *Adolescent romantic relationships: A new look.* Symposium conducted at Society for Research in Child Development, New Orleans.

Feiring, C., & Lewis, M. (1981). Middle class differences in the mother–child interaction and the child's cognitive development. In T. Field (Ed.), *Culture and early interactions* (pp. 63–94). Hillsdale, NJ: Lawrence Erlbaum Associates, Inc.

Feiring, C., & Lewis, M. (1991). The transition from middle childhood to early adolescence: Sex differences in the social network and perceived self-competence. *Sex Roles, 24* (7/8), 489–509.

Feiring, C., & Lewis, M. (1993). Do mothers know their teenagers' friends? Implications for individuation in early adolescence. *Journal of Youth and Adolescence, 22* (4), 1–18.

Furman, W., & Buhrmester, D. (1985). Children's perceptions of the personal relationships in their social networks. *Developmental Psychology, 21,* 1014–1024.

Furman, W., & Wehner, E. A. (1994). Romantic views: Toward a theory of adolescent romantic relationships. In R. Montemayor, G. R. Adams, & T. P. Gullotta (Eds.), *Advances in adolescent development, Vol. 3: Relationships in adolescence* (pp. 168–195). Beverly Hills, CA: Sage.

Gilligan, C. (1982). *In a different voice.* Cambridge, MA: Harvard University Press.

Grinder, R. E. (1966). Relations of social dating attractions to academic orientation and peer relations. *Journal of Educational Psychology, 57,* 27–34.

Hallinan, M. T. (1978–79). The process of friendship formation. *Social Networks, 1,* 193–210.

Hansen, S. L. (1977). Dating choices of high school students. *The Family Coordinator, 26,* 133–138.

Hansen, S. L., & Hicks, M. W. (1980). Sex role attitudes and perceived dating-mating choices of youth. *Adolescence, 15,* 83–90.

Hartup, W. W. (1983). Peer relations. In E. M. Hetherington (Series Ed.) and P. H. Mussen (Vol. Ed.), *Handbook of child psychology, Vol. 4: Socialization, personality, and social development* (pp. 103–196). New York: Wiley.

Hartup, W. W., & Overhauser, S. (1991). Friendships. In R. M. Lerner, A. C. Petersen, & J. Brooks-Gunn (Eds.), *Encyclopedia of adolescence* (pp. 378–384). New York: Garland.

Hatfield, E., & Rapson, R. L. (1987a). Gender differences in love and intimacy: The fantasy vs. reality. In H. Gochros & W. Ricketts (Eds.), *Social work and love*. New York: Hayworth.

Hatfield, E., & Rapson, R. L. (1987b). Passionate love: New directions in research. In W. H. Jones & D. Pearlman (Eds.), *Advances in personal relationships, Vol. 1* (pp. 109–139). Greenwich, CT: JAI.

Hazan, C., & Shaver, P. (1987). Conceptualizing romantic love as an attachment process. *Journal of Personality and Social Psychology, 52,* 511–524.

Hazan, C., & Shaver, P. (1994). Attachment as an organizational framework for research in close relationships. *Psychological Inquiry, 5,* 1–22.

Hill, J. P., & Lynch, M. E. (1983). The intensification of gender-related role expectations during early adolescence. In J. Brooks-Gunn & A. C. Petersen (Eds.), *Girls at puberty: Biological and psychosocial perspectives* (pp. 201–228). New York: Plenum.

Hill, J. P., Thiel, K. S., & Blyth, D. A. (1981). *Grade and gender differences in perceived intimacy with peers among seventh to tenth grade boys and girls.* Unpublished manuscript, Boys Town Center for the Study of Youth Development, Omaha, NE.

Hinde, R. A. (1984). Why do the sexes behave differently in close relationships? *Journal of Social and Personal Relationships, 1,* 471–501.

Husbands, C. T. (1970). Some social and psychological consequences of the American dating system. *Adolescence, 5,* 451–462.

Huston, T. L., & Ashmore, R. D. (1986). Women and men in personal relationships. In R. D. Ashmore & F. K. Del Boca (Eds.), *The social psychology of female–male relations* (pp. 167–210). Orlando, FL: Academic.

Katchadourian, H. (1990). Sexuality. In S. S. Feldman & G. R. Elliott (Eds.), *At the threshold: The developing adolescent* (pp. 330–351). Cambridge, MA: Harvard University Press.

Kerckhoff, A. C., & Davis, K. E. (1962). Value consensus and need complementarity in mate selection. *American Sociological Review, 27,* 295–303.

Lee, J. A. (1977). A typology of style of loving. *Personality and Social Psychology Bulletin, 3,* 172–182.

Lee, J. A. (1988). Love styles. In. R. J. Sternberg & M. Barnes (Eds.), *The psychology of love* (pp. 38–67). New Haven, CT: Yale University Press.

Maddock, J. W. (1973). Sex in adolescence: Its meaning and its future. *Adolescence, 8* (31), 325–342.

McCabe, M. P. (1984). Toward a theory of adolescent dating. *Adolescence, 19* (73), 159–170.

McDaniel, C. O. (1969). Dating roles and reasons for dating. *Journal of Marriage and the Family, 31,* 97–107.

Miller, J. B. (1976). *Toward a new psychology of women.* Boston, MA: Beacon Press.

Murstein, B. I. (1976). *Who will marry whom? Theories and research in marital choice.* New York: Springer.

Neeman, J., Kojetin, B., & Hubbard, J. (1992, March). Looking for love in all the wrong places: A longitudinal study of adjustment and adolescent romantic relationships. In W. Furman (Chair), *Adolescent romantic relationships: Conceptualizations, characterizations, and functions.* Symposium conducted at the meeting of the Society for Research on Adolescence, Washington, DC.

Offer, D. (1969). *The psychological world of the teenager.* New York: Basic.

Padgham, J. J., & Blyth, D. A. (1991). Dating during adolescence. In R. M. Lerner, A. C. Petersen, & J. Brooks-Gunn (Eds.), *Encyclopedia of adolescence* (pp. 196–198). New York: Garland.

Parker, J. G., & Gottman, J. M. (1989). Social and emotional development in a relational context. In T. J. Berndt & G. W. Ladd (Eds.), *Peer relationships in child development* (pp. 95–131). New York: Wiley.

Peplau, L. A. (1983). Roles and gender. In H. H. Kelley, E. Berschied, A. Christensen, J. H. Harvey, T. L. Huston, G. Levinger, E. McClintock, L. A. Peplau, & D. R. Peterson (Eds), *Close relationships* (pp. 220–264). New York: Freeman.

Petersen, A. C., Crockett, L., Richards, M., & Boxer, A. (1988). A self-report measure of pubertal status: Reliability, validity, and initial norms. *Journal of Youth and Adolescence, 17* (2), 117–133.

Rice, F. P. (1975). *The adolescent: Development, relationships and culture.* Boston: Allyn & Bacon.

Rivenbark, W. H. (1971). Self-disclosure patterns among adolescents. *Psychologic Reports, 28,* 35–42.

Savin-Williams, R. C., & Berndt, T. J. (1990). Friendship and peer relations. In S. S. Feldman & G. R. Elliott (eds.), *At the threshold: The developing adolescent* (pp. 277–307). Cambridge, MA: Harvard University Press.

Schofield, J. W. (1981). Complementary and conflicting identities: Images of interaction in an interracial school. In S. A. Asher & J. M. Gottman (Eds.), *The development of children's friendships* (pp. 53–90). New York: Cambridge University Press.

Sharabany, R., Gershoni, R., & Hofman, J. E. (1981). Girlfriend, boyfriend: Age and sex differences in intimate friendship. *Developmental Psychology, 17,* 800–808.

Shaver, P., & Hazan, C. (1988). A biased overview of the study of love. *Journal of Social and Personal Relationships, 5,* 473–501.

Simmons, R. G., Blyth, D. A., & McKinney, K. L. (1983). The social and psychological effects of puberty on White females. In J. Brooks-Gunn & A. C. Petersen (Eds.), *Girls at puberty: Biological and psychosocial perspectives* (pp. 229–272). New York: Plenum.

Skipper, J. K., & Nass, G. (1966). Dating behavior: A framework for analysis and an illustration. *Journal of Marriage and the Family, 28,* 412–420.

Smith, E. A. (1962). *American youth culture: Group life in teenage society.* New York: The Free Press of Glencoe.

Smith, E. A., & Udry, J. R. (1985). Coital and non-coital sexual behaviors of White and Black adolescents. *American Journal of Public Health, 75,* 1200–1203.

Steinberg, L. (1981). Transformations in family relationships at puberty. *Developmental Psychology, 17,* 833–840.

Sternberg, R. J. (1986). A triangular theory of love. *Psychological Review, 93* (2), 119–135.

Sternberg, R. J. (1988). Triangulating love. In R. J. Sternberg & M. Barnes (Eds.), *The psychology of love* (pp. 119–138). New Haven, CT: Yale University Press.

Sullivan, H. S. (1953). *The interpersonal theory of psychiatry.* New York: Norton.

Wechsler, D. (1974). *Wechsler Intelligence Scale for Children–Revised.* San Antonio, TX: Psychological Corporation.

Wehner, E. A. (1992, March). Characteristics of adolescent romantic relationships and links with parent–adolescent relationships and friendships. In W. Furman (Chair), *Adolescent romantic relationships: Conceptualizations, characterizations, and functions.* Symposium conducted at the meeting of the Society for Research on Adolescence, Washington, DC.

Weiss, R. S. (1982). Attachment in adults. In C. M. Parker & J. Stevenson-Hinde (Eds.), *The place of attachment in human behavior* (pp. 171–184). New York: Basic.

Wheeler, L., Reis, H., & Nezlek, J. (1983). Loneliness, social interaction, and sex roles. *Journal of Personality and Social Psychology, 45,* 945–953.

Wright, L. S. (1982). Parental permission to date and its relationship to drug use and suicidal thought among adolescents. *Adolescence, 17,* 409–418.

Youniss, J., & Smollar, J. (1985). *Adolescent relations with mothers, fathers, and friends.* Chicago: University of Chicago Press.

Zelnik, M., & Shah, F. K. (1983). First intercourse among young Americans. *Family Planning Perspectives, 15,* 64–70.

Questions

1. Do romantic relationships meet needs different from those fulfilled by same-sex friendships?
2. Why are adolescent romantic relationships short in duration yet intense?
3. What are the costs and benefits of adolescent romantic relationships?
4. Why do sex differences occur in the qualities adolescents use to describe their romantic attachments?
5. At what age are adolescents ready to enter into romantic relationships?

References and Further Reading

Connolly, J. A., & Johnson, A. M. (1996). Adolescents' romantic relationships and the structure and quality of their close interpersonal ties. *Personal Relationships, 3,* 185–195.

Furman, W., & Wehner, E. A. (1997). Adolescent romantic relationships: A developmental perspective. *New Directions in Child Development, 78,* 21–36.

Levesque, R. (1993). The romantic experience of adolescents in satisfying love relationships. *Journal of Youth and Adolescence, 22,* 219–251.

Chapter 12

School and Work

Early in the twentieth century only a small number of young people continued their education in 4-year high schools, but today 90% of adolescents receive diplomas from high school. Thus schools have taken on an increasingly important role in shaping the lives of adolescents. Considerable debate has taken place during the last century over how to educate youth to best prepare them for adult life. In a review of the history of the junior high school, Fred Hechinger concluded that junior high schools and middle schools have alternated between "sincere efforts to respond to a growing understanding among experts of the special needs of teenagers," and efforts to respond to "a variety of social and economic issues, from competing more effectively with adversaries in international trade to preparing adolescents for admission to college" (Hechinger, 1993, p. 79).

Some educators have faulted schools for failing to understand and address the needs of adolescents and the risks they face in terms of substance abuse, sexual behavior, and involvement in violent behavior. Other educators have faulted schools for failing to educate poor and minority youth who are more likely to underachieve and to drop out of school. Some educators argue that in addition to stressing basic intellectual development, schools should do more to promote vocational development, to break down the barriers between school and work by providing opportunities for adolescents to apply skills they are learning in the classroom to monitored work experiences. Some feel that schools alone cannot provide a complete environment for young people or give students the experiences with real life that will prepare them for adulthood. The role of student is a relatively narrow one, focusing solely on academic skills and learning tasks that are primarily solitary; it does not offer young people a broad range of roles and activities applicable to the "real world."

Debate has also centered on whether early entry into the labor force through part-time work is a positive bridge between the institutional realms of school and work, or whether it draws adolescents away from academic achievement and places them at greater risk. Some researchers have argued that part-time work offers special opportunities for growth at adolescence (see Finch, Mortimer, & Ryu, 1997). The work context can foster thinking about identity and future occupational goals and work preferences, helping to clarify what kind of work adolescents might like to do, and giving feedback about what they are good at. Part-time work helps adolescents learn to manage time, to juggle the multiple roles of student, friend, worker, and family member. Work provides the opportunity for young people to take responsibility; it builds self-reliance, self-discipline, and dependability. Further, for adolescents who grow up in neighborhoods with high rates of poverty and unemployment, part-time work provides a way for them to provide for their own financial needs when families are unable to do so (Reading 7.1), and it enables poor youth to participate in the youth culture by providing funds for dress and recreation. Employment provides a track record for future employment that many poor youth find to be more important than a high school diploma. Finally, adolescents from inner-city neighborhoods who work have less time to spend in their high-risk neighborhoods (Newman, 1996).

Others have argued, however, that part-time work poses risks to adolescents' health and development. If adolescents work long hours, the dual demands of school and part-time work lead to lack of sleep and exercise, and role overload reduces adolescents' investment in homework and academic achievement. The number of hours worked per week, the quality of work, the social meaning of work, and the context in which it occurs are important factors that determine whether the costs will outweigh the benefits of work (Finch, Mortimer, & Ryu, 1997).

Through the contexts of school and work, adolescents are helped to prepare for future vocational and adult roles. The nature of schooling and adolescent involvement in the labor force are likely to continue to evolve in response to changing social and economic pressures and current failures to adequately meet the needs of adolescents.

Additional Resources

References and Suggested Reading

Carnegie Council on Adolescent Development (1989). *Turning points: Preparing American youth for the twenty-first century.* Washington, DC: Carnegie Corporation.

Finch, M. D., Mortimer, J. T., & Ryu, S. (1997). Transition into part-time work: Health risks and opportunities. In J. Schulenberg, J. L. Maggs, & K. Hurrelmann (Eds.), *Health risks and developmental transitions during adolescence* (pp. 321–344). New York: Cambridge University Press.

Hechinger, F. M. (1993). Schools for teenagers: A historical dilemma. In *Adolescence in the 1990s: Risk and opportunity* (pp. 64–81). New York: Teachers College Press.

Mortimer, J. T., & Johnson, M. K. (1998). New perspectives on adolescent work and the transition to adulthood. In R. Jessor, (Ed.) *New perspectives on adolescent risk behavior* (pp. 425–496). Cambridge: Cambridge University Press.

Newman, K. S. (1996). Working poor: Low-wage employment in the lives of Harlem youth. In J. A. Graber, J. Brooks-Gunn, & A. C. Petersen (Eds.), *Transitions through adolescence: Interpersonal domains and context* (pp. 323–343). Mahwah, NJ: Lawrence Erlbaum.

On the Internet

http://www.personal.psu.edu/faculty/n/x/nxd10/schools2.htm
Adolescence: Change & Continuity—Schools

http://www.personal.psu.edu/faculty/n/x/nxd10/balance.htm
Adolescence: Change & Continuity: Work
These two sites were produced by Pennsylvania State University students taking Human Development and Family Studies 433: The Transition to Adulthood, and Human Development and Family Studies 239: Adolescent Development.

http://www.aflcio.rg/publ/newsonline/95sep25/teens.html
AFL-CIO News—Teens Are in Harm's Way on Jobs
This is the Web site of The American Federation of Labor-Congress of Industrial Organizations (AFL-CIO), a voluntary federation of America's unions. The AFL-CIO News Online chronicles labor events.

http://www.ed.gov/PressReleases/09-1994/drop.html
U.S. Department of Education—Press Releases: High School Dropout Rates Decline Over Two Decades

http://www.ed.gov/PressReleases/12-1997/dropout.html
U.S. Department of Education—Press Releases: Dropout Rates Remain Stable Over Last Decade
These two Web sites were produced by the U.S. Department of Education. These press releases are provided by the Office of Public Affairs.

12.1   Jacquelynne S. Eccles, et al., 1996

Schools, Families, and Early Adolescents: What Are We Doing Wrong and What Can We Do Instead?

Jacquelynne S. Eccles, Ph.D., is a professor of education and psychology at the University of Michigan. She teaches developmental and social psychology. She has written and edited extensively on adolescent issues of gender, education, and control.

Over the course of the twentieth century, dissatisfaction with the nature of public schooling has taken many forms. Of current concern is the fact that many adolescents begin a downward spiral marked by declines in motivation and attention in class, in school attendance, and in confidence in intellectual ability, leading eventually to school failure and dropping out of school.

In 1989 the task force of the Carnegie Council on Adolescent Development issued a report finding that the curriculum and organization of middle schools failed to meet the emotional needs of young adolescents (Carnegie Council on Adolescent Development, 1989). The report advocated reorganizing large institutions into smaller units within those schools so that students might become well known to one adult. Consistent with the Carnegie Council report, Jacquelynne Eccles and her colleagues argue that the problems many early adolescents face are heightened by negative experiences in school. They attribute the motivational and behavioral declines, which may lead to academic failure and dropping out, in part to the nature of the learning environment in junior high schools, claiming that a lack of fit exists between the characteristics young adolescents bring to junior high schools and the characteristics of those schools.

Eccles and her colleagues argue that for optimal development to occur there must be a good fit between the needs of early adolescents and the opportunities provided them by their social environments. While adolescents are in need of close relationships with adults outside the home, the structure of junior high schools does not afford them the opportunity to form these personal and positive connections with caring adults. Eccles and her colleagues argue, for example, that compared to elementary schools, junior high schools offer little opportunity for classroom decision making or individualized instruction. Standards of grading often become higher and forms of evaluation more public than in elementary school. Teachers hold negative stereotypes about adolescents and feel less confident in their teaching efficacy. These characteristics have negative effects on students' motivational orientation toward school, and contribute to negative psychological and behavioral outcomes for adolescents.

Abstract Although most individuals pass through adolescence without excessively high levels of "storm and stress," many individuals experience difficulty during this period. Why? Is there something unique about this developmental period that puts individuals at greater risk for difficulty? This paper focuses on these questions and advances the hypothesis that some of the "negative" psychological and behavioral changes associated with adolescent development result from a mismatch between the needs of developing adolescents and their experiences at school and at home. It provides theoretical and empirical examples of how this mismatch develops, how it is linked to negative age-related changes in early adolescents' motivation, self-perceptions, self-evaluations, and psychological competence, and how we could provide more developmentally appropriate social environments, particularly at school. *J Dev Behav Pediatr 17:267–276, 1996.* Index terms: adolescents, schools, family, motivation, mental health, self-concept.

Adolescents today face great risks to their current and future well-being, perhaps greater than at any previous point in our history.[1] As a result, a substantial portion of America's adolescents are not doing very well; between 15 and 30% (depending on ethnic group) drop out of school before completing high school; adolescents have the highest arrest rate of any age group; and increasing numbers of adolescents consume alcohol and other drugs on a regular basis.[2] In addition, academic failure often co-occurs with other problem behaviors, such as disruptive behavior in the classroom, skipping classes, truancy, delinquency, substance abuse, and teenage pregnancy.[3,4] Many of these problems appear to begin during the early adolescent years.[5] Why? Is there something unique about this developmental period that puts individuals at greater risk for difficulty? This paper focuses on this question. Consistent with the view elaborated in the Carnegie Council on Adolescent Development report *Turning Points,*[5] we suggest that the problems of many early adolescents are exacerbated by the kinds of experiences they often have in middle and junior high schools. There is considerable evidence (which we review in some detail) that junior high schools are often too large and impersonal to meet the needs of young adolescents, particularly young adolescents who may already be experiencing problems at school. As a result, these young people can slip through the cracks of adult supervision and monitoring, and their needs can go unnoticed until it is too late. As is argued in *Turning Points,* the junior high school years may be the last best chance to "save" these young people. But for this to occur, junior high schools and middle schools need to provide a different type of social environment for both the teachers and the students. In this paper, we outline some of the characteristics of typical junior high school environments that need to be changed to provide a better social environment for both the young people themselves and the adults who have the responsibility for educating and parenting them through this vulnerable developmental period.

"Problematic" Changes Associated With Early Adolescent Development

Evidence from several sources suggests that the early adolescent years mark the beginning of a downward spiral for some individuals, a downward spiral that leads these adolescents to academic failure and school drop out.[3,6–8] For example, Simmons and Blyth[8] found a marked decline in some early adolescents' school grades as they moved into junior high school, with the magnitude of this decline being predictive of subsequent school failure and drop-out. Similar declines have been documented for such motivational constructs as: interest and feelings of belonging in school,[9,10] intrinsic motivation,[11] and self-concepts/self-perceptions and confidence in one's intellectual abilities, especially after failure.[12–15] There are also age-related increases during early adolescence in such negative motivational and behavioral characteristics as test anxiety,[16] learned helpless responses to failure,[17] and a focus on self-evaluation rather than task mastery.[18]

Similar types of negative changes have also been noted in family interactions. Although the findings are neither universal nor indicative of major disruptions for most adolescents and their families, there does appear to be a temporary increase in family conflict, particularly over issues related to autonomy and control, during the early adolescent years.[19–26] For example, Hill and Steinberg, in both their observational and self-report studies, found increased conflict between mothers and their sons and daughters during the early and middle adolescent years, particularly for early maturing adolescents.[27–29]

Thus, although these types of negative changes are not extreme for most adolescents, there is sufficient evidence of a gradual decline in various indicators of self-perceptions, academic motivation, performance, positive school behaviors, and family functioning as well as a gradual increase in school problems and anti-social behaviors over the early adolescent years to make one wonder what is happening.[6]

A variety of explanations have been offered to explain these "negative" changes. Some have suggested that such declines result from the intrapsychic upheaval assumed to be associated with early adolescent development.[30] Others have concluded that it is the coincidence of the timing of multiple life changes. For example, Simmons and her colleagues have suggested that the concurrent timing of the junior high school transition and pubertal development accounts for the declines in the school-related measures and self-esteem.[8,31] Drawing on cumulative stress theory, they suggest that declines in motivation occur because so many young adolescents must cope with two major transitions: pubertal change and the move to middle or junior high school. To test this hypothesis, Simmons and her colleagues compared the pattern of change on early school-related outcomes for adolescents who moved from sixth to seventh grade in a K–8, 9–12 system with the pattern of change for adolescents who made the same grade transition in a K–6, 7–9, 10–12 school system. This work separated out the effects of age and school transition operating in most developmental studies of this age period. These researchers found clear evidence, especially among girls, of greater negative change among adolescents making the junior high school transition than among adolescents remaining in the same school setting as part of a K–8 school program. But are these differences due to the cumulative impact of school transition and pubertal change for girls who moved to a junior high school at grade 7 or are they due to differences in the nature of the school environments in these two educational structures? Or are the differences due to both of these sets of experiences? Simmons and her colleagues[8] argue for the latter.

Similarly, Eccles and her colleagues have suggested that the *change* in the nature of the learning environment associated with the junior high school transition is a plausible explanation for some of the declines in the school-related measures associated with the junior high school transition.[6,12] Drawing on person-environment fit theory,[32] Eccles and Midgley[6] proposed that these motivational and behavioral declines could result from the fact that many junior high schools do not provide appropriate educational and social environments for early adolescents. According to person-environment fit theory, motivation is influenced by the fit between the characteristics individuals bring to their social environments and the characteristics of these social environments. Individuals are not likely to do very well, or be very motivated, if they are in social environments that do not meet their psychological needs. If the social environments in the typical junior high school do not fit very well with the psychological needs of adolescents, then person-environment fit theory predicts a decline in motivation, interest, performance, and behavior as they move into this environment. This is the perspective elaborated in this current paper. This perspective is also extended to the family context, focusing on the possible mismatch between adolescents' need for great autonomy from parental control and the opportunities for such autonomy provided by many adolescents' parents.

Stage/Environment Fit and School-Related Changes

Various explanations have been offered for the declines in early adolescents' school-related motivational orientations associated with the junior high school transition. In this section, the possible role that the school may play in exacerbating these declines is discussed. To understand this role, two types of evidence regarding school effects are presented: evidence drawn from studies that follow the standard environmental influences approach and evidence from studies that adopt a developmental variant on the person-environment fit paradigm, or as Eccles and Midgley have termed it, the "stage/environment fit" approach.[6]

General Environmental Influences

Work in a variety of areas has documented the impact of several classroom and school environmental characteristics on motivation. For example, the big school/small schools literature has demonstrated the motivational advantages of small schools, especially for marginal students.[33] Similarly, many studies have documented the importance of teacher confidence and positive teacher-student relations for both teachers' and students' motivation.[34-36] Finally, motivational psychologists have demonstrated the importance of participation and self-control on motivation.[37-39] Although this list is by no means exhaustive, there are many characteristics of classrooms and schools that influence students' motivation and attachment to their school. If students experience a change in these characteristics as they move from elementary school into junior high school, then their motivation and interest in school should also change. In fact, evidence (reviewed later) is growing to suggest that there are fairly systematic differences between typical elementary classrooms and schools and typical junior high classrooms and schools. Furthermore, the evidence indicates that many junior high schools exhibit those characteristics usually linked with lowered motivation and interest. For example, they are usually bigger than elementary schools and have less personal and friendly student-teacher relationships. If this is the case, then these types of differences could help explain some of the motivational changes seen among early adolescents as they make the transition into middle or junior high school. If so, then some of the motivational problems seen at early adolescence may be as much a consequence of negative changes in their school environment as a consequence of the pubertal changes that accompany this developmental period (see Higgins and Parsons[40] for a full elaboration of this argument).

Stage-Environment Fit

A slightly different analysis of the possible environmental causes of the motivational changes associated with the junior high school transition draws on the idea of person-environment fit. This perspective leads one to expect negative motivational consequences for individuals when they are in environments that do not fit well with their needs.[32,41] At the most basic level, this perspective suggests the importance of looking at the fit between the needs of early adolescents and the opportunities afforded them in the traditional junior high school environment. A poor fit would help explain the declines in motivation associated with the transition to junior high school.

An even more interesting way to use the person/environment fit perspective is to put it into a developmental framework. Hunt[32] argued for the importance of adopting a developmental perspective on person-environment fit in the classroom and suggested that teachers should provide the optimal level of structure for children's current levels of maturity while providing a sufficiently challenging environment to pull the children along a developmental path toward higher levels of cognitive and social maturity. What is intriguing about this suggestion is its applicability to understanding the motivational declines associated with the junior high school transition. If it is true that different types of educational environments may be needed for different age groups to meet developmental needs and to foster continued developmental growth, then it is also possible that some types of changes in educational environments may be especially inappropriate at certain stages of development. In fact, some types of changes in the educational environment may be "developmentally regressive." Exposure to such changes at the junior high school or middle school transition could lead to a particularly poor person-environment fit and thus help explain some of the declines in motivation seen at this developmental period.

Systematic Changes in School Environments With the Transition into Middle or Junior High School

In essence, we are suggesting that it is the fit between the developmental needs of the adolescent and the educational environment that is important. This hypothesis was discussed at length in *Turning Points*.[5] In this report, the Council argued that educational environments for early adolescents need to be especially designed for the needs of this age period. Furthermore, the Council argued that many of the features of typical junior high schools, such as the impersonal relationships between teachers and students, are not appropriate for early adolescents. We also believe that: (1) there are several classroom organizational, instructional, and climate characteristics such as ability grouping (or tracking) practices, evaluation techniques, motivational strategies, locus of responsibility for learning, and quality of teacher-student and student-student relationships that are likely to undermine early adolescents' academic motivation and confidence and (2) these characteristics are much more common in junior high schools than in elementary schools. If this is true, then these types of changes in school characteristics could help explain the types of negative motivational changes we see in early adolescents as they make the junior high school transition. Although relatively little research has been done comparing elementary school and junior high school classrooms, that which exists provides support for these suggestions.

First, junior high school classrooms, compared with elementary school classrooms, are characterized by a greater emphasis on teacher control and discipline and fewer opportunities for student decision-making, choice, and self-management.[42–45] For example, in our own work, 6th grade elementary school math teachers reported less concern with controlling and disciplining their students than these same students' 7th grade junior high school math teachers reported 1 year later.[43] Similar differences emerged on indicators of student opportunity to participate in decision making regarding their own learning. For example, again in our work, both 7th graders and their teachers in the first year of junior high school reported less opportunity for students to participate in classroom decision-making than did these same students and their 6th grade elementary school teachers 1 year earlier. In addition, using a measure developed by Lee, Statuto, and Kedar-Voivodes[44] to assess the congruence between the adolescents' desire for participation in decision-making and their perception of the opportunities for such participation, Midgley and Feldlaufer[45] found a greater discrepancy between the adolescents' desire for autonomy and their perception of the extent to which their classroom afforded them opportunities to engage in autonomous behavior when the adolescents were in their first year in junior high school than when these same adolescents were in their last year in elementary school.

Second, junior high school classrooms, compared with elementary school classrooms, are characterized by less personal and positive teacher/student relationships.[6] For example, in our work, both students and observers rated junior high school math teachers as less friendly, less supportive, and less caring than the teachers these students had 1 year earlier in the last year of elementary school.[46] In addition, the 7th grade teachers in this study also reported that they trusted the students less than did these students' 6th grade teachers.[43]

Third, the shift to junior high school is associated with an increase in practices such as whole class task organization, between classroom ability grouping (i.e., tracking), and public evaluation of the correctness of work.[6] For example, Rounds and Osaki[47] found that, in comparison to 6th grade classrooms in an elementary school, whole-group instruction was more common, and small-group instruction and individualized instruction were much less common, in 7th grade junior high school classrooms. Similar shifts toward increased use of whole-class instruction with most students working on the same assignments at the same time, using the same textbooks, and completing the same homework assignments were evident in our study of the junior high school transition. In addition, several reports have documented an increased use of between class ability grouping beginning at junior high school.[48]

Changes such as these are likely to increase social comparison, concerns about evaluation, and competitiveness.[12,49] They may also increase the likelihood that teachers will use normative grading criteria and more public forms of evaluation, both of which may have a negative impact on many early adolescents' self-perceptions and motivation. These changes may also make aptitude differences more salient to both teachers and students, leading to increased teacher expectancy effects and decreased feelings of efficacy among teachers.

Fourth, junior high school teachers feel less effective as teachers, especially for low ability students. This was one of the largest differences we found between 6th and 7th grade math teachers despite the fact that the 7th grade math teachers were more likely to be math specialists than the 6th grade math teachers.[43]

Finally, junior high school teachers appear to use a higher standard in judging students' competence and in grading their performance than elementary school teachers.[6] There is no stronger predictor of students' self-confidence and sense of efficacy than the grades they receive. If grades change, then we would expect to see a concomitant shift in adolescents' self-perceptions and academic motivation. There is evidence that junior high school teachers use stricter and more social comparison-based standards than elementary school teachers to assess student competency and to evaluate student performance, leading to a drop in grades for many early adolescents as they make the junior high school transition. For example, Finger and Silverman[50] found that 54% of the students in New York State schools experienced a decline in their grades when they moved into junior high school. Similarly, Simmons and Blyth[8] found a greater drop in grades between 6th and 7th grade for adolescents making the junior high school transition than for adolescents who remained in K–8 schools. Of interest, the decline in grades was not accompanied by a similar decline in the adolescents' scores on standardized achievement tests, which suggests that the decline reflects a change in grading practices rather than a change in the rate of the students' learning.[51]

Developmental Needs of the Adolescent

Changes such as those noted above are likely to have a negative effect on children's motivational orientation toward school at any grade level. But we believe these types of school environment changes are particularly harmful at early adolescence given what is known about psychological development during this stage of life. Early adolescent development is characterized by increases in desire for autonomy and self-determination, peer orientation, self-focus and self-consciousness, salience of identity issues, concern over possible sexual relationships, and capacity for abstract cognitive activity.[8] Simmons and Blyth[8] argued that adolescents need reasonably safe and also intellectually challenging educational environments to adapt to these shifts, environments that provide a "zone of comfort" as well as challenging new opportunities for growth. In light of these needs, the environmental changes often associated with transition to junior high school seem especially harmful in that they emphasize competition, social comparison, and ability to self-assess at a time of heightened self-focus; they decrease decision-making and choice at a time when the desire for control is growing; and they disrupt both peer and adult social networks at a time when adolescents are especially concerned with peer relationships and may be in special need of close adult relationships outside of the home. We believe that the nature of these environmental changes, coupled with the normal course of individual development, results in a developmental mismatch so that the "fit" between the early adolescent and the classroom environment is particularly poor, increasing the risk of negative motivational outcomes, especially for adolescents who are having difficulty succeeding in school academically. In the next section we review research findings relevant to these predictions.

But first it is important to step back and consider briefly why junior high school classrooms might have these characteristics. Several sources have suggested that these characteristics result, in part, from the size and bureaucratic nature of the junior high school as an institution.[5,8,38] For example, these sources argue that such school characteristics as size, connection to the community, and system of governance, as well as such instructional organization characteristics as departmentalized teaching, ability grouping, normative grading, and large student load, undermine the motivation of both teachers and students. It is difficult for teachers to maintain warm, positive relationships with students if they have to teach 25 to 30 different students each hour of the day. Similarly, it is hard for teachers to feel efficacious about (i.e., have confidence in) their ability to monitor and teach all of these students. Finally, it seems likely that teachers will resort to more controlling strategies when they have to supervise such a large number of students.

Each of these consequences of the size and organization of traditional junior high schools on teachers' motivation are likely to be exacerbated by the negative stereotypes about adolescents propagated in this culture by presumed experts and by the mass media.[52] We live in a culture that has a very negative view of early adolescents, and we tend to attribute their behavior to the biological upheaval associated with puberty. Teachers often do not want to teach in junior high schools precisely because of these beliefs. As a result, the best and most motivated teachers often leave junior high schools as soon as openings become available in either elementary or high school, making it even more difficult to maintain high teacher and student morale.

Impact of Classroom Environmental Changes on Early Adolescents' Motivation: The Michigan Study of Adolescent Life Transitions

To test some of these predictions, we conducted a large-scale, 2-year longitudinal study of the impact of changes in the school and classroom environments on early adolescents' achievement-related beliefs, motives, values, and behaviors using The Michigan Study of Adolescent Life Transitions (MSALT). The sample of 1500 adolescents was drawn from 12 school districts located in middle-income communities in southeastern Michigan in which the students moved from the 6th grade in an elementary school into the 7th grade in a junior high school during the course of the study. Because we wanted to test whether it was the transition per se or the specific type of change in classroom characteristics that the students experienced as they made this transition, we selected districts that varied in the nature of the junior high school environment. We were able to find some junior high schools that did not evidence the negative characteristics outlined above. We then compared the changes in the students' attitudes, motivation, and self-confidence depending on the nature of the classroom changes they experienced as they made the junior high school transition. We predicted that we would see the typical negative changes only among the early adolescents who experienced a negative change in the characteristics of their classrooms as they made the junior high school transition. Questionnaires were administered at school during the fall and spring terms of these 2 consecutive school years.

Teacher Efficacy (Confidence in One's Ability to Teach All of One's Students)

One of the largest differences we found between the 6th and 7th grade teacher of our students was in their confidence in their teaching efficacy: the 7th grade teachers reported less confidence than the 6th grade teachers. Given the negative correlations between teachers' sense of efficacy and students' self-concept of ability and self-reliance found in several studies,[34] differences in teachers' sense of efficacy before and after the transition to junior high school could contribute to the decline in early adolescents' beliefs about their academic competency and potential. To test this hypothesis, we divided our adolescent sample into four groups based on median splits of their math teachers' ratings of their personal teaching efficacy.[53] The largest group (559 of the 1329 included in these analyses) moved from a high efficacy 6th grade math teacher to a low efficacy 7th grade math teacher. Another 474 adolescents had low efficacy teachers both years, 117 moved from low to high efficacy teachers, and 179 had high efficacy teachers both years. Thus, fully 78% of the adolescents in our sample moved to a low teacher efficacy math classroom in the 7th grade. The potential impact of such a shift on the motivation and self-perceptions of early adolescents, especially those having difficulty mastering the academic material, is sobering.

As predicted, the adolescents who moved from high efficacy to low efficacy math teachers during the transition (the most common pattern) ended their first year in junior high school with lower expectations for themselves in math, lower perceptions of their performance in math, and higher perceptions of the difficulty of math than the adolescents who experienced no change in teacher efficacy or who moved from low to high efficacy teachers. Also, as predicted, teacher efficacy beliefs had a stronger impact on the low achieving adolescents' beliefs than on the high achieving adolescents' beliefs; by the end of the junior high school year, low achieving adolescents who had moved from high to low efficacy math teachers suffered a dramatic decline in their confidence in their ability to master mathematics. This drop is likely to signal the beginning of the downward spiral in school motivation that eventually leads to school drop out among many low achieving adolescents. It is important to note, however, that this same decline was not characteristic of the low achieving adolescents who moved to high efficacy 7th grade math teachers, suggesting that the decline is neither the result of general early adolescent development or of the junior high school transition per se but rather is a consequence of the change in learning environment experienced by so many early adolescents as they make the junior high school transition.

Teacher/Student Relationships

As reported earlier, we also found that student/teacher relationships deteriorated after the transition to junior high school. Research on the effects of classroom climate indicates that the quality of student/teacher relationships is associated with students' academic motivation and attitudes toward school.[35,36] Consequently, there is reason to believe that transition into a less supportive classroom will have a negative impact on early adolescents' interest in the subject matter being taught in that classroom. To test this prediction, we looked at the effect of differences in perceived teacher support before and after the transition to junior high school on the value early adolescents attach to mathematics.[46] As predicted, those early adolescents who moved from elementary teachers they perceived to be low in support to junior high school math teachers they perceived to be high in support showed an increase in the value they attached to math; in contrast, those early adolescents, particularly the lower achieving students, who moved from teachers they perceived to be high in support to teachers they perceived to be low in support showed a decline in the value they attached to mathematics.

Summary

Each of these two studies demonstrated that the declines often reported in studies of early adolescents' motivational orientation are not inevitably the result of either general developmental changes associated with pubertal development or the junior high school transition per se. Instead, these declines are associated with *specific types of changes* in the nature of the classroom environment experienced by many early adolescents as they make the junior high school transition. The studies also showed that a transition into more positive classrooms can induce positive changes in early adolescents' motivation and self-perceptions. Unfortunately, our findings also indicate that most adolescents experience a negative change in their classroom experiences as they make the junior high school transition.

Person-Environment Fit in Classroom Decision-Making

Both the adolescents and the teachers in MSALT were also asked to rate whether students were allowed to have input into classroom decisions regarding seating arrangements, classwork, homework, class rules, and what to do next and whether students *ought* to have input into each of these decisions. These questions can be used to determine the extent of match or mismatch between the students' preferences and the opportunities actually afforded them in the school environment and to assess the extent to which grade-related changes in this match are related to developmental changes in the adolescents' self-perceptions and school-related motivation.

As noted earlier, both the early adolescents and their teachers reported less opportunity for participation in classroom decision-making in the 7th grade than in the

6th grade. In contrast, the adolescents reported a greater desire for participation in classroom decision-making in the 7th than in the 6th grade. As a consequence of these two divergent patterns, the congruence between early adolescents' desires for participation in classroom decision-making and their perceptions of the opportunities available to them was lower in the 7th grade than in the 6th grade.[45] Person-environment fit theory suggests that the mismatch between young adolescents' desires for autonomy and control and their perceptions of the opportunities in their environments should result in a decline in the adolescents' intrinsic motivation and interest in school. But more critical to note, from a developmental perspective, the exact nature of the mismatch should also be important. As noted earlier, given the normative developmental progression toward increased desire for independence and autonomy during the early adolescent period, adolescents who experience decreased opportunities for participation in classroom decision-making along with an increased desire for greater participation in such decisions (i.e., a "can't but should be able to" mismatch) should be more at risk for negative motivational outcomes than adolescents experiencing other forms of mismatch (such as the "can but shouldn't be able to" mismatch).

In a longitudinal analysis of these items, MacIver and Reuman[54] provided some support for this prediction. They compared the changes in intrinsic interest in mathematics for adolescents reporting different longitudinal patterns in their responses to the actual and preferred decision-making items across the four waves of data. Consistent with the prediction, it was the adolescents who perceived their 7th grade math classrooms as putting greater constraints on their preferred level of participation in classroom decision-making than their 6th grade math classrooms who evidenced the largest and most consistent declines in their intrinsic interest in math as they moved from the 6th grade into the 7th grade. These are the students who experienced a developmentally regressive mismatch as they moved into junior high school. The other students who did not experience a developmentally regressive mismatch as they moved into junior high school did not show the decline in their interest in math. Instead, some of them showed an increase in their interest. Unfortunately, these luckier students were in the minority. The majority of students experienced the developmentally regressive pattern of change.

Broader Consequences of Lack of Fit in School

The research discussed thus far highlights the importance of understanding early adolescents' adjustment in light of both the psychological characteristics salient to adolescents and the school context in which adolescents spend a good portion of their waking hours. A key challenge for adolescents is to develop a coherent personal identity that integrates personal competencies with the expanding social roles and experiences that accompany this developmental period. The contexts in which adolescents develop can either facilitate or undermine their pursuit of this unique and coherent personal identity. We have presented evidence that school environments that do not fit well with the developmental needs of the adolescent have implications for adolescents' motivation for school achievement, academic motivation, and attachment to school. Indeed, our results suggest that many early adolescents experience a junior high school environment that is developmentally regressive and likely to undermine both academic achievement and healthy psychological maturation. Academic achievement is related to personal adjustment during this time and may serve as a protective factor against many of the negative outcomes that are manifest later in adolescence, including problem behaviors and mental health problems.[55–57] Conversely, academic underachievement and alienation in early adolescence may be risk factors for later adjustment. For instance, several authors have discussed the relationships between negative self-perceptions of academic and social competence and internalized and externalized distress.[56] The result of such a poor fit of the school environment to the adolescents' psychological needs can be alienation from the very context that the adolescent needs to promote the growth of competencies critical for success in this society.[57]

Stage-Environment Fit in Perceived Control in the Family

As noted earlier, adolescents' relationships with their parents also undergo a stressful period during early and middle adolescence. Furthermore, this stress is often focused on issues of control and autonomy within the family. Adolescence is a time for renegotiating the power and authority relationships within the family. When they are young, by necessity, children's relationship with their parents is asymmetrical in terms of power and authority. But as children mature, they need to take more and more responsibility for themselves until, ultimately, they leave their natal home and take full responsibility for their own lives. In the optimal situation, parents will reinforce and stimulate this process of growing autonomy, self-determination, and independence. But it is very likely that the renegotiation processes associated with these developmental trajectories will not be smooth. It is not easy for parents to determine the optimal level of autonomy versus control for their children at all ages. And, according to a stage-environment fit perspective, one would predict strained relationships whenever there is a poor fit between the child's desire for increasing autonomy and the opportunities for independence and autonomy provided by the child's parents.

Early adolescence seems a likely developmental period for asynchrony in this dimension to emerge within the family context. Social changes in the world of adolescents substantially increase the opportunity for them to experience independence outside the home. The transition to junior high school, and cultural beliefs regarding "appropriate" amounts of adult supervision for children of different ages, lead to a dramatic increase in the amount of unsupervised age-mate contact during this developmental period.[40] This increase creates the opportunity for adolescents to spend a lot of time in relationships that are likely to be more balanced in terms of interpersonal power and authority. These experiences may lead early adolescents to expect greater equality in their relationships at home as well. The opportunity to be exposed to a broader range of families is also likely to increase with the junior high school transition because these schools typically are larger and draw their attendance from a more diverse range of neighborhoods and communities. This broadened exposure, in turn, may lead early adolescents to question the legitimacy of their parents' rules.[24,25,40] Exposure to a broader range of belief systems, along with increasing cognitive maturity, may also lead adolescents to try to integrate and coordinate diverse social perspectives and to evaluate interpersonal relationships. These changes, in turn, may lead early adolescents to question their parents' authority and to push for a more symmetrical relationship with their parents. Finally, parents, in response to their children's emerging sexuality, may become more concerned about their children's safety and may actually become more restrictive than they were during the period of middle childhood, further exacerbating the perceived asynchrony in the child's mind. However, as the family adjusts to these changes, one would expect new authority relationships to emerge and the strain to decrease over the adolescent years.[22]

We are in the process of examining these issues in our study of adolescent development (The Michigan Study of Adolescent Life Transitions study described earlier). We assessed family decision-making in two ways; both the adolescents and their parents responded to two items derived from the Epstein and McPartland[58] scale of family decision-making (e.g., "In general, how do you and your child arrive at decisions?" [1 = I tell my child just what to do; 3 = We discuss it and then we decide; 5 = I usually let my child decide] and "How often does your child take part in family decisions that concern her/himself?" [1 = never; 4 = always]). The adolescents were also asked to rate how they thought decisions ought to be made in their family and the extent to which they think "their parents treated them more like a kid than like an adult."

Consistent with the analyses reported earlier for schools, we found both an increase over time in adolescents' desire for greater participation in family decision-making and positive associations between the extent of the adolescents' participation in family decision-making and indicators of both intrinsic school motivation and positive self-esteem.[59–64] Even more interesting from the stage-environment fit perspective, the parents reported that they included their children more in family decision-making than the children perceived to be true.[59,62] Furthermore, the discrepancy between the adolescents' and the parents' perception of the opportunities for the adolescents to participate in family decision-making increased over the four data collection points in our study.[62]

Finally, and most importantly, the pattern of changes in early adolescents' self-esteem and intrinsic versus extrinsic motivation for school work were systematically, and predictably, related to changes in their perceptions of the opportunity to participate in family decision-making at home. As our developmental stage-environment fit perspective on adult control implies, the adolescents who reported decreasing opportunities to participate in family decision-making showed a decrease in their self-esteem and intrinsic motivation over the period of this study; the opposite pattern of change occurred for the adolescents who reported increasing opportunities to participate.[60,63] In addition, the opportunity to participate in family decision-making also predicted better adjustment to the junior high school transition.[61] Thus, not only may a mismatch between authority relationships in the home precipitate increased conflict, it may also be detrimental to the adolescents' self-esteem and school-related motivation.

In another study of 1500 families and their 7th grade adolescent, we have demonstrated similar patterns of associations of the negative consequences of "can't but should" mismatch in family decision-making for a broad range of indicators of psychological well-being.[57] Relative to those 7th graders who were satisfied with their involvement in family decision-making, the adolescents who reported that they were not involved in family decision-making as often as they thought they should be and that their parents were too intrusive and overprotective also reported lower self-esteem, more depressive symptomatology (particularly girls), more anger, and less personal resourcefulness. These results are consistent with our hypothesis that a misfit between parents and their adolescents can undermine adolescents' psychological well-being. What these correlational data cannot yet tell us, however, is the direction of effect of the relation of stage-environment mismatch to adolescent mental health. Although we found evidence in other studies that a stage-environment mismatch can lead to negative changes in self-esteem over time, it is possible that characteristics of the child contribute to the perceived mismatch in the family. For example, parents may need to be more protective and intrusive and to provide less opportunity for autonomous decision-making if their child is involved in risk taking or problem behavior or is depressed or immature. Further analyses using longitudinal data will hopefully provide valuable insight into the direction of processes.

Conclusion/Implications

We have argued that optimal development takes place when there is a good fit between the needs of developing individuals and the opportunities afforded them in their social environments. We have provided evidence of the negative effects of the decrease in personal and positive interactions with teachers after the transition to junior high school and have argued that this decline is especially problematic during early adolescence when children are in special need of close relationships with adults outside of their homes. We have also noted the increase in ability grouping (tracking), comparative and public evaluation, and whole class task organization at a time when young adolescents have a heightened concern about their status in relation to their peers. Finally, we discussed, and provided evidence of, the negative consequences of these kinds of developmentally inappropriate environmental changes on early adolescents' school motivation and academic self-concepts.

We also discussed the role of opportunity for self-determination and participation in rule-making, pointing out the particularly important need for a match between the individual's increasing desires for autonomy and self-determination and the opportunities for such autonomy provided in the home and at school. Although adolescents desire more freedom from adult control than children, they do not want total freedom, and they do not want to be emotionally detached from their parents. Instead, they desire a gradual increase in the opportunity for self-determination and participation in decision- and rule-making. Furthermore, evidence suggests that they develop best when these increasing opportunities occur in environments that are emotionally supportive.[57,64,65]

Unfortunately, our research suggests that many early adolescents do not have these experiences in either the school or family setting. After the transition to junior high school, in particular, early adolescents are often confronted with a regressive environmental change. Not surprisingly, there is also a decrease in intrinsic motivation and an increase in school misbehavior associated with this transition, and these changes are most apparent among the adolescents who report experiencing the greatest mismatch between their needs and their opportunities to participate in classroom decision-making. Such motivational changes are not apparent in adolescents who report the more developmentally appropriate increase in opportunity for participation in classroom decision-making.

Although our analysis of the family data is not as complete as our analysis of the classroom data, we have found evidence suggesting that a similar process is occurring in the family. Excessive parental control is linked to lower intrinsic school motivation, to more negative changes in self-esteem after the junior high school transition, to more school misbehavior, and to relatively greater investment in peer social attachments.

Clearly, these results point out the importance of designing educational and family environments for early adolescents that provide a better match to their developing needs and desires. The current situation in traditional junior high schools seems especially problematic. The existing structure of many junior high schools appears to create a climate that undermines both teacher and student motivation. The large size, coupled with departmentalized teaching and large student loads, makes it difficult for teachers and students to form close relationships. In turn, this lack of close relationships, coupled with the generally negative stereotypes about adolescents, could be responsible for the prevalence of low teacher efficacy and high use of controlling motivational strategies in junior high school classrooms. *Turning Points* outlines a variety of changes in the structure of middle grade educational institutions (e.g., junior highs, middle schools, and intermediate schools) that would make it easier for teachers to maintain a high sense of self-efficacy and for both students and teachers alike to have a strong sense of shared community with each other. In turn, these changes could make it easier for teachers to provide a more positive learning environment for early adolescents. Field studies of the more successful middle and junior high schools provide numerous examples of classrooms and schools that have more positive and developmentally appropriate learning environments, for example, higher teacher efficacy, greater opportunity for meaningful student participation in both school and classroom decision-making, and more positive student-teacher relationships.[3,5,6] Young adolescents in these schools do not evidence the same declines in intrinsic motivation and school attachment stereotypically associated with students in junior high schools; they also do not engage in the same amount of school misbehavior as students in more traditional junior high schools. Unfortunately, many junior high schools do not provide such a developmentally appropriate environment.[6] When they do, the early adolescents adjust much better and do not evidence serious declines in their school motivation and interest.

One potential strategy for remediating the impersonal quality of traditional junior high schools involves within-school re-organization based on the middle school teaching philosophy. Some characteristics of the middle school philosophy that have been identified as potentially helpful are small house programs (programs in which groups of students are kept together for most of their courses over the junior high school years), team teaching, and advisory sessions. Future research is needed to determine the beneficial impact of these re-structuralization strategies on students' adjustment.

There is a similar need for developmentally responsive environments in the family. Existing evidence suggests that there is variability in how families adapt to their children's movement into adolescence and that adolescents fare best in family environments that provide a good fit to their increasing need for autonomy. Adolescents fare more poorly in families that respond to their development either by throwing up their hands and relinquishing control or by cracking down too much. Families, like schools, are confronted with a difficult problem, providing an environment that changes in the right way, and at the right pace, to maintain a good fit with their children's developmentally appropriate needs. Unfortunately, we know less about how to help families achieve this balance than we know about how to design schools that help teachers achieve the right balance. There is a great need for programs that will help parents with this difficult task.

The contexts in which adolescents develop can either facilitate or undermine an adolescent's pursuit of a unique and coherent personal identity and sense of competence. Adolescents' perceptions of their school and family environments as satisfying, or thwarting, their developmentally appropriate autonomy needs contribute to their development of competent adjustment. The findings reviewed here also suggest that teachers and parents of early adolescents might not be attuned to the experiences and needs of children making the transition to early adolescence. Although for teachers this diminished sensitivity is probably, in part, due to the ecological set-up of school environments at this time, the low fit may also reflect teachers' and parents' lack of understanding about what early adolescents are up against at this period and about what they need from the adults in their lives.

Health care workers can help ameliorate these negative changes. In many school districts, adolescents are required to get a physical before entering junior high school. This provides the opportunity for the health care provider to do some anticipatory guidance with both the family and the adolescents. Both parents and youth can be alerted to the kinds of changes they may experience as they move into junior high school. Information can be provided about resources the family and youth might turn to if they find the transition to be especially difficult. Parents can be provided with information about danger signs they should pay attention to and about alternative supportive environments they might try to provide for their adolescent after school and on the weekends.

References

1. Takanishi R: The opportunities of adolescence: Research, intervention, and policy. Am Psychol 48: 85–88, 1993

2. Office of Educational Research: Youth indicators. Washington, D.C., U.S. Government Printing Office, 1988

3. Dryfoos JG: Adolescents at Risk: Prevalence and Prevention. Oxford, England. Oxford University Press, 1990

4. Rosenbaum JE: Making Inequality: The Hidden Curriculum of High School Tracking. New York, NY. John Wiley and Sons, 1976

5. Carnegie Council on Adolescent Development: Turning Points: Preparing American Youth for the 21st Century. New York, NY. Carnegie Corporation, 1989

6. Eccles JS. Midgley C: Stage/environment fit: Developmentally appropriate classrooms for early adolescents, in Ames RE, Ames C (eds): Research on Motivation in Education, vol 3. New York, NY, Academic Press, 1989

7. Kazdin AE: Adolescent mental health: Prevention and treatment programs. Am Psychol 48: 127–141, 1993

8. Simmons, RG, Blyth DA: Moving into Adolescence: The Impact of Pubertal Change and School Context. Hawthorn, NY, Aldine de Gruyler, 1987

9. Epstein JL, McPartland JM: The concept and measurement of the quality of school life. Am Educ Res J 13: 15–30, 1976

10. Roeser RW, Midgley CM, Maehr ML: Unfolding and enfolding youth: A development study of school culture and student well-being. Presented at the Society for Research on Adolescence. San Diego, CA, February, 1994.

11. Harter S: A new self-report scale of intrinsic versus extrinsic orientation in the classroom: Motivational and informational components. Dev Psychol 17: 300–312, 1981

12. Eccles JS. Midgley C, Adler T: Grade-related changes in the school environment: Effects on achievement motivation, in Nicholls JG (ed): The Development of Achievement Motivation. Greenwich, CT, JAI Press, 1984, pp 283–331

13. Harter S: The perceived competence scale for children. Child Dev 53: 87–97, 1982

14. Parsons JE, Ruble DN: The development of achievement-related expectancies. Child Dev 48: 1975–1979, 1977

15. Simmons RG, Blyth DA, Van Cleave EF, Bush D: Entry into early adolescence: The impact of school structure, puberty, and early dating on self-esteem. Am Soc Rev 44: 948–967, 1979

16. Hill KT: Motivation, evaluation, and educational test policy, in Fyans LJ (ed): Achievement Motivation: Recent Trends in Theory and Research. New York, NY, Plenum Press, 1980

17. Rholes WS, Blackwell J, Jordan C, Walters C: A developmental study of learned helplessness. Dev Psychol 16: 616–624, 1980

18. Nicholls JG: String to develop and demonstrate ability: An intentional theory of achievement motivation. Presented at the Conference on Attributional Approaches to Human Motivation, Center for Interdisciplinary Studies, University of Bielefeld, West Germany, June, 1980

19. Buchanan CM, Eccles JS, Becker J: Are adolescents the victims of raging hormones? Evidence for the activational effects of hormones on moods behavior at adolescence. Psychol Bull 111: 62–107, 1992

20. Collins WA: Parent-child relationships in the transition to adolescence: Continuity and change in interaction, affect, and cognition, in Montemayor R, Adams G, Gullota T: Advances in Adolescent Development, vol 2: From Childhood to Adolescence: A Transitional Period? Newbury Park, CA, Sage, 1990, pp 85–106

21. Hauser S, Powers SI, Noam GG: Adolescents and their families. New York, NY. The Free Press, 1991

22. Montemayor R: Family variation in parent-adolescent storm and stress. J Early Adolesc 3: 83–103, 1983

23. Paikoff RL, Brooks-Gunn J: Do parent-child relationships change during puberty? Psychol Bull 110: 47–66, 1991

24. Smetana JG: Adolescents' and parents' conceptions of parental authority. Child Dev 59: 321–335, 1988

25. Smetana JG: Concepts of self and social convention: Adolescents' and parents' reasoning about hypothetical and actual family conflicts, in Gunnar M. Collins WA (eds): Development During the Transition to Adolescence: Minnesota Symposia on Child Development, vol 21. Hillsdale, NJ, Erlbaum, 1988b, pp 79–122

26. Steinberg L: Interdependence in the family: Autonomy, conflict, and harmony in the parent-adolescent relationship, in Feldman SS, Elliot GR (eds): At the Threshold: The Developing Adolescent. Cambridge, MA. Harvard University Press, 1990

27. Hill JP: Adapting to menarche: Familial control and conflict, in Gunnar M, Collins WA (eds), Minnesota Symposia on Child Development, vol 21. Hillsdale, NJ, Erlbaum, 1988, pp 43–47

28. Steinberg L: Reciprocal relations between parent-child distance and pubertal maturation. Dev Psychol 24: 122–128, 1981

29. Steinberg L: Interdependence in the family: Autonomy, conflict, and harmony in the parent-adolescent relationship, in Feldman SS, Elliot GR (eds): At the Threshold: The Developing Adolescent. Cambridge, MA, Harvard University Press, 1990

30. Blos P: The initial stage of male adolescence. Psychoanal Study Child 20: 145–164, 1965

31. Blyth DA, Simmons RG, Carlton-Ford S: The adjustment of early adolescents to school transitions. J Early Adolesc 3: 105–120, 1983

32. Hunt DE: Person-environment interaction: A challenge found wanting before it was tried. Rev Educ Res 45: 209–230, 1975

33. Barker R. Gump P: Big school, small school: High school size and student behavior. Stanford, CA, Stanford University Press, 1964

34. Brookover R, Beady C, Flood P, Schweitzer J, Wisenbaker J: School social systems and student achievement: Schools can make a difference. New York, NY, Praeger, 1979

35. Fraser BJ, Fisher DL: Predicting students' outcomes from their perceptions of classroom psychosocial environment. Am Educ Res J 19: 498–515, 1982

36. Moos RH: Evaluating educational environments. San Francisco, CA, Jossey-Bass, 1979

37. deCharms R: The origins of competence and achievement motivation in personal causation, in Fyans LJ Jr. (ed): Achievement Motivation: Recent Trends in Theory and Research. New York, NY, Plenum, 1980, pp 22–23

38. Deci EL, Ryan RM: The support of autonomy and the control of behavior. J Pers Soc Psychol 53: 1024–1037, 1987

39. Deci EL, Ryan RM: Intrinsic Motivation and Self-Determination in Human Behavior, New York, NY, Plenum, 1985

40. Higgins ET, Parons JE: Social cognition and the social life of the child: Stages as subcultures, in Higgins ET, Ruble DW, Hartup WW (eds): Social Cognition and Social Behavior: Developmental Issues. New York, NY, Cambridge University Press, 1983, pp 15–62

41. Lewin K: A Dynamic Theory of Personality. New York, NY, McGraw-Hill, 1935

42. Brophy JE, Everston CM: Learning from Teaching: A Developmental Perspective, Boston, MA, Allyn and Bacon, 1976

43. Midgley C, Feldlaufer H, Eccles JS: The transition to junior high school: Beliefs of pre- and post-transition teachers. J Youth Adolesc 17: 543–562, 1988b

44. Lee P, Statuto C, Kedar-Voivodas G: Elementary school children's perceptions of their actual and ideal school experience: A developmental study. J Educ Psychol 75: 838–847, 1983

45. Midgley C, Feldlaufer H: Students' and teachers' decision-making fit before and after the transition to junior high school. J Early Adolesc 7: 225–241, 1987

46. Midgley C, Feldlaufer H, Eccles JS: Student/teacher relations attitudes toward mathematics before and after the transition to junior high school. Child Dev 60: 375–395, 1988a

47. Rounds TS, Oakes, SY: The Social Organization of Classrooms: An Analysis of Sixth- and Seventh-grade Activity Structures. Report EPSSP-82-5. San Francisco, CA, Far West Laboratory, 1982

48. Oakes J: Tracking policies and practices: School by school summaries. A Study of Schooling: Technical Report No. 25. Los Angeles, CA, University of California Graduate School of Education, 1981

49. Rosenholtz SJ. Simpson C: The formation of ability conceptions: Developmental trend of social construction? Rev Educ Res 54: 301–325, 1984

50. Finger JA, Silverman M: Changes in academic performance in the junior high school Personnel Guidance J 45: 157–164, 1966

51. Kavrell SM, Peterson AC: Patterns of achievement in early adolescence, in Maehr ML (ed): Advances in Motivation and Achievement. Greenwich, CT, JAI Press, 1984, pp 1–35

52. Miller CL, Eccles JS, Flanagan C, et al: Parents' and teachers' beliefs about adolescents: Effects of sex and experience. J Youth Adolesc 19: 363–394, 1990

53. Midgley C, Feldlaufer H, Eccles JS: Change in teacher efficacy and student self- and task-related beliefs during the transition to junior high school. J Educ Psychol 81: 247–258, 1989

54. MacIver D, Reuman DA: Decision-making in the classroom and early adolescents' valuing of mathematics. Presented at the annual meeting of the American Educational Research Association, New Orleans, LA, April, 1988

55. Cowen EL: In pursuit of wellness. Am Psychol 46: 404–408, 1991

56. Rae-Grant N, Thomas H, Offord DR, et al: Risk, protective factors, and the prevalence of behavioral and emotional disorders in children and adolescents. J Am Acad Child Adolesc Psychiatry 28: 262–268, 1989

57. Eccles JS, Lord SE, Roeser RW: Round holes, square pegs, rocky roads, and sore feet, in Cicchetti D, Toth SL (eds): Rochester Symposium on Developmental Psychopathology: Adolescence, Opportunities and Challenges. Rochester, NY, University of Rochester Press, 1996

58. Epstein JL, McPartland JM: The Quality of School Life Scale and Administrative and Technical Manual. Boston, MA, Houghton Mifflin, 1977

59. Flanagan C: Early adolescent needs and family decision-making environments: A study of person-environment fit. Presented at the meeting of the American Educational Research Association, San Francisco, CA, April, 1986

60. Flanagan C: Adolescents' autonomy at home: Effects on self-consciousness and intrinsic motivation at school. Presented at the meeting of the American Educational Research Association, Montreal, Canada, April, 1989

61. Lord SE, Eccles JS, McCarthy K: Surviving the junior high school transition: Family processes and self-perceptions as protective and risk factors. J Early Adolesc 14: 162–199. 1994

62. Yee DK: Participation in family decision-making: Parent and child perspectives. Presented at the meeting of the Society for Research in Child Development, Baltimore, MD, April, 1987

63. Yee DK, Flanagan C: Family environments and self-consciousness in early adolescence. J Early Adolesc 5: 59–68, 1985

64. Baumrind D: Current patterns of parental authority. Dev Psychol Monogr 4: 1, 1971

65. Ryan RM, Lynch JH: Emotional autonomy versus detachment: Revisiting the vicissitudes of adolescence and young adulthood. Child Dev 60: 340–356, 1989

Questions

1. What features in the structure of our junior high schools are problematic for early adolescents? Why?

2. What would a more developmentally appropriate school look like?
3. What difficulties would be encountered in trying to create developmentally appropriate schools?
4. Are schools as currently conceived the best institution to bring youth to adulthood?
5. Why do poor and minority adolescents fare so much worse academically in school than whites and drop out of school more often than whites?

References and Further Reading

Carnegie Council on Adolescent Development (1989). *Turning points: Preparing American youth for the twenty-first century.* Washington, D.C.: Carnegie Corporation.

Comer, J. P. (1988). Educating poor minority children. *Scientific American, 259*(5), 42–48.

Eccles, J. S., Midgley, C., Wigfield, A., Buchanan, C. M., Reuman, D., Flanagan, C., & Iver, D. M. (1993). Development during adolescence: The impact of stage-environment fit on young adolescents' experiences in schools and families. *American Psychologist, 48*(2), 90–101.

Entwisle, D. R. (1990). Schools and the adolescent. In S. Feldman, & G. Elliott (Eds.) *At the threshold: The developing adolescent* (pp. 197–224). Cambridge, MA: Harvard University Press.

12.2   Laurence Steinberg, Suzanne Fegley,
                            and Sanford M. Dornbusch, 1993

Negative Impact of Part-Time Work on Adolescent Adjustment: Evidence From a Longitudinal Study

Laurence Steinberg, Ph.D., is the Distinguished University Professor and Laura H. Carnell Professor of Psychology at Temple University. He is director of the John D. and Catherine T. MacArthur Foundation Research Network on Adolescent Development and Juvenile Justice. Dr. Steinberg is author of numerous books including *Crossing Paths: How Your Child's Adolescence Triggers Your Own Crisis* (with Wendy Steinberg, 1994), *Beyond the Classroom: Why School Reform Has Failed and What Parents Need to Do* (with B. Bradford Brown and Sanford Dornbusch, 1996), and *You and Your Adolescent: A Parent's Guide for Ages 10 to 20* (with Ann Levine, 1997).

Suzanne Fegley, Ph.D., is a lecturer at the University of Pennsylvania Graduate School of Education, teaching in the Interdisciplinary Studies of Human Development program.

Sanford M. Dornbusch, Ph.D., is the Reed-Hodgson Professor of Human Biology and professor emeritus of sociology and education at Stanford University. He currently chairs the advisory board to the Stanford Center on Adolescence. His recent research includes papers on the effects of school tracking; family and school processes that affect school performance and deviance; ethnic differences in family and school processes; and homeless families, youth, and children. He is coauthor (with Christy M. Buchanan and Eleanor E. Maccoby) of *Adolescents After Divorce*, (1996) and coauthor (with Laurence Steinberg and B. Bradford Brown) of *Beyond the Classroom: Why School Reform Has Failed and What Parents Need to Do* (1996).

In the mid-twentieth century, it was rare to find adolescents working part-time while attending school, but by the 1980s, a study of over 70,000 high school seniors found that 75% of the adolescents had entered the workforce in a part-time capacity while going to school (Bachman & Schulenberg, 1993). Given this dramatic shift, research has addressed the advantages and disadvantages of part-time work: how part-time work affects performance and involvement in school, what types of skills are learned through work, and the impact of working on self-esteem and well-being and on involvement in problem behaviors.

Considerable controversy has existed about the costs and benefits of part-time work for adolescents. The consensus is that it is long hours of employment, rather than employment itself, that is associated with negative outcomes. Longer work hours, it has been found, are associated with lower grades in school (Steinberg & Dornbusch, 1991). Bachman and Schulenberg's large-scale national survey of high school students found that longer working hours were associated with a variety of negative outcomes such as increased cigarette, alcohol, and drug use; increased aggressive behavior and theft; victimization; trouble with police: and decreased sleep and exercise (Bachman & Schulenberg, 1993). The strength of the association between longer working hours and negative outcomes was greatly reduced, however, when the backgrounds of adolescents and their educational success prior to working were controlled. Students who do well in school tend to work less hours at part-time jobs. Those working the most hours have a history of poor academic performance throughout high school, are more likely to have been held back a grade, and are less likely to plan to attend college.

Laurence Steinberg, Suzanne Fegley, and Sanford Dornbusch examine the causes of the negative correlates of extensive part-time employment. They carried out a longitudinal study assessing 1,800 high school sophomores and juniors at two points in time a year apart. This methodology enabled the researchers to control for differences in prework history, to determine whether the negative correlates of part-time work were a consequence of prework differences rather than labor force participation. In this study, as in previous studies, adolescents who worked longer hours were found to earn lower grades, hold lower educational expectations, and spend less time on homework. Longer work hours were found to lead to increased delinquency and drug use, and to diminished self-reliance. Steinberg and his colleagues report that despite prework differences, entering the labor force fosters academic disengagement, further distancing adolescents from school. Adolescents doing poorly at school seek longer employment, and that employment in turn increases academic disengagement, lowering class attendance and time spent on homework, and increasing school misconduct. It is important to keep two things in mind in considering the generalizability of these findings. First, the study focuses on extensive part-time employment. The negative outcomes may or may not pertain to low-intensity work. Second, this study followed adolescents over the course of a year during high school, but not over the course of high school or during the college years. The effects of intensive part-time work over a longer period of time or later in adolescence may be different from the outcomes that emerged in this study.

Abstract Researchers disagree over whether negative correlates of extensive part-time employment during adolescence are consequences of working or are due to differential selection into the labor force. This study examines the over-time relation between school-year employment and adjustment in a heterogeneous sample of approximately 1,800 high school sophomores and juniors. Analyses indicate both significant selection effects and negative consequences of employment. Before working, adolescents who later work more than 20 hr per week are less engaged in school and are granted more autonomy by their parents. However, taking on a job for more than 20 hr per week further disengages youngsters from school, increases delinquency and drug use, furthers autonomy from parents, and diminishes self-reliance. Leaving the labor force after working long hours leads to improved school performance but does not reverse the other negative effects.

Many studies of part-time employment during adolescence have shown that work in excess of 15 or 20 hr a week during the school year is associated with a number of problems, including lower academic achievement and school involvement (Barton, 1989; Charner & Fraser, 1987; Damico, 1984; Lillydahl, 1990; McNeil, 1984; Mortimer & Finch, 1986; Steinberg, Greenberger, Garduque, & McAuliffe, 1982; Yasuda, 1990), greater psychological distress and somatic complaints (Greenberger, Steinberg, & Vaux, 1981; Steinberg & Dornbusch, 1991), higher rates of drug and alcohol use (Bachman, Bare, & Frankie, 1986; Bachman & Schulenberg, 1991; Greenberger et al., 1981; Mortimer, Finch, Ryu, & Shanahan, 1991; Steinberg & Dornbusch, 1991, Steinberg, Greenberger, Garduque, Ruggiero, & Vaux, 1982), diminished parental supervision (Greenberger & Steinberg, 1986; Steinberg & Dornbusch, 1991), and more frequent delinquency (Elliott & Wofford, 1991; Ruggiero, 1984; Shannon, 1982; Steinberg & Dornbusch, 1991).[1] Studies suggesting that extensive employment may have deleterious consequences are important, because national surveys indicate that approximately two thirds of all high school juniors and seniors hold jobs in the formal part-time labor force at any specific time during the school year and that over half of all employed U.S. high school seniors work more than 20 hr per week (Bachman & Schulenberg, 1991; Lewin-Epstein, 1981).

Although most researchers agree that the negative correlates of employment are linked to how much, rather than whether, a student works (cf. Bachman et al., 1986; Damico, 1984; Greenberger & Steinberg, 1986; Mortimer & Finch, 1986; Schill, McCartin, & Meyer, 1985; Steinberg & Dornbusch, 1991; Wirtz, Rohrbeck, Charner, & Fraser, 1987), there is considerable controversy over whether the negative correlates of extensive employment are actually caused by youngsters' labor force participation. A number of investigators have suggested that apparent differences between students who do and who do not work long hours may be attributable to prework differences in attitudes, values, and behaviors (e.g., Bachman & Schulenberg, 1991; Barton, 1989; Mortimer et al., 1991). Their argument is that youngsters who work long hours (either by choice or necessity) are, for example, less interested in school than their peers and more inclined to use drugs and alcohol before they enter the labor force, and, accordingly, that any postemployment differences between them and their agemates merely reflect these preemployment differences in orientation. In other words, these researchers caution that the widely observed differences between youngsters who do and who do not work a great deal may be caused by *differential selection* into the workplace and not, as others have argued, to *differential socialization* (e.g., Greenberger & Steinberg, 1986).

Although longitudinal evidence is clearly necessary to distinguish between the selection and socialization arguments, studies that have examined the over-time impact of school-year employment are rare. And, although some of the longitudinal studies of student employment and its effects have indicated that some of the negative correlates of employment may indeed be consequences of working (e.g., Mortimer & Finch, 1986; Shannon, 1982; Steinberg, Greenberger, Garduque, Ruggiero, & Vaux, 1982), others have suggested that there are strong selection effects (e.g., Gottfredson, 1985; Mortimer et al., 1991).

More important, while a handful of studies have taken into account differential selection into the work force (i.e., preemployment differences between youngsters who do and who do not enter the labor force), only one study to date (Mortimer et al., 1991) has considered differential selection into extensive versus modest work hours (i.e., preemployment differences between youngsters who work long hours and those who do not)—a critical consideration given the consensus that it is long hours of employment, rather than employment status, that are potentially injurious. However, the Mortimer et al. (1991) study, which followed students from 9th to 10th grade, did not follow youngsters into their late high school years—the age when most adolescents are likely to work a great deal and the developmental period during which most of the negative correlates of extensive employment have been documented. Thus, although Mortimer et al.'s documentation of differential selection effects is important, their study does not adequately address the question of differential socialization. It is possible, after all, that extensive employment in adolescence may have both psychological antecedents and psychological consequences.

The present study examines the over-time relation between weekly hours of employment during adolescence and many of the variables previously found to be correlated with long work hours in a large heterogeneous sample of high school youth. The prospective longitudinal design used permits an examination of differential selection into the labor force as well as differential selection into long work hours, the over-time consequences of both modest and extensive weekly hours of work, and the effects of changes in work status and work hours.

Specifically, we examine the relation between school-year employment and five sets of behavioral and psychological outcomes: (a) school performance and engagement, including grades, time spent on homework, educational expectations, and various markers of psychological investment in school; (b) problem behavior, including delinquency, drug and alcohol use, and school misconduct; (c) internalized distress, including both psychological and somatic symptoms; (d) adolescent autonomy from parental control, including indexes of family decision making and parental supervision; and (e) psychosocial development, including self-reliance and self-esteem. With respect to differential selection into long work hours, we hypothesize that, before working, adolescents who subsequently work long hours are less involved in school and more prone to use drugs and alcohol than their peers. With respect to the consequences of working, however, we hypothesize that working longer hours—even after taking into account differential selection into the workplace—leads to lowered school performance and school engagement, increased problem behavior, increased internalized distress, and increased autonomy from parental control. Based on previous research (e.g., Bachman et al., 1986; Steinberg & Dornbusch, 1991), we hypothesized that working longer hours has neither a positive nor negative impact on self-esteem or self-reliance.

Method

Subjects

Our sample is drawn from the student bodies of nine high schools in Wisconsin and northern California. The schools were selected to yield a sample of students from different socioeconomic brackets, a variety of ethnic backgrounds, and different types of communities (urban, suburban, and rural). Data for the present analyses were collected during the 1987–1988 and 1988–1989 school years through self-report surveys filled out by the students on 2 days of survey administration each school year. (Because of its length, the survey was divided into two equal parts and administered on 2 separate testing days.)

Procedure

On each day of testing, we explained to all of the students in attendance the purposes of the study and asked them to complete the questionnaires. Informed consent was obtained from all participating students. All of the students' parents had been notified about the study several weeks earlier by first-class mail, and they were asked to call or write to their child's school or our research office if they did not want their child to participate in the study. Fewer than 1% of the adolescents in each of the target schools had their participation withheld by their parents. For each questionnaire administration, out of the total school populations, approximately 5% of the students chose not to participate (or had their participation withheld by parents), approximately 15% were absent from school on the day of the initial questionnaire administration (this figure is comparable to national figures on daily school attendance), and approximately 80% provided completed questionnaires.

The sample on which the present analyses are based is substantially smaller than the initial pool of respondents ($N = 11,257$ for Part 1 of the first survey), for several reasons. First, our longitudinal study sample across the 2 years (i.e., the sample overlap between the 1987–1988 and 1988–1989 questionnaires involving work) included only 4,401 students. Discounting subject loss caused by absence on one or more testing days, the main sources of attrition over the 1-year period were graduation (the 1987–1988 sample completing Part 1 of the first year's survey included 2,538 seniors), movement out of the school district (17% of the sample reported having attended more than one high school, indicative of the high degree of mobility within the population studied), or dropping out of school.

A second source of sample shrinkage was deliberate on our part. Preliminary analyses indicated that very few 9th graders were employed in 1987 and that those who did enter the labor force during the subsequent year were unlikely to be employed for more than 20 hr weekly. Because a main focus of our analysis was on the impact of intensive employment, 9th graders (2,876 of the respondents to Part 1 of the first survey) were dropped from the analysis. This left a potential study sample of 2,845 (i.e., students who were in the 10th or 11th grade in 1987–1988 and who were followed up in 1988–1989). This figure represents 49% of the 5,843 Grade 10 and 11 students who completed Part 1 of the first survey.

Because the questions concerning employment were at the end of each questionnaire, not all students completed these items. Of the 2,845 Grade 10 and 11 students who participated in both years of the study, approximately 1,777 provided complete information concerning their employment status in both years, including the nature of their job and their weekly work hours. (This represents 30% of the 10th and 11th graders who completed Part 1 of the first survey.) As Table 1 indicates, the sample of youngsters on whom we have complete work data is demographically comparable to the initial sample of survey respondents. However, because absence from school was an important source of missing data, our sample in all likelihood is underrepresented with students who are relatively less engaged in school, more prone to problem behavior and internalized distress, and less monitored by their parents (all of which would decrease the probability of school attendance and, hence, study participation).

To examine this possibility, we conducted analyses that contrasted the entire sample of 10th and 11th graders who participated in the study in 1987–1988 but who did not participate in 1988–1989 (or who did not provide sufficient information on their work status in both years of the survey) with their counterparts whose data

Table 1

Characteristics of Study Sample

Variable	Initial sample (%)	Study participants (%)
Sex		
Male	47.3	46.9
Female	52.7	53.1
Grade level		
10th grade	50.0	48.1
11th grade	50.0	51.9
Parental education		
Less than high school	12.6	9.5
High school graduate	15.7	12.9
Some college	30.1	31.6
College graduate	30.5	33.6
Advanced degree	11.1	12.4
Ethnic background		
African-American	8.1	7.3
White	65.4	67.0
Hispanic-American	9.3	8.4
Asian-American	13.6	15.4
Other	3.6	1.9

are analyzed in this report. These contrasts indicated, as expected, that the sample attrition was not random (see also Weinberger, Tublin, Ford, & Feldman, 1990). (Because the groups are demographically comparable and because this is a longitudinal study in which subjects' prior scores are used as controls in the analyses, this selective attrition is less problematic than it might otherwise be.) Nevertheless, consistent with our expectations, students who did not participate fully in the study were, at Time 1, more involved in problem behavior, less engaged in school, less well-monitored by their parents, and less psychosocially competent than students who participated in all phases of the research. In general, the groups did not differ with respect to internalized distress.

More important than these mean differences, however, are differences in the *variability* in our outcome measures between the two samples of youngsters. Virtually without exception, there is significantly less variance in outcome scores among the students who participated fully in the study than among the students who did not. One important ramification of this is that our estimates of the effects of working are likely to be on the conservative side: Because variability in our outcome measures is constrained, it is more difficult to find significant relations between these measures and our independent variables.

Characteristics of the study sample are presented in Table 1, along with characteristics of the initial sample of survey respondents. The study sample is evenly divided by gender and by year in school and is taken from households that vary

Table 2

Number of Participants in Work Status Categories

Work status at Time 1	Work status at Time 2		
	Not Employed	Employed 1–20 hr/week	Employed 21 + hr/week
Not employed	672	359	113
Employed 1–20 hr/week	129	268	94
Employed 21 + hr/week	34	49	59

considerably with respect to parental education levels and that are ethnically diverse (approximately one third non-White).

Measures

Of interest in the present analysis are the questions concerning employment as well as five sets of outcome measures: (a) school performance and engagement, (b) problem behavior, (c) internalized distress, (d) autonomy from parents, and (e) psychosocial development.

Employment Each year, students completed questions asking whether they were employed in a "Regular paying part-time job" (volunteer work was not counted as employment, nor was occasional work) and, if so, the type of job held and the weekly hours worked. The distributions of workers across varying levels of work intensity at Time 1 and at Time 2 are presented in Table 2. The distributions of boys and girls across the nine work status categories shown in Table 2 were not significantly different, consistent with recent surveys indicating comparable rates of employment among adolescent boys and girls (e.g., Bachman & Schulenberg, 1991).

Additional information about the jobs held by the study participants at Time 1 is presented in Table 3 (descriptive data from Time 2 were comparable). As in previous surveys, the vast majority of the working adolescents in this sample are employed in the service industry, with a significant number working in restaurants and retail stores. It is also noteworthy that few employed adolescents are working through programs that award academic credit, that more than a third of the employed adolescents earn in excess of $200 monthly, and that the majority of workers spend the bulk of their earnings on themselves, rather than saving them for future education or using them to defray their families' living expenses (see also Bachman, 1983).

School performance and engagement Nine indexes of school performance and engagement were assessed each year. Students provided information on their current *grade point average* (GPA); their *educational expectations* (how far they expect to go in school, on a scale from "leave school as soon as possible" to complete postgraduate

Table 3

Selected Characteristics of Jobs at Time 1

Variable	%
Job type	
Restaurant work	30.2
Cashier/salesperson	26.4
Babysitting/child care	10.2
Manual labor (e.g., gardening)	9.0
Clerical/office work	8.3
Skilled crafts (e.g., mechanic)	2.5
Technical (e.g., data processing)	2.5
Factory work	1.1
Farming	1.6
Other	8.2
Working in family business	
Yes	14.4
No	85.6
Receiving school credit for work	
Yes	10.4
No	89.6
Monthly income	
Less than $25	6.7
$25–$49	9.2
$50–$99	16.2
$100–$199	29.5
$200–$299	20.2
$300 or more	18.2
Those who use "most" or "all" of monthly earnings	
To save for future education	11.0
To help family pay for living expenses	3.0
To spend on self for immediate expenses	56.6

schooling); the average amount of *time spent on homework each week* for each major subject class (the homework index is averaged across the major subject classes); their *disengagement from school* (a 6-item scale, $\alpha = .69$: sample items include "The best way to get through most days at school is to goof off with my friends" and "I'm losing interest in school because my teachers keep going over the same old thing"; Wehlage, Rutter, Smith, Lesko, & Fernandez, 1989); their frequency of unexcused absence (*cutting class*) for each major subject class (averaged across classes); their frequency of the extent to which they *concentrate* hard in class (averaged across major subject classes) and pay attention in class (averaged across major classes); the extent to which they exert maximum *effort* in class (averaged across major classes); and the extent to which they report *mind wandering* in class (averaged across major classes). In analyses of data from a different sample of 5,000 students attending several of the same schools here, Dornbusch, Ritter, Liederman, Roberts, and Fraleigh (1987) reported that the correlation between self-reported GPA and school-reported GPA was nearly .80.

Behavior problems   Three measures were used to assess behavior problems. First, respondents provided information on their frequency of cigarette, alcohol, marijuana, and other drug use, which was used to form an index of *drug and alcohol use* (α = .86; Greenberger et al., 1981). Second, respondents reported on their frequency of involvement in delinquent activities such as theft, carrying a weapon, vandalism, and using a phony ID card, which was used to form an index of *delinquent activity* (α = .82; Gold, 1970). Finally, information was gathered on respondents' *school misconduct* (cheating, copying homework, and so on; α = .68; Ruggiero, 1984).

Internalized distress   Two indexes of internalized distress were adapted from the Center for Epidemiological Studies Depression Scale (CES-D; Radloff, 1977); *psychological symptoms* (anxiety, depression, tension, fatigue, insomnia, and so on; α = .88), and *somatic symptoms* (headaches, stomachaches, colds, and so on; α = .67).

Autonomy from parents   Two indexes of autonomy from parents were examined in the present analyses. Respondents completed a five-item measure of *parental monitoring* (α = .79), which taps the extent to which the adolescent's parents are familiar with the youngster's activities, whereabouts, and out-of-school experiences (cf. Patterson & Stouthamer-Loeber, 1984), as well as a 13-item measure of family decision making, which is used to compute an index of the extent to which the adolescent is given *decision-making autonomy* over such matters as curfew, money management, dating, and leisure activities (α = .82; see Dornbusch et al., 1985, and Steinberg, 1987, for similar measures).

Psychosocial development   Respondents completed the *self-reliance* subscale of the Psychosocial Maturity Inventory (Form D; Greenberger & Bond, 1976; Greenberger, Josselson, Knerr, & Knerr, 1974; α = .81), as well as a 10-item measure of *self-esteem* adapted from Rosenberg (1965; α = .87).

Plan of Analysis

In light of previous research suggesting that 20 hr per week represents a potentially important breaking point between employment with and without adverse correlates, we distinguished in our analyses among nonworkers (students who were not employed), moderate workers (students employed between 1 and 20 hr weekly), and intensive workers (students employed more than 20 hr weekly). Our analyses were based on three sets of contrasts. First, we contrasted adolescent nonworkers who remained nonemployed over the 1 year with their peers who entered the labor force during the 1-year interval at 20 hr or fewer per week and with those who entered the labor force at more than 20 hr each week. Second, we contrasted adolescent workers who were initially working 20 hr or fewer per week and who remained employed at this level with those who were initially working 20 hr or less weekly and who left the labor force during the 1-year interval, as well as with those who increased their work hours beyond 20 hr weekly. Finally, we contrasted adolescents who initially were working more than 20 hr weekly and who maintained this level of work intensity with those who had been working more than 20 hr weekly and decreased their work hours to 20 hr or less weekly, as well as with those who left the labor force entirely. Taken together, these contrasts allow us to assess the impact of entering the labor force (at either a moderate or high number of hours), the impact of increasing one's work hours from a moderate to a high amount, the impact of decreasing one's work hours from a high level to a moderate level, and the impact of leaving the labor force (from either moderate or high initial work hours).

Within the framework of these contrasts, we examined both selection effects and socialization effects. Selection effects (i.e., differences that predated changes in youngsters' employment status or work intensity) were examined through a series of multiple analyses of variance (MANOVA), in which adolescents' scores on outcome variables at Time 1 were contrasted across groups with different 1-year patterns of employment. Socialization effects (i.e., differences attributable to changing employment status or work hours) were examined through a series of analyses of covariance (ANCOVA), in which adolescents' scores on outcome variables at Time 2—after taking into account their scores on these same variables at Time 1—were contrasted across groups who had experienced different patterns of employment over the 1-year.[2] Significant ANCOVAs were then followed up with paired contrasts between work pattern groups. Controls for Time 1 scores rule out the possibility that observed differences at Time 2 are due to selection effects and point instead to consequences of differential patterns of employment.

Developmental scientists do not agree about the desirability of controlling statistically for background characteristics, such as socioeconomic status, in the analysis of data from nonexperimental studies in which subjects have not been randomly assigned to "treatment" groups (in the present investigation, employment status is the "treatment"). Although in some disciplines (e.g., sociology), such controls are routinely used as a means of taking into account potential confounding factors, a number of developmental methodologists have advised against it, arguing that such controls merely introduce different but unknown confounds (for a discussion, see Appelbaum & McCall, 1983). They argued that it is better to be aware of, and acknowledge, the existence of known confounding factors than to control them statistically and inadvertently introduce a different set of confounds whose effects are indeterminate.

Rather than introducing such uncertain confounds into our analyses, we used respondents' initial scores as covariates in predictions of their follow-up scores. This approach not only controls for selection effects (see earlier) but also takes into account potential confounding factors, because any such factors are likely to be correlated similarly with outcome measures taken just 1 year apart (and, in essence, are controlled along with the Time 1 outcome covariate). To ensure that this was in fact the case, we compared the correlation between socioeconomic status (the most likely confounding variable) and the Time 1 versus Time 2 measure of each of the outcome variables used in the study. In every case, the correlation coefficient was virtually identical at Time 1 and at Time 2. In addition, the relation between socioeconomic status and employment status is identical at Time 1 and Time 2.[3]

Results

Work and School-Related Outcomes

The MANOVA designed to detect selection effects indicated that there indeed are preemployment differences in school-related attitudes and behaviors between nonworkers who remain nonemployed and nonworkers who later decide to enter the labor force, multivariate $F(18, 1784) = 2.43$, $p < .001$. Before they entered the labor force, nonworkers who would eventually take on jobs were earning lower grades, reporting lower future educational expectations, spending less time on homework, and expressing more disengagement from school than their peers who would remain nonworkers (all univariate Fs significant at $p < .01$ or better). However, the groups did not differ at Time 1 with respect to academic effort, class cutting, mind wandering, classroom attention, or classroom concentration. It is interesting to note that no selection effects were found either in contrasts involving youngsters who were working moderate amounts at the beginning of our study (and who remained employed at this level, left the labor force, or increased their work hours) or in contrasts involving youngsters who were working extensive amounts when the study began (and who remained employed at more than 20 hr weekly, reduced their work hours, or left the labor force).

Analyses designed to examine the school-related consequences of entering the labor force suggest, however, that there are effects of working that operate over and above preemployment selection differences. Compared with their counterparts who remained out of the labor force, by the time of the second assessment, adolescents who entered the workplace were spending less time on homework, $F(2, 849) = 7.405$, $p < .001$; cutting class more often, $F(2, 913) = 3.028$, $p < .05$; reporting lower educational expectations, $F(2, 953) = 4.748$, $p < .01$,[4] and were more disengaged from school, $F(2, 937) = 4.046$, $p < .05$, even after taking into account any differences in these variables that preceded their labor force entry. Planned contrasts indicate that adolescents who remained nonworkers had significantly more positive school profiles at the 1-year follow-up than either their peers who had entered the labor force at more than 20 hr weekly (with respect to all four of the aforementioned outcomes) or their peers who had entered the labor force at fewer than 21 hr weekly (with respect to all four outcomes except class cutting). Table 4 presents unadjusted Time 2 means for the three employment status groups and summarizes the results of the paired contrasts for each of the outcome variables that significantly differed among the three groups at the 1-year follow-up after taking into account group differences at Time 1. Although the groups also appeared different with respect to GPA at the Time 2 follow-up, these differences were not significant once preemployment differences in school performance were taken into account.

Contrasts of adolescents who began the study as moderate workers also revealed significant differences in school-related outcomes at the 1-year follow-up as a function of their intervening work experiences, even after taking into account initial group differences (see Table 5). These Time 2 differences were found in the areas of educational expectations, $F(2, 384) = 2.29$, $p < .10$; GPA, $F(2, 375) = 4.904$, $p < .01$; time spent on homework, $F(2,333) = 6.693$, $p < .001$; class cutting, $F(2,365) = 2.389$,

Table 4

Results of Paired Contrasts on Outcomes That Differ Significantly Among Initially Nonemployed Adolescents Who Did and Who Did Not Enter the Labor Force Over the 1-Year Interval

Variable	Remained nonworkers		Entered workforce at 1–19 hr		Entered workforce at 20+ hr		Significant contrast
	M	*SD*	*M*	*SD*	*M*	*SD*	
School outcome							
Educational expectations	5.32	0.88	5.15	0.98	4.78	1.23	1 > 2 > 3[*]
Class cutting	1.32	0.63	1.40	0.68	1.46	0.67	1 < 3[*]
Time on homework	4.09	1.26	3.80	1.27	3.72	1.12	1 > 2, 3[*]
School disengagement	6.29	6.21	7.86	6.97	8.65	7.14	1 > 2, 3[*]
Problem behavior							
Delinquency	1.13	0.31	1.15	0.40	1.35	0.73	1, 2 $\leq$ 3[*]
School misconduct	2.20	0.67	2.30	0.65	2.41	0.77	1 < 3[*]
Alcohol and drug use	1.46	0.65	1.60	0.78	1.92	0.94	1 < 2 < 3[*]
Autonomy from parents							
Decision making[a]	0.45	0.34	0.40	0.70	0.35	1.09	1 > 3[*]
Psychosocial development							
Self-reliance	3.05	0.43	3.08	0.39	2.95	0.48	2 < 3[**]
Self-esteem	3.03	0.50	3.06	0.47	2.93	0.48	2 < 3[*]

Note. Tests of significance of differences in outcomes at 1-year follow-up take into account initial group differences at the beginning of the study. Means and standard deviations reported in the table are unadjusted Time 2 outcomes.

[a]For this variable only, the pattern of unadjusted means (presented in this table) is the reverse of that observed for adjusted means. In the analyses that take into account initial differences in starting points, the Time 2 decision-making scores show that intensive employment increases, not decreases, youthful autonomy.
*$p < .05$. **$p < .10$.

$p = .09$; classroom attention, $F(2,366) = 5,853$, $p < .01$; and mind wandering, $F(2,364) = 6.63$, $p < .001$. The order of the means was identical for all of these variables: Moderate workers who had left the labor force were performing better in school than those who remained employed at moderate work hours, who in turn were performing better than those who increased their work hours. However, these groups did not differ with respect to academic effort, classroom concentration, or school orientation once initial differences were taken into account.

Finally, contrasts of adolescents who began the study as extensive workers showed differences at the 1-year follow-up as a function of their intervening work experiences only in their level of disengagement from school, $F(2, 101) = 3.097$, $p < .05$, once initial differences were taken into account. Here, however, the most negative orientation toward school was reported by adolescents who cut back their work hours from an extensive level to a more moderate level.[5] The most positive orientation

Table 5

Results of Paired Contrasts on Outcomes That Differ Significantly Among Adolescents Initially Working Between 1–19 Hr Weekly Who Left the Labor Force, Remained Employed at This Level, or Increased Work Hours Beyond 20 Hr Weekly Over the 1-Year Interval

School outcome	Became nonworkers		Remained employed 1–19 hr		Increased hours to 20+ hr		Significant contrast
	M	*SD*	*M*	*SD*	*M*	*SD*	
Grade point average	3.23	0.67	2.99	0.72	2.88	0.78	1 > 3*
Educational expectations	5.38	0.81	5.32	0.74	4.89	1.14	2 > 3*
Class cutting	1.40	0.66	1.48	0.60	1.56	0.82	1 < 3**
Classroom attention	4.14	0.67	3.95	0.67	3.80	0.84	1 > 3*
Mind wandering	2.45	0.79	2.52	0.70	2.76	0.82	1, 2 < 3*
Time on homework	4.01	1.26	3.99	1.12	3.44	1.35	1, 2 < 3*

Note. Tests of significance of differences in outcomes at 1-year follow-up take into account initial group differences at the beginning of the study. Means and standard deviations reported in the table are unadjusted Time 2 outcomes.
*$p < .05$. **$p < .10$.

toward school in this group was reported by adolescents who had left the labor force entirely after working in excess of 20 hr weekly.

Taken together, these findings indicate that youngsters who take on part-time jobs are less engaged in school before they enter the labor force but that taking on a part-time job, especially for more than 20 hr weekly, further exacerbates this problem. In addition, the results indicate that among adolescents who are working moderate hours, increasing their work hours beyond 20 hr per week further weakens their investment in school, whereas leaving the labor force leads to an improvement in school performance and orientation.

Work and Problem Behavior

The results of the MANOVA indicate that there also are prework selection effects in the area of problem behavior, multivariate $F(6, 1870) = 2.20$, $p < .001$, but that these effects are limited to minor delinquency, univariate F significant at $p = .06$. Inspection of the group means on this variable indicates that the nonworkers who eventually became workers with moderate work hours reported less delinquency before entering the labor force than their nonworking counterparts who remained nonemployed or their nonworking counterparts who entered the labor force at an extensive level. No significant differences were found in analyses designed to detect similar selection effects in contrasts involving youngsters who were working moderate amounts at Time 1 or in contrasts involving youngsters who were working extensive amounts at Time 1.

Analyses designed to detect consequences of differential work experiences after taking into account initial selection differences indicate, however, that entering the labor force clearly leads to increased problem behavior among adolescents. At the time of the 1-year follow-up, nonworkers who had remained out of the labor force reported less delinquency, $F(2, 930) = 8.897$, $p < .001$;[6] less school misconduct, $F(2, 938) = 2.703$, $p = .06$; and less drug use, $F(2, 928) = 11.056$, $p < .001$, than their peers who entered the work force in excess of 20 hr weekly. The difference in drug use between adolescents who worked long hours and those who worked moderate hours was significant as well. However, similar contrasts were not significant among the adolescents who began the study as moderate workers or as extensive workers.

Considered together, the findings on problem behavior indicate that, before entering the workplace, adolescents who choose to work tend to be engaged in more delinquent activity than their peers, but not in more drug use or school misconduct. However, entering the work force, especially at more than 20 hr weekly, further exacerbates the delinquent inclinations of youngsters who choose to work and also leads to increased drug use and school misconduct. Interestingly, increases or decreases in work hours neither exacerbate nor ameliorate the behavior problems caused by entry into the labor force.

Work and Internalized Distress

The analyses did not indicate any prework selection differences in the domain of internalized distress among adolescents who were nonworkers at Time 1. However, comparable analyses did indicate such differences among adolescents who were working moderate hours at Time 1, multivariate $F(4, 958) = 3.14$, $p < .05$. Univariate analyses indicated significant effects for both psychological and somatic symptoms (both $ps < .05$), and inspection of the means indicated that adolescents who were initially working moderate hours but who left the labor force reported fewer psychological and somatic symptoms at Time 1 than their peers who remained employed (either at the same or at a higher number of hours). No selection effects were found in the domain of internalized distress among youngsters who were working extensively at Time 1.

Analyses designed to examine the effects of working on internalized distress indicated no differences among youngsters as a function of their work status once initial differences had been taken into account. This absence of effects was evident among adolescents who were nonworkers at Time 1, among those who were working moderate hours at Time 1, and among those who were working extensively at Time 1.

Work and Autonomy From Parents

The results of the MANOVA contrasting the Time 1 autonomy scores of initial nonworkers indicate that there are preemployment selection differences among these groups of youngsters, multivariate $F(4,2200) = 4.79$, $p < .001$. Inspection of the means indicates that nonworkers who remained nonemployed tended to have been more closely monitored by their parents at Time 1 than were nonworkers who entered the labor force (either at moderate or extensive time commitments; $p = .07$) and that nonworkers who subsequently would enter the labor force and work extensively were being granted more decision-making freedom at Time 1 than were other non-workers ($p < .001$). No selection effects were found in contrasts designed to examine autonomy-related precursors in contrasts involving youngsters who were working moderate amounts at Time 1 or in contrasts involving youngsters who were working extensive amounts at Time 1.

Analyses designed to detect effects of working on adolescent autonomy after taking into account prework selection differences indicate that at the 1-year follow-up, adolescents' decision-making autonomy varies as a function of their work experience, $F(3, 848) = 2.845$, $p = .06$. Specifically, nonworkers who entered the labor force at more than 20 hr weekly report greater decision-making autonomy than those who remained nonemployed. No differences were found with respect to parental monitoring, however, nor were significant differences found in contrasts among adolescents who began the study as moderate workers or as extensive workers. It appears, then, that adolescents who are inclined to work have more decision-making autonomy than their peers to begin with but that the experience of working further enlarges this difference.

Work and Psychosocial Development

The results of the MANOVA examining psychosocial outcomes do not indicate selection effects on the variables of self-reliance or self-esteem in contrasts among the adolescents who had been nonworkers, who had been working moderately, or who had been working intensively at Time 1. The ANCOVAs indicate a tendency, however, for self-reliance and self-esteem to be negatively affected by working long hours: for self-reliance, $F(2, 937) = 4.05$, $p < .05$, and for self-esteem, $F(2, 931) = 2.45$, $p = .08$. (Interestingly, a significant Work Status × Sex interaction revealed that the negative impact of work on self-reliance was especially true among girls—an opposite finding from that reported in Steinberg, Greenberger, Garduque, Ruggerio, & Vaux, 1982). As Table 4 indicates, nonworkers who entered the labor force at more than 20 hr per week scored lower on each of these indicators at the 1-year follow-up than their peers who entered the labor force at moderate intensity.

Discussion

Previous research has indicated that working more than 20 hr weekly has adverse correlates in adolescent behavior and development, but the majority of these studies have not been able to distinguish between results caused by differential selection into the workplace (and in particular, differential selection into work of more than 20 hr weekly) and those genuinely caused by the consequences of extensive employment. Given the plausibility of the selection hypothesis—that youngsters whose schooling and behavior are already compromised are simply more likely to work long hours, either by choice or necessity—it is important to examine whether working (or working long hours) during the school year actually leads to deleterious consequences among adolescents. The present study suggests that it does.

In the absence of a randomized experimental design, it is of course impossible to demonstrate causality in a correlational study. But the longitudinal nature of the present research and the specific data analytic strategies used permit a more confident assessment of the direction of effects. Even after taking into account initial preemployment differences between adolescents who do and those who do not work (or between those who do and those who do not work long hours), we find that entering the labor force and, in particular, taking on a job for more than 20 hr weekly, diminish youngsters' investment in school, increase delinquency and drug use, further autonomy from parental control, and diminish feelings of self-reliance. Many of these effects are small in magnitude, but the overall pattern is consistent with previous cross-sectional studies and with the little short-term longitudinal evidence that exists on the over-time impact of adolescent employment (e.g., Steinberg, Greenberger, Garduque, Ruggiero, & Vaux, 1982).

There are a number of important limitations inherent in the present study that need to be acknowledged. First, although the interval studied was relatively brief (1 year), there may have been undetected movement in and out of the labor force during the time period that introduced error into our classification of adolescents. Second, as noted earlier, there was selective attrition over the course of the study that led to an attenuation in variability in the outcome measures studied. (Presumably, each of these factors would make it more difficult to detect significant effects.) Finally, the data come from adolescents' self-reports; future studies, especially those examining adolescent school engagement or autonomy from parents, might incorporate information provided by teachers and parents, respectively.

Our finding that taking on a job with long work hours leads to adverse consequences for young people does not contradict the argument that adolescents who work long hours are different from their peers who do not before they enter the labor force (e.g., Bachman & Schulenberg, 1991; Mortimer et al., 1991). Indeed, we find evidence for selection effects, especially in the domain of schooling. Adolescents who enter the labor force—and especially those who work more than 20 hr weekly—are less academically inclined and poorer students to begin with than their peers who do not work. Selection effects are less consistent in other domains, however. Of particular note in this regard is our failure to find support for the contention that adolescents who work are more involved in drug and alcohol use than their peers before entering the labor force, a frequent explanation for the finding that substance use is higher among teenagers with long work hours (e.g., Bachman et al., 1986). Nor do we find that youngsters who are psychologically more responsible than their peers, as indexed by a standardized measure of self-reliance, are more inclined to take on jobs. Rather, our findings concerning differential selection into the workplace point specifically to disengagement from school, broadly defined, as an important precursor of labor force entry.

By the same token, documenting that there are in fact preemployment psychological attributes that distinguish adolescents who do versus those who do not enter the labor force does not counter the claim that working long hours has psychological consequences as well. In the domain of schooling, for example, many of the attributes that differentiate nonworkers who become workers from those who remain nonemployed are also those that appear to be affected by extensive employment. Thus, while academic disengagement impels youngsters toward the workplace, part-time employment further distances adolescents from school. In essence, the operative process is not selection or socialization, but a dynamic and reciprocal process, in which adolescents both actively choose and are at the same time affected by the environments they encounter.

One of the most hotly contested issues in the study of adolescent work is whether extensive part-time employment threatens youngsters' schooling (cf. Barton, 1989; Charner & Fraser, 1987; Greenberger & Steinberg, 1986; Hotchkiss, 1986; Lewin-Epstein, 1981; McNeil, 1984; Mortimer & Finch, 1986; Steinberg & Dornbusch, 1991). This study indicates that working appears to make a bad situation worse, lowering the educational expectations, adversely affecting the school behaviors (specifically, time on homework and class attendance), and souring the school-related attitudes of students who already are achieving less and are more negative toward school than their peers. Our finding that working long hours also tends to increase school misconduct (an index that includes, among other things, cheating and copying homework) provides further evidence for the contention that employment weakens adolescents' attachment to formal education.

Working does not further erode students' grades, however, despite the negative impact it has on class attendance, homework performance, and attitudes toward school. This, we believe, is due to the fact that many working adolescents are able to maintain and protect their grade point average by choosing easier teachers, selecting less challenging courses, or cheating on class tests and assignments (see Greenberger & Steinberg, 1986; McNeil, 1984; Steinberg & Dornbusch, 1991). In this sample, for instance, over one third of the working adolescents admitted to taking easier classes in order to protect their grades from the negative effects of employment. For this reason, grade point average may be the wrong bottom line along which to evaluate the impact of employment on schooling (see also Greenberger & Steinberg, 1986; Steinberg & Dornbusch, 1991).

As in previous studies, we find that working also is associated with higher rates of deviance (Bachman et al., 1986; Elliott & Wofford, 1991; Ruggiero, 1984; Steinberg & Dornbusch, 1991). Specifically, taking on a job for more than 20 hr weekly leads to more delinquency and substance abuse. In the case of drug and alcohol use in particular, the difference attributable to working is not trivial: By the time of the 1-year follow-up, previously nonemployed adolescents who had been working more than 20 hr weekly were using drugs and alcohol 33% more often than their counterparts who had remained nonemployed. (The effect size coefficient for this contrast, $d > 1.0$, is comparable to that reported in other studies of employment and delinquency [Elliott & Wofford, 1991].) Although not studied here, the impact of extensive employment on adolescent drug and alcohol use has been attributed to the fact that adolescents' discretionary income (and hence, opportunity to purchase drugs and alcohol) varies as a direct function of how many hours they are employed each week (e.g., Greenberger & Steinberg, 1986; Steinberg & Dornbusch, 1991).

Two specific findings concerning other domains investigated in this study are noteworthy. First, adolescents whose parents are more permissive are more likely to work long hours than their peers; presumably, extensive employment during the school year is one of the indulgences that these parents permit. In addition, working tends to lead to further independence from parents, at least as indexed by our measure of family decision making. Whether this effect should be viewed in a positive light (i.e., working fosters more egalitarian parent-child relations) or in a negative light (i.e., working undermines parental authority) cannot be determined on the basis of the results reported here, however.

Second, working long hours appears to adversely affect youngsters' self-reliance and, to a lesser extent, self-esteem. Because previous studies of work and psychosocial development have yielded inconsistent results—some report no effects (e.g., Bachman et al., 1986) whereas others report differential effects for boys and girls (e.g., Steinberg, Greenberger, Garduque, Ruggiero, & Vaux, 1982)—it is probably best to view the findings reported in the present study as further confusing an already perplexing picture. Several writers have suggested that the impact of work on adolescent psychosocial development most likely varies as a function of the characteristics of the adolescent's job (e.g., Greenberger & Steinberg, 1986; Mortimer, Finch, Shanahan, & Ryu, 1992; Mortimer, Ryu, Dennehy, & Lee, 1992); unfortunately, however, data were not collected on youngsters' work conditions in the present investigation. Future research should look more closely at differences among adolescents' jobs in their impact on youngsters' development and behavior.

Examining the results of some of the specific contrasts conducted further elucidates the observed patterns of effects. With respect to problem behavior, the clearest effects occur at the point of transition into the labor force, rather than when youngsters adjust their work hours or leave the work force after having been employed. Indeed, when adolescents who are working in excess of 20 hr weekly decrease their work hours or drop out of the labor force entirely, their drug and alcohol use does not immediately decline. This suggests that the increase in drug and alcohol use observed among workers occurs during the first year of employment and may stabilize at the higher level. One hypothesis is that initial employment helps to establish a higher standard of living (so to speak) that is not so easily given up. Consistent with this, we are not able to predict changes in employment status among adolescents already working on the basis of their initial drug and alcohol use. Presumably, such predictions would be possible if tiring with the working person's "life-style" were a reason to cut back one's work hours.

The results in the domain of schooling present a different picture. Here we find effects both of entering the labor force and of changing one's work situation. The findings concerning the over-time school profiles of adolescents who had initially been working for moderate amounts of time are illuminating, and the news is both bad and good. On the negative side, increases in work hours from a moderate to a high level lead to moderate declines in schooling and achievement; on the positive side, however, dropping out of the labor force leads to improved schooling and achievement—in fact, moderately employed adolescents who later left the labor force were earning identical grades at the 1-year follow-up as adolescents who had remained nonemployed during the year (GPA = 3.2 in each case). Unlike the effects of work on drug and alcohol use, then, the adverse effects on schooling appear to be reversible.

As in previous studies (e.g., Steinberg & Dornbusch, 1991), the results of the present investigation do not indicate a clear or consistent threshold beyond which the effects of employment turn from innocuous to harmful. On some outcomes (e.g., homework), the difference between nonworkers and moderate workers was significant, whereas the outcome for moderately and intensively employed workers was equivalent. On others (e.g., delinquency), the critical difference was between adolescents working moderate hours and those working long hours. On others still (e.g., drug use), all three groups differed significantly. Nevertheless, across the outcomes studied, inspection of group means indicated that nonworkers generally were better adjusted than adolescents with moderate work hours, who in turn were better adjusted than adolescents with long work hours. As we concluded in an earlier, cross-sectional report (Steinberg & Dornbusch, 1991), the most prudent interpretation of the data is that the adverse correlates of school-year employment increase as a function of the number of hours a teenager is employed each week. The present study provides evidence that some of these deleterious correlates of working long hours are indeed likely to be consequences.

Notes

1. Although a few studies have suggested that employment in certain types of jobs may hold advantages for young people's long-term occupational development (e.g., Mortimer, Ryu, Dennehy, & Lee, 1992; Stern, Stone, Hopkins, & McMillion, 1990), research on the short-term consequences of school-year employment is more often negative than positive in its implications, and the number of adolescents who work in "good" jobs is very small (Greenberger & Steinberg, 1986).
2. To examine whether the effects of work were different among boys and girls, we also tested for Work Status × Sex interactions in these analyses. Very few interactions (7 out of 54) reached significance, and those that did were seldom readily interpretable. Cases in which the interaction was interpretable are noted in the text.
3. As a precaution, we also ran the analyses with controls for socioeconomic status and found that the results changed very little, particularly in the case of socialization effects. Not surprisingly, the pattern of findings varied somewhat more with and without controls for socioeconomic status when selection effects were examined, but, even still, the change was not dramatic, and the basic pattern of results was identical.
4. A significant Work Status × Sex interaction in the prediction of educational expectations revealed that, although the negative impact of working is evident among both boys and girls, the drop in expectations among girls occurs only in the high work hours group; for boys, the effect is more linear.
5. A significant Work Status × Sex interaction in this case indicated that this pattern was especially true among girls.
6. A significant Work Status × Sex interaction indicated that the impact of work on delinquency, while similar for both sexes, was especially pronounced among boys.

References

Appelbaum, M., & McCall, R. (1983). Design and analysis in developmental psychology. In P. H. Mussen (Series Ed.) & W. Kessen (Vol. Ed.), *Handbook of child psychology: Vol. 1. History, theory, and methods* (4th ed., pp. 415–476). New York: Wiley.

Bachman, J. (1983). Premature affluence: Do high school students earn too much? *Economic Outlook USA, Summer,* 64–67.

Bachman, J. G., Bare, D. E., & Frankie, E. I. (1986). *Correlates of employment among high school seniors* (Monitoring the Future Occasional Paper #20). Ann Arbor, MI: Institute for Social Research.

Bachman, J., & Schulenberg, J. (1991). *Part-time work by high school seniors: Sorting out correlates and possible consequences* (Monitoring the Future Occasional paper #32). Ann Arbor, MI: Institute for Social Research.

Barton, P. (1989). *Earning and learning: The academic achievement of high school juniors with jobs.* Princeton, NJ: National Assessment of Educational Progress, Educational Testing Service.

Charner, I., & Fraser, B. (1987). *Youth and work.* Washington, DC: William T. Grant Foundation Commission on Work, Family and Citizenship.

Damico, R. (1984). Does working in high school impair academic progress? *Sociology of Education, 57,* 157–164.

Dornbusch, S., Carlsmith, J., Bushwall, S., Ritter, P., Leiderman, H., Hastorf, A., & Gross, R. (1985). Single parents, extended households and the control of adolescents. *Child Development, 56,* 326–341.

Dornbusch, S. M., Ritter, P. L., Liederman, P., Roberts, D., & Fraleigh, M. (1987). The relation of parenting style to adolescent school performance. *Child Development, 58,* 1244–1257.

Elliott, D., & Wofford, S. (1991). *Adolescent employment.* [Unpublished report prepared for press release available from the authors]. Boulder, CO: Institute of Behavioral Science, University of Colorado.

Gold, M. (1970). *Delinquent behavior in an American city.* Monterey, CA: Brooks/Cole.

Gottfredson, D. (1985). Youth employment, crime, and schooling: A longitudinal study of a national sample. *Developmental Psychology, 21,* 419–432.

Greenberger, E., & Bond, L. (1976). *Technical manual for the Psychosocial Maturity Inventory.* Unpublished manuscript, Program in Social Ecology, University of California, Irvine.

Greenberger, E., Josselson, R., Knerr, C., & Knerr, B. (1974). The measurement and structure of psychosocial maturity. *Journal of Youth and Adolescence, 4,* 127–143.

Greenberger, E., & Steinberg, L. (1986). *When teenagers work: The psychological and social costs of adolescent employment.* New York: Basic Books.

Greenberger, E., Steinberg, L., & Vaux, A. (1981). Adolescents who work: Health and behavioral consequences of job stress. *Developmental Psychology, 17,* 691–703.

Hotchkiss, L. (1986). Work and schools—complements or competitors? In K. Borman & J. Reisman (Eds.), *Becoming a worker* (pp. 90–115). Norwood, NJ: Ablex.

Lewin-Epstein, N. (1981). *Youth employment during high school.* Washington, DC: National Center for Education Statistics.

Lillydahl, H. (1990). Academic achievement and part-time employment of high school students. *Journal of Economic Education, Summer,* 307–316.

McNeil, L. (1984). Lowering expectations: The impact of student employment on classroom knowledge. Madison, WI: Wisconsin Center for Educational Research.

Mortimer, J. T., & Finch, M. (1986). The effects of part-time work on adolescents self-concept and achievement. In K. Borman & J. Reisman (Eds.), *Becoming a worker* (pp. 66–89). Norwood, NJ: Ablex.

Mortimer, J., Finch, M., Ryu, S., & Shanahan, M. (1991, April). *Evidence from a prospective longitudinal study of work experience and adolescent development.* Paper presented at the biennial meetings of the Society for Research in Child Development, Seattle, WA.

Mortimer, J., Finch, M., Shanahan, M., & Ryu, S. (1992). Work experience, mental health, and behavioral adjustment in adolescence. *Journal of Research on Adolescence, 2,* 25–57.

Mortimer, J., Ryu, S., Dennehy, K., & Lee, C. (1992, October). *Part-time work and occupational value formation in adolescence.* Paper presented at the annual meetings of the American Sociological Association, Pittsburgh, PA.

Patterson, G., & Stouthamer-Loeber, M. (1984). The correlation of family management practices and delinquency. *Child Development, 55,* 1299–1307.

Radloff, L. S. (1977). The CES-D scale: A self-report depression scale for research in the general population. *Applied Psychological Measurement, 1,* 385–401.

Rosenberg, M. (1965). *Society and the adolescent self-image.* Princeton, NJ: Princeton University Press.

Ruggiero, M. (1984). *Work as an impetus to delinquency: An examination of theoretical and empirical connections.* Unpublished doctoral dissertation, University of California, Irvine.

Schill, W., McCartin, R., & Meyer, K. (1985). Youth employment; Its relationship to academic and family variables. *Journal of Vocational Behavior, 26,* 155–163.

Shannon, L. (1982). *Assessing the relationship of adult criminal careers to juvenile careers.* Washington, DC: U.S. Department of Justice (Microfiche No. NCJ 77744, available from the National Criminal Justice Reference Service, Washington, DC).

Steinberg, L. (1987). Single parents, stepparents, and the susceptibility of adolescents to antisocial peer pressure. *Child Development, 58,* 269–275.

Steinberg, L., & Dornbusch, S. (1991). Negative correlates of part-time work in adolescence: Replication and elaboration. *Developmental Psychology, 17,* 304–313.

Steinberg, L., Greenberger, E., Garduque, L., & McAuliffe, S. (1982). High school students in the labor force: Some costs and benefits to schooling and learning. *Educational Evaluation and Policy Analysis, 4,* 363–372.

Steinberg, L., Greenberger, E., Garduque, L., Ruggiero, M., & Vaux, A. (1982). Effects of working on adolescent development. *Developmental Psychology, 18,* 385–395.

Stern, D., Stone, J., Hopkins, C., & McMillion, M. (1990). Quality of students' work experience and orientation toward work. *Youth and Society, 22,* 263–282.

Wehlage, G., Rutter, R., Smith, G., Lesko, N., & Fernandez, R. (1989). *Reducing the risk: Schools as communities of support.* London: Falmer Press.

Weinberger, D., Tublin, S., Ford, M., & Feldman, S. (1990). Preadolescents' social-emotional adjustment and selective attrition in family research. *Child Development, 61,* 1374–1386.

Wirtz, P., Rohrbeck, C., Charner, I., & Fraser, B. (1987). *Intense employment while in high school: Are teachers, guidance counselors, and parents misguiding academically-oriented adolescents?* Washington, DC: George Washington University Graduate Institute for Policy Education and Research.

Yasuda, K. (1990). *Working and schooling decisions: A study of New Hampshire teenage labor market behavior and level of educational attainment* (First and Second Interim Reports). Concord, NH: New Hampshire Department of Economic and Labor Market Information Bureau.

Questions

1. What are the costs and benefits of part-time work?
2. If working more than 20 hours a week threatens schooling, should schools allow students to enroll part time so they can work part time?
3. Why might working longer hours adversely affect self-reliance and self-esteem?
4. Why might working longer hours be associated with more drug use and school misconduct?
5. Would the results of this study generalize to college students?

References and Further Reading

Bachman, J. G., & Schulenberg, J. (1993). How part-time work intensity relates to drug use, problem behavior, time use, and satisfaction among high school seniors: Are these consequences or merely correlates? *Developmental Psychology, 29,* 220–235.

Fine, G. A., Mortimer, J. T., & Roberts, D. F. (1990). Leisure, work, and the mass media. In S. S. Feldman, & G. R. Elliott (1990). *At the threshold: The developing adolescent* (pp. 225–252). Cambridge, MA: Harvard University Press.

Mortimer, J. T., & Johnson, M. K. (1998). New perspectives on adolescent work and the transition to adulthood. In R. Jessor (Ed.), *New perspectives on adolescent risk behavior* (pp. 425–496). Cambridge, U.K.: Cambridge University Press.

Steinberg, L, & Dornbusch, S. M. (1991). Negative correlates of part-time employment during adolescence: Replication and elaboration. *Developmental Psychology, 27,* 304–313.

Chapter 13

Violence and Gangs

Several readings in this book provide frameworks for understanding why adolescents might join together in gangs and engage in criminal and violent behavior. Erikson (Reading 5.1) noted that some youth form a *negative identity,* an "identity perversely based on all those identifications and roles which, at critical stages of development, had been presented to them as most undesirable or dangerous and yet also as most real" (Erikson, 1968, p. 174). From Erikson's perspective, the decision to engage in criminal or violent behavior speaks to deficits in the adolescent's upbringing and social context. Acceptable roles are perceived to be unattainable. Society offers no way for the adolescent to be "somebody," to get respect, admiration, and recognition; the only avenue open to be somebody is through negative means. Erikson argued that adolescents would rather be somebody totally bad than to be "not-quite-somebody."

Bakan (Reading 1.1) suggests that adolescents will behave appropriately if they believe in "the promise" that doing well in school will lead to the realization of success, income, and status. Delinquency and rebellion will predominate when adolescents do not buy into the promise. MacLeod's study of adolescents from low-income families provides empirical support for Bakan's claims (Reading 7.1). MacLeod found that many working-class youth saw little connection between school achievement and their prospects in the workplace, and as a result they disengaged from school and engaged in delinquent activity.

Another framework is offered by psychoanalyst Peter Blos (1971) who noted that as adolescents move from the personal context of family into the wider society, if society offers no stable structures to receive youth, "the maturing child turns, exclusively, to his contemporaries, his peers, in order to create for himself that social extra-familial structure without which he cannot maintain his psychic integrity" (Blos, 1971, p. 975). When adolescents find themselves in a social context in which they feel unsupported by families, schools, and other social institutions, they will turn to others like themselves. When they are growing up in neighborhoods that are poor and unsafe, the peers they are likely to turn to for support are members of gangs, exposing them to involvement in criminal and delinquent activity.

Gangs are not a new phenomena. As early as 1850, over 200 gang wars were taking place in New York City, some lasting for days (Teeter, 1988). Today, more than 90% of large American cities report gang problems, and gangs are appearing in small to medium-size cities and suburban areas as well. While gangs until the mid-1900s were predominantly white and of various European backgrounds, since the 1970s gangs have become predominantly African American, Hispanic, or Asian, and are composed of recently migrated youth of lower social class (Flannery, Huff, & Manos, 1998). Gangs draw their members from poorer households and arise in response to disparities between the aspirations of youth and the opportunities they have to meet those aspirations. Deleterious changes in economic conditions have occurred in many inner-city neighborhoods. Manufacturing jobs have disappeared, and levels of unemployment and underemployment have risen. The erosion of economic opportunities coupled with racial discrimination has led to the institutionalization of gangs and made their appeal hard to resist.

Gangs have become of greater concern today because gang members are engaging in more violent offenses and using more lethal weapons. Gang warfare is marked by the use of guns and impersonal violence carried out in drive-by shootings that affect innocent bystanders as well as rival gang members. Today's inner-city youth have easy access to guns, and those who carry weapons and are involved with drugs are "often impulsive and frequently lack the cognitive problem-solving skills to settle disputes calmly. Fistfights turn into more lethal confrontations because guns are present" (Flannery et al., 1998, p. 184).

The readings in this chapter look at the individual, family, and societal factors that lead to involvement with gangs and violence. They examine the benefits that gangs offer and the needs they meet that are not being met by family, school, or other support networks. Finally, they examine the costs of gang involvement.

Additional Resources

References and Suggested Reading

Blos, P. (1971). The child analyst looks at the young adolescent. *Daedalus,* Fall, 961–978.

Borduin, C. M., & Schaeffer, C. M. (1998). Violent offending in adolescence: Epidemiology, correlates, outcomes, and treatment. In T. P. Gullotta, G. R. Adams, & R. Montemayor (Eds.) *Delinquent violent youth: Theory and interventions* (pp. 144–174). Thousand Oaks, CA: Sage.

Erikson, E. H. (1968). *Identity: Youth and crisis.* New York: W. W. Norton.

Cummings, S., & Monti, D. J. (Eds.). (1993). *Gangs: The origins and impact of contemporary youth gangs in the United States.* Albany: State University of New York Press.

Teeter, R. (1988). Coming of age on the city streets in nineteenth-century America. *Adolescence, 23*(92), 909–912.

On the Internet

http://parentingteens.about.com/parenting/parentingteens/msub56.htm

About.com—Parenting of Adolescents: Gang Violence

http://parentingteens.about.com/parenting/parentingteens/msubmenu1.htm

About.com—Parenting of Adolescents: Youth Violence

These two sites on the About.com Network provide links to information on gang violence and youth violence. The About.com Network consists of over 700 Guide sites covering more than 50,000 subjects with over 1 million links to resources on the Net and a fast-growing archive of original content.

http://www.aacap.org/whatsnew/10point.htm

American Academy of Child & Adolescent Psychiatry—10 Point Plan
This is the Web site of the American Academy of Child & Adolescent Psychiatry. The site is designed as a public service to aid in the understanding and treatment of developmental, behavioral, and mental disorders.

http://www.ama-assn.org/adolhlth/special/school.htm

American Medical Association—Adolescent Health Special Topic, Adolescents and Violence
The American Medical Association's (AMA) Program on Child and Adolescent Health provides this site as a resource on adolescent health issues and for their Guidelines for Adolescent Preventive Services (GAPS) program.

http://www.childrensdefense.org/youthviolence/resources.html

Children's Defense Fund—Youth Violence Resource Center
The Children's Defense Fund Youth Violence Resource Center provides resources through this Web site to better understand the nature of youth violence, the early warning signs that may be a precursor to youth violence, and positive steps that can be taken to reduce youth violence.

http://ojjdp.ncjrs.org/programs/programs.html

Office of Juvenile Justice and Delinquency Prevention—OJJDP Programs
The Office of Juvenile Justice and Delinquency Prevention Web site is designed to provide information and resources on general areas of interest about juvenile justice and delinquency including conferences, funding opportunities, and new publications. It also describes a comprehensive strategy as a framework for communities to combat youth crime.

http://www.ed.gov/offices/OESE/SDFS/safeschools.html

U.S. Department of Education—Keeping Schools And Communities Safe
This is the U.S. Department of Education Web site. It provides information to educators, policy makers, parents, students, researchers, and other citizens with a stake in education.

Gangs, Social Control, and Ethnicity: Ways to Redirect

James Diego Vigil, Ph.D., is a professor of anthropology at the University of California, Los Angeles. He is author of *From Indians to Chicanos: The Dynamics of Mexican American Culture* (1984) and *Barrio Gangs: Street Life and Identity in Southern California* (1988). His research has focused on Mexican and U.S. Southwest ethnohistory, educational anthropology, adolescent acculturation issues, and urban anthropology.

Gangs and violence arise in response to a host of problematic social, economic, and family circumstances that are faced by adolescents in inner cities and increasingly in smaller communities. Gangs more often emerge in poorer communities of immigrants and ethnic minorities. Families living in poverty are under enormous stress due to low income and unstable work. Immigrant families that are nonwhite face barriers that prevent their integration into mainstream America and economic advancement. Economic stresses are associated with poorer parenting skills, an inability to set firm boundaries and to provide supervision for adolescents (Reading 10.2).

Gang members generally do poorly in school and do not receive a positive sense of themselves in the role of student. They find the skills learned in school to be unnecessary in their lives, as a vast discrepancy exists between being street smart and being smart in academic subjects. Schools have little to offer in preparing them for survival in unsafe neighborhoods. Given the high unemployment in their neighborhoods and limited economic and job opportunities, they see the costs of finishing school as greater than the benefits (Reading 7.1).

A gang acts as a surrogate family, school, and even as police where ties with these authorities are problematic. Because gangs are associated with violent and delinquent activity, they have traditionally been viewed in a negative light. But much of gang life does not revolve around fighting and delinquent acts. Positive dimensions exist to the gang experience that many youth cannot find in the family, school, or community. Gang members engage in many conventional activities that serve to create solidarity among themselves and to establish an identity to outsiders. They play, joke, exchange stories, talk about personal and social events. Gangs offer roles in which members can achieve success and "be somebody."

James Vigil argues that in immigrant and ethnic minority communities, gangs have taken over the role of socializing young people, which has formerly been filled by families and schools. He examines the factors that lead adolescents to join gangs and the benefits they offer. Gangs offer security and protection to adolescents who experience pervasive fear in their neighborhoods; strategies for coping with everyday life; friendship; a sense of brotherhood, loyalty, and support; and a way to gain status and respect.

Why do young people join gangs?[1] What roles do ethnicity and gender and the desire for affiliation and achievement play in the formation and maintenance of gang subculture and gang membership? The ethnic traditions of the streets can provide answers to these questions. Although gangs have been an urban problem in the United States since the 19th century, gangs, added new dimensions that placed them in a different light in the late 20th century. Drug use and trafficking, gangbanging, and wanton drive-by shootings raised public alarm to a new level. Specially trained law enforcement "gang" units, probation programs, and court sentencing "crackdowns" took aim at the "gang problem," but to little or no avail. Thus, by the late 1980s, more and more public servants and observers began to rethink how the problem of gangs might be approached and rectified (Huff, 1990; Sahagun, 1990, 1991). Some made a complete turnabout in shifting from law enforcement to socially based solutions to the problem, creating renewed interest in unraveling the causes of gang formation and behavior and the dissolution and redirection of gangs.

Many poor ethnic families, primarily from southeastern Europe, immigrated to the United States in the late 19th century looking for improved working and living conditions. Although adaptation was difficult for all family members, it was the immigrant children who underwent especially intense culture change pressures. When the parents left their traditional culture and rural, peasant ways of life, they had no idea that they would be "doubly" stressing their children by subjecting them to urban slums with deteriorated and substandard housing and to a modern urban culture that placed unfamiliar demands on them. Nor were parents aware that traditional means of social control, anchored in the small community and in close, extended families of the peasant village, would be totally transformed in these new American cities, where public servants, such as schoolteachers and police, would come to dominate their lives.

Instead, what occurred for generation after generation of different ethnic immigrant groups was that the street life of the cities began to affect detrimentally the character of many of the immigrant children, especially by loosening established means of social control and unevenly introducing new ones. Young males lost connections to established social institutions, such as family and schools, and made their own street adaptation. Early on, large portions of these youth formed street gangs from groups that social reformers then referred to as "pavement" children. Through the turn of the century and until the 1940s and 1950s, these European American ethnic gangs caught the eye of both the public media and researchers.

Many social programs then took the form of settlement houses, recreation and social opportunities, and even make-work projects as the public became more open to the social experiments of the Progressive Era and the budding welfare state. Researchers of that era also noted how social and environmental problems caused the gang problem. By mid-century, it was clear there were different types of ghettoes, or urban slums, that produced different kinds of street groups. The ebb and flow of the economy played a role in the development of street gangs. When the economy was relatively strong, increased opportunities for employment helped stabilize the lives of the majority of the European American ethnic children, who could at least expect and get jobs and hope to start a family. Conversely, when the economy faltered, the chances for avenues of employment and a conventional life diminished. With some variations created by the history of immigration, location, and strength and sources of outside influences, the economic downturn of the late 20th century helped create the diversity of gangs across Mexican American, African American, and southeast Asian youth in Los Angeles.[2] . . .

A Framework for Understanding Gangs: Multiple Marginality

Although with some ethnic variations and slightly different ways of incorporating females, all gang cultures in Los Angeles have revolved around how poor immigrants, migrants, or ethnic minorities and their children adapt to the city. The stresses and strains of this adaptation are manifold, and an assessment of them provides insight into what causes gangs and why certain individuals join them.[3]

Because barrios and ghettos and the living and working conditions of their residents stand as appendages to and facets of the remainder of society, this condition can best be characterized as multiple marginality. Applying this framework to the Mexican American case, one notes that there are ecological, economic, sociocultural, and psychological components of marginality. Although the sequence is clear, beginning with where people lived and worked and following with other adjustments, a dynamic action and reaction implicit in the construct account for the interaction among all of the sectors.

The barrio was founded in ecologically inferior areas adjacent to workplaces and separate from neighboring European Americans, which created a spatial and social distance alongside a visual blight of poverty that exacerbated Mexican American integration into society. Coupled with the low-paid, low-skill jobs that were available to barrio residents and the secondary labor market practices that affect permanent employment and retard social mobility, these conditions translated into substandard housing and crowded conditions that placed many families under stress.

Generational changes affected acculturation and the transition from Mexican to mainstream European American–dominated cultural norms. Some people sought total assimilation, while others selected paths in conformance with a bilingual-bicultural style. However, for many individuals, such assimilation was a very stressful, uneven affair, for neither Mexican culture was retained nor a new "American" mainstream culture acquired. Instead, a syncretic culture, midway in a hit-or-miss fashion between the two cultures, created the predicament of a *cholo** label defining the cultural marginals of the population.

With economic dislocations, culture change, and the effects of the streets came a loss of social control within traditional families. Under economic strain, adults lost firm parenting skills; in the family, gender roles shifted, especially when females found work outside the home and males did not. As families became less able to supervise their children and schools failed in developing appropriate learning programs for this population, a breakdown in the key sources of social control took place. Street socialization took over and brought youth into close, negative contact with police.

Because of the marginal, conflicting forces noted earlier, self-identification among barrio youth—especially during the adolescent "psychosocial moratorium," when a marginal status crisis emerged—led young people to street role models. Peers began to compete successfully with the family, school, and other authority figures. Age and gender clarification took on new forms and processes during this time, as a rigid sense of "masculinity" came to be embraced by gang members. Street pressures reinforced a code of toughness for survival.

In short, multiple marginality—combining, adding, and integrating different elements—worked to create disaffiliated, detached youths who grouped together into gangs. With the creation of the gang subculture, there arose a marginal street recruitment force with which youth had to reckon. Because of variations in the degree and intensity of multiple marginality across barrios and ghettos, some poorer and more fragmented than others, different types of gangs as well as gang members emerged.

Street Realities as Socialization

Uniting all gangs, the crucible for the subculture, is the reality of the streets, especially in neighborhoods of older and more established gangs. On unsupervised streets, at-risk youth learn the ways of the gang, contending with new places, times, and modes of socialization. Most of the gang subculture activities occur in empty lots, hallway transits, the back or side porches of homes, alleyways, rooftops of apartments, out-of-view corners and crannies of odd-shaped public parks, and backsides of stores, apartments, and small industrial buildings. Much of the time spent in such locations is during the night. In the dark, symbolically, perhaps, when darker human emotions reign, such places—as well as unoccupied locations such as school yards and recreational facilities—are often taken over by gangs. Youngsters out at night also encounter winos, gangsters, molesters, the homeless, the criminally prone, and, of course, society's street social control specialists, the police.

In the course of such encounters, behavior is shaped by street realities. An attitude of awareness—one of wariness bordering on paranoia, looking over the shoulder, double-checking associates, watching friends, and avoiding danger as best one can by being streetwise—is cultivated.

---

*[This term has evolved to mean those of mixed or pure Indian ancestry who are trying to move up the social and economic ladder—Ed.]

It is in the context of the street that the gang subculture flourishes. Pervading this street reality is fear: fear of hidden places, fear of darker times, and fear of strange behaviors. For children entering street life, peers, older children, and young adults begin to affect their attitudes and shape their behavior in unconventional ways. Prominent in the curriculum of street socialization are how to talk, walk, think, and observe the rituals and ceremonies of the gang. Friendship and protection are important to gang subculture, for emotional security and physical defense from real threats are key to survival.

Gender socialization occurs under the strict auspices of the street codes. Girls are usually subject to male domination, sometimes including molestation and rape. Because of this, brothers and older male relatives of young females constantly admonish them for being "out in the streets," even when they themselves run the streets. Some girls and young women have rejected such supervision and advice and have established a street reputation of their own. However, most of the females reluctantly follow the male directives, avoiding the worst effects of the streets. If they do join the street gang, they usually do so as an auxiliary of the male gang.

Males are a different story. Traditional working-class male values extol the virtues of "masculinity" and showing that one "has balls." Many Mexican Americans and African Americans share this urban working-class background. For those who come from immigrant or migrant backgrounds, however, the changes forced by such street realities can be doubly difficult. Job and work paths for ethnic minorities in urban areas change traditional male maturation patterns from their former rural, small-town base. Coupled with high dropout and unemployment rates that further undermine male developmental experiences, the streets become the "only game in town." Being "a man"—tough, unfeeling, courageous, and daring—limits the role choices available to males forced to adjust and adapt to street realities. To resist this street subcultural requirement is to invite trouble; a person is left unprotected, unaffiliated, and subject to the wills and whims of others.

Street children have to deal with pervasive fear, and if their parents and other authorities cannot help, the gang steps in. Although the media and police reports emphasize peer gang member pressure and intimidation as principal means of recruiting new gang members, one cannot escape the observation that family and school voids—in short, social control breakdowns—are the main reason these children give for being in the streets. In their reality of limited choices, they feel almost compelled to join a gang (Klein, 1968). Many come from female-dominated, single-parent households and must learn to measure up to male rules and expectations in the streets. This socialization is a strange and unsteady arrangement, which gang initiation rituals partially address: Beating up a new gang member helps ensure that all the "femininity" is eliminated and also provides a public showing for fellow gang members to see how a "man" takes a beating.

Contrasts between African Americans' experience with deep-rooted racist and other structural developments and the refugee Vietnamese predicament make for different types of family structures and maladies. For one group it may be a permanently etched blemish, while for another a temporary arrangement that marks the first years of adaptation. Similarly, the Mexican American population's history shows that the economic relationship between two neighbor nations and incessant immigration from the poorer one create troublesome family dynamics. What follows is a general outline that provides a baseline for all of the ethnic groups whose youth are drawn to gang life.

Focusing on social control features is a middle-range analysis that acknowledges macrohistorical (e.g., immigration and racism) and macrostructural (e.g., secondary labor market, underclass, and poverty) causative forces but also attempts to spell out what these factors are and how they can be recaptured by societal efforts and programs in lieu of a major transformation of society or revolution. Four broad areas aid our understanding of the process: attachment, commitment, involvement, and belief.

Attachment emphasizes effective ties that youth form to significant others, such as family, parents, and other role models who become primary socializers for acceptable behavior. When these conventional ties loosen and voids are created, other social units serve this need. With commitment, the key point is aspiration for an acceptable status with well-defined future goals in the offing. Again, if possibilities for affiliation and achievement are missing, other avenues are sought or taught for gaining respect and prestige. Involvement is simply a category that highlights participation in conventional activities that lead to socially valued success and status objectives—in other words, the quality of a youth's time spent on prosocial activities. Finally, belief specifies acceptance of the moral validity of the core social value system, the social rules. The implications of this latter aspect of social control are obvious, especially if a youth recognizes dominant values but may feel disaffiliated because of weakened ties to them. Some researchers refer to "oppositional" culture, in which working-class youth subvert middle-class values (Willis, 1977).

With breakdowns in the social webs, which cause confusion around questions such as whom to look up to for direction, what to do to reach goals, how to spend spare time, and why to accept social rules, it is no wonder that the gang subculture has evolved for just these purposes (Cohen, 1955). A gang is established and persists because it continues to meet the needs of those who follow its creators. With choloization and street socialization frequent products of immigrant adaptation dynamics, the gang subculture serves several functions for many unconventional youths.

Gang members have troubles with school, strained families, and an excess of free, unsupervised time to follow the wrong leaders and actors. The gang fulfills important needs, both personal and social, because of the voids mentioned earlier. If we stretch our minds to say that involvement, attachment, commitment, and belief in conventional social control units have shifted to the gang, then we are better able to appraise what gangs actually do and what potential might lie in empowering and redirecting the energies of gangs. But first we have to ask directly: What does the gang subculture do?

Social Control and the Gang Subculture

One 16-year-old gang member who was asked "Why did you join the gang?" answered, "Fun, adventure, money." Summaries of gang culture have suggested the following as important features: (1) recruitment and initiation, (2) goals and roles, (3) striving for

rank, and (4) positive self-concept (Cartwright, Tomson, & Schwartz, 1975)....
([T]here are important gender differences in the manner in which these features are
enacted. Here, the focus is on male gang members.) Attachment to significant others
is a key facet in gang structures. Commitment is shown to attain status, but in a
street-devised, gang-directed manner. Involvement is unconventional but approximates
what street people consider "socially" acceptable status objectives and use of time. In
the end, belief in social rules revolves around and is constricted by the limited horizons
in which gang members find themselves.

The strongest role played by gangs is in offering friendship, emotional support, and a sense of security and protection in the face of unpredictable, "crazy"
street pressures. Attachment to the gang and gang members is verified in what
gang members do for one another, such as "backing up" each other, retaliating
when a member is killed, providing a place to sleep, and sharing personal resources. Friendships may have started earlier if the youngsters grew up together,
bonding on many different dimensions, but gang affiliation usually entails the use
of fictive kinship terms. Mexican Americans, for example, refer to themselves as
carnales (usually translated as brothers; the word more nearly approximates "of
the [same] flesh"), "homeboys" (same gang or neighborhood), or *camaradas* (comrades) to verbalize, sometimes with great aplomb, the seal and pact that constitute
gang membership. African Americans usually rely on "cuz" (cousin), "bro"
(brother), "blood" (close relative), and homeboy, although in Los Angeles at least
"blood" and "cuz" took on new connotations of particular gang names by the
1990s. Both Mexican American and African American groups feel and say on countless occasions that the gang is like a family (Vigil, 1988b).

The sociopsychological aspects of this attachment dynamic include ego, group,
and role facets. Self-identification within the gang involves observing, mimicking, and
following the attitude and behavior of peers, older relatives who have been in gangs,
and *veteranos* (veterans, experienced gang members) or OGs (original gangsters, in
the African American version). The latter provide examples for how to act, think, and
feel about any number of street realities, such as how to group together for self-
defense. A gang initiation ritual cements these relationships.

Commitment comes from attaining status with the gang goals as the individual
learns to surrender himself to the gang or group. This type of dedication, or release
of individual or significant-other choices, is possible because most gang members have
weak or fragmented self-identities, which makes them particularly vulnerable and
receptive to group pressures and concerns. The trade-off, protection and friendship
from the group, encourages the individual to be loyal and supportive to the group.
Showing care, sharing resources, backing up one's homeboys or *camaradas*, and making
time and expanding energies for all types of gang activities are also ways to attain
status and reach goals designated by the gang.

One important gang goal is defense of the "turf" or barrio from transgressors'
drive-by shootings of homes, cars, and people on the streets. To protect against such
intrusions, there is a need for particularly tough and strong gang members. A valued
gang quality specifically for members of the gang is *locura* (the art of acting or playing
with craziness, or wild and unpredictable behavior). Locos are prized gang members,

and there are some who are in fact loco (crazy). However, many more stretch into the role of loco. Usually, the ingestion of alcohol and drugs aids the role-playing required to demonstrate *locura,* often with one of the older or experienced gang members goading a novitiate into crazy action (e.g., a drive-by shooting). Status, albeit unconventional and antisocial, is striven for and attained by such loco activity. Even the gang initiation ritual is viewed as a public demonstration of one's *locura* capabilities: Can he take it and dish it out or is he a punk?

Street life directs what street children do and how they show their involvement in different types of socially valued successes and status objectives. Obviously, the quantity of time spent on the streets by gang members appears to be endless. However, most of their time is spent in very normal, adolescent youth activities covering play, socializing, love and dating arrangement, drinking and doing drugs, and being entrepreneurial (Taylor, 1990). Such activities are well-spent, quality time, but other, more publicly recognized antisocial, gangbanging habits also receive quality time. Homework or street work, for that matter, may take the form of learning how to plan and prepare a drive-by shooting or retaliation, to arrange a meeting place to "score" drugs or alcohol, and to listen at a gang hangout to *veteranos'* war stories of past battles lost and won.

Many peripheral, temporary, or situational gang members mix conventional and unconventional activities. Some compile fairly decent school records and successfully hold a job while continuing as a gang member. Eventually, many of these individuals mature out of the gang, typically through finding a good-paying, career-ladder occupation or a steady, stabilizing girlfriend or wife. They look back at their gang years as a crazy, disjointed period, sometimes with embarrassment, for they "weren't really themselves." The fact remains, however, that they did spend time on the streets and learned about the gang subculture. Also, for a time, they valued and dedicated their energies to other objectives.

Belief, the last of the social control facets, is very complex. Familiarization with the gang subculture most assuredly leads to a new belief system. Implicit in choloization and street socialization is disruption of the socially acceptable value system and blurring of what constitutes correct values. The streets produce their own realities, which through human adaptation and creativity (or maladaption) lead to new values. Although it might be stretching matters to state that these street youngsters have consciously fashioned an "oppositional" culture to subvert society as rebels of one sort or another, it is clear that a life of instability and of fending for oneself has necessitated the creation of new ways to think, act, and believe. If there is a conscious choice in the matter, as the "fun, adventure, money" response mentioned earlier shows, it is more an ephemeral, spontaneous reaction to life as it is rather than how it should be. Some have suggested that *vatos locos* (crazy dudes who opt for and consistently follow *locura*) have taken an old Mexican and southeastern United States folktale character derived from Native American traditions, the Trickster, and corrupted it. Instead of being Trickster only 1 or 2 days of the year, the *vato loca* has reversed it to mean only 1 or 2 days for normal behavior.

The marginalization and street socialization that ethnic minority youth experience transforms conventional attachment, commitment, involvement, and belief dynamics. In large part integrating these dynamics, gangs have developed broad strategies of street coping. But can society recapture these functions, returning commitment and respect to the family, school, police, and other authorities? More critically, with the creation of a street gang subculture, there are new values and norms that did not exist before; can these new patterns be eliminated, curtailed, redirected, or co-opted or are they here to stay? This question raises another challenge, for any effort to alter these dynamics must of necessity address ways to use potentially functional elements of the gang subculture that street youth have fashioned. Is the subculture something new or really more a fractured, segmented facsimile of what existed previously? . . .

Conclusion

Friendship, protection, security, recreation, courting, and socializing are found within gang subcultural practices and habits. Even with the breakdowns in social control, gang participants still mostly carry out the normal functions and activities found among adolescents and youth. However, the negative and destructive patterns and the aggressions and intimidations are the most alarmingly felt and widely publicized acts of gang subcultural members. It is these deeds and actions that have drawn public attention to the gangs, even though such activities constitute a relatively small percentage of what gangs do every day.

Although the most multiply marginal communities and the most established individual gang members are probably responsible for the initiation and perpetuation of much of the violent and life-threatening activities, it is the fringe and casually connected gang members who get caught up in the momentum—the *locura* binge, if you will—that dominates street life. With nothing else to do except hang around with the *vatos*, making them easily available for gangbanging duties, they are regularly accessible to the influences of "significant others" to carry out deeds that they have not conjured up themselves.

To address this gang problem, our society must reevaluate the complex networks of social control. If family, school, and police goals and purposes have fallen short and have been undermined such that the gang subculture has taken them over, how do we recapture them? Simply stated, attachments, commitments, involvements, and beliefs have to be reengineered within the context of the gang subculture to reconnect with conventional norms and values. This strategy can begin with the understanding that most gang members eventually "mature out" of the gang and discover other sources of direction and support. If outgrowing the gang and ending the psychosocial moratorium commonly occurs, those who have matured out could operate as "shock troops" for social programs aimed toward shepherding and hastening the maturation process for other younger gang members.

The focus on maturation is important for several reasons. First, it is certainly the case that maturing out of the gang has been associated with finding a good job and a steady girlfriend to redirect a person's life (Cartwright, Tomson, & Schwartz, 1975; Moore, 1978, 1991; Sullivan, 1988). Similarly, female gang members often leave the gang through attachment to work and husband or boyfriend. So crucial to all members of society and especially wayward street youth, this act of starting a family and learning how to behave in responsible ways is a marked accelerator for maturing out of the gang. Instead of remaining a gang member well past the normal gang membership age (roughly the late teens and early 20s), a member can be thrust into a new role that requires more conventional habits.

Responsibility from the gang members must be matched by responsibility from society, however. If jobs and programs are lacking to expedite maturation, then only a dead end awaits the former gang member. Maturing out seems to have been stretched and delayed with the early 1990s because of economic restructuring and limited job opportunities; there are more "dinosaurs" (older gang members) today (Hagedorn, 1988; Moore, 1991; Sahagun, 1990).

It is from this group that identification and recruitment of former gang members are crucial. Getting such streetwise, experienced adults to help in turning the gang problem around constitutes a key element to a broadened, community-wide strategy. These individuals know both the attractions and the dangers of gangs. They can help provide community leaders with insights into and information on how gang entrance and exit unfold in particular neighborhoods and gangs. They can offer details to help the public to comprehend the processes and rules of such affiliations and dissociations. Advice from these individuals would help public leaders to focus on the strands of social control that need to be addressed. They could act as the most immediate role models and be empowered with connections to different community resources and agencies geared to hastening gang members' maturation out of the gang. With this leadership role and as members of the community who know the problem firsthand, they could help shape new commitments for status and goals and make arrangements for uses of time in activities that lead to positive, prosocial objectives. They could begin to challenge gang members just where it hurts most: the belief system of the gang subculture that maintains street life leads nowhere except to trouble.

Notes

1. Although the discussion will be dominated by issues and examples from the Mexican American population, the author's ethnographic base of African American and Vietnamese youth experiences will also be included where appropriate. All of the data and evidence are based on fieldwork in Los Angeles and Orange County, a multiethnic metropolitan area with large numbers of street youth and a pervasive gang problem since the early decades of the 20th century.

2. Most of the early work on gangs centered on Chicago; see, for example, writings of the Chicago School of Sociology in the 1920s (Burgess, 1925; Park, 1928; Thrasher, 1926). These and writings that followed after the 1940s consistently pointed to the deficiency of Chicago's social support services for inner-city youth (Cloward & Ohlin, 1960; Shaw & McKay, 1942; Whyte, 1943/1973).

3. A previous work (Vigil, 1988a) elaborates a conceptual framework to highlight most of the elements that contribute to gang formation in barrios and how these elements converge and are reflected in the lives of particular gang members.

References

Burgess, E. W. (1925). The growth of the city: An introduction to a research project. In R. E. Park, E. W. Burgess, & R. O. McKenzie (Eds.) *The city* (pp. 47–62). Chicago: University of Chicago Press.

Cartwright, D. S., Tomson, B., & Schwartz, H. (1975). *Gang delinquency*. Monterey, CA: Brooks/Cole.

Cloward, R. A., & Ohlin, L. B. (1960). *Delinquency and opportunity: A theory of delinquent gangs*. New York: Free Press.

Cohen, A. K. (1955). *Delinquent boys: The culture of the gang*. Glencoe, IL: Free Press.

Hagedorn, J. (1988). *People and folks: Gangs, crime and the underclass in a rustbelt city*. Chicago: Lake View.

Huff, C. R. (Ed.). (1990). *Gangs in America, Diffusion, diversity, and public policy*. Newbury Park, CA: Sage.

Klein, M. W. (1968). Impressions of juvenile gang members. *Adolescence, 3*(9), 53–78.

Moore, J. (1978). *Homeboys: Gangs, drugs, and prison in the barrios of Los Angeles*. Philadelphia: Temple University Press.

Moore, J. (1991). *Going down to the barrio: Homeboys and homegirls in change*. Philadelphia: Temple University Press.

Park, R. E. (1928). Human migration and marginal man. *American Journal of Sociology, 33*, 881–893.

Sahagun, L. (1990, November 11). Fight against gangs turns to social solution. *Los Angeles Times*, pp. A1, A3.

Sahagun, L. (1991, January 16). Sheriffs, officials, community leaders shift gang strategy. *Los Angeles Times*, p. B3.

Shaw, C., & McKay, R. (1942). *Juvenile delinquency and urban areas*. Chicago: University of Chicago Press.

Sullivan, M. (1988). *Getting paid*. Ithaca, NY: Cornell University Press.

Taylor C. (1990). *Dangerous society*. East Lansing, MI: Michigan State University Press.

Thrasher, F. M. (1926). *The gang*. Chicago: University of Chicago Press.

Vigil, J. D. (1988a). *Barrio gangs: Street life and identity in Southern California*. Austin: University of Texas Press.

Whyte, W. F. (1943/1973). *Street corner society*. Chicago: University of Chicago Press.

Willis, P. E. (1977). *Learning to labour*. Farnborough, England: Saxon House.

Questions

1. What family factors contribute to joining a gang? What societal factors contribute to joining a gang? How are the family and societal factors related?
2. What are the benefits of joining a gang? What needs do gangs meet?
3. Could the benefits derived from gangs be achieved in other ways?
4. How well can gangs be explained by Erikson's concept of negative identity?
5. What are the costs to gang membership?

References and Further Reading

Huff, C. R. (Ed.) (1996). *Gangs in America,* (2nd ed.) Thousand Oaks, CA: Sage.

Moore, J. (1991). *Going down to the barrio: Homeboys and homegirls in change*. Philadelphia: Temple University Press.

Vigil, D. (1993). The established gang. In S. Cummings, & D. J. Moore (Eds.), *Gangs: The origin and impact of contemporary youth gangs in the United States* (pp. 95–112). Albany: State University of New York Press.

13.2 Daniel J. Flannery, C. Ronald Huff, and Michael Manos, 1998

Youth Gangs: A Developmental Perspective

Daniel J. Flannery, Ph.D., is an associate professor of Justice Studies and the director of the Institute for the Study and Prevention of Violence at Kent State University. He is coeditor of *Youth Violence: Prevention, Intervention and Social Policy* (with C. Ronald Huff, 1999). His research focuses on developmental psychopathology and youth violence as well as how parent–child and parent–adolescent relationships impact early adolescent problem behavior.

C. Ronald Huff, Ph.D., is a professor and director of the School of Public Policy and Management and of the Criminal Justice Research Center at Ohio State University. He is author or editor of ten books, including *The Gang Intervention Handbook* (1993), *Gangs in America,* 2nd edition (1996), and *Youth Violence: Prevention, Intervention and Social Policy* (co-edited with Daniel J. Flannery, 1999). His current research examines gangs, drugs, and public policy.

Michael Manos, Ph.D., is a professor in the Department of Psychiatry at Case Western Reserve University's University Hospitals of Cleveland. He is clinical director of University Hospital's Attention Deficit Hyperactivity Disorder Program and of the Pediatric Assessment and Evaluation Service. He researches youth gangs and attention deficit hyperactivity disorder.

Peers play an increasingly important role in the lives of adolescents. Peers provide a positive influence on socialization for some adolescents, while for other adolescents peers encourage involvement in high-risk behavior. For adolescents who choose to affiliate with more formally organized gangs, gang membership puts them at risk for delinquent activity and violence.

Daniel Flannery, C. Ronald Huff, and Michael Manos report that "Gangs and gang members are engaging in more violent offenses, experiencing more serious injuries, and using more lethal weapons" (p. 182). In a study of incarcerated gang members, inmates reported that owning and carrying guns was universal in the street environments they had inhabited (Sheley & Wright, 1993). Today gang members claim that they carry guns for self-protection, convinced that they are not safe in schools or in their neighborhoods. Huff (1996) reports that gang members are significantly more likely than nongang youth to engage in a variety of forms of violent behavior, such as drive-by shooting (40.4% versus 2%), assault in the streets (29.8% versus 10.2%), homicide (15.2% versus 0.0%), and in behaviors that could result in violence should a conflict break out, such as bringing guns to school (40.4% versus 10.2%), bringing knives to school (38.3% versus 4.2%), or

489

carrying a concealed weapon (78.7% versus 22.4%). By contrast, in the nineteenth century street gangs fought with only brass knuckles and brick bats (Teeter, 1988).

One of the main questions that psychologists have asked is why adolescents are drawn to gangs, or what factors influence the decision to join a gang. Daniel Flannery and his colleagues look at three types of risk factors associated with gang involvement: individual personality factors, family factors, and environmental factors. They discuss the developmental needs that gangs meet that are not being met by family, school, or other support networks, and the risk of gang membership for a variety of negative outcomes, such as delinquency and victimization from violence.

Developmental Perspective

A developmental perspective of youth gangs needs to ground itself in understanding what is normal for children and adolescents as a framework for understanding how normal development may have gone "awry." Recent advances in research on adolescent violence show promise in this regard. Specifically, the study of individual risk factors has focused recently on understanding the cognitive underpinnings of antisocial behavior (e.g., attitudes, beliefs, and information-processing skills; Kendall & Hollon, 1979) and has moved from a dependence on static, simplistic definitions of outcome to an articulation of the sequence of behaviors that mark increasing risk for chronic and serious antisocial behavior (Loeber & Hay, 1994). An emphasis on how developmental sequences are altered rather than a focus on changing static behavioral outcomes has helped advance our thinking about prevention and intervention (Kellam & Rebok, 1992). Furthermore, there has been a growing recognition of the impact of context on individual risk (Tolan & Loeber, 1993), particularly with emphases on family factors in the etiology of antisocial behavior and how family factors interact with and unfold in specific cultural and community contexts (Henggeler & Borduin, 1990).

There are many developmental tasks and transformations for adolescents that may influence whether a young person joins a gang. For most youth, delinquent and violent behavior does not suddenly emerge in adolescence. Although risk for gang membership is multifactored, multifaceted, and complex in its etiology, there are several factors that exert a great deal of influence on determining who is at highest risk for gang involvement. We briefly review some of the risk factors at the individual, family, and neighborhood levels. Individual risk includes exposure to and victimization from violence. Under family risk, we include a discussion of peer group influence. Macrosocial risk factors are also examined. Gang membership and gang-related violence are strongly associated with local economic, school, and peer group factors that need to be taken into account (Klein, 1995; Spergel, 1991, 1995). Several excellent reviews of risk for youth violence and delinquency are available (Earls, 1994; Fraser, 1996; Reiss & Roth, 1993; Yoshikawa, 1994).

Individual-Level Risk Factors

At the individual level, those youth who exhibit an antisocial personality at an early age are most at risk for becoming delinquent adolescents and antisocial adults (Elliott, 1994; Farrington et al., 1993). Aggressive behavior in kindergarten and first grade is an important predictor of delinquency in adolescence (Huesmann, Eron, Leftkowitz, & Walder, 1984; Tremblay, Masse, Leblanc, Schwartzman, & Ledingham, 1992), and, in one longitudinal study, this relationship persisted until the age of 30 (Eron & Huesmann, 1990). A child's early aggressive behavior interacts with family factors to place young children at high risk for delinquency and gang membership. Children who have histories of coercive, intimidating social relations from a very early age experience limited social opportunities with other children and adults (Kupersmidt & Coie, 1990). Of course, not all aggressive children end up becoming delinquent or gang-involved adolescents (Tolan, Guerra, & Kendall, 1995).

Young children who suffer from a combination of a mood disorder (e.g., major depression, bipolar disorder), conduct disorder, and associated attention deficit hyperactivity disorder are at particularly high risk for criminal offending, school failure, and incarceration as adolescents and young adults (Farrington, 1991; Loeber, 1982). In the longitudinal studies that have followed young children through adolescence and into adulthood, low verbal intelligence has been shown to be the best predictor of aggressive behavior at age 8 (as rated by both teachers and parents), delinquent behavior in adolescence, and violent criminal offending in late adolescence (Huesmann et al., 1984). The effects of IQ on later delinquency remain even after controlling for the effects of socioeconomic status on delinquent behavior. There is also growing evidence of prenatal factors being associated with adolescent delinquency. Low birth weight, being small for gestational age, and anoxia at birth have all been associated with adolescent delinquency and violence (Kandel & Mednick, 1991).

One cannot discuss gangs from an individual developmental perspective without mentioning the significant link between exposure to violence, victimization from violence, and risk for violence perpetration (Martinez & Richters, 1993; Richters & Martinez, 1993), particularly among African American youth (DuRant, Cadenhead, Pendergrast, Slaven, & Linder, 1994; Fitzpatrick & Boldizar, 1993). The developmental impact of chronic exposure to violence and victimization by violence can be significant for children and adolescents (Flannery et al., 1996). In general, males are more likely than females to be victims of assault and violence and to witness violent acts. Furthermore, symptoms of posttraumatic stress are commonly reported among children and adolescents exposed to violence (Bell & Jenkins, 1991; Garbarino, Durbrow, Kostelny, & Pardo, 1992; Singer, Anglin, Song, & Lunghofer, 1995).

Family conflict and assault also have been linked to increases in interpersonal assaultive behavior among youth. Sibling assault is one of the most commonly reported forms of youth victimization (Finkelhor & Dziuba-Leatherman, 1994). Coupled with high family conflict and poor parental management, violence between siblings creates a home environment with high potential for child victimization and exposure to violence, and for learning interaction styles that lead to further violent behavior (Cicchetti & Lynch, 1993). Other family factors related to victimization and violent youth behavior include poor parental monitoring (Patterson et al., 1989; Steinberg, 1987) and accessibility of firearms in the home (Ropp, Visintainer, Uman, & Treloar, 1992).

Research over the past few years has shown consistently that intentional injury victimization increases one's risk of subsequently perpetrating violence. Prothrow-Stith (1995), in her book *Deadly Consequences,* discusses her experience as a young emergency department physician in Boston. She was often faced with young patients who told her that the person who injured them would soon be at the hospital for treatment of his own injuries, usually involving the use of firearms. The consensus is that advances in emergency medical care keep the homicide rates among young people from skyrocketing beyond their already epidemic proportions.

Several theories have been advanced about why individuals sometimes alternate between the role of offender and victim. Singer (1981) argues that victims of crime may become offenders because of norms that justify retaliation. Conversely, offenders may become victims because they hold values that support the initiation of violence to resolve disputes (i.e., "victim precipitation"). Sparks (1982) suggested that offenders make ideal victims because they are likely to be viewed by other offenders as vulnerable targets who are unlikely to call police, as compared to nonoffender victims. Gottfredson (1984) supported the victimogenic potential of offending by showing the relationship between victimization and self-reported criminal behavior.

In their most recent work, Rivara, Shepherd, Farrington, Richmond, and Cannon (1995) examined criminal records of males ages 10 to 24 treated for injuries in emergency departments compared to males treated for unintentional injury. They found that assault patients were significantly more likely in the past to have been formally warned or convicted of a violent crime. In addition, they found that differences between injury groups was most pronounced for males 10 to 16 years old, who had significantly different and less extensive criminal histories than did their older counterparts. Rivara et al. (1995) did find, however, that all of their 10- to 16-year-old offenders had convictions in the year following treatment of an injury. This showed that the incident in which they were injured did not deter them from further criminal activity and supports the risk for an intentional injury victim subsequently perpetrating violence and assault against others.

The relationships between victimization and assault perpetration is particularly salient for gang-involved youth. Huff (1996) found that gang-involved youth in Cleveland were significantly more likely to assault rivals (72% versus 16%) and to be victims of assault (34% versus 0%) than were their nongang peers. Furthermore, gang members were more likely to be assaulted by other members of their own gangs than their at-risk peers were of being assaulted by their peers. The notion that gang membership somehow protects a member from being victimized by violence or from perpetrating assault against others is a dangerous falsehood for young people to endorse. Sanchez-Jankowski (1991) showed that the longer a gang remains viable, the greater the potential for criminal victimization to occur for its members. Savitz, Rosen, and Lalli (1982) also found that membership in a fighting gang was related to increased chances of victimization. Finally, it should be noted that Huff's interviews in Cleveland, south Florida, and Denver consistently revealed that youth are far more likely to be assaulted if they join a gang (as part of the initiation and thereafter) than if they politely refuse to join (Huff, 1995, 1996).

Family-Level and Peer-Related Risk

Patterson and his colleagues have a model of early versus late starters in delinquent activity that incorporates child antisocial behavior as a precursor to early childhood behavior problems and poor parent management. These lead to school failure and rejection by peers, precursors of adolescent delinquency and violence. According to Patterson and Yoerger (1993), there exist two primary routes to delinquency, each with a different set of determinants and long-term outcomes. The critical determinant is age at first arrest. If a child is arrested prior to age 14, he or she is considered an early starter. If arrested after the age of 14, he or she is considered to be a late starter. The primary assumptions of both models is that disrupted parenting practices directly determine a child's antisocial behavior, and that these, in turn, place a child at risk for early arrest (Patterson et al., 1989). Second, it is assumed that the majority of adult criminal offenders are early starters. This latter assumption is consistent with the evidence for the chronicity and stability of aggressive, violent behavior shown across longitudinal studies (Eron & Huesmann, 1990; Farrington, 1991; Patterson, Reid, & Dishion, 1992).

Several other findings and assumptions that underlie their coercion model are important to mention. First is the assumption that, as the frequency of antisocial behavior increases, the severity shifts from the trivial to more severe acts (Patterson & Bank, 1989). Second, Patterson and colleagues have found that parents of antisocial children are noncontingent in many of their interactions with their children. They are essentially ineffective disciplinarians who punish frequently, inconsistently, and ineffectively, and they tend to ignore or fail to reinforce prosocial behaviors. Patterson et al.'s model focuses on five parenting constructs shown to be important predictors of antisocial and delinquent child behavior: discipline, monitoring, family problem solving, involvement, and positive reinforcement (Patterson et al., 1992).

Their program of research has demonstrated how child antisocial behaviors directly determine school failure, rejection by peers, and involvement with deviant peers and indirectly determine depressed mood and substance use. All of these factors place youth at greater risk for gang involvement. In the coercion model, child antisocial behavior is viewed as merely the first step in a long-term dynamic process resulting in adolescent delinquency and adult antisocial behavior. What is crucial, from a developmental perspective, is understanding that early childhood behavior is the marker for who is at risk for early adolescent gang involvement and for participation in the aggressive, criminal, and violent behavior characteristic of many gang-involved youth.

The influence of peers on gang involvement and activity is significant. Goldstein (1991) asserts that establishing a stable sense of identity and striving for peer acceptance are two central features of adolescent development fostered by gang involvement. Contacts with deviant peers are readily available to most adolescents. Cairns and

Cairns (1991) showed that most adolescents develop support networks of some kind. For most adolescents, the peer group provides at least one of those social networks. For some adolescents, the gang becomes the primary support network, made up mostly of other deviant peers and rejected youth who are not attached to school or home, and who live in families where parents are not interested in or are unable to monitor effectively who they are with and what they are doing. In their struggle to establish an identity, the gang can provide a context for establishing a system of values, beliefs, and goals.

Physical, emotional, cognitive, and social developmental tasks merge during early and middle adolescence, forcing young people to cope with many issues, expectations, and responsibilities that they may not yet be capable of handling on their own. For gang-involved youth, it is the peer group that provides both girls and boys with a safe refuge and a surrogate family. Patterson and others have shown that the most antisocial youth are those most committed to a deviant peer group. Being relatively free from adult supervision and free from any attachment to school, religion, or family, hanging out with other rejected youth provides a great deal of opportunity to engage in delinquent activity (Gottfredson & Hirschi, 1990; O'Donnell, Hawkins, & Abbott, 1995). The sooner the antisocial child is out on the streets, the more exposed he or she is to higher levels of antisocial behavior and violence and the more opportunities he or she has to perpetrate criminal acts.

Macrosocial/Community-Level Risk

Several macrosocial or community-level factors contribute to gang membership, gang activity, crime rates, and violence. Examples of macrolevel risk factors include neighborhood resident mobility, levels of disorganization, population density, heterogeneity, unemployment, and income inequality (e.g., the spatial proximity of middle class and poor). Each of these has been related to higher levels of gang activity, crime, and violence (Coulton, Korbin, & Su, in press; Sampson & Lauritsen, 1993). A major dimension of social disorganization relevant to violence is the ability of a community to supervise and control teenage peer groups, particularly gangs (Sampson & Groves, 1989). There is much evidence that adolescent delinquency is most often a group activity, and thus the capacity of the community to control group-level dynamics is a key theoretical mechanism linking community characteristics with crime and gang activity (Sampson & Lauritsen, 1993).

Skogan (1986) reviews some of the "feedback" processes that may further increase levels of crime and gang activity in a community. These include (a) physical and psychological withdrawal from community life, (b) weakening of the informal social control processes that inhibit crime, (c) a decline in the organizational life and mobilization capacity of the neighborhood, (d) deteriorating business conditions, (e) the importation and domestic production of delinquency and deviance, and (f) further dramatic changes in the composition of the population. So, if people shun their neighbors and withdraw from their community, there will be fewer opportunities to form friendship networks that may help provide appropriate adult supervision of youth group activity (Sampson & Lauritsen, 1993).

Implications for Adolescent Development

During adolescence, multiple developmental tasks converge to make this an important time for gang activity and involvement. Gangs can be an attractive alternative to an at-risk youth struggling to fulfill unmet needs and resolve emerging developmental issues. Gang membership jeopardizes adolescent psychosocial development in general and particularly threatens the adequate resolution of primary adolescent developmental tasks, including achieving effective relations with peers of both genders, achieving a masculine or feminine social role, achieving an appropriate body image and becoming competent in using the body, achieving emotional autonomy, preparation for marriage and family life, preparing for an economic career, developing a value-based ideology, and aspiring to participate responsibly in the community (Straus, 1994). Gang membership, which may substitute for an adolescent's desire to be a member of an accepting and supportive social network, cannot replace the support and adequate supervision that a parent can provide. Furthermore, membership in a social network that tolerates and approves of violence is a strong predictor of violent behavior (Callahan & Rivara, 1992; Webster, Gainer, & Champion, 1994). This is a particular irony for those youth who initially join a gang for protection. Females who join a gang for protection from abusive parents have, in most cases, simply placed themselves at greater risk (although perhaps different) for sexual and physical victimization (Portillas & Zatz, 1995). Because victimization leads to an increased risk for perpetrating violence, the attainment of any "normative" developmental tasks in adolescence is problematic at best.

Gang membership places young people at risk for a variety of negative outcomes. Gang membership is highly associated with earlier onset of delinquency and victimization from violence (Widom, 1989). For both genders, gang involvement has been associated with earlier onset of sexual intercourse, unsafe sex, and early pregnancy or the fathering of a child (Morris et al., 1996). Gang members also more frequently report suicidal ideation and suicide attempts, often involving heavy substance abuse.

Recently, researchers have begun to specifically examine outcomes for gang-involved females. Moore and Hagedorn (1996) assert that no matter what the cultural context, and no matter what the economic opportunity structure, there appears to be one constant in the later life of women in gangs. Most of them have children, and children have more effect on women's lives than on men's. For women, but rarely for men, the new responsibilities associated with child rearing may speed up the process of maturing out of the gang. As Chesney-Lind and Brown (in press) point out, in an environment of extreme poverty and deprivation, developmental tasks are subordinate to the imperatives of short-term survival on the streets. There is little hope for the future, especially for females in this environment: Recent data suggest that the future awaiting gang girls is bleak indeed; 94% will go on to have children, and 84% will raise them without spouses. One third of them will be arrested, and the vast majority will be dependent on welfare (Campbell, 1990).

References

Bell, C., & Jenkins, E. (1991). Traumatic stress and children. *Journal of Health Care for the Poor and Underserved, 2,* 175–185.

Cairns, R. B., & Cairns, B. D. (1991). Social cognition and social networks: A developmental perspective. In D. J. Pepler & K. H. Rubin (Eds.), *The development and treatment of childhood aggression* (pp. 249–274). Hillsdale, NJ: Lawrence Erlbaum.

Callahan, C. M., & Rivara, F. P. (1992). Urban high school youth and hand-guns. *Journal of the American Medical Association, 267,* 3038–3042.

Campbell, A. (1990). Female participation in gangs. In C. R. Huff (Ed.), *Gangs in America* (pp. 163–183). Newbury Park, CA: Sage.

Chesney-Lind, M., & Brown, M. (in press). Girls and violence: An overview. In D. Flannery & R. Huff (Eds.), *Youth violence: Prevention, intervention, and social policy.* Washington, DC: American Psychiatric Press.

Chicchetti, D., & Lynch, M. (1993). Toward an ecological/transactional model of community violence and child maltreatment: Consequences for children's development. *Psychiatry, 56,* 96–118.

Coulton, C., Korbin, J., & Su, M. (in press). Measuring neighborhood context for young children in an urban area. *American Journal of Community Psychology.*

DuRant, R., Cadenhead, C., Pendergrast, R., Slaven, G., & Linder, C. W. (1994). Factors associated with the use of violence among urban black adolescents. *American Journal of Public Health, 84,* 612–617.

Earls, F. J. (1994). Violence and today's youth. *Critical Issues for Children and Youth, 4,* 4–23.

Elliot, D. E. (1994). Serious violent offenders: Onset, developmental course, and termination. *Criminology, 32,* 1–21.

Eron, L. D., & Huesmann, R. (1990). The stability of aggressive behavior—Even unto the third generation. In M. Lewis & S. M. Miller (Eds.), *Handbook of developmental psychopathology* (pp. 147–156). New York: Plenum.

Farrington, D. P. (1991). Antisocial personality from childhood to adulthood. *The Psychologist, 4,* 389–394.

Farrington, D. P., Loeber, R., Elliot, D. S., Hawkins, J. D., Kandel, D. B., Lein, M. W., McCord, J., Rowe, D. C., & Tremblay, R. E. (1993). Advancing knowledge about the onset of delinquency and crime. In B. B. Lahey & A. E. Kazdin (Eds.), *Advances in clinical child psychology* (Vol. 12, pp. 283–342). New York: Plenum.

Finkelhor, D., & Dziuba-Leatherman, J. (1994). Victimization of children. *American Psychologist, 49,* 173–183.

Fitzpatrick, K., & Boldizar, J. (1993). The prevalence and consequence of exposure to violence among African American youth. *Journal of the American Academy of Child and Adolescent Psychiatry, 32,* 424–430.

Flannery, D. J., Vazsonyi, A., Embry, D., & Atha, H. (1996). *Longitudinal follow-up of PeaceBuilders violence prevention program* (Centers for Disease Control and Prevention, Cooperative Agreement #U81/CCU513508-01).

Fraser, M. W. (1996). Aggressive behavior in childhood and early adolescence: An ecological-developmental perspective on youth violence. *Social Work, 41,* 347–361.

Garbarino, J., Durbrow, N., Kostelny, K., & Pardo, C. (1992). *Children in danger: Coping with the consequences of community violence.* San Francisco: Jossey-Bass.

Goldstein, A. P. (1991). *Delinquent gangs: A psychological perspective.* Champaign, IL: Research Press.

Gottfredson, M. (1984). *Victims of crime: The dimensions of risk* (Home Office Research Study #81). London: Her Majesty's Stationery Office.

Gottfredson, M., & Hirschi, T. (1990). *A general theory of crime.* Stanford, CA: Stanford University Press.

Henggeler, S. W., & Borduin, C. M. (1990). *Family therapy and beyond: A multi-systemic approach to treating the behavior problems of children and adolescents.* Pacific Grove, CA: Brooks/Cole.

Huesmann, L. R., Eron, L. D., Leftkowitz, M. M., & Walder, L. O. (1984). Stability of aggression over time and generations. *Developmental Psychology, 20,* 1120–1134.

Huff, C. R. (1985). *Final report to the National Institute of Justice regarding the criminal behavior of gang members.* Columbus: Ohio State University Press.

Huff, C. R. (1996). The criminal behavior of gang members and nongang at-risk youth. In C. R. Huff (Ed.), *Gangs in America* (2nd ed., pp. 75–102). Thousand Oaks, CA: Sage.

Kandel, E., & Mednick, S. A. (1991). Perinatal complications predict violent offending. *Criminology, 29,* 519–529.

Kellam, S. G., & Rebok, G. W. (1992). Building developmental and etiological theory through epidemiologically based preventive intervention trials. In J. McCord & R. E. Tremblay (Eds.), *Preventing antisocial behavior: Interventions from birth through adolescence* (pp. 62–195). New York: Guilford.

Kendall, P. C., & Hollon, S. D. (1979). *Cognitive-behavioral interventions: Theory, research, and procedures.* New York: Academic Press.

Klein, M. (1995). *The American street gang: Its nature, prevalence, and control.* New York: Oxford University Press.

Kupersmidt, J. B., & Coie, J. D. (1990). Preadolescent peer status, aggression, and school adjustment as predictors of externalizing problems in adolescence. *Child Development, 61,* 1350–1362.

Loeber, R. (1982). The stability of antisocial and delinquent child behavior: A review. *Child Development, 53,* 1431–1446.

Loeber, R., & Hay, D. F. (1994). Developmental approaches to aggression and conduct problems. In M. Rutter & D. F. Hay (Eds.), *Development through life: A handbook for clinicians* (pp. 288–316). Boston: Blackwell Scientific.

Martinez, P., & Richters, J. E. (1993). The NIMH community violence project: II. Children's distress symptoms associated with violence exposure. *Psychiatry, 56,* 22–35.

Moore, J. W., & Hagedorn, J. M. (1996). What happens to girls in the gang? In C. R. Huff (Ed.), *Gangs in America* (2nd ed., pp. 205–220). Thousand Oaks, CA: Sage.

Morris, R. E., Harrison, E. A., Knox, G. W., Romanjhauser, E., Marques, D. K., & Watts, L. L. (1996). Health risk behavioral survey from 39 juvenile correctional facilities in the United States. *Journal of Adolescent Health, 117,* 334–375.

O'Donnell, J., Hawkins, J. D., & Abbott, R. D. (1995). Predicting serious delinquency and substance use among aggressive boys. *Journal of Consulting and Clinical Psychology, 63.* 529–537.

Patterson, G., DeBaryshe, B., & Ramsey, B. (1989). A developmental perspective on antisocial behavior. *American Psychologist 44,* 329–335.

Patterson, G. R., & Bank, L. (1989). Some amplifying mechanisms for pathologic process in families. In M. R. Gunner & E. Thelem (Eds.), *Systems and development: The Minnesota symposia on child psychology* (Vol. 22, pp. 167–210). Hillsdale, NJ: Lawrence Erlbaum.

Patterson, G. R., & Yoerger, K. (1993). Developmental models for delinquent behavior. In S. Hodgins (Ed.), *Mental disorders and crime* (pp. 140–172). Newbury Park, CA: Sage.

Portillas, E., & Zatz, M. S. (1995, November). *Not to die for: Positive and negative aspects of Chicano youth gangs.* Paper presented at the annual meeting of the American Society of Criminology, Boston.

Prothrow-Stith, D. (1995). *Deadly consequences.* New York: HarperCollins.

Reiss, A. J., Jr., & Roth, J. (1993). *Understanding and preventing violence.* Washington, DC: National Academy Press.

Richters, J., & Martinez, P. (1993). The NIMH community violence project: I. Children as victims of, and witnesses to violence. *Psychiatry, 56,* 7–21.

Rivara, F., Shepherd, J., Farrington, D., Richmond, P. W., & Cannon, P. (1995). Victim as offender in youth violence. *Annals of Emergency Medicine, 26,* 609–615.

Ropp, L., Visintainer, P., Uman, J., & Treloar, D. (1992). Death in the city: An American childhood tragedy. *Journal of the American Medical Association, 267,* 2905–2910.

Sampson, R. J., & Groves, W. B. (1989). Testing social-disorganization theory. *American Journal of Sociology, 94,* 774–802.

Sampson, R. J., & Lauritsen, J. (1993). Violent victimization and offending: Individual, situational, and community-level risk factors. In A. J. Reiss, Jr., & J. A. Roth (Eds.), *Understanding and preventing violence.Vol. 3: Social influences* (pp. 1–114). Washington, DC: National Academy Press.

Savitz, L., Rosen, L., & Lalli, M. (1982). Delinquency and gang membership as related to victimization. *Victimology, 5,* 152–160.

Singer, S. (1981). Homogeneous victim-offender populations: A review and some research implications. *Journal of Criminal Law and Criminology, 72,* 779–788.

Singer, M., Anglin, T., Song, L., & Lunghofer, L. (1995). Adolescents' exposure to violence and associated symptoms of psychological trauma. *Journal of the American Medical Association, 273,* 477–482.

Skogan, W. (1986). Fear of crime and neighborhood change. In A. J. Reiss & M. Tonry (Eds.), *Communities and crime* (pp. 203–229). Chicago; University of Chicago Press.

Sparks, R. (1982). *Research on victims of crime.* Washington, DC: U.S. Government Printing Office.

Spergel, I. A. (1991). *Youth gangs: Problem and response.* Washington, DC: U.S. Department of Justice, Office of Juvenile Justice and Delinquency Prevention.

Spergel, I. A. (1995). *The youth gang problem: A community approach.* New York: Oxford University Press.

Steinberg, L. (1987). Familial factors in delinquency: A developmental perspective. *Journal of Adolescent Research, 2,* 255–268.

Straus, M. (1994). *Violence in the lives of adolescents.* New York: Norton.

Tolan, P., & Guerra, N. (1994). *What works in reducing adolescent violence: An empirical review of the field.* Boulder, CO: Center for the Study and Prevention of Violence.

Tolan, P. H., Guerra, N. G., & Kendall, P. C. (1995). A developmental perspective on antisocial behavior in children and adolescents: Toward a unified risk and intervention framework. *Journal of Consulting and Clinical Psychology, 63,* 579–584.

Tolan, P. J., & Loeber, R. (1993). Antisocial behavior. In P. H. Tolan & B. J. Cohler (Eds.), *Handbook of clinical research and practice with adolescents* (pp. 307–331). New York: John Wiley.

Tremblay, R., Masse, B., Leblanc, M., Schwartzman, A. E., & Ledingham, J. E. (1992). Early disruptive behavior, poor school achievement, delinquent behavior, and delinquent personality: Longitudinal analyses. *Journal of Consulting and Clinical Psychology, 60,* 64–72.

Webster, D. W., Gainer, P. S., & Champion, H. R. (1994). Weapon carrying among inner-city junior high school students: Defensive behavior vs. aggressive delinquency. *American Journal of Public Health, 83,* 1604–1608.

Widom, C. S. (1989). The cycle of violence. *Science, 244,* 160–166.

Yoshikawa, H. (1994). Prevention as cumulative protection: Effects of early family support and education on chronic delinquency and its risks. *Psychological Bulletin, 115,* 28–54.

Questions

1. What problems do gang members have as children?
2. What is the nature of the parenting that gang members experience?
3. How does violence play a role in the family histories of gang members?
4. How does victimization from violence translate into perpetrating violence?
5. What are the characteristics of the communities in which gang members are raised?
6. What is the impact of gang membership on psychosocial development?

References and Further Reading

Huff, C. R. (Ed.) (1990). *Gangs in America: Diffusion, diversity, and public policy.* Newbury Park, CA: Sage.

Huff, C. R. (1996). The criminal behavior of gang members and nongang at-risk youth. In C. R. Huff (Ed.) *Gangs in America* (2nd ed., pp. 75–102). Thousand Oaks, CA: Sage.

Moore, J. (1991). *Going down to the barrio: Homeboys and homegirls in change.* Philadelphia: Temple University Press.

Sheley, J. F., & Wright, J. D. (1993). Gun acquisition and possession in selected juvenile samples. Washington, DC: U.S. Department of Justice, National Institute of Justice, Office of Juvenile Justice and Delinquency Prevention.

Teeter, R. (1988). Coming of age on the city streets in nineteenth century America. *Adolescence, 23*(92), 909–912.

Chapter 14

Teenage Pregnancy

From an anthropological perspective, there is nothing inherently abnormal about bearing a child during the teenage years. In their study of 186 preindustrial cultures, Alice Schlegel and Herbert Barry III (Reading 2.2) report that in the majority of the societies they studied, adolescence ended for girls by about age 16 and the transition to adulthood was marked by marriage, which moved the girls into reproductive relationships. But in preindustrial societies, girls who become mothers do not live in isolated households, and they are raising children with the help of a network of supportive relatives and neighbors. By contrast, in industrialized nations like the United States, many families and communities view teenage pregnancy as problematic and morally wrong. Bearing a child is seen by mainstream society as compromising a young girl's chance for academic and occupational success and successful parenting. In addition, parents are expected to care for their own offspring in separate households without sharing responsibility with other relatives.

Considerable variability exists, however, within our society in terms of the prevalence and acceptance of teenage pregnancy and the family support provided to teenage parents. In some subcultures or communities within this society, such as African American communities in the inner cities, premarital teenage childbearing is widespread and largely accepted. Families and extended families are generally forgiving and are supportive in raising the baby. Girls growing up in these communities often do not find the educational and vocational opportunities offered to more advantaged adolescents, so that bearing a child is not perceived as curtailing future occupational success. Teenage childbearing in these communities is seen as an expected route to adulthood (Cohler & Musick, 1996).

The majority of the research on teenage pregnancy has focused on identifying the medical and psychosocial risks associated with adolescent motherhood and with the offspring of adolescent mothers. The research has demonstrated that teenage mothers are more likely to suffer from anemia and hypertension and to have babies who are premature, have lower birth weights, or suffer from sudden infant death syndrome, accidental trauma, and poisoning. The children of teenage mothers are more likely to experience developmental delays, neglect, behavioral problems, school failure, and withdrawal from school (Stevens-Simon & McAnarney, 1992). These adverse outcomes, however, are not necessarily attributable to the age of the mother. These studies are correlational in nature, and in more recent research the adverse outcomes of teenage pregnancy have been found to be reduced when the socioeconomic status and the race of the mother and the preexisting differences between adolescent mothers and older mothers have been controlled for (Reading 14.2); Stevens-Simon & McAnarney, 1992).

The readings in this chapter look at teenage pregnancy from two perspectives. Musick (Reading 14.1) looks at the psychological factors that motivate adolescent girls growing up in poverty to become pregnant. She looks at how the sociocultural environment shapes family experience, experiences in school, and opportunities for the future, and how these factors impact the identity development of girls who become pregnant as teenagers. Coley and Chase-Lansdale (Reading 14.2) review the research on adolescent pregnancy, the causes and consequences of teenage parenthood, and the policy implications of these data.

Additional Resources

References and Suggested Reading

Bolton, F. G. (1980). *The pregnant adolescent: Problems of premature parenthood.* Beverly Hills, CA: Sage.

Burton, L. (1990). Teenage childbearing as an alternative life-course strategy in multigeneration black families. *Human Nature, 1,* 123–143.

Chase-Lansdale, P. L., & Brooks-Gunn, J. (1994). Correlates of adolescent pregnancy and parenthood. In C. B. Fisher & R. M. Lerner (Eds.) *Applied developmental psychology* (pp. 207–236). New York: McGraw-Hill.

Cohler, B. J., & Musick, J. S. (1996). Adolescent parenthood and the transition to adulthood. In J. Graber, J. Brooks-Gunn, & C. Petersen (Eds.) *Transitions through adolescence: Interpersonal domains and context* (pp. 201–230). Mahwah, NJ: Lawrence Erlbaum.

Hoffman, S. D., Foster, E. M., & Furstenberg, F. F., Jr. (1993). Reevaluating the costs of teenage childbearing. *Demography, 30,* 1–13.

Lancaster, J. B., & Hamburg, B. A. (1986). The biosocial dimensions of school-age pregnancy and parenthood: An introduction. In J. B. Lancaster & B. A. Hamburg (Eds.) *School-age pregnancy and parenthood: Biosocial dimensions* (pp. 3–13). New York: Aldine de Gruyter.

Stevens-Simon, C., & McAnarney, E. R. (1992). Adolescent pregnancy. In E. R. McAnarney, R. E. Kreipe, D. P. Orr, & G. D. Comerci (Eds.) T*extbook of adolescent medicine* (pp. 689–695). Philadelphia: W. B. Saunders.

Super, C. M. (1986). A developmental perspective on school-age parenthood. In J. B. Lancaster & B. A. Hamburg (Eds.) *School-age pregnancy and parenthood: Biosocial dimensions* (pp. 379–386). New York: Aldine de Gruyter.

On the Internet

http://parentingteens.about.com/parenting/parentingteens/msub17.htm
About.com—Parenting of Adolescents: Teen Pregnancy and Parenting
The About.com Network consists of over 700 Guide sites covering more than 50,000 subjects with over 1 million links to resources on the Net and a fast-growing archive of original content. This site provides links to information on teenage pregnancy.

http://www.personal.psu.edu/faculty/n/x/nxd10/adparent2.htm
Adolescence: Change & Continuity—Parenthood
This site was produced by Pennsylvania State University students taking Human Development and Family Studies 433: The Transition to Adulthood, and Human Development and Family Studies 239: Adolescent Development.

http://www.ama-assn.org/adolhlth/special/teenpreg.htm
American Medical Association—Teen Pregnancy Prevention
The American Medical Association's Program on Child and Adolescent Health provides this site as a resource on adolescent health issues and their Guidelines for Adolescent Preventive Services (GAPS) program.

http://www.plannedparenthood.org/library/TEEN-PREGNANCY/
childbearing.htm
Planned Parenthood—Fact Sheet on Pregnancy and Childbearing Among U.S. Teens
Planned Parenthood is a voluntary family planning organization dedicated to the principles that every individual has a fundamental right to decide when or whether or not to have a child and that every child should be wanted and loved. It provides fact sheet resources on its Web site.

http://agi-usa.org/pubs/or_teen_preg_decline.html
The Alan Guttmacher Institute—Why is Teenage Pregnancy Declining?
The Alan Guttmacher Institute is a nonprofit organization that engages in reproductive health research, policy analysis, and public education and provides up-to-date information on adolescent sexual activity, pregnancy, and childbearing.

http://www.tpronline.org/index.cfm
The Prevention Research Online—Summary of Adolescent Pregnancy Research: Implications for Prevention
The Prevention Researcher is a research newsletter published quarterly by Integrated Research Services for prevention professionals looking for the latest research on at-risk youth.

Adolescent Development

Judith S. Musick, Ph.D., is a developmental psychologist and was the first director of the Ounce of Prevention Fund, an initiative for disadvantaged youth and their families. She authored *Young, Poor, and Pregnant: The Psychology of Teenage Motherhood* (1993) and coauthored (with Janet Auint and Joyce Ladner) *Lives of Promise, Lives of Pain: Young Mothers After New Chance* (1994).

The trend among mainstream American women is early entry into the job market, later marriage, and a delay of childbearing often until the late 20s. Thus the decision to bear a child during the teenage years violates the social timetable and at first glance seems difficult to understand. Psychologists have found, however, that bearing a child off-schedule according to prevailing norms may not be ill-timed for adolescents growing up in poverty. In this socioeconomic context, early childbearing is a strategy that proves to be beneficial to personal and social development (Cohler & Musick, 1996).

As a girl struggles to complete the task of identity formation, the identity she will assume will be based on her childhood history as shaped by her family and sociocultural context and on the reworking of that history in the face of the opportunities open to her in society. Girls from poor neighborhoods often have grandmothers, mothers, and sisters who were themselves teenage mothers and modeled this option, as well as friends who are teenage parents. Girls can remain connected to relatives and friends by being like them and following the same path. Friends and relatives who could model or lead girls to the world of work are lacking. Motherhood offers girls membership in adult society and confers a highly valued identity. Girls growing up in poverty have been socialized to view parenthood as the principal realm in which they can meet their needs. Bearing a child matches with their sense of who they are, what they can do, what options are available, and what others expect of them (Cohler & Musick, 1996).

Judith Musick argues that for girls who are poor, adolescent motherhood provides a resolution of the issues of identity. She analyzes the developmental histories of girls raised in poverty and argues that teenage parenthood is a logical outcome of these particular circumstances. These girls tend to have a history of unmet dependency needs and sexual exploitation and to have an impaired sense of industry (Reading 5.1). Having done poorly in school, they have repeatedly gotten the message that they cannot do things well and that they lack the skills to produce something of worth. While lacking in skills valued by schools, these girls may have derived a sense of mastery from the role of caretaker,

503

having been required to do inordinate amounts of caretaking for younger siblings and other family members. When these girls imagine who they are and what they can do well, they may commit to the parent role because it is available, it fits with what they can do, and because they have not been encouraged to develop other skills and strengths.

The Social Context of Development

The psychological histories of many disadvantaged girls are likely to have included at least some of the following conditions: frequent separations from primary attachment figures in early life, which leave residues of vulnerability to threats of abandonment; the absence of appropriately protective fathers or father surrogates, which creates later vulnerability to exploitation by males, particularly older males; and family disorganization or exposure to family violence such as physical and sexual abuse. Finally, there may be little consistent, useful guidance from significant adults and few positive alternative role models, particularly when there is parental absence or failure.

In both the popular and scientific literature there is mounting evidence of the developmentally toxic influences of disadvantage during early childhood. Infants and young children born and reared in poverty are far more likely to die young, are sicker, and fare worse in virtually every aspect of life—from cradle to frequently early grave (see Schorr 1988). Much of this research on younger children has a strong developmental flavor and reflects an awareness of the interaction of environment with the development of competence and individual potential. Why is such awareness all but invisible in regard to the late school years, the period between childhood and adolescence?

Although we may have data on such biosocial phenomena as response to puberty, we still lack some fairly basic knowledge on the relation between the social context and other aspects of development during that period—that is, how the environment shapes the central developmental tasks confronting youth at this time and how these will in turn affect development and psychological functioning later, during adolescent proper. For example, what do we know about continuities in family relations between childhood and adolescence (Steinberg 1988)? Is the history of a girl's relationship to her mother prior to adolescence relevant to their relationship during adolescence? At the same time, early adolescence brings about certain discontinuities with the past because of the shift in role status from child to adolescent. Because these major social changes are superimposed on the profound biological transformations of puberty, their stressful impact is bound to be high (Hamburg 1974; Petersen and Taylor 1980), especially within an environment of risk.

According to Erikson (1968), the principal developmental task of the years before adolescence, especially the latter part of that era, from age 9 or 10 to approximately age 14, is to establish a sense of *industry*. During this period the young person's energy is supposed to be devoted to learning and mastering the basic skills needed to function in society, acquiring fundamental knowledge, coming to take pride in and wanting to do well in the world of work. In our society, for preadolescents the world of work is that of school. In addition to school, the preadolescent world of work usually includes such extracurricular activities as sports, hobbies, and a host of other avocational interests including the arts. These experiences provide the preteen with a sense that she is a person who gets things done and does them well, a person successfully growing up and into the wider world. Such inner resources will be called on shortly to keep her on course and moving forward through the changes of the teen years to follow. They provide the cognitive and emotional anchors to steady her as she makes the transition from child to adolescent and, later, from adolescent to adult. Her sense of industry is her psychological insurance against a sense of inadequacy, hopelessness, inferiority—the sense that she will never amount to much. It is her insurance against identity confusion during adolescence itself.

Whereas a middle-class 10- to 13-year-old's world of work is focused on school and sports and lessons and trips and hobbies, that of her disadvantaged sister is generally quite different. While the former is, in a sense, cared for by her environment, the latter is struggling to take care of herself and frequently of others, as well, such as younger siblings or older family members lost to drink or drugs. She is often being raised by a very young mother with her own poorly resolved developmental issues or a mother who, having started childbearing very young, is now too depressed or hard pressed coping with her own survival to respond sensitively to the needs of her children.

> You know I was a mother when I was younger. I used to take care of my brother. I was 9 going on 10 when he was born. By the time I was 11 or 12 I would take him everywhere. I never had a childhood. I was a mother to my brother and then a mother to my children. Another reason was my mother. I didn't have a father figure, he left when I was 10. After that my mother was never home. She had her own social life. I guess she was trying to gain back the freedom she lost when she was with my father. She neglected us kids.... I grew up in the streets with my friends. That's where I learned about sex. If my mother had been there, I don't think I would have started exploring so soon. My friends were my family.... If you don't have any love at home you find it in a man or in the streets.

Having to compete with too many siblings for her mother's limited time and attention or being compelled to assume adult responsibilities prematurely and inappropriately requires psychological adaptations that may be at the cost of the preteen's personal development. Coping strategies that were initially useful or even beneficial under these circumstances may become maladaptive if she uses them indiscriminantly during adolescence (Hauser and Bowlds 1990).

In addition to taking care of immature parents and younger siblings, at the very first sign of budding sexual maturity—and often well before—many preadolescent girls become prey for predatory older males in their homes, families, and communities:[1]

> I had a sexual experience with my mother's boyfriend. He made me suck on his penis and he made me kiss him. I was 12 years old.

> I am a 17-year-old with two babies.... My son's father is 28 and has been my boyfriend on and off since I was 11.

Without the presence of protective fathers or father figures, young girls in disadvantaged communities are far more vulnerable to sexual exploitation. In our research on the prevalence of a history of sexual abuse among pregnant and parenting teens (Gershenson et al. 1989; Ruch-Ross, Stucki, and Musick 1990), my colleagues and I found that the average age of first abuse was 11.6 years. The youngest abusers tended to be in their late teens, but most were older. Could one possibly call the pairings of 11-year-old girls and 25-year-old men "dates"?

How does an 11- or 12-year-old girl handle her changing body and her emerging sexuality in a home where she is nightly faced with her young mother's active sexual life? How does she make sense of these psychological and physical changes within the context of her sexual exploitation at the hands of her mother's temporary lovers or older males in her family environment? Does she conclude that she has no right to or control over her own body, that she and her body are somehow tainted and not worth protecting?

> Girls, I think they don't give a care if they are alive because they get sexually abused and they will go around just jumping into any other guy's bed.... After it happens they feel so cheap and fleezy and they don't care about their life anymore. "They are hurting me so why shouldn't I hurt myself? ... *They* don't care. Why should I care?" So they will go out and, you know, ruin their life more.

What messages does she get about what it means to be female when her mother fails to protect her from such victimization?

> When we got up our nerve to tell my mom what he was doing [she and her sister were abused for years by their mother's boyfriend] she didn't believe us.... I even thought it was a dream since she didn't believe us and he was still in her life ... and my mom had a baby from him.

Do such experiences tell the girl that her well-being is less important to her mother than having a man; that females are powerless when it comes to males?

> Mothers should be real careful about the people they date or people they plan to get married with ... and don't ever choose a man over your own flesh and blood.

Where will the 12- and 13-year-old girl in these circumstances find the psychic energy to invest in school, considering what she is trying to cope with in her relationships? How do such emotional burdens interact with the educational limitations conferred by her home life and the less-than-adequate schools of her community? What compensatory psychological benefits can she derive from doing well in school, and what are the chances of her finding other arenas for developing a sense of industry or other adults to act as mentors and models of alternative life-styles? Unless she has some striking gift or talent, the chances are pretty slim.

Consider another sphere in which the interaction of development and social context can lead to difficulties for early adolescent girls. The early adolescent sense of self tends to be highly dependent on the attitudes, real or perceived, of others. This helps to explain the power of the peer group over the individual, particularly during the early teen years. Although the relationship between child and parent undergoes a variety of transformations, the girls' parents are still vitally important influences on her life (Blos 1979; Grotevant and Cooper 1983, 1986; Youniss and Smollar 1985; Steinberg 1988, 1989). During these years, girls from more nurturing family environments are in the process of transforming their earlier dependent relationships with their parents while continuing to feel a need for their guidance and support. What happens to the girl who must distance herself emotionally in order to survive? What added power might that girl's peer group or boyfriends have when she needs them to fulfill the roles and functions her parents are unable or unwilling to carry out?[2] As one of these young women said, they will be the ones she turns to; they will become her family.

The preadolescent girl cannot have it all. If the social context of her life forces her to divert her energies from the developmental tasks that confer a sense of industry, personal efficacy, and pride in self, the price will be high, and she may well spend the rest of her life paying it.

> I was 13 when I had sex for the first time. I was scared, I really didn't want to, but in a way I thought I was ready and now when I look back I wasn't ready. And the guy I was with wasn't the person I wanted to be with. I wish now that I would have been with somebody I really loved and cared about. It would have been a lot better. I just wish I would have waited till I was older. In my opinion no girls at 13 should be having sex. They should be doing other things.

> I feel so sick for the way I grew up. There are so many things I've been through that I never should have. I always feel like going back to the age of 12 and doing it all over again . . . I hate the fact of having sex so young. I would like to forget that part of my life. Too bad I can't. I should have stayed in school and went to college and went on to be somebody.

The experiences of preadolescence shape the girl's self-image and concepts about who she is and what she can do. If these experiences teach her that she exists merely to be used by or to do for others, her desire and ability to achieve will be diminished. Instead of an inner assurance that she can make things happen, she will be convinced that she cannot. In place of competence, she will feel defeat before she begins. A girl who enters adolescence with these feelings has nothing better to do with her future than to have children. Having resolved the industry versus inferiority crisis (Erikson 1968) in favor of inferiority, she lacks the portfolio of motives and skills that are the best protection against pregnancy and thus is much more likely to drift—or drive herself—into unprotected sex and premature motherhood.

Problems of the Self

Clinicians and researchers alike have pointed to a cluster of self-related problems as predisposing factors for adolescent motherhood: girls who are insecure, who have low self-esteem, and who rely heavily on others for approbation are thought to be at high risk for too-early childbearing. But knowledge of what underlies such ostensibly self-defeating or self-destructive behavior is sorely lacking. What are the antecedents and the functional significance of these problems during pre- and early adolescence? How are such developmentally induced or mediated problems created, and how do they magnify or potentiate other risk factors? What particular self-concepts make early adolescent girls especially vulnerable and unprepared to cope with the socially imposed tasks of the middle and later adolescent years? By what paths and processes do these concepts reduce the motivation and capacity for change?

The phrase "low self-esteem" has often been used in explaining such phenomena as adolescent pregnancy. But what does low self-esteem denote in operational terms, and how does it actually influence behavior? Preadolescent and early adolescent girls typically feel insecure from time to time, and most experience fluctuations in self-esteem. Indeed, some researchers have noted a normative drop in self-esteem during early adolescence (Simmons et al. 1979; Petersen and Taylor 1980; Rosenberg 1986). Also, as Brooks-Gunn and Reiter (1990) note, early adolescence may be a time of heightened vulnerability to psychological distress, especially depression, for girls. Rare is the adolescent girls who does not turn to the outside world, especially to males, for self-validation and mirroring. These personal vicissitudes are part of adolescence, part of what makes this a time of anxiety and disequilibrium for many young people. How do such feelings come to exert power over the lives of poor adolescent girls—drawing them toward early, unprotected sex and away from other means of self-enhancement? Many middle-class girls grow up in unhappy, even dysfunctional families, in homes marked by turmoil or neglect. But most of these young women will eventually move into productive adult life, albeit not without pain or problems. Why are dysfunctional families so lethal for poor youth? Why do only the exceptional escape and, even then, only with a good deal of help and at great personal cost to themselves or their children?

When the girl's past and current life experiences combine to lead to a distorted or defeated sense of who she is and what she can do, the meanings she ascribes to the events of her life and the actions she takes or fails to take will reflect that distortion or defeat. The meanings are not simply attitudes she holds; the actions are not merely spur-of-the-moment behaviors. Neither are wholly reactions to the pressures and lack of options in her environment. They have a deeper and more complex history in the development of her self and its adaptations to her environment.

A 14-year-old runs away from home and, in spite of involvement in various youth service programs, repeatedly finds herself in self-destructive relationships. These eventually lead to far more serious troubles.

A 16-year-old mother drops out of school and then abandons her counseling and general equivalent degree (GED) programs. Later she appears to lose job after job and have baby after baby, "deliberately."

When such personal failures take place, it is not simply that the environment has offered few realistic or appropriate alternatives for these adolescents, although this is probably the case. It is not just that the institutions in the community are insensitive or unresponsive to their needs, although most likely they are. Certainly, there are real obstacles in the way; but there are sometimes opportunities as well—people who want to help, chances to start again. These go unheeded or unused.

Many such teens do not trust people to be sources of help. For others, the psychological burdens of their histories lead them to put their trust in the wrong people, those who will hold them back or betray them again and again. Such people fit easily into these girls' working models of themselves. They fulfill familiar roles and serve functions similar to those of people the girls have come to know all too well in the years before adolescence.

> When I was 5 years old I had to go and stay with an aunt. She was very bad with me, and then I had to go to another aunt and she was even worse.... One day my mother appeared and picked us up. It's not fair that you have to be going from place to place even if it's with your family, and it's bad when somebody from your family doesn't have pity on you, like you didn't have the same blood, but that happened to me. They did not have pity on me. They did not care for me. They did not defend me. I was so small I could not defend myself against adults.... I always ask myself how come God gave me this punishment. What had I done to deserve all this suffering?

> When I was small I got so many disappointments with friends and family that it is hard to trust someone again.... When I was small I don't know why but I was scared of big people.... Today I feel afraid like if someone is chasing me or something is going to happen to me. I usually have this awful feeling.... I hope I can make it disappear someday.

> It is hard to trust anyone because I am still feeling like people are trying to sexual abuse me and I think that about other people.

The sense of self a girl brings to adolescence has developed and will continue to develop within an interpersonal matrix, but it affects far more than her interpersonal relationships. Weaknesses or vulnerabilities in overall self-esteem and the various aspects of the self may interfere with the emergence and resolution of normal identity issues during middle and later adolescence. Without mastery of these issues, a core task of adolescence—the formation of a new identity to bring to adulthood—is left unfulfilled. Without a sense of self-acceptance and worth as a person, the girl is poorly prepared to meet, let alone master, the premier challenge of adolescence....

Sixteen in the Mainstream: Struggles and Supports

> When I was fifteen, I felt it coming; now I was sixteen, and it hit. My feet had imperceptibly been set on a new path, a fast path into a long tunnel.... I wandered witlessly forward and found myself going down.... There wasn't a whole lot I could do about it, or about anything. I was going to hell in a handcart, that was all, and I knew it and everyone around me knew it, and there it was. I was growing and thinning, as if pulled. I was getting angry, as if pushed.... My feelings deepened and lingered. The swift moods of early childhood—each formed by and suited to its occasion—vanished. Now feelings lasted so long they left stains. They arose from nowhere, like winds or waves, and battered at me or engulfed me.

> Annie Dillard, *An American Childhood*

This is how the Pulitzer Prize-winning writer Annie Dillard describes her emotionally stormy adolescence. Raised in the 1940s by a strong, loving (and well-to-do) two-parent family rooted in the past and current life of their community, Dillard made mistakes and took risks, but the foolishness of her adolescence could be weathered and its experiences successfully integrated as part of her developing self, without pulling her down forever.[3] But there are other, vastly different American childhoods, ones that have more serious and lasting effects both on the young woman's sense of identity and on the kind of life she may well be forced to lead for many years to come. Because of the pressures and constraints of adolescence in a risk-packed environment, the mistakes of her youth may be her companions for life.

Most adults in society's mainstream recognize that adolescence is a major crossroads, a time of life when a young person's future life-course begins to be set in earnest. As Steinberg (1991) points out, "adolescence is a period of preparation, defined less by its own essence than what it is followed by—maturity." The process of achieving maturity has its own particular challenges in current U.S. society, but it is a process that most adolescents undergo with reasonable success. For most mainstream girls, entry into the period of adolescence takes place against a backdrop of psychic strength and integrity, gained from the successful execution of the basic developmental tasks of childhood. As identity is being re-tested and re-formed during adolescence and relational skills and practical competencies are being built, there is normally a core of emotional and intellectual wholeness. In addition, parents and numerous other social supports are likely to be available to help the adolescent overcome her problems and to be activated if there is too much adolescent turbulence or too little achievement. Parents and teachers are generally concerned, for example, when a formerly motivated girl suddenly seems to lose interest or fails in school. The significant adults in such a girls' life recognize that for some reason she is not able to handle the various pressures of adolescence and to balance its often conflicting internal and external pulls.

Adults will be concerned, if not alarmed, if a girl begins to act out sexually in response to such problems as the loss of a father or to family discord, which leave her without the emotional support and guidance she needs to cope with her unfolding sexuality. Adults (and often peers) worry about the girl who seeks to resolve identity conflicts by involving herself in a series of destructive relationships. Such behavior is felt to portend future problems with men.

When parents are not able or willing to help, a good-quality school, with caring, involving teachers and guidance counselors, can be lifesaving, literally as well as figuratively, for an adolescent who is troubled or in crisis. As an external support system, the school can serve as a model, encouraging and reinforcing an adolescent's coping efforts and demonstrating positive values (Rutter 1979). Those who have studied stress resistance in adolescence find that resilient adolescents usually have extensive contacts outside their immediate families, with concerned and caring teachers, ministers, and older friends (Hauser et al. 1985; Werner and Smith 1982).

A mainstream girl whose sexual acting out results in a pregnancy will probably have an abortion. If this is not possible or acceptable to her, she will be far more likely to relinquish her child for adoption than will her disadvantaged counterpart

(Musick et al. 1984; Hayes 1987; Kalmuss, Namerow and Cushman 1991). In those comparatively rare cases where a girl from a working-class or middle-class background does elect to keep and raise her baby, she has a greater chance to marry than her disadvantaged counterpart, greater material resources, and, even if she is a high school dropout, greater likelihood of eventually getting a job.

As difficult and potentially damaging as adolescent developmental tribulations can be, they are far less likely to have lasting negative effects if the girl has social and economic advantages. The more privileged adolescent's parents may provide her with therapy, find her a tutor, or even send her to a private school when the going gets too rough. Should her parents be unwilling or unable to do this, the schools in her more affluent community will almost certainly offer counseling or a special program designed for youth experiencing educational and emotional difficulties.

Thus, for the middle-class girl, temporary psychological vulnerability need not inevitably result in permanent disability. For the travails of a troubled youth, there are the cushions and buffers of middle-class life. Where there is social and economic advantage, a "wasted youth" does not automatically lead to a wasted life.

Sixteen, Female, and Poor: A Different Experience, A Different Identity

For adolescent girls raised in severe poverty, reality is different in every dimension. These girls frequently have grown up in damaged and damaging family situations where the basic developmental foundation has been poorly laid or is lacking altogether. In addition, the environment in which they live—at home, in school, and in the community—is often highly threatening. Surely more of these teens, when compared with their more advantaged counterparts, are highly stressed if not deeply troubled. At the same time, their external supports and their opportunities to find alternative models of coping are fewer and far less adequate.

What happens to one of these teenage girls when confronted with the challenges of adolescence? If she engages in sexual acting-out, finds and involves herself with males who exploit or abuse her, or fails in school, she is more often than not drawn into a vortex from which there is little chance of escape.

The difficulties that regularly face such a young woman can range from overt threats of random and unpredictable violence to subtle but ubiquitous pressure to engage in risky sexual behavior. All these work against any effort of hers to make something of herself or to work toward a better life. Beyond that, there is frequently a deeper problem. These girls handle the transformations in relations with family, peers, and the community that accompany adolescence quite differently than their mainstream counterparts. Even if, in the short term, the ways they handle these transformations are adaptive, in the long term they may be quite damaging.

For example, typical mainstream adolescent girls are struggling to come to grips with such questions as: Who am I? What are these feelings I'm feeling? Do my parents understand me? Are they listening to me? What do they know? I'm old enough, why won't they let me do what I want? What should I do about my sexual attractiveness to boys? How do I feel about sex? How do I balance my social and school lives? And, especially in the middle to later adolescent years, will I go to college? If so, where? What will I do with my life—will I have a career, or marry and raise children, or both?[4]

On the other hand, many girls who come of age in underclass communities—especially those in single-parent, father-absent families—are struggling with different questions. They, too, are asking "Who am I?" but from a psychological perspective that belongs to an earlier period of development. For these girls, the issues of identity often are not predominantly those of redefining and renegotiating family relationships, searching for a sense of where one is headed in the future, and envisioning the place one will take in the broader society. Rather, identity-related issues may still be grounded in the questions of early childhood: Who cares about me? Whom can I trust? Whom can I depend on? Where and how can I find security and safety?

The self's voice in these young women may remain fixed on one basic set of questions: What do I need to do, and who do I need to be, to find someone who will stay close to me and care for me as I wish my mother had done? What do I need to do, and who do I need to be, to find a man who won't abandon me, as the men in my life and my mother's life have done?

If an adolescent's psychological energies are too strongly focused on defensive and security measures, much of her time and effort will be focused on trying to resolve her unmet dependency needs, searching for and trying to maintain attachments. When this occurs, her attention and energies are diverted from the critical developmental tasks that undergird adolescent and, later, adult competence in our society. Girls for whom basic acceptance and love are the primary motivating forces have little interest or emotional energy to invest in school or work-related activities unless they are exceptionally bright or talented. Even then, the pull of unmet affiliative or dependency needs may be more powerful than anything the worlds of school or work have to offer, particularly when these offerings are as inadequate and inconsistent as those typically found in poverty communities.

Fighting the Odds

The adolescent girls most likely to be struggling with the developmental tasks of childhood are those who have been forced to adapt to family and other environments that provide too little care and protection for children and youth. In searching for the acceptance and love they crave, these girls will take many risks and few precautions. The capacity for self-care is, after all, predicated on a history of being cared for and protected by others. While growth-thwarting personal histories are by no means exclusive to impoverished communities, they are more predominant there for a variety of reasons, and their effects are far more lethal.[5]

Noxious early childhood and preadolescent life experiences not only foster bad attitudes and actions; they act to shape an inadequate sense of self, an identity that prohibits forward movement in positive, self-enhancing ways. Such experiences leave girls developmentally unprepared for the rapid and extensive physical and psychosocial changes of adolescence. There are too few "stakes in the ground" to help these girls withstand the strong winds of adolescence. The internal and external pressures of the teen years find them psychologically unprepared and overwhelm their psyches.

Certain experiences, especially within the family, take a heavy toll on development, affecting intellectual as well as social emotional functions: "I had a terrible young life. So many things I made sure they were not in my mind. I would black them out. When he hit her he would hit me. I lost a lost of my memory."

Most important, traumatic experiences leave a residue of emotional discontinuities—breaks between present and past, between thought and feeling, between actions and intentions. Mental health professionals generally refer to such discontinuities as forms of dissociation, psychological defenses used to retain a sense of self under traumatic or brutalizing conditions. When this happens, the girl is functionally the prisoner of the disavowed and unacknowledged pain of her past (Miller 1983; 1986). She is caught between the security-seeking behavior that experience has taught her to engage in and want, on the one hand, and the security-threatening results of that behavior, on the other. She cannot easily learn from these repeated "mistakes" because the feelings and perceptions are not related to each other. For psychic self-protection, she has developed a pattern of compartmentalizing, so that what appears to her to be functional (even rational) survival-oriented behavior is not psychically related to its invariably negative outcomes. She has learned to perceive her participation in self-injurious interactions that cannot be avoided as, in effect, a positive skill and thus has come to insulate her emotions from the normally associated pain.

Emotional discontinuities between what she does and what she intended to do are likely to be intensified by the normal adolescent tendency to be somewhat oblivious to the internal reasons for one's actions. Thus the stage has been set for a series of personal crises that the girl has instigated, either actively or passively, but about which she appears to be bewildered. "How did this happen to me?" "How did I get pregnant?" "How did I get kicked out of school?" "How did I lose the job? I didn't do anything wrong." "How did I get involved with a (another) guy who takes advantage of me, who beats me up and abuses my kids?" "Why did the state take my kids away?"

For those who question why a disadvantaged adolescent, even one in an intervention program, continues to seek and find more trouble, it is well to remember that defensive patterns of behavior are usually grounded in necessary, perhaps even life-saving, adaptations to terrible life circumstances. Because such adaptations initially (and repeatedly) "worked" they are deeply entrenched in self and identity and strongly resistant to change. Few of the young women who participate in intervention programs could be said to be mentally ill or to have serious personality or character pathology. Indeed, many have remarkable strengths and resilience. Still, seriously and continuously depriving experiences are rarely without psychological consequences, which interfere with the ability to negotiate the critical tasks of this transitional period and create additional vulnerability that magnify the effects of risk factors in the environment. When this happens, the adolescent is left without the personal resources and coping skills she most needs to withstand the multiple pressures of her daily life or to thrust herself up and out of poverty. It is fate's cruel trick that in order to move beyond a life of poverty, today's disadvantaged adolescent needs to possess not just good psychosocial resources and skills but extraordinarily good ones; not just an adequate self-concept but one that is invincible.

Notes

1. As Steinberg (1991) notes, "One of the effects of the salience of physical changes associated with puberty is the tendency (and, at times, the danger) of extrapolating from the physical to the psychological." Clinical and anecdotal data clearly indicate that this is what happens with many early maturing preadolescent girls: males assume they are "ready for sex" because of their physical appearance. On the other hand, some men prefer having sex with prepubescent girls.

    Carol Gilligan (personal communication) has a thought-provoking interpretation of the motivation for this behavior. She believes that men who sexually abuse preadolescent girls are responding not so much to emerging female sexuality, but rather to the spirit and feistiness that characterizes girls at this age. According to Gilligan, sexual exploitation is a negative response to female assertiveness; a male's way of putting a woman (albeit a young one) in her place and asserting his power over her. Considering that the men who victimize these girls are often marginal and powerless themselves, this is a plausible explanation. It may also be that they abuse preadolescent girls because they can get away with it more easily than with older, and less naive, adolescent women.

2. In general, girls are more likely than boys to be swayed by the actual or presumed sexual behavior of their peers, especially their best friends and their boyfriends (Billy and Udry 1983; Cvetkovich and Grote 1980). However, white girls are more susceptible to peer influences than their African-American counterparts.

3. For another revealing picture of a turbulent but fruitful adolescence, see Simon 1986.

4. Some of the best sources of information on normal adolescent development can be found in Feldman and Elliott 1990. I thank Shirley Feldman, of Stanford University, for generously providing me with copies of chapters in progress; they were invaluable for this work. I also thank Dr. Ruby Takanishi of the Carnegie Council on Adolescent Development for directing me to this work and to Professor Feldman.

5. The work of Robert Halpern (1990a, 1990b), William Julius Wilson (1987, 1989), and David Ellwood (1988) provides a sense of the cumulative effects of poverty on the family. Halpern deals more with family functioning—specifically parenting—whereas Wilson and Ellwood are more concerned with structural issues such as family formation.

Questions

1. What are the early family experiences of girls growing up in poverty that contribute to their becoming pregnant as adolescents?
2. What messages have some teenage mothers gotten about themselves from school? From their families?
3. How might a history of sexual exploitation contribute to teenage childbearing?
4. Why does teenage childbearing make sense for girls growing up in poverty? What issues does it resolve? What needs does it fulfill?
5. Can teenage mothers be considered to be adults?

References and Further Reading

Burton, L. (1990). Teenage childbearing as an alternative life-course strategy in multi-generation black families. *Human Nature, 1,* 123–143.

Cohler, B., & Musick, J. S. (1996). Adolescent parenthood and the transition to adulthood. In J. Graber, J. Brooks-Gunn, & C. Petersen (Eds.) *Transitions through adolescence: Interpersonal domains and context.* Mahwah, NJ: Lawrence Erlbaum.

Musick, J. (1993). *Young, poor and pregnant: The psychology of teenage motherhood.* New Haven, CT: Yale University Press.

14.2   Rebekah Levine Coley and
                            P. Lindsay Chase-Lansdale, 1998

Adolescent Pregnancy and Parenthood: Recent Evidence and Future Directions

Rebekah Levine Coley is a research associate at Harvard's John F. Kennedy School of Government's Malcolm Wiener Center for Social Policy. She works in the Joblessness and Urban Poverty Research Program.

P. Lindsay Chase-Lansdale, Ph.D., is a professor at Northwestern University's School of Education and Social Policy. Her research interests include public policy and adolescent development, consequences of poverty and welfare reform on children and families, and family functioning.

Young people who have not yet resolved the developmental tasks of adolescence have been seen as inadequately prepared for assuming the role of parent, perhaps the most demanding and complex adult social role. Adolescent parents are viewed as cognitively and emotionally immature, too egocentric to adequately assume responsibility for the care of another person, to truly understand a baby's emotional and physical needs, and to separate a baby's feelings from their own (Reading 4.2). Young adolescents may fail to realize how difficult and time consuming a baby can be and are distressed to discover how different an actual baby can be from the one who they fantasized would offer them unconditional love. Adolescents may lack the psychological well-being and resources to enable them to negotiate the challenges posed by a newborn infant. Finally, adolescent parenthood is seen as costly to adolescent girls themselves. Adolescent mothers become more dependent on families and on public assistance at a time when other adolescents are moving toward greater autonomy. Adolescent pregnancy causes girls to foreclose on their identities (Reading 5.2), limiting prospects for further identity exploration, and curtailing girls' opportunities to complete their education, thereby limiting their vocational opportunities.

Rebekah Levine Coley and P. Lindsay Chase-Lansdale review the research on the causes of teenage childbearing and consequences for both parent and child. New research reveals that many of the negative outcomes that were previously ascribed to parental age precede rather than stem from early parenthood. If teenage mothers are less likely to complete high school, this may be due to their lower educational attainment before the pregnancy rather than to the pregnancy itself. Many of the earlier studies did not control for social class, and research now shows that many negative outcomes that have been attributed to the age of the mother can be better explained by the effects of poverty. Coley and Chase-Lansdale examine the scarce research on teenage fathers, their involvement with their children and the mothers of their children, and their financial contribution. Unfortunately little research exists on the impact of fatherhood on the teenage fathers themselves. Coley and Chase-Lansdale provide an overview of the types of programs that have been created to prevent the occurrence of teenage pregnancy or to improve the goals or life chances of the teenage mother. Finally, they discuss the possible implications of welfare reform and the Personal Responsibility and Work Opportunity Reconciliation Act of 1996 for teenage mothers.

Abstract An overview of recent research on adolescent sexual activity, pregnancy, and parenthood is presented, with a focus on the dearth of knowledge concerning psychological precursors and consequences. Although the rate of teenage childbearing has decreased substantially this century, increasing rates of sexual activity, illegitimacy, and welfare receipt raise public concerns. New research is discussed that suggests that many negative outcomes previously ascribed to mothers' age are as much causes or correlates of teenage pregnancy as effects of it, although this claim is less substantiated regarding effects on children of teenager mothers. Literature on fathers and grandmothers is summarized, and suggestions are made for furthering this research. An overview is given of recent successes among intervention programs, and policy implications of the new federal welfare law are considered for teenage mothers and their children.

Adolescent pregnancy has long been a societal concern, but in the past decade, this issue has become one of the most frequently cited examples of the perceived societal decay in the United States (U.S. House of Representatives, 1996). In 1990,

1,040,000 adolescents under the age of 20 became pregnant, approximately 530,000 (51%) of whom gave birth (Alan Guttmacher Institute, 1994). Ironically, the rate of births to teenagers is much lower now than it has been throughout much of the 20th century. Between 1960 and 1985, the rate of births to female adolescents declined substantially, falling from 89.1 births per 1,000 teenagers ages 15–19 in 1960 to 51.0 in 1985. In the late 1980s, the rate increased to a recent high of 62.1 in 1991 but then declined again in the 1990s to 56.8 birth per 1,000 15–19 year-olds in 1995 (U.S. Department of Health and Human Services, 1995; Ventura, Martin, Curtin, & Mathews, 1997). Most of the births to teenagers are concentrated in the later years of adolescence: Rates for 18–19-year-olds are more than double those for 15–17-year-olds. The rates for those under 15 years of age are too low to provide detailed statistics in most reports (1.3 per 1,000 10–14-year-olds in 1995; Rosenberg, Ventura, Maurer, Heuser, & Freedman, 1996; Ventura et al., 1997).

There are also large differences among female adolescents of different racial and ethnic groups. Whites[1] have considerably lower rates of adolescent births (39.3 per 1,000 15–19-year-olds in 1995) than Hispanics[2] (106.7) or African Americans (99.3; Ventura et al., 1997). Whereas childbearing rates in White and African American adolescents have shown substantial declines, rates for Hispanic adolescents have risen steadily in the past 15 years. Although Latina adolescents have lower rates of early sexual experience, they are less likely to use birth control and, once pregnant, are less likely to abort than are White or African American adolescents (Perez & Duany, 1992).

Although adolescent birthrates in the United States have declined in recent decades, they remain high in stark contrast to those in other industrialized nations. Even though American teenagers do not exhibit significantly different patterns of sexual activity as compared with adolescents in many industrialized countries, they use contraception less consistently and effectively; thus, birthrates are much higher in the United States than they are elsewhere. In fact, at the beginning of this decade, the rate of teenage births was almost twice as high in the United States as in the country with the next highest rate, Great Britain; more than 4 times greater than those of Sweden and Spain; 7 times greater than those of Denmark and the Netherlands; and 15 times greater than that of Japan (United Nations, 1991). Although some researchers argue that ethnic diversity is largely responsible for these differences, the birthrate of White adolescents in the United States still easily surpasses that of adolescents in every other industrialized nation (United Nations, 1991).

If birthrates to adolescents are significantly lower now than they were in the 1960s and the 1970s, why has teenager pregnancy become such a major policy concern in the past decade? Two reasons are paramount: links with (a) nonmarital childbearing and (b) welfare dependence. First, although the total rate of births to teenagers has decreased substantially since midcentury, the percentage of non-marital teenager births has soared, from a small minority of 15% of all births to teenagers ages 15–19 in 1960 to a strong majority of 75% in 1995. This percentage is significantly higher for African Americans (95% in 1995) than for Whites (68%) and Hispanics (67%; Ventura et al., 1997). Teenagers who become unwed mothers are also likely to have additional children outside of wedlock in their 20s, adding to the growing proportion of births that are nonmarital (Foster & Hoffman, 1996). Second, the United States has become increasingly concerned about families' use of welfare (Temporary Assistance for Needy Families [TANF]) and persistent childhood poverty (U.S. House of Representatives, 1996). A sizable portion of teenage mothers are poor, and they are also likely to spend extended spells of time on welfare (Bane & Ellwood, 1986). Because of these long spells, teenage mothers receive a disproportionate amount of welfare funding over their life course. For example, although teenage mothers represent only a minority of the welfare caseload at any particular time, overall, 53% of welfare funding is spent on families formed by teenage births (Alan Guttmacher Institute, 1994).

We draw attention, however, to the fact that both of these concerns can be seen as slightly misguided when directed solely at adolescents. Although teenagers accounted for 30% of nonmarital births in 1992 and those under age 18 for only 13%, women in their 20s accounted for 54% of nonmarital births. Similarly, 73% of never-married teenage mothers go on welfare within 5 years of giving birth but so do 66% of never-married mothers in their early 20s (Foster & Hoffman, 1996; Koppelman, 1994).

Causes and Correlates of Teen Pregnancies

Individual, Family, and Neighborhood Characteristics

Numerous individual, family, and neighborhood characteristics predispose girls to become young single mothers. Female adolescents who are poor students with low educational aspirations are more likely to become teenage mothers than are their high-achieving peers; in fact, one-third of teenage mothers drop out of school before becoming pregnant (Maynard, 1995). Teenage pregnancy is also linked to other problematic adolescent behaviors such as alcohol and drug use and, not surprisingly, to early initiation of sexual activity. (Horwitz, Klerman, Kuo, & Jekel, 1991a; Paikoff, 1995; Peterson & Crockett, 1992; Urdy, Kovenock, & Morris, 1996). Female adolescents who are raised in poverty by single parents and by parents with low educational attainment are also prone to teenage parenthood (Brewster, Billy, & Grady, 1993; Cherlin, Kiernan, & Chase-Lansdale, 1995; Furstenberg & Teitler, 1994; Maynard, 1995). Indeed, in 1988, 60% of adolescent mothers lived in poverty at the time of the birth of their babies (Alan Guttmacher Institute, 1994). Finally, teenagers who reside in communities with high rates of poverty, welfare use, and single-mother households are also at higher risk (Wilson, 1987).

The reasons and processes behind these correlations are numerous but are often hypothesized to revolve around experiences of poverty and resulting perceptions of limited life options and choices. (Brewster et al., 1993; Luker, 1996; Wilson, 1987). Life experiences associated with poverty, such as alienation at school, prevalent models of unmarried parenthood and unemployment, and lack of educational opportunities and stable career prospects all serve to lower the perceived costs of early motherhood (Brewster et al., 1993; Luker, 1996; Moore, Morrison, & Glei, 1995). Similarly, structural issues also play a role. The U.S. economy has lost most of its low-skill, high-paying manufacturing jobs, and higher education is increasingly necessary for living-wage employment (Wilson, 1996). This change not only has affected the stability of inner cities and the working poor but also has changed the face of the teenage years and the early 20s, such that the median ages of school completion, marriage, and childbearing have increased substantially for the middle-class population (Cherlin, 1992; Rosenheim & Testa, 1992). However, low-income populations have not adapted to these critical changes by delaying their family formation activities (Rosenheim & Testa, 1992). Thus, adolescent childbearing, which earlier occurred mostly in the context of marriage with an employed husband, is now occurring in unmarried teenagers who, because of their impoverished backgrounds, have few immediate prospects for economic security.

Sexuality Decisions

In addition to such background characteristics and structural issues, individual choices and actions also play a role in adolescent childbearing. Some see the road to parenthood as one that includes numerous decision steps (Hardy & Zabin, 1991). One must have sexual intercourse; use or not use effective contraception; once pregnant, decide whether to abort or not; and, once the child is born, choose to raise the child or to put the child up for adoption (cf. Morrison, 1985). Changes have occurred in recent decades regarding all four of these decision points.

First, the risk period for young childbearing has increased substantially through both decreasing age at first intercourse and rising age at marriage (Cherlin, 1992). For example, in the late 1950s, 46% of female adolescents were sexually active by age 19. This proportion increased to 53% in the early 1970s, 66% in the 1980s, and 76% in 1995 (Abma, Chandra, Mosher, Peterson, & Piccinino, 1997; Ventura et al., 1997). Although adolescents' use of contraceptives, especially condoms, has also increased, it has not been adequate to stem the rate of pregnancy. Data from 1990 to 1995 indicate that 33% of teenagers did not use contraception at first intercourse, and the rates are higher for younger teens than for older teens (Abma et al., 1997). Adolescents also tend to use contraception sporadically and ineffectively. However, this is not to imply that teenagers are trying to become pregnant. The disparity between not wanting to become pregnant and not effectively using contraception has multiple roots, including a lack of knowledge about reproduction and contraception, limited access to family-planning and health services, and inadequate ability to foresee and to be prepared for protected sexual activity (Morrison, 1985; W. L. Robinson, Watkins-Ferrell, Davis-Scott, & Ruchs-Ross, 1993). Many of these factors improve significantly with age. In fact, age is one of the strongest predictors of birth control use (Moore & Peterson, 1989). In addition, adolescents' views of invulnerability and egocentrism, leading to beliefs that pregnancy could never happen to them and thus to ineffective preventive practices, may also play a role, especially for high-risk teenagers (Elkind, 1978; Keating, 1990; Quadrel, Fischhoff, & Davis, 1993). Second, teenagers' use of abortion and adoption have decreased in recent years, as have rates of marriage for pregnant teens (Ventura et al., 1997). Together, these changes have resulted in rising rates of unwed adolescent childbirth among low-income teenagers.

Psychological Processes

Although knowledge is growing concerning the demographics of teenage sexuality and childbearing, relatively little research has addressed the psychological variables and processes that predict the occurrence of teenage births. Exceptions include work on influences of general social competence on teenage sexuality decisions (Allen, Philliber, Herrling, & Kuperminc, 1997); Paikoff's (1995) work on preadolescents' understanding and appraisals of sexual situations; and research on an emotional deprivation model of adolescent pregnancy, which asserts that adolescents who lack adequate emotional support and stability may look to early sex and motherhood to provide emotional closeness (Horwitz et al., 1991a; Musick, 1993). Research on the psychological contributors to teenage sexuality and pregnancy needs to be continued and expanded.

Sexuality Issues Among Male Adolescents

Many of the factors that have played a part in increasing births to female adolescents have also affected male adolescents and men. The age of sexual onset has decreased for male adolescents in recent decades, and the use of contraceptives has risen. For example, the proportion of sexually experienced male adolescents at age 18 rose from 55% in the early 1970s to 64% in the mid-1980s (U.S. Department of Health and Human Services, 1995). At the same time, among urban male 17–19-year olds, the rate of condom use at last intercourse increased from 20% in 1979 to 54% in 1988 (U.S. Department of Health and Human Services, 1995). However, many aspects of male adolescents' roles in teenage births are not well understood. For example, the role of male partners in making abortion and adoption decisions has received negligible research attention. A number of structural arguments, such as the loss of stable blue-collar jobs in urban areas, have been posed as explanations for the decreasing rates of marriage and financial responsibility of male adolescents and young men for the young women they impregnate and the babies they father (e.g., Wilson, 1987, 1996). In contrast, the psychological processes behind these choices have not been adequately explored (see below). Finally, a newly discovered trend raises disturbing questions concerning the male role in teenage pregnancy. Recent studies have reported that a large proportion of teenage mothers have experienced sexual abuse and forced sexual intercourse prior to their early initiation of sex and teenage pregnancy (Boyner & Fine, 1992; Butler & Burton, 1990; Moore et al., 1995). Further research is needed to explore this issue in representative samples and in comparison groups of nonparenting adolescents.

Consequences of Parenthood for Teenage Mothers

Teenagers who give birth during their adolescent years tend to function less effectively in numerous realms than their peers who delay childbearing. Recent research has indicated that many of the negative outcomes of adolescent motherhood, such as low educational achievement and poverty, precede rather than stem from early parenthood. Nevertheless, teenage childbearing also adds to the limited prospects of already disadvantaged adolescents. These outcomes include poorer psychological functioning, lower rates of school completion, lower levels of marital stability and additional non-marital births, less stable employment, greater welfare use, higher rates of poverty, and slightly greater rates of health problems for both mothers and children as compared with peers who postpone childbearing (Chase-Lansdale & Brooks-Gunn, 1994; Hayes, 1987). We address each of these areas in turn.

Psychological Processes

A number of psychological tasks of adolescence may be impeded by early parenthood. During the adolescent years, teenagers face the challenges of solidifying their sense of identity (Hauser, 1991; Hauser & Bowlds, 1990) and developing autonomy and independence from parents (Chase-Lansdale, Wakschlag, & Brooks-Gunn, 1995; Feldman & Elliott, 1990; Wakschlag, Chase-Lansdale, & Brooks-Gunn, 1996). Parenthood, with its continual demands and responsibilities, can leave little time for exploration and appropriate individuation in areas of normative teen concern such as peer relations, dating, schooling, and career choices. Young mothers may react to such conflicting demands with psychological distress, perhaps expressed through depressive symptomatology (Carter, Osofsky, & Hann, 1991; Wasserman, Brunelli, & Rauh, 1990). Overall, relatively little recent research has addressed the psychological effects of unplanned early parenthood or the processes that allow some adolescent mothers to overcome the disruptive experiences of this situation.

Educational Attainment

Until recently, most studies on adolescent mothers concluded that early parenthood had a strong negative effect on their educational attainment, such that young mothers were unlikely to continue their education after childbirth and thus obtained lower total levels of education than their peers who delayed childbirth (e.g., Moore & Waite, 1977). However, recent studies have found that this gap is narrowing, in part, because of increasing general equivalency degree (GED) programs, schooling requirements for welfare receipt, and more progressive school policies on accepting pregnant students. In addition, new methodologies have revealed that much of the difference in educational attainment seen between adolescent mothers and older mothers may be due not to teenage motherhood itself but rather to preexisting differences between the groups (Hoffman, Foster, & Furstenberg, 1993; Hotz, McElroy, & Sanders, 1997; Moore et al., 1993).

Several innovative methodological techniques have been developed to attempt to separate out the effects of background characteristics that influence both the probability of teenage birth and the future functioning of young mothers from the effects of early childbearing. For example, a number of studies have compared sets of sisters, one of whom had a child as a teenager and one of whom delayed childbearing until adulthood, to control for differences in family background characteristics commonly found between teenagers who do and do not become young parents. Fixed-effects regression techniques, which control for unmeasured differences between families, also have been used (Geronimus & Korenman, 1992; Hoffman et al., 1993). Such studies have found that the effects of teenage childbearing on high school completion and total educational attainment are much smaller than previous studies had indicated but are still significant. For example, Hoffman et al. found that postponing childbirth to after the age of 20 increased total educational attainment by 0.38 years.

These studies have been criticized for their failure to control for unmeasured differences between sisters that may affect both the decision to become a young mother and other functioning outcomes (influences such as motivation, academic ability, etc.; Klepinger, Lundberg, & Plotnick, 1995). To attend to such concerns, in a recent study, Hotz et al. (1997) compared two groups of pregnant teenagers: One group gave birth as teenagers, and the other group became pregnant but miscarried. Such a comparison, the authors claimed, controls for many unmeasured individual characteristics that might influence the behaviors and decisions leading to adolescent pregnancy (Hotz et al., 1997). This study found that having a child before the age of 18 significantly reduced the likelihood of graduation from high school but increased the likelihood of obtaining a GED, with both birth and miscarriage groups showing a high school completion (diploma or GED) rate of slightly more than 50%. However, because a GED may carry a lower return in future earnings than a high school diploma (Cameron & Heckman, 1993), these differences remain disturbing.

The effects of teenage childbearing on educational attainment are also moderated by other variables, such as birth spacing and the decision to drop out of school. For example, if teenage mothers stay in school, they are almost as likely to graduate from high school (73%) as are their nonparent peers (77%). In contrast, dropping out of high school is a strong risk factor for pregnancy, and of adolescents who drop out of school either before or shortly after childbirth, only 30% return and eventually graduate, about half the rate of nonmother dropouts (Upchurch & McCarthy, 1990).

Marital Patterns

In addition to effects on educational attainment, teenage childbearing is also linked to different marital patterns. Although teenage mothers have higher rates of early marriage than later childbearers, their marriage rates drop off quickly in their 20s and 30s to rates lower than those of the nonteenage-mother population. Young mothers are also more likely to divorce; thus, overall, teenage mothers spend more of their parenting years as single mothers than do women who delay childbearing (Bennett, Bloom, & Miller, 1995; Furstenberg, Brooks-Gunn, & Morgan, 1987; Hayes, 1987; Hotz et al., 1997; Moore et al., 1993; U.S. Department of Health and Human Services, 1995). Teenage mothers also have slightly more children, often in quick succession, than do teenagers who postpone parenthood (Hotz et al, 1997; Moore et al., 1993). The psychological processes behind these marital and family formation choices are not well understood. It is possible that female adolescents who do not expect to marry choose instead to have an unwed birth, but research to date indicates that this relationship likely functions in the other direction, that is, that early unwed births lead to a lower likelihood of marriage (Bennett et al., 1995). Whether this decreased propensity to marry is due to lowered marriage incentives for young mothers, less opportunity, or other reasons is still being debated (Bennett et al., 1995; Wilson, 1987, 1996).

Economic Outcomes

In large part because of low educational attainment and low marital stability, coupled with the poverty endemic to young parenthood, teenage mothers have lower incomes as adults and are more likely to be on welfare than their peers who delay childbirth (Moore et al., 1993). For example, the study by Hoffman et al. (1993) that compared sets of sisters found that a teenage birth nearly doubled the likelihood that a woman would be poor at ages 21–33, increasing the rate of poverty from 16% to 28%. Other studies have questioned whether these differences are attributable to the early birth itself or solely to preexisting factors. The study by Hotz et al. (1997) that compared teenage mothers with those who had miscarried during their adolescent years found that teenage mothers actually had slightly greater earnings than their peers and similar rates of welfare receipt during their 20s. Although teenage mothers' use of welfare is higher and their incomes are lower in the years immediately after birth, they make up for this by increased employment and earnings in their late 20s and beyond, when their children reach school age and employment tends to be more lucrative (Furstenberg et al., 1987; Hotz et al., 1997). The work of Hotz et al. has been criticized on numerous methodological and theoretical fronts, including, for example, assertions that because not all miscarriages are random (e.g., some are caused by smoking or drinking during pregnancy) and because some female adolescents who miscarried would have had abortions, miscarriages are not true exogenous occurrences. However, further analytic work by Hotz, Mullin, and Sanders (in press) reinforced the validity of their results claiming that for non-African American women, teenage childbearing actually increases the labor market earnings and hours worked compared with what they would have been had women delayed childbearing. Whether these differences will continue over the long term is not yet known.

Health Outcomes

Adolescent mothers experience more pregnancy and delivery problems and have less healthy babies overall than do older mothers, but these differences are becoming less notable in recent research. First, the absolute size of these differences seems to be decreasing in recent studies, perhaps because of increased health services for young mothers. Second, new work indicates that deleterious health outcomes are related more to the poverty and lack of prenatal care common to pregnant teenagers than to age per se (there seems to be an exception for female adolescents under the age of 15; for reviews and a meta-analysis, see Klerman, 1993; Scholl, Hediger, & Belsky, 1994). Moreover, the frequency of negative maternal health outcomes is greatly reduced for teenagers who receive comprehensive prenatal care (Klerman, 1993).

Racial Differences

Much of the research on adolescent mothers also considers whether teenage parent outcomes differ by race and ethnicity. In general, the negative effects of teenage childbearing on later income and poverty rates are less severe for African Americans than for Whites and Hispanics. It has been proposed that this difference is due to the high rates of single parenthood and poverty among all African American families, such that families headed by teenage mothers are not that different from African American families with older mothers (Astone, 1993; Moore et al., 1993). In addition, young White mothers are most likely to marry, followed by Hispanics and African Americans (U.S. Department of Health and Human Services, 1995), whereas African American teenage mothers are more likely than Whites or Hispanics to stay in their family home, continue in school, and delay marriage, practices that likely serve to increase their access to family help with child rearing and financial support (Rosenheim & Testa, 1992). Finally, Geronimus (1987) proposed that early childbearing may be an adaptive practice for African Americans, especially in relation to their physical health. Termed the *weathering hypothesis,* this argument claims that because African Americans tend to experience high rates of health problems, such as elevated blood pressure and diabetes, in their late 20s and beyond, and because they are more likely to receive aid from both their families and the government during their teen years than when they are adults, early childbearing is a logical and adaptive practice for this group (Geronimus, 1987, 1992). The weathering hypothesis remains controversial and is in need of further research.

Individual Differences

Finally, longitudinal research on adolescent mothers points to the importance of considering individual differences and diversity in the long-term outcomes of teenage mothers and their children. For example, in the Baltimore Study, a longitudinal study of more than 300 low-income Black mothers who were pregnant as teenagers in the late 1960s, a 17-year follow-up showed much more promising functioning than short-term studies had predicted (Furstenberg et al., 1987). More than one third of the women had received some education past high school, and almost three quarters were employed. Approximately 25% had achieved middle-class standing by means of marriage, employment, or a combination of the two. However, the women's marriages had high rates of dissolution, and their children appeared to be faring less well than their counterparts with older mothers. Similarly, a 20-year follow-up of adolescent mothers enrolled in the Young Mother Program in the late 1960s indicated that 62% of the sample had achieved "long-term success," defined by the authors as economic self-sufficiency and completion of a high school degree (Horwitz, Klerman, Kuo, & Jekel, 1991b). However, these mothers also experienced low levels of life satisfaction and a preponderance of stressful life events.

What caused these different trajectories? Being at grade level when one became pregnant, coming from a smaller family of origin not on public assistance, and having high expectations from both one's family and oneself were all predictors of long-term success for these young mothers (Furstenberg et al., 1987; Horwitz et al., 1991b). However, it is important to note that although the economic and educational outcomes of these young mothers were somewhat better than expected, their psychological and family functioning appears more bleak over the long run. Further research needs to more clearly address such differences and how they interact.

Summary

In sum, study of the effects of teenage childbearing on maternal functioning continues to receive a large amount of increasingly sophisticated research attention. New methodologies including innovative comparison groups and statistical techniques are providing more precise estimates of the impact of young childbearing, controlling for many of the selection factors that both lead to teenage pregnancy in the first place and continue to exert effects on young mothers and children. This work needs to continue with current cohorts of young people. Much of the work discussed above involves women who gave birth as adolescents in the 1960s and the 1970s. Whether such findings will hold for current cohorts of teenagers remains to be seen.

A second challenge to research on teenage motherhood must be highlighted. The study of life trajectories of adolescent mothers has been the province of economics, sociology, and demography. Yet, psychological theory and methods are essential for understanding key developmental processes associated with the causes and consequences of adolescent childbearing. For example, developmental transformations that occur during adolescence, such as individuation, identity formation, and the ability to form mature, intimate relationships (Feldman & Elliott, 1990), may be affected by early parenthood (Brooks-Gunn & Chase-Lansdale, 1995). However, this developmental knowledge has rarely been applied to the study of teenage pregnancy, in large part because longitudinal, national data sets tend to focus on demographic components such as educational and employment outcomes and to neglect psychological functioning. Virtually no longitudinal and prospective studies have examined whether psychological variables such as self-esteem, individuation, and depression influence and are influenced by sexual activity and early childbearing, a notable omission in the literature. Although new research indicates that effects of early childbearing on economic outcomes are not as negative as previously thought, once predisposing characteristics and poverty are accounted for, the same may not be true for psychological and family functioning.

Parenting Practices and Consequences of Teenage Childbearing for Children

New research has made substantial gains in its consideration of the effects of early childbearing on the functioning and well-being of young mothers. However, the same level of attention has not been directed toward the study of the children of teen mothers. Although many longitudinal, national studies contain basic child-functioning measures, the innovative comparison group and statistical techniques discussed above have not been used to assess effects of teenage childbearing on child development or on maternal parenting practices.

Parenting Practices

The transition to parenting can be a stressful time for all parents, regardless of age and background (Cowan & Cowan, 1992). For teen mothers, this stress may be compounded by their typically underprivileged and impoverished backgrounds as well as by the addition of other normative changes that occur during adolescence, such as identity formation and the renegotiation of relationships with one's family of origin (Chase-Lansdale & Brooks-Gunn, 1994; Feldman & Elliott, 1990). In addition, young mothers rarely marry and tend to have additional children in quick succession; these factors increase the already substantial difficulties such mothers may have balancing child-care, educational, and work responsibilities. Thus, it seems reasonable to predict that adolescents will have more difficulty with parenting than will older mothers.

Teenage mothers have been found to be just as warm but less verbal, less sensitive, and less responsive to their infants than older mothers (Culp, Appelbaum, Osofsky, & Levy, 1988), factors that may be related to their greater levels of depressive symptomatology in the year following childbirth (Wasserman et al., 1990). Young mothers also tend to provide a less stimulating home environment (Luster & Dubow, 1990; Moore, Morrison, & Greene, 1997), to perceive their infants as being more difficult, and to have unrealistic expectations (for reviews, see Brooks-Gunn & Chase-Lansdale, 1995; Brooks-Gunn & Furstenberg, 1986). However, it is important to consider the methodologies of these studies and the comparison groups they use. For example, many studies compare the parenting practices of teenage mothers with those of significantly older, middle-class mothers who may not constitute a reasonable comparison group. Relatedly, many of these studies do not adequately take into account background and socioeconomic differences between older and younger mothers, and when these variables are controlled, the strength of the differences diminishes significantly although the differences do not appear altogether (see Klerman, 1993). Similarly, in studies that use more similar comparison groups, such as mothers in their early 20s who also live in poverty, few differences are found in parenting styles (Benasich & Brooks-Gunn, 1996; Chase-Lansdale, Brooks-Gunn, & Zamsky, 1994; Wakschlag et al., 1996).

In addition, the vast majority of research on the parenting practices of adolescent mothers studies only the first year or two of parenting. Whether teen's parenting behaviors change over time relative to those of older mothers is unknown. Considering the findings (see below) that child functioning appears to worsen over time in children of adolescent mothers, the hypothesis remains that adolescent mothers' parenting may decrease in quality or effectiveness as their children grow into adolescents. Overall, more research is needed that considers the psychological and family processes that are responsible for the patterns of parenting found over time in teenage mothers, with more closely matched comparison groups and with designs that include more extensive and sophisticated measures than are typically found in large data sets.

It is also important to raise a more general cautionary note concerning measurement in studies of teenage parents. Many studies of adolescent mothers involve samples of low-income, mostly minority families (Brooks-Gunn & Furstenberg, 1986). The measures used, however, are often developed and normed on middle-class, White, married samples and, thus, may not correctly capture the assumed constructs and behaviors (Benasich & Brooks-Gunn, 1996; Brooks-Gunn & Chase-Lansdale, 1995). Hence, more work is needed on the applicability of measures for different samples of mothers and children.

Child Functioning

Numerous small-scale studies have examined the cognitive and behavioral functioning of children of teenage mothers, although the majority of these studies have considered only the infancy and preschool periods (for reviews, see Brooks-Gunn & Furstenberg, 1986; Chase-Lansdale & Brooks-Gunn, 1994; Chase-Lansdale, Brooks-Gunn, & Paikoff, 1991). Few differences have been found in infancy between children of teenagers and children of older mothers. In the preschool years, delays in cognitive development begin to emerge and continue into the school years (Furstenberg et al., 1987; Moore, 1986; Moore et al., 1997). Preschoolers of teenage mothers also tend to show behavior problems, including higher levels of aggression and lower impulse control than their peers born to older mothers. In adolescence, children of teenagers experience higher rates of grade failure, delinquency, incarceration (for male adolescents), and early sexual activity and pregnancy than their peers born to older mothers (Furstenberg et al., 1987; Furstenberg, Hughes, & Brooks-Gunn, 1992; Grogger, 1997; Haveman, Wolfe, & Peterson, 1997; Horwitz et al., 1991a; Moore et al., 1997).

However, there are a few important caveats to this seemingly bleak picture. One is that children, like their mothers, show diversity in their functioning. For example, although there is a perception that all children of teenage mothers are at high risk of early pregnancy themselves, most adolescents do not repeat their mothers' childbearing patterns. In the Baltimore Study, one third of the daughters became teenage mothers (Furstenberg et al., 1987), whereas the follow-up of the Young Mothers Program showed that one quarter of the daughters and 11% of the sons of participants became teen parents (Horwitz et al., 1991a). In addition, as for teenage mothers themselves, socioeconomic status and poverty appear to be more important predictors of children's and adolescents' functioning than is maternal age at birth (Brooks-Gunn & Furstenberg, 1986).

In contrast to research on educational and behavioral outcomes of children born to teenage mothers, little research has considered their psychological functioning. In infancy, babies born to teenage mothers appear no more likely to experience attachment problems than children of comparable high-risk older mothers (Benn & Saltz, 1989; Hann, Osofsky, Stringer, & Carter, 1988; Spieker & Bensley, 1994). However, children of teenage mothers are more likely to be recipients of reported child abuse and neglect and are more likely to be placed in foster care than are children of older mothers. This effect is stronger for later-born than for firstborn children of young mothers (Goerge & Lee, 1997). More research is needed on the socioemotional development of children of teenage mothers during their preschool and childhood years.

A plethora of questions remain concerning the effects of early parenthood on the children of teenage mothers. (a) Why do problems in cognitive and behavioral functioning seem to increase with children's age? Hypothesized explanations include the effects of accumulated stress, increasing demands of parenting older children and adolescents, cumulative effects of long-term poverty, changes in living arrangements, and the transition to school. (b) What about the later-born children of teen mothers; do they fare better than firstborns because of more experienced mothering, or do they fare worse, perhaps because of lower social support and cumulative stress? (c) What parenting and contextual variables are responsible for these patterns of child functioning? Numerous factors could play a role: If adolescent mothers work more than their older counterparts in the early years of their children's lives, as Hotz et al. (1997) suggested, mothers may have less time to spend with their children and, thus, may provide less warmth, stimulation, and supervision; the low marriage rates and high marital instability in families with teenage mothers likely lead to lower paternal involvement in children's lives; and early motherhood may bring with it special psychological stresses whose effects and processes are yet to be delineated. Overall, it seems that today's children of teenage mothers, faced with differing educational and employment demands of a changing global market, may fare worse, in fact, than longitudinal studies of previous cohorts of young mothers might imply.

Finally, methodological considerations of research on children of adolescent mothers deserve attention. Like earlier studies of teenage mothers themselves, many of the studies of child outcomes suffer from serious methodological difficulties and lack adequate controls for background characteristics. In light of how much of the problematic long-term outcomes of teenage mothers have been attributed to preexisting background characteristics and not to early childbearing per se, research on child functioning in families with young mothers deserves the same careful attention. In particular, it is important to distinguish effects of poverty from effects of mothers' age at birth on child development. For example, a large research base details the negative effects of poverty on family and child functioning, effects such as harsh parenting and parental depression, and for children, school failure, early sexuality, and delinquency (Duncan & Brooks-Gunn, 1997; Duncan, Brooks-Gunn, & Klebanov, 1994; McLoyd, 1990). As these outcomes are strikingly similar to the outcomes of teenage parenthood described above, it seems plausible that poverty may account for much of the impact on children previously ascribed to teenage childbearing, but firm conclusions along these lines cannot be made. A stronger focus on individual differences, especially concerning coping and adaptation, is needed.

Involvement and Impact of Fathers

Who Are Teenage Fathers?

Overall, detailed and thorough information on fathers of children born to teenage mothers is rare. Most data sets gather information only from the mothers and in many cases do not include even basic demographic information on the fathers. From the information that is available, it is generally agreed that fathers tend to be 2 to 3 years older, on average, than teenage mothers, a fact that has caused concern among some researchers and policymakers (Coley & Chase-Lansdale, 1997; Landry & Forrest, 1995; B. E. Robinson, 1988). However, it is instructive to note that in American society, older male partners are normative: Partners of mothers in their 20s and 30s at the time of childbirth also average 3 years older than mothers (Lindberg, Sonenstein, Ku, & Martinez, 1997). Like teenage mothers, the male adolescents and men who father their children tend to be poor, are often continuing an intergenerational practice (many are from families who experienced teenage childbearing and welfare receipt), live in low-income communities, and have low educational achievement (Lerman, 1993). In addition, like early motherhood, early fatherhood appears to have negative consequences on future functioning, although this issue needs more attention. Adolescent fathers appear to work more hours and earn more money than their nonparent peers in the first years following the birth, but perhaps because of this commitment, they obtain less education and, thus, have lower long-term labor market activity and earnings than their counterparts who delay parenthood (Brien & Willis, 1997; Marsiglio, 1986).

Financial Contributions

Because of their own typically impoverished backgrounds, young fathers are rarely strong sources of financial support for teen mothers and their children. Although most start out with a desire to provide for their children, their child support contributions are extremely low. Historically, this has been exacerbated by the low rates of paternity establishment and legal child support arrangements made by mothers. However, both of these are now increasing substantially because of the Family Support Act of 1988 (Chase-Lansdale & Vinovskis, 1995), and further increases are expected in reaction to the 1996 welfare reform legislation (see below). In addition, smaller and more qualitative studies of young fathers have found substantially higher levels of financial contributions than formal census figures show, perhaps because of the prevalence of unreported, irregular, and in-kind contributions (Coley & Chase-Lansdale, 1997). Finally, it is important to keep in mind that the financial status of young fathers tends to improve over time, and thus enforcement of child support payments could, in the long run, make a relatively large contribution to the care of children born to teenager mothers (Chase-Lansdale & Vinovskis, 1993).

Fathers' Involvement

The amount of contact that young fathers have with their children is also quite variable. Somewhat surprisingly, given the low rates of marriage and high incidence of divorce among teenage mothers and their partners, 50% of teenage fathers live with their children sometime after birth, although this situation often does not last long (Marsiglio, 1987). Rates vary greatly by race: White fathers have the highest rates of cohabitation, followed by Hispanics, and then African Americans. Many young fathers regularly see their children, at least for the first few years. In a nationally representative sample, Lerman (1993) found that almost half of new young fathers visited their children weekly, and almost 25% had daily contact. Smaller studies have found similar results (e.g., Coley & Chase-Lansdale, 1997). However, these rates decrease over time, such that fewer than a quarter of fathers see their school-age children weekly (Lerman, 1993).

What predicts fathers' involvement? African American fathers have very low rates of marriage and cohabitation, but they tend to remain more involved with their children over time than do White or Hispanic fathers (Lerman, 1993; Marsiglio, 1987). Unstable or hostile mother–father bonds seem to interfere with unmarried fathers' positive involvement with their children, whereas positive intrafamilial relationships appear to support greater involvement by fathers (Coley & Chase-Lansdale, 1997; Furstenberg, 1995; Furstenberg & Harris, 1993). Mother–father relations also mediate the relationship between father–child contact and child functioning (Amato & Rezac, 1994). Although most research on young fathers, like work with broader samples of unmarried men, tends to focus on simplistic measures of fathers' involvement, such as visitation frequency and child support, new research is beginning to address more qualitative and psychological aspects of fathering and more expansive measures incorporating such constructs as paternal responsibility, types and frequency of interactions, and emotional relationships between fathers and children (Coley, in press; Coley & Chase-Lansdale, 1997). Intervention programs are also starting to address whether steps can be taken to increase the involvement of young fathers with their children.

Effects of Young Fathers on Children

Although many questions remain unanswered concerning the quality and extent of father–child bonds in families of young mothers, even more remains unknown about how such relations affect children. In a 20-year follow-up of children of the Baltimore Study teenage mothers, Furstenberg and Harris (1993) found that for adolescents who lived with their biological fathers or stepfathers, those with strong attachments showed better educational, behavioral, and emotional functioning than adolescents with weak paternal bonds. In contrast, having highly involved fathers early on who then decreased their involvement or having poor relationships with fathers were more detrimental than having no relationship at all. A myriad of questions remain concerning young fathers and their children, including how fathers' availability, involvement, and interactions with their children affect child development.

Psychological Functioning

The psychological functioning of young fathers is another area that has been almost completely ignored in research. Little is known about the psychological predictors of adolescent fatherhood, except that adolescent fathers, in comparison with nonfathers, tend to be more accepting of teenage pregnancy and of abortion (B. E. Robinson, 1988). The impact of young fatherhood on the fathers themselves has also received scant attention, although teenage fathers, like teenage mothers, seem to have unrealistic expectations and difficulties adjusting to teenage parenthood (B. E. Robinson, 1988). The effects of early fatherhood on male adolescents' emotional functioning is clearly deserving of further attention, especially as new welfare and child support laws are likely to increase fathers' active participation and roles in parenthood.

Involvement and Impact of Grandmothers

Effects of Grandmothers' Involvement on Young Mothers

Research on adolescent parenthood is moving from a field where teenage mothers and their children were studied relatively context-free to one in which context, including family, race, socioeconomic status, and neighborhood, is often taken into account and directly addressed. One particular area in which this change is obvious is that of three-generational family systems. A number of recent research studies have carefully considered the roles that grandmothers[3] play in coparenting, housing, and supporting young mothers and children and how these activities, in turn, affect family functioning (East & Felice, 1996; Spieker & Bensley, 1994; Unger & Cooley, 1992). For example, through extensive observational and interview information from three-generational families, Wakschlag et al. (1996) determined young mothers' individuation, that is, autonomy from and communication with grandmothers, to be the most important aspect of mother–grandmother relations in predicting positive parenting practices, especially for noncoresiding adolescent mothers. Relatedly, Apfel and Seitz (1991) determined a pattern of shared child rearing in which grandmothers aided their daughters and modeled appropriate parenting behaviors (but neither disengaged nor took total control of parenting responsibilities) was most appropriate for providing young mothers with both the support and the autonomy they needed to effectively assume healthy primary parental responsibility.

In addition, recent studies on the effects of coresidence have provided somewhat surprising findings. Although earlier research indicated that coresidence was protective for teenage mothers and their children, at least during the early years of the children's lives (Furstenberg et al., 1987; Horwitz et al., 1991a), newer studies disagree. In research with three-generational African American families with three-year-old children, Chase-Lansdale et al. (1994) found that both mothers' and grandmothers' parenting practices were of lower quality (less supportive and authoritative, more negative and disengaged) when young mothers coresided with grandmothers. In families where mothers were in their early teens when they gave birth, however, coresidence predicted warmer and more positive parenting by grandmothers. Similarly, East and Felice (1996) found that coresidence among adolescent mothers and grandmothers was linked with higher mother–grandmother conflict and poorer child functioning. From this still sparse research base, it appears that teenage mothers, at least older teenagers, may provide the most effective parenting and their children function best when they live apart from the grandmothers but receive high levels of grandmother support or child care (East & Felice, 1996; Spieker & Bensley, 1994). These findings present important implications for new welfare policies that require teenage mothers to reside at home to receive welfare benefits. The implications of forced coresidence should be a top priority for research (Gordon, Chase-Lansdale, Matjasko, & Brooks-Gunn, 1997).

Effects on Grandmothers

Teenage parenthood also can directly affect grandmothers. Early entry into grandmotherhood and coresidence with grandchildren can create difficulties for grandmothers, who often provide scarce monetary resources, time, and emotional support to daughters and grandchildren, thus leaving little time and energy for their own challenges and tasks (Burton, 1990; Burton & Bengtson, 1985). More work is needed to understand the effects of these experiences on grandmothers (who are often just recovering from early parenthood themselves; Chase-Lansdale et al., 1991) and to address long-term functioning and life-course pathways of young grandmothers.

Intervention Programs

As public and political attention has become increasingly focused on teenage child-bearing, efforts to prevent the occurrence of teenage pregnancy and to ameliorate its consequences have proliferated. Several detailed reviews on teenage pregnancy prevention and intervention programs are available (e.g., Frost & Forrest, 1995; Kirby, 1994; Maynard, 1995; Miller, Card, Paikoff, & Peterson, 1992; Miller & Paikoff, 1992); here, we cover only the most significant new programs and issues and then turn to policy considerations.

Sexuality and Pregnancy Reduction Programs

Programs aimed at delaying or reducing sexual activity have taken a number of tactics: providing knowledge of sexual reproduction and access to contraceptives; reinforcing values and teaching abstinence; building decision-making and social skills; and increasing other life options (Maynard, 1995; Miller et al., 1992). Programs most successful in delaying sexual activity and increasing contraceptive use among adolescents generally contain a two-pronged approach of (a) teaching that abstinence is best for preteens and young adolescents and (b) providing information and access to contraceptives for older teens (Frost & Forrest, 1995). Other key program elements include developing clear and specific program goals, appropriately targeting services by developmental and experience level, and providing comprehensive services with a variety of components (see Frost & Forrest, 1995; Kirby, 1994; Maynard, 1995; Miller et al., 1992; Miller & Paikoff, 1992).

Among high-risk teenagers, comprehensive health-oriented services seem to be the most promising avenue for decreasing the rate of pregnancy. For example, one of the most successful programs to date, the Johns Hopkins Pregnancy Prevention Program, incorporated comprehensive medical care and contraceptive services, social services, and parenting education in a school-linked, coordinated system. This program postponed the age of sexual onset; increased contraception use; reduced the frequency of sex; and, most strikingly, reduced the pregnancy rate by 30% while comparison school rates rose by 58% (Hardy & Zabin, 1991).

Another success is the Teen Outreach Program, which focuses on enhancing social development among adolescents through structured volunteer community service combined with classroom discussions on future life choices, careers, and relationships (see Allen et al., 1997). This program is based on a developmentally oriented approach that addresses the broader psychological processes underlying all adolescent problem behaviors (of which early sexuality and pregnancy are just two examples), with the expectation that improved social competence and connections to adults will lead to enhanced psychological functioning and decreased problem behaviors (Donovan, Jessor, & Costa, 1988). A national evaluation found significantly lower rates of sexual intercourse (as well as school suspension and course failure) among adolescents in the program as compared with controls (Allen et al., 1997). Although the success of the Teen Outreach Program illustrates the importance of psychological processes, more work is needed to see if the program is equally effective in persistently poor neighborhoods and if program effects endure over time.

Thus, a few recent interventions have shown significant progress in efforts to delay sexual initiation, increase contraceptive use, and decrease pregnancy among adolescents. However, a great many programs are unsuccessful, and there are numerous avenues for improvement. For example, many school-based programs deal only with abstinence and are not allowed to discuss contraceptive choices, a narrow focus that has been shown to have little measurable effect on reducing sexual activity or pregnancy for most groups of adolescents (Kirby, 1994). Nevertheless, in 1996, the U.S. Congress allocated $250 million to fund abstinence-only programs over the next five years (Illinois Caucus for Adolescent Health, 1997). Clearly, a greater commitment is needed to funding scientifically rigorous evaluations of programs and replications of those that are most successful.

Programs for Parenting Teenagers

Intervention programs that target parenting teenagers in an effort to build their human and social capital and to improve their goals and life chances also have had predominantly disappointing results. Many of these programs specifically target teenage parents on welfare or those who have dropped out of school, and these programs often include an impressive array of services such as education and job training, free child care and transportation, and other support services. A number of programs have increased participants' educational attainment, but most of this increase has been in achievement of a GED, rather than a high school completion or a college education. In addition, few programs have increased teenage mothers' rates of employment or earnings or decreased their use of welfare, and some have experienced increases in repeat pregnancies and births (see Maynard, 1995, for a review). However, results may improve in future years, as the effects of the interventions have time to mature.

Why are the results of these interventions so disappointing? First, the young mothers whom these programs serve are often multiply disadvantaged. In addition, to being young parents and living in poverty, these teenagers often lack basic educational skills. For example, the Teenage Parent Welfare Demonstration found that one third of its adolescents had reading skills below the sixth-grade level (Maynard, 1995; Quint, Polit, Bos, & Cave, 1994). Such low basic academic skills often prohibit adolescent mothers from accessing job training and further educational services. Participants with higher education or skills at entry generally benefit more from such programs (Warrick, Christianson, Walruff, & Cook, 1993). Second, although programs attempt to coordinate a multitude of services, the services themselves are often of low quality or have requirements, such as minimum educational standards, that the teenagers do not meet.

A striking and disturbing commonality in almost all of these programs and interventions is their inattention to the children of teenage mothers. Although most programs presumably believe that by aiding the prospects of teenage mothers, they will in turn aid the outcomes of their children, very few programs or evaluations directly address this, either through services specifically for children or evaluations of program effects on children (New Chance is an exception; Polit, 1989; Quint, Musick, & Ladner, 1994). Thus there is very little information about whether intervention programs, especially welfare reform programs (which often include sanctions on welfare grants that could seriously limit children's access to adequate food, shelter, and clothing: Long, Gueron, Wood, Fisher, & Fellerath, 1996; Maynard, 1995), might negatively or positively affect children's development, an urgent question in this era of policy changes.

Summary

Numerous lessons can be derived from the plethora of intervention programs assessed to date. One is the need to direct programs to the developmental needs of the participants and to intervene at multiple points in time. For example, programs that promote abstinence have the best response with youth who are virgins at the start of the program, whereas contraceptive information is most useful for teenagers who are beginning or at least thinking about sexual activity. Second, stronger links between services for mothers and children are needed (Chase-Lansdale et al., 1991; Smith, 1995). Third, programs for children of adolescent mothers should go beyond infancy and the preschool years. Although existing research indicates more negative outcomes for older versus younger children of teenager mothers, this finding is not reflected in child-oriented services. Fourth, programmatic perspectives do not take a family systems approach. For example, very few services include fathers or other family members nor directly target grandmothers or other primary caregivers.

Policy Implications: A Focus on Welfare Reform

The most relevant and compelling current policy issue related to teenage pregnancy is welfare reform. The passage of the Personal Responsibility and Work Opportunity Reconciliation Act of 1996 is an extraordinary event in U.S. social policy toward impoverished children and their families, especially adolescent mothers and their offspring. This unprecedented antipoverty legislation stems, in part, from long-standing concern on the part of the public and policymakers that the former welfare system caused families to rely on government cash aid rather than to seek employment and become financially self-sufficient. However, it was the intersection of this concern regarding welfare dependency with reactions to high rates of nonmarital and adolescent childbearing that truly galvanized support for the 1996 legislation.

Given these concerns, the new welfare legislation was designed specifically to address adolescent and out-of-wedlock pregnancies and births. Because the majority of teenage mothers use welfare at some point during the early years of their children's lives and often use it as their major source of support for long periods, these changes are likely to have far-reaching effects in this population. The main provisions of the bill that are likely to have a large impact on young mothers are as follows: (a) Entitlement to cash welfare benefits is abolished; (b) families can receive benefits for no longer than five years over their lifetimes (shorter at state discretion; longer if states use their own funds); (c) recipients are required to work 20–30 hours per week after two years of TANF receipt; (d) minor mothers are required to live with a parent or a legal guardian and to stay in school; and (e) mothers are required to identify the fathers of their children and to cooperate with child support enforcement. States also may impose a family cap, that is, give no additional money for children born while the mothers are on welfare (Leven-Epstein, 1996; U.S. House of Representatives, 1996).

Each of these provisions is likely to affect young mothers. First, as many teenage mothers receive welfare for 10 years or more (Bane & Ellwood, 1986), time limits present a major challenge, and an economic recession may lead states to close down eligibility for new recipients of public aid. The positive argument behind welfare reform for adolescent mothers is largely an economic one: With a time-limited opportunity to raise children at home with governmental support, female adolescents will no longer have monetary incentives for pregnancy and disincentives for employment or marriage. Similarly, school and work requirements may provide a necessary incentive to aid some young mothers in finishing their education and obtaining employment, possibly leading to improved self-esteem and better psychological functioning and, thus, the ability to provide better parenting to their children. Opponents of welfare reform argue that mothers who enter the workforce or stay in school may have difficulty locating quality child care and may experience added stress from increased time demands. For other mothers who are unable to acquire stable jobs, their families thus could slide deeper into poverty, possibly inducing homelessness or increases in child abuse and neglect.

The implications of the new coresidency requirement were discussed above. It is possible that forced coresidency may increase tensions between some mothers and grandmothers and lead to poorer parenting, especially for older teenagers. Finally, the provisions concerning fathers will increase the number of legally recognized father–child relationships and possibly will increase fathers' monetary contributions to their children and also may improve the amount of interaction and the emotional bonds between fathers and their children. However, for some women and children, fathers may be a destructive presence. It is also possible that these increased paternal demands may actually decrease fathers' contributions and presence by interfering with private parental agreements.

The intense focus on teenage mothers and out-of-wedlock births in the new legislation is evidenced by several other provisions. Up to five states per year will each receive a $20-million "bonus" if they show a decline in both "illegitimacy" and abortion rates (U.S. House of Representatives, 1996, p. 15). As mentioned previously, substantial funds have been set aside for new abstinence education programs for adolescents. However, no TANF funds are targeted for family planning or other types of programs to prevent teenage pregnancy (Leven-Epstein, 1996).

Overall, the new policies are likely to produce significant changes in the lives of many teenage mothers and their children. The direction and meaning of these changes are unknown at this time because the new programs are just beginning to be implemented. It is likely that effects will not be simple and unidirectional but rather that subsets of mothers will react in different ways. For example, for young mothers with high school degrees and work experience, the benefit changes and time limits may provide the needed incentive to obtain and maintain stable employment. Mothers with low education skills and poor functioning or with other family problems such as a disabled child may have great difficulty maintaining stable employment and thus may suffer a substantial loss in income, as the research to date has suggested (Long et al., 1996; Maynard, 1995). Finally, disturbingly little attention has been paid to the possible effects of welfare reform on the children of adolescent mothers; these effects may be substantial (cf. Chase-Lansdale & Brooks-Gunn, 1995).

Conclusion

The most striking conclusion to be drawn from this review of basic and applied research, evaluation studies, and program and policy implications concerning teenage pregnancy and parenthood is that a strong psychological perspective is lacking, in particular, a perspective that emphasizes development. Psychologists have an extremely important role to play in this broad field. Understanding and documenting normative sexual development and behavior is well underway, but much more extensive psychological research is needed to examine the antecedents, correlates, and consequences of teenage pregnancy and childbearing. Currently, the central discourse addressing the causes and consequences of teenage pregnancy—including widely accepted ideas for reducing nonmarital births and requiring young mothers to be self-sufficient—is based on an economic model, namely, that the primary reasons adolescents become pregnant are financial. To ensure that the crucial psychological factors surrounding adolescent pregnancy and parenthood are better understood and accorded their proper role, psychologists must forge a stronger presence in research paradigms, methods, interventions, and policy settings.

Notes

1. Throughout this article, we use the term *Whites* to refer to non-Hispanic Caucasians and the term *Hispanics* to refer to those of any race.
2. There is also great variation within Hispanic subgroups. For example, in 1989, 22% of all births to Puerto Ricans were to women under the age of 20, whereas teen births accounted for 17% of Mexican American births, 8% of Central and South American births in the United States, and 7% of Cuban American births.
3. In this article, we use the term *grandmother* to refer to the biological mother or the mother-figure of the teenage mother.

References

Abma, J., Chandra, A., Mosher, W., Peterson, L., & Piccinino, L. (1997). Fertility, family planning, and women's health: New data from the 1995 National Survey of Family Growth. *Vital Health Statistics, 23* (19). Hyattsville, MD: National Center for Health Statistics.

Alan Guttmacher Institute. (1994). *Sex and America's teenagers.* New York: Author.

Allen, J. P., Philliber, S., Herrling, S., & Kuperminc, G. P. (1997). Preventing teen pregnancy and academic failure: Experimental evaluation of a developmentally based approach. *Child Development, 64,* 729–742.

Amato, P. R., & Rezac, S. J. (1994). Contact with nonresidential parents, interparental conflict, and children's behavior. *Journal of Family Issues, 15,* 191–207.

Apfel, N. H., & Seitz, V. (1991). Four models of adolescent mother–grandmother relationships in Black inner-city families. *Family Relations, 40,* 421–429.

Astone, N. M. (1993). Are adolescent mothers just single mothers? *Journal of Research on Adolescence, 3,* 353–372.

Bane, M. J., & Ellwood, D. T. (1986). Slipping into and out of poverty: The dynamics of spells. *Journal of Human Resources, 21,* 1–23.

Benasich, A. A., & Brooks-Gunn, J. (1996). Enhancing maternal knowledge and child-rearing concepts: Results from an early intervention program. *Child Development, 67,* 1186–1205.

Benn, R., & Saltz, E. (1989, April). *The effects of grandmother support on teen parenting and infant attachment patterns within the family.* Paper presented at the meeting of the Society for Research in Child Development, Kansas City, MO.

Bennett, N. G., Bloom, D. E., & Miller, C. K. (1995). The influence of nonmarital child-bearing on the formation of first marriages. *Demography, 32,* 47–62.

Boyner, D., & Fine, D. (1992). Sexual abuse as a factor in adolescent pregnancy and child maltreatment. *Family Planning Perspectives, 24,* 4–11.

Brewster, K. L., Billy, J. O. G., & Grady, W. R. (1993). Social context and adolescent behavior: The impact of community on the transition to sexual activity. *Social Forces, 71,* 713–740.

Brien, M. J., & Willis, R. J. (1997). Costs and consequences for the fathers. In R. A. Maynard (Eds.), *Kids having kids: Economic costs and social consequences of teen pregnancy* (pp. 95–144). Washington, DC: Urban Institute Press.

Brooks-Gunn, J., & Chase-Lansdale, P. L. (1995). Adolescent parenthood. In M. H. Bornstein (Ed.), *Handbook of parenting: Vol. 3. Status and social conditions of parenting* (pp. 113–149). Mahwah, NJ: Erlbaum.

Brooks-Gunn, J., & Furstenberg, F. F., Jr. (1986). The children of adolescent mothers. Physical, academic, and psychological outcomes. *Developmental Review, 6,* 224–151.

Burton, L. (1990). Teenager childbearing as an alternative life-course strategy in multi-generation Black families. *Human Nature, 1,* 123–143.

Burton, L., & Bengtson, V. (1985). Black grandmothers: Issues of timing and continuity of roles. In V. Bengtson & J. Robertson (Eds.), *Grandparenthood* (pp. 61–78). Newbury Park, CA: Sage.

Butler, J. R., & Burton, L. M. (1990). Rethinking teenage childbearing: Is sexual abuse a missing link? *Family Relations, 39,* 73–80.

Cameron, S., & Heckman, J. (1993). The nonequivalence of high school equivalents. *Journal of Labor Economics, 11,* 1–47.

Carter, S. L., Osofsky, J. D., & Hann, D. M. (1991). Speaking for the baby: A therapeutic intervention with adolescent mothers and their infants. *Infant Mental Health Journal, 12,* 291–301.

Chase-Lansdale, P. L., & Brooks-Gunn, J. (1994). Correlates of adolescent pregnancy and parenthood. In C. B. Fisher & R. M. Lerner (Eds.), *Applied developmental psychology* (pp. 207–236). New York: McGraw-Hill.

Chase-Lansdale, P. L., & Brooks-Gunn, J. (Eds.). (1995). *Escape from poverty: What makes a difference for children?* New York: Cambridge University Press.

Chase-Lansdale, P. L., & Brooks-Gunn, J., & Paikoff, R. (1991). Research and programs for adolescent mothers: Missing links and future promises. *Family Relations, 40,* 1–8.

Chase-Lansdale, P. L., Brooks-Gunn, J., & Zamsky, E. S. (1994). Young African-American multigenerational families in poverty: Quality of mothering and grandmothering. *Child Development, 65,* 373–393.

Chase-Lansdale, P. L., & Vinovskis, M. A. (1993). Adolescent pregnancy and child support. In R. Wollons (Ed.), *Children at risk in America* (pp. 202–229). Albany: State University of New York Press.

Chase-Lansdale, P. L., & Vinovskis, M. A. (1995). Whose responsibility? An historical analysis of the changing roles of mothers, fathers, and society. In P. L. Chase-Lansdale & J. Brooks-Gunn (Eds.), *Escape from poverty: What makes a difference for children?* (pp. 11–37). New York: Cambridge University Press.

Chase-Lansdale, P. L., Wakschlag, L. S., & Brooks-Gunn, J. (1995). A psychological perspective on the development of caring in children and youth: The role of the family. *Journal of Adolescence, 18,* 515–556.

Cherlin, A. C. (1992). *Marriage, divorce and remarriage* (Rev. and enlarged ed.), Cambridge, MA: Harvard University Press.

Cherlin, A. C., Kiernan, K. E., & Chase-Lansdale, P. L. (1995). Parental divorce in childhood and demographic outcomes in young adulthood. *Demography, 32,* 299–318.

Coley, R. L. (in press). Children's socialization experiences and functioning in single-mother households: The importance of fathers and other men. *Child Development.*

Coley, R. L., & Chase-Lansdale, P. L. (1997). *Young African American fathers' involvement in the birth and early years of their children.* Manuscript submitted for publication.

Cowan, C. P., & Cowan, P. A. (1992). *When partners become parents: The big life change for couples.* New York: Basic Books.

Culp, R. E., Appelbaum, M. I., Osofsky, D. D., & Levy, J. A. (1988). Adolescent and older mothers: Comparison between prenatal maternal variables and newborn interaction measures. *Infant Behavior and Development, 11,* 353–362.

Donovan, J. E., Jessor, R., & Costa, F. M. (1988). Syndrome of problem behavior in adolescence: A replication. *Journal of Consulting and Clinical Psychology, 56,* 762–765.

Duncan, G., & Brooks-Gunn, J. (Eds.). (1997). *Consequences of growing up poor.* New York: Russell Sage Foundation.

Duncan, G., Brooks-Gunn, J., & Klebanov, P. (1994). Economic deprivation and early-childhood development. *Child Development, 65,* 296–318.

East, P. L., & Felice, M. E. (1996). *Adolescent pregnancy and parenting: Findings from a racially diverse sample.* Mahwah, NJ: Erlbaum.

Elkind, D. (1978). Understanding the young adolescent. *Adolescence, 13,* 127–134.

Feldman, S., & Elliott, G. (Eds.). (1990). *At the threshold: The developing adolescent.* Cambridge, MA: Harvard University Press.

Foster, E. M., & Hoffman, S. D. (1996). Nonmarital childbearing in the 1980's: Assessing the importance of women 25 and older. *Family Planning Perspectives, 28,* 117–119.

Frost, J. J., & Forrest, J. D. (1995). Understanding the impact of effective teenage pregnancy prevention programs. *Family Planning Perspectives, 27,* 188–195.

Furstenberg, F. F., Jr. (1995). Fathering in the inner city: Paternal participation and public policy. In W. Marsiglio (Ed.), *Fatherhood: Contemporary theory, research, and social policy* (pp. 119–147). Thousand Oaks, CA: Sage.

Furstenberg, F. F., Jr., Brooks-Gunn, J., & Morgan, S. P. (1987). *Adolescent mothers in later life.* New York: Cambridge University Press.

Furstenberg, F. F., Jr., & Harris, K. M. (1993). When and why fathers matter: Impacts of father involvement on children of adolescent mothers. In R. I. Lerman & T. J. Ooms (Eds.), *Young unwed fathers* (pp. 117–138). Philadelphia: Temple University Press.

Furstenberg, F. F., Jr., Hughes, M. E., & Brooks-Gunn, J. (1992). The next generation: Children of teenage mothers grow up. In M. K. Rosenheim & M. F. Testa (Eds.), *Early parenthood* (pp. 113–135). New Brunswick, NJ: Rutgers University Press.

Furstenberg, F. F., Jr., & Teitler, J. O. (1994). Welfare benefits, economic opportunities, and out-of-wedlock births among Black teenage girls. *Demography, 27,* 519–535.

Geronimus, A. (1987). On teenage childbearing and neonatal mortality in the United States. *Population and Developmental Review, 13,* 245–280.

Geronimus, A. (1992). The weathering hypothesis and the health of African American women and infants: Evidence and speculations. *Ethnicity and Disease, 2,* 207–221.

Geronimus, A., & Korenman, S. (1992). The socioeconomic consequences of teen childbearing reconsidered. *Quarterly Journal of Economics, 107,* 1187–1214.

Goerge, R. M., & Lee, B. J. (1997). Abuse and neglect of the children. In R. A. Maynard (Ed.), *Kids having kids: Economic costs and social consequences of teen pregnancy* (pp. 205–230). Washington, DC: Urban Institute Press.

Gordon, R. A., Chase-Lansdale, P. L., Matjasko, J. L., & Brooks-Gunn, J. (1997). Young mothers living with grandmothers and living apart: How neighborhood and household contexts relate to multigenerational coresidence in African American families. *Applied Developmental Science, 1,* 89–106.

Grogger, J. (1997). Incarceration-related costs of early childbearing. In R. A. Maynard (Ed.), *Kids having kids: Economic costs and social consequences of teen pregnancy* (pp. 231–256). Washington, DC: Urban Institute Press.

Hann, D. M., Osofsky, J. D., Stringer, S. S., & Carter, S. S. (1988, April). *Affective contributions of adolescent mothers and infants to the quality of attachment.* Paper presented at the International Conference on Infant Studies. Washington, DC.

Hardy, J. B., & Zabin, L. S. (1991). *Adolescent pregnancy in an urban environment: Issues, programs, and evaluation.* Baltimore: Urban & Schwarzenberg.

Hauser, S. T. (1991). *Adolescents and their families.* New York: Free Press.

Hauser, S. T., & Bowlds, M. K. (1990). Stress, coping, and adaptation. In S. S. Feldman & G. R. Elliott (Eds.), *At the threshold: The developing adolescent* (pp. 388–413). Cambridge, MA: Harvard University Press.

Haveman, R. H., Wolfe, B., & Peterson, E. (1997). Children of early childbearers as young adults. In R. A. Maynard (Ed.), *Kids having kids: Economic costs and social consequences of teen pregnancy* (pp. 257–284). Washington, DC: Urban Institute Press.

Hayes, C. D. (Ed.). (1987). *Risking the future: Adolescent sexuality, pregnancy, and childbearing* (Vol. 1). Washington, DC: National Academy of Sciences Press.

Hoffman, S. D., Foster, E. M., & Furstenberg, F. F., Jr. (1993). Reevaluating the costs of teenage childbearing. *Demography, 30,* 1–13.

Horwitz, S. M., Klerman, L. V., Kuo, H. S., & Jekel, J. F. (1991a). Intergenerational transmissions of school-age parenthood. *Family Planning Perspectives, 23,* 168–172, 177.

Horwitz, S. M., Klerman, L. V., Kuo, H. S., & Jekel, J. F. (1991b). School-age mothers: Predictors of long-term education and economic outcomes. *Pediatrics, 87,* 862–867.

Hotz, V. J., McElroy, S. W., & Sanders, S. G. (1997). The costs and consequences of teenage childbearing for mothers. In R. A. Maynard (Ed.), *Kids having kids: Economic costs and social consequences of teen pregnancy* (pp. 55–94). Washington, DC: Urban Institute Press.

Hotz, V. J., Mullin, C. H., & Sanders, S. G. (in press). Bounding causal effects using data from a contaminated natural experiment: Analyzing the effects of teenage childbearing. *Review of Economic Studies.*

Illinois Caucus for Adolescent Health. (1997, May). *Issue brief.* Chicago: Author.

Keating, D. (1990). Adolescent thinking. In S. S. Feldman & G. R. Elliott (Eds.), *At the threshold: The developing adolescent* (pp. 54–92). Cambridge, MA: Harvard University Press.

Kirby, D. (1994). *Sex education in the schools.* Menlo Park, CA: Henry J. Kaiser Family Foundation.

Klepinger, D. H., Lundberg, S., & Plotnick, R. D. (1995). Adolescent fertility and the educational attainment of young women. *Family Planning Perspectives, 27,* 23–28.

Klerman, L. V. (1993, March). *Adolescent pregnancy and parenting: Controversies of the past and lessons for the future.* Gallagher Lecture presented at the annual meeting of the Society of Adolescent Medicine, Chicago.

Koppelman, J. (1994). *Reducing teen pregnancy and childbearing in America: What is the federal role?* (Issue Brief No. 654). Washington, DC: National Health Policy Forum.

Landry, D. J., & Forrest, J. D. (1995). How old are U.S. fathers? *Family Planning Perspectives, 27,* 159–165.

Lerman, R. I. (1993). A national profile of young unwed fathers. In R. I. Lerman & T. J. Ooms (Eds.), *Young unwed fathers* (pp. 27–51). Philadelphia: Temple University Press.

Leven-Epstein, J. (1996). *Teen parent provisions in the new law.* Washington, DC: Center for Law and Social Policy.

Lindberg, L. D., Sonenstein, F. L., Ku, L., & Martinez, G. (1997). Age differences between minors who give birth and their adult partners. *Family Planning Perspectives, 29,* 61–66.

Long, D., Gueron, J. M., Wood, R. G., Fisher, R., & Fellerath, V. (1996). *LEAP: Three year impacts of Ohio's welfare initiative to improve school attendance among teenage parents.* New York: Manpower Demonstration Research Corporation.

Luker, K. (1996). *Dubious conceptions: The politics of teenage pregnancy.* Cambridge, MA: Harvard University Press.

Luster, T., & Dubow, E. (1990). Predictors of the quality of the home environment that adolescent mothers provide for their school-aged children. *Journal of Youth and Adolescence, 19,* 475–495.

Marsiglio, W. (1986). Teenage fatherhood: High school completion and educational attainment. In A. B. Elster & M. E. Lamb (Eds.), *Adolescent fatherhood.* Hillsdale, NJ: Erlbaum.

Marsiglio, W. (1987). Adolescent fathers in the United States: Their initial living arrangements, marital experience and educational outcomes. *Family Planning Perspectives, 19,* 240–251.

Maynard, R. (1995). Teenage childbearing and welfare reform: Lessons from a decade of demonstration and evaluation research. *Children and Youth Services Reviews, 17,* 309–332.

McLoyd, V. C. (1990). The impact of economic hardship on Black families and children: Psychological distress, parenting, socioemotional development, *Child Development, 61,* 311–346.

Miller, B. C., Card, J. J., Paikoff, R. L., & Peterson, J. L. (Eds.). (1992). *Preventing adolescent pregnancy.* Newbury Park, CA: Sage.

Miller, B. C., & Paikoff, R. L. (1992). Comparing adolescent pregnancy prevention programs: Methods and results. In B. C. Miller, J. J. Card, R. L. Paikoff, & J. L. Peterson (Eds.), *Preventing adolescent pregnancy* (pp. 265–284). Newbury Park, CA: Sage.

Moore, K. A. (1986). Children of teen parents: Heterogeneity of outcomes. *Final Report to the Center for Population Research, NICHD.* Washington, DC: Child Trends.

Moore, K. A., Morrison, D. R., & Glei, D. A. (1995). Welfare and adolescent sex: The effects of family history, benefit levels, and community context. *Journal of Family and Economic Issues, 16,* 207–237.

Moore, K. A., Morrison, D. R., & Greene, A. D. (1997). Effects on the children born to adolescent mothers. In R. A. Maynard (Eds.), *Kids having kids: Economic costs and social consequences of teen pregnancy* (pp. 145–180). Washington, DC: Urban Institute Press.

Moore, K. A., Myers, D. E., Morrison, D. R., Nord, C. W., Brown, B., & Edmonston, B. (1993). Age at first childbirth and later poverty. *Journal of Research on Adolescence, 3,* 393–422.

Moore, K. A., & Peterson, J. (1989). *The consequences of teenage pregnancy: Final report.* Washington, DC: Child Trends.

Moore, K. A., & Waite, L. J. (1977). Early childbearing and educational attainment. *Family Planning Perspectives, 9,* 221–225.

Morrison, D. M. (1985). Adolescent contraceptive behavior: A review. *Psychological Bulletin, 98,* 538–568.

Musick, J. S. (1993). *Young, poor, and pregnant: The psychology of teenage motherhood.* New Haven, CT: Yale University Press.

Paikoff, R. L. (1995). Early heterosexual debut: Situations of sexual possibility during the transition to adolescence. *American Journal of Orthopsychiatry, 65,* 389–401.

Perez, S. M., & Duany, L. A. (1992). *Reducing Hispanic teenage pregnancy and family poverty: A replication guide.* Washington, DC: National Council of La Raza.

Peterson, A. C., & Crockett, L. J. (1992). Adolescent sexuality, pregnancy, and child rearing: Developmental perspectives. In M. K. Rosenheim & M. F. Testa (Eds.), *Early parenthood and coming of age in the 1990's* (pp. 34–45). New Brunswick, NJ: Rutgers University Press.

Polit, D. F. (1989). Effects of a comprehensive program for teenage parents: Five years after Project Redirection. *Family Planning Perspectives, 21,* 164–168, 187.

Quadrel, M. J., Fischhoff, B., & Davis, W. (1993). Adolescent (in)vulnerability. *American Psychologist, 48,* 102–116.

Quint, J. C., Musick, J. S., & Ladner, J. A. (1994). *Lives of promise, lives of pain: Young mothers after New Chance.* New York: Manpower Demonstration Research Corporation.

Quint, J. C., Polit, D. F., Bos, H., & Cave, G. (1994). *New Chance: Interim findings on a comprehensive program for disadvantaged young mothers and their children.* New York: Manpower Demonstration Research Corporation.

Robinson, B. E. (1988). Teenage pregnancy from the father's perspective. *American Journal of Orthopsychiatry, 58,* 46–51.

Robinson, W. L., Watkins-Ferrell, P., Davis-Scott, P., & Ruchs-Ross, H. (1993). Preventing teenage pregnancy. In D. S. Glenwick & L. A. Jason (Eds.), *Promoting health and mental health in children, youth, and families* (pp. 99–124). New York: Springer.

Rosenberg, H. M., Ventura, S. J., Maurer, J. D., Heuser, R. L., & Freedman, M. A. (1996). Births and deaths: United States, 1995. *Monthly Vital Statistics Report, 45* (3, Suppl. 2). Hyattsville, MD: National Center for Health Statistics.

Rosenheim, M. K., & Testa, M. F. (Eds.). (1992). *Early parenthood and coming of age in the 1990's.* New Brunswick, NJ: Rutgers University Press.

Scholl, T. O., Hediger, M. L., & Belsky, D. H. (1994). Prenatal care and maternal health during adolescent pregnancy: A review and meta-analysis. *Journal of Adolescent Health, 15,* 444–456.

Smith, S. (1995). *Two generation programs for families in poverty.* Norwood, NJ: Ablex.

Spieker, S. J., & Bensley, L. (1994). Roles of living arrangements and grandmother social support in adolescent mothering and infant attachment. *Developmental Psychology, 30,* 102–111.

Unger, D., & Cooley, M. (1992). Partner and grandmother contact in Black and White teen parent families. *Journal of Adolescent Health, 13,* 546–552.

United Nations. (1991). *Demographic yearbook.* New York: Author.

Upchurch, D. M., & McCarthy, J. (1990). The timing of first birth and high school completion. *American Sociological Review, 55,* 224–234.

Urdy, J. R., Kovenock, J., & Morris, N. M. (1996). Early predictors of nonmarital first pregnancy and abortion. *Family Planning Perspectives, 28,* 113–116.

U.S. Department of Health and Human Services. (1995). *Report to Congress on out-of-wedlock childbearing.* Hyattsville, MD: Author.

U.S. House of Representatives. (1996). *Personal Responsibility and Work Opportunity Reconciliation Act of 1996* (Conference Report H.R. 3734, Report No. 104-725). Washington, DC: U.S. Government Printing Office.

Ventura, S. J., Martin, J. A., Curtin, S. C., & Mathews, T. J. (1997). Report of final natality statistics, 1995. *Monthly Vital Statistics Report, 45*(11, Suppl. 2). Hyattsville, MD: National Center for Health Statistics.

Wakschlag, L. S., Chase-Lansdale, P. L., & Brooks-Gunn, J. (1996). Not just "ghosts in the nursery": Contemporaneous intergenerational relationships and parenting in young African-American families. *Child Development, 67,* 2131–2147.

Warrick, L., Christianson, J. B., Walruff, J., & Cook, P. C. (1993). Educational outcomes in teenage pregnancy and parenting programs: Results from a demonstration. *Family Planning Perspectives, 25,* 148–155.

Wasserman, G. A., Brunelli, S. A., & Rauh, V. A. (1990). Social supports and living arrangements of adolescent and adult mothers. *Journal of Adolescent Research, 5,* 54–66.

Wilson, W. J. (1987). *The truly disadvantaged: The inner city, the underclass, and public policy.* Chicago: University of Chicago Press.

Wilson, W. J. (1996). *When work disappears: The world of the new urban poor.* New York: Knopf.

Questions

1. What are the causes of teenage pregnancy?
2. What are the outcomes for mother and child of teenage parenthood?
3. What factors account for the negative outcomes for mother and child?
4. Is teenage pregnancy a problem?
5. What is the impact of fathers?
6. What are the costs and benefits of welfare reform for teenage mothers?
7. Are adolescents emotionally equipped to become parents?

References and Further Reading

Brooks-Gunn, J. & Chase-Lansdale, P. L. (1995). Adolescent parenthood. In M. H. Bornstein (Ed.) *Handbook of parenting: Status and social conditions of parenting* (Vol. 3) (pp. 113–149). Mahwah, NJ: Lawrence Erlbaum.

Burton, L. (1990). Teenage childbearing as an alternative life-course strategy in multi-generation black families. *Human Nature, 1,* 123–143.

Fraiberg, S. (1982). The mother and her infant. *Adolescent Psychiatry, 10,* 7–23.

Holz, V. J., McElroy, S.W., & Sanders, S. G. (1997). The costs and consequences of teenage childbearing for mothers. In R. A. Maynard (Ed.) *Kids having kids: Economic costs and social consequences of teen pregnancy* (pp. 55–94). Washington, DC: Urban Institute Press.

Chapter 15

Eating Disorders

The two most common forms of eating disorders that exist today are anorexia nervosa and bulimia nervosa. According to the *Diagnostic and Statistical Manual of Mental Disorders,* fourth edition (American Psychiatric Association, 1994), anorexia is diagnosed based on four criteria. First, there is a refusal to keep body weight at a normal level for one's height and age, and body weight drops to 15% below normal. Second, a person experiences an intense fear of gaining weight. Third, the experience of one's body image is distorted and an overemphasis is placed on body weight in self-evaluation. Finally, for women past puberty, at least three consecutive menstrual cycles have been missed. Bulimia is diagnosed based on five criteria. The first two criteria include recurrent episodes of binge eating and recurrent use of purging (vomiting, misuse of laxatives and diuretics), fasting, or excessive exercise to prevent weight gain. Third, binging and purging must take place on average at least twice a week over the course of three months. Fourth, one's self-evaluation is unduly influenced by body shape and weight. Finally, the symptoms of bulimia do not take place principally during occurrences of anorexia. While most adolescents will never fully meet the criteria for the diagnosis of either anorexia or bulimia (only 1% to 3% meet the diagnostic criteria), many adolescents meet some but not all of the diagnostic criteria and suffer from symptoms of disordered eating such as recurrent binge eating. (Smolak, Levine, & Striegel-Moore, 1996).

Eating disorders commonly begin at adolescence and are most prevalent among women. As one progresses from childhood to adolescence, awareness of societal gender role expectations increases (chapter 8). Puberty is associated with weight gain, and this weight gain puts girls at odds with cultural expectations that include unrealistic standards of thinness as criteria of attractiveness for women. The pressure to conform to the thin ideal, along with pubertal weight gain, may lead to body dissatisfaction, negative body images, and disordered eating in an attempt to reach this ideal.

Standards and attitudes about the body, however, have been found to differ by race, ethnicity, and sexual orientation, as has the incidence of eating disorders. African American women, for example, report higher ideal body weights than do white women, are less likely to report themselves to be overweight, and show less of a discrepancy between their actual and ideal body images than white women (Dawson, 1988; Molloy & Herzberger, 1998). African Americans have also shown a lower incidence of eating disorders, and it is African Americans who are successful in traditionally white domains who have been found to be at the greatest risk for eating disorders. Individuals outside the dominant culture may be less affected by its standards for thinness.

Many researchers believe that mass media contributes significantly to the prevalence of eating disorders, promoting standards for beauty that are unrealistic and dangerously thin (Levine & Smolak, 1996). Content analyses clearly demonstrate that the media (magazines, television programming, and advertising) presents images of thinness and standards of beauty that are artificially enhanced and virtually unattainable. Images of women in the media have changed over time, shifting toward a thinner ideal, and the number of articles in popular magazines about diet and exercise have increased over time (Levine & Smolak, 1996). These studies, however, provide no evidence that images in the media have an impact on viewers' self-concepts or eating behaviors. In a review of the literature on the impact of the media on eating disorders, Michael Levine and Linda Smolak conclude, "data from experimental studies in general provide precious little evidence that exposure . . . immediately increases body dissatisfaction in females who are not already processing the content in terms of well-established weight and shape concerns." (Levine & Smolak, 1996, p. 253). The effect of long-term, repeated exposure to media images has not been determined.

Eating disorders are multidetermined and depend upon a biological vulnerability, a psychological disposition, and a particular social climate. Researchers have looked at numerous individual factors that may predispose an adolescent to eating disorders, for example, personality dispositions such as perfectionism and low self-esteem, and internalization of societal messages about the importance of thinness and attractiveness to female success. They have also examined family and societal contributions. The readings in this chapter address societal changes over the course of this century that have increased pressure on women to be unrealistically thin (Reading 15.1). They also examine the cultural, psychological, physiological, and family factors that contribute to the development of eating disorders (Reading 15.2).

Additional Resources

References and Further Reading

Bergeron, S. M., & Senn, C. Y. (1998). Body image and sociocultural norms: A comparison of heterosexual and lesbian women. *Psychology of Women Quarterly, 22*(3), 385–401.

Dawson, D. (1988). Ethnic differences in female overweight: Data from the 1985 National Health Interview Survey. *American Journal of Public Health, 78,* 1326–1329.

Heinberg, L. J., & Thompson, J. K. (1995). Body image and televised images of thinness and attractiveness: A controlled laboratory investigation. *Journal of Social and Clinical Psychology, 4,* 325–338.

Levine, M. P., & Smolak, L. (1996). Media as a context for the development of disordered eating. In L. Smolak, M. P. Levine, & R. Striegel-Moore (Eds.) *The developmental psychopathology of eating disorders* (pp. 235–257). Mahwah, NJ: Lawrence Erlbaum.

Molloy, B. L., & Herzberger, S. D. (1998). Body image and self-esteem: A comparison of African-American and Caucasian women. *Sex Roles, 38*(7/8), 631–643.

Posavac, H. D., Posavac, S. S., & Posavac, E. J. (1998). Exposure to media images of female attractiveness and concern with body weight among young women. *Sex Roles, 38*(3/4), 187–201.

Smolak, L., Levine, M. P., & Striegel-Moore, R. (Eds.). (1996). *The developmental psychopathology of eating disorders.* Mahwah, NJ: Lawrence Erlbaum.

Striegel-Moore, R. H., & Cachelin, F. M. (1999). Body image concerns and disordered eating in adolescent girls: Risk and protective factors. In N. G. Johnson, M. C. Roberts, & J. Worell (Eds.) *Beyond appearance: A new look at adolescent girls* (pp. 85–108). Washington, DC: American Psychological Association.

Thompson, J. K., & Heinberg, L. J. (1999). The media's influence on body image disturbance and eating disorders: We've reviled them, now can we rehabilitate them? *Journal of Social Issues, 55*(2), 339–353.

Wiseman, C. V., Gray, J. J., Mosimann, J. E., & Ahrens, A. H. (1992). Cultural expectations of thinness in women: An update. *International Journal of Eating Disorders, 11,* 85–89.

On the Internet

http://AboutOurKids.org/mh/eating_frame.html

About Our Kids.org—Eating Disorders
This is the New York University Child Study Center Web site. It makes materials available for educational purposes to raise general awareness of mental health issues affecting children.

http://www.addictions.net/eating.htm

Addictions & More—Eating Disorders
Addictions & More maintains this Web site to provide information and education about ADD-ADHD and addictions, including eating disorders, teen substance abuse, and gambling.

http://www.apa.org/monitor/mar97/gender.html

Body-Image Problems Affect All Groups
This is the American Psychological Association Web site. This article is from the American Psychological Association publication, *The Monitor.*

http://eating-disorders.com/

The Center for Eating Disorders
This is the Web site of The Center for Eating Disorders at St. Joseph Medical Center in Towson, Maryland. The center provides comprehensive treatment

programs for anorexia and bulimia. The site provides information on eating disorders for educational purposes.

Joan Jacobs Brumberg, 1988

Modern Dieting

Joan Jacobs Brumberg, Ph.D., is a professor at Cornell University's Department of Human Development and Family Studies. She teaches American women's history, family history, and social history of medicine. She has written about the changing historical experience of adolescent girls in her books *Fasting Girls: A History of Anorexia Nervosa* (1988) and *The Body Project: An Intimate History of American Girls* (1998).

Anorexia today is a modern form of food-refusing behavior that has existed through the centuries. Women and girls have engaged in rigid control of appetite and food dating back to the medieval world (Brumberg, 1988). This is not to say that the fasting of medieval women could be traced to the same causes as anorexia or bulimia today. Appetite control takes on new meaning in different historical periods. The symptoms of and motivating factors for anorexia change with the changing sociocultural environment. Young women with anorexia provide a window into contemporary values. Joan Jacobs Brumberg argues that "From the vantage point of the historian, anorexia nervosa appears to be a secular addition to a new kind of perfectionism, one that links personal salvation to the achievement of an external body configuration rather than an internal spiritual state" (Brumberg, 1989, p. 7).

Americans became aware of anorexia in the 1970s when the popular press began to focus on the disease, and since that time cases of the disorder have been increasing. Although only a very small portion of the population may be diagnosed with anorexia, its prevalence on college campuses has been estimated at close to 20% (Brumberg, 1989). Anorexia is a disease that strikes primarily white females of higher socioeconomic status. Researchers have struggled to explain why young, attractive, affluent girls from well-educated and successful families should increasingly fall ill from this disorder, losing 15% of their original body weight with no known medical illness to precipitate that weight loss.

In the selection that follows, historian Joan Jacobs Brumberg examines the history of modern dieting and the changes that occurred over the first half of the twentieth century that have led to the centrality of dieting and appetite control in the lives of American women. She provides an account of the development of the fashion, cosmetic, and dieting industries and examines the pressures they have placed on women to attain unrealistic standards of thinness. She traces the shift to the increasingly slender ideal and argues that the imperative to diet has intensified as the ideal body size has become thinner and the slender figure has become a criterion for success and self-esteem for women.

Beauty and Guilt

Within the first two decades of the twentieth century, even before the advent of the flapper, the voice of American women revealed that the female struggle with weight was under way and was becoming intensely personal. As early as 1907 an *Atlantic Monthly* article described the reaction of a woman trying on a dress she had not worn for over a year: "The gown was neither more [n]or less than anticipated. But I . . . *the fault was on me* . . . I was more! Gasping I hooked it together. The gown was hopeless, and I . . . I am fat." (Italics added.)[1] While Progressive Era ideology fostered an expectation of personal responsibility for the body in both sexes, women began to internalize the responsibility for weight maintenance in ways that men did not. Although some people in the Victorian era subscribed to the doctrine that "satiety was a conviction of sin," a nineteenth-century woman whose body was large was generally not indicted for lack of self-control.[2] By the twentieth century, however, overweight in women was not only a physical liability, it was a character flaw and a social impediment.[3]

Early in the century elite American women began to take body weight seriously as fat became an aesthetic liability for those who followed the world of haute couture. Since the mid-nineteenth century wealthy Americans—the wives of J. P. Morgan, Cornelius Vanderbilt, and Harry Harkness Flagler, for instance—had traveled to Paris to purchase the latest creations from couturier collections such as those on view at Maison Worth on the famed rue de la Paix. The couturier was not just a dressmaker who made clothes for an individual woman; rather, the couturier fashioned "a look" or a collection of dresses for an abstraction—the stylish woman. In order to be stylish and wear couturier clothes, a woman's body had to conform to the dress rather than the dress to the body, as had been the case when the traditional dressmaker fitted each garment.[4]

In 1908 the world of women's fashion was revolutionized by Paul Poiret, whose new silhouette was slim and straight. Poiret's style, dubbed *le vague* because of its looseness, eliminated the wasp waist, the hips, and the derriere in favor of a high-waisted, small-breasted Empire line. Poiret's "restructuring" of the female body continued into the teens, when his collections featured long, narrow sheaths covered by tunics of different lengths. Almost immediately women of style began to purchase new kinds of undergarments that would make Poiret's look possible; for example, the traditional hourglass corset was cast aside for a rubber girdle to retract the hips.

After World War I the French continued to set the fashion standard for style-conscious American women. In 1922 Jeanne Lanvin's chemise, a straight frock with a simple bateau neckline, was transformed by Gabrielle Chanel into the uniform of the flapper. Chanel dropped the waistline to the hips and began to expose more of the leg: in 1922 she moved her hemlines to midcalf, and in 1926–27 the ideal hem was raised to just below the knee. In order to look good in Chanel's fashionable little dress, its wearer had to think not only about the appearance of her legs but about the smoothness of her form.[5] Women who wore the flapper uniform turned to flattening brassieres constructed of shoulder straps and a single band of material that encased the body from chest to waist. In 1914 a French physician commented on the revised dimensions of women's bodies: "nowadays it is not the fashion to be corpulent; the proper thing is to have a slight, graceful figure far removed from embonpoint, and *a fortiori* from obesity. For once, the physician is called upon to interest himself in the question of feminine aesthetics."[6]

The slenderized fashion image of the French was picked up and promoted by America's burgeoning ready-to-wear garment industry.[7] Stimulated by the popularity of the Gibson girl and the shirtwaist craze of the 1890s, ready-to-wear production in the United States accelerated in the first two decades of the twentieth century. Chanel's chemise dress was a further boon to the garment industry. Because of its simple cut, the chemise was easy to copy and produce, realities that explain its quick adoption as the uniform of the 1920s. According to a 1923 *Vogue,* the American ready-to-wear industry successfully democratized French fashion: "Today, the mode which originates in Paris is a factor in the lives of women of every rank, from the highest to the lowest."[8]

In order to market ready-to-wear clothing, the industry turned in the 1920s to standard sizing, an innovation that put increased emphasis on personal body size and gave legitimacy to the idea of a normative size range. For women, shopping for ready-to-wear clothes in the bustling department stores of the early twentieth century fostered heightened concern about body size.[9] With a dressmaker, every style was theoretically available to every body; with standard sizing, items of clothing could be identified as desirable, only to be rejected on the grounds of fit. (For women the cost of altering a ready-made garment was an "add-on"; for men it was not.) Female figure flaws became a source of frustration and embarrassment, not easily hidden from those who accompanied the shopper or from salesclerks. Experiences in department-store dressing rooms created a host of new anxieties for women and girls who could not fit into stylish clothing. In a 1924 testimonial for an obesity cure, a formerly overweight woman articulated the power of dress size in her thinking about dieting and about herself: "My heart seemed to beat with joy at the prospect of getting into one of the chic ready-made dresses at a store."[10]

Ironically, standard sizing created an unexpected experience of frustration in a marketplace that otherwise was offering a continually expansive opportunity for gratification via purchasable goods. Because many manufacturers of stylish women's garments did not make clothing in large sizes, heavy women were at the greatest disadvantage. In addition to the moral cachet of overweight, the standardization of garment production precluded fat women's participation in the mainstream of fashion.

This situation became worse as the century progressed. Fashion photography was professionalized, a development that paralleled the growth of modern advertising, and models became slimmer both to compensate for the distortions of the camera and to accommodate the new merchandising canon—modern fashion was best displayed on a lean body.[11]

The appearance in 1918 of America's first best-selling weight-control book confirmed that weight was a source of anxiety among women and that fat was out of fashion. *Diet and Health with a Key to the Calories* by Lulu Hunt Peters was directed at a female audience and based on the assumption that most readers wanted to lose rather than gain weight. "How anyone can want to be anything but thin is beyond my intelligence," wrote Peters, a Los Angeles physician and former chair of the Public Health Committee of the California Federation of Women's Clubs.[12] A devotee of scientific nutrition, Peters attempted to "stimulate . . . an interest in dietetics" and recommended books by nutritionists Mary Swartz Rose and Belle Wood-Comstock, as well as Wilbur Atwater's famous Department of Agriculture bulletin #142.

Peters was also a spokesperson for the new quantitative vocabulary. "You should know and also use the word calorie as frequently, or more frequently, than you use the words foot, yard, quart, gallon and so forth . . . Hereafter you are going to eat calories of food. Instead of saying one slice of bread, or a piece of pie, you will say 100 calories of bread, 350 calories of pie."[13]

Peters' book was popular because it was personal and timely. Her 1918 appeal was related to food shortages caused by the exigencies of the war in Europe. Peters told her readers that it was "more important than ever to reduce" and recommended the formation of local Watch Your Weight Anti-Kaiser Classes. "There are hundreds of thousands of individuals all over America who are hoarding food," she wrote. "They have vast amounts of this valuable commodity stored away in their own anatomy." In good-humored fashion Peters portrayed her own calorie counting as both an act of patriotism and humanitarianism:

> I am reducing and the money that I can save will help keep a child from starving . . . [I am explaining to my friends] that for every pang of hunger we feel we can have a double joy, that of knowing we are saving worse pangs in some little children, and that of knowing that for every pang we feel we lose a pound. A pang's a pound the world around we'll say.[14]

But Peters showed herself to be more than simply an informative and patriotic physician. Confessing that she once weighed as much as 200 pounds, the author also understood that heavy women were ashamed of their bulk and unlikely to reveal their actual weight. Peters observed that it was not a happy situation for fat women. "You are viewed with distrust, suspicion, and even aversion," she told her overweight readers.

Although she tried to make light of the hunger pains suffered by dieters and adorned her book with playful illustrations, Peters' point was clear: dieting was a lonely struggle that involved renunciation and psychological pain. For some women, such as herself, the struggle was for a lifetime. Although she was able to control her weight at 150 pounds, the author confessed it was not easy. "No matter how hard I work—no matter how much I exercise, no matter what I suffer," lamented Peters, "I will always have to watch my weight, I will always have to count my calories."[15]

Peters' book was among the first to articulate the new secular credo of physical denial: modern women suffered to be beautiful (thin) rather than pious. Peters' language and thinking reverberated with references to religious ideas of temptation and sin. For the modern female dieter, sweets, particularly chocolate, were the ultimate temptation. Eating chocolate violated the morality of the dieter and her dedication to her ideal, a slim body. Peters joked about her cravings ("My idea of heaven is a place with me and mine on a cloud of whipped cream") but she was adamant about the fact that indulgence must ultimately be paid for. "If you think you will die unless you have some chocolate creams [go on a] *debauch*," she advised. " 'Eat 10 or so' but then *repent* with a 50-calorie dinner of bouillon and crackers." (Italics added.)[16]

Although the damage done by chocolate creams could be mediated by either fasting or more rigid dieting, Peters explained that there was a psychological cost in yielding to the temptation of candy or rich desserts. Like so many modern dieters, Peters wrote about the issue of guilt followed by redemption through parsimonious eating: "Every supposed pleasure in sin [eating] will furnish more than its equivalent of pain [dieting]." But appetite control was not only a question of learning to delay gratification, it was also an issue of self-esteem. "You will be tempted quite frequently, and you will have to choose whether you will enjoy yourself hugely in the twenty minutes or so that you will be consuming the excess calories, or whether you will dislike yourself cordially for the two or three days you lose by your lack of will power." For Peters dieting had as much to do with the mind as with the body. "There is a great deal of psychology to reducing," she wrote astutely.[17] In fact, with the popularization of the concept of calorie counting, physical features once regarded as natural—such as appetite and body weight—were designated as objects of conscious control. The notion of weight control through restriction of calories implied that overweight resulted solely from lack of control; to be a fat woman constituted a failure of personal morality.[18]

The tendency to talk about female dieting as a moral issue was particularly strong among the popular beauty experts, that is, those in the fashion and cosmetics industry who sold scientific advice on how to become and stay beautiful. Many early-twentieth-century beauty culturists, including Grace Peckham Murray, Helena Rubenstein, and Hazel Bishop, studied chemistry and medical specialties such as dermatology.[19] The creams and lotions they created, as well as the electrical gadgets they promoted, were intended to bring the findings of modern chemistry and physiology to the problem of female beauty. Nevertheless, women could not rely entirely on scientifically achieved results. The beauty experts also preached the credo of self-denial: to be beautiful, most women must suffer.

Because they regarded fat women as an affront to their faith, some were willing to criminalize as well as medicalize obesity. In 1902 *Vogue* speculated, "To judge by the efforts of the majority of women to attain slender and sylph-like proportions, one would fancy it a crime to be fat." By 1918 the message was more distinct: "There is one crime against the modern ethics of beauty which is unpardonable; far better it is to commit any number of petty crimes than to be guilty of the sin of growing fat."

By 1930 there was no turning back. Helena Rubenstein, a high priestess of the faith, articulated in *The Art of Feminine Beauty* the moral and aesthetic dictum that would govern the lives of subsequent generations of women: "An abundance of fat is something repulsive and not in accord with the principles that rule our conception of the beautiful."[20]

Success and Security

In the 1920s the imperative to diet intensified not only because of medical advice and the flapper style but because of major social changes in the lives of women. In the wake of World War I, American women experienced something of a revolution in their social and political status, a revolution not at all dissimilar to what we have experienced since the 1960s. In both cases, the 1920s and more recently, affluence accompanied social change. In both cases, cultural messages about reducing the body accelerated. This history confirms the thesis of anthropologist Mary Douglas that rapid social change and disintegrating social boundaries stimulate both greater external and greater internal control of the physical body. In short, disorder in the body politic has implications for the individual body.[21]

For women the 1920s were a time of heady optimism and the perception of many new personal and material choices. Prosperity was in the air. In addition to gaining the franchise in 1920, more women worked outside their homes. More American girls were attending high school, as colleges and universities admitted ever larger numbers of women students (who, as a group, were more ethnically diverse than ever before). Advertising and motion pictures stimulated the development of a new mass culture that set styles and sold goods, especially among youth. And many young women—delighted with the prospect of greater personal freedom and more fun—discarded the sexual baggage of the Victorians and pronounced themselves travelers on a new road to increased sexual pleasure and equality with men.[22]

In the fast-paced environment of the 1920s, most women wanted a slim body because of the positive messages it conveyed. Such a body was not only an instrument of fashion, it was also a statement about the social and sexual orientation of the individual. A woman with a slender body distinguished herself from the plump Victorian matron and her old-fashioned ideals of nurturance, service, and self-sacrifice. The body of the "new woman" was a sign of modernity that marked her for more than traditional motherhood and domesticity.

Ironically, the new slim body, with its small breasts and narrow hips, symbolized increased rather than diminished sexuality. Although doctors worried about the consequences of dieting for women's reproductive potential, the new woman pursued svelteness in the name of her sexuality. A lithe figure was an emblem that also marked a woman as separate from the sex-segregated or homosocial world of the Victorians and from the notion of woman's asexuality, a characteristic associated with prudish married women as well as unmarried feminists.[23] Sexual interest and experimentation were novel luxuries, related in part to the availability of birth control, particularly the diaphragm and the condom.[24] In a world where sexuality and reproduction could be separated, a slender body and the willingness to wear more revealing clothes were taken as signs of increased sexual confidence, freedom, and enjoyment. A svelte female figure became, for the first time, the ultimate sign and symbol of heterosexual interest and success.

In the early twentieth century no individual better expressed this idea than Annette Kellerman, the young Australian swimmer who became a star in American silent films.[25] In the new moving pictures, form and grace of movement were particularly important, making slenderness a considerable asset. (Other early female film stars such as Irene Dunne, Clara Bow, Louise Brooks, Billie Burke, and Lillian and Dorothy Gish were all quite slim.) Kellerman's celebrity status was based not only on her swimming (she won the championship of New South Wales and set the record for women's efforts at the English Channel) but on the perfection of her body and her willingness to display it. In the 1916 film *Daughter of the Gods* she appeared nearly au naturel in a series of scenes in vine-covered pools, on coral reefs, amid powerful rapids, and in the fanciful harem of a sultan's palace. What the *New York Times* called Kellerman's "novelties of nudity and natation" spoke to a variety of different interests and symbolized American women's new freedom in manners and morals.[26]

Kellerman was proud of her 5-foot-3¾-inch, 137-pound body. She alleged that Dudley A. Sargent, director of physical training at Harvard, thought her figure "nearer the correct proportions than any he had ever seen." Although Kellerman's weight and measurements (35-26-37) seem quite ample by today's standards, she was an avid campaigner against fat. In *Physical Beauty,* a statement of her own personal beauty code, Kellerman declared:

> "Fat" is a short and ugly word. But "stoutness," "plumpness," "fleshiness," "obesity" and "embonpoint" are only softpedal euphemisms. It is fat just the same, and just as clumsy, as unhealthy, as ugly and awkward spelled with ten letters as with three.[27]

Just as the scientific beauty experts did, Kellerman subscribed to the credo of self-denial, proclaiming "eternal vigilance . . . the price of health and beauty." [28] In order to keep a careful focus on the body, Kellerman advocated daily exercise in the nude before a full-length mirror.

An advocate of the physical culture movement, Kellerman was always more than willing to tell the women's magazines how she used swimming to reach bodily perfection, and she wrote many detailed articles on why and how girls should learn to swim. In this respect she and the movement she represented were important advocates of a healthy female athleticism.[29] Kellerman's magazine lessons always included some version of the following: "Don't wear any more clothes than you need. They hinder your movements and make the body much heavier." Kellerman's popular advocacy of women's swimming had an unintended but critical consequence: by encouraging women to disrobe for more efficient swimming Kellerman set the stage for the transformation of the female bathing suit into an icon of sexual attractiveness.[30] Beginning in the 1920s, female beauty pageants made bathing suit competitions a centerpiece of their contests, a procedure that underscored the primacy of the body in the definition of feminine good looks. Kellerman reinforced this priority when she declared the figure "even more essential" than the face.[31]

Intensity of interest in the female body was rooted in social insecurity as well as in the physical culturists' credo of self-affirmation. Heterosexual relationships in the 1920s were in transition, much as they are today. Pursuit of the body beautiful was linked to a major dimension of modern social change, the rising rate of divorce. By the late 1920s marital dissolutions were obviously on the rise, a fact that reflected changing expectations of marriage.[32] Personal happiness and satisfaction had replaced duty and sacrifice as the glue that made marriage work; couples came to expect both romance and sexuality in their experience of conjugal love. These attitudinal developments underwrote Annette Kellerman's claim that a great deal of contemporary divorce was the result of the married woman's inattention to her physique. "We should find that in 7 cases out of 10 [cases] the wife had lost her physical charm for her husband," she wrote.[33]

Firmer control of the female body was Kellerman's answer to increasing family insecurity. Instead of challenging the new marital ethic and the heightened legitimacy it gave to male sexual prerogatives, Kellerman urged women to improve themselves by spending more time in the cultivation of good looks. To charges of self-indulgence, Kellerman adamantly replied: "The old lie that the cultivation of feminine beauty is wicked wrecks more homes than poverty, and kills more loves than downright immorality. The new and true gospel of a woman's right to remain beautiful will save more marriages than all the anti-divorce sermons ever preached."[34] Kellerman was not alone in her emphasis on the physical side of marriage. Films by Cecil B. DeMille, such as *Old Wives for New* (1918), and *Why Change Your Wife?* (1920), presented visual tableaux contrasting the frumpy wife with the one who understood appearance as the key to modern marriage.[35] Women were told, often by other women, that their failure to meet the sexual challenge of modern marriage led to divorce court.

Annette Kellerman articulated a basic precept of twentieth-century femininity: to get and hold a man, women needed to preserve their youth and their physical attractiveness. Married women were no longer exempt from such concerns. Traditional wifely virtues, such as excellence in domesticity and a kind heart, could no longer guarantee the success of a marriage—but a beautiful body could. Kellerman, declared, "[Beauty] is a more potent sermon on 'How to Keep Your Husband' than all the issues of The Homely Ladies' Journal which tries to answer that question with a lot of drivel about 'tact' and 'sympathy' and 'warmed slippers' and 'attractive dishes from leftovers.'"[36] In effect, by the 1920s outward appearance was more important than inner character because allure had replaced spirituality as woman's "shining ornament."[37]

For individual women this innovative cultural prescription was a decidedly mixed blessing. Although it held out the promise of sexual liberation, it also generated a psychological dilemma that echoed Calvinist religious struggles: How could salvation (that is, beauty) be achieved? Was beauty a state of being, achievable through self-exertion and denial, or was it a commodity, available to be bought? If beauty could be purchased, then consumption was a form of self-improvement rather than self-indulgence. If beauty could be earned, then a righteous woman could achieve it through her "good works": careful attention to complexion, hair, and clothing as well as healthful exercise and, most important, restrained eating.[38]

Not all women could handle these pressures with equanimity.[39] Many internalized the notion that the size and shape of the body was a measure of self-worth; many believed that the process of losing weight would bring spiritual as well as physical transformation. By the 1920s calorie counting was everywhere on the increase and some women turned to bulimic behavior. At the Adult Weight Conference of 1926, a well-known physician reported, "I discovered that many of our flappers have mastered the art of eating their cake and yet not having it, inducing regurgitation, after a plentiful meal, either by drugs or mechanical means."[40] Apparently many women took frequent "high colonic irrigations" (enemas), cathartics, and iodine in the effort to reduce. It was evident that the new woman faced a complicated problem in how to relate to the beauty imperatives of a modern capitalist society. Because weight control was regarded as so important to beauty, women came to feel increasingly at odds with their appetite.

Younger and Thinner

Because of the exigencies of the Great Depression and World War II, women in the 1930s and 1940s involved themselves with major external, collective issues of survival, protection, and work. The canon of style in these decades continued to project a slim image, yet dieting seemed an inappropriate and silly preoccupation in the midst of scarcity and a compelling national emergency.[41] Popular literature on how to reduce never entirely disappeared during this era, but the growth of the diet industry was slowed by other, more pressing national and local concerns, including problems of food shortage and distribution. During the war women who waited in line for a weekly ration of butter and sugar were more likely to savor than to reject items made from these hard-to-get ingredients.

Despite the political and economic emergency that directed attention away from the individual body, the 1940s saw a subtle but important change in the history of modern dieting. Beginning in that decade adolescent girls, known as subdebs, were targeted as an audience for diet information and literature. The post–World War II popularization of adolescent weight control, a phenomenon that set the stage for our contemporary difficulties with anorexia nervosa, had two sources: parents and physicians newly alert to childhood obesity as a pathology, and commercial interests intent on selling to girls the same beauty concerns (and products) that absorbed the attention of their mothers.

Before 1940 the overweight child was mentioned only occasionally in the clinical literature or in popular medical writing.[42] Since the early part of the century, pediatricians and parents had shared a common concern for problems of childhood nutrition, focusing particularly on the poor eater. Underweight was the central problem because of its association with the wasting diseases. As medicine made significant gains in the treatment of these once-devastating illnesses, however, underweight became less of a liability in children.[43] Parents and physicians began to fear for their children what they feared for themselves—overweight. Yet in the 1920s and 1930s, when the first studies of overweight children appeared, most people still regarded overweight in children as a nonproblem. Overweight was simply "baby fat," destined to disappear as children matured into adolescence.

Medicine and psychology were building a different interpretation. They saw the problem of childhood obesity as more serious, complex, and enduring. In 1924 Bird T. Baldwin, a physician at the Iowa Child Welfare Research Station and codesigner of an influential set of height and weight tables for children, wrote, "The decidedly overweight child should be as much a subject of pathologic study as the underweight child."[44] In "Comparative Psychology of the Overweight Child," a doctoral thesis written at Teacher's College, Columbia University, overweight children were reported to be more fearful and less happy than either underweight or normal-weight youngsters.[45] In the mid-1930s Hilde Bruch also began to study obese children. Trained in psychoanalysis, she emphasized the fat child's early development and emotional life within the family. Bruch first gained prominence in 1939 by eliminating a disease of boys, Fröhlich's syndrome, which consisted of excessive obesity, small genitalia, and sluggish behavior. She rejected the idea of a pituitary disturbance and demonstrated that overeating and underactivity were the cause; moreover, boys with Fröhlich's syndrome could be treated with psychotherapy. In a series of influential articles Bruch asserted that the hunger of fat children was deep, psychic, and rooted in the pathology of individual families. And in the first edition of *The Common Sense Book of Baby and Child Care* (1945), Benjamin Spock told concerned parents that "fatness is a complicated problem" and that overeating in children was often a symptom of loneliness or maladjustment.[46] By the close of World War II these ideas were circulating among the middle-class parents who read child-raising literature. Fat children were now a medical, psychological, and social problem.

In adolescence fat was considered a particular liability because of the social strains associated with that stage of life. In the 1940s articles with titles such as "What to Do about the Fat Child at Puberty," "Reducing the Adolescent," and "Should the Teens Diet?" captured the rising interest in adolescent weight control.[47] Women's magazines, reflecting the concerns of mothers anxious to save their daughters from social ostracism, for the first time promoted diets for young girls. According to the *Ladies' Home Journal:* "Appearance plays too important a part in a girl's life not to have her grow up to be beauty-conscious. Girls should be encouraged to take an interest in their appearance when they are very young." Advice to teenagers warned "Not too many fudge sundaes!" and "Resist the three s's: Sundaes, Sodas, and Second Helpings."[48]

Adolescent weight control was also promoted by popular magazines hoping to sell products to young women. As early as the 1920s American business had turned its attention to the youth market.[49] Sales were stimulated by the existence of a youth subculture fostered by a massive increase in school enrollments at the high school and college levels. Between 1900 and 1930 the high school population grew by 650 percent, and colleges and universities experienced a threefold increase in the number of students.[50] In high school and college, young people were exposed to a peer group that generated its own priorities and rules of conduct. In both settings relations between the sexes became a focal point of both student energies and faculty concern.

Heterosexual popularity and sexual allure required a certain level of stylistic conformity. High school and college girls, following the model of adult women, adopted beauty and fashion as the coin of the realm.

Advertisers and merchants were heartened by the American girl's devotion to fashion and her insistence on having the best. They also portrayed a young woman's entrance into the consumer culture as an important rite of passage: "No mere man can understand the revolution that takes place in the life of a girl around the ages of eighteen to twenty. For the first time she is buying things for herself on an extensive scale, and yields herself to new fancies, new impressions, new styles . . . She is on the alert to discover the latest and smartest—as they reveal her personality in fashion's setting." In short, "having money to spend on the self was intimately connected to breaking out of the family circle."[51]

By the close of World War II, younger, middle-class high school girls living at home emerged as a discrete new market.[52] These were girls with their own allowances to spend and full-time mothers to escort them on shopping trips. Entrepreneurs embraced popular theories of adolescent development which suggested that girls like these, on the brink of maturity, needed special help in weathering the trials and tribulations of modern adolescence. Advertisements for soaps and skin creams to prevent adolescent acne and displays of attractive clothing to build social confidence were part of the newest marketing strategy. These ideas about adolescence and the hope of profits spawned *Seventeen* magazine, which made its first appearance at the start of the school year in September 1944. Helen Valentine, the first editor, proclaimed, "*Seventeen* is your magazine, High School Girls of America!"[53] The magazine built its success on its ability to sell fashion and beauty products to teenage girls.

Seventeen's adoption of the cause of weight control confirmed that slimness was a critical dimension of adolescent beauty and that a new constituency, high school girls, was learning how to diet. From 1944 to 1948, *Seventeen* had published a full complement of articles on nutrition but almost nothing on weight control. Following the mode of earlier home economists and scientific nutritionists, the magazine had presented basic information about food groups and the importance of each in the daily diet; balance but not calories had been the initial focus. In 1948, however, *Seventeen* proclaimed overweight a medical problem and began educating its young readers about calories and the psychology of eating. Adolescent girls were warned against using eating as a form of emotional expression (do not "pamper your blues" with food) and were given practical tips on how to avoid food binging. No mention was made of the new "diet pills" (amphetamines) introduced in the 1930s for clinical treatment of obesity. Instead, teenagers were encouraged to go on "sensible" and "well-rounded" diets of between 1,200 and 1,800 calories. By the 1950s advertisements for "diet foods" such as Ry-Krisp were offering assistance as they told the readership "Nobody Loves a Fat Girl."[54] Girls, much as adult women, were expected to tame the natural appetite.

Although adolescent girls were consistently warned against weight reduction without medical supervision, dieting was always cast as a worthwhile endeavor with transforming powers. "Diets can do wonderful things. When dispensed or approved by your physician . . . all you have to do is follow whither the chart leads."[55] The process of metamorphosis from fat to thin always provided a narrative of uplift and interest. "The Fattest Girl in the Class" was the autobiographical account of Jane, an obese girl who, after suffering the social stigma associated with teenage overweight, went on a diet and found happiness.[56] Being thin was tied to attractiveness, popularity with the opposite sex, and self-esteem—all primary ingredients in adolescent culture. Nonfiction accounts of "make-overs" became a popular formula in all the beauty magazines of the postwar period and provided a tantalizing fantasy of psychological and spiritual transformation for mature and adolescent women alike.[57]

The popularization of adolescent female weight control in the postwar era is a prime component of the modern dieting story and a critical factor in explaining anorexia nervosa as we know it today. In the 1980s dieting is a central motif in the lives of women of nearly all ages; at least 50 percent of American women are on a diet at any given time.[58] And across the twentieth century the age of those controlling the appetite in the name of beauty has declined. Sadly, recent studies suggest that close to 80 percent of prepubescent girls—sometimes at ages as young as eight or nine—restrict their eating in the interest of not getting fat.[59] The fact that young girls, but not young boys, have such precocious concerns about attractiveness is compelling evidence for the power of sex-role socialization and the potency of the diet message.

* * * *

The history of the diet industry in America (as yet unwritten) probably represents one of the most astounding triumphs of twentieth-century capitalist enterprise. In 1985 the American people spent over $5 billion on the effort to lose weight. The diet industry is an entrepreneur's delight because the market is self-generating and intrinsically expansive. Predicated on failure (dieters regain weight and must diet again and again), the interest in diet strategies, techniques, and products seems unlimited.[60] For nearly a decade one "diet book" or another has been a fixture on the list of the nation's best-sellers. Moreover, weight control is now a formal scientific subspecialty in American medicine. The American Society of Bariatric Physicians, an association with over six hundred members, describes itself as a group specializing in the treatment of obesity.[61] The existence of bariatrics confirms the fact that many in our society, not just young women, are in hot pursuit of day-to-day assistance and medical guidance on the issue of appetite and weight control.

Since the 1960s the dieting imperative has intensified in two noticeable and important ways that have consequences for anorexia nervosa. First, the ideal female body size has become considerably slimmer. After a brief flirtation with full-breasted, curvaceous female figures in the politically conservative postwar recovery of the 1950s, our collective taste returned to an ideal of extreme thinness and an androgynous, if not childlike, figure.[62] A series of well-known studies point to the declining weight since the 1950s of fashion models, Miss America contestants, and *Playboy* centerfolds.[63] Neither bosoms, hips, nor buttocks are currently in fashion as young and old alike attempt to meet the new aesthetic standard. A Bloomingdale's ad posits, "Bean lean, slender as the night, narrow as an arrow, pencil thin, get the point?"[64] It is appropriate to recall Annette Kellerman who, at 5 feet 3¾ inches and 137 pounds, epitomized the body beautiful of 1918. Obviously, our cultural tolerance for body fat has diminished over the intervening years.

Second, notably since the middle to late 1970s, a new emphasis on physical fitness and athleticism has intensified cultural pressures on the individual for control and mastery of the body. For women this means that fitness has been added to slimness as a criterion of perfection.[65] Experts on the subject, such as Jane Fonda, encourage women to strive for a lean body with musculature. The incredible popularity among women of aerobics, conditioning programs, and jogging does testify to the satisfactions that come with gaining physical strength through self-discipline, but it also expresses our current urgency about the physical body. Many who are caught up in the exercise cult equate physical fitness and slimness with a higher moral state.

More often than not, those who strive for physical perfection are concerned about what they eat. In the 1960s and 1970s many Americans began to change their diet in the interest of fitness and health. (In 1984 we ate more vegetables, fruits, and cereals and less beef and pork than we did in the 1970s.) This interest in a lighter diet sprang from both the social critique of food processing associated with counter-cultural dietary practices and the powerful medical suggestion that consumption of fats and sodium is linked to coronary disease and perhaps cancer. Given these relationships, many people chose to eliminate from their diet either a particular ingredient (butter, salt, white sugar) or a category of food (meat). Simultaneously, some became food zealots, exalting certain foods or vitamins (bran, cabbage, lecithin, vitamins C and E) for their special properties and proclaiming their own bodily purity. The anorectic's devotion to the ideal of thinness, her elaborate espousal of food theories, and the narrowing of her food repertoire to only the lightest of food is part and parcel of this *mentalité*.[66] In essence, food once again is central to holiness.

According to psychologist Rita Freedman, the contemporary emphasis on fitness and exercise is a double-edged sword. On the one hand, women are profiting in terms of both psychological and physical health from the new athleticism that has accompanied the contemporary women's movement. On the other hand, a "narcissism based on health" is not essentially different from one based on beauty.[67] In fact, spokespersons for the new credo of female fitness espouse the same principles of vanity, self-sacrifice, and physical and spiritual transformation that characterized the beauty zealots of the early twentieth century. What is different is that compulsive exercising and chronic dieting have been joined as twin obsessions.

Notes

1. "On Growing Fat," *Atlantic Monthly* (March 1907), 430–431.
2. In *Eating and Drinking* (New York, 1871), George M. Beard complained that many Americans still had Puritan ideas about subduing the appetite. He rejected the idea of satiety as "a conviction of sin" (p. v).
3. Overweight was associated with promiscuity and infanticide in female criminals. See Caesar Lombroso and William Ferrero, *The Female Offender* (New York, 1899). Among juvenile delinquents overweight was associated with girls, underweight with boys.
4. For the history of couture fashion I rely on Michael Batterberry and Ariane Batterberry, *Mirror Mirror: A Social History of Fashion* (New York, 1977); Diana DeMarly, *The History of Haute Couture, 1850–1950* (New York, 1980); Jo Ann Olian, *The House of Worth: The*

Gilded Age, 1860–1919 (New York, 1982). Abrams, "Thinning of America," chap. 2, first provided me with the basic progression of events described here. Charles Frederick Worth is credited with having transformed the craft of dressmaking into the art of haute couture. He was the first to present a collection of dresses that could be ordered by individual customers and the first to sign his work with labels (Olian, *House of Worth*, p. 1).

5. DeMarly, *History of Haute Couture*, pp. 81–83; Batterberry and Batterberry, *Mirror Mirror*, pp. 286–297. For Poiret see *The Autobiography of Paul Poiret* (Philadelphia, 1931). On Chanel see Edmonde Charles-Roux, *Chanel: Her Life, Her World, and the Woman behind the Legend She Herself Created* (New York, 1975). Banner, *American Beauty*, pp. 214, 218, reports the use of depilatories by 1918.

6. P. Rostaine, "How to Get Thin," *Medical Press and Circular* 149 (December 23, 1914), 643–644. Rostaine, clinical director of the Faculty of Medicine in Paris, approved of the emphasis on slenderness because of the connection between fat and high mortality.

7. On the ready-to-wear industry and its "leveling" consequences see Stuart Ewen and Elizabeth Ewen, *Channels of Desire: Mass Images and the Shaping of American Consciousness* (New York, 1982), esp. pt. 4; Claudia Kidwell and Margaret C. Christman, *Suiting Everyone: The Democratization of Clothing in America* (Washington, D.C., 1974); Margaret Walsh, "The Democratization of Fashion: The Emergence of the Women's Dress Pattern Industry," *Journal of American History* 66 (September 1979); Boorstin, *Democratic Experience*, pp. 100, 188–189. In *Democracy and Social Ethics* (New York, 1902), Jane Addams portrayed clothing as a great leveler: "Have we worked out our democracy further in regard to clothes than anything else?" (p. 36).

8. *Vogue* (January 1, 1923), 63.

9. Banner, *American Beauty*, p. 262; Ewen and Ewen, *Channels of Desire*, pp. 193–198. On women and the late-nineteenth-century and early-twentieth-century department store see William R. Leach, "Transformations in a Culture of Consumption: Women and Department Stores, 1890–1925," *Journal of American History* 71 (September 1984), 319–342; Susan Porter Benson, *Counter Culture: Saleswomen, Managers, and Customers in American Department Stores, 1890–1940* (Champaign, Ill., 1986); Elaine S. Abelson, " 'When Ladies Go A-Thieving': The Department Store, Shoplifting, and the Contradictions of Consumerism, 1870–1914," Ph.D. diss., New York University, 1986.

10. Quoted in " 'San-gri-na': Another Fake Cure," *Journal of the American Medical Association* 83: 21 (1924), 1703.

11. Banner, *American Beauty*, p. 287; Anne Hollander, *Seeing through Clothes* (New York, 1975). Hollander argues not so much that the camera distorts reality as that photographs are read differently than three-dimensional bodies.

12. Peters, *Diet and Health*, p. 11. Peters' book, which between 1918 and 1922 went through seventeen editions, was dedicated to Herbert Hoover, then head of the effort for recovery in Europe. In 1924, and in 1925, it was number one on the nation's nonfiction best-seller list. See Alice Payne Hackett and James Henry Burke, *Eighty Years of Best Sellers, 1895–1975* (New York, 1977), pp. 97, 99.

13. Peters, *Diet and Health*, pp. 24, 39.

14. Ibid., pp. 12, 104, 110.

15. Ibid., pp. 12–13, 109.

16. Ibid., pp. 85, 94.

17. Ibid., pp. 85, 93, 94.

18. The foremost critic of calorie counting as a diet technique is Dr. William Bennett. See William Bennett, "Dieting: Ideology versus Physiology," *Psychiatric Clinics of North America* 7 (June 1984), 321–334, and idem, "Dietary Treatments of Obesity," unpublished.

19. Banner, *American Beauty*, pp. 214–216, makes this point.

20. "On Her Dressing Table," *Vogue* (April 24, 1902), 413, and ibid. (July 1, 1918), 78; Helena Rubenstein, *The Art of Feminine Beauty* (New York, 1930), p. 133.

21. Mary Douglas, *Purity and Danger* (London, 1970). An important discussion of the body in relation to social theory is that of Bryan Turner, *The Body and Society: Explorations in Social Theory* (Oxford, 1984). Turner argues for the relationship between dietary management and capitalist society's need for increasing social control of bodies. Michael Featherstone, "The Body in Consumer Culture," *Theory, Culture and Society* 1: 2 (1982), 18–33, hypothesizes that contemporary patterns of dieting and body maintenance are regarded as vehicles to release the temptations of the flesh (rather than as a defense against them).

22. On women in the 1920s see Mary Ryan, *Womanhood in America from Colonial Times to the Present,* 2nd ed. (New York, 1975), pp. 151–182; William Chafe, *The American Woman: Her Changing Social, Economic, and Political Roles, 1920–1970* (New York, 1972); Paula S. Fass, *The Damned and the Beautiful: American Youth in the 1920s* (New York, 1977); Ewen and Ewen, *Channels of Desire,* esp. pt. 3.

23. On the primacy of nineteenth-century women's relationships with one another, see Carroll Smith-Rosenberg, "The Female World of Love and Ritual: Relations between Women in Nineteenth Century America," *Signs* 1 (Autumn 1975), 1–29; and Martha Vicinus, *Independent Women: Work and Community for Single Women, 1850–1920* (Chicago, 1985). On the sexuality of nineteenth-century women see Peter Cominos, "Late Victorian Sexual Respectability and the Social System," *International Review of Social History* 8 (1963), 18–48, 216–251; Carl Degler, "What Ought to Be, and What Was: Woman's Sexuality in the Nineteenth Century," *American Historical Review* 79 (December 1974), 1467–90; John S. Haller and Robin M. Haller, *The Physician and Sexuality in Victorian America* (Urbana, Ill,, 1974); Nancy Cott, "Passionlessness: An Interpretation of Victorian Sexual Ideology, 1790–1850," *Signs* 4 (Winter 1978), 219–236.

24. On the history of birth control in the United States see Linda Gordon, *Women's Bodies, Women's Rights* (New York, 1976); Daniel Scott Smith, "The Dating of the American Sexual Revolution: Evidence and Interpretation," in *The American Family in Social-Historical Perspective,* ed. Michael Gordon (New York, 1974), pp. 328–332.

25. On Kellerman see the portraits in *Bookman* 47 (May 1918), 314–315; *Cosmopolitan* (June 1910), 86; *Harper's Weekly* (January 27, 1912), 19. See also Banner, *American Beauty,* pp. 207, 267, 341. According to Robert Grau, *Forty Years Observation of Music and Drama* (New York, 1909),. Kellerman's success was based on the "extraordinary sensationalism" of her publicity (p. 40).

26. See the review of "Daughter of the Gods," *New York Times Film Reviews* 9 (October 9, 1916), 1. James R. McGovern, "The American Woman's Pre–World War I Freedom in Manners and Morals," *Journal of American History* 55 (September 1968), 315–333, suggests that the sexual revolution occurred before 1920.

27. Annette Kellerman, *Physical Beauty* (New York, 1918), p. 23.

28. Ibid., p. 50.

29. Physical culturists such as Bernarr A. McFadden, editor of the monthly *Physical Culture* magazine, promoted strength, fitness, and sexuality. In particular, McFadden viewed intercourse as a healthy, recreative function, not simply a procreative technique. See Green, *Fit for America,* pp. 245–251, for an excellent discussion of the physical culture movement.

30. Annette Kellerman, "Why and How Girls Should Swim," *Ladies' Home Journal* 27 (August 1910), 11. Green, *Fit for America,* makes the point that "health and sex were intimately linked" in the physical culture movement and that publications such as *Physical Culture* catered to middle-class males by displaying nubile young women in revealing outfits (pp. 245–251).

31. On the history of beauty pageants see Banner, *American Beauty,* pp. 249–270, and Kellerman, *Physical Beauty,* p. 17.

32. Elaine Tyler May, *Great Expectations: Marriage and Divorce in Post Victorian America* (Chicago, 1980); Michael Gordon, "From an Unfortunate Necessity to a Cult of Mutual Orgasm: Sex in Marital Education Literature, 1830–1940," in James Henslin, ed., *Studies in the Sociology of Sex* (New York, 1971), pp. 53–80.

33. Kellerman, *Physical Beauty,* p. 15.

34. Ibid., p. 16.

35. Ewen and Ewen, *Channels of Desire,* pp. 100–101.

36. Kellerman, *Physical Beauty,* p. 16.

37. See Mary Ryan, "The Projection of a New Womanhood: The Movie Moderns in the 1920s," in *Our American Sisters: Women in American Life and Thought,* ed. Jean E. Friedman and William G. Shade, 2nd ed. (Boston, 1976), pp. 366–384, for a discussion of early films and the rise of sexual allure; and Ewen and Ewen, *Channels of Desire,* pp. 97–99, for a description of Theda Bara and her personification of the "Vamp."

38. In *Advertising the American Dream* (Berkeley, 1985), Roland Marchand argues that advertising campaigns of the 1920s and 1930s made beauty a "duty" (pp. 176–179).

39. The emphasis on personal appearance translated into a preoccupation with having certain material goods, especially the accoutrements of current fashion. On working-class girls see Addams, *Democracy and Social Ethics,* pp. 34–36. In "Ladies Go A-Thieving" Abelson ties middle-class women's escalating consumer desires to the origins of kleptomania.

40. Harlow Brooks, "The Price of a Boyish Form," in Fishbein, *Your Weight,* p. 32.

41. On women in the 1930s and 1940s, see Ryan, *Womanhood,* pp. 183–198; Chafe, *The American Woman;* Winifred Wandersee Bolin, "The Economics of Middle Income Family Life: Working Women during the Great Depression," *Journal of American History* 65 (June 1978), 60–74; Susan Ware, *Holding Their Own: American Women in the 1930s* (Boston, 1982); Susan Hartman, *The Home Front and Beyond: American Women in the 1940s* (Boston, 1982); D'Ann Campbell, *Women at War with America: Private Lives in a Patriotic Era* (Cambridge, Mass., 1984). It is interesting to note how views of female body configuration have changed since the 1930s. Images of women in the Depression era, captured by Works Progress Administration photographers, seemed horrific at the time because the women were so gaunt and thin. Today their bodies would not be an issue; in fact, they look rather like those of contemporary fashion models.

42. Schwartz, *Never Satisfied,* p. 269, writes that American anxieties about overweight and obesity settled in the 1940s and 1950s on adolescents; in the 1960s, on grade-schoolers; and in the 1970s, on toddlers, infants, and newborns.

43. On the improvement in child mortality in this period, see Cone, *American Pediatrics,* pp. 159–160, 171–179, 202. According to Cone, the most significant decline in childhood tuberculosis and child mortality occurred after 1925.

44. Bird T. Baldwin, "Use and Abuse of Weight-Height-Age Tables as Indexes of Health and Nutrition," *Journal of the American Medical Association* 92, (1924), 1–4.

45. Kathryn McHale, "Comparative Psychology of the Overweight Child," Ph.D. diss., Columbia University, 1926, p. 89.

46. In the 1930s Bruch was the first to emphasize the importance of emotional problems within the families of fat children over any endocrinologic or glandular abnormality. Among a number of articles written in this period the best-known is Hilde Bruch and Grace Touraine, "Obesity in Childhood, V: The Family Frame of Obese Children," *Psychomatic Medicine* 2 (1940), 141–206. Related articles by Bruch were published in the *American Journal of the Diseases of Children, Journal of Pediatrics, American Journal of Orthopsychiatry, American Journal of Psychiatry,* and *Nervous Child.* Bruch's thinking on the subject of obesity and the problems it creates were synthesized in her *Importance of Overweight* (New York, 1957); Benjamin Spock, *The Common Sense Book of Baby and Child Care* (New York, 1945), pp. 359–360.

47. Literature typical of the late 1930s and the 1940s includes Mildred H. Bryan, "Don't Let Your Child Get Fat!" *Hygeia* 15 (1937), 801–803; G.D. Schultz, "Forget That Clean-Plate Bogey!" *Better Homes and Gardens* 21 (September 1942), 24; J. H. Kenyon, "Don't Let Your Child Get Fat," *Good Housekeeping* 121 (October 1945), 62. On adolescents see Regina J. Woody, "Reducing the Adolescent," *Hygeia* 19 (1941), 476–482; F. W. Schultz,

"What to Do about the Fat Child at Puberty," *Journal of Pediatrics* 19 (1941), 376–381; Lulu Graves, "Should the Teens Diet?" *Parents' Magazine* 15 (April 1940), 76.

48. Louise Paine Benjamin, "I Have Three Growing Daughters," *Ladies' Home Journal* 57 (June 1940), 74. Benjamin had her three daughters, all under fifteen years of age, doing posture exercises in order to guard against "protruding derrières and tummy bulges." See also the monthly "Sub-Deb" column of *Ladies' Home Journal* for expressions of concern about beauty and overweight.

49. See for example a market research study conducted for *Photoplay* magazine, *The Age Factor in Selling and Advertising: A Study in a New Phase of Advertising* (Chicago, 1922), frontispiece and pp. 9, 43–44, 96.

50. Fass, *The Damned and the Beautiful,* p. 124 and chaps. 3 and 4.

51. *The Age Factor,* p. 18; Ewen and Ewen, *Channels of Desire,* p. 94.

52. James A. Gilbert, *A Cycle of Outrage: America's Reaction to Juvenile Delinquency in the 1950s* (New York, 1986), pp. 204–207.

53. Helen Valentine, "Seventeen Says Hello," *Seventeen* (September 1944), 33.

54. The material cited is from "You'll Eat It Up at Noon," *Seventeen* (September 1946), 21–22; Irma M. Phorylles, "The Lost Waistline" ibid. (March 1948), 124; "Overweight?" ibid. (August 1948), 184. On drugs in dieting see Johnston, "Double Bind," p. 55. See *New Republic* (August 1937) on the "miracle drug" (alpha-dinitrophenol); *Time* (August 23, 1943) on "Weight Reducing Made Easy" (dextroamphetamine); *Newsweek* (September 15, 1947) on benzedrine.

55. Phorylles, "Lost Waistline," p. 124.

56. "Fattest Girl in the Class," *Seventeen* (January 1948), 21–22.

57. In the "Psychology of Dieting," *Ladies' Home Journal* (January 1965), 66, the editors explained: "Everybody knows that it is bad to be overweight, that it is unattractive, is a social and psychological handicap and even a threat to health. Still, this is not reason enough to reduce. You must know what difference it will make if you change your weight."

58. *USA Today,* August 11, 1986.

59. Jeffrey Zaslow, "Fourth Grade Girls These Days Ponder Weighty Matters," *Wall Street Journal,* February 11, 1986; "Dieting: The Losing Game," *Time* (January 20, 1986), 54. Both the *Wall Street Journal* and *Time* reported results from a University of California study. Dieting peaks, however, at the onset of middle age. See Jeremy Schlosberg, "The Demographics of Dieting," *American Demographics* 9 (July 1987), 35–37, 61–62.

60. Bennett and Gurin, *Dieter's Dilemma,* is the best statement about the ineffectiveness of dieting. See also *USA Today,* August 11, 1986, and *Time* (January 1, 1986), 54. Over 37 percent of all adults are dieting at any given time. According to the Calorie Control Council, an association of diet food producers, most people on diets cut out high-calorie foods (81 percent); increase exercise (78.5 percent); use special low-calorie foods (67 percent); or skip meals (31.5 percent).

61. Founded in 1961, the National Glandular Society in 1972 became the American Society of Bariatric Physicians.

62. Banner, *American Beauty,* pp. 283–285, points out that in the 1950s the asexual adolescent and the voluptuous beauty both held sway. In teen magazines, such as *Seventeen,* and on television the ideal for adolescent girls was the ingenue epitomized in petite women such as Sandra Dee and Debbie Reynolds.

63. See, as an example, David M. Garner et al., "Cultural Expectations of Thinness in Women," *Psychological Reports,* 47 (1980), 483–491.

64. Quoted in Rita Freedman, *Beauty Bound* (New York, 1986), p. 150.

65. See "Coming on Strong: The New Ideal of Beauty," *Time* (August 30, 1982), 72–77, for a comprehensive overview of the ways in which American women are reshaping their bodies. Freedman, *Beauty Bound,* chap. 7, deals with the psychological impact of the "obsession with food and fitness."

66. On the move from countercuisine to a lighter diet see Warren Belasco, "Lite Economics: Less Food, More Profit," *Radical History Review* 28–30 (September 1984), 254–278. For a journalistic report on the shift in American diet, see *U.S. News and World Report* 96 (April 30, 1984), 20. Hilde Bruch was attuned to the role of food faddism in American culture; see her "The Allure of Food Cults and Nutrition Quackery," *Journal of the American Dietetic Association* 57 (October 1970), 316–320.
67. Freedman, *Beauty Bound*, pp. 166–167.

Questions

1. How do the fashion, cosmetic, and dieting industries contribute to eating disorders?
2. How have cultural values about the qualities of the ideal woman changed over the course of the century?
3. Why has our society placed increasing emphasis on what the body looks like?
4. Why are eating disorders more prevalent in women? What men are most likely to be affected?
5. Which individuals are most likely to be adversely impacted by societal pressures to be thin? Which individuals are least likely to be adversely impacted by societal pressures to be thin?

References and Further Reading

Brumberg, J. J. (1988). *Fasting girls: A history of anorexia nervosa.* Cambridge, MA: Harvard University Press.
Brumberg, J. J. (1997). *The body project: An intimate history of American girls.* New York: Vintage Books.
Casper, R. C. (1992). Risk factors for the development of eating disorders. *Adolescent Psychiatry, 18,* 91–103.

15.2   Peter J. Fagan and Arnold E. Andersen, 1990

Sexuality and Eating Disorders in Adolescence

Peter J. Fagan, Ph.D., is an assistant professor of medical psychology and the director of the Sexual Behaviors Consultation Unit at the Johns Hopkins Medical Institution. He also serves as the clinical director of the Johns Hopkins Bayview Physicians Uniformed Service Family Health Plan in the Department of Psychiatry, Baltimore, Maryland. He researches the clinical characteristics of individuals with sexual disorders.

Arnold E. Andersen, M.D., is clinical director of the Eating Disorders Unit at the University of Iowa Hospital. He is author of numerous books including *Practical Comprehensive Treatment of Anorexia Nervosa and Bulimia* (1985), *Males with Eating Disorders* (1990), and *Eating Disorders: A Guide to Medical Care and Complications* (1999).

Researchers have looked at psychological and societal factors that put adolescents at risk for the development of eating disorders. Particular personality traits are associated with anorexia and bulimia. Anorexics tend to be shy, retiring, inhibited, and perfectionistic, whereas bulimics tend to be more emotional, volatile, expressive, and socially adept (Casper, 1992). The internalization of societal standards of beauty has been identified as an important risk factor for the development of disordered eating. Dieting, even if it becomes life threatening, may not be an unreasonable choice for adolescents who are surrounded by mothers and female adults who diet, who are exposed to media images of unrealistically thin models, who have identified with the female sex role, who believe in the importance of thinness to attractiveness, or who are trying to meet societal expectations of female adulthood (Striegel-Moore & Cachelin, 1999).

Because eating disorders have their onset at adolescence, Peter Fagan and Arnold Andersen argue that eating disorders may be an attempt to cope with changing demands placed on adolescents as they prepare for adulthood. They argue that eating disorders represent a defense against change. As one leaves childhood, new expectations come into play about relationships with parents and peers. Leaving childhood implies evolving from dependency to autonomy from parents (chapter 10), and developing a sexual identity (chapter 9). Fagan and Andersen contend that eating disorders prevent or retard both differentiation from parents and the development of a sexual identity, and the authors examine the cultural factors that contribute to making these developmental transitions difficult.

While all adolescents face these developmental transitions, not all of them develop eating disorders, though many develop disordered eating. Thus, other factors must play a role in increasing the risk for the development of an eating disorder. Fagan and Andersen go on to examine a variety of additional risk factors for eating disorders,—genetic, physiological, and family factors that predispose certain adolescents to eating disorders.

The motivated behaviors of sexuality and eating share many of the same psychological, physiological and social determinants. The factors that cause an anorectic adolescent to restrict food intake also deter sexual development. The impulsive bulimic is frequently impulsive in sexual behavior. The body image problem in obesity often contributes to a poor sex role image. In conceptualizing the relationship between sexuality and eating disorders in adolescents, the therapist may rely upon these generalizations and miss the subtleties of the interactions of the etiological factors in the individual. When this happens the adolescent in the clinical setting may be hidden behind a stereotype (albeit valid) that prevents both understanding and treatment. The purpose of this [selection] is to present the varieties of relationships between sexuality and eating disorders in adolescents in the hope that it will serve to develop in the therapist an informed but still somewhat uncertain curiosity about his or her individual patients.

Eating Disorders as Developmental Disorders

Eating disorders that have their onset in adolescence—especially in early adolescence—can in most instances be seen as developmental disorders (Bruch, 1981) or developmental "breakdowns" (Laufer & Laufer, 1984). Assuming two major developmental tasks of adolescence, namely to differentiate from parents (Blos, 1979) and to secure a sexual identity (Erikson, 1968), we find that eating disorders in adolescence prevent or retard both. In adopting a patient role, the young person with an eating disorder retains an enmeshed relationship with parents (Minuchin, Baker, Rosman, Liebman, Milman, & Todd, 1975). Eating disorders retard the achievement of sexual identity. As is witnessed most clearly in anorexia, the eating disorder inhibits the development of secondary sexual characteristics, lowers the adolescent's sexual drive, and reduces social and psychological interaction with the opposite sex.

A Defense Against Change

Eating disorders in young adolescents are a defense against the primary event of adolescence: change. Change during adolescence results in loss or threatened loss of that which was perceived in prepubescence to be stable: a sense of untested autonomy within the security of family. An adolescent is aware on some level of consciousness of this loss. The potential for low mood is never far from actualization. The chronic dysthymia of eating disordered adolescents may be due not only to affective disorder (as will be mentioned below) but also to their sensitivity and vulnerability to the repeated losses of adolescence.

Granted that the change of adolescence is signaled by emergent sexuality and bodily mutations, it is, nevertheless, *change itself* that is so terrifying to the eating disordered adolescent.

> The changes of pubescence, the increase in size, shape and weight, menstruation with its bleeding and new, undefinable sensations, all represent danger, the threat of complete loss of control. The frantic preoccupation with weight is an attempt to counteract this fear, and rigid dieting is the dimension through which they try to keep their maturing bodies in check. (Bruch, 1981, p. 216)

Anorectics "freeze" their bodies not only with lowered temperatures but also in a somatic cast of emaciation. They attempt to preserve prepubescent morphology in a time warp of perceived childhood stability. The more attractive they were prior to puberty the more at risk they are for lowered self-esteem (Zakin, Blythe, & Simmons, 1984). Changes in physiology, the emergence of abstract thought processes (Piaget, 1952) as well as familial and cultural expectations (to grow up) represent further evidence of something always subliminally suspected by premorbid eating disordered adolescents: that they have little control over life.

An eating disorder is a desperate defensive attempt to exert control over the changes in early adolescence that represent to the young person a loss of control. Thus the anorectic seeks to control weight more than to achieve some stable body weight (even at an emaciated level). It "feels better" *losing* weight than to have lost weight. There is a greater sense of control (over change) in losing weight than in the passive state of achieved weight level in which any fluctuation represents loss or threatened loss of control. The adolescent whose obesity is of prepubescent onset retreats from the anxiety of change by incessant recourse to oral gratification in hopes of quieting indistinguishable needs, emotions, and desires (Bruch, 1981).

Both the obese and the anorectic adolescent attempt to control the change that sexual development would bring to their body image by achieving a body that is as sexually neutral as possible. The round or skinny kid is not androgynous; he/she is sexually undifferentiated (Bem, 1974) and as such strives to ward off the change that definite sexual morphology would bring. In their study of anorexia in males and females, Crisp, Burns, and Bhat (1986) found that both sexes are similar in terms of premorbid characteristics and illness features. They concluded that "(anorexia) is a regressed and diminished state of body and mind characterized by loss of identity and desperation—even the differences between male and female have become blurred."

Bulimic adolescents are most frequently "failed anorectics." Control over the changes brought by adolescence is initially sought through dieting and food restriction. Failure to control change through diet results in decreased control and self-esteem. In addition, extroverted personality characteristics, that are exquisitely sensitive to external cues, coupled with a poor internal locus of control result in a greater ambivalence in the bulimic about adolescent developmental changes. Being loved by parents and significant others is perceived as conditional, based upon a demand to achieve a precocious maturation: to separate from family *now;* to attain the highest scholastic or career goals; and to conform to the (perceived) sexual requests of one's peers or, occasionally, one's parents. The extroverted bulimic is caught straddling unrealistic conditions for love and acceptance with limited inner psychological resources, including the defense of food restriction, by which an artificial sense of control might be effected. The impulsive eating behavior is a regressive collapse which attempts to satiate temporarily a sense of inner emptiness with an engorgement of food.

The tripartite division of obesity made by Bruch (1941, 1957) and supported empirically among adolescent girls by Zakus and Solomon (1973) remains a useful model for us.

1. The constitutionally obese individual has a physiological tendency to be overweight. If the "weight set point" theory is valid, then for this group the point would be set far above normal.

2. The developmentally obese person is overweight because of disturbances in the developmental process—most probably during the oral stage. The obesity is chronic and expressive of an unresolved dependency upon oral gratification and maternal protectiveness.

3. The reactively obese person represents a regression in response to external pressures. An obese youth who had normal body size until the advent of puberty would be considered reactively obese unless some pathophysiology was discovered. The reactive group most closely parallels anorexia and bulimia as an adolescent developmental disorder. It is primarily this group of obese adolescents along with the anorectics and bulimics to which we are referring when we employ the phrase eating disordered adolescents.

As the adolescent draws attention to the eating disorder as a potentially serious medical condition, the role of patient is assumed, which further reinforces bonds of dependency with parents. The emaciation of the anorectic which may require repeated medical or psychiatric hospitalizations is a visible sign that separation from parents is being resisted. Even when marriage ensues at an older age, the anorectic often selects a spouse who will tolerate her dependency needs, make minimum requests for a vibrant sexual life, and not have a strong desire for children. Scapegoated as the "problem child" or the "sick child," the eating disordered adolescent assumes a fixed place in the family system which prevents the active separation from family. The bulimic may make some attempts at independence, but these are usually unsuccessful and are marked with self-destructive behavior, for example, drug and alcohol abuse, sexual activity that puts one at risk for sexually transmitted diseases.

Problems in Sexual Identity

The second major developmental task of adolescence is the achievement of a stable sexual identity (Erikson, 1968). As early as 1963, King noted "sex disgust" in anorectics compared with controls during pubertal years. While disgust may be present at an unconscious level, what is clinically obvious is a disinterest in sex in most anorectics.

Among early adolescents one would expect to find masturbatory activity and a central masturbation fantasy that assist in the gradual replacement of forbidden oedipal objects of sexual desire (Scharff, 1982). Among anorectics it is common to hear "I have never masturbated" from both males and females.

Dating is either nonexistent or limited to "must attend" functions such as proms. There is no ongoing romantic involvement—usually explained away with the rationalization that the anorectic is too busy with other more important matters, for example, wrestling team, performance dance, scholastic achievement. For a female anorectic, the mere thought of pregnancy and its gross effects on body shape is terrifying. The thought of pregnancy is relatively rare, however, because of the cessation of ovulation and other asexual defenses she typically employs.

Among male adolescent anorectics treated in our inpatient unit, we have found the incidence of homosexual orientation to be about 25%—nearly twice that of the general population. Others have reported the presence of homosexual conflict preceding the onset of anorexia in males (Crisp and Toms, 1972; Dally, 1969). While the etiologies of male homosexuality still remain controversial (Isay, 1986), a greater than expected portion of our patients are stereotypically effeminate and report histories of alienation from father and identification with mother. The adolescent male anorectic's bodily habitus perpetuates this negative oedipal configuration by evoking the rejection of the father and the protection of the mother toward her son "who is just not understood."

Bulimics tend to be more sexually active than anorectics; indeed, as has been noted previously, their sexual behaviors can frequently be impulsive. Sexual activity in the bulimic should not be *a priori* evidence of the achievement of stable sexual identity or even the minimal integration of genital sexuality. Just as the binge eating is devoid of gustatory pleasure, so the sexual activity of the bulimic is frequently without pleasure. Among those who have coitus, anorgasmia in women and delayed ejaculation in men have been observed clinically. The sexual relationships themselves often have a sadomasochistic flavor to them. Yellowlees (1985) noted that among the sample studied 40% of the bulimics (N = 15) reported a frequent desire to vomit associated with a feeling of revulsion during sexual activity. It is not surprising that there is a striking parallel between the behaviors of eating and sex in bulimics: both are often terminated leaving the person feeling disgusted about the activity; revulsed about the self; and, in the adolescent, insecure about sexual identity.

There is little reported about obesity and adolescent sexual development. Our impressions are similar to those of Bruch (1981) and Zakus and Solomon (1973) concerning the forms of obesity that are not primarily pathophysiological in origin (Kolodny, Masters, & Johnson, 1979). Adolescent obesity that is developmental, that is, due to faulty development in the mother-child interaction in the oral stage, results in an adolescent whose passivity, dependency, and lack of individuation prevent pubertal sexual exploration with peers and the development of pseudointimacy in dating. Masturbatory activity with poorly developed fantasy in terms of age-appropriate objects is often the entire sexual repertoire of developmentally obese adolescents.

Obesity in adolescents which is reactive to the onset of puberty is a defense against sexual development. Research is needed on the sexual behaviors of reactively obese adolescents—especially boys. Zakus and Solomon (1973) have observed that adolescent girls with reactive obesity are more likely to come from a disruptive parental relationship in which the role of woman, wife, and mother is poorly modelled. The sexual behavior of these girls is not easily categorized. One would expect to find cases of asexuality and self-injurious promiscuity among the more severely impaired obese adolescent girls.

In conclusion, in this section we have attempted to describe eating disorders in adolescents as developmental disorders that inhibit the twofold adolescent task of separating from parents and stabilizing a sexual identity. We have described with sweeping lines the general experiences of anorectic, bulimic, and obese adolescents as they attempt to negotiate these developmental tasks. In doing so, we may have restated the obvious for many of our readers.

We now examine some of the contributing factors to eating disorders especially as they relate to adolescent sexuality. Here we strive to avoid the problem of the obvious because in most patients the etiology of the disorder is multifactorial. Each eating disordered adolescent is affected by the separate factors with a different valency.

Factors in Sexual Behaviors of Adolescents with Eating Disorders

Cultural Factors

The most striking cultural factor that influences the sexual behavior of eating disordered adolescents is the norm for women that thinner is better. Mazur (1986) has described the evolution of feminine beauty in the United States in which the changing cultural image of the beautiful woman now emphasizes a slender body with trim hips. After reviewing trends in popular art, Miss America contests, and advertising, Mazur agrees with Garner, Garfinkel, Schwartz and Thompson (1980) and Polhemus (1978) and concludes that "there is little doubt that the overall trend in self-starvation has been produced by our culture's increasing idealization of slenderness as the model for feminine beauty."

The full-breasted adolescent girl risks being at odds with the cultural ideal. A recent newspaper article, for example, told of a high school girl who was rejected as a cheerleader because her breasts were too big. The anorectic prevents this feared rejection by her self-starvation. The bulimic girl, who often has a normal body and secondary sex characteristics, typically feels that her breasts are gross embarrassments to her. She is uncomfortable speaking about her breasts. When she must speak about them, she will refer to her "chest" (denial) or to her "tits" (devaluation). The obese adolescent body, far from the cultural ideal, is a chronic source of poor self-image and social alienation (Stunkard & Burt, 1967; Stunkard & Mendelson, 1967). It is important to remember that a poor body image is not merely an intrapsychic phenomenon that causes poor self-image and alienation. In reality adolescents shun association and identification with "fat" schoolmates. A cultural ideal *does exist* in society and not solely in the object relations mentation of the obese adolescent. Compensatory social skills are needed in adolescents who are obese. Unfortunately, they often are developed in a larger than life manner, as seen in the "funny fat man" or "big bully."

A second cultural factor affecting the sexual behavior of adolescents is the current preoccupation with physical fitness. Normal adolescent narcissism with its cathexis on the body has become a cultural phenomenon that knows no chronological limits. A narcissistic concern with the body, necessary in the development of sexual identity and adolescent psychosocial relatedness, is now pervasive in the mainstream adult Western culture. The effect that this has on eating disordered adolescents is to exacerbate their body image vulnerabilities. A pimple is not just a pimple. The intensity of the cathexis is increased and so is the likelihood of distortions of body size (often of delusional proportions) and resultant emotional lability. In adolescence the normal narcissism with its focus upon the body is ultimately at the service of social and sexual relatedness. One must preen the feathers before the mating dance ensues. However, with the entire culture in the throes of body-oriented narcissism, the adolescent with an eating disorder is less able to set limits on the attention to self and cannot begin in earnest to develop intimacy with another. The preening, in the form of self-starvation or obsession with body, a narcissistic feature, deters object relatedness.

A final cultural factor that impinges upon the sexual development of eating disordered adolescents is the general sexual permissiveness in society. A high proportion of United States college-aged adolescents report engaging in intercourse and the rate for females has increased more rapidly than that for males (Darling, Kallen & VanDusen, 1984). A West German study (Clement, Schmidt, & Kruse, 1984) involving over 5,000 students reported liberalization of all forms of sexuality since 1966, but specifically age at first coitus, coital incidence, and frequency.

Eating disordered adolescents, together with their peers, are invited/required to be sexually active. The specific problem for these adolescents is that in complying with the cultural norm, they are attempting to relate to the body of another person without a "good enough" relationship to their own body. The anorectic, bulimic, or obese youth seeks to gain from the other what is felt to be lacking: a sense of self. Scharff (1982) has described the liabilities of premature intercourse from an object relations viewpoint. "When intercourse is an early substitute for masturbation, reliance on the other person is often prematurely substituted for the individual adolescent's working out of his own narcissistic struggles" (p. 95). This is particularly apt for the eating disordered adolescent for whom masturbation and sexual fantasy life are restricted or impoverished.

To summarize the cultural factors affecting the sexual development of the eating disordered adolescent, the following is suggested: the normal narcissism of adolescence, with its cathexis upon the sexualized body, is reinforced by the mainstream culture. The psychological vulnerabilities underlying perception of body image found in eating disordered adolescents are further compromised by the cultural pressures cited above. The result is that adolescence becomes a greater "change" demand, and the defenses of eating disorders are employed against these changes.

Genetic and Physiological Factors

Gershon et al. (1984) and Strober and Katz (1988) have noted the increased incidences of affective disorders in the families of patients with anorexia nervosa or bulimia. The link between these two disorders has not been completely clarified, but the correlation of eating disorders and mood disorders is four to six times greater than that expected by chance.

Andersen (1986) has examined the multiple interactions between eating disorders and depression. Starvation by itself and binge-eating lead to depressive symptoms that respond to restoration of normal weight and interruption of binge/purge activity, respectively. A more subtle relationship has recently been appreciated. Eating disorders, especially binge activity and to some extent starvation, may be self-treatments for lowered mood. This may help to explain the increased incidence of mood disorders in patients with anorexia nervosa or bulimia. On a genetic basis, the family may contribute a lowered mood which in our culture is self-medicated by the eating disorder. Finally, the family may contribute a sensitive, perfectionistic personality which is more frequently present in families with affective spectrum disorder, and on this basis predisposed to anorexia nervosa or bulimia. Walsh, Stewart, Roose, Gladis, and Glassman (1984) and Pope and Hudson (1984) have both explored the possible contributions of antidepressant medication to the treatment of bulimia.

Genetic or hormonal conditions that lead to obesity should be ruled out initially. But regardless of the etiology of the obesity, one can presume that it has had a negative psychological affect upon the adolescent and will therefore challenge adolescent psychosexual development. It is, of course, imperative to assist these patients in knowing what they are responsible for and what is beyond control and must be adapted to and accepted. While body weight may be only minimally and temporarily responsive to alteration, obese adolescents may be assisted in developing ego strength to enable them to progress through adolescence *in spite of* the obesity.

A recent report on 540 adult adoptees by Stunkard et al. (1986) suggests that individuals raised apart from their families of origin conform more to their biologic than to their adoptive parents in weight. The Midtown Manhattan studies (Goldblatt, Moore, & Stunkard, 1965) suggest that social class plays an important role in determining weight with obesity found more commonly in the lower socioeconomic classes.

Holland, Hall, Murray, Russell, and Crisp (1984) compared the incidence of anorexia in identical and dizygotic twins. Nine of 16 of the monozygotic pairs were concordant for anorexia nervosa while only 1 out of 14 of the dizygotic pairs were concordant. Whether there is a direct or indirect genetic vulnerability to anorexia nervosa, these and other twin studies suggest that familial contributions based on genetic factors may play a role in the origin and development of anorexia nervosa. The mechanisms remain uncertain.

There have been some studies of physiological factors which have associated obesity with hypogonadism and sexual and menstrual dysfunction (Kolodny et al., 1979). Abnormality of reproductive hormone functioning has always been an important part of the criteria for the diagnosis of anorexia nervosa. The female hormonal milieu is characterized by hypothylamic hypogonadism, with lowering of both luteinizing (LH) and follicle stimulating hormones (FSH) as well as decreased estrogen. The picture in males with anorexia nervosa shows a linear response to starvation, with a decrease in testosterone proportional to the degree of starvation (Andersen, Wirth, & Strahlman, 1982). In starvation, sexual desire is below the threshold of experience. When males with anorexia nervosa regain weight, the increase in sexual thoughts and functioning is positively correlated with improvement in testosterone level.

As body weight increases, sexual desire (and whatever conflicts that may bring with it) emerges (Crisp et al., 1986). Just as starvation prevents sexual desire from being experienced, the condition also depletes the person of conflict-generated anxiety that is necessary for psychotherapy. For this reason we believe that no uncovering or expressive psychotherapy is possible while the patient remains in a starvation condition. Ego-supportive therapies are the appropriate choices with starvation-afflicted patients. . . .

Familial Factors

We are indebted to the pioneering work of Minuchin et al. (1975) for describing the etiological roles family systems play in the development of eating disorders, as well as for offering helpful treatment strategies. In general, family system theorists hold that eating disorders (as well as other psychiatric disorders) are the result of an enmeshed family system in which the boundaries between individuals have become blurred. The eating disordered adolescent has become scapegoated as the "sick one" in the family and colludes in this role. The treatment is to reestablish a proper family hierarchy with the parents in the position of authority and to assist the children (especially the "sick" child) gradually to achieve independence according to age and abilities. Hedblom, Hubbard, and Andersen (1981) examined more than 60 families with anorexia nervosa to test Minuchin's hypothesis about the etiological role of family systems in the development of eating disorders. They found that while many families were enmeshed, a substantial minority was disengaged, and about 15% were normal with no significant pathology in either direction.

Bruch (1981) described the family dynamics of obese adolescents as being more manifestly tense and disturbed than those of anorectics and bulimics. In the latter two groups, the families give the appearance of relative order and harmony between the parents and the family. Only as the situation is brought under scrutiny, such as occurs in therapy, will it become apparent that there is distance and disillusionment between spouses and disorder within the entire familial system.

Root, Fallon and Friedrich (1986) conceptualize that in bulimia there is a problem with the adolescent and the family about the movement forward into independent young adulthood, that these families have boundary problems, and that there are three types of families in which bulimia occurs—perfect, chaotic, and overprotective.

In terms of sexual development, Yellowlees (1985) reported that among the sample studied (N = 32) one third of the bulimics, but none of the anorectics (non-bingers), claimed "sexual interference" during childhood by either adults or older children. Our clinical impressions are that frequently fathers of female bulimic adolescents are overinvolved in the sexual lives of their daughters, while mothers are correspondingly distant and subtly competitive with their daughters. Root et al. (1986) reported a victimization experience (physical or sexual abuse) in over 66% of a sample of female bulimics. It remains for future research to determine the actual incidence of incest among eating disordered persons. Hypothetically, one would suspect that bulimic adolescents are the eating disordered group that has the greatest likelihood of having been victims of incest; their symptomatology is expressive of the ambivalence they experienced during the sexual abuse.

Finally, eating disordered adolescents need modelling of expressive affection between adults as do all adolescents. If there is any deficit in the family system, any repression of sexuality, affection, or emotional warmth, the eating disordered adolescent's vulnerabilities will be affected. We might even suggest that a normal "good enough" family system is not good enough for the anorectic, bulimic, or obese youth in his/her integration of sexual identity and role. Resources outside the family, for example, family therapy, are often required both to remedy deficits and to develop strategies such as modelling of sexual roles. . . .

Summary

Eating disorders in adolescence are disorders of development. Separation from family and establishment of a stable sexual identity as a man or woman are changes which pose serious threats to the anorectic, bulimic, or reactively obese youth. The eating disordered defend against the resultant anxiety. Preoedipal defenses and traits predominate. The incorporation of genital sexuality is as poorly achieved by these adolescents as their incorporation of food. The treatment of the sexual issues of these afflicted youths is first to treat the medical problems which are present and then to address in psychotherapy the characterological and developmental issues.

References

Andersen, A., Wirth, J., & Strahlman, E. (1982). Reversible weight-related increase in plasma testosterone during treatment of male and female patients with anorexia nervosa. *International Journal of Eating Disorders, 1,* 74–83.

Andersen, A. E. (1985). *Practical comprehensive treatment of anorexia nervosa and bulimia.* Baltimore: Johns Hopkins University.

Andersen, A. E. (1986). Anorexia nervosa, bulimia, and depression: multiple interactions. In F. F. Flach (Ed.), *Directions in psychiatry* (Vol. 6). New York: Hatherleigh.

Bem, S. L. (1974). The measurement of psychological androgyny. *Journal of Consulting and Clinical Psychology, 42,* 155–162.

Blos, P. (1979). *The adolescent passage.* New York: International Universities.

Bruch, H. (1941). Obesity in childhood and personality development. *American Journal of Orthopsychiatry, 11,* 467–474.

Bruch, H. (1957). *The importance of overweight.* New York: W. W. Norton.

Bruch, H. (1981). Developmental considerations of anorexia nervosa and obesity. *Canadian Journal of Psychiatry, 26,* 212–217.

Casper, R. C., Eckert, E. D., Halmi, K. A., Goldberg, S. C., & Davis, J. M. (1980). The incidence and clinical significance of bulimia in patients with anorexia nervosa. *Archives of General Psychiatry, 37,* 1030–1035.

Clement, U., Schmidt, G., & Kruse, M. (1984). Changes in sex differences in sexual behavior: A replication of a study on West German students (1966–1981). *Archives of Sexual Behavior, 13,* 99–120.

Crisp, A. H., & Toms, D. A. (1972). Primary anorexia nervosa or weight phobia in the male: Report on 13 cases. *British Medical Journal, 1,* 334–338.

Crisp, A. H., Burns, T., & Bhat, A. V. (1986). Primary anorexia nervosa in the male and female: A comparison of clinical features and prognosis. *British Journal of Medical Psychology, 59,* 123–132.

Dally, P. (1969). *Anorexia nervosa.* London: Heineman.

Darling, C. A., Kallen, D. J., & VanDusen, J. E. (1984). Sex in transition, 1900–1980. *Journal of Youth and Adolescence, 13,* 385–398.

Erikson, E. H. (1968). *Identity: Youth and Crisis.* New York: W. W. Norton.

Fagan, P. J., Meyer, J. K., & Schmidt, C. W., Jr. (1986). Sexual dysfunction in an adult developmental perspective. *Journal of Sex and Marital Therapy, 12,* 1–12.

Garfinkel, P. E., Moldofsky, H., & Garner, D. M. (1980). The heterogeneity of anorexia nervosa: Bulimia as a distinct subgroup. *Archives of General Psychiatry, 37,* 1036–1040.

Garner, D., Garfinkel, P., Schwartz, D., & Thompson, M. (1980). Cultural expectation of thinness of women. *Psychological Reports, 47*, 483–491.

Gershon, E. S., Schreiber, J. L., Hamovit, J. R., Dibble, E. D., Kaye, W., Nurnberg, J. I., Andersen, A. E., & Ebert, M. (1984). Clinical findings in patients with anorexia nervosa and affective illness in their relatives. *American Journal of Psychiatry, 141*, 1419–1422.

Goldblatt, P. B., Moore, M. E., & Stunkard, A. J. (1965). Social factors in obesity. *Journal of the American Medical Association, 192*, 1039–1044.

Halmi, K. A. (1983). *Diverse courses of bingeing and fasting anorexics.* Paper presented at the Seventh World Congress of Psychiatry, Vienna.

Hedblom, J. E., Hubbard, F. A., & Andersen, A. E. (1981). Anorexia nervosa: a multidisciplinary treatment program for patient and family. *Social Work in Heath Care, 7*, 67–86.

Holland, A. J., Hall, A., Murray, R., Russell, G. F. M., & Crisp, A. H. (1984). Anorexia nervosa: A study of 34 twin pairs and one set of triplets. *British Journal of Psychiatry, 145*, 414–419.

Isay, R. (1986). Homosexuality in homosexual and heterosexual men: Some distinctions and implications for treatment. In G. I. Fogel, F. M. Lane, R. S. Liebert (Eds.), *The psychology of men.* New York: Basic Books.

Jacobson, E. (1964). *The self and the object world.* New York: International Universities.

King, A. (1963). Primary and secondary anorexia nervosa syndromes. *British Journal of Psychiatry, 109*, 470–479.

Kolodny, R. C., Masters, W. H., & Johnson, V. E. (1979). *Textbook of sexual medicine.* Boston: Little, Brown.

Laufer, M., & Laufer, M. E. (1984). *Adolescence and developmental breakdown: A psychoanalytic view.* New Haven: Yale University.

Mahler, M. S. (1974). Symbiosis and individuation: The psychological birth of the human infant. *Psychoanalytic Study of the Child, 29*, 89–106.

Mazur, A. (1986). U.S. trends in feminine beauty and overadaptation. *The Journal of Sex Research, 22*, 281–303.

Minuchin, S., Baker, L., Rosman, B. L., Liebman, R., Milman, L., & Todd, T. C. (1975). A conceptual model of psychosomatic illness in children. *Archives of General Psychiatry, 32*, 1031–1038.

Piaget, J. (1952). *The origins of intelligence in children.* New York: International Universities.

Polhemus, T. (1978). *The body reader.* New York: Pantheon.

Pope, H. G., & Hudson, J. I. (1984). *New hope for binge eaters.* Cambridge, MA: Harper and Row.

Root, M. P. P., Fallon, P., & Friedrich, W. N. (1986). *Bulimia: A systems approach to treatment.* New York: W. W. Norton.

Scharff, D. E. (1982). *The sexual relationships: An object relations view of sex and the family.* Boston: Routledge and Kegan Paul.

Strober, M., & Katz, J. (1988). Depression in the eating disorders: A review and analysis of descriptive family and biological findings. In D. M. Garner & P. E. Garfinkel (Eds.), *Diagnostic issues in anorexia nervosa and bulimia nervosa.* New York: Brunner/Mazel.

Stunkard, A., & Mendelson, M. (1967). Obesity and body image: I Characteristics of disturbance in the body image of some obese persons. *American Journal of Psychiatry, 123*, 1296–1300.

Stunkard, A., & Burt, V. (1967). Obesity and body image: II Age at onset of disturbances in the body image. *American Journal of Psychiatry, 123*, 1443–1447.

Stunkard, A. J., Sorensen, T. I., Hanis, C., Teasdale, T. W., Chakbraborty, R., Schull, W. J., & Schulsinger, F. (1986). An adoption study of human obesity. *New England Journal of Medicine, 314*, 193–198.

Sugar, M., & Gates, G. (1979). Artificial gastric distention and neonatal feeding and hunger reflexes. *Child Psychiatry and Human Development, 9*, 206–209.

Walsh, B. T., Stewart, J. W., Roose, S. P., Gladis, M., & Glassman, A. H. (1984). Treatment of bulimia with phenelzine: A double-blind placebo-controlled study. *Archives of General Psychiatry, 41,* 1105–1109.

Yellowlees, A. J. (1985). Anorexia and bulimia in anorexia nervosa: A study of psychosocial functioning and associated psychiatric symptomatology. *British Journal of Psychiatry, 146,* 648–652.

Zakin, D. F., Blythe, D. A., & Simmons, R. G. (1984). Physical attractiveness as a mediator of the impact of early pubertal changes for girls. *Journal of Youth and Adolescence, 13,* 439–450.

Zakus, G., & Solomon, M. (1973). The family situations of obese adolescent girls. *Adolescence, 29,* 33–42.

Questions

1. How does an eating disorder help an adolescent cope with becoming a sexual person?
2. How does an eating disorder help an adolescent cope with individuating from parents?
3. What cultural factors make the development of a sexual identity difficult?
4. What is the relationship between eating disorders and depression? Do eating disorders lead to depression, or does depression lead to eating disorders?
5. What family factors contribute to the development of anorexia?

References and Further Reading

Brumberg, J. J. (1997). *The body project: An intimate history of American girls.* New York: Vintage Books.

Casper, R. C. (1992). Risk factors for the development of eating disorders. *Adolescent Psychiatry, 18,* 91–103.

Smolak, L, & Levine, M. P. (1996). Adolescent transitions and development of eating problems. In L. Smolak, M. P. Levine, & R. Striegel-Moore (Eds.) *The developmental psychopathology of eating disorders* (pp. 207–233). Mahwah, NJ: Lawrence Erlbaum.

Striegel-Moore, R. H. (1997). Risk factors for eating disorders. In M. S. Jacobson, N. H. Golden, & C. E. Irwin (Eds.) *Adolescent nutritional disorders: Prevention and treatment* (pp. 98–109). New York: New York Academy of Sciences.

Striegel-Moore, R. H., & Cachelin, F. M. (1999). Body image concerns and disordered eating in adolescent girls: Risk and protective factors. In N. G. Johnson, M. C. Robertsk, & J. Worell (Eds.) *Beyond appearance: A new look at adolescent girls* (pp. 85–108). Washington, DC: American Psychological Association.

Acknowledgments

Chapter 1

Reading 1.1
David Bakan, "Adolescence in America: From Idea to Social Fact." *Dædalus, Journal of the American Academy of Arts and Sciences,* from the issue entitled "Twelve to Sixteen: Early Adolescence," Fall 1971, Vol. 100, No. 4. Reprinted by permission.

Reading 1.2
Michael Mitterauer, "Puberty—Adolescence—Youth." *A History of Youth* (Oxford, UK: Blackwell, 1992). Copyright © 1993 by Basil Blackwell Ltd. Reprinted by permission of Blackwell Publishers.

Chapter 2

Reading 2.1
Ruth Benedict, "Continuities and Discontinuities in Cultural Conditioning." *Psychiatry: Interpersonal and Biological Processes,* 1938, 1:161-167. Reprinted by permission of the Guilford Press.

Reading 2.2
Alice Schlegel and Herbert Barry III, "Looking at Adolescence Across Cultures." *Adolescence: An Anthropological Inquiry* (New York: The Free Press, 1991). Copyright © 1991 by Alice Schlegel and Herbert Barry III. Reprinted by permission of the authors.

Reading 2.3
James E. Côté, "Coming of Age in Contemporary Samoa." *Adolescent Storm and Stress: An Evaluation of the Mead-Freeman Controversy* (Hillsdale, NJ: Lawrence Erlbaum Associates, 1994). Copyright © 1994 by Lawrence Erlbaum Associates, Inc. Reprinted by permission of the author and publisher.

Chapter 3

Reading 3.1
Reed Larson and Maryse H. Richards, *Divergent Realities: The Emotional Lives of Mothers, Fathers, and Adolescents* (New York: Basic Books, 1994). Copyright © 1994 by Reed Larson and Maryse H. Richards. Reprinted by permission of Basic Books, a member of Perseus Books, L.L.C. Notes omitted.

Reading 3.2
Mary A. Carskadon, Cecilia Vieira and Christine Acebo, "Association Between Puberty and Delayed Phase Preference." *Sleep,* 1993, Vol. 16, No. 3, pp. 258–262. Reprinted by permission of the journal *Sleep.*

Reading 3.3
Laurence Steinberg, "Reciprocal Relation Between Parent-Child Distance and Pubertal Maturation." *Developmental Psychology,* 1988, Vol. 24, No. 1, pp. 122–128. Copyright © 1988 by the American Psychological Association. Reprinted by permission of the American Psychological Association and the author.

Chapter 4

Reading 4.1
Jerome Kagan, "A Conception of Early Adolescence." *Dædalus, Journal of the American Academy of Arts and Sciences,* from the issue entitled "Twelve to Sixteen: Early Adolescence," Fall 1971, Vol. 100, No. 4. Reprinted by permission.

Reading 4.2
David Elkind, "Egocentrism in Adolescence." *Child Development,* 1967, Vol. 38, pp. 1025–1034. Reprinted by permission.

Chapter 13

Chapter 14

Chapter 15